59th Yearbook of the National Reading Conference

Edited by

Robert T. Jiménez
Victoria J. Risko

Melanie K. Hundley
Deborah Wells Rowe
Vanderbilt University

With the editorial assistance of

Christopher Stewart Keyes
Vanderbilt University

Christopher Roper, *Executive Director*
Technical Enterprises, Inc.

Jenny Kasza, *Editor*
Technical Enterprises, Inc.

Nancy Herrick, *Assistant Editor*
Technical Enterprises, Inc.

Michelle Majerus-Uelmen, *Graphic Designer*
Technical Enterprises, Inc.

Published by
National Reading Conference, Inc.
Oak Creek, Wisconsin

2010

NRC Yearbook is published annually by the National Reading Conference, Inc., 7044 South 13th Street, Oak Creek, WI 53154, Tel: (414) 908-4924.

POSTMASTER:
Send address changes to NRC Yearbook, 7044 South 13th Street, Oak Creek, WI 53154.

SUBSCRIPTIONS:
Institutions: $80 domestic or $90 foreign (surface), per year. Individuals who are NRC members in good standing as of October 1, 2010 will receive the *Yearbook* as part of their membership. Quantity discounts available for use in university or college courses. Write for information.

PERMISSION TO QUOTE OR REPRINT:
Quotations of 500 words or longer or reproductions of any portion of a table, figure, or graph, require written permission from the National Reading Conference, and must include proper credit to the organization. A fee may be charged for use of the material, and permission of the first author will be secured.

PHOTOCOPIES:
Individuals may photocopy single articles without permission for nonprofit one-time classroom or library use. Other nonprofit educational copying, including repeated use of an individual article, must be registered with the Copyright Clearance Center, Academic Permission Service, 27 Congress Street, Salem, MA 01970, USA. *The fee is $1.25USD per article, or any portion, or any portion thereof, to be paid through the Center. The fee is waived for individual members of the National Reading Conference.* Consent to photocopy does not extend to items identified as reprinted by permission of other publishers, nor to copying for general distribution, for advertising or promotion, or for resale unless written permission is obtained from the National Reading Conference.

Microfiche copy is available from ERIC Reproduction Service, 3900 Wheeler Avenue, Alexandria, VA 22304. The YEARBOOK is indexed in *Psychological Abstracts, Index to Social Sciences & Humanities Proceedings and Educational Research Information Clearing House.* The NRC Yearbook is a refereed publication. Manuscripts must be original works that have been presented at the Annual Meeting of the National Reading Conference, and that have not been published elsewhere.

ISSN
ISBN 1-893591-12-3
Printed in the United States of America

National Reading Conference

Editorial Advisory Review Board

59th Yearbook of the National Reading Conference

Amy Seely Flint
Georgia State University

Judith Franzak
New Mexico State University

Lee Freeman
The University of Alabama

Jesse Gainer
Texas State University-San Marcos

Heriberto Godina
The University of Texas at El Paso

Ernest Goetz
Texas A&M University

Jorge Gonzalez
Texas A&M University

Michael F. Graves
University of Minnesota

Priscilla Griffith
University of Oklahoma

Stephanie Grote-Garcia
The University of the Incarnate Word

Juliet Halladay
University of Vermont

Lara J. Handsfield
Illinois State University

Janis M. Harmon
The University of Texas at San Antonio

Kathleen Hinchman
Syracuse University

Jim Hoffman
The University of Texas at Austin

Teri Holbrook
Georgia State University

Deborah Horan
The University of Texas at Austin

Rosalind Horowitz
The University of Texas at San Antonio

Amy C. Hutchison
Iowa State University

Chinwe Ikpeze
St. John Fisher College

Julie Ellison Justice
University of North Carolina at Chapel Hill

Ted Kesler
Queens College, City University of New York

Sharon B. Kletzien
West Chester University of Pennsylvania

Linda Kucan
University of Pittsburgh

Diane Lapp
San Diego State University

Judson Laughter
University of Tennessee

Kristin Lems
National-Louis University

Xiaoming Liu
Towson University

Sarah Lohnes Watulak
Towson University

Minda Morren López
Texas State University-San Marcos

Judith Lysaker
Butler University

Donna Mahar
Empire State College, State University of New York

Beth Maloch
The University of Texas at Austin

Joyce E. Many
Georgia State University

Patrick Manyak
University of Wyoming

Prisca Martens
Towson University

Mona W. Matthews
Georgia State University

Laura A. May
Georgia State University

Kathy G. Short
University of Arizona

Marjorie Siegel
Teachers College, Columbia University

Sunita Singh
Le Moyne College

Allison Skerrett
The University of Texas at Austin

Patrick H. Smith
The University of Texas at El Paso

Sheelah Sweeny
Northeastern University

Brad Teague
INTERLINK Language Center, UNC-Greensboro

Dianna Townsend
University of Nevada, Reno

Guy Trainin
University of Nebraska at Lincoln

Jennifer D. Turner
University of Maryland, College Park

Patricia Vadasy
Washington Research Institute, Seattle, WA

Carolyn Walker
Ball State University

Nancy Walker
University of La Verne

Allison E. Ward
Winthrop University

Patricia A. Watson
Texas Tech University

Linda Wedwick
Illinois State University

Courtney West
Texas A&M Health Science Center

Dana J. Wilber
Montclair State University

Joan Williams
Sam Houston State University

Nance Wilson
University of Central Florida

Linda S. Wold
Loyola University Chicago

Thomas DeVere Wolsey
Walden University

Jo Worthy
The University of Texas at Austin

Shelley Hong Xu
California State University, Long Beach

Janet Young
Brigham Young University

Kristien Zenkov
George Mason University

Student Editorial Advisory Board
59th Yearbook of the National Reading Conference

Amy B. Spiker
University of Wyoming

Nancy Stevens
Marquette University

Cheryl Taliaferro
University of North Texas

F. Blake Tenore
Vanderbilt University

Susan Toma-Berge
University of San Diego

Victor Villarreal
Texas A&M University

Christine M. Wiggins
The University of Utah

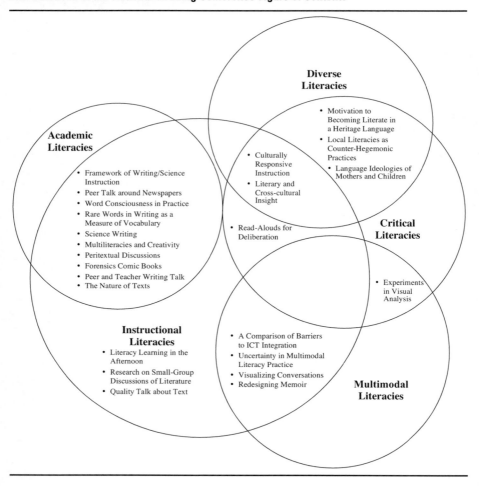

Diverse Literacies

- Motivation to Becoming Literate in a Heritage Language
- Local Literacies as Counter-Hegemonic Practices
- Language Ideologies of Mothers and Children

Academic Literacies

- Framework of Writing/Science Instruction
- Peer Talk around Newspapers
- Word Consciousness in Practice
- Rare Words in Writing as a Measure of Vocabulary
- Science Writing
- Multiliteracies and Creativity
- Peritextual Discussions
- Forensics Comic Books
- Peer and Teacher Writing Talk
- The Nature of Texts

- Culturally Responsive Instruction
- Literary and Cross-cultural Insight

- Read-Alouds for Deliberation

Critical Literacies

- Experiments in Visual Analysis

Instructional Literacies

- Literacy Learning in the Afternoon
- Research on Small-Group Discussions of Literature
- Quality Talk about Text

- A Comparison of Barriers to ICT Integration
- Uncertainty in Multimodal Literacy Practice
- Visualizing Conversations
- Redesigning Memoir

Multimodal Literacies

59th Yearbook of the National Reading Conference

PREFACE

SUMMARY OF THE
59TH NRC ANNUAL MEETING

AWARDS

Albert J. Kingston Award
Oscar S. Causey Award

PRESIDENTIAL ADDRESS

INVITED ADDRESS

AWARD ADDRESS

STUDENT AWARD

ARTICLES

LEGEND

DL DIVERSE LITERACIES

AL ACADEMIC LITERACIES

CL CRITICAL LITERACIES

IL INSTRUCTIONAL LITERACIES

ML MULTIMODAL LITERACIES

Mapping and categorizing the articles accepted to the *Yearbook* is an imprecise and difficult process. There are certainly many categories that are not included, as well as many ways these articles could be mapped. Academic Literacies (AL) refer to work done around school and academic practices. Instructional Literacies (IL) are concerned with the actual instruction of literacy. Critical Literacies (CL) bring a critical lens to literacy, while Diverse Literacies (DL) focus on diverse populations. Multimodal Literacies (ML) are those that employ an array of modes or technologies.

LEGEND

DL DIVERSE LITERACIES

AL ACADEMIC LITERACIES

CL CRITICAL LITERACIES

IL INSTRUCTIONAL LITERACIES

ML MULTIMODAL LITERACIES

Preface

59th Yearbook of the National Reading Conference

The editorial team at Vanderbilt University takes great pride in presenting this edition of the *Yearbook* to the National Reading Conference. We thank all of you for having given us the honor to serve you in this way. As most already know, this is our final year as editors, and we hope that you have found the *Yearbook* to be as useful, interesting, and thought provoking as we have. In addition to our roles as lead editors this year, Vicki Risko and I are working with a group of middle school students near our campus and we are reading with them the young adult novel, *Brothers in Arms* by Paul Langan and Ben Alirez. While we have not had to endure anything like the problems faced by the novel's protagonist, whose little brother is shot and killed, our four years as editors have allowed us to get to know our fellow editors as 'colleagues in arms.' These colleagues for this year included Deborah Wells Rowe and Melanie Hundley. In addition, over the past four years, we have profited from the collegial and expert contributions from our fellow Vanderbilt faculty members, Don Compton, David Dickinson, and Kevin Leander. Also, Youb Kim, now at Pennsylvania State University, added her considerable talents to our labor. Working with each of these individuals through a series of constant deadlines beginning in February of each year and ending sometime in June has been intensely satisfying and an incredible pleasure (especially when we finish!).

Last year's meeting carried the banner, *Literacy Research Past, Present, and Future: Multiple Paths to a Better World*. This year's contributions nicely reflected that theme by including research on literacies for diverse groups; multimodal literacies; teaching literacies; writing, learning and instruction; and children's and young adult literature. Over the past four years, we have consistently received around 100 manuscripts each February and we have published between 20 to 30 of these papers. This year we received 103 and we published 24. We wish to extend our deepest gratitude to all who submitted a manuscript to be published in the *Yearbook*. Your thoughtful contributions move us all a bit closer to a better world of literacy research. We also want to thank all 129 of our fellow members who so very generously gave of their time to review all of these manuscripts. Your help was absolutely essential in what is always a difficult selection process. NRC is indeed fortunate to have so many caring, informed, and generous members.

In addition, we extend our thanks to Chris Keyes, this year's lead editorial assistant, whose excellent work continued the tradition established by our previous assistants of keeping our entire editorial enterprise on track, organized, and on time. He and his fellow doctoral students, Tara Alvey, Emily Bigelow, Nathan Phillips, Kelly Puzio, and Blaine Smith, impressed us with their good cheer, careful editing, thoughtfulness, and energy. We look forward to continuing to work with them in the future. Finally, we thank the Dean of Peabody College, Camilla Benbow, whose vision for supporting the greater research endeavor allowed us to undertake this task.

Please let us know your thoughts about the *59th Yearbook of the National Reading Conference*. We look forward to hearing from you!

Robert T. Jiménez
Victoria J. Risko
NRC Yearbook Lead Editors

A Summary of the 59ᵗʰ Meeting of the National Reading Conference

December 2 – December 5, 2009 * Albuquerque, New Mexico

The 59ᵗʰ Annual Meeting of the National Reading Conference marked several firsts for the organization. Prominently, it was the first conference held after a vote of the membership in 2008 to change the name of the organization from the National Reading Conference (NRC) to the Literacy Research Association (LRA). Because the change of name took effect legally between the 2008 and 2009 conferences and because a period of transition was considered necessary and prudent, the 2009 conference was held under the NRC banner. However, attendees and the organization's leadership at this conference began to use the acronym LRA nearly as often as NRC when referring to the organization and to future conferences.

The 59ᵗʰ Annual Meeting was also the first conference to be held in Albuquerque; the first to have two official hotels, rather than a single hotel as in past years; the first to use a convention center for the conference; and the first to have snow. In fact, the temperature in Albuquerque matched an all-time low of 15 degrees Fahrenheit during the conference. Although Albuquerque was expected to be somewhat colder than the warm climates typical of NRC meetings, the record-low temperatures created an unfamiliar sight for longtime attendees—overcoats, hats, and gloves.

The conference program, too, had some new features:

- The conference theme, *Literacy Research Past, Present, and Future: Multiple Paths to a Better World*, was announced shortly after the previous conference. Submitters of proposals for the conference were encouraged to connect their papers or sessions to that theme. Approximately a quarter of the accepted proposals made such connections and these papers or sessions were noted in the conference program.

- Chairs of each Area to which proposals were submitted (see a subsequent listing of Areas and Chairs) selected a paper or session in their respective areas for an "Area Chair Award," based on the reviews. These award-winning sessions were noted in the conference program.

- All paper sessions were assigned discussants.

- Prior to the conference, an e-mail was sent to attendees that provided background about the two invited plenary speakers (Gloria Ladson-Billings, University of Wisconsin; Charles M. Payne, University of Chicago). Attached to the e-mail were two publications, each of which the speakers had recommended as good preparation for their respective talks.

- A scheme was initiated whereby Chairs in each odd-numbered Area were invited to submit a proposal to the conference chair for a sponsored session, which included a small budget as needed. In subsequent years odd- and even-numbered Areas would be allowed to submit such proposals corresponding to odd- or even-numbered years.

- All presenters, particularly at paper sessions, were strongly urged to provide attendees at their sessions with access to prepared papers, ideally by uploading them to the organization's Web site where they would be archived and accessible.

There were also several new special events on the conference program:

- Thursday a brown-bag lunch was held to highlight NRC's major initiative to mentor scholars of color. The Ethnicity, Race, and Multilingual Committee sponsored that initiative, which is referred to as Scholars of Color Transitioning Into Academic Research Institutions (STAR).

- A luncheon with Distinguished Scholars was held on Saturday. A Distinguished Scholar at each table met with up to 10 attendees who had registered in advance for this event.

- Traditionally, the plenary session on Saturday morning is a presentation by an NRC scholar who reviews an area of research. However, for the 2009 conference two teams of senior scholars debated a resolution pertaining to the role of research in providing explicit guidance for practitioners and policy makers. The debate included opening statements, several rounds during which a team provided cases supporting its position, followed by a rebuttal from the other team, and closing statements. After each round and after the closing statements the audience, using wireless devices, voted which team had made the more convincing argument. Results were displayed immediately on a large screen for all to see.

The following new winners of several NRC awards were also announced and recognized at one of the plenary sessions:

Oscar S. Causey Award
>Barbara M. Taylor, *University of Minnesota*

Albert J. Kingston Award
>Diane Barone, *University of Nevada, Reno*
>Cathy Roller

Edward B. Fry Book Award
>Leila Christenbury, *Virginia Commonwealth University*
>Randy Bomer, *The University of Texas at Austin*
>Peter Smagorinsky, *University of Georgia*

Student Outstanding Research Award
>Susan E. Bickerstaff, *University of Pennsylvania*

Early Career Achievement Award
>Misty Sailors, *The University of Texas at San Antonio*

Distinguished Scholar Lifetime Achievement Award
>Walter Kintsch, *University of Colorado at Boulder*

J. Michael Parker Award
>Holly Hungerford-Kresser, *The University of Texas at Arlington*

The conference's vital statistics did not change dramatically from the most recent preceding years (2008 numbers in parentheses), but they are perhaps worth noting for the record:

Total attendees: 1178 (1240)

Proposals submitted: 733 (645)

Proposals accepted: 553 (484)

Acceptance rate: 75.44% (75.04%)

Session Type

>Paper 307 (272)
>Roundtable 127 (104)
>Symposium 65 (62)
>Alternative 39 (31)
>Study group 15 (15)

There are several individuals who merit special recognition for their contributions to the 2009 conference.

Foremost, I wish to recognize Christopher Roper, NRC's Executive Director, who provided phenomenal attention to detail, unsurpassed organizational skills, savvy knowledge of the hospitality business, and deep knowledge of NRC's management. Patty Anders, University of Arizona, as conference co-chair, was a valued assistant in planning the program. George Hruby, Utah State University, was the conference social chair and assisted with local arrangements. Diane Tracey, Kean College, coordinated the New Scholars luncheon. Diane Schallert, The University of Texas, moderated the Saturday debate and worked closely with me and with the two debate teams to coordinate many complex details and resolve many issues associated with that event. Jamie Colwell, my doctoral student at Clemson University, assisted with many tasks. Finally, the quality of the annual conference program is the result of the diligent and substantial efforts of the Area Chairs who manage all aspects of the review process. NRC owes a debt of gratitude to the Area Chairs for the 59th Annual Meeting whose names and affiliations follow:

Area 1: Pre-Service Teacher Education in Literacy
    Julie Kidd, *George Mason University*
    Karen Spector, *The University of Alabama*
    Kristien Zenkov, *George Mason University*

Area 2: In-Service Teacher Education/Professional Development in Literacy
    Cheryl Dozier, *SUNY Albany*
    Ellen McIntyre, *North Carolina State University*
    Katherine Stahl, *New York University*
    Ruth Wharton-McDonald, *University of New Hampshire*

Area 3: Literacy Instruction and Literacy Learning
    Valerie Robnolt, *Virginia Commonwealth University*
    Amy Seely Flint, *Georgia State University*
    Jennifer Jones, *Radford University*

Area 4: Literacy Assessment, Evaluation, and Public Policy
    Les Burns, *University of Kentucky*
    Mary Applegate, *Saint Joseph's University*
    Courtney Zmach, *American Institutes for Research*

Area 5: Early and Elementary Literacy Processes
    Barbara Bradley, *University of Kansas*
    Kelly Cartwright, *Christopher Newport University*
    Kevin Flanigan, *West Chester University*

Area 6: Adolescent, College, and Adult Literacy Processes
    Stergios G. Botzakis, *University of Tennessee*
    Heidi Hallman, *University of Kansas*
    David Gallagher, *Mount Saint Mary College*

Area 7: Social, Cultural, and Political Issues of Literacy Practices In and Out of School
    Kristiina Montero, *Syracuse University*
    Gwendolyn McMillon, *Oakland University*
    Rachelle Washington, *Clemson University*

Area 8: Literacy Learning and Practice in Multi-Lingual and Multi-Cultural Settings
Lori Assaf, *Texas State University - San Marcos*
Xiufang Chen, *Rowan University*
Julia Lopez-Robertson, *University of South Carolina*

Area 9: Text Analysis/Children's, Young Adult, and Adult Literature
Cyndi Giorgis, *University of Nevada Las Vegas*
Miriam Martinez, *The University of Texas San Antonio*
Janelle Mathis, *University of North Texas*

Area 10: Literacy Technology and Media
Erica Boling, *Rutgers University*
David Lund, *Southern Utah State University*
Liqing Tao, *City University of New York*

Area 11: Study Groups
Laurie Henry, *University of Kentucky*
Nina Nilsson, *Saint Joseph's University*

Area 12: Other Topics
Jackie Malloy, *George Mason University*
Nadjwa Norton, *City University of New York*
Lisa Simon, *City University of New York*

David Reinking
President, National Reading Conference
2009-2010

Diane M. Barone

Albert J. Kingston Award

The annual Albert J. Kingston Service Award honors an NRC member for distinguished contributions of service to the National Reading Conference. Established in 1985, the award was designed to honor the work of NRC's 1965-'66 president, Albert J. Kingston. Professor Kingston, an educational psychologist and reading specialist, played a major role in the development of the National Reading Conference. In 2009 the committee selected two deserving members of NRC for this award: Diane Barone and Cathy Roller.

Dr. Diane M. Barone, Foundation Professor of Literacy Studies at the University of Nevada, Reno, exemplifies what it means to serve the profession. She began her teaching career in the primary grades after graduation from Case Western (B.A.) and Kent State (M.Ed. in Early Childhood Education). She later received a doctorate from the University of Nevada, Reno. After holding faculty positions at the University of California Bakersfield and University of Nevada, Las Vegas (UNLV), Diane returned to her alma mater, the University of Nevada, Reno, where since 1984 she has taught a variety of classes in literacy and research methods. Professor Barone is well known for her scholarship on the literacy development of young children and particularly for her research focused on children of poverty and drug-exposed young children. An author of numerous books, including *Narrowing the Literacy Gap*, Dr. Barone also has published extensively in peer-reviewed journals, including *The Reading Teacher, Reading Research Quarterly,* and *Journal of Literacy Research.*

Professor Barone exemplifies commitment to serving others not only as a teacher and scholar, but also in service to professional organizations. She has been an active member of the International Reading Association throughout her career serving on a number of committees, as editor of the *Reading Research Quarterly,* and as a member of the Board of Directors. However, it is her long-standing service to the National Reading Conference that is perhaps most noteworthy. From 1989 to present, Diane has reviewed proposals for the annual conference, presented numerous papers, and chaired dozens of sessions. She also has served as a reviewer for the *Yearbook* and *Journal of Reading Behavior/Journal of Literacy Research (JRB/JLR)* for more than 20 years. In addition, Dr. Barone served as the Publications Chair (2004-2006) and on the Board of Directors (2003-2006). We extend our thanks and congratulations to Diane M. Barone, recipient of the 2009 Albert J. Kingston Award, on a much-deserved recognition for her many contributions to NRC.

Diane Corcoran Nielsen, Chair
Albert J. Kingston Award Committee
December 2009

Cathy M. Roller

Albert J. Kingston Award

Dr. Cathy M. Roller has a long and distinguished career as a teacher, scholar, and leader in the literacy community. After receiving a B.A. in English from Mount Union College, Cathy began her career in education as a high school English teacher. She soon turned her focus to reading, completing an M.A. in Reading at the University of Tulsa, and serving as a reading specialist in Oklahoma and Montana. After completing her Ph.D. in Reading, Psychology, and Statistics at the University of Minnesota, Dr. Roller was on the faculty at the University of Iowa for 20 years. She served as the Director of Research and Policy for the International Reading Association for more than a decade, retiring in 2009. Dr. Roller has an extensive record of scholarship, including numerous publications on issues related to struggling readers and more recently teacher preparation.

Dr. Roller is equally well known for her contributions to and leadership within professional organizations. An active and long-standing member of NRC, she served on numerous committees, the editorial boards of both the *Journal* and *Yearbook*, and as a member of the Board of Directors (1996-'98). In addition, and most noteworthy, is Dr. Roller's leadership as Director of Research and Policy for the International Reading Association (IRA). In that role, she promoted and facilitated collaboration between the efforts of NRC and IRA and involved reading researchers of NRC in the IRA Annual Research Conference and on policy and research-award committees. Whether it is between IRA and NRC or other professional groups, Dr. Roller is known for bringing scholars of disparate viewpoints together to use research to inform standards and practice. We thank Dr. Roller for her many contributions and extend our congratulations on receiving the 2009 Albert J. Kingston Award in recognition of distinguished service to NRC.

Diane Corcoran Nielsen, Chair
Albert J. Kingston Award Committee
December 2009

Barbara Taylor

Oscar S. Causey Award

The Oscar S. Causey Award is presented each year at the annual conference to honor outstanding contributions to literacy research. Dr. Oscar S. Causey, the founder of the National Reading Conference, was Chair of the Executive Committee for several years, and served as President from 1952 to 1959. Individuals who are honored with this prestigious award have conducted and published research that generates new knowledge and is deemed substantial, significant, and original. The individual is also recognized as a leader in the conduct and promotion of literacy research.

Barbara Taylor, the 2010 recipient of the Oscar S. Causey Award for outstanding contributions to literacy research, has been on the faculty of the University of Minnesota since 1978. She held the Guy Bond Professor of Reading chair and served as founder and Director of the Minnesota Center for Reading Research. Her research lines are distinguished by both their relevance and rigor, reflecting a systematic, significant, and prolific contribution to the field.

Dr. Taylor conducted instructional studies to improve comprehension of informational text. She developed and studied an Early Intervention using a balanced approach designed to be taught by teachers within their own classrooms and limited time constraints; it has been exceptionally effective for students at risk for early failure. She has conducted research on understanding and improving the nature and quality of instruction in low-income schools, as part of the Center for the Improvement of Early Reading Achievement (CIERA), then as Principal Investigator of Minnesota's Reading Excellence and Reading First initiatives. Her site-based, grass-roots approach to reading reform runs counter to the national trend toward top-down, pre-packaged reforms and has demonstrated achievement gains consistently more impressive than those achieved through more Draconian means. Her instructional model emphasizes active student response, student-centered pedagogy, and tasks with high levels of cognitive challenge and engagement. Her approach to professional learning emphasizes creating and maintaining a professional community with grass-roots decision-making.

In terms of rigor, Dr. Taylor uses the most careful approaches to quasi-experimental design available for work in educational settings where random assignment is not possible. Using careful experimental and statistical controls, at least modest levels of causal explanation can be made, especially as one examines the accumulation of trends over several years. She includes multiple measures of student achievement and one of the most elaborate and "disinterested" of observational systems currently in use. She uses sophisticated statistical tools (e.g., hierarchical linear modeling) to tease out the effects of the intervention across sites and levels.

Dr. Taylor is committed not only to producing important research, but to seeing that her findings have a positive impact on the learning of a significant number of disadvantaged students. Her work is available to both literacy researchers and literacy practitioners publishing in prestigious refereed research journals as well as in chapters, articles, and books accessible to practitioners. Dr. Taylor epitomizes the Oscar S. Causey Award for a lifetime of contributions to understanding literacy theory, research, and practice and impacting the lives of countless literacy professionals who have, in turn, changed the lives of tens of thousands of children.

Deborah R. Dillon, Chair
Oscar S. Causey Award Committee
December 2009

Literacy Identities of Youth Identified for Special Education: Who Is Responsible?

Kathleen A. Hinchman
Syracuse University

In the spirit of many past National Reading Conference presidential addresses, this paper takes an advocacy stance to answer the question raised in the title. In it I share experiences to outline ways that mainstream literacy educators, including me, have excluded individuals identified for special education from their work. I then draw on disabilities studies (Biklen, 2005; Kliewer, Biklen, & Kasa-Hendrikson, 2006) and sociocultural perspectives toward literacy (O'Brien, 2003; Street, 1995) to attend to video representations of the literacy identities of three young people who were identified for special education services. Finally, I invite National Reading Conference (NRC) members to join me in assuming responsibility for conducting the various kinds of research needed to improve literacy instruction for all young people, including those with identified disabilities.

Why is this important? When a teacher encounters a student who struggles with literacy instruction, she can find an increasing number of recommendations in the mainstream literacy literature for initial instructional interventions (Johnston, 2010; Lipson & Wixson, 2010). It is far more difficult to find satisfactory instructional advice for those for whom preliminary interventions do not work, as can be the case for individuals with severe learning disabilities, autism spectrum disorders, or intellectual disabilities. Some students are even assumed to be unable to benefit from literacy instruction on the basis of their labels or indecipherable communication. Even more specialized research literature recommends only rudimentary sight word instruction or other emergent literacy activities, with little said about developing decoding, comprehension, or writing. The classroom reality is that limited literacy instruction occurs, if any (Duffy, 2009; Kliewer, Biklen, & Kasa-Hendrickson, 2006; Mirenda, 2003).

However, as more schools move toward including all students in classrooms regardless of identified disabilities, parents, teachers, the community, and students themselves will demand productive literacy instruction for all (Yell, Drasgow, & Lowrey, 2005). A growing body of literature suggests that such engagement is possible but that more work is needed to direct our efforts (Chandler-Olcott & Kluth, 2009; Dickinson, McCabe, & Essex, 2006; Erickson, Clendon, Abraham, Roy, & Van de Carr, 2005; Farrell & Elkins, 1995; Kliewer & Biklen, 2006; Koppenhaver & Erickson, 2003; Lemons & Fuchs, 2010; Mirenda, 2003). Because of NRC members' expertise and varied perspectives toward literacy, we are well positioned to address this need.

EXPERIENCES THAT BROUGHT ME TO THIS ISSUE

Despite my long interest in young people's perspectives toward in- and out-of-school literacies (Hinchman, Payne-Bourcy, Sheridan-Thomas, & Chandler-Olcott, 2002), I have only recently begun explicitly conducting research with young people identified for special education services (Greenleaf & Hinchman, 2009; Hinchman 2008). I previously limited my work to students who participated in regular education settings, overlooking those who were excluded from such settings. My decisions embody larger social constructions that have limited many literacy researchers' attentions to the needs of such learners. In the following section, I trace the history of this decision-making to make such social constructions more explicit.

Fostering Literacy, Or Not, Under P.L. 94-142

I began teaching English in a junior high school near Syracuse in the mid-1970s, and my college roommate went into secondary special education. My roommate argued that she was making a difference for young people about whom few cared, and I thought that I was sharing my love of literature and writing. Why her students would not have appeared on my first class rosters did not occur to me. This was at the same time that U.S. Public Law 94-142, the Education for All Handicapped Children Act, was beginning to be implemented in schools across the country. This new law "guaranteed a free, appropriate public education to each child with a disability in every state and locality across the country" (United States Department of Education, 2007). By the time I realized the implications of this law for my life as an English teacher, I had also realized that not every junior high school student shared my love of literature and writing.

When I moved into a reading specialist position at the same school, the special education teacher, school psychologist, and I initially implemented P.L. 94-142 by negotiating who would provide instruction to our most severely disabled readers. We shared an approach to problem solving that began with identifying potential causes of students' literacy difficulties without realizing that our reference to this causal model might restrict how we viewed young people's potential (Hinchman & Michel, 1999; Johnston & Allington, 1991). I did not even know that some severely disabled readers in our attendance zone did not attend our school because they were bused to a regional educational facility.

Influential to our decisions were reading expectancy formulas (Harris & Sipay, 1975). This causal model calculation compared young people's mental ages to reading grade equivalents to determine potential to benefit from reading instruction. Young people with measured intelligence that was lower than average were said to be working at capacity when their reading achievement was less than that of peers, and instructional expectations were lowered as a result. Such formulas were to help reading specialists attend to students who could make the most gains, referring others to special education.

As P.L. 94-142 was tested in courts, its provision for "access for children with disabilities" (USDE, 2007, p. 3) was increasingly interpreted to mean access to all activities—even when activities were undifferentiated and did little to address children's needs. Special education teachers helped students complete schoolwork, sometimes by reading, dictating, or writing it for them, and leaving little time for literacy instruction (Allington & McGill-Franzen, 1989).

Fostering Literacy, Or Not, As a Literacy Education Professor

After my doctoral studies I was sometimes asked to teach elementary reading methods classes. Without suitable teaching experience, I referred to the table of contents in a bestselling textbook to organize my syllabus. I was comforted when its organization referred to causes of reading disability. I gained the most confidence from this sentence:

> Because most children have the intelligence, motivation, emotional stability, and physical health necessary to learn to read and to enjoy reading and because most schools have good teachers, good instructional materials, and good conditions for

learning, most children in our country learn to read with relatively little difficulty.
(Smith & Johnson, 1976, p. 28)

As a result, I thought that the text's contents represented the necessary and sufficient information to suit preservice teachers' needs (Snow, Griffin, & Burns, 2005). That the statement excluded many young people did not occur to me or my earliest methods students.

I also worked as a project director for several adult literacy projects in collaboration with Laubach Literacy and Literacy Volunteers, both of which were founded in Syracuse. I had the chance to see how these organizations struggled at their fiftieth anniversaries when adults seeking services brought a history of special education. These students were learning to read even though they had usually attended segregated schools, although in several cases they were actual former students whom my colleagues and I had failed. I was humbled when a Student-of-the-Year pointed to me during a talk, saying, "I am here because I didn't pay attention to my reading teachers. Look, there's one in the back of the room! Miss Hinchman, I am sorry I didn't listen to you when I had the chance."

When I moved into my current literacy education faculty position at Syracuse, I abandoned my dependence on tables of contents and organized classes to balance literature-based inquiry with methods of teaching literacy skills and strategies (Duffy & Roehler, 1993; Leu & Kinzer, 1995). By helping my students to enhance the literacy understandings of their students, I was confident they could deliver suitable instruction, at least in the rudimentary fashion expected of beginning teachers (Snow, Griffin, & Burns, 2005). In response, I was sometimes confronted by impatient 20-year-olds who responded to our new program's inclusive ideology with considerable enthusiasm, implicitly calling me out on the parameters of my enculturation:

Student: Dr. Hinchman, there's a fifth grader in my classroom who can't read at all!!

KH: Is he labeled?

Student: What difference would that make?

That my students could not interact with individuals in segregated facilities did not occur to me until my students pointed it out. My interactions with such insightful students helped me to deconstruct assumptions that children's special education status somehow indicated whether they would benefit from literacy instruction. I even began to look for students with special needs at my research sites rather assume they were someone else' concern.

Another of my standing teaching assignments, a summer literacy education MS practicum, added to my understanding regarding the needs of students identified for special education. With prompting from doctoral students, I began to solicit tutees identified for special education services. One young man came to our practicum through a high school guidance counselor; I have written about him elsewhere as a highly motivated young adult who grew excited when learning word patterns extended his ability to read interesting materials (Hinchman, 2008). Another had a label of severely mentally retarded changed to learning disabled when her tutor gave her fidget toys to help her focus while she learned to read. Still another grew confident in defending opinions in book club discussions—progress that encouraged his school district to augment literacy professional development for special education teachers.

This school district, like others, was also encouraged to help special education teachers provide literacy instruction because of the reauthorized Individuals with Disabilities Education Act and the Elementary and Secondary Education Act, known as No Child Left Behind. The two laws required states to have goals for the performance of children with disabilities that were the same as the State's objectives for adequate yearly progress by all children, and that addressed graduation and dropout rates, as well as other goals and standards for children established by the state. The new laws also asked school districts to report reading performance of all students, disaggregated by subpopulations that included special education status, and special education students were allowed fewer testing accommodations. Many school districts have been embarrassed by resultant revelations about special education students' literacy achievement. Whether such requirements were the most viable solution to tracking individuals' needs and progress was debatable, yet the requirements clearly caused schools to pay attention to all students' literacy progress in new ways (Darling-Hammond, 2007; USDE 2004).

Soon after these changes, like many NRC members, I began to work with local schools seeking advice for improving literacy achievement of special education students. I referred them to the growing body of research-based interventions that might preclude identification, such as those described by Clay (1993), Blachman and Tangel (2008), Vellutino and Scanlon (2002), Deshler and Schumaker (1988), and Schoenbach and colleagues (1999). But according to Lipson and Wixson (2009), many schools are steering clear of teacher-dependent problem-solving in favor of standardized commercial interventions to alleviate concerns that students' failure could too often be caused by poor teaching. It's problematic that such interventions are prescribed for students who are categorized by test score or special education label with the assumption that all their needs are alike. The truth is actually quite different: There is "no quick fix," especially for individuals who experience the world in nonmainstream ways (Allington & Walmsley, 2007). Research-based instructional recommendations that take such differences into account are hard to find.

Most IDEA and NCLB stipulations remain in new Race to the Top initiatives, as well as in anticipated Elementary and Secondary Education Act reauthorization. However, education experts suggest use of individual growth modeling to document students' individual progress rather than comparison of individuals' performance to standard cut scores, changes that would well serve students with special needs. Cut score models have been dubbed "hurdle models" by some, resulting in what Pearson called "perverse incentives" to school districts to provide instruction only to students closest to making the cut (Pearson, 2009)—yet another reason that the literacy learning needs of students with significant disability labels have been ignored.

WHAT DISABILITY STUDIES AND SOCIOCULTURAL PERSPECTIVES SUGGEST ABOUT LITERACY IDENTITIES OF YOUNG PEOPLE IDENTIFIED FOR SPECIAL EDUCATION

Analyses that reach beyond the preceding narrative are needed to better understand literacy instruction that has been or could be provided to individuals identified with reading, learning, communicative, and intellectual disabilities. Described in the following section, disabilities studies and sociocultural perspectives toward literacy can help us to understand, dismantle, and reconstruct beliefs about literacy and identity. Such excavation is one kind of research that can help us develop alternative literacy pedagogies that appreciate and respond to all young people's literacy initiations in newly productive ways.

The Disability Studies Perspective

The disabilities studies perspective begins with the idea that "disability" is a way that society positions people relative to a society's constructions of normal. This sociocultural perspective was developed to theorize, understand, and advocate for individuals who are constructed as disabled. The perspective does not dispute that individuals viewed as disabled may experience the world in ways that differ from other people. Instead, scholarship from this perspective explores how social constructions concerned with disability are enacted, as well as how various identities related to disability are inscribed on some bodies and not others. The slash in dis/ability that is sometimes used by those who work from this perspective is to call attention to the false binary of either/or social categories that are often used to classify people and instruction relative to such individuals, such as dis/abled and special/regular education (Biklen, 2005; Kliewer, Biklen, & Kasa-Hendrikson, 2006).

The disabilities studies perspective is not to be confused with the reading disabilities perspective that prevailed in literacy instruction for much of the last century and that was a focus of my reading specialist training (Harris & Sipay, 1975). Johnston and Allington's (1991) *Handbook of Reading Research* chapter, "Remediation," contains a thorough discussion of the reading disabilities perspective. From this perspective, differences in individuals' literacy development were attributed to such factors as background, education, physical and mental health, language processing, and cognitive ability.

The reading disabilities perspective has often been described as representing a "medical model" worldview because of its implication that if one somehow addressed, or treated, the causes of reading disability, one could achieve more effective instructional results. The source of reading disability was located within the individual, and individual performance was judged according to such socially constructed criteria as what it means to be meeting sixth-grade standards or reading at a third-grade level. This worldview is typically juxtaposed with a more contemporary notion of literacy instruction that begins, instead, with young people's existing ideas and insights about the workings of literacy rather than their history (Clay, 1993).

That discussion of reading disability focused on individuals' deficits relative to socially constructed standards aligns this perspective with other, deficit-oriented perspectives critiqued by disabilities studies scholars. Various analyses tell us that the dawning of the twentieth century abounded with psychologists who tested various constructs, such as intelligence and reading comprehension, by comparing individual performance against average (Gould, 1981). Individuals like Edmund Burke Huey, called the father of the psychology of reading, and Goddard, the father of American intelligence testing and special education, employed such techniques in their work (Hartman, 2007; Zenderland, 1998).

It is now commonly accepted, even beyond the disabilities studies community, that the most brutal form of sort-and-select historically occurred for individuals with what were thought to be the most severe mental disabilities. Prior to the 1960s, parents of infants born with Down syndrome, a chromosomal abnormality that yields observable physical markers along with cognitive manifestations, were told by physicians to place their children in institutions, often despite desires to raise such children with family. Other behaviors that could result in a child's institutionalization included inability to speak, hear, see, learn, or act in what were seen as normal ways. Burton Blatt, a former School of Education Dean at Syracuse University, was a Massachusetts state education department official who visited state mental institutions with a photographer in the mid 1960s to reveal the tragedies in how such places treated people (Blatt & Kaplan, 1966). Their photographs, combined with Blatt's testimony before the Supreme Court in the mid 1970s, led to passage of P.L. 94-142, which brought young people with severe disabilities from institutions to schools (USDE, 2007).

However successful such advocacy was at closing institutions, the kinds of schools individuals with significant disabilities were allowed to attend varied widely, as was the instruction offered. As I have noted elsewhere in this paper, many young people with some kinds of disabilities have received minimal or no literacy instruction. Only within the last few years have researchers begun documenting literacy learning by individuals with significant intellectual or communicative disabilities in ways that hint there is more to be understood about this important area (Biklen, 2005; Chandler-Olcott & Kluth, 2009; Colasent & Griffith, 1998; Kliewer,1998; Kliewer, et al., 2004; Koppenhaver & Erickson, 2003; Lemon & Fuchs, 2010; Mirenda, 2003).

We brought young people with significant disabilities to public schools in the 1970s, though not much was offered to them in the way of literacy instruction. In the meantime, students with significant high-incidence learning disabilities were often placed together in resource rooms with students with emotional difficulties and low-incidence intellectual or communicative disabilities. Their special education teachers could not offer suitable literacy instructional to all the students in such challenging settings (Katims, 2000). One wonders how many literacy initiations of students with various kinds of disabilities have been overlooked, ignored, or attended to in inappropriate ways in such settings, data that are unavailable because so many young people were historically excluded from assessment.

Sociocultural Views of Literacy

Sociocultural views of literacy hold that our meaning construction is situated in particular institutional, historical, and societal contexts that mediate and are mediated by the social world (Lewis, Enciso, & Moje, 2007). One version of this theory holds that, in an age when communicative media and social groups evolve rapidly and vary widely, our multimodal literacies allow us to communicate as we move from home to work, and to various other affinity groups (New London Group, 1996; Street, 1995). Use of the plural, literacies, is intended to move the discussion from a view of literacy as singular, autonomous, universal reading and writing skills to the multiple, interwoven, multimodal skills and strategies specific to particular social contexts, each embedded with power relations and invoking texts representing multiple modalities (O'Brien, 2003; Alvermann, 2008).

Scholars have begun to explore communication strategies deployed within and across these various literacies, including those involving individuals' use of assistive technologies, as well as others demonstrated by individuals who struggled with or were not invited to explore academic literacies (Kliewer, 1998; 2008). The idea of multiple literacies provides a way to understand the communicative transactions of individuals whose literacies were not historically recognized. Chandler-Olcott and Kluth (2009) point out:

Such a conceptualization invites participation by a wider range of learners, including those who have traditionally been seen as at risk (O'Brien, 2003), and makes visible strengths and interests that might otherwise be lost as resources for literacy instruction. (p. 14)

Kliewer and Biklen (2007) reviewed commonalities in literacy demonstrations by significantly developmentally disabled individuals to find that, when local understandings included expectations that such individuals desired communication and appreciated unconventional initiations, these individuals demonstrated a variety of literacy initiations—despite previous diagnoses that asserted that literacy demonstrations would be impossible. Similarly, Chandler-Olcott and Kluth (2009) explored how individuals with autism spectrum disorders demonstrated multiple literacies. Both lines of work suggest that it is easier to recognize literacy development in such individuals when interactions begin with a presumption of competence and desire to communicate, even though communication may not be demonstrated in typical ways (Biklen, 2005).

Sociocultural scholars have suggested that the intersection of literacy and identity is important to study because people's identities shape and are shaped by the texts they read, produce, and talk about (Gee, 2001; McCarthey & Moje, 2002). Such scholars have drawn on wide-ranging theorists, including but not limited to Mead (1934), Anzaldúa (1999), Bakhtin (1981), and Bourdieu (1992). Lewis and delValle (2009) explained that work in this area has considered identity as made up of stable characteristics constructed through cultural affiliation, explored performance of literacy practices mediating identity in social settings, and, most recently looked at identity as "hybrid, metadiscursive, and spatial," in connection with literacy practices "networked within local and global flows of activity" (p. 317). Moje and Luke (2009) added that, "Learning, from a social and cultural perspective, involves people in participation, interaction, relationships, and contexts, all of which have implications for how people make sense of themselves and others, identify, and are identified" (p. 416).

Noting the proliferation of literacy-and-identity studies, Moje and Luke (2009) caution those who conduct research in this area to seek precision in their use of these constructs, and they posit five metaphors to capture the various conceptualizations of identity invoked by these studies. The identity-as-difference metaphor is used in analyses that focus on how individuals identify with and use literacy practices that are situated within sense of self as tied to a social group. Studies utilizing the identity-as-self metaphor represent a range of perspectives regarding constitution of self, including how one deploys various texts and literacy practices to be certain kinds of people, or not. Analyses that draw on identity-as-mind or -consciousness metaphor hold that literacy is a tool for developing mind. Identity-as-narrative work explores what and how literacy practices are performed in stories people tell to represent themselves. The identity-as-position metaphor is employed by those studies exploring how individuals enact or resist literacy practices and tools that order, or position, individuals relative to one another in space.

These five metaphors also give us a way to conceptualize studies into how literacy resonates in the lives of individuals identified with disabilities that have historically minimized their opportunities for literacy instruction. For instance, a third-grader's resistance to assigned literacy tasks that make him look stupid may be telling us how literacy positions her in her classroom. That a middle school student asks for help with unconventional spelling and sentence structure to blog is telling us about his sense of self and desire to communicate in a digital world. When a young woman chooses a trade book that seems too difficult, plowing through with dictionary in hand, she is enacting agency in ways that are important to understand.

Clay (1966) long ago suggested that young people demonstrate nascent understandings of literacy before they are able to read or write, and that these initiations lay the groundwork for literacy development. Research since then has explored various aspects of these initiations, much of which considered the sociocultural view that children's literacy initiations stemmed from their recognition of functions of print in social contexts (Teale & Sulzby, 1986). More recently, researchers have explored demonstrations of multiple literacies and identities represented in these initiations (Siegel, Kontovourki, Schmier, & Enriquez, 2008).

Other research emphasizes the role of oral language in emergent literacy (Snow, Griffin, & Burns, 1998), suggesting that "children who were identified as having oral language impairments in preschool were at greater risk for oral and written language impairment as they progressed through school, even if their language impairments appeared to have been remediated by the time they entered kindergarten" (Rhyner, 2009, p. 2). Of course it is important for educators to ameliorate such difficulties when they can. However, we also need literacy instruction that decouples oral language and print literacy for students with oral difficulties. Yet single-minded focus on oral language remediation may cause caregivers and educators to miss opportunities that present themselves in young people's demonstrations of literacy and identity, especially when demonstrations are unconventional (Chandler-Olcott & Kluth, 2009).

Literacy Identities: Three Cases

Developing understandings of unconventional and multimodal demonstrations of literacy and identity, as well as of suitable instructional responses to such various demonstrations—even when they are not likely to yield passing scores on high-stakes tests—is an important focus for research. Melding the terms "literacies" and "identities"—both plural—into a single term, "literacy identities" gives researchers a way to recognize all young people's literacy initiations, in various modalities, without limiting observations to oral-to-written language or academic traditions. Such a term could allow educators to presume competence, that is, assume that young people communicate as they can, and that each demonstration provides important insight. Such a term may also invite young people to consider how they might position themselves relative to developing competence in various representational modes suited to their aspirations.

In this section, I share transcripts from video representations of three young people who were identified for special education services. These individuals, Susan, Peter, and Terrance, have been identified with autism spectrum disorder, Down syndrome, and a learning disability, respectively. These video representations are limited; they are included to hint of the kind of research that might be possible to explore the literacy identities such enact on a day-to-day basis, hints that need to be more systematically understood with additional literacy research so that appropriate instructional responses can be designed.

Example 1: Susan

Consider Susan, a young woman with autism who was the focus of the Academy Award-nominated documentary, *Autism is a World* (Rubin & Wurzburg, 2004), a film that should be seen in its entirely to understand Susan better. As you scan the following transcript excerpts, consider: Who was Susan's most important teacher? How were her literacy instructional needs likely dealt with in school before and after she learned to communicate? How have her enactments of literacy identities evolved over time?

Susan's written words were read by a narrator throughout the film, as in the excerpts included below. Her mother is also interviewed in the included excerpts.

> My name is Sue Rubin. I am 26 years old. I have written these thoughts about my life because I don't really talk. This is not my voice but these are my words. I have autism. And until the age of 13, everyone assumed I was also retarded. Now I live on my own with assistance from others...

> I certainly understand why I was assumed to be retarded. All of my very awkward movements and all my nonsense sounds made me appear retarded. Perhaps I was. Voices floated over me. I heard sounds but not words. It wasn't until I had a communication system that I was able to make sense out of the sounds. When I was 13, Jackie, my educational psychologist, called my mother and said that she had seen someone with autism, who was like me, start to communicate using a keyboard in support...

> Progress was slow at first. I was a terrible subject because of my behaviors, but my mom insisted that I practice every day. As I began to type, my mind began to wake up...

> Susan's mother: I asked her if she could type three vegetables. And you can see it was really difficult for her to get anything and it just looked like gibberish to me. I saw that she was doing S-P, S-I, S-P-I, and so I said to her, do you mean spinach. And then she got it. She typed "spinach." And then I said to her one more and you can go. She typed "kale." K-A-L-E. I have no idea where that came from because I never buy kale. I don't like kale. I don't make kale. She never had kale. But anyway, she typed kale.

> When she started communicating, she was reassessed and she had another psychological examination and, where before she had tested at the two and a half year level, which is about a 29 I.Q. for someone who is 13, she ended up testing 133 I.Q. So when it came time for her to go to high school, we knew she had to be in regular classes in an academic program.

Susan graduated from high school and was a junior in college at the time the film was made; the film documents her participation in a college class, typing answers to the professor's questions to be read by her assistant as other students scrambled to locate answers in their notebooks. Her mother was one of her most important teachers, teaching Susan to type her thoughts on a keyboard. The kind of one-to-one help that Ms. Rubin's mother was able to provide, responding to Susan's initiations, has not typically been available in school. Her mother presumed competence, figured out ways to unlock Susan's communication abilities, and Susan flourished as a result. Learning to read and write the language she had been hearing and not comprehending helped Susan to enact literacies and identities in important new ways.

Example 2: Peter

Peter was a nine-year-old boy with Down's syndrome at the time the film, *Educating Peter*, was made (Wurzburg, 1992), another film that should be viewed in its entirety for added insight. First shown on HBO, this Academy Award-winning film chronicled Peter's third-grade year in a newly inclusive classroom. As you read the classroom excerpts included below, ask yourself how Peter's enactments of literacy identities evolved throughout the school year. How did this teacher respond to his literacy initiations, and how did Peter respond to her in turn?

The following excerpt is a classroom sequence from early in the school year.

Peter: [Looking up from his writing] Miss Dice? I stupid.

Teacher: No you're not. Just get to work. You're doing fine. [She moves to help another student.]

Peter: Miss Dice. Miss Dice. Miss Dice. I stupid.

Teacher: Just a minute, just a minute. [Coming to Peter's desk] What? Your pictures? Are they glued on yet?

Peter: I stupid.

Teacher: Let's not talk about being stupid. You're a smart little boy. Good. Are you ready to do your pictures? Good [as Peter picks up his pencil].

Student: Peter, you're not stupid.

Peter: Stupid.

Teacher: [To other students] Nah. He's just trying to get us going this morning, isn't he? Why don't you finish this sheet and do your journal so you can do the science experiment with the group. Do you want to do the science experiment?

Peter: Yeah.

Teacher: Good.

In a narrative clip, the teacher explained, "I think he felt a little lost, you know. He knew we were doing some things that he couldn't do. He knew he was basically out of place for a while." A part of the film from later in the school year illustrates how much more Peter was a part of classroom activities. The segment includes a classmate helping Peter as he stands in front of the class holding up a sentence strip for the class to read.

Student: OK, let's go. 1, 2, 3. Say 1, 2, 3. Peter?

Peter: 1, 2, 3.

Class: [Reading from the sentence strip as Peter faces them, holding it up.] I made a cake for dinner.

Peter: [Putting the strip on the floor, peering closely and pointing to words as he reads] I made a cake for dinner.

Teacher: [As the class applauds] Wow. Good job, Peter! [Peter smiles and moves to take his seat.]

Peter realized early in the year that he wasn't doing the same activities as the other children, and he recognized the hierarchical positioning this suggested. His teacher worked to understand

and respond to his literacy initiations, and Peter figured out how to engage in classroom activities in ways that he and others saw as productive. His teacher presumed Peter's competence, and Peter's enactments of literacy identities evolved in response.

Example 3: Terrance

Terrance (pseudonym) is a ninth-grader in a Reading Apprenticeship classroom, a young man about whom Cynthia Greenleaf and I have written elsewhere (Greenleaf & Hinchman, 2009). Terrance was identified for special education services as a learning disabled student when he was in elementary school. As you read his words, captured in an interview and think-aloud conducted by Cindy Litman, one of Greenleaf's colleagues, ask yourself: Who were Terrance's most important teachers? How have his enactments of literacy identities likely changed over time? What responsibilities does he seem to have assumed for his own literacy development?

> It actually was hard for me to like comprehend reading when I was like first and second grade because I couldn't understand any of what I was reading, but I knew that I was reading something. So now I like really understand what I'm reading since I practice like every night and all day, like reading on the internet and stuff, so now I really understand what I'm reading…

> Teachers and my momma and my friends and family helped me actually understand what I was reading… They got me to read books and stuff like that and my momma put me up in an afterschool program where they helped me read up in there, so I actually know how to read by my family and friends…

> A lot of it took place in school, too, because they got me in support classes where the teacher actually helps me with my work and projects and homework and stuff, so I do a lot of reading in there on the internet and do projects and she helped me read and understand everything like that.

Litman also asked Terrance to read and discuss a newspaper article. The article described a court case involving the American Civil Liberties Union defense of a group of high school students who had received permission to hold a peaceful anti-war protest only to have the principal withdraw her permission and suspend the student leaders. A portion of Terrance's interpretation follows:

> I just think the students are just trying to use their right to freedom of speech because they don't like the war and they're against the war. The students are having a anti-war rally and the principal don't like that. Well, the principal is using that freedom of speech too, as well, because she don't, she don't want the students to have the rally so she's actually telling them they can't have it. But the students are using theirs, too, in the same way, because they want to have the rally for the anti-war message.

Terrance came to see himself as a reader capable of completing sophisticated reading tasks; in other portions of the interview Terrance explains the many digital and print sources he reads each day. He was willing to tackle the reading and interpreting of a newspaper article on videotape, and he produced a reasonable initial interpretation.

Each of these individuals made progress because others responded to their desire for literacy. Susan's mother helped her learn to communicate through typing, Peter's teachers helped him to learn structures and practices that allowed his print literacy to emerge, and Terrance used scaffolded and independent reading experiences to develop the ability to interpret sophisticated text. Presumed competence and instruction enabled them to extend their literacy identities, along with their hopes, dreams and aspirations, in new directions.

CONCLUSION

Who is responsible for the literacy identities of youth identified for special education? Sue, Peter, and Terrance would likely argue that, ultimately, they are. Even though my excerpts are limited representations, they hint of these individuals' pride regarding their literacy-related accomplishments. These accomplishments were enhanced when knowing others also assumed responsibility by presuming they were competent, despite their disabilities, and by exploring ways to enhance their literacy initiations.

Yet we know little about fostering such agency, about literacy identities that are or could be constructed by such individuals, or about how everyone would be shaped by these individuals in turn. Any one of these students might be ignored by most literacy researchers as not being representative enough for the purposive sampling of qualitative research, or because defining behaviors are not easily specified for the large-scale sampling of experimental or quasi-experimental design. Literacy researchers might also argue that development of these individuals' identities is the purview of special educators, although literature from this community seems not to have offered satisfying solutions to their needs either. Without clear guidance from research, extant intervention often uses commercial materials, resulting in indiscriminant programming that is unlikely to position young people favorably as citizens in the ways Susan's mom or Peter's or Terrance's teachers seem to have done.

As I also argued at the outset of this paper, members of the National Reading Conference can assume responsibility for addressing the literacy instructional concerns of young people identified for special education services. Publishing our work in mainstream outlets will, by itself, help other educators begin to include such individuals in their gaze. We can explore the literacy identities of such individuals in far more nuanced ways than are hinted in the video excerpts that I was able to include in this paper, and we can conduct other kinds of research to provide insights into competence and instruction. No one is better equipped than NRC members to explore such issues.

REFERENCES

Allington, R., & McGill-Franzen, A. (1989). School response to reading failure: Instruction for Chapter 1 and special education students in grades 2, 4, and 8. *Elementary School Journal, 89,* 529-542.

Allington, R., & Walmsley, S. (2007). *No quick fix, the RTI edition.* New York, NY: Teachers College Press.

Alvermann, D. E. (2008). Why bother theorizing adolescents' online literacies for classroom practice and research. *Journal of Adolescent and Adult Literacy, 52,* 8-19.

Anzaldúa, G. (1999). *Borderlands/La frontera: The new mestiza* (2nd. ed.). San Francisco, CA: Aunt Lute.

Bakhtin, M. M. (1981). *The dialogic imagination.* Austin, TX: University of Texas Press.

Biklen, D. (2005). *Autism and the myth of the person alone.* New York, NY: New York University Press.

Blachman, B., & Tangel, D. (2008). *Road to reading.* Baltimore, MD: Brookes Publishing.

Blatt, B., & Kaplan, F. (1966). *Christmas in purgatory: A photographic essay on mental retardation.* New York, NY: Allyn and Bacon.

Bourdieu, P. (1992). *The logic of practice.* Stanford, CA: Stanford University Press.

Chandler-Olcott, K., & Kluth, P. (2009). "Mother's voice was the main source of learning": Parents' role in supporting the literacy development of students with autism. *Journal of Literacy Research, 40,* 1-32.

Clay, M. (1966). *Emergent reading behavior.* Unpublished doctoral dissertation, University of Auckland, NZ.

Clay, M. (1993). *Reading recovery: A guidebook for teachers in training.* Portsmouth, NH: Heinemann.

Colasent, R., & Griffith, P. L. (1998). Autism and literacy: Looking into the classroom with rabbit stories. *The Reading Teacher, 51*, 414–420.

Darling-Hammond, L. (2007, May 21). Evaluating "No Child Left Behind." *The Nation.* Retrieved March 3, 2010 from http://www.thenation.com/doc/20070521/darling-hammond.

Deshler, D. D., & Schumaker, J. B. (1988). An instructional model for teaching students how to learn. In J. L. Graden, J. E. Zins, & M. J. Curtis (Eds.), *Alternative educational delivery systems: Enhancing instructional options for all students* (pp. 391-411). Washington, DC: NASP.

Dickinson, D. K., McCabe, A., & Essex, M. J. (2006). A window of opportunity we must open to all: The case for preschool with high-quality support for language and literacy. In D. K. Dickinson & S. B. Neuman (Eds.), *Handbook of early literacy research* (Vol. 2, pp. 11-28). New York, NY: Guilford Press.

Duffy, G., & Roehler, L. (1993). *Improving classroom reading instruction: A decision-making approach.* New York, NY: McGraw Hill.

Duffy, M. (2009, December). *Literacy instruction for students with moderate to severe cognitive disabilities: An analysis of parents' descriptions and perspectives.* Paper presented at the annual meeting of the National Reading Conference, Albuquerque, NM.

Erickson, K. A., Clendon, S., Abraham, L., Roy, V., & Van de Carr, H. (2005). Toward positive literacy outcomes for students with significant developmental disabilities. *Assistive Technology Outcomes Benefits, 2*, 45-54.

Farrell, M., & Elkins, J. (1995). Literacy for all? The case of Down syndrome. *Journal of Reading, 38*(4), 270–280.

Gee, J. P. (2001). Identity as an analytic lens for research in education. *Review of Research in Education, 25*, 99–125.

Gould, S. J. (1981). *The mismeasure of man.* New York, NY: W. W. Norton & Company.

Greenleaf, C., & Hinchman, K. A. (2009). Reimaging our inexperienced adolescent readers: From struggling, striving, marginalized and reluctant to thriving. *Journal of Adolescent and Adult Literacy, 53*, 4-13.

Harris, A. J., & Sipay, E. (1975). *How to increase reading ability: A guide to developmental and remedial methods* (6th ed.). Philadelphia, PA: David McKay Publishers.

Hartman, D. K., (2007). *One hundred years of reading research—1908-2008—From Edmund B. Huey to the present.* A research review address presented at the 57th Annual Meeting of the National Reading Conference, Austin, TX.

Hinchman, K. A. (2008). Intervening when older youth struggle with reading: Teach me what I need to know next. In M. Conley (Ed.), *Meeting the challenge of adolescent literacy: Research we have and research we need* (pp. 11-35). New York, NY: Guilford.

Hinchman, K. A., & Michel, P. (1999). Reconciling polarity: Toward a responsive model of evaluating literacy performance. *The Reading Teacher, 52*, 578-587.

Hinchman, K. A., Payne-Bourcy, L., Thomas, H., & Chandler-Olcott, K. (2002). Representing adolescents' literacies: Case studies of three white males. *Reading Research and Instruction, 41*, 229-46.

Johnston, P. (2010). *RTI in literacy: Responsive and comprehensive.* Newark, DE: International Reading Association.

Johnston, P., & Allington, R. L. (1991). Remediation. In R. Barr, P. Mosenthal, M. Kamil, & P. D. Pearson (Eds.), *Handbook of reading research* (pp. 984-1012). New York, NY: Longman.

Katims, D. S. (2000). Literacy instruction for people with mental retardation: Historical highlights and contemporary analysis. *Education and Training in Mental Retardation & Developmental Disabilities, 35*, 3-15.

Kliewer, C. (2008). Joining the literacy flow: Fostering symbol and written language learning in young children with significant developmental disabilities. *Research and Practice for Persons with Severe Disabilities, 33*, 103-121.

Kliewer, C. (1998). *Schooling children with Down syndrome.* New York, NY: Teachers College Press.

Kliewer, C., & Biklen, D. (2007). Enacting literacy: Local understanding, significant disability, and a new frame for educational opportunity. *Teachers College Record, 109*, 2579–2600.

Kliewer, C., & Biklen, D. (2001). School's not really a place for reading: A research synthesis of the literate lives of children with severe disabilities. *Journal of the Association for Persons with Severe Handicaps, 26*, 1–12.

Kliewer, C., Biklen, D., & Kasa-Hendrickson, C. (2006). Who may be literate? Disability and resistance to the cultural denial of competence. *American Educational Research Journal, 43*, 163–192.

Kliewer, C., Fitzgerald, L. M., Mayer-Mork, J., Hartman, P., English-Sand, P., & Raschke, D. (2004). Citizenship for all in the literate community: An ethnography of young children with significant disabilities in inclusive early childhood settings. *Harvard Educational Review, 74*, 373–403.

Koppenhaver, D., & Erickson, K. (2003). Natural emergent literacy supports for preschoolers with autism and severe communication impairments. *Topics in Language Disorders, 23*(4), 283–292.

Lemons, C., & Fuchs, D. (2010). Modeling response to intervention in children with Down syndrome: An examination of predictors of differential growth. *Reading Research Quarterly, 45,* 134-168.

Leu, D. J., & Kinzer, C. K. (1995). *Effective reading instruction K-8.* Columbus, OH: Merrill Publishing.

Lewis, C., & delValle, A. (2009). Literacy and identity: Implications for research and practice. In L. Christianbury, R. Bomer, & P. Smagorinsky (Eds.), *Handbook of adolescent literacy research* (pp. 307-322). New York, NY: Guilford.

Lewis, C., Enciso, P., & Moje, E. (2007). *Reframing sociocultural research on literacy.* New York, NY: Erlbaum.

Lipson, M., & Wixson, K. (2009). *Response to intervention: Promises, possibilities, and potential problems for reading professionals.* Paper delivered at the annual meeting of the International Reading Association, Minneapolis, MN.

Lipson, M., & Wixson, K. (2010). *Successful approaches to rti: Collaborative practices for improving K-12 literacy.* Newark, DE: International Reading Association.

McCarthey, S. and Moje, E. B. (2002). Identity matters. *Reading Research Quarterly, 37,* 228-237.

Mead, G. H. (1934). *Mind, self, and society: From the standpoint of a social behaviorist.* Chicago, IL: University of Chicago Press.

Mirenda, P. (2003). "He's not really a reader": Perspectives on supporting literacy development in individuals with autism. *Topics in Language Disorders, 23*(4), 270–281.

New London Group. (1996). A pedagogy of multiliteracies: designing social futures. *Harvard Educational Review, 66,* 60-92.

O'Brien, D. (2003, March). Juxtaposing traditional and intermedial literacies to redefine the competence of struggling adolescents. *Reading Online, 6*(7). Retrieved February 1, 2007, from http://www.readingonline.org/newliteracies/lit_index.asp?HREF=obrien2/

Pearson, P. D. (2009). *Teaching reading in a time of promise: What we can expect of the Obama years.* Paper delivered at the annual meeting of the International Reading Association, Minneapolis, MN.

Rhyner, P. (2009). Introduction. In P. Rhyner (Ed.), *Emergent literacy and language development: Promoting learning in early childhood.* New York, NY: Guilford.

Rubin, S., & Wurzburg, G. (2004). *Autism is a world.* Washington, DC: CNN Productions and State of the Art.

Schoenbach, R., Greenleaf, C., Cziko, C., & Hurwitz, L. (1999). *Reading for understanding: A guide to improving reading in middle and high school classrooms.* San Francisco, CA: Jossey Bass.

Siegel, M., Kontovourki, S., Schmier, S., & Enriquez, G. (2008). Literacy in motion: Case study of a shape-shifting kindergartener. *Language Arts, 86,* 89-98.

Smith, R., & Johnson, D. (1976). *Teaching children to read.* Reading, MA: Addison Wesley.

Snow, C., Burns, M. S., & Griffin, P. (1998). *Preventing reading difficulties in young children.* Washington, DC: National Academy Press.

Snow, C., Griffin, P., & Burns, M. S. (2005). *Knowledge to support the teaching of reading: Preparing teachers for a changing world.* San Francisco, CA: Jossey Bass.

Street, B. (1995). *Social literacies: Critical approaches to literacy development, ethnography, and education.* New York, NY: Addison Wesley.

Teale, William, & Sulzby, Elizabeth. (1986). *Emergent literacy: Writing and reading.* Norwood, NJ: Ablex Publishing Corporation.

United States Department of Education (USDE). (2004). *Building the legacy: IDEA 2004.* Washington DC: United States Department of Education. Retrieved March 1, 2010, from idea.ed.gov/

United States Department of Education (USDE). (2007). *History of educating children with disabilities through IDEA.* Washington, DC: United States Department of Education Office of Special Education Programs. Retrieved March 1, 2010, from www2.ed.gov/policy/speced/leg/idea/history.pdf.

Vellutino, F., & Scanlon, D. (2002). The interactive strategies approach to reading intervention. *Contemporary Educational Psychology, 27,* 573-635.

Wurzburg, G. (1992). *Educating Peter.* Washington, DC: State of the Art.

Yell, M., Drasgow, E., & Lowry, K. A. (2005). No Child Left Behind and students with autism spectrum disorders. *Focus on Autism and Other Developmental Disorders, 20*(3), 30–39.

Zenderland, L. (1998). *Measuring minds: Henry Herbert Goddard and the history of intelligence testing in the United States.* Cambridge, UK: Cambridge University Press.

"Why Can't We Read Something Good?" How "Standards," "Testing," and Scripted Curricula Impoverish Urban Students

Gloria Ladson-Billings
University of Wisconsin-Madison

I must confess I always feel like something of an imposter when I come to present at literacy and/or English conferences. My own true disciplinary home is history, but like many middle school social studies teachers I was "given" some sections of English to teach and there was a presumption that I could do it because I had a minor in English. I learned a series of painful lessons about how to get students engaged in English/literacy. I also feel a bit fraudulent at these meetings because I came running to this community after a very public falling out with the social studies organization. Without dragging out that tortured story, suffice it to say that I left the social studies association with a very bad taste in my mouth about the lack of commitment to issues of equity and social justice. So, with those caveats I take on the task of saying something meaningful to you about what is happening in the area of literacy in urban schools.

Urban schools—we all have the image firmly imprinted in our minds. The physical plant is crumbling, the roof is leaking, the bathrooms are unsanitary, the furniture is falling apart, the common spaces such as the cafeteria, the auditorium, and the corridors are inadequate. The schools are horribly dangerous and people are always on guard for their lives. The teachers are all burnouts except for the handful of new idealistic teachers and they will be either be burnouts or dropouts before the year ends. This notion of urban school is so pervasive that Hollywood has been able to bank on it as a genre. We all know the titles—*Blackboard Jungle* (Brooks, 1955), *Up the Down Staircase* (Pakula & Mulligan, 1967), *To Sir, with Love* (Clavell, 1967), *Stand and Deliver* (Law & Menéndez, 1988) *Dangerous Minds* (Guinzberg & Smith, 1995), *Music of the Heart* (Weinstein & Craven, 1995), *Freedom Writers* (DeVito & LaGravenese, 1997), and the list goes on. The storyline rarely changes—a bunch of misfit children from dysfunctional families (generally, belligerent and ignorant mothers) attend a school where no one cares about them except one, lone, heroic teacher. And, like *Rumpelstiltskin* (Zelinsky, 1996) this teacher can spin straw into gold, or in this case, turn total failures into huge successes. The storyline is so trite and so predictable it is a wonder that we keep seeing it over and over again. But I don't want to talk about Michelle Pfeiffer putting on a leather jacket and talking tough to a bunch of Black and Latino students (Guinzberg & Smith, 1995) or Hillary Swank pulling out a strand of pearls and convincing everyone to write the story of their lives (DeVito & LaGravenese, 1997). Instead I want to talk about a very different kind of violence that is occurring in urban schools (actually in most schools—except it has more serious ramifications in urban schools)—the violence being perpetrated on the minds of young people in the name of rigor, high standards, and accountability.

Every years millions of young people enter our schools and classrooms and find themselves subjected to a curriculum, a pedagogy, and a set of required texts that do little more than push them further away from our so-called stated goal—to educate all students so that they can, as the late Ted Sizer (1984) said, "use their minds well." My challenge in this talk is to attempt to reinvigorate leaders of the literacy community to stand against the derogation of the field and its role in developing thinking citizens, prepared to fully participate in a democratic and multicultural society. At a family literacy conference last fall a scholar shared the comments of many freshmen students about how much they disliked reading Nathaniel Hawthorne's (1850) *The Scarlet Letter*. My initial response to the students' comments was, "Of course, urban students would dislike *The Scarlet Letter*." However, the presenter was quick to correct my internal dialogue by pointing out that the comments were from middle-class, mostly White, college-bound students. So it is not merely "urban" students who resisted reading canonical literature—most students find it inaccessible and irrelevant to the lives they are living. And why wouldn't they? Hawthorne, Melville, Twain, Shakespeare, and all of those writers were not writing books for adolescents. They wrote adult books with adult themes for adult readers.

As I prepared for this address I began to peruse the Internet for freshmen English syllabi and I was amazed at the uniformity. All across the nation students are still asked to read *The Scarlet Letter* (Hawthorne, 1850), *Romeo and Juliet*, *To Kill a Mockingbird* (Lee, 1960), *Lord of the Flies* (Golding, 1954), and *The Adventures of Huckleberry Finn* (Twain, 1948)—the same set of texts that I read as a teenager. Now I am not attempting to argue against the literary merit of any of these texts. Rather, I want to raise questions about how these canonical texts seem to have the opposite effect of their stated intent. And yet, there is a literary genre emerging that urban youth are embracing as a form of counter story, counter-revolution, and counter culture. In the remainder of this discussion I want to briefly describe the literary choices of adolescents—both suburban and urban—and the way current so-called reforms are working against the literacy development of young adults.

WIZARDS, DRAGONS, AND VAMPIRES

It is not difficult to determine what White, suburban, mostly middle-class young adults are reading. Because of their numbers they command the attention of booksellers and have a large impact on the market. According to goodreads.com, books with themes of wizards, dragons, and vampires top the list of best-selling books for young adults. Stephanie Meyer's *Twilight* (2005), *New Moon* (2006), *Eclipse* (2007), and *Breaking Dawn* (2008) have captivated the imagination and pocketbooks of young adult females. Close behind are the *Harry Potter* books of J. K. Rowling (1998, 1999, 2000, 2003, 2005, 2007). Rounding out the top sellers is Christopher Paolini's *Eragon* (2003).

At the next level are a series of books seemingly targeted at the particular angst felt by young adult females. They include titles such as Scott Westerfeld's trilogy, *Uglies* (2005), *Pretties* (2005), and *Specials* (2006), Laurie Halse Anderson's, *Speak* (1999) and Ann Brashares' *The Sisterhood of the Traveling Pants* (2001). These titles are specifically aimed at young adults and young adults read them. The 2001 Report of the Federal Interagency Forum on Child and Family Statistics indicates that 28% of 13-year-olds and 25% of 17-year-olds report reading independently on a daily basis. The National Education Association reports that over 41% of teens report reading more than 15 books.

Among White, suburban young adult males the graphic novel has become the text of choice. These texts represent an extension of comic books and carry themes that speak to young males—

superheroes, science fiction, and futurism. An interesting development in this genre is its appeal among urban male students of color—especially Black and Latino. Perhaps their appeal is linked to the connection between the narratives that emerge from video and computer games and Japanese anime. Titles such as Abel, Sorria, and Pleece's *Life Sucks* (2008), Hinako Ashihara's *Sand Chronicles* (2008), and Clevinger and Wegener's *Atomic Robo: Atomic Robo and the Fightin' Scientists of Tesladyne* (2008) are hugely popular among adolescent boys.

The genre known as "Afro-futurism" is a somewhat new genre that is a "literary and cultural aesthetic that combines elements of science fiction, historical fiction, fantasy and magic realism… in order to critique not only the present-day dilemmas of people of color, but also to revise, interrogate, and re-examine the historical events of the past" (Dery, 1994). Cultural critic (and supposed founder of the term) Mark Dery adds that it is a "Speculative fiction that treats African-American themes and addresses African-American concerns in the context of 20th century technoculture— and more generally, African American signification that appropriates images of technology and a prosthetically enhanced future" (Dery, 1994).

Unlike some of the other wizard, dragon, and vampire literature previously referenced, Afro-futurism pulls from both older, "official" texts such as Toni Cade Bambara's, *The Salt Eaters* (1980) or Octavia Butler's *Kindred* (1979), and Ralph Ellison's *Invisible Man* (1952) as well as more recent publications such as Tananarive Due's *Joplin's Ghost* (2005) that opens with these words:

Someone rapped on the hotel room door.

Gloria squealed, laughing, "He's still there, Phee."

"Shhhh, it's not funny." Phoenix wasn't in the mood for any fan bullshit.

If this was the same boy, he'd been outside their hotel suite two solid hours, knocking softly every half hour to let them know he hadn't gone anywhere. What had been amusing at ten was annoying at midnight.

Phoenix pulled a velvet throw pillow from her cousin's bed across her eyes. Before the last knock, Gloria had been flipping through *The Source*, fantasizing about which men she'd like to hook up with when they had a chance to shop backstage at the Grammy's of the MTV Music Awards—It's a tough choice between Tyrese and 50 Cent, huh?

Phoenix's only fantasy right then was to have the strength to walk to her master bedroom across the hall, brush her teeth, and go to bed. The OutKast CD sounded tinny and awful from the cheap CD player that doubled as a clock radio, and Phoenix knew she had to be tired if OutKast couldn't wake her up. She couldn't remember being this trashed on the road before, even when she had a band hauling instruments and amps.

Yes, adolescents do read. They just don't always read what we think they should read. In addition to the wizards, dragons, vampires, graphic novels, anime, and Afro-futurism there is at least one more genre that few teachers employ in their classrooms.

URBAN LIT—READING HIP HOP

The latest genre that seems to have captivated urban students, particularly urban African-American female students is urban literature. Urban lit, also known as Street lit, is a literary genre in a city landscape that depends on the race and culture of the characters as well as the dark settings and profane language. The stories are primarily about the underside of urban life with lots of sex and violence and explicit anger and derogation of Whites. While Claude Brown's *Manchild in the Promise Land* (1999) and *The Autobiography of Malcolm X* (X & Haley, 1987) represent early examples of the genre, more recent examples of this genre include Omar Tyree's *Flyy Girl* (1997), Sister Souljah's *The Coldest Winter Ever* (1999), and Kole Black's *The Chance She Took* (2007) and *The Risk of Chance* (2008). In each of these books we find African-American female protagonists who use their sexuality to get ahead and to define themselves. The language is coarse, the situations are vulgar, and the lifestyles described in the texts are unfamiliar to the typical English teacher. Yet, these books are exactly about the lives their Black female students live and/or observe. Sapphire's *Push* (1996) that has been adapted for the feature film, and *Precious* (Siegel-Magness, Magness & McGuigan, 2009), is an example of this genre. It is raw, gritty, and uncomfortable to read/watch, but urban Black female adolescents find it compelling and read it in out-of-school settings.

Interestingly, the tension over urban lit is not only between Black teens and the White school establishment (i.e. teachers, administrators, librarians, school board members), but is more pointed between Black teens and Black adults who are proponents of what they consider "real" Black literature such as that written by Toni Morrison, Alice Walker, Richard Wright, Ralph Ellison, James Baldwin, and Zora Neale Hurston. What is undeniable is that urban or ghetto lit sells. A book like *Project Chick* outsells Toni Morrison's *Love* (2003) by 3 to 1 and many of the literati lament this phenomenon. However, others argue that Danielle Steele, Tom Clancy, and Barbara Bradford Taylor are not critiqued for reaching large popular audiences and no one suggests that they represent quality literature. Acclaimed author Walter Mosley says, "Obviously, there can be an art to ghetto lit. I would never dismiss it out of hand. But I'm an American who believes in freedom of speech and freedom of thought. I may not read it, but I can't make a moral decision for someone else." More importantly, Mosley says, "Reading is a good thing. "You might read this hip-hop book, and next year, read Mosley or even Mark Twain," he continued. "It's not about the book—it's the idea that reading becomes an important part of your life."

READING BECOMES AN IMPORTANT PART OF YOUR LIFE

It is that last sentiment, "reading becomes an important part of your life," that leads me to the final point of this discussion. What is happening to young people in classrooms throughout this nation is working directly against having reading become an important part of their lives. We are stripping every single joy out of reading and language and that is the opposite of what we are charged to do. Of course this is not true of every individual teachers, in fact it is probably not true of most English/Language Arts teachers. But it is true of the system to which we are acquiescing.

The movement to create common standards has enlisted 46 of the 50 states with only Alaska, Missouri, South Carolina, and Texas failing to sign on. The early draft of the Standards for Reading Informational and Literary Texts proposes a set of Core Standards that the right rejects because they say they are without substance and the left rejects because they say they are too prescriptive. The typical classroom English/Language Arts teacher has some vision of what to do with a text and does not need to be told what to teach and how to teach it. However, in a district where my son teaches, teachers are required to list on the board each day what curriculum strand and content standard they are teaching. [He describes himself as teaching in a "Stepford" District.] The district standards then list the task analysis or prerequisite knowledge the students must have to complete the standard. So for example the document says, *"Curriculum Strand Three: Literary Response and Analysis: The students will read and respond to historically or culturally significant works of literature that reflect and enhance their studies of history and social science. They conduct in-depth analyses of recurrent patterns and themes. The selections in [name of district] core, supplementary, and extended reading lists illustrate the quality and complexity of the materials to be read by the students.*

The Content Standard states:

> The students will: determine characters' traits by what the characters say about themselves in narration, dialogue, dramatic monologue, and soliloquy.

The Task Analysis/Prerequisite Knowledge states:

> Can the students: (1) understand the function and purpose of dramatic monologue and soliloquy? (2) recognize how narration and dialogue reveal character?

The Suggested Benchmarks/Assessment states:

> Reread Act 1, Scene I of the play *Romeo and Juliet*. Examine what Romeo's use of oxymorons in lines 173-180 reveals about his state of mind. Use "Interactive Reading," p. 60 ("Thank you M'am" chart) and p. 61 (Standards Review Exam).

I decided to go into my curriculum library to see if I could find the text the standards reference and I did. I have to say I was bewildered by the fact that these anthologies are about 1,100 pages and in the section that contains *Romeo and Juliet* there is a textbook-like rendering of this classic filled with "features," photographs, and vocabulary explanations. Nothing about the presentation of the play said, "You are a reader who is likely to read for pleasure and for your own information. Instead it implied you are not smart enough to read this play so your textbook will digest it and feed it to you. Incidentally, your teacher is not smart enough to really teach it to you.

The next slide is a copy of the assessment activity that is paired with this standard. One must ask oneself, "Who reads a text in this way?" The answer is simple—people who we do not intend to be readers, who read because it is an assignment and who we will do everything we can to discourage their love of reading.

Unfortunately, this is one of the less offensive things we are seeing in the teaching and learning of literacy. We are asking teachers and their students to be so focused on assessments that we do not care if they actually read texts as long as they know the test answers. In one California district the school board decided that the only class that would receive actual books were the seniors (Johnson, 2005). Everyone else would receive anthologies. The teachers were so infuriated that they begin a protest of standing outside of the school each morning at 7:00 am reading the stories and novels aloud. When I was contacted to lend support, I recall sending a message that read, "In the 60s we were protesting the content of the books we were asked to read. Who knew that in the 21ˢᵗ century we would have to protest to read ANY book?" Perhaps the most salient comment about what is happening in our classrooms is that offered by educator and social critic Herb Kohl (2009):

> People who insult and denigrate teachers by forcing scripted curriculum on them are perfectly aware that they are forcing teachers to act against their conscience and students to close down their minds. What must be raised and answered for is the moral cost of creating joyless schools that resemble panopticons.

> ..."the irony is that even with the imposition of so-called "teacher-proof" curriculum, teachers are evaluated on the effectiveness of their student's performance on tests relating to material they have no control over. No one evaluates Open Court or other such curriculum when students fail. It is the powerless "proofed" teachers who take the hit. This is morally reprehensible and yet the question of the values underlying this kind of teaching and evaluation is neglected when experts discuss educational issues.

For those of us who understand high levels of literacy as the most powerful skills one can have in a democratic, global society, Kohl's observations are distressing, perhaps even depressing. Our students DO want to read. All the evidence points to it. They just want to read something good!

REFERENCES

Abel, J., Soria, G., & Pleece, W. (2008). *Life Sucks*. New York, NY: First Second Press.
Anderson, L.H. (1999). *Speak*. New York, NY: Penguin Group.
Ashihara, H. (2008). *Sand Chronicles, vol 1*. San Fransisco, CA: Viz Media.
Ashihara, H. (2008). *Sand Chronicles, vol 2*. San Fransisco, CA: Viz Media.
Ashihara, H. (2008). *Sand Chronicles, vol 3*. San Fransisco, CA: Viz Media.
Bambara, T. C. (1980). *The Salt Eaters*. New York, NY: Random House.
Black, K. (2007). *The Chance She Took*. Spaulden Publishing.
Black, K. (2008). *The Risk of Chance*. Spaulden Publishing.
Brooks, R. (Producer & Director). (1955). *Blackboard Jungle* [Motion picture]. United States: Metro Goldwyn Mayer.
Brown, C. (1999). *Manchild in the Promised Land*. New York, NY: Touchstone Press.
Brashares, A. (2001). *The Sisterhood of the Traveling Pants*. New York, NY: Delacorte Press.
Butler, O. E. (1979). *Kindred*. Boston, MA: Beacon Press.
Clavell, J. (Proucer & Director). (1967). *To Sir With Love* [Motion picture]. United States: Columbia Pictures Corporation.
Clevinger, B., & Wegener, S. (2008). *Atomic Robo: Atomic Robo and the Fightin' Scientists of Tesladyne*. Red 5 Comics. Calgary, Alberta: Red 5 Comics.
Dery, M. (1994). *Flame Wars*. Durham, NC: Duke University Press
DeVito, D. (Producer), & LaGravenese, R. (1997). *Freedom Writers* [Motion picture]. United States: Paramount Pictures.
Due, T. (2005). *Joplin's Ghost*. New York, NY: Washington Square Press.
Ellison, R. (1952). *Invisible Man*. New York, NY: Vintage Books.
Federal Interagency Forum on Child and Family Statistics. (2001). *America's Children: Key National Indicators of Well-Being, 2001*. Washington, DC.: U.S. Government Printing Office.
Golding, W. (1954). *Lord of the Flies*. New York, NY: Berkley Publishing Group.
Guinzberg, K. (Producer), & Smith, J. N. (Director). (1995). *Dangerous Minds* [Motion picture]. United States: Hollywood Pictures.
Hawthorne, N. (1850). *The Scarlet Letter*. New York, NY: Bantam Dell.
Johnson, C. (2005, May 27). Teachers fight scripted curriculum. *San Francisco Chronicle*, p. B-1.

Kohl, H. (2009, Jan. 8). The educational panopticon. *Teachers College Record* (retrieved electronically from http://www.tcrecord.org ID number15477.

Law, L. (Producer), & Menéndez, R. (Director). (1988). *Stand and Deliver* [Motion picture]. United States: American Playhouse.

Lee, H. (1960). *To Kill a Mockingbird*. New York, NY: Harper Collins.

Meyer, S. (2005). *Twilight*. New York, NY: Little Brown and Company.

Meyer, S. (2006). *New Moon*. New York, NY: Little Brown and Company.

Meyer, S. (2007). *Eclipse*. New York, NY: Little Brown and Company.

Meyer, S. (2008). *Breaking Dawn*. New York, NY: Little Brown and Company.

Morrison, T. (2003). *Love*. New York, NY: Alfred A. Knopf.

Pakula, A. J. (Producer), & Mulligan, R. (Director). (1967). *Up the Down Staircase* [Motion picture]. United States: Park Pace Production.

Paolini, C. (2003). *Eragon*. New York, NY: Alfred A. Knopf.

Rowling, J.K. (1998). *Harry Potter and the Sorcerer's Stone*. New York, NY: Scholastic.

Rowling, J.K. (1999). *Harry Potter and the Chamber of Secrets*. New York, NY: Scholastic.

Rowling, J.K. (1999). *Harry Potter and the Prisoner of Azkaban*. New York, NY: Scholastic.

Rowling, J.K. (2000). *Harry Potter and the Goblet of the Fire*. New York, NY: Scholastic.

Rowling, J.K. (2003). *Harry Potter and the Order of the Phoenix*. New York, NY: Scholastic.

Rowling, J.K. (2005). *Harry Potter and the Half-Blood Prince*. New York, NY: Scholastic.

Rowling, J.K. (2007). *Harry Potter and the Deathly Hallows*. New York, NY: Scholastic.

Sapphire (1996). *Push*. New York, NY: Vintage.

Siegel-Magness, S., & Magness, G. (Producers) & McGuigan, P. (Director). (2009). *Precious* [Motion picture]. United States: Summit Entertainment.

Sizer, T. R. (1984). *Horace's Compromise: The Dilemma of the American High School*. New York, NY: Houghton Mifflin.

Souljah, S. (1999). *The Coldest Winter Ever*. New York, NY: Simon & Schuster, Inc.

Twain, M. (1948). *The Adventures of Huckleberry Finn*. New York, NY: Grosset & Dunlap.

Tyree, O. (1997). *Flyy Girl*. New York, NY: Simon & Schuster, Inc.

Weinstein, B. (Producer), & Craven, W. (Director). (1999). *Music of the Heart* [Motion picture]. United States: Craven-Maddalena Films.

Westerfield, S. (2005). *Uglies*. New York, NY: Simon Pulse.

Westerfield, S. (2005). *Pretties*. New York, NY: Simon Pulse.

Westerfield, S. (2006). *Specials*. New York, NY: Simon Pulse.

X, Malcom, & Haley, A. (1987). *The Autobiography of Malcolm X: As told to Alex Haley*. New York, NY: Ballantine.

Zelinsky, P. O. (1996). *Rumpelstiltskin*. London, UK: Puffin Books.

Defying Gravity: Literacy Reform in Urban Schools

Taffy E. Raphael
University of Illinois at Chicago

For the past eight years, I've been working on a collaborative effort with key personnel within the Chicago Public Schools and faculty members from several Chicago-area universities. The project was supported by a grant from the Searle Funds of The Chicago Community Trust. The goal of the project, initially conceptualized by the late Becky Barr in conversations with Terry Mazany and Peggy Mueller from The Trust, was to build capacity in Chicago Public Schools for improving literacy teaching and learning, with a specific emphasis on low-performing schools (ARDDP, 2008). The close collaboration with district leaders was in response to what was seen as the failure of the Annenburg initiative—a multiyear and multimillion-dollar project—to sustain effective practices once the funding period ended.

Having just arrived in Chicago, I was tapped by our dean, Vicki Chou, to lead the University of Illinois at Chicago (UIC) portion of the new project. Not only had I no school contacts in the city, I'd never been involved in a project of this scope in my career as a literacy instructional researcher. Not surprisingly, I felt that I was in over my head. Many metaphors came to mind as I was preparing this Oscar S. Causey presentation: initially, drowning was at the top of my list! But, I kept gravitating (pardon the pun) to "defying gravity" as the most hopeful and, in fact, the one that best captured my feelings over the project's eight years.

I liked *the idea* that it conveyed, both literally and figuratively. Literally, human beings have been defying gravity for centuries, beginning in the 1780s with the first hot air balloon flight carrying a duck, a sheep, and a rooster, continuing into the turn of the last century with the first manned airplane flight, and ongoing today with routine air travel and maintaining a multi-national space station. Those who defied gravity in the literal sense had a vision of the future where the challenges holding us down were overcome. In Chicago, we defy gravity figuratively when we overcome challenges that hold us back from sustainable, high-quality literacy education for all students.

In 2001, when we began this work, my colleagues and I knew a lot about differences between more and less effective schools, but not much about turning around public, neighborhood, urban schools, working with the existing administration, faculty, and staff members. Over time, I saw that the things I knew and thought might be helpful from 30 years as a researcher studying literacy instruction—strategy instruction, QAR (Question Answer Relationship), Book Club, volunteer teacher networks like the Teachers Learning Collaborative—turned out not to be the things that have mattered most.

It's been a steep learning curve. It started when I learned what it meant to have a pilot project in Chicago schools—I imagined a pilot meant working closely for a year or two in one school, and if successful, scaling to another one or two. When I shared my plan with our dean, Vicki responded, "That's not the way it works in Chicago." I heard words to that effect repeated over the past eight years. In contrast to my version of a pilot study, my collaborators and I, from the beginning, have worked with at least 10 schools each year. All the schools serve students living in poverty, with over 95% eligible for free or reduced lunch. Each year our project has supported at least 10 principals,

12 literacy coaches, and 360 classroom teachers working with over 8000 students, primarily African American or Latino. What a contrast from where I started—researching the effects of my teaching small groups of randomly assigned fourth-, sixth-, and eighth-graders about QAR (Raphael & Pearson, 1985).

From research I've read about school reform, and based on our own extensive data collection, I stand convinced that if we work together, we *can* create new cultures for schooling and improve opportunities for literacy learning for urban students in high-poverty settings. However, *it takes a focused and sustained effort.* It *requires a team with members who cut across traditional work groups.* And, most of all, *it is fragile.* Gravity—or school failure—can be successfully overcome, at least for a time. But we must be mindful that our efforts can easily and all too quickly come crashing down.

I've organized this paper into four sections. First, I present some background about school reform in literacy. Second, I describe the reform approach, developed by Kathy Au (2005), that my colleagues and I adapted for our work in Chicago. Third, I describe how our work scaling Kathy's approach to Chicago was embedded in a longer history of school reform in the city, what Charles Payne and others (Payne, 2008; Simmons, 2006) have characterized as a play in three acts. Act IV began in fall 2009, marked by the hire of a new superintendent replacing Arne Duncan. The changes this new superintendent is enacting have helped crystallize lessons we've learned, the focus of the fourth section.

BACKGROUND FOR SCHOOL REFORM IN LITERACY

Considering just the contributions of members of our organization to understanding literacy teaching and learning, it is an understatement to assert that we know a great deal. Together, we have created a research-based body of knowledge for high-quality literacy instruction—what to teach, how to teach it, how to prepare teachers to teach it, how to support practicing teachers, and how to monitor our progress. But, despite all that we know, when we look at the results in terms of the achievement gap, it is frustrating. The knowledge we have generated, the programs we have produced, and the coursework we have provided have not closed the gap between our high- and low-achieving students. If history is any indication, this gap is tenacious, and from many indications, is not going away. Its tenacity can be traced to an array of factors.

A number of scholars—David Berliner (2006) and the late Gerald Bracey (2009) among them—point to poverty and all the factors associated with poverty that impact students' ability to learn, such as high stress, poor health and lack of health care, family relations, nutritional quality, exposure to pollutants, and the summer loss that is not seen in students who do not live in poverty. Bracey (2009) argued that simply saying that 'all children can learn' ignores the factors that challenge some children and not others. He pointed to the tendency in the public press to pit the "education establishment"—those of us who recognize that school reform is embedded in this larger context—against those labeled "reformers" by public commentators such as David Brooks in his *New York Times* column on May 7, 2009. "Reformers" view schools as *the* solution to societal improvement. Educators are characterized as part of the problem, when we are simply pointing out that education alone is unlikely to lead to sustainable improvements for all children.

Within this context, we also see solutions recommended that do not address the problems—within and beyond the school boundaries. For example, we've seen demands for rigorous content standards but without accompanying opportunity to learn content associated with the standards, including both allocation of resources and support for *meaningful* professional development. This misuse of standards has been a consistent problem and one unlikely to change based on the newest federal agendas. Glass (2008) points out that requiring rigorous standards can convey the appearance of doing something while not really allocating significant resources where it could make a difference—professional development, better schooling conditions, improving the lives of those living in poverty. How many times have we, in literacy education, seen the push to more rigorous standards and the implementation of new tests? They have not solved the problem in the past and I do not think they are the solution for the future.

A second problem stems from what Newmann, Bryk, and their colleagues (Newmann, Smith, Allenworth, & Bryk, 2001)—along with literacy educators such as Dick Allington (Allington & Walmsley, 1995)—describe as the fallacy of the 'quick fix.' This plays out in various ways in Chicago. For example, we've observed district administrators requiring schools to enact what they call 'quick wins:' implementing quickly what they suggest are 'easy' solutions. I've heard quick wins refer to everything from posting standards on the classroom walls to establishing a leadership team to enacting Writers Workshop to using QAR. Yet, we know there are no quick fixes—if there were, they would have been enacted already.

Further, those items identified as quick fixes—often programs brought in to solve specific problems from discipline to comprehension—end up leading to what Newmann and colleagues have termed Christmas tree schools. In Chicago, a Christmas tree school is one that has amassed many different programs, just like a family might collect many unique ornaments for their tree. Family members needn't worry if new ones fit in with the others. Some may even reflect very different perspectives on holiday decorations.

In a Christmas tree school, like ornaments, each program is separate and stands alone. Unfortunately, what may be great for the Christmas tree is not so good for the school. Newmann and his colleagues argue that instead, a curriculum must be coherent, with consistency within grade levels and progression in depth and complexity across grade levels, building each and every year toward a clear vision of excellent readers and writers. Such coherence is particularly critical for students living in poverty who depend on school for learning. The Chicago Consortium's research has shown curricular coherence is not common in Chicago schools.

In short, these problems drag us down, and solutions such as changing standards, bringing in a new test, specifying national standards, or adopting a new program don't do much to address the challenges.

OUR APPROACH: THE STANDARDS-BASED CHANGE PROCESS

Fortunately, my colleagues and I did not have to start from scratch. Kathy Au, my colleague and friend of many years, had developed an approach to whole-school reform that aligned with The Chicago Community Trust's vision (Au, 2005; Au, Raphael, & Mooney, 2008). Consistent with The Trust, Kathy had taken the approach of building schools' capacity to engage in reform, helping each school create its own set of solutions. The process she developed and tested in Hawaii—the Standards Based Change (or SBC) Process—was based on schools' developing their own coherent curriculum, strategically selecting resources and programs based on their students' needs (Au, 2005, 2010). The curriculum builds from year to year like a staircase, each step representing a grade level, with stairs that are steep enough to achieve the vision of the graduate, and with no gaps between stairs through which children might fall.

Instead of bringing in programs developed by outsiders to be followed with fidelity, Kathy's SBC approach uses a change process that could be adapted by insiders within the school to build on strengths and correct weaknesses. Through networks and on-site support, Kathy used a gradual release of responsibility model applied to the professional learning of the participating adults— teachers, administrators, and staff.

Kathy and I saw our collaboration as mutually beneficial, and my colleagues in Chicago (such as Susan Goldman) agreed. Scaling Kathy's approach to Chicago gave us a head start in laying out our scope of work, an obvious benefit. In turn, Kathy believed that Chicago would provide a rigorous test of the approach in a very different context, and the opportunity to extend the work in what we all hoped would be interesting ways. Our 8-year collaboration on school literacy reform spans the 10th and 3rd largest districts in the United States, with schools from the highest poverty settings to the most affluent, and using conventional to language immersion curricula. Our work builds on a long history of research on school reform in general and literacy in particular.

SCHOOL REFORM RESEARCH BASE

When I first started reading about school reform, I was reminded of Sheila Valencia and Karen Wixson's NRC 2001 review of research on policy and literacy—they found that the two areas barely intersected, with scholars in each publishing in almost totally different venues and participating in completely separate organizations. For school reform researchers, the *subject area* of the reform is almost incidental; in turn, literacy researchers certainly recognize that our work is nested within classrooms, grade-level teams, schools, and districts—the very focus of school reform researchers, but for us, the reform itself is not an emphasis—witness the lack of a chapter on school reform in literacy in any of the first three volumes of the *Handbook of Reading Research*.

As we moved deeper into the project, we read the literature on school reform extensively. Eventually Kathy and I teamed with Barbara Taylor to create the first chapter on this topic for the upcoming fourth volume of the *Handbook of Reading Research*. Barbara, Kathy, and I used three categories to distinguish the research literature on school reform. The earliest and probably most extensive body of research is that on *effective schools*, addressing the question, "What distinguishes effective from unsuccessful schools?" (e.g., Brookover & Lezotte, 1979; Edmonds, 1979; Purkey & Smith, 1983). The second category contains studies of *curriculum reform*. This research focuses on promoting coherence through the adoption or implementation of defined programs or organizational frameworks. Examples include Comprehensive School Reform programs like *Success for All* and *America's Choice* (e.g., Borman, Slavin, et al., 2007; CPRE, 2002). The third and most recent category emphasizes reform through professional development—how to move unsuccessful schools to become successful, effective sites for literacy teaching and learning (e.g., Au, 2005;

Lipson, Mosenthal, Mekkelsen, & Rush, 2004; Taylor, Pearson, Peterson, & Rodriguez, 2003, 2005).

Effective Schools Research

Effective schools research identifies features that distinguish successful from failing schools: (1) strong principal leadership, (2) high expectations for teachers and students, (3) teaching emphasis on cognitive development and warmth toward students, (4) teach choice in approaches, (5) teacher-developed tests and teacher judgment, and (6) students' self-efficacy, all brought about through policy, changes in teachers knowledge and practices, and changes in leadership approaches and school organization. But, while the features may be clear, this body of research was not designed to, and thus, could not demonstrate how these features could be developed in sites where they did not exist. Further, Purkey and Smith (1983, p. 439), in their review of effective schools research, noted that "it is one thing to demand that all schools be effective; it is an entirely different matter to assume . . . that what has positive effects in one setting will invariably have the same effects in another." In fact, in studies of the effect of Michigan's changing policies to improve literacy teaching and learning, Dutro, Wixson, and their colleagues (Dutro, Fix, Koch, Roop, & Wixson, 2002) demonstrated that enacting policies does not unequivocally, nor uniformly, change practice in desired directions.

Curriculum Driven Reform

The second section of our review, on curriculum-based reform, found that the Comprehensive School Reform initiatives had both strengths and weaknesses (CPRE, 2002). These programs do provide stability, are relatively easy to implement, and have built-in accountability. But, even when gains are demonstrated in student achievement levels, students who had been at low levels tend to remain below national norms. Further, sustainability is a problem—even initially strong implementation tends to deteriorate over time, which Linda Darling-Hammond (2003) hypothesizes may be due to lack of teacher ownership. The programs lack flexibility, and this reduces the ability of the program to adapt to particular needs of schools, teachers, and students.

Professional Development-Driven Reform

The effective schools and curriculum reform research gave us the pieces of the puzzle, but it was in this third category, reform based in professional development, that researchers focused on determining how these various pieces come together. Research in this area includes those studies conducted by Jim Mosenthal and Marge Lipson's (Lipson, et al., 2004; Mosenthal, Lipson, Mekkelsen, & Thompson, 2003; Mosenthal, Lipson, Torncello, et al., 2004) studies in Vermont, Barbara Taylor and David Pearson's within the Beat the Odds studies of the Center for the Improvement of Early Reading Achievement (Taylor, et al., 2003, 2005), Kathy Au's work in Hawaii (Au, 2005, 2010), Doug Fisher and Nancy Frey's in San Diego (Fisher & Frey, 2007), and Stuart McNaughton (Lai, McNaughton, Amituanai-Toloa, et al., 2009; McNaughton, MacDonald, Amituanai-Toloa, et al., 2006), and Helen Timperly and Judy Parr's in New Zealand (Timperly & Parr, 2007). All of these projects focused on how to move unsuccessful schools to become successful, effective sites for literacy teaching and learning, and all focused primarily on professional development.

These literacy researchers confirmed and extended existing research unpacking challenges faced by schools attempting reform—problems Payne (2008) outlines so powerfully in his book, *So Much Reform; So Little Change.* Across these studies, researchers asked:

1. How can you scale what worked in one setting to others, whether very similar or significantly different? and

2. How can you move a school that does not have the characteristics of effective schools to develop what it needs to become successful?

The data from studies that have attempted to address these questions suggest the importance of six features. First, external partners provided some of the professional development on effective literacy curriculum and instruction. Second, schools developed school-based learning communities. Third, within this community, professional learning was ongoing, deliberate, and well planned. Fourth, there was an emphasis on reflection on practice to inform instructional change. Fifth, professional learning was tailored to schools' unique needs, and sixth, there was an emphasis on ongoing learning for literacy leaders.

SCHOOL REFORM IN CHICAGO

Chicago, one of the most researched districts in the nation, has engaged in reform since 1987. I begin with some demographics to give you a feel of the city's school district, and then describe the acts that frame the reform focus (Payne, 2008; Simmons, 2006) and influence what happens today.

In terms of demographics—the sheer scale of the school district is mind-boggling when I think about the level of support needed for effective reform. It *is* the third largest district in the country with 482 elementary schools and 122 high schools. In Chicago, elementary is defined as pre-K through eighth grades. Elementary schools enroll nearly 242,000 students, 45% of whom are African American, 41% Latino, with the remaining 12% White, Asian/Pacific Islander or Native American. Eighty-five percent of the students are from low-income families. The district employs over 23,000 teachers—one-third of whom are African American, almost half White, and 15% Latino. For the 2009-2010 school year, its budget exceeded 4 billion dollars (Chicago Public Schools, 2009).

Reform in Three Acts

As described in accounts of school reform in Chicago (e.g., Payne, 2008; Simmons, 20006), Act I of Chicago's school reform—the 1980s through 1994—was the era of *decentralization.* The era established 12-member Local School Councils: 6 parents, 2 community members, 2 teachers, the principal, and a student. The Local School Council legacy remains today. This first Act raised the need for school accountability; however, only about a third of the schools benefited from increased local control. Many of those that did not were in low-income areas with parents and community members lacking the skill set needed to make informed decisions about school practices, position hires, and so forth.

Act II, orchestrated by the 1995 mayoral appointee, Superintendent Paul Vallas, (now head of the New Orleans schools), was known as the era of accountability. Vallas' accountability reform left a legacy, which includes high-stakes testing and threats of school closure if students are consistently low performing.

Act III began in 2001, led by Barbara Eason-Watkins following Arne Duncan's appointment as superintendent. This act focused on curriculum and instructional support within the district, "the synthesis—leadership that comes in talking the language of human-capital development and instruction and organizational transparency" (Payne, 2008, p. 13). This is where most of our project was situated between 2002 and 2009.

Act IV: The Current Context

Act IV began in spring 2009, led by Ron Huberman—a former policeman, then the Chicago mayor's Chief of Staff, and most recently, head of the Chicago Transit Authority—who is now our superintendent. His approach is grounded in Performance Management Review, using hard evidence of student achievement from our state's achievement test, the ISAT. Unfortunately, like many of the state tests, the ISAT overestimates students' achievement levels when compared to the national assessment (NAEP, 2009). As Valencia (personal communication, e-mail November 2009) has noted, "depending on a single measure … is problematic, and there is good reason to worry about relying on only a high-stakes state test, especially one that reports significantly more kids at proficient level that does the NAEP." Our project is completing its final academic year (2009-2010), as Huberman does not believe The Chicago Community Trust-sponsored effort and district collaboration with area university literacy faculty align with district needs. So, perhaps we should not be surprised at what Payne (2008, p. 4) has had to say about school reform. "After a couple of decades of being energetically reformed, most schools, especially the bottom-tier schools, and most school systems seem to be pretty much the same kind of organizations they were at the beginning."

As I mentioned earlier, during Act III we began our work with the first 10 participating Chicago schools. Since we believe that higher expectations are necessary, but not sufficient, our reform effort focuses on addressing those factors that facilitate and those that can impede what it takes to meet higher expectations.

ENACTING THE STANDARDS-BASED CHANGE PROCESS IN CHICAGO

Our approach consists of: (1) the Standards-Based Change Process for guiding schools in their reform effort, (2) a set of dimensions that schools must address, and (3) progress levels that can be used to identify components of the process to focus on in a given academic year.

The Process

Conceptually, the process is simple and straightforward. All members of the school's professional community—administrators, teachers, and other staff—collaborate to construct a vision of their excellent graduating reader or writer—this vision is the top of the staircase. With the overall goal in place, each grade level or school subject team constructs its end-of-year goals or benchmarks, in effect its step on the staircase to the vision of the graduate. The benchmarks capture each group's responsible contribution to student progress. The teams then develop common assessments to form a monitoring system for tracking students' progress and informing instructional decisions throughout the year. Progress and instructional decisions are shared with the whole school at the beginning, the middle, and end of the school year to inform school-wide planning, identify issues, and examine progress (Au, et al., 2008).

Figure 1. Standards-Based Change Process "To Do Cycle"

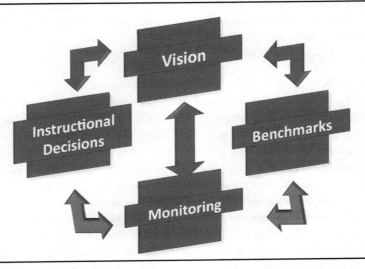

The Dimensions

To do this work effectively, schools focus on the core dimensions critical to sustainable change (Raphael, et al., 2009). Figure 2 conveys the relationship among the essential areas of infrastructure, classroom practices, and student outcomes.

First, schools construct an infrastructure that includes attending to the way the school is organized for collaborative work, the administrative and curriculum leadership to support the work, the professional learning community and relevant work teams, and the quality and coherence of

Figure 2. Dimensions for Successful School Change

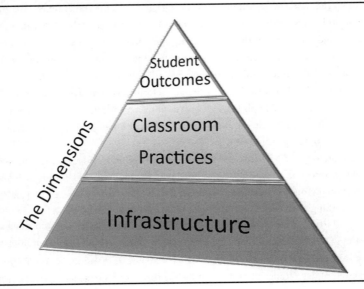

in-school professional development. With this foundation in place they can focus on the form, quality, and coherence of their classroom practices—assessment, instruction, and curriculum resources—for improving literacy teaching and learning. Student outcomes focus on both student engagement and achievement.

The Seven-Level Model

Documentation across schools in both Hawaii and Chicago helped us refine Kathy's original model of school progress. Kathy, Susan Goldman, and I described the seven-level Developmental Model of school change in our chapter in Jim Hoffman & Yetta Goodman's edited book published by Routledge (Raphael, Au, & Goldman, 2009). In the chapter, we describe the three phases of research that led to its construction.

The first phase began with Kathy's research in schools in Hawaii (Au, 2005) that detailed four levels that capture schools' progress beginning with their work through the To Do Cycle conveyed in Figure 1. The second phase began when we scaled the Standards-Based Change (SBC) Process to Chicago. Over a period of 3 years, we observed, interviewed participants, videotaped, and gathered artifacts of our school's attempts to engage in the SBC Process. Together with colleagues from the other Chicago-area university projects (ARDDP, 2005), we identified a set of indicators that conveyed what schools needed to put into place (i.e., the infrastructure) before they could begin to sustain the reform activities required for creating a coherent literacy curriculum (i.e., the To Do Cycle). As a result of what we learned from the second phase of research, we expanded the original SBC Process developmental model (Au, 2005) to its current seven-level version.

In the third phase of our research, we worked with principals, literacy coaches, and teachers in Hawaii and Chicago to test and establish the construct validity of the model. The seven levels frame what the staff members work on to create and use what Kathy termed the school's Staircase Literacy Curriculum. The levels are: (a) recognizing the need for change, (b) organizing for change, (c) working on the building blocks, (d) pulling the whole school together, (e) sharing results, implementing the staircase curriculum, and (f) engaging students and families (Au, 2010). Schools with few or no leaders and/or staff who see any need for change or those that do not believe that curricular change is possible in their schools (e.g., too many discipline problems to consider work on curriculum, despair that their school may be closed no matter what they do) are not placed on the developmental continuum and thus appear as a "0" in school ratings. Data from initial needs assessments from 27 schools working on literacy reform revealed that urban schools like ours in Chicago tend to start 1 to 2 levels below those in suburban and small-town settings on their overall ratings (scale from 0–7) across the dimensions (Urban Schools [n=12]: 1.58; Rural [n=2]: 2.00; Suburban/Small Town [n=13]: 2.75).

For a more detailed window into the developmental model, I describe four of the levels in terms of what educators say and do, and how our staff supports them within each level. *Emerging Schools* are working on Levels 1 and 2; *Aspiring Schools* are working on Levels 3 and 4; *Progressing Schools* are working on Levels 5 and 6; *Inspiring Schools* are working at Level 7.

Emerging schools. Educators in Level 1 schools make comments such as, "What we are doing isn't working," "I don't know what to do," and even, "This will be too much work." They work mostly on infrastructure: a first-time literacy coach who is learning about her position and how to be effective; establishing a leadership team that for the first time has teacher representatives on it. And critically important, the principal is often learning what it means to lead in a more constructivist way, take a more active role as an instructional leader, and learn new ways of engaging with his or her staff.

Overall, these educators are working to establish a new culture in the school emphasizing teacher voice, ownership, and responsibility for instructional decisions. They are overcoming less productive approaches, such as requiring teachers to faithfully follow the many programs adopted for the school. Blaming the students if they didn't succeed, with little to no reflection about using evidence to guide needed adjustments in their own classroom practices. Our support for these schools focused on guiding infrastructure development and helping the participants learn how to be effective in new roles.

Aspiring schools. Educators in schools at the Aspiring levels tend to ask questions about improving their infrastructure and working as a whole school community, such as, "How do we make the leadership team more effective" and "Does our vision of the graduating reader represent the highest levels of achievement?" They are starting to use their infrastructure to develop their components of the SBC Process, from vision of the graduate through the monitoring system. Adjacent grade levels are particularly focused on alignment between the end-of-year expectations at one grade level and the beginning of the year expectations at the next. Our professional development support focuses on knowledge building about the SBC Process, about literacy, and about leadership strategies.

Progressing schools. Comments from educators in schools at Progressing levels focus on the need for more time, examples, and specific strategies as they work to make their benchmarks and monitoring system components more rigorous. They are using their infrastructure and systems to monitor students' progress and use this information to adjust classroom practices. Grade level and disciplinary subject teams are active within their groups and across the whole-school sharing sessions. They focus on both within grade level team and vertical curriculum alignment. Professional development support at these levels focuses on rigor for benchmark alignment, monitoring system components, and instructional decision-making based on student data. At Level 6, teacher ownership of the curriculum is established and stable.

Inspiring schools. In Chicago, no school has yet reached Level 7, although schools from suburbs and small towns in Hawaii have. Comments from educators in these schools reflect their sense of independence and control (e.g., "We manage to balance our own goals and district mandates.") and their satisfaction with their work environment (e.g., "I love my job! We are a great faculty."). Educators focus on reflection and revision, and involving parents in their children's learning. While these efforts begin earlier in the process, they are formalized at Level 7 through student portfolios, students leading parent conferences, and so forth. Support for Level 7 schools emphasizes student portfolios and helping bring teachers new to the school up to speed.

SCALING THE STANDARDS-BASED CHANGE PROCESS TO CHICAGO

As should now be clear, it takes a team working together to bring these changes about. From UIC, core team members included Kate Weber, MariAnne George, Susan Goldman, Erin Koning, Jackie Popp, Mary Pat Sullivan, Shelby Cosner, and Kay Fujiyoshi. Also on the core team was Susan

McMahon from National Louis University. Over three dozen other educators have contributed to the work. Staff has changed as graduate students completed their degrees and moved into academic positions or moved onto different projects, while various representatives from CPS have worked with us as interns or liaisons from the district curriculum and school services offices.

Though we were funded primarily as a service project, we had a small amount of support for documentation, justified because it provided critical information to inform next steps and improve our service to the schools. In any given year 10–14 of us engaged in service and documentation activities.

We used Kathy's SBC Process approach (Au, 2005) because of its potential to address problems related to instructional practices in Chicago. Researchers from the Consortium on Chicago School Research, formerly headed by Tony Bryk (now at Carnegie), had found that too frequently the same topics were being taught year after year, without appropriate development in content, depth, or complexity. Instructional tasks focused primarily on review and repetition, rather than reasoning, thinking, or problem solving. And, faculty members neither shared in the overall conception of their schools' instructional program, nor had a clear sense of their own responsibilities for students' progress. Three foci of the SBC Process directly address these issues: development of a coherent, shared, school-wide vision of the graduating student; vertical alignment of the curriculum; and the use of evidence of student progress in instructional planning and decision making.

Thus, knowledge building was key to our capacity-building charge. We worked in two primary sites. First, we organized monthly network meetings for participants in key roles: principals, literacy coaches, and teacher leaders. These meetings focused on developing knowledge of the SBC Process, of literacy, and of leadership. Second, we worked on-site in each school, collaborating with literacy coaches, supporting the leadership team and grade-level meetings, and providing or co-leading professional development sessions on restructured and professional development days.

When we began working with our schools, we found fairly consistent patterns of: (1) low student performance on standardized tests, (2) school infrastructures that reflected a top-down system emphasizing delivery of district mandates, (3) professional development comprised of one-shot workshops, (4) infrequent grade-level team meetings or none at all, and (5) non-functioning or non-existent leadership teams. Many of these schools had not been particularly interested in the reform aspect of the work, but joined the project for some of the resources it provided to their schools (e.g., a half-time literacy coach). However, in the latter four years of the project, as schools discontinued and new schools joined the project, we have seen a specific desire on a key school leaders' part to work with the SBC Process to improve their students' literacy achievement.

Over eight years, we have worked with 30 schools, continuing to average about 10 a year; with variation in how long any one school participated, from 1 to 8 years. Figure 3 provides a snapshot of schools per year, looking vertically. Looking horizontally lays out the length of time with each individual school. The number in each cell indicates school's level on the SBC Process Developmental Model for that year, with a few schools joining the project but without engaging in the reform activities indicated with a '0.' All school names are pseudonyms.

Our project has had three funding cycles, each with a slightly different goal. The first two years—the lightest shading on the chart—focused primarily on adaptations of Kathy's approach for urban schools; learning for example, about our schools' need to begin with a strong and comprehensive focus on infrastructure. The second cycle—the middle years on the chart—involved elaborating on how to best guide schools through the SBC activities within the relevant levels. In the third cycle, the district's Area structure became very relevant. Each Area, headed at the time by

Figure 3. Chart of School Participation

School	2002-03	2003-04	2004-05	2005-06	2006-07	2007-08	2008-09	2009-10
Saylor			2	3	4	4	5	5
Denver				1	2	4	4.67	5.33
Chambers				1	1.67	2	4	5
Somerset	1	2	2	3	4	4	2.67	2.67
Landon	2	3	4	4.67	4.67			
Weldon	1	1.67	2	2	0			
Reid			1	1.67	2	2.67	2.67	
Sheffield				2	2	2	2	
Barnes	0	1	1.33					
Damon	0	0	0					
Parsons	0	1	3					
Renalde	1	2	2					
Temple	0	0	0					
Williams	1	1	1					
Nexus	1	2				2		
Newman				1	1			
Piper				0				
Sears				0				
Danbury						2	2	3.33
Britt						1	1	2.67
Mulberry						1.67	2.67	3.33
Melville						2	2.33	2.67
Hartley						1	2	3.33
McMac						2	2	
Farmer						1	2	3.33
Tarrington						0	0	
Helms						0	0	
Pine							2	3
Avery							2	3
Jeffrey							2	2

Figure 4. Data Streams

Interviews	Classroom Visits	Professional Development Events	School Updates
22 Literacy Coordinator: Interviews (n = 76)	Classroom observations (n = 60)	Whole School Data Sharing (i.e., "Gallery Walks") 3 times per year (n = 90)	Initial Analysis of School (i.e., Needs Assessments) (n = 10) Annual School Reports, 2006 – 2007) (n = 20)
292 Teachers: Interviews (n = 72) Surveys (n = 248)	Partnership READ Environmental Snapshot: 2 times / year 2004 – 2008; all schools, all classrooms (n = 2000)		Network Monthly Seminars: (1) principals, (2) literacy coaches, (3) "Fellows" (i.e., selected teachers): 8 each per year X 5 years (principals, teachers) and 7 years (literacy coaches)
19 Principals: Interviews (n = 66)			Monthly updates for each school during staff and documentation meetings.

the Area Instructional Officer, consists of about 30 schools. Schools receive support from Area staff like the Reading and the Math Coaches. In this cycle of work, we were asked to scale up within the Area, working with Area staff in anticipation of turning the initiative over to the district as the Trust scaled back on their support.

We used four primary data streams, and as Figure 4 suggests, our biggest challenge has been data reduction with 8 years of data within and across these different streams.

We analyzed data using primarily qualitative methods, with quantitative used as appropriate. Qualitative methods applied follow conventions of constant comparative methods; within, then across data streams depending on the question addressed (Glaser & Strauss, 1967; Strauss & Corbin, 1994). Overall, we created an audit trail of data analyses conducted by small teams (2-4 people) from the project staff (Creswell, 1998; Merriam, 1998). Each team constructed thick descriptions laying out the overall themes identified within their data stream. Each team engaged in multiple passes through their data set to: (a) compare/define emerging categories within data streams, (b) analyze the degree of support, and (c) identify non-examples. Teams then met for cross-team data analyses to: (a) compare/contrast categories across streams, (b) define school progress levels across time, and (c) examine role enactment across time within and across roles.

We used quantitative lenses to examine trends and patterns in data sets such as a teacher survey, and the ISAT data. For teacher survey data, we used frequency counts and simple t-tests where appropriate; while for all students for whom we had permission, we examined trends in achievement. For students, we focused on trend data within schools across years, using students' scores on the ISAT, because in Chicago that remains the gold standard. We first examined patterns of students' achievement for each school participating during 2008-2009, tracking the percentage of students over four years who met or exceeded expectations for their grade level. This analysis included students who may or may not have been present during the four years, however, as it used publicly available group data from the state Web site, rather than individual student data from each school. While the trends were generally positive—the longer the school worked with the SBC Process, the more improvement was visible in their ISAT schools, we were curious as to whether the trend would be reduced or magnified if we controlled for the students' actual presence during the time the school engaged with the SBC Process, since mobility rates for students were rather high. In a single year, student turnover in participating schools ranged from 11.1% to almost 24%; over four years mobility rates within a single cohort of students ranged from 25% to 36%.

Because of limited resources, we could not obtain the individual student data for all schools, so selected two that represented the demographics of schools in the larger pool for further examination. For these two schools (Saylor, Denver), we identified students who were present during the period of time that the SBC Process was used in the school. Those students in grades 3 through 5 for the first year of the school's engagement with the SBC Process formed the cohort that was then tracked using their ISAT scores each year for a total of four years, at the end of which the cohort of students were in middle school, grades 6 through 8.

What We Learned

As I've noted above, we derived three key findings from the data: it can be done, it takes a team, but it's fragile. I will discuss each, in turn.

It can be done: school progress. Analysis of our data streams indicates that literacy reform efforts in urban schools can help schools move from lower to higher levels of success looking at school progress and at student achievement levels. To examine school progress, we tracked individual schools on their movement through the SBC Process 7-Level Developmental Model. To examine students' achievement, we used the percentage of students meeting or exceeding grade level expectations based on ISAT scores.

Despite all the challenges that faced our schools, about one-third of our schools experienced steady growth across years reflected in their rise in levels on the developmental model for the SBC Process (see Figure 5).

Figure 5. School Progress: Continuing Schools

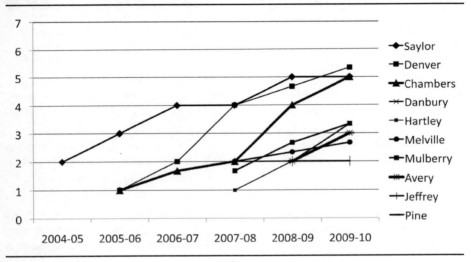

Note that for individual schools, specific patterns of growth across the levels varied. Some schools show steady progress each year, moving through the development of their infrastructure to working through the To Do Cycle, to sharing their results and analyzing student evidence for trends and patterns within and across grade levels. No Chicago schools have yet to begin Level 6 work, constructing their grade level's curriculum guides and developing a system for mentoring new teachers though several are on track to do so in the coming year.

However, steady progress was not characteristic for two-thirds of the schools that discontinued their activities within the project after a few months to a few years of efforts.

We have identified four primary causes for school attrition, visible in varying combinations within each school. First, there are failures in school leadership (e.g., a principal who defined his job as bringing the most possible programs to his school; a literacy coach who told us, with pride, that she would be hard to work with; literacy coaches who described having no support within their schools). Some schools are rated at the 0 level, as they actually never really began to participate in any way other than superficially (e.g., assigning someone in the school to attend network seminar meetings, accepting the funds for a literacy coach but assigning them to duties outside the realm of

Figure 6. School Progress: Schools that Discontinued

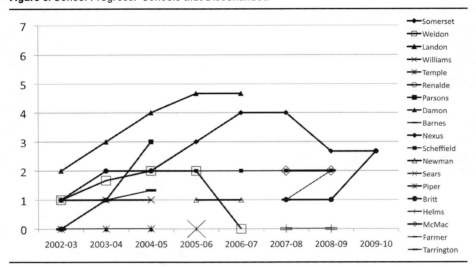

literacy work, such as substituting for absent teachers or lunchroom duties). Others show a flat line at lower levels on the developmental model (e.g., multiple years at Level 1).

Second, there are the ever-present competing mandates (e.g., schools that want to continue but find themselves at odds with their Area leaders; schools who want to continue but in the end, decide to follow the dictates of an adopted basal reading program or a required set of district- or area-mandated assessments). Such schools show patterns of growth followed by decline in level of progress. Third, over the course of the eight years, our project has had shifting priorities impacting funding for individual schools. For example, some schools were making progress but lost funding for key personnel to lead the initiative in the Area Scale Up year, since they were located in Areas no longer within the UIC project's boundaries. Their progress lines look similar to those who ended because of shifting mandates described above.

Fourth, some schools were simply dysfunctional, with such fundamental problems that they were unable to see their way to focusing on curriculum (e.g., severe discipline problems, likelihood of school closure, extensive distrust among the staff). These schools had patterns that typically showed initial growth as an infrastructure was created, but little to no progress thereafter as the infrastructure was not able to be used to support collaborative work groups and existed primarily on paper.

It can be done: student progress. I turn now to student achievement and our cohort analysis, drawing on findings from two of our schools, Saylor and Denver, represented by the first two lines in Figure 5. The bar graphs on Figures 7 and 8 represent the achievement gains of a cohort of students from each school—both PreK through 8th grades—over the four most recent years of their work with us. Saylor is one of the largest elementary schools in Illinois, with just under 2000 students. Denver is one of the smallest ones. The two schools represent the demographic populations of the district. Within each school's graph, each bar represents the same students as they move through from intermediate grades to middle school.

Figure 7 shows the progress of Saylor School's students across four years, beginning when students were in intermediate grades, 3 through 5. Prior to working with us (not pictured on the graph), less than half (46.5%) of Saylor's students were meeting or exceeding expectations.

Figure 7. Cohort Analysis: Saylor

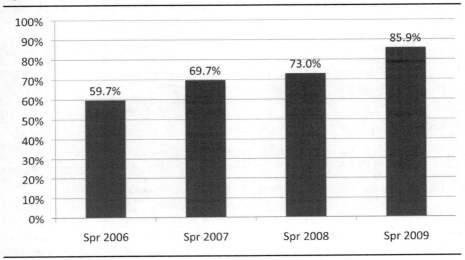

By Spring 2006, they had already experienced one bump up, with almost 60% of the intermediate grade cohort meeting or exceeding expectations. Four years later, in Spring 2009, almost 86% of the students in this same group, now in middle school, grades 6 through 8, were meeting or exceeding expectations. A similar pattern is seen in Denver's cohort analysis, a pattern that Kathy also saw in her work in Hawaii as reported in her 2005 *Journal of Literacy Research* article.

Figure 8. Cohort Analysis: Denver

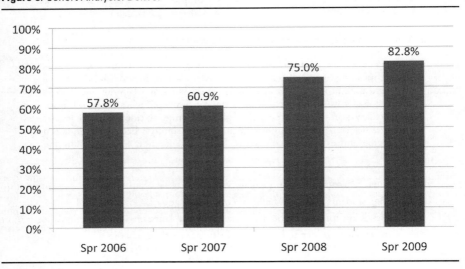

It takes a team. The second major area of findings relates to the critical importance of the team—within the school, and between the school and the external partner—us. Quotes from interviews and comments made in reflective journals reflect differences in the nature of the collaborative environment in the emerging and progressing schools. Teachers in emerging schools, for example, saw grade-level teams as wasted time and felt they lacked voice in school policies and decisions. The following entry into one teachers' reflective journal was typical,

> "Teachers in my grade level team do not feel that we have a voice in what the meetings should be about. We are not asked what we would like in the agenda and our meetings are led by either the principal or reading coach. Due to this, we as teachers dread to be in the meetings and have a negative attitude when we have our grade level meetings." (Fellow Reflective Journal, 11/5/08)

AND

> "I have been in countless grade level meetings when I have felt like there has been a large amount of wasted time. Instead of discussing ideas related to instruction and curriculum, much time is focused on less important topics like where should we hold the eighth grade luncheon?" (Fellow Reflective Journal, 11/5/08)

Literacy coaches note a lack of coherence in the work, consistent with findings from the Chicago Consortium researchers. They saw a need to come together, but efforts to do so had not yet come to fruition. This is reflected in a principal's description of "a significant divide in teachers" (Interview, 9/08).

In contrast, comments made by educators in progressing schools reflect the functioning infrastructure and progress toward teacher and student ownership and responsibility for high-quality literacy teaching and learning. For example, a teacher from Saylor noted that:

> "Teamwork is key at Saylor. Since our staff is so large, meeting with our grade level teams help us to give everyone a chance to have their voice heard. It also allows us to communicate our ideas and reflect on our instruction and assessment. This teamwork allows teachers to take ownership of their ideas, count on one another, as well as to achieve goals." (Fellow Reflective Journal, 11/5/08)

And from Denver, a teacher wrote in his reflective journal,

> "Through our weekly grade cluster meetings, we are able to co-construct agendas that are meaningful and directed to our needs as a learning community. There are a handful of people anyone can turn to in the building when they are in need of additional help or support. They include fellow colleagues, administrators, and ancillary staff. No one person is given the role or title of leader at our school; rather it invokes an ethos of shared responsibility where professionalism is respected and expertise is invited to be shared." (Fellow Reflective Journal, 11/5/08)

Similarly, literacy coaches and principals value the collaborative professional community focused on insuring students achieve at high levels (Weber, Raphael, Goldman, Sullivan, & George, 2010). And while all are concerned about the state test, the language in these schools focuses on their vision of the excellent reader and writer graduating from their school.

Success is fragile. And, like successfully defying gravity, we know that success is fragile. In this article, I hope to have underscored the extensive collaboration among schools and between schools and the university partners. Given limitations of time and space, I didn't even touch on the collaboration among the partner universities (e.g., National Louis University, Roosevelt University), The Chicago Community Trust project officers, and the Area- and District-level personnel. Throughout our project, the emphasis has been on ownership at every level—from the Trust's mandate that our projects all focus on capacity building, not dependence; to our work with schools engaging parents, students, and the community. Our approach emphasizes schools' responsibility and power to devise solutions to their problems, scaffolding educators at different levels as they engage the whole staff in this effort. We emphasize rigor in working toward goals of high levels of literacy, including attention to the allocation of resources to support the unique needs of each school and the individuals within.

Summer 2009 marked the end of Act III and its emphasis on curriculum and instruction at the district level. It marked the end of a collaborative relationship that valued district-university partnerships toward improving literacy teaching and learning in the district. It has been replaced by a return to decentralization—this time at the Area level. The emphasis is on accountability through performance management review from the district to Area to individual schools. The district's curriculum offices have been largely dismantled. The Area Instruction Officer position no longer exists. It became the Chief Area Officer—the removal of Instruction from the title quite deliberate.

We are no longer collecting data from our schools or the Area, so I turn now to simply sharing my own personal experiences. Admittedly, in the midst of change it is difficult to bring a neutral, analytic eye to interpret what I am seeing. Thus, I would be the first to say it is too early to tell the impact these changes and resulting approaches may have. I share with you three different approaches I have observed in conversations with Chief Area Officers and school personnel.

One Area is beginning what the Chief Area Officer (CAO) sees as the start a 10-year plan that emphasizes attention from birth through high school. The Officer is explicit in emphasizing the importance of and support for high-quality teaching, the involvement of local community organizations, and building a technology infrastructure. Throughout the document, we find an emphasis on the construct of developing talent, resonating with The Trust's and our commitment to building capacity. This CAO is using what is called within the district a "vendor approach" where each school may select from a pool of identified service providers to support their efforts to improve.

A second Chief Area Officer is drawing on the logic of building a *team theory of action*. The Area team—consisting of the Chief and staff members such as the Area math and literacy coaches— has visited every school within their Area, gathering information to inform the Area action plan. The plan addresses three components. The first is improving each school's core instructional program. The Area's action plan promotes instruction based in standards, a foundational set of instructional strategies (e.g., scaffolded instruction, models of differentiation), and attention to instructional time and materials. The second is improving the school's system for professional development, which includes helping school leaders establish their own theories of action for their schools and developing related plans for improvement. The third component is improving school environments from better access to technology to a consistent approach to behavior issues. If designed appropriately, the Area Officer believes these action plans will result in much-needed gains in literacy, language acquisition, and learning of school subjects such as science.

In a third Area, following visits to each of the Area schools, the Chief Area Officer distributed a checklist of expectations to all principals, including items such as posting class schedule and standards addressed; lesson plans opened to current lesson; guided reading, shared reading, active word walls, writing journals, workshop approach: folders or notebooks, workshop approach: teacher-made charts; some prompt writing. The principals, in turn, have shared the checklist with their staff, with the explanation that items on the checklist must be in place by March 1. In some cases, principals were told that if these items are not in place, the principal will be fired and the school will move into what is called 'turnaround.' This means that the school can be taken over by the Area, the principal and staff replaced, and new approaches enacted, ranging from changes to programs to redistricting. One principal has been removed as warned.

The opposite of the Standards-Based Change Process—as well as the approaches enacted in the first two Areas I described—is to treat all schools the same, present goals and standards without looking at support needed to achieve them, and use a transmission model for delivery without interpretation, construction, or adaptation of the process. This is what the research literature suggests we have been defying in large urban districts…this is not unusual—it's how it has always been. But when we see signs of this returning in *our* district and in some of the Areas we have worked with over the years, we see the fragility of school reform.

CONCLUSION

What do I take away from this experience as a literacy researcher primarily focused on instruction? First, I believe sustainable school reform requires working with a unit that is neither too small nor too large, but just right. For sustainable reform—reform that is desperately needed in many urban schools serving children who depend on them totally for their education, my thinking has changed—I now believe that the classroom or the teacher unit is just too small. For years I believed in 'going with the goers'—insuring that students at least get some great years of the best education possible. This is not enough. The district, however—especially when it's as huge as Chicago—is just too large. The right unit to me is the school, ideally with support from its next unit up—the Area in Chicago, perhaps the district in a smaller geographic region. We've seen it can be done, and it can be sustained across years.

Second, I believe it takes a team that involves members both internal and external to the school, working closely together; we saw benefits from working directly with a combination of administrators, curriculum leaders, and teachers. We understand and appreciate the unique role that each group plays, and their unique contributions.

Third, I see the fragility—how quickly a reform effort can simply go away. I remain optimistic for some of our schools—especially those in the first two Areas I described. My observations of schools in the third is that they are currently backtracking—driven by top-down, externally mandated foci and a focus on maintaining their employment or finding another job, rather than continuing their work to improve the school's literacy curriculum.

In closing, decades of instructional research have given us a vision of wonderful classrooms—children who can think creatively, respect one other, and so forth. Making these classrooms a reality, especially for children in high-poverty urban schools, won't happen by instructional researchers alone. We have to think more strategically about partnerships, ownership, reaching out to policy-makers, and programs that educate administrators. And while this is challenging, to say the least, it can be done.

REFERENCES

Allington, R. L., & Walmsley, S. A. (1995). *No quick fix.* New York, NY: Teachers College Press.

ARDDP. (2008). Partnerships for improving literacy in urban schools: Advanced Reading Development Demonstration Project. *The Reading Teacher, 61*(8), 674-680.

Au, K. A. (2005). Negotiating the slippery slope: School change and literacy achievement. *Journal of Literacy Research, 37*(3), 267-288.

Au, K. (2010). Real schools, real success: A roadmap for change. *Reading Forum New Zealand, 25*(1), 25-35.

Au, K. H., Raphael, T. E., & Mooney, K. (2008). Improving reading achievement in elementary schools: Guiding change in a time of standards. In S. B. Wepner & D. S. Strickland (Eds.), *Supervision of reading programs* (4th ed., pp. 71-89). New York, NY: Teachers College Press.

Berliner, D. C. (2006). Our impoverished view of educational research. *Teachers College Record, 108*(6), 949-995.

Borman, G., Slavin, R., Cheung, A., Chamberlain, A., Madden, N., & Chambers, B. (2007). Final reading outcomes of the national randomized field trial of Success for All. *American Educational Research Journal, 44*(3), 701-731.

Bracey, G. (2009). *The Bracey Report on the Condition of Public Education.* Boulder and Tempe: Education and the Public Interest Center & Education Policy Research Unit. Retrieved 11/17/09 from http://epicpolicy.org/publication/Bracey-Report

Brookover, W. B., & Lezotte, L. W. (1979). *Changes in school characteristics coincident with changes in student achievement* (No. ERIC Document Reproduction Service No. ED 181005). East Lansing: Institute for Research on Teaching, Michigan State University.

Brooks, D. (2009, May 7, 2009). The Harlem miracle. *New York Times,* p. 31. Retrieved 11/17/09 from http://www.nytimes.com/2009/05/08/opinion/08brooks.html

Chicago Public Schools (2009). Webpage: *At-A-Glance,* retrieved 11/18/09 from http://www.cps.edu/About_CPS/At-a-glance/Pages/Stats_and_facts.aspx.

Consortium for Policy Research in Education (2002). *America's Choice school design: A research-based model.* Washington DC: National Center on Education and the Economy.

Creswell, J. W. (1998). *Qualitative inquiry and research design: Choosing among five traditions.* Thousand Oaks, CA: Sage.

Darling-Hammond, L. (February 16, 2003). Standards and assessments: Where we are and what we need. Retrieved 11/27 3:11:41 PM, from http://www.tcrecord.org ID 11109

Dutro, E., Fisk, M. C., Koch, R., Roop, L. J., & Wixson, K. (2002). When state policies meet local district contexts: Standards-based professional development as a means to individual agency and collective ownership. *Teachers College Record, 104*(4), 787-811.

Edmonds, R. (1979). Effective schools for the urban poor. *Educational Leadership, 37*(1), 15-24.

Fisher, D., & Frey, N. (2007). Implementing a school wide literacy framework: Improving achievement in an urban elementary school. *The Reading Teacher, 61*(1), 32-43.

Glaser, B., & Strauss, A. (1967). *The discovery of grounded theory: Strategies for qualitative research.* Chicago, IL: Aldine.

Glass, G. (2008). *Fertilizers, pills, and magnetic strips: The fate of public education in America.* Charlotte, NC: Information Age Publishing.

Lai, M., McNaughton, S., Amituanai-Toloa, M., Turner, R., & Hsiao, S. (2009) Sustained acceleration of achievement in reading comprehension: The New Zealand Experience. *Reading Research Quarterly, 44*(1), 30–56.

Lipson, M. L., Mosenthal, J. H., Mekkelsen, J., & Russ, B. (2004). Building knowledege and fashioning success one school at a time. *The Reading Teacher, 57*(6), 534-542.

McNaughton, S., MacDonald, S., Amituanai-Toloa, M., Lai, M., MacDonald, S., & Farry, S. (2006). *Enhnaced teaching and learning of comprehension in Year 4-9: Mangere Schools.* Auckland, New Zealand: Uniservices Ltd.

Merriam, S. B. (1998). *Qualitative research and case study applications in education: Revised and expanded from case study research in education.* San Francisco, CA: Jossey-Bass.

Mosenthal, J., Lipson, M., Mekkelsen, J., & Thompson, E. (2003). The dynamic environment of success: Representing school improvement in literacy learning and instruction. *Yearbook of the National Reading Conference, 52*, 308-320.

Mosenthal, J., Lipson, M., Torncello, S., Russ, B., & Mekkelsen, J. (2004). Contexts and practices of six schools successful in obtaining reading achievement. *The Elementary School Journal, 104*(5), 343-367.

(NAEP), National Assessment of Educational Progress (2009). *Grade 4 average scale scores between jurisdictions for all students.* Retrieved May 16, 2010, 2010, from http://nces.ed.gov/nationsreportcard/NDEGraphicsGenerator/scmaphost.aspx?TableID=14301.

Newmann, F. M., Smith, B. S., Allenworth, E., & Bryk, A. S. (2001). Instructional program coherence: What it is and why it should guide school improvement policy. *Education, Evaluation, and Policy Analysis, 23*(4), 297-321.

Payne, C. (2008). *So much reform, so little change: The persistence of failure in urban schools.* Cambridge, MA: Harvard Education Press.

Purkey, S. C., & Smith, M. S. (1983). Effective schools: A review. *The Elementary School Journal, 83*(4), 427-452.

Raphael, T. E., Au, K. H., & Goldman, S. R. (2009). Whole school instructional improvement through the Standards-Based Change Process: A developmental model. In J. Hoffman & Y. Goodman (Eds.), *Changing literacies for changing times* (pp. 198-229). New York, NY: Routledge/Taylor Frances Group.

Raphael, T. E., & Pearson, P. D. (1985). Increasing student's awareness of sources of information for answering questions. *American Educational Research Journal, 22*(2), 217-236.

Simmons, J. (2006). *Breaking through: Transforming urban school districts.* New York, NY: Teachers College Press.

Strauss, A. L., & Corbin, J. (1994). *Basics of qualitative research: Grounded theory procedures and techniques.* Newbury Park CA: Sage.

Taylor, B. M., Pearson, P. D., Peterson, D. S., & Rodriguez, M. C. (2003). Reading growth in high-poverty classrooms: The influence of teacher practices that encourage cognitive engagement in literacy learning. *Elementary School Journal. 104*, 3-28.

Taylor, B. M., Pearson, P. D., Peterson, D. P., & Rodriguez, M. C. (2005). The CIERA School Change Framework: An evidenced-based approach to professional development and school reading improvement. *Reading Research Quarterly, 40*(1), 40-69.

Timperley, H. S., & Parr, J. M. (2007). Closing the achievement gap through evidence-based inquiry at multiple levels of the education system. *Journal of Advanced Academics, 19*(1), 90-115.

Valencia, S. W., & Wixson, K. K. (2001). Literacy policy and policy research that make a difference. In J. V. Hoffman, D. I. Schallert, C. M. Fairbanks, J. Worthy & B. Maloch (Eds.), *50th Yearbook of the National Reading Conference* (pp. 21-43). Oak Creek, WI: National Reading Conference.

Weber, C. M., Raphael, T. E., Goldman, S. R., Sullivan, M. P., & George, M. A. (2010, May). *Roles and responsibilities of instructional leaders in urban reform: A seven-year longitudinal study of literacy coaches.* Paper presented at the American Educational Research Association, Denver.

Authoring Lives: Youth Returning to School Narrate Past, Present, and Future Selves

Susan Bickerstaff

University of Pennsylvania

High school attrition is a critical issue in the ongoing effort to reduce disparities in access and equity, particularly as students of color and English language learners are grossly overrepresented in the number of high school dropouts (Balfanz & Legters, 2004; Laird, DeBell, & Chapman, 2006; Orfield, 2004). In October 2004, an estimated 3.8 million 16- to 24-year-olds in the United States were out of school without a high school diploma or equivalent degree (Laird, et al., 2006). Yet for many students leaving high school is not a permanent decision; instead, it is a well-accepted fact that many high school dropouts cycle in and out of adult education programs, often intermittently throughout much of their lives. Several recent studies indicate that the number of 16- to 20-year-olds in alternative schools, GED classes, Daylight-Twilight programs, community colleges, and other adult education settings is growing (e.g., Flugman, Perin, & Spiegel, 2003; Welch & DiTommaso, 2004). Despite the relatively large body of scholarly work on high school attrition and ongoing efforts toward dropout prevention, surprisingly little is known about the experiences of students who leave and subsequently return to school.

Using a post-structuralist narrative lens, this paper offers analysis of the identity constructions embedded in the stories of young people who left high school and later returned to a college-based alternative high school diploma program. Through close examination of their oral and written narratives, a nuanced portrait emerges of the lived experiences of youth who have persisted in education despite their "failure" to graduate from a traditional high school.

This project builds on and extends existing qualitative research on high school dropouts (e.g., Fine, 1991; Rymes, 2001) that suggests that students return to school with a range of experiences both in and out of high school and that these experiences may not be merely reflective of "disengagement" or "resistance," but instead constitute learning, growth, and the development of identity. In the tradition of Luttrell (1997), Robinson (2007), and others, I worked to record the stories of participants to learn something about their self-understandings. In this way, my aim was to uncover the "storied selves" (Luttrell, 1997) of the young adults in this program. As Rymes (2001) demonstrated, students' dropout stories can have profound implications for pedagogy and school reform.

THEORETICAL PERSPECTIVES

Grounded in a sociocultural literacy framework, this study utilizes post-structuralist understandings of identity (e.g., Kamler, 2001) and the "possible selves" framework (e.g., Oyserman & Markus, 1990) to make sense of the narratives of young people returning to school. Work by Bruner (1990), Labov, and Waletzsky (1967) and others have laid the theoretical foundation for the use of narrative as a lens of interpretation in education and social sciences. Memories, both individual and collective, as well as experiences, norms, values, thoughts, and feelings manifest in the ways in which people choose to narrate their lives (e.g., Bell, 2002). The study of narratives gives insight into the way individuals make sense of experiences over time, and therefore is a particularly appropriate frame for an inquiry into the experiences of students leaving and subsequently returning to school. Feminist and post-structuralist influences on narrative research over the past two decades have resulted in a "shift from mining biographies for actual events in individual's lives toward understanding how people interpret their actions and represent themselves" (Hull, Jury, & Zacher, 2007, p. 301). Thus an analysis of a participant's story may or may not reveal the "facts" about her experiences, but is likely to reveal the way she is positioning herself in the world. Personal narratives offer particular representations of memories that are affected by dominant discourses, local contextual factors, and cultural conventions (Pavlenko, 2002).

The production of narratives, both written and oral, is a complex literacy activity in which the author creates a text drawing upon multiple sources, offering a representation of events, and positioning herself and the listener/reader in relation to dominant discourses. In the framing of this project, I self-consciously use the term "youth literacies" to mark a particular theorization of the literacies of adolescence and young adulthood. Although the literacy of high school leavers is frequently considered from a school-based deficit perspective, sociocultural studies of youth have revealed the ways in which even "marginalized readers" (Franzak, 2006) engage in intricate literacy practices. Decades of youth literacy research have demonstrated the rich and varied writing lives of adolescents in out-of-school settings (e.g., Cintron, 1991; Hull & Schultz, 2002; Mahiri, 2004). Broadened definitions of literacy and text under this framework represent a sharp break from traditional notions of literacy as an autonomous set of skills used to make meaning from decontextualized written text. Drawing on the early work of Scribner and Cole (1981) and Heath (1983) and more recent pieces like Kress and van Leeuwen (2001) and Gee, Hull, and Lankshear (1996), this project understands literacy practices as embedded in local context, instrumental in the maintenance of power and privilege, and inextricably linked to the enactment of identity. Youth literacies offers a conceptual lens for understanding the ways in which young adults manipulate and interpret a wide range of semiotic resources, including locally produced and mass mediated multimodal texts in order to enact identities, narrate their lives, and take up social positions in the world (e.g., Alvermann, 2006; Moje, 2000).

Closely related to work on narrative constructions of self is the notion of "possible selves" developed by Markus and Nurius (1986). Possible selves are temporally constructed ideations of future identity and are frequently categorized into "hoped-for selves," "feared selves," and "expected selves." One of the affordances of the possible selves framework is its implications for methodology and its connection to narrative. This research project is influenced by the conceptual framing of a number of studies that combine narrative methods and theories of possible selves to uncover the ways adolescents and young adults view their present and future identities (e.g., Gadsden, Wortham & Turner, 2003; King & Raspin, 2004). Recently, this theoretical construct has also been applied to the multiple, contextual, and "continuously revised" (Giddens, 1991) identities enacted by adolescents and young adults (e.g., Halverson, 2005; Shepard, 2004). Despite its rich potential to further illuminate the literate lives of young adults, possible selves has rarely been used in conjunction with a youth literacies framework.

CONTEXT AND METHODOLOGY

Located in a large metropolitan center, the Pathways program at City Community College (CCC) serves youth, ages 16 to 21, who have withdrawn from one of the city's public high schools (program and participant names are pseudonyms). Most Pathways students attended and subsequently left high-poverty low-performing high schools. In 2002, 61% of this city's high schools graduated less than one-half of the freshman class within four years (Balfanz & Letgers, 2004). In 2006, 79% of the district's students were eligible to receive free or reduced lunch. Pathways enrolls just over 100 students, of whom 54% identify as Black, 9% identify as Hispanic or Latino/a, and 34% identify as White.

Pathways is a dual-enrollment program that allows students to simultaneously work toward a high school diploma and earn credits toward an associate's degree. During their first semester students take courses that are specifically designed for Pathways students, but are taught by CCC faculty and are nearly identical to developmental (remedial) courses required of many regular CCC students. Upon successful completion of their first semester, Pathways students matriculate into the general college population and enroll independently in a variety of college courses depending on their missing high school credits and their educational goals. Some Pathways courses, particularly those taken during their first semester, only count for high school credit, but as students progress, many of their courses count for both high school and college credits. Once a student earns enough credits to fulfill the school district's requirements for graduation, a high school diploma is issued from the high school the student last attended. Although students' courses are taught by college faculty, Pathways employs a number of staff members to support its students, including a number of counselors who mentor, advise, and counsel students.

Using a critical case-study methodology, I spent one year at Pathways, following a group of nine students from their first day in the program through three semesters. The nine students, three males and six females, identify as either Black, Latino/a, or biracial and range in age from 17 to 20 years old. I employed a number of ethnographic-focused methods including semi-structured interviews and conversation groups, classroom and program observations, and document analysis.

I approached this project with a critical-constructivist epistemological lens, meaning the methods for collection and analysis were selected and employed with an eye toward avoiding practices that might silence or disempower participants. By considering the data through a post-structuralist lens, I hoped to reject positivist claims which frequently reinscribe existing power structures and privilege the researcher's voice over the voices of the researched. Inherent in this inquiry is the assumption that "all thought is fundamentally mediated by power relationships" (Kincheloe & McLaren, 1994, p. 139), and thus my epistemology assumes that the knowledge generated from this study must be considered inherently "situated, embodied, and partial" (Richardson, 1997, p. 58). In the conceptualization of the study, its design and execution, and in the writing of this paper, I endeavored to keep my process transparent, include the participants in frank discussions about my research, and give back to the people and program who hosted me.

The data presented here are drawn from four sources: fieldnotes taken during classroom and program observations (approximately 100 hours), transcriptions of nine monthly conversation groups and four rounds of individual interviews with the nine students (approximately 45 minutes each), and writing samples participants shared with me, including poetry, song lyrics, short stories, journal entries, and essays for their coursework. Analysis was ongoing and recursive. Using Erickson's (1992) stages of qualitative analysis as an overarching guide, I began by reviewing fieldnotes and transcripts holistically, and then identifying segments and features of organization and participation structures within those segments. Once selections of data were coded and analyzed in detail, as Erickson suggests, I looked across the larger data set for themes, paying special attention to discrepant cases.

During the first months of data collection, I systematically coded fieldnotes using Miles and Huberman's (1994) first-level coding method. These codes were largely descriptive and "low-inference" (Carspecken, 1996). About six months into the study, I began applying a similar coding method to student writing and the transcripts of interviews and conversation groups, often using "in vivo codes" (Strauss & Corbin, 1990). For high-inference pattern coding, Carspecken's (1996) critical method of interpretive analysis was useful in uncovering underlying objective, normative, subjective, and identity claims. With its focus on uncovering tacit claims of normativity (what participants think of as normal or proper) and identity, his four-pronged approach was particularly applicable to my question about identity construction and the relevance of dominant narratives. Working with pieces of transcripts or student writing samples, I employed this method to discover, for example, what implicit claims speakers or writers made about what is valued and how those speakers or writers positioned themselves in relationship to these values.

Using Toma's (2006) framework for rigorous qualitative research, I employed a number of validation strategies, including member checks, triangulation, and regular analysis sessions with a critical peer, to bolster this study's credibility, transferability, dependability, and confirmability. Richardson (1997) writes that "postmodernist culture permits us—indeed, encourages us—to doubt that any method of knowing or telling can claim authoritative truth" (p. 168), and thus I do not presume to eliminate bias or reactivity in pursuit of an objective reality. It would be unwise for me to understate the implications of a White middle class graduate student asking low-income students of color about their experiences with education and their thoughts on success and failure. However, throughout the research process, from the formulation of the questions through the data collection and analysis, I worked to remain "reflexive" (Hammersley & Atkinson, 1995), recording and writing about my own assumptions and subject positions and their effect on my interactions in the setting and my interpretations of the data.

FINDINGS

The findings of this study support previous empirical research that has found students leave school because of a lack of caring relationships with teachers, low standards, and an unengaging curriculum (e.g., Hondo, Gardiner & Sapien, 2008; Smyth & Hattum, 2003). Participants offered eloquent critiques of the schools they attended, the school district's structures, which systematically excluded them from the city's few well-resourced schools, and larger social and institutional factors including poverty, racism, and a lack of meaningful employment and advancement opportunities in their communities. Like many students who leave high school, participants also shared stories of personal tragedies including mental and physical illness, incarceration and death of loved ones, and family, sexual, and community violence.

Yet despite participants' personal experiences with hardship, exclusion, and oppression, they exhibited almost unwavering optimism as they imagined their futures: "I feel confident that it will come true.... I'm resolute about it." As one young woman stated when I probed her about the possibility of a setback on her educational journey: "I don't see that, I really don't. That's not even something I speak into existence."

In an effort to further understand how students reconciled what might be understood as a contradiction—hope for the future in the face of past struggles—I conducted a close analysis of students' talk and writing about their pasts and futures. Three themes emerged that demonstrate how students frame past stories of struggle and future expectations of success. Firstly, as part of their talk about negative high school experiences, participants crafted narratives of exceptionalism in which they position themselves as different from typical high school students and traditional high school dropouts. Secondly, via narratives of self-reliance, participants constructed strong independent identities as individuals who could persevere despite uncertain resources and unreliable support networks. Finally, analysis of student writing revealed that participants in this study engage in out-of-school writing practices that give voice to their hopes and expectations for the future. In their writing, past hardship is understood as an essential element of their journey toward future success. In the following sections, I explore these themes in detail, foregrounding the students' voices whenever possible. This paper concludes with a discussion of the implications of these findings for practitioners and literacy researchers.

Narratives of Exceptionalism

The post-structuralist narrative framework implies that much can be learned about a speaker's understanding of his or her current and future selves from close analysis of the stories he or she tells. I term the stories in this section "narratives of exceptionalism" because in these stories participants represent themselves as atypical or unusual in comparison to their peers. Narratives of exceptionalism highlighted participants' desire to learn and their talents, intelligence, and maturity; these stories focused both on the ways in which those characteristics made participants different from other high school students and on the ways in which they therefore defied school and societal expectations. These stories reveal much about the work of Pathways students to reject dominant cultural narratives about youth and specifically about dropouts. In their narratives of exceptionalism, participants resist the subjectivities imposed on them by school and society, and thus instead imagine for themselves a prosperous and hopeful future.

Narratives of exceptionalism operate as counternarratives to dominant discourses about dropouts as less intelligent or less motivated than their peers. Pathways students resisted such positioning vigorously, and in so doing employed descriptions of "typical" high school students. Through their stories about other students and other dropouts, participants framed their exceptional identities. These attempts at counternarrative work speak to the power of discourses about low-income high school students and dropouts; for in their descriptions of self as exceptional, typical high school students were portrayed as unmotivated, deviant, and unintelligent:

> So they come in all late, looking a mess, just you know, being all rude and disrespectful because they know it takes nothing to get the grade there. All you gotta do is show up. So, yeah, that's the type of kids that were there.

This excerpt, in which a young woman named Lady describes her peers, implicates the school in promoting negative behavior because "it takes nothing to get a grade there." Ultimately, however, the focus is on her fellow students, as later in the interview she says, "I've always been respectful, that was never an issue for me." Critiques of school in relationship to students' exceptionalism were frequent: "Something about school growing up that never brought the talent out of me that I've had."

The idea that they had always valued education was central to participants' stories about previous school experiences. For example, Talia's ambivalence about school stood in sharp contrast to her certainty about her devotion to reading and learning: "I mean I always always been interested in learning, because like I'm a book worm. I read to go to sleep. Really I do. But, it's just, school, I don't know." Likewise, in telling high school stories, participants emphasized their intelligence ("And I was very bright; the only thing that wasn't so bright was that I never did homework"), respectfulness ("I don't walk around and act all loud and stuff like these girls do") and goal orientation ("I'm talking about going to college and everybody's like what?").

Just as participants represented themselves as different than typical high school students, they positioned themselves as different from most dropouts who, as described by participants in interviews with me, leave school "because they weren't properly prepared" because of "problems at home," or a "lack of support." By contrast, in most cases, participants saw their own stories as different from and more complex than their imagined story of a typical dropout. For some students, like Mercedes, leaving high school was part of an effort to find a more conducive learning environment with less violence and a better social atmosphere:

> People hype [high school] up and they make it their whole life and I guess I just wasn't one of the people who made high school my whole life. I kind of knew from the beginning I wasn't gonna be a high school person.

Two participants recalled crying at their middle school graduations because they didn't want to go to high school. For these students, high school represented a place where they never fit in or never wanted to attend. Therefore, dropout is not understood to be an indication of academic failure or the result of problems at home, but rather an attempt to find a better learning environment.

Even when acknowledging that their own narrative was similar to that of a "traditional dropout," participants distinguished themselves. A young woman named Chanel who was asked to leave a magnet school explains:

> I felt like even if I wouldn't have slacked off and failed I feel like I would have left anyway, because I was becoming so increasingly upset with the school and feelings of alienation were just like overwhelming. So I felt untraditional in the sense of I would have left for those reasons if I wasn't asked to leave.

In this excerpt, Chanel acknowledges that while she "slacked off and failed"—reasons students traditionally leave school—she would have left the school anyway for what she understands to be an untraditional reason, her feelings of alienation.

The power of dominant discourses about poor students, Black and Latino students, and high school dropouts was evident in these narratives. These dominant discourses were sometimes mentioned explicitly, as they were in a lively conversation group: "[They say] either we gotta be a singer or a basketball player or otherwise, we're not going to make it." More often, though, they were referenced implicitly in participants' talk about their high school teachers. One of the main critiques of high school was that teachers and schools positioned participants as unexceptional. Lady explained: "In high school you're assumed to be a statistic, you know, you're a dropout, you're no good." Students regularly recounted frustrating incidents, like this one shared by Cleveland, in which teachers treated them like the other students: "He treated everybody the same, not in a good way. As in, everybody was bad, everybody was doing wrong. And it really wasn't a good thing, because I wouldn't be doing something wrong." Stories like these about participants' experiences with low expectations, in which every student is assumed to be a dropout, a criminal, or another statistic, demonstrate the extent to which these narratives of exceptionalism are essential to students' visions of their own successful futures.

Narratives of Self-Reliance

Just as participants portrayed themselves as exceptional and therefore capable of transcending expectations for dropouts, they also positioned themselves as possessing the inner strength, motivation, and determination to succeed in the face of any obstacle. In students' narratives of exceptionalism, they issued implicit critiques of dominant discourses about poor youth of color. Similarly, their narratives of self-reliance operate as tacit critiques of the uncertain or unreliable support networks in their lives.

Students talked about self-reliance in relationship to their current achievements in the Pathways program. In describing the ways in which he has grown and changed since high school, Cleveland stated:

> I don't want to say I did it on my own or anything, 'cause I know there are other people that I probably didn't think about that helped me along the way, but I changed a lot of what I needed to change on my own.

This excerpt is emblematic of many students' self-reliance narratives in the way that he takes responsibility both for his past problems (things that needed to be changed) and his current success. Students, like Chanel, talked about personal traits like "independence" and "individualism" as central to their past and future success:

> Growing up like I was just like alone a lot. I was really a loner. So I think that partially made me like a huge nerd, which worked out better in life, but it also helped me be really independent.

Later, Chanel goes on to extol the value of independence, which she sees as one of the traits that contributes to her success in Pathways. In this story, Chanel also reveals her ideas about the connections between previous challenges and current success. Being a loner, which she describes as painful, is understood to be crucial to her potential to achieve in the future.

Within these stories of self-reliance, internal or intrinsic characteristics were cited as major factors in past successes: "It just depends on how strong your will is." As students looked to the future, they anticipated that achieving their goals would be possible because, as one student explained: "I know my drive will get me there." Just as challenges were represented as necessary for the strengthening of their self-reliance ("If I didn't have any obstacles in life, I couldn't be as strong as I was today"), those who used external obstacles as an excuse for poor performance were deemed "weak-minded." In a conversation about poverty and racism a participant asserted: "It doesn't matter what you might face every day, you should not let that hold you back." Even in critical discussions about the school district, students highlighted the primacy of an individual's will to work hard and succeed: "I don't necessarily believe like, okay, you change the school system, it would make things better. It's more resources, but I think it's within the individual." Thus while participants identified structural inequities and barriers to resources, they positioned themselves as capable of transcending these obstacles (in part because they were exceptional and in part because past hardships made them stronger) and therefore were able to stay optimistic.

These narratives of self-reliance, in which the participants position themselves as intrinsically motivated, seemingly indicate an individualistic understanding of success. Yet while apparently endorsing the meritocratic myth that success is predicated upon one's motivation, in their narratives of self-reliance, participants also offer implicit critiques of social and educational structures that have failed them. In their stories about high school, students reported reaching out to teachers and other staff who offered little support. In a conversation group, one student described an exchange with a high school teacher that was familiar to many other participants: "I think that was the worst thing I ever heard when I was in school: 'It doesn't matter if you pass or fail, I'm still getting paid.' And I heard that from most of my teachers." Likewise, high schools were portrayed as places where counselors were unavailable, where expectations were low, and where "there's not really any preparation for the future."

Social support networks outside of school were similarly represented as uncertain or unreliable. Friends were often portrayed as "bad influences" or as failing to take participants' efforts to get a high school diploma "seriously." Participants also talked about family members who demonstrated inadequate support of their educational goals. Talia reported that although her mother gave her money to get to school, she wanted a different form of intellectual and emotional support:

> My mom, she proud of me, but mmm, and she support me... but she don't really ask me like oh, how was your day, or what did you learn and stuff like that.

In addition to providing inadequate support, families were cited as sources of stress and distraction, as participants frequently complained about children "running around screaming all day" and assorted other "family drama." Importantly, Pathways students also talked about the ways in which family, friends, program staff, neighbors, and former and current teachers served as important sources of encouragement and support. Yet the narratives of self-reliance are noteworthy because of the work they do in positioning students as prepared for future success.

Fellow Pathways students were also represented as uncertain sources of support and as potential distractions. In her third semester in the program, Chanel described her relationships with her classmates: "But it's like I'll get so worried about hanging around with them or doing whatever that I won't really do what I have to do." Lady stated that she preferred to work alone or seek out official channels of support: "I'd rather see a tutor than buddy up with someone [in my class] because everybody is human and they have their own personal issues that could possibly get in the way." Instead of relying on support networks composed of peers or family, participants largely agreed with the sentiment: "I came by myself, I'm leaving by myself, and that's really it."

Each of the nine young people I worked with told stories of situations in which he or she had succeeded independently. Narratives of self-reliance offered hope for the future because they demonstrated the ways in which participants could make changes and improve their situations without the support of others.

Writing a Hoped-For Future

The oral narratives explored in the previous two sections offer important insights into how students maintain optimism in the face of personal challenges and societal inequities. Analysis of student writing reveals the similar and different ways in which participants' out-of-school writing practices offered a mode through which students made sense of past struggle and envisioned a successful future.

Six of the nine participants in this study engaged in a wide range of writing and self-publishing practices. These writing practices, which included writing short stories, poetry, song lyrics, fanfiction, posts for their MySpace pages, new ideas for video games, and personal reflections, were developed in childhood, high school, or during their time out of school. Despite Pathways' demanding schedule and its exclusive focus on academic writing (e.g., persuasive essays), most participants were able to maintain these writing habits during their time in the program. I asked participants to show me samples of their writing during our interviews. Many were kept in journals or notebooks, but about half of the participants also published thoughts, stories, and poetry on their MySpace pages.

Students' out-of-school writing was future-oriented, but filled with allusions to struggles of the past. Past suffering and future success or happiness were held in tension, particularly in student written poetry. For example, in an interview, Cleveland talked about his proclivity for the dark and light imagery in his writing: "A lot of the times I write more of the good things or the bad things or transformation between the two." In a poem entitled "Unsure Heroes Soon to Be Villains" he wrote: *"Eyes scarred by the light, see no light. So by working through the darkness the eyes are restored. A villain is laid to rest and a hero is reborn."* The juxtaposing images of heroes, villains, darkness, and light in this piece highlight the relationships—salient in much of Cleveland's work—between affliction and hope.

While some participants used writing primarily as a way to document past struggles, even the direst pieces of student work contained references to a hopeful future. Mercedes' autobiographical poem, "Diary of a Fallen Angel," chronicles her experiences with isolation, betrayal, and illness:

> *Steadily trying to make my way in this life/ Seems like no matter what I do I get blindsided by strife/ Hoping one day I grow up to be someone's mother and wife*

In this section, in the midst of describing the challenges she has faced and continues to face, Mercedes records one hoped-for self—to become "someone's mother and wife."

In another poem by Mercedes entitled "Floating," she writes: *"I wonder how far this river goes and will it lead me out to sea."* Here, as she describes floating on a river, she indicates that despite her uncertainty about where she is headed, she senses that life is leading her in a positive direction: *"Not really sure how I got here, but I'm sure it's for good reason."* Fate and destiny were frequently invoked in student poetry as an explanation for past struggles. Talia, who plans to become a professional lyricist and artist someday, crafted a remarkably similar line conveying the same sentiment: *"I try to keep my hope alive, believing there's a reason for everything.* " In Talia's line, the idea that "everything happens for a reason" is a source of comfort when hope is dwindling. In Mercedes' poem, the idea of destiny offers comfort when the future is uncertain.

In oral narratives about past experiences, students also alluded to fate or destiny, particularly as they accounted for how life circumstances had brought them to Pathways. As Lady explained, her failure to gain admission to a magnet school likely led to her dropping out of the poorly managed comprehensive high school she attended. However, in retrospect this was understood to be fortuitous: "I had a D on my report card so I couldn't get in to [the magnet school]. So I kind of was upset… but I believe everything happens for a reason. If I would have went to that school, I probably wouldn't be here." Similarly, Mercedes looked back on her gang involvement as an important part of her journey of growth and development:

> And I think being in a gang taught me a lot. A lot of people take that as a bad experience. I think it was a really good one because I saw how the real world works… All these bad things led up to something good because I think I turned out pretty well.

In this interview excerpt, hardship is understood to be part the journey to adulthood. A poem by Talia entitled "Life Thus Far" includes similar themes:

> *I feel like I'm blessed and at peace with myself/ But first had to go through hell/ First, lost in my very own entity/ Didn't know which way to go/ But as the years have passed me by, grown older, much wiser*

Just as in students' self-reliance narratives, in which hardships fostered motivation, strength, and independence, in this selection, going through hell is presented here as prerequisite for obtaining wisdom, maturity, and a sense of peace. This idea was echoed by students in interviews and conversation groups: "If everything is handed to you, you don't know how to live life." Students questioned the extent to which they would be as mature, as worldly, or as dedicated to their current educational goals without those negative past experiences.

As evidenced from transcripts cited above, Pathways students made similar rhetorical moves in their talk about their past and future lives. However, out-of-school writing offered a particular opportunity for six of the participants in this study to explore various hoped-for selves. For example, Cleveland, who kept a notebook full of ideas for new characters for his favorite television shows and video games, described his writing this way: "I think all of the characters are parts of my personality. The crazy side of me. The person that I would like to be. The person I'm not, but people see me as." In describing a short story he wrote about a battle between angels in heaven and on earth, he reflected on how his writing served as an inspiration to him: "Just my desire to be free. Cause I see myself with those wings and flying and so I just was seeing the character with the wings, me with the wings." Other examples of participants using writing to author the future included Mercedes' piece of futuristic fiction that featured a gay president (because "I kind of hope that one day somebody who's homosexual will be president"), Lady's poetry about marriage and other things she has not yet experienced, and Talia's profile posts on MySpace that allow her to "open up emotionally" and combat the feeling of being "in a prison." Both through their writing and through their oral narratives, these young adults make sense of personal tragedies and unjust social systems by framing struggle as intimately connected to strength and by imagining and authoring an optimistic future.

DISCUSSION

Inherent in this inquiry is an acknowledgement that schools are inadequately serving large segments of the student population. The young adults in Pathways who shared their stories and their writing represent a largely understudied, yet growing population of adolescents seeking alternative pathways to the high school diploma. Despite the wealth of research on the literacies of out-of-school youth, rarely have student writing practices been investigated in the context of youth returning to school. Understanding more about young adults who leave high school and subsequently return to school is of great importance for literacy researchers, for practitioners working with youth transitioning back to school, and for leaders seeking to increase and sustain student engagement and retention in traditional K-12 settings.

The subjectivities students adopt—as exceptional, independent learners—offer new and interesting insights for the ways in which programs and practitioners think about and engage returning students. These findings raise questions about the extent to which alternative programs and traditional high schools support and foster the resiliency and persistence exhibited in these students' stories. While the narratives in this paper contrast sharply with images of dropouts with poor academic self-concepts and low self-esteem, they also reveal an uncertainty among participants about their place in a world in which youth like them are considered "statistics." The tensions in these narratives, particularly their pride and confidence contrasted with their feelings of isolation, speak to the lack of consistent support networks in their high schools and the construction of deviance as a norm for youth.

Educators have much to learn from listening to the stories of students who work to reconcile the various and often conflicting messages they receive about their abilities to succeed and the likelihood that they will fail. The ways in which participants negotiated normative cultural images of poor youth of color and high school dropouts offer commentary on the strength and pervasiveness of those images. Interestingly, despite their critical commentary on high schools that failed to engage them, participants' personal narratives largely did not "penetrate" (Willis, 1977) dominant discourses about deviant youth. Instead, their narratives of exceptionalism allowed them to craft identities as untraditional dropouts, and thus ideas about what it means to be a dropout or an urban adolescent were unchallenged. Likewise, participants' differentiation from "typical" dropouts served as a tacit indictment of those who leave high schools for traditional reasons, thus implicitly relieving schools of their responsibilities to effectively educate students. These narratives and the associated narratives about independence, drive, and motivation have important implications for the possibilities of critical literacy and critical pedagogy and the roles schools and programs play in fostering particular understandings of success and failure. These data also raise questions about the extent to which critical or "penetrating" perspectives on race, class, meritocracy, and opportunity are compatible with optimism and hope.

The analytic frames for this study—post-structural understandings of narrative and theories of identity drawn from the possible selves literature—offer possibilities for opening new conversations to complement and contribute to the wealth of youth literacy research. One of the projects of the post-structuralists has been an attempt to show the ways in which "our identities and subjectivities are multiple, changing and always constructed in relation to others" (Maher, 2001, p. 28). In these data, this lens calls attention to the intended and potential audiences for the oral and written narratives produced by participants. Narratives of exceptionalism and self-reliance were largely crafted for me in interviews and in conversation groups with fellow Pathways participants. Student writing, some of which was published on MySpace and thus intended for a wider audience, displayed similar optimistic themes but was less likely to position authors in relation to other students or dropouts.

Hesford (1999) writes that autobiographical acts should be examined "as social signifying practices shaped by and enacted within particular institutional contexts and their histories" (p. xxiii). As such, the context for these conversations, a college-based high school diploma program, also cannot be overlooked. Narratives of exceptionalism and self-reliance and students' hope for the future were, in part, shaped by participants' status as students in the Pathways program and their adopted subject positions were part of larger discourses circulated by the program's staff. It is also worth noting, that while a major theme in students' talk and writing was their self-reliance, their out-of-school writing lives were tied to social relationships with family and friends. Participants' literacy lives were built around experiences with literacy mentors, co-authors, and audience members, who they sought out either in person or via MySpace. These data demonstrate the various ways in which students construct contextually dependent identities via the narrative work they do on paper, online, and in formal and informal conversations.

It is worth reiterating that the participants in this study were pushed out, kicked out, or dropped out of high school. Yet in spite of, or perhaps because of, these negative school experiences, their writing practices flourished. This raises questions about the ways in which traditional high school classrooms foster or constrain students' writerly identities. Previous research has long pointed to the potential for teachers to invite students' out-of-school writing lives into the classroom. These data specifically indicate that writing classrooms can also be places for rich discussions about issues of representation, audience, and voice. Likewise, Pathways students' literacy practices highlight the potential for autobiographical writing prompts, digital stories, self-publishing technologies, and other forms of authorship in which explicit attention is paid to self-reflection and self-representation.

REFERENCES

Alvermann, D. (2006). Ned and Kevin: An online discussion that challenges the 'not yet adult' cultural model. In K. Pahl and J. Rowsell (Eds.), *Travel notes from the New Literacy Studies: Instances of practice* (pp. 39-56). Clevedon, UK: Multilingual Matters Ltd.

Balfanz, R., & Legters, N. E. (2004). Locating the dropout crisis: Which high schools produce the nation's dropouts? In G. Orfield (Ed.), *Dropouts in America* (pp. 57-84). Cambridge, MA: Harvard Education Press.

Bell, J. S. (2002). Narrative inquiry: More than just telling stories. *TESOL Quarterly, 36*(2), 207-213.

Bruner, J. (1990). *Acts of meaning.* Cambridge, MA: Harvard University Press.

Carspecken, P. F. (1996). *Critical ethnography in educational research: A theoretical and practical guide.* New York, NY: Routledge.

Cintron, R. (1991). Reading and writing graffiti: A reading. *The Quarterly Newsletter of the Laboratory of Comparative Human Cognition, 13*(1), 21-24.

Erickson, F. (1992). Ethnographic micro-analysis of interaction. In M. LeCompte, W. Millroy, and J. Preissle (Eds.), *The handbook of qualitative research in education* (pp. 201-225). San Diego, CA: Academic Press.

Fine, M. (1991). *Framing dropouts.* Albany: SUNY Press.

Flugman, B., Perin, D., Spiegel, S. (2003). An exploratory case study of 16-20 year old students in adult education programs. Center for Advanced Study in Education. Retrieved March 13, 2007, from http://www.16to20AE.org

Franzak, J. (2006). Zoom: A review of the literature on marginalized adolescent readers, literacy theory, and policy implications. *Review of Educational Research, 76*(2), 209-248.

Gadsden, V., Wortham, S., & Turner, H. (2003). Situated identities of young African American fathers in low-income settings: Perspectives on home, street, and the system. *Family Court Review, 41*(3), 381-399.

Gee, J. P., Hull, G., & Lankshear, C. (1996). *The new work order: Behind the language of the new capitalism.* Boulder, CO: Westview.

Giddens, A. (1991). *Modernity and self-identity: Self and society in the late modern age.* Cambridge, UK: Polity Press.

Halverson, E. R. (2005). InsideOut: Facilitating gay youth identity development through a performance-based youth organization. *Identity: An International Journal of Theory and Research, 5*(1), 67-90.

Hammersley, M., & Atkinson, P. (1995). *Ethnography: Principles in practice.* New York, NY: Routledge.

Heath, S. B. (1983). *Ways with words: Language, life and work in communities and classrooms.* New York, NY: Cambridge University Press.

Hesford, W. (1999). *Framing identities: Autobiography and the politics of pedagogy.* Minneapolis, MN: University of Minnesota Press.

Hondo, C., Gardiner, M., & Sapien, Y. (2008). *Latino dropouts in rural America: Realities and possibilities.* Albany, NY: SUNY Press.

Hull, G., Jury, M., & Zacher, J. (2007). Possible selves: Literacy, identity, and development in work, school, and community. In A. Belzer (Ed.), *Toward defining and improving quality in adult basic education* (pp. 299-318). Mahwah, NJ: Lawrence Erlbaum Associates.

Hull, G., & Schultz, K. (Eds.). (2002). *School's out: Bridging out-of-school literacies with classroom practices.* New York, NY: Teachers College Press.

Kamler, B. (2001). *Relocating the personal: A critical writing pedagogy.* Albany, NY: SUNY Press

Kincheloe, J. L., & McLaren, P. L. (1994). Rethinking critical theory and qualitative research. In N. K. Denzin and Y. S. Lincoln. (Eds.), *Handbook of Qualitative Research,* Thousand Oaks, CA: Sage.

King, L., & Raspain, C. (2004). Lost and found possible selves, subjective well-being, and ego development in divorced women. *Journal of Personality, 72,* 602-632.

Kress, G., & van Leeuwen, T. (2001). *Multimodal discourse: The modes and media of contemporary communication.* London, UK: Edward Arnold.

Labov, W., & Waletzsky, J. (1967). Narrative analysis: Oral versions of personal experience. In J. Helm (Ed.), *Essays on the verbal and visual arts* (pp. 12-44). Seattle, WA: University of Washington Press.

Laird, J., DeBell, M., & Chapman, C. (2006). Dropout rates in the United States: 2004 (NCES 2007-024). U.S. Department of Education. Washington, DC: National Center for Education Statistics. Retrieved June 6, 2007, from http://nces.ed.gov/pubs2007/2007024.pdf

Luttrell, W. (1997). *Schoolsmart and motherwise: Working class women's identity and schooling.* New York, NY: Routledge.

Maher, F. (2001). John Dewey, progressive education, and feminist pedagogies: Issues in gender and authority. In K. Weiler (Ed.), *Feminist engagements: Reading, resisting, and envisioning male theorists in education and cultural studies.* New York, NY: Routledge.

Mahiri, J. (Ed.). (2004). *What they don't learn in school: Literacy in the lives of urban youth.* New York, NY: Peter Lang.

Markus, H., & Nurius, P. (1986). Possible selves. *American Psychologist, 41,* 954-969.

Miles, M., & Huberman, A. M. (1994). *Qualitative data analysis.* Thousand Oaks, CA: Sage Publications.

Markus, H., & Nurius, P. (1986). Possible selves. *American Psychologist, 41,* 954-969.

Moje, E. (2000). 'To be part of the story': The literacy practices of gangsta adolescents. *Teachers College Record, 102*(3), 651-690.

Orfield, G. (Ed.) (2004). *Dropouts in America.* Cambridge, MA: Harvard Education Press.

Oyserman, D., & Markus, H. (1990). Possible selves and delinquency. *Journal of Personality and Social Psychology, 59*(1), 112-125.

Pavlenko, A. (2002). Narrative story: Whose study is it anyway? *TESOL Quarterly, 36*(2), 213-218

Richardson, L. (1997). *Fields of play: Constructing an academic life.* New Brunswick, NJ: Rutgers University Press.

Robinson, C. (2007) From the classroom to the corner: Female dropouts' reflections on their school years. New York, NY: Peter Lang.

Rymes, B. (2001). *Conversational borderlands: Language and identity in an alternative urban high school.* New York, NY: Teachers College Press.

Scribner, S., & Cole, M. (1981). *The psychology of literacy.* Cambridge, MA: Harvard University Press.

Shepard, B. (2004). In search of self: A qualitative study of the life-career development of rural young women. *Canadian Journal of Counselling, 38*(2), 75-90.

Smyth, J., & Hattam, R. (2004). *'Dropping out,' drifting off, being excluded: Becoming somebody without school.* New York, NY: Peter Lang.

Strauss, A., & Corbin, J. (1990). *Basics of qualitative research: Grounded theory procedures and techniques.* Thousand Oaks, CA: Sage.

Toma, J. D. (2006). Approaching rigor in applied qualitative research. In C. F. Conrad and R. C. Serlin (Eds.), *The Sage handbook for research in education: Engaging ideas and enriching inquiry* (pp. 405-423). Thousand Oaks, CA: Sage Publications.

Welch, J., & DiTommaso, K. (2004). Youth in ABE: The numbers. *Focus on the Basics, 7*(A), Retrieved March 13, 2007, from NCSALL: http://www.ncsall.net/?id=123

Willis, P. (1977). *Learning to labor: How working class kids get working class jobs.* New York, NY: Columbia University Press.

Research on Small-Group Discussions of Literature—Past, Present, and Future: An Analysis of Three Decades

Susan King Fullerton
Jamie Colwell
Clemson University

From the 1980s to the early 2000s, literature response received much attention. This burgeoning interest was reflected in comprehensive reviews (e.g., Beach & Hynds, 1991; Galda & Beach, 2001; Marshall, 2000; Martinez & Roser, 2003) and a large number of investigations (more than 100) conducted between 1978 and 2000 (Martinez & Roser, 2001). Unfortunately, in the National Reading Panel Report (2000), literature response and discussion was another "neglected pillar" (see Allington, 2005 for his list). As Nystrand (2006) asserts, the role of discussion is an essential component of language arts and reading comprehension instruction. Nystrand cautions that given "current research and policy climates calling for 'evidence-based' pedagogy, we would do well, as researchers and educators in language and literacy education, to assess just what we know, where we are, and how best to respond to these challenges" (p. 393). In this article, we attempt to respond to the first two needs in relation to literature discussion group research within elementary classrooms. As researchers, we are interested in literature response as well as the learning potential of small-group collaborative settings. We view literary development as an important form of comprehension and literacy development.

As research on response to literature has evolved, it has become clear that response is more than a transaction between reader and text. Within sociocultural contexts, response is also a construction of meaning and stances (Galda & Beach, 2001). While the previous decade provided much new knowledge about response, reviewers have called for more attention to the various constructs and contexts related to response, particularly the collaborative nature of literature study and the role of teachers and students (Marshall, 2000; Martinez & Roser, 2001; 2003). We sought to explore one example of a collaborative context, literature response in small-group discussions. We used qualitative data analysis, specifically ethnographic content analysis (Altheide, 1996), to: a) identify perspectives, themes, and trends, and b) to determine whether particular themes or foci changed in elementary-based literature discussion group research of the last 30 years, since the publication of Eeds and Wells' (1989) "Grand Conversations." For analysis purposes, we defined small group as 3-8 students, although most groups within the studies were larger than three and less than eight.

Ethnographic Content Analysis (ECA) has been commonly used to track media reports and their impact, but Altheide (1996) suggests that ECA methodology may also extend our ability to study public discourse and change. We posit that in education, our accessible "public discourse" is primarily reflected in professional publications. In agreement with this stance, Gaffney and Anderson (2000) contended that *"the words people use reveal the assumptions they make"* (p. 55), referring to their content analysis. Conversely, Altheide emphasized that attention must also be given to the words that are not used. Using ECA, we set out to systematically investigate how points of view, trends, and themes "arose" and "traveled" (Altheide, p. 69) within and across our professional discourse. Such exploration will develop new understandings of collaborative, small-group literature discussions in relation to both teacher and student learning.

Like many of the researchers in these studies, our views are grounded in the notion that social interaction is foundational to learning. Knowledge develops through interaction with others (Vygotsky, 1978; Wells, 1997), and talk is the primary tool for this constructive process (Luria, 1979; Mercer, 1995). Thus, we believe literary thought has the potential to develop literate minds (Langer, 1995), as response to literature is a social, cultural, and situated activity (Galda & Beach, 2001; Rosenblatt, 1985; 2004). As an ethnographer's lens may influence an investigation, these theoretical perspectives (or biases) are the lens through which we read and analyzed the documents in this ethnographic content analysis.

PROCEDURES

A common view in ethnography or anthropology is that "the proper understanding or interpretation of people's words and actions can only be achieved if these are related to the wider context in which they have been used or happened" (Gibbs, 2002, p. 2). Our purpose for this investigation was to use ECA (Altheide, 1996), to systematically explore the "wider context" and determine points of view, trends, and themes in literature discussion documents from 1989-2009. As with constant comparison but unlike traditional content analysis, ECA allows for concepts and information to emerge; information may be presented qualitatively as narrative information. Given our choice of analysis, our role as researchers may be compared to an ethnographer who attempts to study, analyze, and interpret a case. In this context, a document is the case. For each case, a protocol or template is used to record information, somewhat analogous to field notes.

Search and Inclusion Criteria

To locate documents, we searched Academic Premier, Education Research Complete, ERIC, and PsychInfo databases, using the terms literature, discussion(s), and reading from 1989 through 2009. We excluded dissertations and non-English documents. We also used adult, college, and secondary as exclusion terms since we were interested in elementary (K-5) discussion groups. The search yielded 1,896 documents. From this pool, we narrowed the results by using the subject term, discussion (teaching technique). This search identified 171 articles. Using the same databases, we conducted a separate search using the term literature discussion group(s), which yielded 66 documents. We combined these searches to identify peer-reviewed publications. In addition, we used Social Sciences Citation Index to conduct cited reference searches. We also used the reference lists of articles and syntheses/reviews (Almasi & Garas-York, 2009; Galda & Beach, 2001; Marshall, 2000; Martinez & Roser, 2001, 2003) to identify additional documents. The results of these electronic and hand searches produced 77 peer-reviewed investigations of elementary-age (K-5) literature discussion groups. In cases of grades 5 *and* 6, the study was included in the analysis.

To ensure inclusion of full research reports and to make in-depth analysis more feasible, we established further practical and methodological screening criteria (Fink, 2005). Our first step was to carefully examine studies to determine adequate representation of research. In a number of articles, authors made reference to their research and reported aspects of procedures or findings, but in most cases, the methodology was not fully represented. It is important to acknowledge, however, that a fully developed research report was not necessarily the intent; in most cases, the primary focus was presentation of the investigation's instructional implications and innovative procedures. In some cases, we were unable to retrieve the full document, so the study was eliminated. Together we reached agreement on the remaining documents and retained 46 studies for analysis, noted with an asterisk in the references.

Analysis

Within Ethnographic Content Analysis (ECA), it is important to look at primary sources as well as "surrounding" documents to gain perspective. Therefore, the practitioner-oriented articles as well as the syntheses and reviews previously mentioned became important "surrounding" resources. In addition, a part of the ECA process is balancing micro and macro analysis procedures; such macro and micro analysis strategies (Miles & Huberman, 1994) were necessary given the number of documents and our goals. The first level, or macro analysis, involved reading the abstract, or in many cases, returning to the article, to briefly categorize each investigation in terms of the purpose, findings, design, context, and participants. The information was organized on a grid. Our second level, or micro analysis, involved the selection of a group of "focal studies" which we analyzed again in more detail. (Such selection of focal cases or participants is often an ethnographic tool.) Based upon our initial macro analysis, we selected a pool of "influential" studies from each decade that would be large enough to compare, contrast, and establish patterns, but small enough to support in-depth analysis. We considered highly regarded, "tier one" type publications (Williams, Hammer, Pierczynski-Ward, & Henson, 2007), and we also determined, whenever possible, the most frequently cited documents within each decade, recognizing that more recent articles would likely garner fewer citations. At the same time, we were mindful of the difficulties outlined by Shanahan and Neuman (1997) in defining "influential." As we reflected upon the results of our analyses thus far and reviewed the studies considering the aforementioned factors as well as representativeness, we reached agreement on inclusion through joint discussion. However, we also considered a tenet from content analysis methodology—look for what is not there or is less common. Table 1 provides a summary of the fourteen focal investigations by decade.

As outlined by Altheide (1996), we created a protocol for analysis by rereading a few of the focal documents several times in order to become more aware of the context, identifying in a broad and preliminary manner, key aspects of the documents that would guide us in tracking trends and themes. A preliminary analysis protocol was trialed and revised as we reread documents. The process continued, resulting in a final protocol that provided: 1) a standardized form for abstracting data from documents, and 2) a record of constructs and themes that were identified within each document. Both researchers read all focal studies and reviewed each protocol to ensure agreement.

These protocols served as the foundation for inductive analysis to establish thematic or conceptual categories (Miles & Huberman, 1994; Strauss & Corbin, 1998). A final step in the process required entering the protocols into NVivo 8 (QSR International, 2008) for further coding and synthesis. NVivo is a qualitative data management and analysis software tool (Gibbs, 2002). We used it to assist us in categorizing data and in facilitating identification of patterns. As is typical in NVivo, an iterative process provided ways to transform codes into representative constructs and themes. In addition, we entered documents into NVivo for text mining (Leech & Onwuegbuzie,

2008) of constructs (as examples, social constructivism, Vygotsky, scaffolding). These final processes aided the synthesis of findings across the studies.

FINDINGS AND DISCUSSION

Literature discussion has never made the "What's Hot, What's Not" list (e.g., Cassidy & Cassidy, 2008) in *Reading Today,* a newspaper published by the International Reading Association. Each yearly list presents reading professionals' prognostications about current interest in reading topics. Yet, literature discussion, and more specifically, literature discussion groups (also called conversational discussion groups, literature study groups, literature circles, and book clubs) have remained a consistent part of literacy research and instruction for at least three decades.

As a way of providing background to the Eeds and Wells (1989) investigation as well as others that followed, we wish to highlight some precursors, previous work that provided a foundation for the onset of "grand conversations." Applebee's (1978) representation of the child's concept of story broke new ground, yet the work was somewhat constrained by the collection methods. In the 1980s, researchers such as Hickman (1981) argued for "research to include the wider range of evidence that can be gathered in naturalistic settings" (p. 344); she pointed out that many questions of both theoretical and pedagogical concern could not be answered with empirical approaches. Hickman provided examples of these important questions:

> "What happens . . . when response is not directly solicited? What forms of response do children use when they deal with stories on their own, or when they interact with each other? Do they seem to organize their thinking in the same ways? Do the developmental stages identified in research function in non-research settings? Does response remain constant when the immediate social context changes?" (p. 344).

Hickman set out to answer these questions by using an ethnographic research design, spending several months in a K-5 setting following 90 children, studying their literary responses. Her study is one of the earliest to use research methods not typically employed in educational research. The investigation foreshadows what would follow by establishing a foundation of asking questions integral to practice, but nonetheless, a foundation that would not become fully accepted or commonly practiced until later. In fact, the questions that Hickman asked have remained a part of the professional discourse throughout the last three decades.

With the Eeds and Wells (1989) study's promising phrase of "grand conversations," an idea was launched; others echoed this term (for example, McGee, 1992; 1994). It is interesting that Eeds and Wells' investigation was conducted with teachers in training. In fact, the researchers acknowledged that some of the conversations were less than grand, a sentiment later echoed by Roller and Beed (1994) in their title, "Sometimes the conversations were grand, and sometimes . . . ." These articles represent an example of cross-pollination of constructs within the professional discourse (albeit a fairly simple one). The notion of "grand conversations" arose, traveled, and shifted as researchers and educators appropriated the term. Soon after Eeds and Wells' study was published, other investigations began to focus on literature and discussion as an important part of the reading instructional program (Raphael, et al., 1991).

Within this section, we refer to findings from the micro analysis of focal studies and in some cases, the macro analysis of other investigations. Related practitioner articles are also cited in some instances. Based on the results of our analysis, we arrived at four broad and interrelated themes: (a) the social construction of understanding, (b) the role of the teacher, (c) authority, and (d) diversity and social justice within literature discussion groups.

The Social Construction of Understanding

Most of the early research characterized children's responses from a developmental perspective (Martinez & Roser, 2001; 2003). Often these characterizations were Piagetian in nature (e.g., Applebee, 1978). Our results indicated that response type was also explored in literature discussion groups during the 1990s, often through varied classification frameworks. For example, McGee (1992) developed a categorization scheme to represent first grader's grand conversations after read-alouds. Earlier work frequently framed the research in relation to Rosenblatt's theories (1978; 1985). However, during the early to mid-1990s, researchers began to shift their primary theoretical focus to Vygotskian theories. (A few referred to both Rosenblatt and Vygotsky.) Determined through text mining of the focal studies, Vygotsky (1978) was the most frequently cited, and as is often the case in professional discourse, there was much variation in referencing Vygotsky's theories (e.g., sociohistorical, sociocultural, and social constructivist). These results correspond to those of Gaffney & Anderson (2000), who found increased use of sociocultural-related terms across literacy research in general, peaking in 1991-1995. In the context of literature discussion groups, this shift seems logical. As focus on response moved away from a developmental perspective and an individual's response and transactions with text (though often aggregated in the research) researchers began to attend to the socially situated nature of meaning-making within a small-group context. In this article, we give much attention to the social construction of understanding as it was represented in all focal studies. Table 1 provides summaries of the 14 focal studies.

During the last two decades, literature discussion research and instruction have built upon the notion that a knowledgeable other (peer or teacher) models or scaffolds higher cognitive functions (Vygotsky, 1978) such as literary interpretations and understandings. Over time, these processes become internalized by individual learners helping them to guide their own learning. Contextualized within sociocultural or social constructivist environments, many of these studies looked at the nature and role of talk, particularly in relation to how understandings are constructed. Commeyras and Sumner (1998) found that students were empowered when given the opportunity to ask their own questions, engaged by peers' questions, and productively responded to questions to build understandings. In Almasi's (1995) research, students in the peer-led discussions provided higher-level responses than those in teacher-led groups. Through exploration of sociocognitive conflicts in literature discussions, she determined that there are distinct patterns of discourse associated with different episodes of conflict.

Conflict or argument was also a focus in studies of "Collaborative Reasoning" (CR) (Anderson, et al., 2001, Chinn, Anderson, & Waggoner, 2001; Li, et al., 2007; Reznitskaya, Anderson, McNurlen, Nguyen-Jahiel, Archodidou, & Kim, 2001), a small-group framework that teaches students to critically analyze text as well as their own and peers' thinking. These researchers also found that conflict or argument is an important aspect of discussion discourse. Through their analyses, Anderson et al. (2001) found that arguments that occurred within extended talk could

Table 1. Focal Studies within Research on Small-Group Discussions of Literature by Decade in Chronological Order 1989-2009

1989

Study	Purpose	Theoretical perspectives	Design/ Methodology	Discussion format	Context/ Participants	Findings
Eeds & Wells (1989)	To explore what happened when children and teachers gathered to talk about a work they had all read	Sociocultural	Quantitative and qualitative case studies	Peer-led literature discussion groups with college students as facilitators	5-7 twice weekly discussions; 17 college students enrolled in a methods course and fifth- and sixth-grade students	Talk about literature helped students confirm, extend, or modify individual interpretations and created better understandings of text.

1990-1999

Study	Purpose	Theoretical perspectives	Design/ Methodology	Discussion format	Context/ Participants	Findings
Almasi (1995)	To explore and describe the nature of episodes of sociocognitive conflict among fourth-grade readers in peer-led and teacher-led discussions of narrative text	Sociocognitive Reader response Sociocultural	Quantitative and qualitative	Peer-led and teacher-led literature discussion groups	Eleven-week study; six classroom teachers; 97 fourth-grade students	Students in peer-led contexts were better able to recognize and resolve episodes of conflict, whereas students in teacher-led contexts were better able to recognize the person experiencing conflict. Student responses in peer-led groups were of higher complexity than those of teacher-led groups. Students in peer-led groups were better able to recognize and resolve episodes of sociocognitive conflict than students in teacher-led groups.
Commeyras & Sumner (1998)	To explore what researchers and students learned when student-generated questions served as the core of the literature discussions.	Social constructivist Dialogic	Qualitative	Dialogical-thinking discussions and peer-led literature discussions	One-year study; 18 second-grade students	Encouraging and valuing student questions supported students' intrinsic motivation. Directing students to respond to questions with reading experiences was educationally valuable.
Goatley, Brock, & Raphael (1995)	To explore the literacy learning of diverse students within a literature-based reading program in a regular education fifth-grade classroom.	Sociocultural Social constructivist	Qualitative ethnography	Peer-led Book Club discussion groups	Three-week study (14 discussion sessions); 5 fifth-grade students	Individual diversity provided rich cultural and linguistic sources of information for discussion. Diverse learners successfully drew on their backgrounds and experiences to create an environment for developing rich and meaningful understandings of literature.

Table 1 ctd.

Study	Purpose	Theoretical perspectives	Design/ Methodology	Discussion format	Context/ Participants	Findings
Lewis (1997)	To examine the influence of power and status on peer-led discussions.	Performance Positioning	Qualitative ethnography	Peer-led literature discussion groups	One-year study; fifth-/ sixth-grade multi-age classroom of 25 students; 5 focal students	Social conditions worked to position students as more or less successful in relation to others within the classroom culture. Less successful students were marginalized in peer-led discussion, leaving power in the hands of high-status or more successful students.
McMahon & Goatley (1995)	To investigate how students with prior experience in leading their own small-group discussions provided support for those new to Book Club.	Social constructivist	Qualitative	Peer-led Book Club discussion groups	Focused on three days during the 2nd year of a three-year study; 5 culturally and academically diverse fifth-grade students	Students facilitated one another's learning in peer-led literature discussion, but the teacher had an important role in monitoring student discourse and planning instruction that met emerging needs.

2000-2009

Study	Purpose	Theoretical perspectives	Design/ Methodology	Discussion format	Context/ Participants	Findings
Almasi, O'Flahavan, & Arya (2001)	To examine more and less proficient peer discussions of literature to determine what makes some discussions effective and others less effective.	Transactional Sociocultural Dialogic	Qualitative	Peer-led literature discussion with the teacher as a facilitator	Four-month study; 49 fourth-grade students; 6 classroom teachers	Recursivity and embedded topics contributed to coherence in discussion which was important to conversational competence. Too much metatalk in literature discussion was debilitating.
Chinn, Anderson, & Waggoner (2001)	To examine how the discourse of children and teachers is affected by the use of two different instructional frames, recitations, and Collaborative Reasoning.	Reader response Collaborative Reasoning	Quantitative	Teacher-led literature discussion (recitation and CR)	Seven-week study (12 discussions); 84 students in 4 fourth-grade classrooms; 4 teachers	When students were given greater control over interpretation, turn taking, and topic, engagement was enhanced and this resulted in greater use of beneficial cognitive processes.
Evans (2002)	To investigate students' perceptions of their experiences when participating in peer-led literature discussion groups.	Social constructivist Constructivist	Qualitative	Peer-led literature discussion groups with teacher and researcher as facilitators	One-year study; 22 students (11 females and 11 males) in a fifth-grade classroom; one classroom teacher, Marcy	Students had a well-developed sense of the conditions necessary to promote effective discussion.

Table 1 ctd.

Study	Purpose	Theoretical perspectives	Design/ Methodology	Discussion format	Context/ Participants	Findings
Li et al. (2007)	To investigate leadership in small groups engaging in Collaborative Reasoning.	Collaborative Reasoning Schema (leadership)	Qualitative	Peer-led literature discussion with teacher facilitator	Five-week study with twice weekly discussions (120 total discussions); 35 males and 41 females in 4 fourth-grade classrooms; 4 teachers	When children were given social and intellectual space to operate on their own, many emerged as leaders in classroom discussion groups. Collaborative Reasoning discussions provided an environment conducive to the emergence of child leaders and leadership schemas.
Maloch (2002)	To examine the multiple roles of the teacher and the relationship between the teacher's role and student participation in literature discussion groups.	Sociocultural	Qualitative Discourse analysis	Peer-led literature discussion with teacher as facilitator	Five-month study; 29 students in a third-grade classroom	Transition to student-centered discussion formats required scaffolding. Microanalysis of teacher-student participation patterns indicated that teacher facilitation was dynamic as students progressed in their development of conversational strategies and exploratory talk.
Maloch (2005)	To explore two students' shifting participations and constructions of self across a variety of literacy events in their classroom.	Social constructivist Positioning Cultural capital	Qualitative case studies	Peer-led literature discussion with teacher as facilitator	Five-month study; third-grade classroom; two African-American males, Antwan & Chris, as focal students	Participation structures that were more decentralized and offered more opportunities for flexible student involvement allowed students to gain cultural capital and reconstruct their personal identities.
McIntyre, Kyle, & Moore (2006)	To describe how one primary-grade teacher scaffolded learners' participation in dialogue about books, construction of meaning, and literary concepts in a second-grade classroom of primarily at-risk students.	Dialogic Transactional Cultural historical activity	Qualitative grounded theory and collaborative teacher action research	Peer-led literature discussion with teacher as a facilitator	Four-day study; 24 students in a multi-age first-/second-grade classroom; experienced teacher, Gayle	Primary-grade children were able to engage in dialogue about books in meaningful ways through supports such as teacher-fronted classroom discourse and a democratic classroom environment.
Möller (2004)	To show how one struggling reader, Ashley, interacted with her teachers and a group of six classmates in their heterogeneous literature discussion group.	Social constructivist	Qualitative case study	Peer-led literature discussion with teacher and researcher as facilitators/ participants	One-year study; 22 students in a fourth-grade classroom; one focal student, Ashley	Ashley was supported with empowering spaces and was able to demonstrate and enhance her competencies as she explored the possibilities that exist to learn from others, to learn with others, and to teach others.

be broken into patterns of discourse that they categorized as "argument strategems" (p. 2). Such discourse patterns had a "snowballing," or spreading activation effect on other participants. Li et al. (2007) noted the same snowballing effect for leadership schemas that developed as students learned to control discussions. Across studies, the CR researchers found that discourse and interactional factors related to argument and leadership influenced turn-taking and engagement. As a result, students were more likely to participate with increased frequency in such productive cognitive events. Taken as a whole, studies that incorporated dialogic frameworks demonstrated that learners are able to serve as more knowledgeable others, are able to tussle with competing perspectives, and are more likely to have increased opportunities for talk.

Though some investigators did not use the specific term, the notion of exploratory talk was investigated and/or discussed in a large number of studies. Appearing in research and pedagogical articles in the 1990s (e.g., Leal, 1993; Pierce, 1995), interest in exploratory talk barely waned in the last decade. Leal described exploratory talk as "talking without fully intact answers" (p. 117), and as such, it emphasizes the process of learning rather than the product. Mercer (1995) defined exploratory talk as "a way of using language effectively for joint, explicit, collaborative reasoning" (p. 103). Many researchers have given thoughtful consideration to the contextual parameters that promote exploratory talk and have described what happens during the discussions. Once again, classifying talk was important, but the focus had shifted—researchers were interested in how talk became a tool for constructing knowledge within the collective group. For example, Almasi, O'Flahavan, & Arya (2001) examined the quality of talk during peer-led conversational discussion groups (O'Flahavan, 1989), comparing more and less proficient fourth-graders. While earlier investigations primarily analyzed distinct and defined meaning units of talk to categorize response, these investigators looked at the underlying structure of the entire conversation to see how the talk cohered and how understandings were negotiated. The researchers stressed that peer discussions are key to increased opportunities to negotiate procedures, conventions, and interactions. Unlike cooperative models (e.g., literature circles, Daniels, 1994) in which students maintain specified roles within the discussion, in conversational peer discussions, students' roles are open to change. In this more dynamic context, the researchers suggested that teachers or peers may have more direct as well as incidental opportunities for scaffolding interactions.

As this example typifies, across the last two decades, a majority of studies focused on small-group discussions were, in essence, examining the influence of peer-led discussions on students and teachers. In agreement with the Almasi et al. (2001) findings, there is consensus among researchers that the teacher's decision-making and interactions are critical to the development of quality exploratory talk. Clearly, there has been consistent interest in the role of the teacher, which is the second broad theme we identified.

The Role of the Teacher

Shortly after literature discussion group instruction was initially implemented and researched, authors were already discussing the difficulties in the teacher's ability to engage students and ensure productive discussions. Foundational to these concerns is the role of the teacher. Many studies set out to determine how the teacher might support quality literature discussions. Examples of questions included: How might the teacher scaffold? (e.g., Maloch, 2002, 2004). Can students perform the role of more knowledgeable other? What happens when students develop their own questions? (e.g., Commeyras & Sumner, 1998). Several experts suggested ways to structure talk and interactions so that students could differentiate growth in interpretations as well as in their interactions (O'Flahavan, 1994; Wiencek & O'Flahavan, 1994).

Across the decades, it appears that two primary factors relative to the teacher's role influenced discussion interpretations and interactions. The first, teacher focus, was instrumental in influencing student engagement and interaction as well as the quality of discussions. For instance, McMahon (1992) noted that learner interactions changed as a result of the teacher's instructional focus, and responses varied based on whether the teacher focused on personal response or reading skills and strategies. "What counts as knowledge and understanding in any given classroom is largely shaped by the questions teachers ask, how they respond to their students, and how they structure small-group and other pedagogical activities" (Nystrand, 2006, p. 400). As Nystrand's quote suggests, the second influence, teacher interactions, is related to teacher focus. Teacher decision-making about the focus of talk and teacher interactions with the group clearly influence group interpretations and interactions. Almasi et. al. (2001) found that students were more proficient in managing group processes and sustaining quality conversations when the teacher had a less intrusive role in the discussions; in turn, the other teacher's increased interactions with the less proficient group resulted in decreased student responsibility.

Across all studies, the teacher's role may be represented through a continuum. Stronger teacher involvement or control, indicated by the teacher generating questions to discuss (sometimes beforehand) and/or fully participating in discussions, represented one end of the continuum. Moderate or minimal involvement was exhibited by the teacher's listening in to facilitate, to model a response, or to briefly scaffold the group's interactions or interpretations. On the other end of the continuum, there was little or no teacher involvement with peers almost entirely directing the talk and interactions of the group. In the latter, some of the teachers recorded the discussions and listened to them afterwards. In certain cases, it is unclear if non-participation was an explicit part of the teacher's decision-making or if the groups were peer-led by default because of the teacher's inability to support multiple group discussions simultaneously. What is reflected at times, and at both ends of the continuum, are difficulties that occur, often in relation to interactions.

In cases where it was possible to examine a series of articles or a strand of research by the same researcher (e.g., Maloch, 2000, 2002, 2004, 2005) it became apparent that a number of researchers were grappling with the notion of scaffolding. Maloch's (2002) study serves as an exemplar of the difficulties that students face when transitioning from teacher-led to peer-led discussions, especially in taking on more active roles. The study also focused on teacher responsiveness, examining the nature of teacher scaffolding as the teacher, Ms. P., intervened to support students' interactional difficulties. In this investigation, the teacher explicitly modeled talk as a way of highlighting particular interactional patterns. Initially, students attempted to use the interactional tools in a formulaic manner, but eventually, they appropriated these tools and used them more effectively.

In much the same way, Gayle, the second-grade teacher of a group of poor, working-class students (McIntyre, Kyle, and Moore, 2006), front-loaded what was to be learned. Gayle used "heavy teacher-fronted discourse, emphasizing telling, defining, and modeling at the beginning of her lessons" (p. 37); yet, her responses were also "carefully measured" (p. 41) and characterized by intently listening and thinking about the students' ideas. The researchers suggested that Gayle's interactional responses—her slow, deliberate speech, her proximity to the children, her use of gestures, body language, paraphrase, and repetition of information created a low-risk environment for these students to become more comfortable with "academic talk" (p. 61). They proposed that the classroom culture cultivated by Gayle "enabled the dialogue to develop once she put the instructional conversation structures into place" (p. 61).

These descriptions suggest that researchers' views of the teacher's role seemed to be subtly debated across the decades. It is clear from the research that the teacher needs to have a facilitative role, but to what degree and in what context are still important concerns. What the work of both Maloch (2002) and McIntyre et al. (2006) put forward is that the nature of teacher responses and interactions is highly contextualized. The rich, thick descriptions provided in many of the qualitative investigations allow for closer examination of the teacher(s), learners, and instructional contexts, helping us to sort through some of the complexity. The role of the teacher is also a part of the next theme, the examination of authority.

Authority

In classrooms with dialogic discussions, there is typically the view that multiple interpretations exist for a text (Rosenblatt, 2004). With the transition from teacher-led to peer-led discussions, theoretically, the teacher is not the authority, or the arbiter of what goes on in terms of talk or interactions. Such a view acknowledges that peers can perform the role of knowledgeable other. Furthermore, opportunities for student talk, such as that in peer-led discussions, have been advocated to promote democratic classroom cultures. Many experts suggested that such structures for learning potentially emancipate the learner and give voice to all learners (see Knoeller, 1998). However, from this shift came some surprising results. The interactions of the groups did not always facilitate democratic discussions. For example, Almasi and Russell (1998) found that students appropriated language and behaviors of the teacher in order to gain authority. There was the potential for backlash from other students when learners attempted to move toward interpretive authority (e.g., Evans, 1996), and students competed to gain authority within the groups (e.g., Lewis, 1997). Evan's (1996) study revealed that facilitative roles can be abused when students position themselves and others in ways that allow verbal domination. Gender and power merged as the boys in the group controlled and silenced one of the female participants. Clearly, such unintended consequences were a concern for Evans; in her 2002 investigation, she explored students' perceptions of their literature discussion groups. An important follow-up, Evans (2002) found that the fifth-graders she observed and interviewed had a well-developed sense of the factors and conditions that impact discussions; nevertheless, the students found it difficult to enact some of the conditions when participating in mixed-gender groups. From a research stance as well as a pedagogical view, this study suggests the importance of gathering information from informants, in this case students. Such information offers important instructional considerations for teacher planning and decision-making.

In spite of the thorny issues that may occur in literature discussion groups, our analyses suggest that interactions that promote ownership and risk-taking in relation to interpretations give students important opportunities to grow as learners, to try out ideas, and to take on leadership roles with peers (Almasi, 1995; Chinn, et al., 2001, McMahon & Goatley, 1995; Möller, 2004; Li, et al., 2007). As a particularly compelling example, Möller's (2004) description of a young girl who takes advantage of teacher assistance to grow in leadership and literacy knowledge represents the potential of scaffolding and transference of understandings in discussion group contexts. On the other hand, Li et al. (2007) characterized the major finding of their study as "the striking extent to which child leaders emerged in classroom discussion groups when the teacher stepped back and gave children the social and intellectual space to operate on their own" (p. 105). Again, the role of the teacher is integrally related to interpretive authority and group management authority. The findings of Möller as well as Li and colleagues speak to the complexity of teacher decision-making that must occur in discussion contexts. With too much teacher control, students may become disenfranchised and passive; on the other hand, when teachers are not involved at all, the conversations may be unproductive or even socially unjust. Our findings suggest that when groups are carefully scaffolded (Maloch, 2002; Möller, 2004) or receive front-loading through explicit demonstration and clear expectations, or are prepared to use particular discourse structures such as argument strategems (Anderson, et al., 2001; Li, et al., 2007), some disadvantageous interactional issues are ameliorated.

Diversity and Social Justice

Much of the preceding discussion of democratic cultures, positioning, and authority is strongly linked to diversity and the related construct, social justice. While we found fewer investigations focused on this theme, a pattern emerged in the 1990s and became stronger in the last decade— concerns about diversity and social justice within literature discussion groups. Evans provided a glimpse into gender issues and positioning as early as 1996, as did Lewis (1997) shortly after. Lewis noted that ability, age, and gender surfaced repeatedly as she analyzed her data. Her findings suggest that the differential power and status that are a part of the overall classroom structure are re-enacted in peer-led discussion groups.

A number of studies represented the challenges that come as gender, ability, race, and class intersect with authority and power. Some of these investigations reported negative effects that occurred when these issues become a source of tension within groups (e.g., Evans, 1996, 2002; Lewis, 1997). However, as Möeller's case study of Ashley suggests, it is possible for the teacher's scaffolding to mediate and support a disenfranchised learner, assisting her in becoming an integral part of the group. As a result, the injustices within her own life gave Ashley the experiences to position herself as a source of authority and knowledge, lifting her peers' understandings of text and social justice in ways that might not have been possible otherwise.

With a view toward group diversity, Goatley and her colleagues (e.g., Goatley, Brock, and Raphael, 1995; McMahon & Goatley, 1995) examined participation in student-led Book Clubs (Raphael & McMahon, 1994). They found that through the support of peers, diverse learners (in this case, learning disabled and English language learners) were successful in literature discussions. At the time, the role of peer support was a particularly important finding, suggesting that learners can take on roles that assist peers in discussing and understanding text.

While peers provided the necessary scaffolds in the previous study, the teacher provided the necessary scaffolding in Maloch's (2005) case studies of two boys who were culturally and linguistically diverse. The boys attended resource and positioned themselves as struggling and were likewise classified by peers. Changes in their positioning and cultural capital were achieved as the teacher (Ms. P., also studied in Maloch, 2002, 2004) made decisions to offer choice, to give support in varied ways, and to help them learn the conversational norms of the group. This study is yet another example that speaks to instructional focus and teacher interactions for scaffolding. Through such changes the two learners were able to participate equally with peers.

The work of Goatley et al. (1995) is an early example of research focused on the participation of culturally diverse students including English language learners. We noted increased attention to this topic in the last decade. For example, the research of Martinez-Roldan (2003, 2005) provided insights into ways that children in bilingual settings navigate small-group literature discussions. Within a few studies, attention was focused on multicultural literature and literature dealing with social justice issues. Typically, the intent was to study learners' responses to cultural differences and societal concerns (e.g., DeNicolo, & Franquiz, 2006; Martínez-Roldán & López-Robertson, 1999).

CONCLUSIONS AND IMPLICATIONS

In the previous discussion, we represented our analysis of past and present research. Here we provide a brief summation of key findings related to each theme and suggest a few implications for future research and instruction. As we arrived at the four primary constructs, the social construction of knowledge, the role of the teacher, authority, and diversity and social justice, we realized how interwoven they are. Such complexity may help to explain why our analysis of small-group literature discussion research suggested mixed results in terms of instructional effectiveness, also recently noted by Almasi & Garas-York (2009). Clearly, sorting out the varied aspects of small-group instruction is challenging for teachers and for researchers.

In relation to the social construction of understanding, our analyses of the research suggested that learners can benefit from small-group discussions and that peers can function as more knowledgeable others. Talk that is exploratory and includes argument or conflict appears to aid learners as they work collaboratively to construct new understandings and ways of interacting. The potential represented by a number of these investigations is promising. To build upon the promising rather than mixed results, we highlight two important points for future consideration. As research in this area began, a number of prominent studies used quasi-experimental designs. Reports of such studies typically do not offer strong contextualizations. We wondered if the shift toward qualitative methods responded to a need within the research, to provide in-depth analyses and understandings of the behaviors and responses that occur within varied contexts. Research tools were selected as a means to answer many of the whys and hows that both researchers and practitioners were asking after "Grand Conversations" was published. Nystrand (2006) maintained that effective classroom discourse should not be studied as an "executed instructional 'treatment' " but as a "medium for instruction" (p. 393). Furthermore, if we want to understand, "moments by which change is made" (as Maloch's title suggests), we must study moment by moment talk, interactions, and decision-making in these richly contextualized settings to see what occurs and how it changes. This idea of closely examining contexts and gradual change is related to our second point. It is not a new idea, but it deserves emphasis—more longitudinal studies are needed. Our findings suggest that in most of the studies, change came slowly. To understand and effect change, teachers and learners need time. Many of our focal studies demonstrated the value of studying contexts and participants for extended periods of time as well as the value of focusing descriptions and analyses on key participants. We hope to see continued study of focal students across time, even school years, and more detailed analyses of teachers' moment by moment decisions, similar to those provided in a few focal studies.

These implications are also relevant in relation to the role of the teacher. Our earlier discussion of results related to teacher decision-making and interactions indicate conflicting findings. In sum, some studies suggested that groups operated better and students learned more when peers functioned autonomously or there was less intrusion from the teacher. On the other hand, some investigations described positive changes that occurred when the teacher intervened with adroit scaffolding. It appears that such interactions are most needed when individuals within the groups have difficulties. More research is needed to determine how and when teachers might mediate group interaction. What is clear is that teacher-learner interactional patterns are one of the most critical and confounding elements in discussions.

We noted previously the shift in qualitative methods. We also found, particularly in the last decade, that many of the researchers essentially became teacher researchers (e.g., Commeyras, Möller). In some cases, the researcher and classroom teachers were co-teaching while in others, the researcher took the primary role of teacher. We highlight these examples as a continuing and promising trend. Why the researcher took on the role of teacher was not explained, but it provided an opportunity to become more attuned to the context of the classroom. Moreover, such involvement offers opportunities to conceptualize and influence change in real time.

Within our discussion of the final themes, authority, diversity and social justice, we identified troubling issues related to the research. As reflected in Lewis (1997), small-group discussions serve as a microcosm of the larger classroom setting. When groups functioned unsuccessfully, difficulties were frequently attributed to issues of gender, race, class, and ability. Students vied for authority, and learners positioned themselves and were positioned by others in relation to their cultural, linguistic, and academic differences. Findings suggested that responsive teachers could meet the needs of diverse and disenfranchised learners by carefully scaffolding and providing the kinds of assistance that help them gain cultural capital. While more attention was given to diversity in the last decade, more research is needed. By highlighting diverse learners, particularly through case studies and other rich narratives, we can more fully develop exemplars for understanding how individuals and groups best construct knowledge.

Recently, Israel & Duffy (2009) noted a "sense of impending change" (p. 674) within research on reading comprehension; we suggest that the same may be true for literature discussion research and instruction. As we read and analyzed these studies, we were struck by how seldom the word comprehension was used. From our perspective, engaging in conflicting points of view, grappling with confusions, pondering a character's motivations, and critically thinking about and interpreting texts are acts of comprehension. We are fairly certain that researchers focused on response would agree. However, as these documents representing our professional discourse suggest, the words we use matter. Comprehension is receiving renewed attention in research, and hopefully increased attention in classrooms as well. We would like to see literature discussion share some of that attention. Perhaps by incorporating comprehension into our language as we discuss what occurs during literature discussions, we may influence a closer connection between the two in assessment and instruction.

REFERENCES

*Allen, J., Moller, K. J., & Stroup, D. (2003). "Is this some kind of soap opera?": A tale of two readers across four literature discussion contexts. *Reading & Writing Quarterly, 19,* 225-251.

Allington, R. L. (2005). The other five "pillars" of effective reading instruction. *Reading Today, 22*(6), 3.

*Almasi, J. F. (1995). The nature of fourth graders' sociocognitive conflicts in peer-led and teacher-led discussions of literature. *Reading Research Quarterly, 30,* 314-351.

Almasi, J. F., & Garas-York, K. (2009). Comprehension and discussion of text. In S. E. Israel & G. G. Duffy (Eds.) *Handbook of research on reading comprehension* (pp. 470-493). New York, NY: Routledge.

*Almasi, J. F., O'Flahavan, J. F., & Arya, P. (2001). A comparative analysis of student and teacher development in more and less proficient discussions of literature. *Reading Research Quarterly, 36,* 96-120.

Almasi, J. F., & Russell, W. S. (November, 2000). *Positioning for power: The female pariah in peer discussions of text.* Paper presented at the 50th annual meeting of the National Reading Conference, Scottsdale, AZ.

Altheide, D. L. (1996). *Qualitative media analysis.* Thousand Oaks, CA: Sage Publications.

*Anderson, R. C., Nguyen-Jahiel, K., McNurlen, B., Archodidou, A., Kim, S., Reznitskaya, A., Gilbert, L. (2001). The snowball phenomenon: Spread of ways of talking and ways of thinking across groups of children. *Cognition and Instruction, 19*(1), 1-46.

Applebee, A. N. (1978). *The child's concept of story: Ages two to seventeen.* Chicago, IL: The University of Chicago Press.

*Barajas, K. E. (2008). Beyond stereotypes?: Talking about gender in school booktalk. *Ethnography and Education, 3*(2), 129-144.

Beach, R., & Hynds, S. (1991). Research on response to literature. In R. Barr, M. L. Kamil, P. B. Mosenthal, & P. D. Pearson (Eds.), *Handbook of reading research* (pp. 453-489). White Plains, NY: Longman.

*Bobola, K. (2003). Children's minds at work: How understanding of rich narrative text emerges in fourth-grade classrooms that combine peer group discussion and journal writing. In C. M. Fairbanks, J. Worthy, B. Maloch, J. V. Hoffman, & D. L. Schallert (Eds.), *52nd Yearbook of the National Reading Conference* (pp. 66-84). Oak Creek, Wisconsin: National Reading Conference.

Cassidy, J., & Cassidy, D. (2008, February/March). What's hot, what's not for 2008. *Reading Today,* pp. 1, 10-11.

*Celani, K., McIntyre, E., Rightmyer, E. C. (2006). Knowing the text, knowing the learner: Literature discussions with fifth grade struggling readers. *Reading Horizons, 47*(2), 97-119.

*Chinn, C. A., Anderson, R. C., & Waggoner, M. A. (2001). Patterns of discourse in two kinds of literature discussion. *Reading Research Quarterly, 36*(4), 378-411.

*Chinn, C. A., & Anderson, R. C. (1999). The structure of discussions that promote reasoning. *Teachers College Record, 100,* 315-368.

*Clark, K. (2009). The nature and influence of comprehension strategy use during peer-led literature discussions: An analysis of intermediate grade students' practices. *Literacy Research and Instruction, 48,* 95-119.

*Commeyras, M., & Sumner, G. (1998). Literature questions children want to discuss: What teachers and students learned in a second-grade classroom. *The Elementary School Journal, 99*(2), 129-152.

Daniels, H. (1994). *Literature circles: Voice and choice in the student-centered classroom.* Markham, Ontario: Pembroke.

*Danielson, K. E. (1992). Literature groups and literature logs: Responding to literature in a community of learners. *Reading Horizons, 32*(5), 372-382.

DeNicolo, C. P., & Franquiz, M. E. (2006). "Do I have to say it?": Critical encounters with multicultural children's literature. *Language Arts, 84*(2), 157-170.

Duffy, G. G., & Israel, S. E. (2009). Where to from here? Themes, trends, and questions. In S. E. Israel & G. G. Duffy, (Eds.), *Handbook of research on reading comprehension.* (pp. 668-675). New York, NY: Routledge.

*Eeds, M., & Wells, D. (1989). Grand conversations: An exploration of meaning construction in literature study groups. *Research in the Teaching of English, 23*(10), 4-29.

*Evans, K. S. (1996). Negotiating roles in collaborative literacy research: Re-examining issues of power and equity. *Language Arts, 77,* 128-136.

*Evans, K. S. (2002). Fifth-grade students' perceptions of how they experience literature discussion groups. *Reading Research Quarterly, 37*(1), 46-69.

*Evans, K. S., Alvermann, D., Anders, P. L. (1998). Literature discussion groups: An examination of gender roles, *Reading Research and Instruction, 37*(2), 107-122.

Fink, A. (2005). *Conducting research literature reviews: From the internet to paper.* Thousand Oaks, CA: Sage.

*Frank, C. R., Dixon, C. N., & Brandts, L. R. (1998). "Dear book club": A sociolinguistic and ethnographic analysis of literature discussion groups in second grade. *47th Yearbook of the National Reading Conference,* pp. 105-115. Oak Creek, WI: National Reading Conference.

Gaffney, J., & Anderson, R. C. (2000). Trends in reading research in the United States: Changing intellectual currents over thirty years. In M. L. Kamil, P. B. Mosenthal, P. D. Pearson, & R. Barr (Eds.) *Handbook of Reading Research* (pp. 53-74). New York, NY: Erlbaum.

Galda, L., & Beach, R. (2001). Theory into practice: Response to literature as a cultural activity. *Reading Research Quarterly, 36*(1), 64-73.

Gibbs, G. R. (2002). *Qualitative data analysis: Explorations with NVivo.* New York, NY: Open University Press.

*Goatley, V. J. (1996). The participation of a student identified as learning disabled in a regular education book club: The case of Stark. *Reading and Writing Quarterly,* 12, 195-214.

*Goatley, V. J., Brock, C. H., & Raphael, T. E. (1995). Diverse learners participating in regular education "Book Clubs." *Reading Research Quarterly, 30*(3), 352-380.

*Godinho, S., & Shrimpton, B. (2003). Boys' and girls' use of linguistic space in small-group discussions: Whose talk dominates? *Australian Journal of Language and Literacy, 26*(3), 28-43.

Hickman, J. (1981). A new perspective on response to literature: Research in an elementary school setting. *Research in the Teaching of English, 15*(4), 343-354.

*Hollingsworth, L. (2008). Complicated conversations: Exploring race and ideology in an elementary classroom. *Urban Education, 44*(1), 30-58.

Israel, S. E., & Duffy, G. G. (Eds.) (2009). *Handbook of research on reading comprehension.* New York, NY: Routledge.

*Keefer, M. W., Zeitz, C. M., & Resnick, L. B. (2000). Judging the quality of peer-led student dialogues. *Cognition & Instruction, 18*(1), 53-81.

Knoeller, C. (1998). *Voicing ourselves: Whose words we use when we talk about books.* Albany, NY: SUNY Press.

Langer, J. A. (1995). *Envisioning literature: Literary understanding and literature instruction.* New York, NY: Teacher College Press and Newark, DE: International Reading Association.

Leal, D. J. (1993). The power of literary peer-group discussions: How children collaboratively negotiate meaning. *The Reading Teacher, 47*(2), 114-120.

Leech, N. L., & Onwuegbuzie, A. J. (2008). Qualitative data analysis: A compendium of techniques and a framework for selection for school psychology research and beyond. *School Psychology Quarterly, 23*(4), 587-604.

*Lewis, C. (1997). The social drama of literature discussions in a fifth/sixth-grade classroom. *Research in the Teaching of English, 31*(2), 163-204.

*Li, Y., Anderson, R. C., Nguyen-Jahiel, K., Dong, T., Archodidou, A., Kim, I., Miller, B. (2007). Emergent leadership in children's discussion groups. *Cognition and Instruction, 25*(1), 75-111.

Luria, A. (1979). *The making of mind.* Cambridge, MA: Harvard University Press.

*Maloch, B. (2000). Shifting roles of responsibility: Scaffolding students' talk during literature discussion groups. In T. Shanahan & F. V. Rodriguez-Brown (Eds.), *Forty-ninth Yearbook of the National Reading Conference* (pp. 222-234). Chicago, IL: National Reading Conference.

*Maloch, B. (2002). Scaffolding student talk: One teacher's role in literature discussion groups. *Reading Research Quarterly, 37*(1), 94-112.

*Maloch, B. (2004). On the road to literature discussion groups: Teacher scaffolding during preparatory experiences. *Reading Research and Instruction, 44*(2), 1-20.

*Maloch, B. (2005). Moments by which change is made: A cross-case exploration of teacher mediation and student participation in literacy events. *Journal of Literacy Research, 37*(1), 95-142.

*Many, J. E. (2002). An exhibition and analysis of verbal tapestries: Understanding how scaffolding is woven into the fabric of instructional conversations. *Reading Research Quarterly, 37*(4), 376-407.

Marshall, J. D. (2000). Research on response to literature. In M. L. Kamil, P. B. Mosenthal, P. D. Pearson, & R. Barr (Eds.), *Handbook of reading research* (Vol. 3, pp. 381-402). Mahwah, NJ: Erlbaum.

Martinez, M. G., & Roser, N. L. (2003). Children's responses to literature. In J. Flood, D. Lapp, J. R. Squire & J. M. Jensen, (Eds.), *Handbook of research on teaching the English language arts* (2nd ed.) (pp. 799-813). Mahwah, NJ: Lawrence Erlbaum Associates.

Martinez, M. G., & Roser, N. L. (2001). A review of research on children's responses to literature. In J. V. Hoffman, D. L. Schallert, C. M. Fairbanks, J. Worthy, & B. Maloch (Eds.), *50th Yearbook of the National Reading Conference* (pp. 409-418). Oak Creek, WI: National Reading Conference.

*Martinez-Roldan, C. M. (2003). Building worlds and identities: A case study of the role of narratives in bilingual literature discussions. *Research in the Teaching of English, 37*(4), 491-526.

*Martinez-Roldan, C. M. (2005). Examining bilingual children's gender ideologies through critical discourse analysis. *Critical Inquiry in Language Studies: An International Journal, 2*(3), 157-178.

Martínez-Roldán, C. M., & López-Robertson, J. M. (1999). Initiating literature circles in a first-grade classroom. *The Reading Teacher, 53*, 270-281.

*McGee, L. M. (1992). An exploration of meaning construction in first graders' grand conversations. In C. K. Kinzer & D. J. Leu (Eds.), *41st Yearbook of the National Reading Conference* (pp. 177-186) Oak Creek, WI: National Reading Conference.

*McGee, L. M., Courtney, L., & Lomax, R. (1994). Supporting first graders' responses to literature: An analysis of teachers' roles in grand conversations. In C. K. Kinzer & D. J. Leu (Eds.), *Multidimensional aspects of literacy research, theory, and practice: 43rd Yearbook of the National Reading Conference* (pp. 517-526), Oak Creek, WI: National Reading Conference.

*McIntyre, E., Kyle, D. W., & Moore, G. H. (2006). A primary grade teacher's guidance toward small-group dialogue. *Reading Research Quarterly, 41*(1), 36-66.

McMahon, S. I. (1992). *A group of five students as they participate in their student-led book club.* Unpublished doctoral dissertation. Michigan State University: East Lansing.

*McMahon, S. I. (1994). Student-led book clubs: Transversing a river of interpretation. *New Advocate, 7*(2), 109-125.

*McMahon, S. I., & Goatley, V. J. (1995). Fifth graders helping peers discuss texts in student-led groups. *Journal of Educational Research, 89*(1), 23-34.

Mercer, N. (1995). *The guided construction of knowledge: Talk amongst teachers and learners.* Bristol, PA: Multilingual Matters.

Miles, M. B., & Huberman, A. M. (1994). *Qualitative data analysis.* Thousand Oaks, CA: Sage.

*Möller, K. J. (2004). Creating zones of possibility for struggling readers: A study of one fourth grader's shifting roles in literature discussions. *Journal of Literacy Research, 36*(4), 419-460.

National Reading Panel (2000). Teaching children to read: An evidence-based assessment of the scientific research literature on reading and its implications for reading instruction. http://www.nichd.nih.gov/publications/nrp/report.cfm.

NVivo 8. (2008). Doncaster, Victoria, Australia: QSR International Pty. Ltd.

O'Flahavan, J. F. (1989). Second graders' social, intellectual, and affective development in varied group discussions about literature: An exploration of participation structure. Unpublished doctoral dissertation, University of Illinois, Urbana-Champaign.

O'Flahavan, J. F. (1994). Teacher role options in peer discussions about literature. *The Reading Teacher, 48*(4), 354-356.

*Pantaleo, S. (2002). Grade 1 students meet David Wiesner's "Three Pigs." *Journal of Children's Literature, 28*(2), 72-84.

Pierce, K. M. (1995). A plan for learning. Creating a place for exploratory talk. *Primary Voices, 3*(1), 16-29.

*Porter, S. B. (2006). Learning about learners: Struggling readers in a fourth grade literature discussion group. In P. E. Linder, M. B. Sampson, J. R. Dugan, B. A. Brancato (Eds.), *Building Bridges to Literacy, The Twelfth Yearbook of the College Reading Association,* Readyville, TN: College Reading Association.

*Raphael, T. E., & Brock, C. H. (1993). Mei: Learning the literacy culture in an urban elementary school. In D. J. Leu & C. K. Kinzer (Eds.), *42nd Yearbook of the National Reading Conference* (pp. 179-188). Oak Creek, WI: National Reading Conference.

*Raphael, T. E., Gavelek, J. R., & Daniels, V. (1998). Developing students' talk about text: Analyses in a fifth-grade classroom. *47th Yearbook of the National Reading Conference Yearbook,* (pp. 116, 128). Oak Creek, WI: National Reading Conference.

Raphael, T. E., & McMahon, S. I. (1994). Book club: An alternative framework for reading instruction. *The Reading Teacher, 48,* 102–116.

Raphael, T. E., McMahon, S. I, Goatley, V. J., Bentley, J.L., Boyd, F. B., Pardo, L. S., & Woodman, D.A. (1991). *Reading instruction reconsidered: Literature and discussion in the reading program* (Elementary Subjects

Center Series No. 47). East Lansing: Michigan State University, Center for the Learning and Teaching of Elementary Subjects.

*Reznitskaya, A., Anderson, R. C., McNurlen, B., Nguyen-Jahiel, K., Archodidou, A., & Kim, S. (2001). Influence of oral discussion on written argument. *Discourse Processes, 32*(2/3), 155-175.

Roller, C., & Beed, P. (1994). Sometimes the conversations were grand, and sometimes . . . *Language Arts, 71*, 509-515.

Rosenblatt, L. M. (1978). *The reader, the text, the poem: The transactional theory of the literary work.* Carbondale, IL: Southern Illinois University Press.

Rosenblatt, L. M. (1985). Viewpoints: Transaction versus interaction—a terminological rescue operation. *Research in the Teaching of English, 19*, 96-107.

Rosenblatt, L. M. (2004). The transactional theory of reading and writing. In R. B. Ruddell & N. J. Unrau, (Eds.), *Theoretical models and processes of reading* (5th ed.). (pp. 1363-1398). Newark, DE: International Reading Association.

*Scharer, P. L., & Peters, D. (1996). An exploration of literature discussions conducted by two teachers moving toward literature-based reading instruction. *Reading Research & Instruction, 36*(1), 33-50.

Shanahan, T., & Neuman, S. (1997). Literacy research that makes a difference. *Reading Research Quarterly, 32*(2), 202-210.

*Short, K. G. (1992). Intertextuality: Searching for patterns that connect. In C. K. Kinzer & D. J. Leu (Eds.), *41st Yearbook of the National Reading Conference* (pp. 187-197). Oak Creek, WI: National Reading Conference.

Strauss, A., & Corbin, J. (1998). *Basics of qualitative research.* Thousand Oaks, CA: Sage.

*Villaume, S. K., & Hopkins, L. (1995). A transactional and sociocultural view of response in a fourth-grade literature discussion group. *Reading Research and Instruction, 34*(3), 190-203.

Vygotsky, L. S. (1978). *Mind in society.* Cambridge, MA: Harvard University Press.

Weincek, J., & O'Flahavan, J. (1994). From teacher-led to peer discussions about literature: Suggestions for making the shift. *Language Arts, 71*, 488-489.

Wells, G. (1997). Dialogic inquiry in education: Building on the legacy of Vygotsky. In C. D. Lee & P. Smagorinsky (Eds.), *Vygotskian perspectives on literacy research: Constructing meaning through collaborative inquiry* (pp. 51-85). New York, NY: Cambridge University Press.

*Williams, B. G. (1999). Emergent readers and literature circle discussions. *College Reading Association Yearbook, 21*, 183-200.

Williams, P., Hammer, M., Pierczynski-Ward, & Henson, K. (2007). Straight from the editors' mouths . . .pens. *The Delta Kappa Gamma Bulletin, 73*(3), 13-20.

Note: An asterisk before a reference represents studies included in the macro analysis.

Peer-to-Peer Talk about Newspaper Articles: Supporting Knowledge and Comprehension of an Authentic Informational Genre

Michelle E. Jordan
Arizona State University

Michael G. Massad, Sr.
Austin Independent School District

Researchers increasingly recognize that different text types present different cognitive demands on readers (Park, 2008; Purcell-Gates, Duke, & Martineau, 2007). Informational texts are especially variable in their structures, features, and functions, making demands that students learn diverse strategies for engaging in practices with informational genres. However, when curriculum guidelines calling for students to be familiar with a variety of literary genres are coupled with standardized testing, they can easily lend themselves to instructional practices that emphasize recognizing and naming structures and functions, rather than those that also support ongoing, repeated exposure to and authentic engagement with single genres and their associated practices (Bomer, 2005; Cruz & Pollack, 2004). Relatively little is known about how young students learn to comprehend genres of informational text or about instructional practices that support students' acquisition of appropriate literacy skills with such texts (Maloch, 2008; Palmer & Stewart, 2003). In particular, the affordances and challenges of peer-to-peer interaction around authentic informational texts have not yet received adequate attention in the research literature.

We undertook a qualitative investigation into how students in one third-grade class repeatedly encountered the informational genre of newspaper articles, focusing on how students' peer-to-peer interactions aided them in navigating and comprehending this text type. The daily routine of *In the News* occurred at the beginning of each instructional day throughout the school year. Two students were assigned the role of *reporters* each week, working each day to select, read, summarize, and prepare to present an article from that day's edition of the local newspaper. The class was then called together to listen to the reporters present their summary and to participate in a discussion led by the reporters with the teacher's help. By the end of the year, each student had served as a reporter multiple times with different partners. The teacher hoped that peer-to-peer interaction facilitated by this student-centered structure would improve students' reading comprehension and summarization skills by encouraging students to make their thinking overt and explicit. For this report, we concentrate on the discursive interactions of the pairs of student reporters. We were interested in two questions: (a) how did partners support each other in navigating articles and the newspaper texts in which they were embedded, and (b) how did partners support each other in comprehending article content?

THEORETICAL FRAMEWORKS

As one of the most widely accessible printed text types across the world, the genre of newspapers may be important to study in terms of its affordances as a classroom informational text. The practitioner literature reflects attention to how teachers can use newspapers across the curriculum (see for example Cheyney, 1992; Lambley, 1992; Oldendorf & Calloway, 2008; Sibley, 1999). Also, Newspapers in Education (NIE), an international program, has actively promoted the use of newspapers in K-12 schools since 1955. However, we could find no peer-reviewed case studies of elementary instruction around newspaper texts. We consider three strands of research particularly relevant to our study: authentic classroom practices with authentic texts, comprehension of informational texts, and peer-to-peer talk about texts.

Authentic Practices with Authentic Informational Texts

Authentic classroom texts are "like texts that are used by readers and writers outside of a learning-to-read-or-write context" (Duke, Purcell-Gates, Hall, & Tower, 2006/2007, p. 346). However, the authenticity of classroom literacy practice hinges not only on the texts themselves, but also on the activities through which students interact with texts. Literacy learning is facilitated when classroom activities match or reproduce reading and writing activities in which people participate outside of a literacy learning context (Delpit, 1992; New London Group, 1996). Rather than simply being used to teach skills or content, authentic literacy activities also perform a genuine communicative function (Duke, et al., 2006/2007).

Newspapers are authentic texts, prominent in civic and family life (Duke & Purcell-Gates, 2003). Because of this, they provide ready relationships between the literacy practices in students' homes and communities and the literacy practices of school (Heath, 1982; Street, 1993). Newspapers have long been conveyors of public discourse with the power to shape social ideas and events (Kress, 1983). Even at a time when the newspaper industry is in flux, its future business model unknown and uncertain, it seems unlikely that newspaper journalism—nor newspaper texts—will disappear. The *In the News* activity observed in this study can be considered authentic classroom literacy practice because it provided students with repeated exposure to an authentic informational genre through a non-graded activity structure where students could share and respond to self-selected newspaper articles in much the same way adult readers do. The reading had an authentic real-world purpose communicated by the teacher—to help students keep up with current events in their community, nation, and world, thus becoming more informed citizens.

Comprehension of Informational Texts

Informational texts are notoriously difficult for students across grade levels (Cervetti & Barber, 2009), with high vocabulary requirements (Duke & Billman, 2009) and diverse and unpredictable text structures (Hall, Sabey & McClellen, 2005). Much has been made in recent years of the problems that difficult texts can present, especially for low readers, and the affordances of matching texts and readers. Independent-level texts often are recommended for independent reading as opposed to more difficult frustration-level or instructional-level texts (Billman, Hilden, & Halladay, 2009). In contrast to the calls for matching texts and readers, some researchers see failures to expose children to complex language and rich content in difficult texts as missed opportunities for developing powerful word and world knowledge that could support reading comprehension in higher grades (Chall, 1983). Others have asserted that teachers should deliberately promote mismatches between students and tasks in order to provide students opportunities to develop adaptive learning strategies (Rohrkemper & Corno, 1988).

Although we did not establish the reading level of the articles students read during the *In the News* activity, it is almost certainly true that the majority fell beyond the independent reading level for most of these third grade students. Written primarily for an adult audience, newspaper articles typically have high lexile levels (Smith & Smith, 1984). Newspaper articles are complicated in their semantics, syntax, and vocabulary, and the content often is unfamiliar to young readers. Furthermore, articles are embedded in a complicated text type with multiple genres in the same text and even on the same page (e.g., advertisements, comics, opinion pieces).

We recognize and respect the need to match readers and texts as an important part of a comprehensive literacy program. But we also wonder about the affordances of difficult texts for learning. For instance, newspaper articles contain a plethora of diverse informational content related to multiple academic disciplines, and thereby present opportunities for acquiring content knowledge and content literacy skills and for making interdisciplinary connections. Furthermore, experiences with newspapers may help students develop effective strategies for navigating complicated multimodal and multi-genred texts and for finding and selecting information, including information in online environments (Dreher, 2002; Eagleton & Guinee, 2002). In today's textual milieu, where students are likely to have access to online texts of varying difficulty, they will often encounter texts that are beyond their present reading ability. Additionally, many students choose to read texts considered too difficult for them (Halladay, 2008; Kragler, 2000). These realities beg the question: *What should teachers do when texts do not match readers?*

Our interest was in the kinds of scaffolding that support students' encounters with difficult informational texts. Vygotsky's (1978) concept of a zone of proximal development posits that the mark of a child's ability is what s/he can do with support. Scaffolding of students' text comprehension and participation in the literacy practices associated with the *In the News* activity came from three sources: paired reading between two student reporters, the interaction between the reporters and the teacher, and the whole-class interaction during which the teacher also participated. In this report, we concentrate on the peer-to-peer interaction that occurred between student reporters because we expected that the challenge of reading the newspaper, difficult for most third graders, would offer an uncommon opportunity for peers to support each other's knowledge-building and comprehension-construction.

Peer Interaction around Texts

Various structures for peer-to-peer talk have been found to be successful for engaging students about texts (see for example Brown & Palincsar, 1989; Chinn & Anderson, 1998; Heller, 2006; Raphael, Florio-Ruane, George, Hasty, & Highfield, 2004). Benefits of peer-to-peer talk include opportunities to understand and appreciate text ideas (Kucan & Beck, 1997), develop oral language skills (Almasi, 1995), and practice applying comprehension processes (Berne & Clark, 2006). These and other benefits can accrue to students of diverse backgrounds and skill levels (Martínez-Roldán & López-Robertson, 2000), whether conversational partners are equal in skill or one is more knowledgeable than the other (Rogoff, 1998).

These and other findings have been documented primarily with classroom activities around fiction genres. There is a need to validate findings with diverse informational genres. Additionally, although peer-to-peer talk has been found to be most beneficial to low readers (Hiebert, 2009), it is an interesting question as to the benefits of activities in which on-grade-level partners are working with a difficult text. All students in the class observed for this study read at or above grade level, as indicated by their scores on their state's standardized reading assessment. Thus, this class provided a good context in which to explore this issue.

METHOD

Participants and Context

Data were collected in a third grade classroom located in an urban public school in the southwest United States. One of us, the second author, was the teacher of the class. He saw his participation in the research presented here as an opportunity to improve his teaching practice. At the time of the study, he had 15 years of teaching experience, National Board Certification, and was an instructional leader in his district. Having designed the *In the News* activity the previous year, he was implementing it fully for the first time from the beginning of the school year. There were 18 students in the class: 9 boys and 9 girls; 15 White, 1 African American and 2 Hispanic. For the purposes of the study, we focused on nine students assigned in seven pairs as *In the News* reporters. Each pair was observed for one week (four to five days). Four of these students were assigned to more than one pair and so were observed for two or three weeks. Reporters were purposefully selected to represent a diversity of pairings on multiple dimensions (see Table 1). All names are pseudonyms, including people and places in articles.

Table 1. Characteristics of Pairs of Reporters

Month	September	September	November	November	February	February	May
Reporters	Jacob Eric	Rebecca Curtis	Eric Alysha	Rebecca Tanya	Aaron Amanda	Curtis Jenny	Rebecca Alysha
Gender*	M/M	F/M	M/F	F/F	M/F	M/F	F/F
Ethnicity**	H/W	W/W	H/AA	W/W	W/W	W/W	W/AA
Academic achievement	High/High	High/High	High/Low	High/Low	Low/Middle	High/Middle	High/Low
Selected articles	-pollution of local creek -local hotel being built	-repair of local dams -gas pipeline bursts	-local restaurant owner dies -results of school testing	-study on human brain -mayoral election in nearby city	-Australian wildfire -satellites collide over Australia	-space debris over city -local food market stocks decline	-fire destroys building -comedian honors athlete

*M = Male; F = Female ** W = White; H = Hispanic; AA = African American

The *In the News* activity took place within the context of a comprehensive literacy program that included guided and independent reading, literature circles, authentic writing across the curriculum, and web-based research. The teacher introduced the *In the News* routine the first week of school as he introduced other literacy-related routines. He began by describing and illustrating the features, structures, and functions of newspaper texts and articles. The class then analyzed sample articles. The teacher warned students that newspaper articles were challenging texts; students would likely encounter vocabulary and concepts that were unfamiliar and would need to use the word-attack strategies they were learning. His goal was to reinforce that newspaper articles are informational texts with real-world ties to concepts learned in class.

During the reporters' sessions that were the focus of this study, two student reporters sat at a table with the local newspaper while the teacher met with small reading groups and other students did independent reading. The reporters were assigned to work together to complete four interrelated tasks each day: selecting, reading, summarizing, and presenting an article. The teacher checked in with reporters periodically, monitoring article choice, comprehension, and task completion. A description of each task and the teacher's roles can be found in Table 2.

Table 2. Students' Reporter Tasks During the In the News Activity

Task	Description of Student Activity	Teacher Roles
Select an article	Scanned headlines looking for topics they were interested in and with which they could make a personal connection	Checked with student reporters during or directly after the selection process; questioned students to gauge adequate prior knowledge to understand the article; advised students on how to proceed based on initial assessment
Read the selected article	Took turns reading aloud to reinforce the concept of paragraph structure and to encourage partners to remain engaged; helped each other with unknown words; orally summarized the big ideas; highlighted important information	Checked in periodically to monitor comprehension, provide information, and model reading strategies
Summarize the article for presentation	Filled out a summary sheet with the five Ws & H: Who, What, When, Where, Why, and How	Emphasized the purpose of the summary sheet was to help prepare to present the article to the class; encouraged student reporters to practice their presentation
Present article & lead discussion	Presented the article to classmates by reading from the summary sheet, reading from the article, or speaking extemporaneously; led a whole-class discussion	Scaffolded student reporters' facilitation of turn taking and expanded on their explanations with clarification or additional information

Data Collection

The first author had approached the second author when she learned by word of mouth about his instructional routine involving newspaper articles. Her interests in the activity were in the use of newspapers as non-traditional texts in elementary classrooms and also in peer-to-peer talk in academic settings. She observed, took field notes, and audio- and video-recorded all activity associated with *In the News* four to five days a week for three consecutive weeks, in September, and two weeks in each of three more months: November, February, and May (30 total observations).

Transcripts later were created of each of the observed sessions. Written summary pages and article clippings were collected from every reporter session. Short, informal interviews followed many of the peer-led discussions and were recorded and transcribed.

Data Analysis

Our analysis was inductive and interpretive, using the constant-comparative method (Corbin & Strauss, 2008) and sociolinguistic analysis of classroom discourse (Cazden, 2001; Mercer, 1995, 2000). We met periodically throughout data collection. After our first few passes through the data in which we jointly identified themes emerging from the data, we independently examined the data prior to each meeting, coding field notes and transcripts, and making theoretical notes. We reviewed the research purpose and questions at the beginning of each meeting in order to ensure that our discussion was guided by them. We worked to improve our sense of the data by comparing notes, making extensive theoretical memos, negotiating consensus, and identifying, organizing, and refining emerging categories and themes. Iterating this process several times, we tried to take advantage of our different perspectives and also develop intersubjectivity about our shared context and goals.

Focusing on two randomly selected transcripts from each of seven pairs of reporters (a total of 14 sessions), we first identified segments of the transcripts in which students were engaged in each of their four interrelated tasks, noting overlap and interweaving of tasks. Then, turn by turn, we examined students' peer-to-peer discourse moves and interaction patterns related to those tasks. We looked for evidence and counterevidence of students supporting one another's navigation through the text and comprehension of content. We excluded from this analysis talk that occurred in the presence of the teacher.

Finally, collapsing and clustering emergent categories, we generated codes related to two issues: (1) peer-to-peer talk about the text structures and features by each pair of students (e.g., headlines, maps, continuations, pyramid structure), and (2) the types of knowledge to which students referred during peer-to-peer talk (i.e., school knowledge, local or outside knowledge, connections to media and parents, hypothesizing/conjecturing about the text, use of and explicit reference to reading strategies, and critical literacy moves). Collecting short episodes of discourse surrounding these issues in two tables, we compared talk across pairs of students and within pairs across tasks and across days. We eventually identified four overarching themes related to students' tasks and talk: two related to peer-to-peer talk that supported navigation of the texts, and two related to peer-to-peer talk that supported comprehension of article content.

Finally, we returned to all 30 reporter sessions for our focal pairs to check preliminary hypotheses. Simultaneously, we identified and categorized the teacher's instructional techniques. Due to space constraints, we do not report the results of the analysis of teacher moves.

FINDINGS

We organized our findings in terms of our two research questions. We first present findings related to how students supported each another's navigation of newspaper texts, and then present results on how students supported each other's comprehension of content.

Learning about the Text: Navigating a Complicated Genre

When encountering newspaper texts, students had to manage a genre with complicated structures and features at macro and micro levels. We identified two means by which students supported one another's use of genre knowledge to navigate the texts successfully. First, reporters used their knowledge of text structures and features to help each other simultaneously and iteratively navigate multiple levels of a complicated text. Second, students came to recognize and reinforce through their talk the types of information privileged by newspaper articles.

Recognizing structures and features at multiple levels. At a macro-structural level, the *newspaper article* was only one of many genres embedded in a complicated text type. On a single page of newspaper, one may find many unconnected texts of multiple genres. Although students rarely had trouble differentiating articles from other genres, we noted several instances when one partner was distracted by text unrelated to the mission of selecting an article. Peer interaction often effectively re-directed attention. For example, when Aaron became sidetracked by an interesting advertisement, he re-focused his attention on the task at Amanda's polite request, "Let's look at real articles so we can make it faster."

Students learned to use the fact that newspapers are organized into topical sections to manage their article selection task. Early in the year, peer talk about sections was limited to differentiating among them and recognizing that they contained information about different topics (e.g., Alysha identified the A section, as the one with "the presidents"). As the year progressed, students began expressing preferences and developing affinities for particular sections of the newspaper, using those affinities to narrow and inform their article choices and influence their partner (e.g., "I want to do Sports"; "Let's go to Life & Arts").

Concurrent with their navigation of the macrostructure of the texts, students used their knowledge of text features of newspaper articles to navigate micro-structural aspects of the text as they made their daily selection. Early in the year, students often had trouble identifying all the parts of text that pertained to a selected article (e.g., photos, charts, jump tags). They invariably came to show a facility with this task after repeated experiences, supporting each other by calling and pointing out text features. Headlines, cutlines, and photos played prominent roles in students' evaluation and selection of articles. Students skimmed headlines as they chose from among the many articles in a newspaper, using this text feature to evaluate whether they could make connections with a story. Most partners began by flipping through two different sections of the newspaper, occasionally reading headlines aloud to each other to weigh the potential appeal of an article. Once his or her partner responded with interest and joint attention was established, a reporter often went on to read aloud from the photo cutline or the first paragraph of the article.

At an even more micro-structural level, students navigated the structure of articles. In whole-group instruction, the teacher had emphasized the pyramid structure of hard-news stories. Students supported each other's understanding of articles by reminding one another of this structure. Most of the evidence that students were internalizing expectations about this text structure lay in the fact that articles not following the expected pyramid structure often confused students. For example, Eric and Alysha chose an article for which the lead sentence read, "Decades ago when 12-year-old Joe Stanley took his first job at Burger Heaven, his father paid him 50 cents a day to bus tables." After much exposure to hard-news articles, these two students were confused by this more loosely structured feature article. Even after presenting the article to their classmates, neither student reporter seemed to grasp fully that it was written because the restaurant owner had died. Because both peers were confused by the unexpected and unfamiliar structure, they had difficulty helping one another navigate this text.

Recognizing the dynamic nature of information. Important in how students navigated this informational genre was the fact that newspaper articles tend to follow ongoing stories unfolding over time rather than focus on more static, accepted bodies of knowledge as do most textbooks and trade books. Through repeated exposure supported by peer-to-peer talk, students came to recognize that articles privilege evolving knowledge and understandings of a dynamic world. Each day there was the possibility that questions unanswerable in previous editions of the newspaper would be resolved in a subsequent article as new evidence came to light, for instance, the source of an apartment fire, or as events unfolded as in the 2008 presidential election.

During their daily task of selecting an article, reporters frequently engaged each other in talk about connections between articles, most of which were due to the genre's privileging of dynamic information. For instance, students discussed similarities in content between articles (e.g., "That's the same as yesterday's hotel article"), hypothesized relationships between information in different articles (e.g., "I wonder if it has something to do with the hurricane"), sought out follow-ups stories of interest (e.g., "I can't find the Salmonella article. I don't know why, because eight people died"), and hypothesized about future articles (e.g., "Maybe there'll be a follow-up"). By noticing and calling their partner's attention to connections between articles, reporters narrowed their choices in texts containing a plethora of information.

Learning From the Text: Supporting Comprehension of Diverse Content

When working together to complete their tasks, reporters encountered information about a broad array of topics (e.g., economic issues, cultural conflicts, natural disasters, political elections, entertainment events). We expected to find that students supported each other's comprehension of articles by explicitly providing information about content that filled in each other's knowledge gaps. We did not find much evidence of this. Instead, our second theme reveals how students helped one another comprehend and summarize articles by sharing personal experiences to make intertextual connections and by shaping and refining their understanding of the text together through cumulative and exploratory talk, what we called *idea-smithing*.

Sharing intertextual connections. Newspaper articles tend to privilege information about events that are *current* and *local*. These characteristics led students to share intertextual connections that increased their understanding of, and their interest in, article content. First, when students encountered newspaper articles related to local landmarks with which they were familiar (i.e., parks, schools) or local sports teams with whom they identified, they used this familiarity to create and sustain interest in topics by discussing their shared knowledge of their neighborhood and city. This type of intertextuality is rarely presented by traditional third grade texts because the audiences for these texts span an extensive geographic area. Its affordance in newspaper texts comes as a result of the somewhat unique function of newspapers to serve local communities. Second, because newspaper articles usually concern current events, things taking place close in time to their being read, students had opportunities to share with one another intertextual connections they made between a particular newspaper article and other media sources (namely television news programs) or between an article and conversations they had participated in or overheard in their families (e.g., "I heard my mom talking about that").

Sharing intertextual connections facilitated by newspapers' partiality toward local and current events alleviated some of the difficulties that students' limited background knowledge presented for comprehension. The majority of these connections were made during the article selection process, helping reporters organize their search and influencing which articles students considered for selection. Sharing intertextual connections with each other did not play a direct role in increasing students' comprehension of content; rather it facilitated the generation of interest that indirectly influenced comprehension of article content by enabling students to persist in reading articles about topics for which they otherwise had little experience.

Idea-smithing through cumulative and exploratory talk. Most of the peer-to-peer support for comprehension came in the form of working out textual meanings together, what we called *idea-smithing*. Much like a blacksmith turning a piece of iron over and over with a hammer and anvil, re-working it into a familiar and useful shape, students turned a challenging text over and over, using peer-to-peer talk to re-work their understanding of information in articles, thereby rendering it familiar, comprehensible, and useful. In essence, idea-smithing occurred when students "thought out loud" jointly to make sense of what they were reading. Idea-smithing involved each partner sharing his or her current understanding, offering it for joint consideration and evaluation. Thus, helping one's partner come to initial understanding merely by repeating information from the text or from prior experience, defining unknown vocabulary, or offering aid with decoding, do not fit into our definition of this construct. Idea-smithing was carried out in four different types of talk: marking, accumulating, grappling, and going beyond the text.

One way of initiating idea-smithing was through *marking*. Marking occurred most often during the task of selecting an article or as students were highlighting the text. It was enacted when one partner called attention to part of the text, either because it was interesting to him or her personally (e.g., "Do you know where this is!?"), because he or she felt it was important for the summary sheet (e.g., "Oh, listen to this. 'Green Grocery...' "), or because it was potentially a point of interest to the audience (e.g., "Let's underline that"). Marking could also be enacted simply by highlighting without speaking. Through marking, reporters invited their partner to re-consider a part of the text and also allowed themselves to check their own evaluation of its importance by gauging the reaction of their partner. In this way, students' negotiated the amount of attention allotted to different textual content. Marking itself is not idea-smithing, but was the initiator of idea-smithing when it was followed up with sustained joint attention to particular information and working out of textual understandings. Many markings went by without response beyond a glance toward the specified text, and thus were not instances of idea-smithing.

Students also participated in idea-smithing through what we categorized as *cumulative talk*, described by Mercer (2000) as talk in which students "build on each other's contributions, add information of their own and in a mutually supportive, uncritical way construct together a body of shared knowledge and understanding" (p. 97). By bundling or clustering bits of knowledge and understanding, partners compiled their individual understanding, thereby creating a shared retelling of an article or portion of an article. The example below occurred as Aaron and Amanda were practicing to present an article about a wildfire. ("..." indicates a pause)

Aaron: So the main things we're going to say is...//

Amanda: //all this stuff. [pointing to their highlighted article]

Aaron: Sydney Australia had a wildfire.

Amanda: The main things that got burned//

Aaron: //and killed... at least 750 homes were destroyed. Some tried to escape by cars, but car doors//

Amanda: //were flung open and hit other people...

Aaron: and fire got inside of the cars.

In large part, the impetus for the peer-to-peer talk in this segment was the audience these students would soon face. The goal of their talk was not to build, work out, or evaluate meaning, but to review, organize their thinking, and practice their presentation. That may be why they simply gathered information together in a joint retelling of the text rather than exploring other meaning.

Two additional types of talk associated with idea-smithing required greater investment and intentionality by both partners: *grappling with the text* and *going beyond the text*. These would both likely be categorized by Mercer (2000) as *exploratory talk* in which "partners engage critically but constructively with each other's ideas... Agreement is sought as a basis for joint progress. Knowledge is made publically accountable and reasoning is visible in the talk" (p. 98).

Grappling with the text occurred when students pressed one another for explanations or accuracy in order to increase their understanding of article content. *Grappling with the text* required at minimum one initiating comment and one response, and occurred in one of two ways: (1) by one partner making an initiating comment presenting an idea, followed by his or her partner responding with a comment that confirmed, built on, refined, or countered that idea; or (2) by the initiating partner asking a question that was responded to with attempts to answer the question, either by referring back to the text or to one's own understanding. This type of idea-smithing could change one or both partners' understanding of the text.

Going beyond the text occurred when peer-to-peer talk involved hypothesis-making, conjecturing, or imagining hypothetical situations. *Going beyond the text* was full of "What ifs" and "I wonders" and called on prior knowledge to substantiate one's inferences (e.g., "It couldn't have been just a wing, because when stuff's out in space it crumples up in a ball, like from gravity"). This type of idea-smithing involved making sense of unfamiliar content by making connections to ideas that were more familiar. It occurred less frequently than *grappling with the text*, but was powerful for meaning making and cognitive engagement.

Neither *grappling with the text* nor *going beyond the text* always resulted in accurate comprehension of an article's content. Partners sometimes engaged in exploratory talk about article content that was too far beyond their experience or contradicted their previous knowledge and could not be connected or reconciled with it. However, we argue that even when such talk did not lead to complete understanding, students still benefited from following logical thinking sequences and inquiry processes (Hammer, 1995; Moss, 2008) and from making their thinking explicit to themselves and pushing each other to deeper thinking than they might have done alone. For example, Jenny and Curtis were not able to make complete sense of an article about declining stock prices of a grocery store chain when their personal experience of the term *sales* interfered with the usage of the term in their selected article. Curtis initiated the following exchange with a question that invited grappling with the text he had just read out loud:

Curtis: What does that mean?" So they… like before this happened, it kept going up instead of going down, I guess.

Jenny: It's going down 'cause when you go down more people come and say, "Oh, looky there, the price went down, I changed my mind about that." They don't have such big prices, so they go… [trailing off]

Curtis: No, I think, um, I think they mean when it went down, the profit went down, how much money they get from people because people are trying to cut down on spending their money.

Jenny: Dropping sales to get more customers, but that doesn't leave much money.

Curtis: Yeah, so they are forced to close down some stores.

Jenny: And then they get even less money and then one day they might be really left with a couple dollars//

Curtis: //and finally one day all the stores close and they get off the market. So they're trying to do stuff like offer them coupons and like lowering sales.

Jenny: Yeah, that's what it said.

Through *grappling with the text* (the first five comments) and *going beyond the text* (the next two comments), these students attempted to reduce the confusion they felt when the knowledge they brought to the text (knowledge they thought was relevant) did not bring them resolution.

The summary sheet was an important tool for enabling peer-to-peer talk through which incremental changes to comprehension were enacted, and idea-smithing often occurred while students summarized the text. Idea-smithing did not occur when students simply copied and inserted information directly from an article. Rather, it happened when students used integrating and synthesizing strategies, building incrementally on each other's comments to invent summary statements. In this example, Rebecca and Curtis discuss an article about the city repairing local dams. Curtis had been reading the article while Rebecca began filling out the summary sheet.

Rebecca: Did "what"? [looking at the summary sheet]

Curtis: Repair the dams so they won't break.

Rebecca: The builders, the builders are repairing the dams, so they won't– because if they break… [trailing off]

Curtis: They haven't repaired all the dams. Why don't we just say they're building dams?

Rebecca: They're building dams.

Curtis: Why don't we just say they're building dams better so they won't flood?//

Rebecca: Upgrading.

Curtis: Upgrading the dams so they won't flood.

Rebecca: Upgrading dams… [repeating as she writes]

Idea-smithing took place as Rebecca and Curtis tried out the idea of *repairing* dams, and then shifted to *building,* before deciding on *upgrading* dams. These shifts of verbs that clearly have different meanings indicate that this pair was modifying and clarifying their comprehension of the article through their joint attention. Additionally, these students (re)constructed a logical sequence of causal linkages based on the information they had gathered from the article, connecting the probable past with present ongoing events and possible, hopefully-to-be avoided future. The dams were being upgraded so that they would not break, so that there would not be a flood. Curtis was the first of the pair to articulate each of these ideas. However, Rebecca's uncertain tone, and repetition of Curtis's ideas seemed to encourage both partners' sustained attention to this causal chain. A prerequisite for idea-smithing is willingness to entertain another's ruminations.

Reporter pairs differed widely in the quantity and quality of their idea-smithing conversation. Although we found all four types of idea-smithing talk in nearly every group on at least one day (going beyond the text being the rarest), the frequency, span, and depth with which they occurred varied considerably between pairs, and less so, within pairs on different days.

DISCUSSION

The results of our analysis revealed that student reporters helped one another navigate newspaper texts by sharing their genre knowledge and by recognizing the dynamic nature of information privileged in newspaper articles. Students helped one another comprehend article content by sharing intertextual connections and participating in *idea-smithing*. Additionally, we noted that the dynamic, current and local nature of newspaper content provided prior knowledge hooks that facilitated and encouraged peer-to-peer talk. These characteristics helped students make intertextual connections between different articles, between articles and other sources (e.g., news, family, community, and world), and between one another.

The presence of a classmate willing to engage in talk around a difficult text enabled students to persist in engaged, sustained interaction with an authentic informational genre in the face of comprehension and decoding struggles. Even though students were not always able to work out complete comprehension of content, they remained largely engaged with informational text for sustained periods (20 to 40 minutes) during the *In the News* activity, as evidenced both in informal interviews with the student reporters and by the infrequency of off-task talk in the transcripts of reporter sessions. Although we have no comparison data to back such a claim, we assert the likelihood that peer-to-peer talk enabled better comprehension of this authentic genre than most of these third graders would have achieved working alone with such high level texts.

Although students often took up or created opportunities to help one another navigate and comprehend articles, there were also times they failed to respond to opportunities to do so and times they resisted doing so. Previous research has identified problems also associated with peer-to-peer talk, such as that social inequalities are often re-enacted as powerful students dominate and others are marginalized (Evans, 1996; Lewis, 2001), and that students have difficulty assessing and correcting each other's comprehension and creating a shared social context (Palinscsar & Herrenkohl, 2002). We found evidence of similar problems. For example, Rebecca and Curtis spent many minutes in silence, Rebecca resisting Curtis' attempts jointly to construct knowledge about the text by withholding response to his comments and questions. However, even seemingly cooperative behavior did not in and of itself lead to quality comprehension outcomes. Eric and

Alysha worked hard to cooperate with each other; their talk, however, was sometimes limited to consideration of practical task completion and was not as facilitative of comprehension as the talk of some more openly contentious pairs of reporters.

We also wish to call attention to the fact that peer-to-peer talk took place within a context that encompassed additional scaffolds. Beyond the tools for comprehension (e.g., the summary page, the strategy of highlighting), teacher intervention was critical to students' identification of comprehension failures and to the correction of those failures. Across our observations, the teacher played differential roles for different pairs of students, adapting his interventions in their tasks and talk based on his assessment of their needs. For example, the teacher provided background information, explained concepts, and modeled recognition of the text structure and word-attack skills. Further analysis is needed to ascertain the impact of his intervention on the peer-to-peer interactions described in this report. The whole-class discussion also was likely an important scaffold for comprehension. Although its effects cannot be assessed given the limitations of the analysis reported here, audience questions and connections likely informed student reporters as to the accuracy or completeness of their summary, encouraging re-processing and new attempts to summarize. A continuation of this study could be to observe how the group interaction compares to the idea-smithing that occurred between the reporters.

Implications for Practice and Research

We share Moss' (2008) belief that "reading to learn from text, whether textbooks, newspapers, trade books, or the Internet, is critical to student survival in the Information Age" (p. 211). Thus, teachers are urged to increase the authentic use of informational texts in their classrooms and the variety of authentic informational genres to which their students have repeated exposure. We believe the study results described here will be helpful to teachers as they attempt to use authentic texts and authentic literacy practices in their classrooms and to facilitate peer-to-peer talk around informational texts. The findings illuminate the potential value of on-grade-level peers sharing personal connections and prior knowledge as part of a conversational construct to negotiate meaning of difficult informational texts publically. They also provide teachers with building blocks for creating their own strategies and activities, based on sharing intertextual connections and idea-smithing, that can be used across multiple tasks involving comprehension of informational text. We caution that the same kinds of peer-to-peer talk would likely not occur with below-grade-level students or with students below third grade because of the weighty decoding demands of most newspaper texts.

From a research perspective, the importance of our study is related to the need to identify and describe practices that support young students' meaningful experiences with diverse genres of authentic informational texts. Also, because students are likely to encounter many difficult texts in the current information age and to select difficult texts often when given a choice in reading material, there is a need to understand how to help students deal effectively with texts that are largely beyond their present reading capabilities. Although it could be argued that school is one place in which students should be protected from texts that are overly challenging, we argue that school is a perfect place for students to encounter difficult informational texts so that they can be supported as they learn to manage and make meaning of such texts.

REFERENCES

Almasi, J. F. (1995). The nature of fourth graders' sociocognitive conflicts in peer-led and teacher-led discussions of literature. *Reading Research Quarterly, 30*(3), 314–351.

Berne, J. I., & Clark, K. F. (2008). Focusing literature discussion groups on comprehension. *The Reading Teacher, 62*(1), 74-79.

Billman, A. K., Hilden, K., & Halladay, J. L. (2009). When the "right texts" are difficult for struggling readers In E. H. Hiebert & M. Sailors (Eds). *Finding the right texts: What works for beginning and struggling readers.* (pp. 203-226). New York, NY: Guilford Press.

Bomer, K. (2005). *Writing a life: Teaching memoir to sharpen insight, shape meaning—and triumph over tests.* Portsmouth, NH: Heinemann.

Brown, A. L., & Palincsar, A. S. (1989). Guided cooperative learning and individual knowledge acquisition. In L.B. Resnick (Ed.), *Knowing, learning and instruction. Essays in honor of Robert Glaser* (pp. 395-451). Hillsdale, NJ: Lawrence Erlbaum.

Cazden, C. (2001). *Classroom Discourse* (2nd edition). Portsmouth, NH: Heinemann.

Cervetti, G. N., & Barber, J. (2009). Text in hands-on science. In E. H. Hiebert & M. Sailors (EDs). *Finding the right texts: What works for beginning and struggling readers.* (pp 89-108). New York, NY: Guilford Press.

Chall, J. S. (1983). *Stages of reading development.* New York, NY: McGraw-Hill.

Cheyney, A. (1992). *Teaching reading skills through the newspaper.* Newark, NJ: IRA.

Chinn C. A., & Anderson, R. C. (1998). The structure of discussions that promote reasoning. *Teachers College Record, 100,* 315-368.

Corbin, J. M., & Strauss, A. L. (2008). *Basics of Qualitative Research.* London, UK: Sage.

Cruz, M. C., & Pollack, K. B. (2004). Stepping into the wardrobe: A fantasy genre study. *Language Arts, 81*(3), 184-195.

Delpit, L. D. (1992). Acquisition of literate discourse: Bowing before the master? *Theory Into Practice, 31,* 296–302.

Dreher, M. J. (2002). Children searching and using information text: A critical part of comprehension. In C.C. Block & M. Pressley (Eds.), *Comprehension instruction: Research-based best practices* (pp. 289–304). New York, NY: Guilford.

Duke, N. K., & Billman, A. K. (2009). Informational text difficulty for beginning readers. In E. H. Hiebert & M. Sailors (EDs). *Finding the right texts: What works for beginning and struggling readers.* (pp. 109-128). New York, NY: Guilford Press.

Duke, N. K., & Purcell-Gates, V. (2003). Genres at home and at school: Bridging the known to the new. *The Reading Teacher, 57*(1), 30-38.

Duke, N., Purcell-Gates, V. Hall, L.A., & Tower, C. (2006/2007). Authentic literacy practices for developing comprehension and writing. *The Reading Teacher, 60*(4), 344-355.

Eagleton, M. B., & Guinee, K. (2002). Strategies for supporting student internet inquiry. *New England Reading Association Journal, 38*(2), 39–47.

Evans, K. (1996). Creating spaces for equity? The role of positioning in peer-led literature discussions. *Language Arts, 73,* 194-203.

Hall, K. M., Sabey, B. L., & McClellan, M. (2005). Expository text comprehension: Helping primary-grade teachers use expository texts to full advantage. *Reading Psychology, 26,* 211-234.

Halladay, J. L. (2008). Difficult texts and the Students who choose them: The role of second graders' text choices and independent reading experiences. (Doctoral dissertation, Michigan State University, 2008). *Dissertation Abstracts International, AAT3348113.*

Hammer, D. (1996). Student inquiry in a physics class discussion. *Cognition & Instruction, 13,* 401-430.

Heath, S. (1982). What no bedtime story means: Narrative skills at home and at school. *Language in society, 11*(1), 49-76.

Heller, M. F. (2006). Telling stories and talking facts: First graders' engagement in a nonfiction book club. *The Reading Teacher, 60,* 358-369.

Hiebert, E. H. (2009). The (mis)match between texts and students who depend on schools to become literate. In E. H. Hiebert & M. Sailors (EDs) *Finding the right texts: What works for beginning and struggling readers.* (pp. 1 – 22). New York, NY: Guilford Press.

Kragler, S. (2000). Choosing books for reading: An analysis of three types of readers. *Journal of Research in Childhood Education, 14*(2), 113-141.

Kress, G. (1983). Linguistic processes and the mediation of 'reality': the politics of newspaper language. *International Journal of the Sociology of Language, 40,* 43-57.

Kucan, L., & Beck, I. (1997). Thinking aloud and reading comprehension research: Inquiry, instruction, and social interaction. *Review of Educational Research, 67*(3), 271–299.

Lambley, H. (1992). The newspaper: A learning tool for teacher trainees and pupils in the development of literacy skills. *Reading, 26*(3), 37-39.

Lewis, C. (2001). *Literary practices as social acts: Power, status, and cultural norms in the classroom.* Mahwah, NJ: Erlbaum.

Maloch, B. (2008). Beyond exposure: The uses of informational texts in a second grade classroom. *Research in the Teaching of English, 42*(3), 318-365.

Martínez-Roldán, C., & López-Robertson, J. (1999). Initiating literature circles in a first-grade bilingual classroom. *The Reading Teacher, 53*(4), 270-281.

Mercer, N. (1995). *The guided construction of knowledge: Talk amongst teachers and learners.* Clevedon, UK: Multilingual Matters Ltd.

Mercer, N. (2000). *Words and Minds: How we use language to think together.* New York, NY: Routledge.

Moss, B. (2008). Facts that matter: Teaching students to read informational Text. In P. Lapp, & J. Flood (Eds). *Content Area Reading and Learning.* (pp. 209-235). New York, NY: Lawrence Erlbaum.

New London Group. (1996). A pedagogy of multiliteracies: Designing social futures. *Harvard Educational Review, 66,* 60–92.

Oldendorf, S. B., & Calloway, A. (2008). Connecting children to a bigger world: Reading newspapers in the second grade. *Social Studies and the Young Learner, 21*(2), 17-19.

Palinscsar, A. S., & Herrenkohl, L. R. (2002). Designing collaborative learning contexts. *Theory into Practice, 41*(1), 26-32.

Palmer, R. G., & Stewart, R. (2003). Nonfiction trade book use in primary grades. *Reading Teacher, 57,* 38-48.

Park, Y. (2008, December). *Patterns in and predictors of informational reading performance.* Paper presented at the National Reading Conference meeting, Orlando, FL.

Purcell-Gates, V., Duke, N. K., & Martineau, J. A. (2007). Learning to read and write genre-specific text: Roles of authentic experience and explicit teaching. *Reading Research Quarterly, 42*(1), 8-45.

Raphael, T. E., Florio-Ruane, S., George, M., Hasty, N. L., & Highfield, K. (2004). *Book club plus! A literacy framework for the primary grades.* Lawrence, MA: Small Planet.

Rohrkemper; M., & Corno. L. (1988). Success and failure on classroom tasks: Adaptive learning and classroom teaching. *The Elementary School Journal, 88*(3) 296-312.

Rogoff, B. (1998). Cognition as a collaborative process. In W. Damon, D. Kuhn, & R. Siegler (Eds.), *Handbook of child psychology,* Vol. 2 (5th ed., pp. 679–744). New York, NY: Wiley.

Sibley, R. (1999). What is in the daily news? Problem-solving opportunities. *Teaching children Mathematics, 5*(7), 90-94.

Smith, R. F., & Smith, K. L. (1984). A comparison of readability formulae as applied to newspaper stories. *Journal of Reading, 28*(1), 20-23.

Street, B. (1993). *Cross-cultural approaches to literacy.* Cambridge University Press.

Vygotsky, L. S. (1978). *Mind in society.* Cambridge, MA: Harvard University Press.

A Content Analysis of Forensics Comic Books and Graphic Novels: Implications for Science Instruction

Barbara Guzzetti

Arizona State University

Literacy researchers have identified the importance of examining students' interactions with popular-culture texts (e.g., Alvermann, Moon, & Hagood, 1999; Xu, Sawyer, & Zunich, 2005). Adolescents' interactions with media texts influence students' perceptions of themselves as readers and what reading can do for them (Alvermann, Hagood, & Williams, 2001). These everyday texts can help to position those who are considered literacy outsiders in schools as literacy insiders who select and interact with a variety of alternative texts for their own purposes.

Despite calls for exploring the possibilities of incorporating popular culture texts into instruction (Alvermann & Xu, 2003; Hull & Schultz, 2002), few systematic attempts have been made to determine the utility and allure of media texts for content teaching. Identifying relevant subject-matter concepts and the appealing elements of alternative texts could assist teachers to justify the use of appealing and relevant popular culture texts in instruction. A systematic analysis of the conceptual content of everyday texts could help teachers in designing instructional activities that are motivating for today's students growing up in a generation surrounded by a plethora of media texts (Alvermann, Moon & Hagood, 1999).

Comic Books and Graphic Novels

Comic books are one of the most popular types of media texts among young people. Comic books and graphic novels (comic books with lengthy and complex storylines) are known and read by a wide variety of students (Parsons & Smith, 1993). Comic books are of high interest to adolescents and have been used as vehicles for increasing students' motivation to engage in literacy (Ranker, 2007). Comic books and graphic novels contain unique and interesting combinations of text and graphics that engage students, particularly struggling adolescent readers (Smetana, Odelson, Burns, & Grisham, 2009).

These everyday texts are thought to promote better reading skills and improve comprehension (Frey & Fisher, 2004), particularly for special populations. They have been used as alternative texts in high school English classes with Deaf students to appeal to the visual learners of today who are surrounded by popular culture media (Smetana, Odelson, Burns, & Grisham, 2009). Comic books have been read to English language learners to develop their ability to recognize text features, such as dialogue and narrative structures (Ranker, 2007).

Despite these benefits of incorporating comic books or graphic novels into instruction, these texts have been under-researched for their conceptual content that could be useful in teaching content topics. These everyday texts have been analyzed more for their effects on students' literacy engagement by researchers like Schwartz and Rubinstein-Avila (2006) and Smetana and colleagues (2009) than for their treatment of ideas that relate to the school's curriculum or for their features that might enhance students' academic learning. Little is known about the potential utility of comic books and graphic novels for facilitating students' conceptual learning or the subject-matter concepts contained in them. Researchers also have not yet fully explored the appealing features of these alternative texts that could motivate students in content learning.

One recognized way to analyze the conceptual content in a text is by examining its vocabulary. In academic disciplines, concepts are represented by content vocabulary (Alvermann, Phelps, & Gillis, 2010). Mastery of academic vocabulary is crucial to comprehending content area texts (Pearson, Hiebert, & Kamil, 2007). Wide reading and multiple exposures to words can help students expand their vocabulary (Blachowicz, Fisher, Olge, & Watts-Taffe, 2006). Students who master academic vocabulary are enabled to talk and write like members of a discipline (Nagy & Scott, 2000).

Some evidence does exist that the vocabulary and structure of comic books and graphic novels may be useful for teaching concepts in content areas. For example, comic books like *The X-Men* have been used to discuss and critique business ethics and social issues in management (Gerde & Foster, 2007). Students in foreign language and social studies classes have learned Japanese culture and customs by reading anime or Japanese comics (Fukunaga, 2006). Manga (Japanese graphic novels) have taken up topics of Japanese culture and social issues that other media have not (Schwartz & Rubinstein-Avila, 2006).

Alternative Texts in Science Instruction

Among the content areas, science is perhaps the most frequently identified subject that researchers have identified as appropriate for literacy-based instruction to incorporate multiple and alternative texts (e.g., Lapp, Flood & Ranck-Buhr, 1995; Shanahan, 2003). A plethora of calls have been made to incorporate literacy into science instruction and to teach science as a language-based process (e.g., Lemke, 1990, 2004; Saul, 2004; Hand, et al., 2003). Science instruction should provide opportunities for reading, writing, and discussing scientific concepts in a wide range of textual forms since learners both form and represent their ideas through language (Vygotsky, 1978).

Students' responses to surveys conducted in their science classes confirm this theoretical stance taken by researchers. Adolescents articulate their desire for relevant and motivating texts that link scientific concepts to ordinary life (Guzzetti, 2002). Young people report interacting with a wide variety of texts outside of school that provide them with academic knowledge they relate to their in-school instruction (Guzzetti, 2009).

Recently, secondary students have become motivated to learn scientific ideas and procedures by the media texts of forensic dramas on television, such as *CSI, CSI New York, CSI Miami, Numb3rs, The New Detectives,* and *Forensic Files* (Guzzetti, 2009). As a result, school districts across the nation have begun offering classes in forensics in high schools as science or elective credits. These classes have become some of the most popular courses that high schools offer (Angier, 2009; Guzzetti & Bang, in press).

This sudden popularity of forensics television programs has resulted in the publication of other new texts. Academic textbooks in forensic science that are appropriate for secondary schools have recently been published to support the forensic curriculum (e.g., Saferstein, 2008). New popular culture texts, such as forensic video games, comic books, and graphic novels, have been developed that engage adolescents with scientific processes and ideas. Many of these forensic comic books and graphic novels can be found on LibraryThing.com (www.librarything.com). Some of the most popular of these forensic comic books and graphic novels are *The ChrusherComix* series (www.chrusher.com) and the *CSI* comic books and graphic novels (http://CSI.wetpaint.com/page/CSI+Comic+Book).

PURPOSE

This investigation was stimulated by the popularity of forensic media texts and the need to infuse literacy into science instruction through the use of multiple texts. The purpose of this study was to identify the science concepts in and features of forensic-related comic books and graphic novels to determine their utility for science instruction. The research questions were: How useful are forensics-related comic books and graphic novels for teaching science? What science concepts might students learn from these everyday texts? What are the narrative elements and format features of forensic comics that may motivate adolescents to learn science?

THEORETICAL FRAMEWORKS

This study was conducted from two complementary frameworks. The first of these was literacy as a social practice (Gee, 2003; Street, 1995). This view of literacy recognizes that literacy practices always occur in situated specific contexts (Street, 1995), that students have a literate life outside the classroom, and that students engage with others in their own explorations of literacy.

The complementary perspective of the New Literacies studies (New London Group, 1996; Gee, 2003) also informed this study. This perspective expands the definition of what counts as text to include visual images, as well as oral, written or electronic messages. This view complements the theory of literacy as a social practice by recognizing the multiple texts that students read in and out of school in various social settings. These texts include the visual, digital, and print texts that students interact with in their everyday lives. This theory also recognizes the interrelationships between the literacy skill and knowledge used in interactions with texts in both school and outside-of-school settings (Gee, 2003).

METHODS

Data Collection

To explore the utility of comic books and graphic novels for teaching science, I focused on those that were forensics-related due to the recent addition of forensic science to the curriculum in secondary schools (Guzzetti, 2009). To determine the utility and appeal of these everyday texts for instruction, I gathered a convenience sample of these texts by selecting nine current forensic stories in the *CSI: Crime Scene Investigation* series (*CSI, CSI Miami,* and *CSI New York*). These fictional stories were similar to those shown on the widely viewed *CSI* television dramas and depicted and illustrated the characters shown on these TV programs.

I selected these titles for their recent publication dates (those published over the most recent three-year period) and for their availability in local comic book stores. The usual publication format of these stories was to appear as a continuing episode with an installment of the story in each comic book that was published monthly for five months. A total of five comic books in the series represented a complete story and were eventually bound together as a graphic novel.

The texts that I analyzed included two comic book titles that had been originally published as a series of five comic books, *CSI: Secret Identity* (Grant, 2006) and *CSI: Dying in the Gutters* (Grant, 2005). I procured these as 10 single comic books. Another of the titles, *CSI NY: Bloody Murder* (Collins, 2006) was billed by the publisher as a graphic novella. Three other graphic novels were bound together as one book, *CSI: Miami* (Mariotte, 2005). The graphic novels in this compendium included *CSI Miami: Smoking Gun* (Mariotte, 2005); *CSI Miami: Thou Shalt Not* (Oprisko, 2005), and *CSI Miami: Blood/Money* (Oprisko, 2005). Another three graphic novels, *CSI: Serial* (Collins, 2006); *CSI: Bad Rap* (Collins, 2006), and *CSI: Demon House* (Collins, 2004), represented the first three *CSI* comic books that were published in a series form and later compiled into one volume, *CSI: Case Files* (Collins, Rodriguez, & Wood, 2006).

To supplement the content analyses of these texts, I also interviewed a purposive sample of one adolescent girl, Lizzy (a pseudonym). Lizzy was an upper-middle class, Caucasian 11th grader who was an avid reader of the *CSI* graphic novels. I saw her reading these texts in school during the time when I was conducting a study of a literacy-based forensics unit in her chemistry class (Guzzetti & Bang, in press). I had been in Lizzy's class observing her teacher implementing a curriculum unit she had developed to address state standards for chemistry by using forensic science activities. I first noticed Lizzy reading *CSI* graphic novels during this class while she was waiting for science experiments to be completed or while waiting for others in her group to finish lab assignments.

Although Lizzy typically read these books outside of school, she also read them during times of instructional transitions while waiting for lab equipment to be set up or for experiments to finish. These periods of relative inactivity gave me the opportunity to interview her in-situ while she was reading these texts. In addition, I conducted one semi-structured and audio-recorded interview with her in person, and supplemented these with periodic informal interviews with her by electronic mail. My interview questions focused on her reasons for selecting these graphic novels, her reactions to them, and the connections that she made from these texts to her chemistry instruction.

Data Analysis

I examined the *CSI* comic books and graphic novels to determine their utility as supplementary materials for literacy-based science instruction in secondary schools. To determine their usefulness for teaching concepts in forensic chemistry, I conducted a content analysis of these texts. In this analysis, I identified the occurrence and frequency of vocabulary terms from forensic science that represented major ideas or supporting details in these stories.

In doing so, I noted specific terms in the comic books that are commonly found in forensic curriculum materials and lesson plans, including those available online from the Shodor Educational Foundation (www.shodor.org/succeed-1.0/forensic) and Tru TV (www.trutv.com/forensics_curriculum). I also noted the vocabulary terms in the graphic novels that had been introduced in the forensic unit in the chemistry classes that I had observed in a prior study (Guzzetti & Bang, in press). Finally, I noted the context in which these terms were introduced.

To determine the potential appeal of these comic books and graphic novels to secondary students, I analyzed the narratives for their format and content. First, I searched for topics that are currently popular among adolescents that might help to draw students into science; my informant assisted in directing me to these. Second, I examined the narratives for referents to other media texts that enhanced the comic book's storylines, and for the authors' devices that facilitated predictability or the reader's resolution of the problem that could give students practice with inductive and deductive reasoning or inquiry skills. Finally, I examined format features by describing any additional texts or textual features included in the comic books aside from the main story.

I analyzed these data through matrix analysis (Miles & Huberman, 1994). I began the analysis by first reading through each comic book or graphic novel in its entirety. I then reread the texts, searching for vocabulary that represented the forensic concepts found in forensic curriculum, listing the forensic terms that were used in the storylines. By reading and rereading these lists, I discovered categories that represented distinct types of forensic terms. I then placed these terms within their respective categories and tallied their frequency within these classifications.

To discover potentially appealing features of these comic books and graphic novels, I reread the stories looking for artistic features and narrative elements that further developed forensic concepts and enhanced the storylines. I made notations of topics and settings, the central problems or issues, and the main elements of the plots. In doing so, I listed these features and elements in categories and I constructed frequency tallies within those categories.

To supplement these analyses, I analyzed the interview data with my participant through thematic analysis (Spradley, 1999). In this analysis, I read and reread the in-person interview transcriptions of the audio-recorded interviews, the in-situ interviews recorded in field notes, and the informal interviews printed out from e-mail. I annotated these data and assigned codes and categories. Reoccurring categories resulted in themes or major assertions.

FINDINGS

Content Vocabulary

There were three types of conceptual vocabulary related to forensic science that were found in the graphic novels and comic books. These included terms related to forensic evidence, forensic processes, and forensic technology or equipment. These are discussed below.

Forensic Evidence

The most common type of vocabulary was those terms that represented forensic evidence. Nearly one half of the scientific terms (44%) were words that related to forensic evidence commonly found at crime scenes. There were 34 forensic evidence terms that appeared 76 times across the nine titles for a total of 2,584 occurrences. The most frequently occurring of these were fibers and fingerprints, types of evidence that were included in seven of the nine titles.

These terms represented forensic evidence relevant to forensic science curriculum. Nine of the terms related to forensic evidence (i.e., footprints, fibers, fingerprints, soil samples, bite wounds, dental impressions, blood, soil, and arterial blood spatter) were types of evidence analyzed in chemistry labs during the forensic unit I observed. All of these terms appeared in the forensic curriculum guides and lesson plans found online.

Forensic Processes

There were 21 terms that represented forensic processes that appeared 36 times for a total of 756 occurrences across the nine titles. Eight of these processes (i.e., fingerprint dusting, print casting, dental impressions, fingerprint lifting, particle analysis, chain-of–evidence, mixture analysis, and lab analysis) were addressed both in the forensic curriculum found online and in chemistry instruction. Each of these processes was enacted in laboratory activities in the forensic unit.

Three of these terms, however, (i.e., DNA analysis, Luco crystal violet or LCV analysis, and autopsy) were introduced only in the comic books and graphic novels. These terms did not appear in curriculum guides, nor were they forensic processes used as activities or explained in classroom instruction. These terms represented types of forensic analyses that are typically not conducted in secondary schools for pragmatic reasons.

Forensic Technology and Tools

There were 23 forensic technology or equipment terms that appeared 26 times across the nine titles for a total of 598 occurrences. Two of these terms (mass spectrometer and gas chromatography) were technologies that were included in the curriculum guides and observed in forensic-science instruction. These were techniques used during labs to analyze mixtures found in soil samples taken from a fictional murder scene set up in the chemistry classes.

This type of forensic terminology was less likely than other types of forensic terms to appear in curriculum guides or to be referred to in classroom instruction. Many of these terms, (such as electron microscopy, electrostatic print lifter, automated fingerprint identification system or AFIS, and genetic analyzer) were forensic technologies or tools not readily available in secondary schools. Hence, they had little relevance to the secondary school forensic-science curriculum.

Linking Terms in Forensic Texts to Academic Instruction

Scientific terms of forensic science were introduced in the graphic novels, but they were not defined or described in these texts. Despite the absence of definitions or explanations of these forensic terms within the comic books and graphic novels, Lizzy found that the texts' mention of these scientific terms was motivating. She reported that reading these terms within the context of a forensic graphic novel increased her interest in forensic science and was reinforcing to her academic learning.

Lizzy was often able to discern the general meanings of forensic terms by inferring from the context of the storyline and the graphics. For example, In *CSI: NY: Bloody Murder* (Collins, 2006), the reader is enabled to understand that a genetic analyzer is a machine that analyzes blood samples; readers can infer both from the illustration and from the text that these procedures are steps in a DNA analysis. The book illustrates a forensic scientist using the lights and equipment of these machines and the accompanying text reads, "Danny is running blood samples...through the genetic analyzer" (p. 79).

Even without definitions or explanations, the mere mention of forensic terminology in these texts in instances like the one described previously provided the reader with some working familiarity of their relation to forensic science. While reading the graphic novel, *CSI: Double Dealer* (Collins, 2006), Lizzie stated that she enjoyed reading forensic novels like this one because the forensic terms used in them alerted her to pay attention to these key concepts that were discussed in her chemistry class. The forensic terms used within the context of a crime story provided her with some degree of prior knowledge of the kinds of forensic clues and procedures discussed in her class. Lizzy stated that reading the *CSI* graphic novels allowed her to "go in with a little bit of knowledge and work the forensic problem out" when trying to resolve crime scenes or stories in class.

The forensic terms that Lizzy encountered within the narratives signaled important forensic evidence and procedures that helped her to distinguish the processes, clues, and tools to resolve forensic problems. She perceived that focusing on these terms helped her to develop her inquiry skills and resolve fictional crime stories and scenes in her chemistry class. Reading graphic novels gave her additional practice in using inductive and deductive reasoning to determine resolutions to crime stories other than the fictional crime scenes that she was required to solve in class.

Storylines

There were three reoccurring features within storylines. These included stories that contained high-interest settings or story elements that had current appeal for adolescents, referents to other related media texts, and predictable plots or hints that facilitated the reader's prediction and problem solving. Each of the comic books and graphic novels incorporated these features and are discussed below.

High-interest settings and story elements. The graphic novels and comic books contained a plethora of issues that are popular among adolescent readers. These included settings or topics of youth culture, including comic book conventions, music venues, haunted houses, and custom car shops. High-interest topics taken up in these graphic novels included manga, anime, video gaming, rap, punk rock, hip hop, gangs, skateboarding, shopping, drugs, and vampires. To appeal to younger readers, the protagonists and characters are easily relatable ones for adolescents, such as middle-school teachers and college students who appeared as victims or perpetuators of the fictional crimes.

Related media. The mention of related media enhanced the plots. These media referred to in the storylines represented a range of textual forms. These included trade books, films, paintings, music, newspaper columns, documents, dining guides, video games, television programs, comic books, Web sites such as ComicBookResources.com (www.comicbookresources.com), and graphic novels. Many of these would be recognizable to adolescents who are comic book fans, such as the titles *Spiderman* and *The X Men*.

Other referents, however, alluded to past generations. For example, in *CSI Bloody Murder* (Collins, 2006) the text discussed the bygone eras of the Depression and its bank robbers like John Dillinger, and The Golden Age with films starring actors like Jimmy Cagney, Edward G. Robinson, and George Raft. To enhance the plot line of a man-beast killer, the author recounted past sightings of a monster that has been the subject of many trade books, Yeti, Sasquatch or Big Foot. Many of these referents likely would be unfamiliar to today's adolescents, but as in Lizzy's case, could stimulate students' independent research online to understand the storylines and acquire related background knowledge.

Familiar plots. An analysis of the plot devices revealed that familiar plots were used to assist the reader in problem solving and plot prediction. One of these devices was the author's activation of the reader's schema for knowledge of specific genres of crimes, such as serial killings, ritual slayings, copy-cat killings, and drive-by shootings. These familiar plots provided some degree of predictability to help students resolve fictional crimes.

Advice and hints to the reader. Direct advice from the author to the reader constituted another popular literary device in these fictional texts. For example, in *Bloody Murder: CSI NY* (Collins, 2006), the resolution of the crime paralleled a fictional play about a murder that was part of the storyline. Readers were provided with advice by the author to solve the crime, such as directives to "keep that urban legend [about werewolves] in mind... so if we spot that grain of truth we will recognize it" (p. 21) when referring to the possibility of werewolves living in the sewers of New York City. In *CSI: Serial* (Collins, 2008) readers were provided with a hint to assist them in predicting the outcome by the author's revelation that the crime paralleled the storyline of *Jack the Ripper*. In *CSI: Bad Rap* (Collins, 2008) and *CSI: Blood Money:* (Oprisko, 2005) readers were provided with the fictional detectives' working assumptions about and anticipated resolutions to the crime which could be used for comparison to their own hypotheses. For example, in *CSI: Demon House* (Collins, 2006) readers were offered advice to "follow the evidence" (p. 49) and rely on their knowledge of copy-cat crimes.

Format Features

Photographs and illustrations. Perhaps the most appealing elements of these comic books and graphic novels were the illustrations and photographs. All of the comic books had covers with photographs of the *CSI, CSI NY, and CSI Miami* actors from the television series. The graphics in the comic books and graphic novels were multi colored and well-crafted illustrations of the main characters portrayed on these television dramas. The exception was the compendium of three graphic novels, *CSI: Case Files* (Collins, 2006), reprinted texts with black and white illustrations. The characters in these stories were familiar to readers who followed the television series. The characters' appearances in illustrations reflected the way they looked on television, and their dialogues were consistent with their TV personalities and interrelationships.

These illustrations promoted inferential comprehension due to their lack of accompanying narrative explanations. The lack of narrative elaboration that is commonly found in comic books provided a useful context for promoting critical thinking and reading through inferential thinking (Ivey, 2008). Readers were required to infer the artist's intentions by closely examining the details in the drawings since the text often lacked narrative explanations. The promotion of this skill was evidenced in *Issue One* of *CSI NY: Bloody Murder* (Collins, 2006), a story of a murder where witnesses reported sightings of a beast-like attacker, prompting the recounting of a local urban legend of werewolves living in the sewers of the city. This graphic novel contained numerous pages where the illustrations fostered inductive reasoning and assisted the reader to anticipate a resolution to the crime. For example, one illustration depicted a murder victim with short and deep slashes on her arms, a drawing that prompted the reader to infer that an animal with claws had attacked the victim. Drawings of paw prints at the crime scene required the reader's inference about the type of animal that could have killed the victim. A tattoo on the victim's arm identified as a pentagram (explained as the sign of a werewolf) furthered the reader's inferential thinking to identify the culprit.

Interactive text and immersive media. The single issues of the comic books differed in their formats from the graphic novels. Advertisements that were absent in the bound series and graphic novels were prevalent in the individual issues of the comic books. Each of the five comic books in a series contained ads for other comic books, such as the ads in *Issue Two* of *CSI: Dying in the Gutters* for three current titles in their IDW's *30 Days of Night* comic-book mini series, their publication of a collection of 75 years of *Dick Tracy* comic strips, and their action adventure trade paperbacks. *Issue One* of *Demon House: CSI* advertised *CSI* merchandise and apparel while *Issue Five* of *CSI: Secret Identity* advertised action figures for *Buffy the Vampire Slayer.* These ads promoted wider reading and interactions with graphics by snowballing across textual forms.

Other features in the individual comic books constituted either interactive text or immersive media. Interactive text was evidenced in *Issue Two* of *CSI: Secret Identity* with its letters to the editor page. This column invited readers to communicate with the creators of the comic books and enter a contest to create a title for the column (later named by the winner as *Post Mortem,* appearing in *Issue One* of *CSI NY Bloody Murder*). Some of these letters were clearly from older adolescents who were high school or college students as evidenced by *Post Mortem* comments like the ones in *Issue Five* of *CSI Secret Identity* (Grant, 2005), "as a junior at Turlane Western [pseudonym] high school my mind was on Bigbutt not Bigfoot" (p. 29); and, "I do real good in college actually" (p. 29).

Readers wrote to the editors and the authors to provide their feedback and share their reactions to the comic books' topics like Bigfoot. Fans asked questions about forthcoming titles, author's intentions for future issues, and availability of current issues. This column provided a space for readers to express their fandom with comments by readers posted in this issue like, "I await with giddy anticipation for the next issue..." (p. 30). The motivating power of these interactive features was evidenced by a reader who wrote:

> I'm gonna continue to pick up IDW books. Though to be honest I think I'm compelled to pick them up more due to our correspondence than due to the books themselves (p. 29).

Immersive media were those additional texts that supplemented or extended the readers' interests in forensics. These included other short stories, textual features, and references to additional forms of media. For example, *CSI: Dying in the Gutters: Issue Two* (Grant, 2006) contained a preview of a five-part comic book miniseries, *Spike Asylum* (Lynch & Urru, 2006). Issue One of *CSI: Demon House* (Collins, 2004) provided an interview with one of the actors on the *CSI* television series, Paul Guifoyle, who portrayed the fictional character Captain Brass, who appeared in the *CSI* comic books. In this interview, Guifoyle commented on his character and his role in creating the *CSI* videogame that features the voices and likenesses of the *CSI* cast. Issue Five of *CSI: Secret Identity* (Grant, 2005) provided a short story, *Neighbors,* by Joshua Hale Fialkov, another forensic mystery.

This snowballing across textual forms through immersive media and interactive formats has been identified as an effective strategy for promoting students' engagement with literacy (Guzzetti, 2009). Publishers recognize that other media products and textual forms promote the building of community among fans of a particular genre of media (Hyman, 2004). Adolescents are enabled to extend their engagement with authors and characters by their interactions with these alternative textual forms and features.

DISCUSSION

Findings from this study support the utility of using comic books and graphic novels as supplemental texts in the science curriculum in several ways. First, this study demonstrates that these everyday texts offer readers contextual familiarity with and a degree of prior knowledge of the tools, technologies, evidence, and processes used in forensic science. Second, the appearance of forensic vocabulary in these texts alerts readers to key ideas and important supporting concepts in the forensic science curriculum. Comic books and graphic novels also offer potential for incidental learning acquired from the vocabulary used to describe settings, characters, and plots. Finally, these texts provide readers with opportunities for practicing the skills of comprehension through inferring details from illustrations and predicting plot lines. These fictional texts with their story lines can help to develop students' inquiry skills by fostering their inductive reasoning as scientific inquirers.

Most of all, comic books and graphic novels provide alternative ways to engage adolescents at a range of ability levels from struggling readers to high achievers by providing relevant and motivating topics related to the everyday lives of today's media generation. Incorporating popular culture materials such as comic books and graphic novels helps to bridge the gap between students' literacy pursuits and popular culture interests outside of school and their in-school instruction that they often view as unrelated to the real world (Morrison, Bryan, & Chilcoat, 2002). The use of everyday texts as supplemental reading assists in updating the curriculum to appeal to today's adolescent.

The greatest instructional potential of forensic comic books and graphic novels, however, may be their ability to help adolescents develop their identities as members of the communities of scientific thinkers and literacy practioners. These everyday texts can assist in positioning students as insiders to scientific knowledge through their contextual use of content terms. Students are enabled to learn to think, read, and talk like forensic scientists through contextual familiarity with forensic vocabulary provided by these ordinary texts.

Finally, the use of comic books and graphic novels in the science curriculum can help to alleviate the sense of alienation that many adolescents feel in school by engaging them in literate practice that is both academically and avocationally relevant. Bringing these everyday texts into classroom instruction acknowledges students' immersion in popular culture and their changing perceptions of literacy (Williams, 2009). These alternative texts have powerful potential and benefits that should not be underestimated when considering the incorporation of popular culture materials in the science classroom.

REFERENCES

Alvermann, D. E., Hagood, M., & Williams, K. E. (2001, June). Image, language and sound: Making meaning with popular culture texts. *Reading Online,* 4, (11). Retrieved February 7, 2010 from http://www. readingonline.org/newliteracies/ lit_index.asap?HREF=newliteracies/action/alvermann/index.html.

Alvermann, D. E., Phelps, S. E., & Gillis. V. R. (2010). *Content area reading and literacy: Succeeding in today's diverse classrooms.* Boston, MA: Allyn & Bacon.

Alvermann, D. E., & Xu, S. H. (2003). Children's everyday literacies: intersections of popular culture and language arts instruction across the curriculum. *Language Arts,* 81, 45-54.

Alvermann, D. E., Moon, J. S., & Hagood, M. C. (1999). *Popular culture in the classroom: Teaching and researching critical media literacy.* Newark, DE: International Reading Association.

Angier, N. (2009, May 11). A hit in school, maggots and all. *The New York Times*. Retrieved from http://www. nytimes.com/2009/5/12/science/12angi.html?_r=1&scp=48a9=forensics&5+=cse

Blachowicz, C. L. Z., Fisher, P. J., Ogle, D., & Watts-Taffe, S. (2006). Vocabulary: Questions from the classroom. *Reading Research Quarterly, 41*(4), 524-539.

Collins, M. A. (2004). *CSI: Demon house*. San Diego, CA: IDW Publishing.

Collins, M. A. (2004). *CSI: Double dealer*. San Diego, CA: IDW Publishing.

Collins, M. A., (2006). CSI: *Bad rap*. San Diego, CA: IDW Publishing.

Collins, M. A. (2006). *CSI NY: Bloody murder*. San Diego, CA: IDW Publishing.

Collins, M. A. (2006) *CSI: Serial*. San Diego, CA: IDW Publishing.

Collins, M. A. (2006). *CSI: Case files*. San Diego, CA: IDW Publishing

Fialkov, J. H. (2005). Neighbors. In S. Grant, *CSI: Secret identity*, p. 25-27. San Diego, CA: IDW Publishing.

Frey, N., & Fisher, D. (Eds.) (2004). *Teaching visual literacy: Using comic books, graphic novels, anime, and more to develop comprehension and thinking skills*. Thousand Oaks, CA: Corwin Press.

Fukunaga, N. (2006). "Those anime students": Foreign language literacy development through Japanese popular culture. *Journal of Adolescent and Adult Literacy, 50*(3), 206-222.

Gee, J. P. (2003). *What video games have to teach us about learning and literacy*. New York, NY: Palgrave Macmillian.

Gerde, V. W., & Foster, S. K. (2007). X-Men ethics: Using comic books to teach business ethics. *Journal of Business Ethics, 77*, 3, 245-258.

Grant, S. (2006). *CSI: Dying in the gutters*. San Diego, CA: IDW Publishing.

Grant, S. (2005). CSI: *Secret identity*. San Diego, CA: IDW Publishing.

Guzzetti, B. J. (2002, September). "This place has no atmosphere": Secondary students' reports of and suggestions for literacy in science. Paper presented at the *International Conference on Science and Literacy: Ontological, Epistemological, Linguistic, and Pedagological Considerations of Language and Science Literacy: Empowering Research and Informing Instruction*, Victoria, BC: Canada.

Guzzetti, B. J. (2009). Thinking like a forensic scientist: Learning with academic and everyday texts. *Journal of Adolescent and Adult Literacy, 53*(3), 192-203.

Guzzetti, B. J., & Bang, E. J. (in press). The impact of a literacy-based forensic unit on secondary students' attitudes and achievement in science. *Literacy Research and Instruction*.

Hand, B., Alvermann, D. E., Gee, J. P., Guzzetti, B. J., Norris, S., Phillips, L. M., Prain, V., & Yore, L. D. (2003). Message from The Island Group: What is literacy in science literacy? *Journal of Research in Science Teaching, 40*(7), 607-615.

Hull, & Schultz, K. (2002). *School's out: Bridging out of school literacies and classroom practice*. New York, NY: Teachers College Press.

Hyman, P. (2004). *Video game companies encourage "modders."* Retrieved July 27, 2009 from http://www/ hollywoodreporter.com/hr/search/articledisplay.jap?

Ivey, G. (2008). Intervening when older youth struggle with reading. In K. A. Hinchman & H. K. Sheridan-Thomas (Eds.), *Best practices in adolescent literacy instruction*, (pp. 247-260). New York, NY: The Guilford Press.

Lapp, D., Flood, J., & Ranck-Buhr, W. (1995). Using multiple textual forms to explore scientific phenomenon in middle school. *Reading and Writing Quarterly, 11*(2), 173-186.

Lemke, J. (1990). *Talking science: Language, learning and values*. Norwood, NJ: Ablex.

Lemke, J, (2004). The literacies of science. In W. Saul (Ed.), *Crossing borders in literacy and science instruction: Perspectives on theory and practice*, (pp. 33-47). Newark, DE: International Reading Association.

Lynch, B., & Urru, F. (2006). *Spike asylum*. In S. Grant, *Dying in the gutters*, p. 26. San Diego, CA: IDW Publishing.

Mariotte, J. (2005). *CSI Miami: Smoking gun*. San Diego, CA: IDW Publishing.

Miles, M. B., & Huberman, M. (1994). *Qualitative data analysis: An expanded sourcebook, 2nd ed*. Thousand Oaks, CA Sage.

Morrison, T. G., Bryan, G., & Chilcoat, G. (2002). Using student generated comic books in the classroom. *Journal of Adolescent & Adult Literacy, 45*(8), 758-767.

Nagy, W., & Scott, J. (2000). Vocabulary processes. In M. Kamil, P. Mosenthal, P. D. Pearson (Eds.), *Handbook of Reading Research, Volume III*, (pp. 269-284) Mahwah, NJ: Erlbaum.

New London Group (1996). A pedagogy of multiliteracies: Designing social features. *Harvard Educational Review, 46*, 60-92.l

Oprisko, K (2005*)* *CSI Miami: Blood/money.* San Diego, CA: IDW Publishing.

Oprisko, K (2005). *CSI: Thou shalt not.* San Diego, CA: IDW Publishing.

Parsons, J., & Smith, K. (1993). *Using comic books to teach.* ERIC Document Reproduction Service ED 363892.

Pearson, P. D., Hiebert, E. H., & Kamil, M. L. (2007). Vocabulary assessment: What we know, what we need to learn. *Reading Research Quarterly, 42*(2), 282-296.

Ranker, J. (2007). Using comic books as read-alouds: Insights on reading instruction from an English as a Second Language Classroom. *The Reading Teacher, 6,* 296-305.

Saferstein, R. (2008). *Forensic science: An introduction.* Upper Saddle River, NJ: Pearson/Prentice Hall.

Saul, W. (2004). *Crossing borders in literacy and science instruction: Perspectives on literacy and practice.* Newark, DE: International Reading Association.

Schwartz, A., & Rubinstein-Avila, E. (2006). Understanding the manga hype: Uncovering the multimodality of comic book literacies. *Journal of Adolescent and Adult Literacy, 50*(1), 46-48.

Shanahan, C. (2003, December). *Using multiple texts to teach content.* Learning Point Associates: North Central Regional Educational Laboratory. Retrieved February 7, 2010 from http://www.learningpt.org/pdfs/literacy/shanahan.pdf

Smetana, L., Odelson, D., Burns, H., & Grisham, D. L. (2009). Using graphic novels in the high school classroom: Engaging deaf students with a new genre. *Journal of Adolescent and Adult Literacy, 53*(3), 228-241.

Spradley, J. P. (1979). *The ethnographic interview.* New York, NY: Wadsworth/Thompson Learning.

Street, B. V. (1995). *Social literacies.* New York, NY: Longman.

Vygotsky, L. (1978). *Mind in Society.* Cambridge, MA: Harvard University Press.

Williams, B. (2009). *Shimmering literacies: Popular culture and reading and writing online.* New York, NY: Peter Lang.

Xu, S. H., Sawyer, R., & Zunich, L. (2005). *Trading cards to comic strips: Popular culture texts and literacy learning in grades K-8.* Newark, DE: International Reading Association.

Read-Alouds as Spaces for the Deliberation of Public Sphere Issues

Rebecca Rogers
The University of Missouri-St. Louis

Melissa Mosley
The University of Texas at Austin

INTRODUCTION

What happens when the same read-aloud is used to deliberate the public sphere issues of race, racism, and anti-racism with second graders and with teacher education students? In this paper, we illustrate how the read-aloud and associated discussion of *Mr. Lincoln's Way* (Polacco, 2001) in two classrooms across the lifespan created space for collective engagement around racial narratives. These narratives included those offered in the book and narratives that were constructed in the two classrooms through discussion. We argue that read-alouds, both in their content and in their interactional processes, hold the potential to cultivate a range of discursive and symbolic tools necessary for building and sustaining the public sphere.

As people engage with public sphere issues that impact their life choices, freedoms, opportunities, and happiness, they draw on literacy and other social practices to deliberate and act (Bomer & Bomer, 2001; Giroux, 1988). Deliberating public sphere issues, we argue, is particularly important in an era where "public space" is shrinking—both in terms of literal spaces (schools, social services, parks, and sidewalks) as well as forums for encouraging dialogue and debate (McLaren, Martin, Farahmandpur, & Jaramillo, 2004; Prendergast, 2003). We worry about the status of public space because the diminishment of public spaces represents "the erosion of the public forums in which decisions with social consequence can be democratically resolved" (Lipman, 2007, pp. 14). As we think about literacy classrooms, the spaces for deliberation that fill spaces with dialogue, tension, and dynamic movement are shrinking as well (R. Rogers, Mosley, & Folkes, 2009). It is within this context that we rethink the social practices of a common classroom practice, the read-aloud.

Read-alouds are increasingly used in classrooms in narrow and prescriptive ways—to build vocabulary and teach the elements of story. The tendency is to use literature as a *bridge* to vocabulary development or to build reading strategies. These uses of text deviate from the intent of the author, who writes to entertain, inform, or to inspire dreaming. "Authors do not write books for readers to answer comprehension questions or to do 'exercises' to learn 'reading skills.' They write books because they want the reader to enjoy a good story and ... they have some important ideas about what they want readers to think about" (Wolk, 2009, p. 664). Bomer & Bomer (2001) posit that the whole-class shared read-aloud is a public space, in which "the class is experiencing something together, feeling together, knowing that the others in the room are thinking and feeling similar things, understanding, too, that others are thinking slightly differently from oneself. Each participant knows that the others know the same story" (p. 73).

Read-alouds bring together two literate traditions: literacy and orality. Oral literacy is situational and additive as people share their own experiences in the telling of the story, and print literacy is abstract and objective, transcending the boundaries of time and place (Ong, 1982). Both oral and written stories are artifacts of social activity (Wertsch, 1991). The read-aloud brings orality together with print literacy: as people listen to stories, they call upon their own stories in a transactional sense (Beach, 2000; Rosenblatt, 1978/1994). If there is a space for telling, the read-aloud holds potential for interpretations that transcend boundaries and yet are rooted in everyday concerns. The story in print, interpreted by the reader and the listener, interweaves with the orality of the read-aloud context and presents the possibility of expanded interpretive possibilities.

USING READ-ALOUDS TO DELIBERATE PUBLIC SPHERE ISSUES

We are not the first researchers to investigate the interrogation of public sphere issues using literature. Read-alouds, book clubs, and literature circles have, for some time now, been used to dialogue about important social issues such as race (Tyson, 1999; Zacher, 2008), social class (Jones, 2006), immigration (Gutierrez, 2008), and gender (Martinez-Roldan, 2005; Young, 2000). Talk about literature is a cultural activity in which learning occurs through interaction (Galda & Beach, 2001). Students experience the same story, share interpretations (i.e. the poem), reflect on different understandings, and arrive at deeper meaning (Beach, 2000; Nystrand, 1997, 2006). Nystrand described this work as dialogic interaction where tension and struggle often govern conversation. Classroom talk about social issues in response to literature produces a context in which students come to new understandings by thinking through multiple perspectives.

However, looking across studies of read-alouds and response to literature, we find that most studies of student learning during read-aloud events in elementary classrooms center on the meaning-making of the individual child within the context of the classroom (Almasi & McKeown, 1996; Barrentine, 1996; Sipe, 2000). Reader response is often used as a framework for understanding the exchange that occurs between the reader, the text, and the new text created through the readers' experience (Rosenblatt, 1978/1994). Research focuses on the interaction of reader attributes, readers' strategies, interests, orientations, and texts. For example, Sipe (2000) described three ways in which students orally made meaning in a classroom study of first and second graders' responses to read-alouds in the social environment of the classroom, particularly how students used textual analysis, intertextual connections, personal connections, and engaged in the story world with their own world, and used the text as a platform towards creative expression. This area of research positions students as active meaning-makers, as we see how a child's worlds merge with text worlds as they listen to a read-aloud.

However, looking only at the individual student can mask the power of engagements with literature in classrooms. A look at dialogic spaces and interactions is where we can see the critical reflection that results in altering one's perspective and responses (Rogers, 1999; Rosenblatt, 1978/1994). In this particular study, we were interested in the public sphere issue of race in racially diverse contexts (Bell, 1992; Delgato-Gaitan, 1994; Moje & Lewis, 2007; Pollock, 2008; Willis, 2003). It is important to note that the theoretical perspective that shapes our analysis comes from our studies of racial literacy in these contexts (Mosley, in press; Rogers & Mosley, 2006, 2008).

Racial literacy is a framework for understanding interactions about race in public settings. It is "a set of tools (psychological, conceptual, discursive, material) that individuals (both people of color and White people) use to describe, interpret, explain, and act on the constellation of practices (e.g., historical, economic, psychological, interactional) that comprise racism and anti-racism" (Rogers & Mosley, 2008, p. 126). There are three parts to this framework. First, racial literacy is an interactive *process* in which race, as well as the ways in which gender, class, and geography intersect with race, are used as lenses to examine social action. Second, racial literacy practices recognize that race is a historically constructed category and functions to maintain privilege, hierarchical relationships within social institutions, and economic outcomes (Bell, 1980; Guinier, 2004; Shapiro, 2004). Finally, racial literacy explores how anti-racism and activism have been employed to take action in social contexts where racism is a factor. This framework of racial literacy shapes our analysis of the read-aloud in two different classroom spaces.

RESEARCH DESIGN

This study is one part of an experiment with our teaching that lasted two years (2002-2003 and 2005-2006) where we placed social problems such as classism and racism, war and peace at the center of our literacy teaching. We drew on the tradition of teacher research (Cochran-Smith & Lytle, 1998; Mohr, Rogers, Sanford, Nocerino, & Clawson, 2004; R. Rogers, Mosley, & Kramer, 2009) to pose problems, collect and analyze data, and refine our practices in two settings: first in a second grade classroom where Melissa was the lead teacher and then in the teacher education classroom where Rebecca was the lead teacher. In both classrooms, we rotated in our roles as teacher-researcher. We are both European-American teacher educators who have committed ourselves to integrating anti-racist practices in our teacher education work. During our first study, we were collaborators in a teacher-research group that focused on literacy practices and social justice and came together around our interests in peer learning within working-class communities like the ones where we grew up, and were interested in the relationship between class, race, schooling, and literacy. During the second study, Melissa was a student working on her doctorate and co-teaching with Rebecca to learn the practices of teacher education in literacy. In this context we designed a study that took up many of the same issues we had explored in the second grade classroom around racial literacy; this time, however, was with teacher education students. In total, we worked together to design two, year-long curricula around equity and justice issues within the context of literacy education.

We designed both studies in a way that would rotate between watching, asking, and analyzing in an iterative manner that informed our teaching. We collected data in the form of video- and audio-recordings, fieldnotes, interviews, and document collection on the following class activities: seminar discussions, tutoring sessions, small group discussions, book club discussions, and pre- and post-interviews. We took ethnographic field notes and recorded each other's teaching and then transcribed, debriefed, and analyzed the data together (Carspecken, 1996).

Contexts

The elementary school where this study took place is located in St. Francis, part of the same metropolis where the university is located. The participants were Melissa's second graders who lived in a community that can be described as working class based on the occupations and median income of residents. The community and school were racially diverse (primarily European American and African American). She taught second grade for three years prior to this study and was formally a student in this community for her K-12 schooling.

The second grade classroom centered themes of social action, civil rights, war, and freedom. Students participated in guided reading groups (Fountas & Pinnell, 1996), reading and writer's workshop (Atwell, 2007), and used critical literacy to deconstruct and compose texts. Rebecca was a learner in the classroom without an insider perspective on the community or the pedagogical practices of the school. Melissa was a learner both in terms of the frameworks of racial literacy as well as pedagogy in teacher education. Our relationship developed through conversations, reflections, and years of poring over transcripts and writing with one another. In our design of the curriculum in this classroom, we focused on critical social issues, especially racism, because the study was located in a city with a contested history of race relations (for a detailed history of this community, see Rogers & Mosley, 2006).

The classroom was organized around mini-lessons and individual/group projects in most subject areas. During the literacy block, which lasted the entire morning, Melissa would introduce certain skills or projects with the whole group, read a story aloud, and then the students would rotate through centers while she gathered ability and interest groups in one corner of the room for guided reading and book clubs. When Rebecca was in the classroom, she often led guided reading groups as well. Literacy centers included choices such as perusing text sets, listening and talking about books at the listening center, writing in writers' notebooks, practicing spelling using magnetic letters, and reading with a friend or alone.

The participants in the second context were enrolled in a teacher education program at a midwestern university. The guiding principles of the teacher education program stated that graduates of this program will be committed to equitable and just education for all students, will know the subjects they teach well and know how to teach, and will enact the role of inquirer. Our class included four graduate students and eleven undergraduates. Fourteen students were European American. There was one African American woman enrolled in class. Thirteen of the students were women, and two of the students were men. When we asked the students to write their cultural autobiographies, we learned that they were diverse in terms of their geographic, religious and socio-economic backgrounds (McCarthy, 2003). The program followed a cohort model and the students took three literacy courses together. Two of the literacy courses were located at an urban elementary school and included a practicum component. Every Tuesday, the teacher education students met at an urban elementary school in an African American community near the university. The teacher education classroom focused on reading and writing instruction using critical literacy and accelerative literacy approaches (Dozier, Johnston, & Rogers, 2006; Dozier & Rutten, 2005; Lewison, Flint, & Van Sluys, 2002). As in the second grade classroom, we focused our teaching on race and critical literacy because the school served, and in many ways, underserved historically marginalized students (Wells & Crain, 1997). The school was located in a district close to losing accreditation that had adopted a scripted reading program that had all but eliminated culturally responsive literacy instruction in the schools.

For the purposes of this paper, we have drawn on a similar literacy event, the read-aloud of *Mr. Lincoln's Way* (Polacco, 2001), in the second grade classroom and in the teacher education classroom to answer our question: in what ways might read-alouds build the space necessary for deliberation of important public sphere issues? It is important to note that read-alouds are but one slice into the activity in both classrooms. Our interpretation of the classroom discourse of this event is contextualized within our analysis of a larger project, which we report on elsewhere (Mosley, in press; Mosley & Rogers, 2008; Rogers & Mosley, 2004, 2006, 2008).

The read-aloud. The book, Mr. Lincoln's Way (Polacco, 2001), is about a European-American boy named Eugene (a.k.a. "Mean Gene"), who is a bully and has internalized racist actions from his father. In the story, Mr. Lincoln, an African-American elementary school principal connects with Eugene over their love of birds. Eugene has a grandfather who also loves birds and is not racist, and Mr. Lincoln identifies him as an ally who could also help Eugene. A problem arises in the book as Eugene realizes that the ducklings they have watched together will not be able to find water because the atrium walls of the schools enclose the nest. Mr. Lincoln replies, "You'll think of something, Eugene. I know you will." Eugene does find a way out for the ducklings, and people from the community including Eugene's grandfather come to watch. The story ends as Eugene comments, "you showed me the way out, Mr. Lincoln" and as Polacco shows that Eugene will go on to become a fifth grade teacher, too, and love all of his students.

We believed the read-aloud would raise questions around racism, anti-racism, and white privilege and support the development of racial literacy (Rogers & Mosley, 2008). The book features a collaboration between an African American principal, White student, and a White grandfather who come together to solve a problem around racism. However, the book focuses on an individual notion of racism—Mean Gene is "troubled" because of his father's racism and acts out in ways that harm others. Racism is not explored beyond the definition of having "ugly names" for people who are different. The children who are harmed—children of color—do not have a voice in the story or any power to collectively resist the racism in their school. As we discuss in our findings, we did not take up or trouble how the construct of *racism* was represented in the story with our students while reading this book, and as a result, the discussions reflected at times an acritical read of the story.

DATA ANALYSIS

In both classrooms, the read-aloud was video-recorded and fieldnotes were taken of the event. Situated within the larger data set, the video and the audio supported our transcription of the verbal record. First, we conducted open coding of the transcripts of themes in the talk and roles participants took in talking about the text. For example, in the teacher education transcript, we collapsed codes under the themes of "Whiteness" (i.e. White privilege), "White allies" (i.e. as a support system), "school desegregation," and "voices" (i.e. questioning peers). We captured still frames from the video to view alongside each transcript during the construction of these themes to see how participants used body language, gestures, and other nonverbal communication to make meanings.

We analyzed each transcript using the tools of discourse analysis and multimodal analysis (Fairclough, 1993; Kress, 2009; Norris, 2004; R. Rogers, in press, 2011). At this level we used a framework that includes "ways of interacting," "ways of representing" and "ways of being." We kept the linguistic codes from each level in mind as we coded each domain. In terms of genre we noted linguistic aspects such as repetitions, singing, parallel structure, and storytelling. In terms of discourse, we noted frequently occurring themes. In terms of style, we noted use of pronouns, active and passive construction, and positive or negative cognitive statements about self. We also considered the multimodal dimensions of each interaction. Our findings from the discourse analysis were re-situated in the findings of a larger study. The discussions of *Mr. Lincoln's Way* lasted 37 minutes in the second grade classroom and 30 in the teacher education classroom. Both classroom discussions were at times student or teacher-led.

THE SAME READ-ALOUD, TWO DIFFERENT CLASSES

Building Spaces for Exploring Racism in a Second Grade Classroom

In the middle of a unit of study on African-American history and civil rights, in the early spring of the academic year, Melissa introduced *Mr. Lincoln's Way* by writing "racism" on the board and asking the students if they had seen this word before. In class, the students had discussed equity in terms of discrimination, slavery, and Jim Crow, but had not explicitly talked about racism. Benny, an African-American student, set the tone for the discussion by equating racism with noticing race. He stated, "It's like if I was walking with my friends and I walk up to this person and say, 'Oooh, look at that black person.'" As he says, "Oooh," Benny scrunched his face as if tasting or smelling something pungent. Benny's comment, couched in an imagined dialogue, suggested that he understands racism as verbal comments made against people based on obvious phenotypic differences—in this case, skin color.

With the students gathered on the carpet facing her, Melissa began to read *Mr. Lincoln's Way*, posing wonderings about the storyline every few pages such as, "What do you think he was thinking?" and "Mr. Lincoln found out he does like birds, doesn't he?" She asked students for multiple perspectives and interpretations of the storyline. For example, the students constructed Mean Gene's racism as "meanness" as a result of "unhappiness." Melissa used chosen phrases to encourage their theorizing, for example, "Does anybody have a different reason or another reason?" She also asked students to make personal connections, "Think about people you know like Mean Gene" to build a narrative about racism in the present day.

As Melissa read about the relationship between Mean Gene and Mr. Lincoln, the African-American principal, she asked the students to imagine them spending long hours together in the atrium of the school. The students became increasingly engaged as the story takes a turn: "Mean Gene" makes a comeback and uses racial epithets in the lunch line. Prompted by questions, the students guessed why Eugene used racist language. One student wondered if Eugene's peers were making him feel badly. The students turn and talk, and guess that someone in Eugene's family is making him feel sad or perhaps something happened to the birds in the atrium. Like Mean Gene, the students thought about the complexity of their lives, the multiple influences on their thinking, and their developing notions of justice.

At this moment, the narrative of racism in the present day is explicit in the story, and Melissa wanted to make sure all her students were able to engage in this narrative. They had all been facing her, so she asked them to change their seating arrangement and sit next to each other around the outside of the carpet. She addressed the class:

> Let's sit around the room since there are not many of us here now. That way we could see each other when we talk. We're going to find out what makes Eugene sad on this next page. And it's not what anybody else said would make them sad. It's something different. Somebody at home does make him feel sad. It's his father that made him feel sad.

This move functioned in a way that allowed the students to hear and see each other, to socialize the students to attend to facial expressions, emotionality, and body language. Indeed, relationships are a key part of building understandings together (Goldstein & Freedman, 2003).

Melissa revealed that "Mean Gene" was back because Eugene's father berated him for spending time with Mr. Lincoln. She read, "Then Eugene began to cry. 'My old man got real mad when I got home late from helping you.' He sobbed. 'He said you're not our kind." She lengthened her stopping points for the students' responses at this point in the read-aloud, simultaneously addressing the existence of contemporary racism and the emotions of shame and guilt that Eugene might experience. She posed an open-ended question, "So what do you think is happening between Mr. Lincoln and Mean Gene?"

The students built on one another in seven turns, posing possibilities such as "They're starting to be friends," and "I think he's happy because he seen the birds and Mr. Lincoln is trying to help him and the other thing is I don't think he wants to tell anyone he likes birds."

Melissa asked her students to step into the role of a character in the story and to engage in discussions with those roles in mind. There were invitations to imagine the words and actions that go along with such roles, for example, when Melissa paused as Mean Gene calls a student from Mexico a "brown skinned toad." She asked, "Have you seen any of that in your school, in your classroom?"

It was becoming clear that there were direct connections between the students' definitions of racism and the storyline of *Mr. Lincoln's Way* that revealed the affordances and shortcomings of the racial understandings put forward in the book. The book afforded students an opportunity to think about racism in the present day, as the book appeared to occur close to now. Melissa called on this affordance when she asked, "Have you heard ugly names for people who are different?" However, the book also limited the ways that racism could be defined or understood in society. Eugene's father used racial epithets for what Eugene describes in the book as "everybody that is different from us." In the book, and in Benny's comment at the introduction of the book ("Oooh. Look at that black person"), racism is defined as calling out "difference." Melissa perpetuated this uncomplicated way of defining racism at various points in the read-aloud. She read several pages without pausing longer than to model a wondering, but also made space for students to turn and talk to discuss the plot of the story.

An example of how students took up this narrative of racism occurred when Vanessa, a White student, told a story about how a "Black boy" liked a "little White girl," which caused people to make fun of the girl.

Jackson, an African-American student, replied, "I don't think they should be talking about her because White people and Black people are all the same. And they are treated right and loved right." Jackson put forth an understanding that all people are equal, drawing on the emotion and moral dimensions of interpersonal relationships, and took a position in relation to Vanessa's story.

In the story, Eugene and Mr. Lincoln's relationship continues to build, as they work together on a project to help hatched ducklings from the atrium to a nearby pond. The relationship is a major turning point for Eugene, who decides he has the power to make change in the world. At the same time, the book puts forward a simplistic notion that his relationship with Mr. Lincoln—and their collective engagement in a project—can counter the racism embedded in the fabric of his family.

The students make interesting observations and predictions about the project, engaged in this storyline and the vivid illustrations in the book. Towards the end of the story, the students discovered that Eugene may go to live with his grandfather who loves birds instead of his father who used racial language. The movement to the parameters of the shared space of the floor continued to open up possibilities for exploratory dialogue around race and racism. Melissa read, "Eugene turned toward him. Had Mr. Lincoln something to do with this miracle, with his gramps being here? Now the old man shook Mr. Lincoln's hand heartily." She wondered aloud, "So does Eugene's grandpa feel the same way as Eugene's dad does about people who are different?"

One student replies, "No," and Melissa affirmed, "No, because he wouldn't have shook his hand would he?"

In the illustrations Melissa held before the students, Mr. Lincoln is a man with rich, dark skin, and his hands envelop Eugene's grandfather's hand, his pink fingers wrapped around Mr. Lincoln's. Grandpa's other hand is wrapped around Eugene in a tight embrace. Here and in their guided reading groups the students practiced critically analyzing how race was represented in illustrations (Rogers & Mosley, 2006). Melissa guided the students to talk to a person sitting nearby, "Eugene tells him he wants to stay with him again. Why do you think Eugene wants to stay with him? Why does he want to stay with his grandpa?"

As she drew the students back around her, they again posed multiple possibilities, such as "So he could learn more about birds," and "His grandpa is a nice man."

The conversation drew closer to the narrative of racism in the present day as Melissa asked, "His grandpa's a nice man and you think his dad isn't?"

Two students replied, "No. Not to people that aren't his color," and "I think he wants to get away from his dad because his dad is a mean man." Finally, the students explored the motives for Eugene's bullying. Previously in the conversation, and also in the book, racism was an interpersonal construct that described what people do when they are "not getting along." Here, the students began to see racism as a more embedded part of Eugene's life and the ongoing struggle that he may have in his life. They also are provided with a vision of Eugene as an adult, continuing to value the diversity that Mr. Lincoln and his grandfather taught him.

Taking positions in a teacher education classroom. Two years later, we decided to experiment again with our teaching. This time we were engaged in a year-long project with our teacher education students studying the integration of culturally relevant, multicultural, and anti-racist pedagogy into the literacy curriculum. The read-aloud in the teacher education classroom, similar to the second grade classroom, began with a book introduction. Sitting atop a table, holding her notebook, Rebecca addressed the class with a mini-lesson on White privilege and the development of anti-racist identities (Helms, 1997). She quoted authors who write about anti-racist pedagogy and actions (Ladson-Billings, 1999; Stokes Brown, 2002). She prompted the students to consider the lack of White allies in literature as she read, "You might ask yourself: Who are some examples of White allies either presently or in a historical context? If you can't name some, what might that mean?"

The reading commenced and like Melissa in the second grade classroom, Rebecca asked the teacher education students to think about the story in an analytic manner, drawing them in to textual analysis with questions such as, "How is Eugene feeling now? Why is he feeling what he is feeling?" and making space for small group discussions. She prompted the discussion at the level of multimodal textual analysis (i.e. "What do you think Polacco is trying to communicate with this illustration?") to deepen the talk.

Rebecca interrupted the discussion to ask students to consider how Eugene's grandfather is portrayed in the book. Her prompt allows for an opportunity missed in Melissa's classroom—the opening of spaces to critically analyze how racism or anti-racism is portrayed in *Mr. Lincoln's Way*. The students, when given time to talk, made personal connections. For example, Rex, a White student from a small, rural Midwestern town, constructed a narrative with the colleagues sitting at his table about the people he grew up with and their racist behaviors.

A discussion about White privilege and its presence in society developed in the small groups. During another stopping point in the read-aloud, Jonah, a Jewish-American student, started a discussion with Rex, a European-American student, and Tonya, an African-American student, about how to dismantle White privilege. Jonah began, "I guess part of it is recognizing the habit of how you are participating in it. We can find ways to alter, for instance, how we teach history so we do not white wash history."

Tonya replied, "White privilege runs throughout society. It has to do with White people benefiting from other people's misfortunes. It also is rejecting White privilege which is why..."

Rex interrupted Tonya, asking, "What are all the instances of White privilege? Where are all of the instances where White privilege exists?"

Before Tonya could reply, Jonah, perhaps recognizing the irony in a White man asking a Black woman for examples of White privilege, stated, "Well, that's one of the big issues."

Tonya's next turn overlapped with Jonah's response. She posed her own challenge, "Well let's deconstruct that, Rex. What do you think?"

Rex attempted to close the discussion, with a direct challenge to Tonya: "Well do it. I'd like you to."

In this example, we heard academic language, questioning, and White talk used to evade the real question of how one participates in White privilege. Tonya did not let Rex close the conversation. She answered, drawing on a narrative of how people of color have been denied educational opportunities and explains how inequities in society are reconstructed. She also drew on a personal narrative to explicate what Bell (1980) refers to as the "unspoken covenant" in the U.S. following Brown v. Board, a set of unspoken agreements which continue to deny educational equity to African-American children and families while at the same time guaranteeing the undeserved benefits of education, and by association, property, to their White counterparts. Tonya's narrative evoked the thoughts of Shapiro (2004), who wrote, "Connecting the thorny dots of racial inequality means no less than confronting our historical legacy of vast material inequality, massive residential segregation, and wide gaps in educational conditions" (p. 183). Following Tonya's example, several people at the table discussed the institutional nature of racism exemplified in the vast inequalities between schools where their internships are located.

Such discursive threads as this discussion of White privilege and the preservice teachers' associated identities were part of the narrative they co-constructed. The preservice teachers engaged in deliberating the public sphere issues of White privilege and racism through the read-aloud. The second graders engaged in constructing a similar narrative of racism in society without focusing on White privilege but instead, on the actions that accompany racism in their present-day context. However, particularly in the teacher education classroom, some identities and meanings were taken up and others silenced. The read-aloud prompted the students to think about their own racial identities and the ones offered in the book (Eugene's grandfather and the principal as allies), whereas the second graders focused on racist actions associated with Eugene and his father.

This conversation from the read-aloud continued online for the next week. Lisa, another preservice teacher, brought the following question to her classmates on the online discussion board:

> One thing that Andrea pointed out is that children often have goals but not roles [in children's literature]. Eugene didn't have a positive role to fit into until Mr. Lincoln gave him one. [...] I don't have an answer to what whiteness means to me. Would anyone like to share what whiteness means to them? [...] someone asked how do we not participate in White privilege and that'd be a good question here. Any thoughts?

Lisa continued a conversation she participated in the week before, questioning the roles available for White students when reading texts, or in Sipe's (2000) terms, their opportunities for personal connections or reading their world within the world of the text. This was an interesting question to consider in the context of their discussion about White privilege.

Jonah responded to Lisa, further reading the text through a lens of racial literacy:

> I agree with you Lisa when you pointed out that the author does not really give any practical examples or evidence of how to overcome these issues. I think I do understand why it was not included. If she went more in depth into the issue it would have changed into a different kind of book. By not giving direct evidence on how to approach the issue, the author allows the reader to make his or her own interpretations on how he or she might solve the problems presented. (Jonah, online discussion, February 21)

Jonah repeated and clarified some of his earlier ideas about White privilege and most importantly, what the read-aloud afforded him as a reader and his group—the opportunity to construct an understanding of the text within the context of the social world in which he lives, works, and goes to school.

Tonya, similar to the class discussion, closed the discussion thread with a critical reading of what occurred in the classroom. She reinforced Jonah's perspective that Whites need to examine their own privilege before working to dismantle racism. She then raised an issue not yet addressed: our cohort of pre-service teachers was predominantly White and the university was not producing teachers of color. Tonya's posting did not receive a response, which alerted us to the broader context of practicing racial literacy in teacher education. As teacher educators, we have examined the public space of the read-aloud to think about the ways in which spaces were opened for the students to construct understandings of race and racism, as well as Whiteness. However, our own position as European-American teacher researchers may not have allowed us to see the limitations of using a book like *Mr. Lincoln's Way* in this particular context. Tonya recognized the conversations that were *not* occurring perhaps because of the overwhelming focus on Whiteness, White privilege, and White allies in our treatment of the narrative in the book.

LOOKING ACROSS THE READ-ALOUDS

In both classrooms, the read-aloud of *Mr. Lincoln's Way* was an entry point for a more extended analysis of racism, anti-racism, and/or White privilege. The emphasis in the second grade classroom was on understanding racism whereas the focus in the teacher education classroom was on White privilege. It is important to note that Melissa assumed the second grade students participate in a racialized narrative and Rebecca offered anti-racist identities for the teacher education students. As teachers, we drew on our toolkit of instructional strategies to engage with race. We stopped at key points in the story to encourage students' text-to-life connections, bringing racism into the present day. In the second grade classroom, Melissa thought aloud using a variety of rhetorical tools to bring the private, inner thoughts of a person to the public discourse and build the collective discursive resources of the classroom community. Their physical reactions and words became part of the public sphere in a circle on the rug. She emphasized that deliberation is supported by individual ideas when she wondered, "Mean Gene. He doesn't look very happy, does he?" in which the "does he," does not beg for an answer. By bringing the framework of White allies to the book, the preservice teachers were asked to consider their own racial identities and White privilege, moving from the interpersonal to the social and political.

We asked students to engage with the racial narratives in the storybook and to generate their own theories and narratives concerning race, racism, and anti-racism. In both classrooms, we drew on the frames that Polacco, the author, provided for understanding racism. Polacco portrays racism as direct actions (racial epithets) and anti-racism as friendship between people of different races (Eugene and Mr. Lincoln) as well as solidarity and support between White people (grandpa and Eugene). We engaged with the frame of "racism" with the second graders and "White allies" with the teacher education students, both of which were partial readings. Indeed, Eugene's character represents someone working through the tensions of racism *and* anti-racism. While all readings are partial, a more thorough treatment of this book in both classes would have included a return and reread of the text through both frames of anti-racism and racism.

It is important to emphasize that part of the read-aloud of *Mr. Lincoln's Way* is a visual narrative depicted through the illustrations in the text, and the performance of the read-aloud by the teacher that includes the design of the classroom space. Much of the read-aloud is performed through body language and nonverbals—our tone and intonation, use of space and timing, gaze and body language. In both classrooms, the event of the read-aloud literally brings people together to share an experience. In the case of the second grade classroom, the students move to a new space, the carpet, and occupy the same space. In the teacher education classroom, the students remain in their seats at round tables, but their focus and gaze all turns to the book and the reader. These visual narratives are largely implicit but read, nonetheless by the students and, in turn, by us as teachers and researchers. In both classes, we ask our students to consider and analyze the visual narratives in the book through a multimodal analysis of the illustrations.

The students also made important discursive moves that we could not have anticipated. In both classrooms, we noticed that the students engaged in a process of coming to understand who is in the room and then modifying their ideas and stances accordingly. This requires recognition that relationships are central in learning to live with the ambiguity and conflict associated with democracy (Palmer, 2007). Through the read-aloud, the students in both classrooms related their own stories to *Mr. Lincoln's Way*, constructing a new text that then could be read by others. Rosenblatt (1938) writes, "the study of literature can have a very real, and even central relation to the points of growth in the social and culture life of a democracy" (pp. v.) The read-alouds offered a space for students to create and share their own narratives around race.

For students in the teacher education class, their racial narratives were more thoroughly rehearsed and ingrained as a result of living for two decades in a racialized society. Some of them, like Jonah, had experience building a narrative that recognized his role as a White person. Others, like Rex, had created a narrative full of colorblind discourses and the disavowal that White privilege and racism exist. Too often, these narratives are not recognized and thus, the dialogue around race is silenced (Greene & Abt-Perkins, 2003; Ladson-Billings, 1994).

The second grade students' racial narratives are less rigid and have shorter histories. Before *Mr. Lincoln's Way*, we heard only that the second graders believed that racism happened "long ago," in the context of the civil rights movement. But by telling stories and counter-stories, they constructed new racial understandings. Students made personal connections to the text, relaying stories of bullying, talking about race, and talking about relationships across racial lines. Through stories they explored examples of racism in their day-to-day lives as Melissa asked students to imagine being in a position that a character occupied, if just for a second. It was not the case that every student participated in building talk around positions, and it was not the case that consensus was valued. Instead, value was placed on taking a position, stepping in to the story, and using the story to make sense of the world and hear how others are doing the same.

CONCLUSIONS

Read-alouds offer the possibility to engage with issues that touch our lives as social beings. Through the collective sharing of a text, meaning-making moves from a personal to community pursuit because people are privy to a range of ideas, perspectives and interpretations. When contrasting ideas come into contact, difference becomes centralized, expanding the range of meanings. Perhaps the most difficult part of any analysis is reflexivity: reading our own teaching and learning as we participated in patterns of talk that did or did not expand meaningful deliberations. Consider Benny (the second grade student) and Tonya (the teacher education student), both of whom are African American and participated in the read-aloud discussions. Benny opened the talk in the second grade classroom around racism, posing the definition of racism that guided the conversation: Racism is treating a person differently because of the color of their skin. Tonya, on the other hand, closed the conversation by asking her classmates why her voice was the only one of a person of color in the discussion. These and other moments caused us to reflect on how we could have moved more deeply into how racism operates in the contemporary public sphere, the ways in which White privilege operates in society from the perspective of a person of color, and, finally, the disruption of particular conceptions of racism and privilege. We did not always participate in ways that brought deliberative discourse to the surface, instead moving the discussion along by picking up the text and continuing to read. We could have engaged our classes in a closer examination of the contexts of our classrooms: the segregation of the public schools or the discourse of colorblindness that led Rex to resist reflecting on his own White privilege and insisting that a woman of color provide examples for him. In many places, we wondered: how might we have extended the meaning-making around the literature to promote actions that arise out of critical reflection?

Our pedagogy is an example of how we also continually test our own readings of race relations in the public sphere. Through the insights and challenges of the people in our classes we modify, change, and outgrow our own positions. Our collaborative teaching and research has been a space to design practices that include a multiplicity of perspectives, close readings, and deliberative analysis and reflection. In our analysis, we slow down the conversations that took place in our classrooms and linger over words, images, and moments. This helps us extend the interpretive possibilities of any singular literacy event. As we unravel the meanings being made in the classroom interactions, we open up a space for further meanings.

In an era of shrinking public spaces (Dewey, 1927) it is of paramount concern that educators and researchers renew their commitment to public sphere activities that encourage citizens to participate in multiple perspectives and then make up their own mind. We have learned that how readers learn to enact democratic values depends on how literature is considered in the classroom, more so than the text itself. As we unravel the meanings being made in the classroom interactions, we open a space for intervening in the public sphere of the classroom and community in ways that might make a difference.

Stories help us understand and make sense of human experiences. Read-alouds are but one literacy event that can contribute to a broader collection of teaching and learning in the public interest. Both in their content and in their interactional processes, read-alouds are spaces of meaning-making but also hold the potential to create a range of discursive and symbolic tools that are necessary to the public sphere.

REFERENCES

Almasi, J. F., & McKeown, M. G. (1996). The nature of engaged reading in classroom discussions of literature *Journal of Literacy Research, 28*(1), 107-146.

Atwell, N. (2007). *The reading zone: How to help kids become skilled, passionate, habitual, and critical readers.* New York, NY: Heinemann.

Barrentine, S. J. (1996). Engaging with reading through interactive read-alouds. *The Reading Teacher, 50*(36-43).

Beach, R. (2000). Critical Issues: Reading and Responding to Literature at the Level of Activity. *Journal of Literacy Research, 32*(2), 237-251.

Bell, D. (1980). Brown v. Board of Education and the interest-convergence dilemma. *Harvard Law Review, 93*(3), 518-533.

Bell, D. (1992). *Faces at the Bottom of the Well: The Permanence of Racism.* New York, NY: Basic Books.

Bomer, R., & Bomer, K. (2001). *For a better world: Reading and writing for social action.* New York, NY: Heinemann.

Carspecken, P. F. (1996). *Critical ethnography in educational research: A theoretical and practical guide*. New York, NY: Routledge.

Cochran-Smith, M., & Lytle, S. L. (1998). Teacher research: The question that persists. *International Journal of Leadership in Education, 1*(1), 19-36.

Delgato Gaitan, C. (1994). Consejos: The Power of Cultural Narrative. *Anthropology & Education Quarterly, 25*(3), 298-316.

Dewey, J. (1927). *The public and its problems*. Chicago, IL: Swallow.

Dozier, C., Johnston, P., & Rogers, R. (2006). *Critical literacy/critical teaching: Tools for preparing responsive teachers*. New York, NY: Teachers College Press.

Dozier, C., & Rutten, I. (2005). Responsive teaching toward responsive teachers: Mediating transfer through intentionality, enactment, and articulation. *Journal of Literacy Research, 37*(4), 459-492.

Fairclough, N. (1993). *Discourse and social change*. Cambridge, MA: Blackwell.

Fountas, I. C., & Pinnell, G. S. (1996). *Guided reading: Good first teaching for all children*. Portsmouth, NH: Heinemann.

Galda, L., & Beach, R. (2001). Response to literature as a cultural activity. *Reading Research Quarterly, 36*(1), 64-73.

Giroux, H. A. (1988). *Schooling and the struggle for public life: Critical pedagogy in the modern age*. Minneapolis, MN: University of Minnesota Press.

Goldstein, L., & Freedman, D. (2003). Challenges enacting caring teacher education. *Journal of Teacher Education, 54*(5), 441-454.

Greene, S., & Abt-Perkins, D. (2003). *Making race visible: Literacy research for cultural understanding*. New York, NY: Teachers College Press.

Guinier, L. (2004). From racial liberalism to racial literacy: Brown v. Board of Education and the interest divergence dilemma. *Journal of American History, 91* (1), 92-118.

Gutierrez, K. D. (2008). Developing a sociocritical literacy in the third space. *Reading Research Quarterly, 43*(2), 148-164.

Helms, J. E. (1997). Toward a model of white racial identity development. In K. D. Arnold & I. C. King (Eds.), *College student development and academic life: Psychological, intellectual, social, and moral issues* (pp. 207-224). New York, NY: Garland Publishing, Inc.

Jones, S. (2006). *Girls, Social Class, and Literacy: What Teachers Can Do to Make a Difference*. New York, NY: Heinemann.

Kress, G. (2009). *Multimodility: A social semiotic approach to contemporary communication*. London, Routledge.

Ladson-Billings, G. (1994). *The dreamkeepers: Successful teachers of African American children* (1st ed.). San Francisco, CA: Jossey-Bass Publishers.

Ladson-Billings, G. (1999). Preparing teachers for diverse student populations: A critical race theory perspective. *Review of Research in Education, 24*, 211-247.

Lewison, M., Flint, A. S., & Van Sluys, K. (2002). Taking on critical literacy: The journey of newcomers and novices. *Language Arts, 79*(5), 382-392.

Martinez-Roldan, C. (2005). Examining bilingual children's gender ideologies through critical discourse analysis. *Critical Inquiry in Language Studies: An International Journal, 2*(3), 312-337.

McCarthy, C. (2003). Contradictions of power and identity: Whiteness studies and the call of teacher education. *International Journal of Qualitative Studies in Education, 16*(1), 127-133.

McLaren, P., Martin, G., Farahmandpur, R., & Jaramillo, N. (2004). Teaching in and against the Empire: Critical Pedagogy as Revolutionary Praxis. *Teacher Education Quarterly, 13*(1), 131-153.

Mohr, M., Rogers, C., Sanford, B., Nocerino, M. A., & Clawson, S. (2004). *Teacher research for better schools*. New York, NY: Teachers College Press.

Moje, E. B., & Lewis, C. (2007). Examining opportunities to learn literacy: The role of critical sociocultural literacy research. In C. Lewis, P. Enciso, & E. B. Moje (Eds.), *Reframing sociocultural research on literacy: Identity, Agency, and Power* (pp. 15-48). Malwah, NJ: Routledge.

Mosley, M. (in press). "That really hit me hard": Moving beyond passive anti-racism to engage with critical race literacy pedagogy," *Race Ethnicity and Education*.

Mosley, M., & Rogers, R. (2008). Posing, Enacting, and Solving Local Problems in a Second-Grade Classroom: Critical Literacy and Multimodality. In C. Compton-Lilly (Ed.), *Breaking the silence: Recognizing the Social and Cultural Resources Students Bring to the Classroom* (pp. 92-108). New York, NY: International Reading Association.

Norris, S. (2004). *Analyzing Multimodal Interaction: A Methodological Framework*. London, UK: Routledge.

Nystrand, M. (1997). Dialogic instruction: When recitation becomes conversation. In M. Nystrand (Ed.), *Opening dialogue: Understanding the dynamics of language and learning in the English classroom* (pp. 1-). New York, NY: Teachers College Press.

Nystrand, M. (2006). Classroom discourse and reading comprehension. *Research in the Teaching of English, 40*, 392-412.

Ong, W. (1982). *Orality and litearcy: The technologizing of the word*. London, UK: Methuen.

Palmer, P. (2007). America's Democratic Experiment: Holding the Tension Between Reality and Possibility: The Commonwealth Club of California.

Polacco, P. (2001). *Mr. Lincoln's Way*. New York, NY: Philomel.

Pollock, M. (2008). *Because of race: How Americans debate harm and opportunity in our schools*. Princeton, NJ: Princeton University Press.

Prendergast, C. (2003). *Literacy and racial justice: The politics of learning after Brown v. Board of Education*. Carbondale, IL: Southern Illinois University Press.

Rogers, R. (in press, 2011) (Ed.) *An Introduction to Critical Discourse Analysis in Education* (2nd edition.) New York, NY: Routledge.

Rogers, R., & Mosley, M. (2004). Learning to be just: Peer learning in a working class classroom. In E. Gregory, S. Long & D. Volk (Eds.), *Many pathways to literacy: Learning with siblings, peers, grandparents, and in community settings* (pp. 142-154). New York, NY: Routledge.

Rogers, R., & Mosley, M. (2006). Racial Literacy in a second-grade classroom: Critical race theory, whiteness studies, and literacy research. *Reading Research Quarterly, 41*(4), 462-495.

Rogers, R., & Mosley, M. (2008). A critical discourse analysis of racial literacy in teacher education. *Linguistics and Education: An International Research Journal, 19*(2), 107-131.

Rogers, R., Mosley, M., & Folkes, A. (2009). Standing up to neoliberalism through critical literacy education. *Language Arts, 87*(2), 127-138.

Rogers, R., Mosley, M., & Kramer, M. A. (2009). *Designing Socially Just Communities: Critical Literacy Education across the Lifespan*. New York, NY: Routledge.

Rogers, T. (1999). Literary theory and children's literature: Interpreting ourselves and our worlds. *Theory into Practice, 38*(3), 138-146.

Rosenblatt, L. M. (1978/1994). *The reader, the text, the poem: The transactional theory of the literary work*. Carbondale, IL: Southern Illinois University Press.

Shapiro, T. (2004). *The Hidden Cost of Being African American: How Wealth Perpetuates Inequality*. New York, NY: Oxford University Press.

Sipe, L. R. (2000). The construction of literary understanding by first and second graders in oral response to picture storybook read-alouds. *Reading Research Quarterly, 25*(2), 252-275.

Stokes Brown, C. (2002). *Refusing racism: white allies and the struggle for civil rights*. New York, NY: Teachers College Press.

Tyson, C. A. (1999). "Shut my mouth wide open": Realistic fiction and social action. *Theory into Practice, 38*(3), 155-159.

Wells, A. S., & Crain, R. L. (1997). *Stepping over the color line: African-American students in white suburban schools*. New Haven, CT: Yale University Press.

Wertsch, J. V. (1991). *Voices of the mind: a sociocultural approach to mediated action*. Cambridge, MA: Harvard University Press.

Willis, A. I. (2003). Parallax: Addressing race in preservice literacy education. In S. Greene & D. Abt-Perkins (Eds.), *Making race visible* (pp. 51-69). New York, NY: Teachers College Press.

Wolk, S. (2009). Reading for a better world: Teaching for social responsibility with young adult literature. *Journal of Adolescent & Adult Literacy, 52*(8), 664-673.

Young, J. P. (2000). Boy Talk: Critical Literacy and Masculinities. *Reading Research Quarterly, 35*(3), 312-337.

Zacher, J. C. (2008). Analyzing Children's Social Positioning and Struggles for Recognition in a Classroom Literacy Event. *Research in the Teaching of English, 43*(1), 12-41.

Exploring the Influence of Science Writing Instruction on Fourth-Graders' Writing Development

Jennifer L. Tilson
Jill Castek
Megan Goss
University of California, Berkeley

The purpose of this study was to investigate the possibility that teaching writing as an authentic part of inquiry science could benefit students in their ability to organize and express scientific ideas. To that end, we examined fourth-grade students' informational writing development in the context of an eight week integrated science-literacy unit. An experimental group received a science-literacy unit that included scaffolded instruction on science writing, while a control group received content comparable science-only instruction. All students completed an open-ended writing prompt as a pre/post assessment. This assessment was analyzed using a specially designed rubric that included seven dimensions: science content, use of evidence, introduction, clarity, conclusion, vocabulary usage, and a count of topic-specific vocabulary words used in the piece. Writing assessments from students in the experimental group were compared with those of students in the control group to determine the extent to which seven elements of informational writing were acquired. Results indicated that students in the experimental condition outperformed students in the control condition on all but two of the dimensions of science writing (conclusion and vocabulary usage).

NATURE OF THE PROBLEM

In order to address the pressing challenges that face us as global citizens, educators need to cultivate students who are highly literate problem solvers (Moje, 2007). Academic and workplace achievement is increasingly dependent on the ability to write, read, and speak in sophisticated ways (Alexander & Jetton, 2002; Bransford, Brown, & Cocking, 2004). However, current efforts to increase students' literacy achievement are falling short (Grigg, Lauko, & Brockway, 2006). This is particularly evident in content areas such as science that require a high degree of domain-specific literacy (Carnegie Council on Advancing Adolescent Literacy [CCAAL], 2010). For instance, one indicator of students' science learning, the Trends in International Mathematics and Science Study (TIMSS), reveals that students in the U.S. consistently score below their international peers (Martin, Mullis, Gonzalez, & Chrostowski, 2004). Similar patterns of low achievement among U.S. students have been documented over the past several years (National Center for Education Statistics [NCES], 2006; NCES, 2007; NCES, 2010). Recent research (Greenleaf & Hinchman, 2009; Pearson, Moje, & Greenleaf, 2010) suggests the most promising way to address these concerns is to infuse literacy into content area instruction.

Scientific literacy goes beyond familiarity with a corpus of information. Developing domain-specific knowledge requires a firm grasp of the skills needed to both process and communicate about the ideas that are central to conceptual understanding. In science, paramount among these skills are the ability to reason, interpret, and evaluate information and to make evidence-based explanations (Driver, Newton, & Osborne, 2000; Lemke, 1990). Writing is a key practice that scientists engage in to communicate their findings and explanations with the scientific community and to advance the field (Osborne, 2010; Yore, Hand, & Prain, 2002). However, in science classes at all levels, writing in the form of note taking or short answers is often expected, and more extensive scientific writing is rarely taught explicitly. We contend that providing students with explicit, scaffolded instruction in informational writing in the elementary grades will increase their achievement in both science and literacy and move us closer to the goal of creating more scientifically literate citizens. Morrow, Pressley, Smith, & Smith (1997) contend that teaching informational writing in elementary school is an essential part of jump-starting these efforts, and that the explicit and scaffolded teaching of writing strategies is necessary for students to learn how to write effectively and fluently (Graham & Perin, 2007).

Examining the content and form of students' writing is an especially important area for continued research. Recent studies have called attention to writing as the "Neglected R." Reports from the National Commission on Writing in America's Schools and Colleges (2003) assert that writing does not get nearly as much funding or attention as reading and math do, and that we pay for this neglect as a society, since much of the success in later schooling and in work is contingent upon solid writing skills. Moreover, Bereiter and Scardamalia (2003) suggest that writing enhances content learning because it allows students to call on higher forms of thinking in order to process and express ideas. Writing may also be a central mode through which students make sense of what they are learning (The National Commission on Writing, 2003). As a result, informational writing must become a central focus of content area instruction in classrooms (Cutler & Graham, 2008).

Recent research (e.g., Cervetti, Pearson, Bravo, & Barber, 2006) has shown that integrated science-literacy instruction increases students' proficiency with both content knowledge as well as literacy processes. Additional evidence suggests that students who learn to write well within one content area, such as science, may ultimately gain an understanding of the common characteristics of informational writing in general and will be better able to effectively communicate important ideas across content areas (Holliday, Yore, & Alvermann, 1994). And, writing has been demonstrated to be an effective tool for student learning, particularly in content areas such as science (Graham & Perin, 2007; Klentschy & Molina-De La Torre, 2004; Prain & Hand, 1996). Therefore, teaching writing in the context of science seems to be a promising way to help students gain the skills needed to communicate complex ideas.

THEORETICAL FRAMEWORK

Like many educators and educational researchers, (e.g., Draper & Siebert, 2009; Guthrie, Anderson, Alao, & Rinehart, 1999; Moje, Ciechanowski, Kramer, Ellis, Carrillo, & Collazo, 2004; Shanahan & Shanahan, 2008; Vitale & Romance, 2007) we adopt the perspective that literacy is an essential tool for learning and recognize there is a reciprocal relationship between literacy development and content knowledge. Pearson (2009) points out that to make literacy instruction optimally purposeful, students need to read, write, and talk about content. He goes on to suggest that the more students acquire conceptual understanding about a topic, the more capably they can express their ideas in writing and speaking, and, in turn, the more they can understand what they read about. Knowledge is a foundation on which future learning rests, and literacy is a means towards acquiring this knowledge. This stance—recognizing literacy as the vehicle by which students will accomplish learning about a particular domain—grounds our thinking about reading instruction and writing instruction.

LITERATURE REVIEW

Early work from the 1980s and 1990s examined the overlapping cognitive demands required to be successful in both science and literacy (Carin & Sund, 1985; Holliday, Yore & Alvermann, 1994). Since that time, educators in both fields have acknowledged the critical role that language plays in science on the one hand, and the central importance of content-area knowledge in supporting the development of literacy on the other. For instance, Palinscar and Magnussen (2001) developed and tested a curriculum in which texts were designed to support inquiry by providing data and experiences that were difficult to gain firsthand in the classroom. They found that this approach enhanced the students' understandings of difficult science concepts. Romance and Vitale (1991, 2002), as well as Guthrie and colleagues (1999, 2002), suggest that integration of science and literacy leads to significant gains for students in both domains.

Earlier work on science and literacy integration focused on the connection between reading and scientific reasoning (Hanrahan, 1999; Yore, Hand, Goldman, Hildebrand, Osborne, Treagust, & Wallace, 2004). Researchers have also examined the use of student science notebooks as a means of developing science content knowledge (e.g., Palincsar and Magnusson, 2001). Findings from this study showed that science notebooks were a key component that could be used to link students' experiences in reading and classroom science experiences. When writing was made into a central component linking reading and investigations, students gained greater access to science content. However, this study did not examine students' writing development over the course of the intervention, nor were written products scored on how well students expressed and organized their ideas.

Some researchers have focused on writing as a both vehicle for promoting content understanding as well as a skill set that students can develop. Notably, Klentschy and Molina-De La Torre (2004) found that students' use of science notebooks as an authentic extension of inquiry improved their informational writing in a variety of important ways and also showed benefits for content learning.

A more focused area of research on science writing addressed the need for students to understand the specific writing demands of a given content area and include these characteristics in their own writing (Cervetti, Pearson, Barber & Bravo, 2006; Daniels, Zemelman, & Steineke, 2007; Pappas & Varelas, 2004). Research has suggested that involving students in writing science texts can heighten their awareness of how such texts are created (Littlefair, 1992) and increase their understanding of why and when to use them (Moss, 2005). Over time, students developed the ability to read such texts as writers and to use these pieces for scientific evidence they could include in their own writing. In this way, they were able to create their own texts based upon what they gathered from the model texts they read (Pappas, Kiefer, & Levstik, 1999). Krajcik and McNeill (2007) focused on one important type of science writing—the scientific explanation. Their research suggests that a scaffolded approach to teaching scientific explanation writing led to students' increased ability to make claims, cite relevant supporting evidence, and express their scientific understanding in written form. However, this work was focused on middle school students, and centered on the analysis of science content through students' written products.

Recent work by Lee and Spratley (2010) and Schoenbach and Greenleaf (2009) recognizes the important role that content knowledge plays in literacy development. These researchers suggest that content knowledge and literacy development are highly connected. Developing deep content knowledge essential for helping students develop expert reading and writing skills and strategies, but learning the literacy practices of disciplines such as science is also key for students' success in later schooling.

Although studies of science-literacy integration have shown promising results in terms of student learning outcomes (Cervetti, Pearson, Barber & Bravo, 2006; Guthrie, et al., 1999; Guthrie & Ozgungar, 2002; Palinscar & Magnusson, 2001; Romance & Vitale, 1992, 2001; Wang & Herman, 2005), questions remain about the effectiveness of various elements of integrated instruction. An important question in this area is whether students' writing development improves when learning to write is a part of science instruction (Alvermann, Swafford, & Montero, 2004). Our work on an integrated science-literacy curriculum development and research project (see Pearson & Cervetti, 2005) suggests that learning the written discourse of science is key in enabling students to understand and express scientific understandings. Thus, in this study we aimed to answer the question: *Do students who are taught scientific writing in the context of an integrated science-literacy unit make greater gains in writing than students who are taught science separate from literacy?* To this end, the research reported in this paper examines pre/post scores from an assessment of science writing administered to fourth-grade students.

METHODS

Participants

Ninety-four fourth-grade classrooms in 48 schools were recruited and volunteered to participate in this study. Each classroom was located in the same Southern state, and was comprised of near equal numbers of boys and girls (n=2144). In our sample, 47 classrooms were randomly assigned to the experimental condition (n=215) that taught the integrated science and literacy unit, and 47 classrooms were randomly assigned to the control condition (n=241) that taught a content-comparable science unit. Demographic information from school districts about student participants was only available for 45% of the sample. As a result, in the sections that follow, we report available student demographics, as well as percentages of missing data, in order to characterize the population involved in the study as completely as possible.

Experimental group. At the school level, we examined socio-economic information that was available from the Great Schools nationwide database. A classroom was considered to come from a low-SES school if more than 50% of the students at that school were eligible for free or reduced lunch. By this criterion, 24 of the classrooms in the experimental group came from low-SES schools and 17 of the classrooms did not. For six of the classrooms, information describing the level of economics was not available. Of the 47% if students whose demographics were available, 22%

were White, 18% were African American, and 4% were Hispanic. The remaining 3% of students were Asian (1.6%) and Multiracial (1.4%). Approximately 4% of students were English language learners (ELLs).

Control group. School-level socio-economic information from Great Schools was also examined for the control group (using the same criterion referenced above for low-SES classrooms). Forty-one of control classrooms came from low-SES schools and eight of the classrooms did not. For five of the classrooms, information describing SES was not available. Of the 44% if students whose demographics were available, 18% were White, 18% were African American and 4% were Hispanic. The remaining 4% of students were Asian (2.7%), Multiracial (1%), and American Indian (.3%). About one percent of students were English language learners.

Equivalency of groups. A comparison of the student demographics indicated that the two groups were composed of near-equal amounts of ethnically and linguistically diverse students, but that there were there were fewer numbers of low-SES students in the experimental group and fewer English language learners in the control group. To determine the extent to which these differences may have indicated pre-existing differences among the groups, we examined two standardized student achievement measures. The first was a statewide criterion-referenced content test (CRCT) of English Language Arts that was administered to all fourth-graders in the state in 2007, just prior to the beginning of the study. An independent samples t-test was run to compare the mean scores for each group. The results indicated there were no statistical differences between the groups: t (400) =.86, $p < .39$. The second measure was a statewide criterion-referenced test of general science content that was administered to all fourth-graders in 2007. The results indicated that there was a statistically significant mean difference favoring the control group: t (646) =2.37, $p < .02$. Table 1 includes the descriptive statistics for the criterion-referenced tests and Table 2 contains the mean comparison statistics.

Table 1. Descriptive Statistics Summarizing Pre-existing Differences Between Groups on Criterion-referenced Tests

	Group	N	Mean	Std. Deviation	Std. Error of the Mean
CRCT English Language Arts (ELA) 2007	Experimental	180	820.86	25.68	1.91
	Control	222	823.06	25.68	1.72
CRCT Science 2007	Experimental	317	813.75	35.25	1.98
	Control	331	820.33	35.56	1.96

INSTRUCTION IN THE EXPERIMENTAL CONDITION

Students in the experimental group were taught an integrated science-literacy unit composed of forty 60-minute sessions. The unit was designed to build students' science knowledge about physical science concepts related to light and energy. The curriculum unit was developed at the Lawrence Hall of Science at the University of California, Berkeley by a team of science and literacy educators, including the authors of this paper. The unit included a detailed teacher's guide, student books, and a kit of materials for hands-on investigations. These components were mailed to teachers in the experimental group in advance of the study.

Table 2. Independent Samples (t-test) Mean Comparisons Between Groups on Criterion-referenced Tests

			t-test for Equality of Means				
	t	df	Sig. (2-tailed)	Mean Difference	Std. Error Difference	95% Confidence Interval of the Difference	
						Lower	Upper
CRCT English Language Arts (ELA) 2007	.855	400	.39	2.20	2.58	-2.86	7.27
CRCT Science 2007	2.37	646	*.02	6.58	2.78	1.12	12.05

* $p < .05$

Instructional activities in the unit included a balance of both science- and literacy-focused sessions: approximately 40% of instructional time was spent on literacy activities (reading, writing, and listening/speaking), 40% on hands-on, inquiry science (including discussions of data and findings from students' investigations), and approximately 20% of instructional time was spent on reviewing concepts and assessing students understanding through embedded formative assessment. Topics covered included: the characteristics of light, how light interacts with materials (such as reflecting or refracting), light as a form of energy, and energy transformations.

Instruction was designed so that reading, writing, discussion and hands-on experiences were mutually supportive of student learning. For example, students investigated reflection by testing a set of materials (such as foil, felt, and wood) to see if they reflected light from a flashlight. They discussed their findings and made a table displaying their data. They then referred to a text from the unit that provided additional data about the materials. Students used the data in this book to resolve disagreements about which materials reflected light, as well as to draw inferences about the amount of light reflected by classes of materials (such as *fabric* or *metal*). In this sequence of lessons, students used reading, writing, and oral language skills in support of learning both science content and the discourse of science.

Students were given frequent, explicit instruction on using evidence to support their explanations and arguments in both discussion and in writing. As students gathered more information about which materials reflect light, they debated, revised their findings, and then wrote explanations to express their understanding about the concept *All materials reflect light* using the evidence they had amassed. In the process of writing explanations, students learned that evidence can come from both firsthand investigations and information found in texts.

Throughout the unit, students wrote in various forms for different purposes. For example, students recorded information and data from their investigations, responded to informational texts they read, prepared for small-group discussions, and reflected in writing on what they had learned. Although class time was provided for writing to learn in these ways, instructional time was also focused on teaching a common structure for communicating scientific understandings in written form. The unit incorporated lessons on paragraph writing, including the construction of topic sentences, the inclusion of supporting evidence, and using scientific vocabulary to express ideas in a precise way. These key elements were introduced, modeled, and became the focus each time students were asked to write.

Instruction in scientific writing employed a gradual release of responsibility model (Pearson & Gallagher, 1983), in which the teacher led students to accomplish scientific writing through scaffolded practice that tapered off over time. At the beginning of the unit, the teacher modeled writing an entire piece with student input. As the unit progressed, there was less teacher modeling and more student independence. For example, during the second week of the unit, the class wrote a topic sentence together, which all students used to begin their piece. The teacher directed students to use specific resources (books students had read and notes from firsthand investigations they conducted) to gather evidence for writing, and modeled the use of a graphic organizer to collect information. Students worked in pairs to gather information; then the teacher aided students in transforming their notes into supporting sentences comprising the rest of their paragraphs. Throughout the unit, scaffolds such as graphic organizers and partnered discussion were used before writing to help students focus on essential concepts, generate ideas, and organize information. In addition to several sessions devoted entirely to writing instruction, students had a number of opportunities to write to explain their thinking after they conducted scientific investigations.

Instruction in the Control Condition

Information about instruction in these classrooms was collected using a pre- and post-survey. The survey asked teachers to describe what topics they taught and how instruction was planned, organized, and delivered. Survey results indicated that teachers in the control condition used various materials to teach about light and energy including published textbooks, trade books, inquiry-science units, and teacher-made units involving hands-on science experiences. Although many of the control group classrooms read and wrote during science time, in none of the control classrooms was literacy instruction systematically integrated with science. However, the control and the experimental groups were taught the same concepts about light and energy as expressed in their state science standards.

Assessments Administered in Experimental and Control Conditions

The writing assessment was part of a battery of pre/post measures that accompanied the unit. Teachers administered the writing assessment in their own classrooms using an administration protocol with standardized directions and time limits. The prompt *How does light interact with materials? Give three examples* was pre-printed in an examination booklet provided by the researchers. All students wrote their responses in the space provided and were instructed to stop when the allotted time was up. This prompt was used as both the pre- and post-assessment.

The writing prompt emphasized science content from the state science standards and was given in both the experimental and control conditions. We hypothesized that students who were part of the experimental condition that received scaffolded writing instruction in conjunction with science would be more proficient in developing their ideas, including evidence to support them, organizing their writing, and using the language of science with a higher degree of precision. This proficiency would take the form of using evidence more effectively to support ideas, greater logic and organization, and expressing science content more accurately. In addition, we posited that students in the experimental group would integrate a greater number of science vocabulary words within their writing, and use these words more accurately than students in the control condition.

Rubric Development

Development of the writing rubric involved several stages of collaborative work. The first stage involved reading 65 randomly selected student papers. This first reading was used to determine which aspects of writing were central to an expertly crafted response. Those characteristics were then classified into six dimensions—evidence, introduction, clarity, conclusion, vocabulary, and language use. In addition to this development, science assessment specialists also developed a rubric that was used to score the science content of students' writing in terms of depth and accuracy of understanding.

Developing the score point descriptions for each dimension involved a systematic, iterative process of reading papers, detailing their characteristics, and evaluating writing using the descriptors. As researchers read and discussed papers, aspects that made a response well written were described in the highest score point of the rubric. The Use of Evidence dimension measured how well the evidence the student included supported and explicated the main points in the piece. The Introduction dimension examined the initial statement that prefaced the content that followed. The Conclusion dimension looked at final statement and how effectively it wrapped up the piece. The Clarity dimension looked at how well the ideas in the piece were expressed. Vocabulary Usage examined how words were used and defined in context. Vocabulary Count was an indicator measuring how many of the 32 science words targeted during instruction were included in students' writing. The dimensions on the rubric were scaled from 1-4 with the exception of the clarity dimension, which was scaled from 1-3. Vocabulary count was a frequency count ranging from 0 to 32. The Science Content and Writing Rubric can be accessed online at http://sciencewritingrubrics. wikispaces.com/ and is also included in Appendix A.

Before the initial rounds of scoring, the rubric was refined by the paper's authors and calibrated using exemplars of student work. To establish inter-rater reliability, two trained scorers evaluated a random sample of 20% of the total number of writing papers. Inter-rater reliability for these two scorers was calculated at .85 at pretest and .79 at posttest. When the rubric was ultimately finalized, a single trained scorer evaluated the remaining 80% of student papers independently. The index of dependability for the single scorer was calculated at .81 at pretest and .75 at posttest.

To determine whether students' writing scores were comparable at pretest, a t-test was conducted to compare student performance between the experimental and control groups. Results indicated that there were no statistically significant differences between the groups on any dimension on the rubric at pretest. Table 3 includes the descriptive statistics summarizing differences between groups on the writing pretest. Table 4 contains the writing pretest mean comparisons.

Table 3. Descriptive Statistics Summarizing Pretest Differences Between Groups on the Writing Pretest

	Group	N	Mean	Std. Deviation	Std. Error of the Mean
Science Content (range 0-4)	Experimental	215	1.71	.74	.05
	Control	241	1.75	.70	.05
Use of Evidence (range 0-4)	Experimental	215	1.53	.85	.06
	Control	241	1.59	.84	.05
Introduction (range 0-4)	Experimental	215	2.04	.84	.06
	Control	241	2.02	.74	.05
Conclusion (range 0-4)	Experimental	215	1.92	.75	.05
	Control	241	1.87	.59	.04
Clarity (range 0-3)	Experimental	215	1.73	.79	.05
	Control	241	1.69	.74	.05
Vocabulary Usage (range 0-4)	Experimental	215	1.43	.90	.06
	Control	241	1.53	.92	.06
Vocabulary Count (range 0-32)	Experimental	215	2.27	1.32	.09
	Control	241	2.33	1.34	.09

Table 4. Independent Samples (t-test) Mean Comparisons Between Groups on Writing Pretest

	t-test for Equality of Means						
	t	df	Sig. (2-tailed)	Mean Difference	Std. Error Difference	95% Confidence Interval of the Difference	
						Lower	Upper
Science Content	.55	454	.59	.04	.07	-.10	.17
Use of Evidence	.77	454	.44	.06	.08	-.09	.22
Introduction	-.28	454	.78	-.02	.07	-.17	.13
Conclusion	-.80	454	.42	-.05	.06	-.17	.07
Clarity	-.53	454	.60	-.04	.07	-.18	.10
Vocabulary Usage	1.15	454	.25	.10	.09	-.07	.27
Vocabulary Count	.50	454	.62	.06	.13	-.18	.31

RESULTS

To address the research question, *Do students who are taught scientific writing in the context of an integrated science/literacy unit make greater gains in writing than students who are taught science separate from literacy?* posttest scores on the writing prompt were analyzed. Before interpreting the t-test statistics, Levene's test for equality of variance was examined and determined to be significant in three cases, indicating that there were variance differences between the two groups on Science Content, Use of Evidence, and Introduction. According to Moser, Stevens, & Watts (1989) and Ruxton (2006), the equal variance not assumed statistic makes conservative adjustments for unequal group variances and is therefore an interpretable statistic. The unequal variance statistic was therefore examined, interpreted, and reported in these three cases.

A Bonferroni adjustment was made to control for Type I error rate due to the fact that multiple comparisons were made. Statistically significant differences between groups were found on five dimensions of the writing rubric including Science Content t (414.02) = -7.17, p < .00, Use of Evidence t (412.66) = -3.61, p < .00, Introduction t (437.34) = -4.86, p < .00, Clarity t (454) = -4.63, p < .00, and Vocabulary Count t (454) = -9.39, p < .00. An examination of mean differences indicated that the experimental group outperformed the control condition.

Two additional dimensions measured on the rubric, Vocabulary Usage t (454) = -1.74, p < .08 and Conclusion t (454) = -1.47, p < .14 did not yield a statistically significant mean difference. Table 5 includes the descriptive statistics associated with the analysis of post-test differences between groups and Table 6 contains the mean comparisons between groups.

A composite score, (a total score made up of sub-scores on each of the seven dimensions that were used to assess students' writing), was generated and analyzed using an independent samples t-test. An overall Cohen's d effect size was calculated at .69. Cohen's rules of thumb for characterizing the strength of the effect sizes (Cohen, 1988) indicate a medium-size effect.

Table 5. Descriptive Statistics Summarizing Differences Between Groups on Writing Posttest

	Group	N	Mean	Std. Dev.	Std. Error of the Mean
Science Content (range 0-4)	Experimental	215	2.7	.97	.07
	Control	241	2.10	.79	.05
Use of Evidence (range 0-4)	Experimental	215	2.22	1.24	.09
	Control	241	1.83	1.01	.07
Introduction (range 0-4)	Experimental	215	2.73	.93	.06
	Control	241	2.32	.86	.06
Conclusion (range 0-4)	Experimental	215	2.05	.56	.04
	Control	241	1.97	.60	.04
Clarity (range 0-3)	Experimental	215	2.14	.76	.05
	Control	241	1.82	.75	.05
Vocabulary Usage (range 0-4)	Experimental	215	2.21	1.10	.07
	Control	241	2.03	1.13	.07
Vocabulary Count (range 0-32)	Experimental	215	4.20	1.79	.12
	Control	241	2.71	1.63	.11

Table 6. Independent Samples (t-test) Mean Comparisons Between Groups on Writing Posttest

	t	df	Sig. (2-tailed)	Mean Difference	Std. Error Difference	95% Confidence Interval of the Difference	
t-test for Equality of Means							
						Lower	Upper
Science Content	-7.17	414.02	**.00	-.60	.08	-.76	-.43
Use of Evidence	-3.61	412.66	**.00	-.39	.11	-.59	-.018
Introduction	-4.86	437.34	**.00	-.41	.80	-.58	-.24
Conclusion	-1.47	454	.14	-.08	.06	-.19	.03
Clarity	-4.63	454	**.00	-.33	.07	-.47	-.19
Vocabulary Usage	-1.74	454	.08	-.18	.10	-.38	-.02
Vocabulary Count	-9.39	454	**.00	-1.50	.16	-1.82	-1.19

** $p < .001$

DISCUSSION

The performance of the students in the experimental condition demonstrates that integrated science and literacy instruction was generally successful in improving students' science writing. The findings suggest that when informational writing is taught in an integrated way, students make gains in the areas of science content, use of evidence, using an introduction, writing with clarity, and using scientific vocabulary in their writing. However, when it came to including definitions or examples to explain the scientific vocabulary students used (vocabulary usage), as well as ending their scientific writing with a conclusion, there was no statistically significant difference between the experimental and control groups.

In interpreting the results of this study, it is worth noting that, even though students were not prompted by the teacher to organize their writing in any particular way during the assessment, they still made gains in producing pieces of scientific writing that conveyed ideas clearly. This was additional evidence for the supposition that the integrated curriculum improved students' writing organization and expression of science ideas.

Another interesting finding involved students' use of vocabulary in their writing, which was measured in two ways. The intent of these two dimensions of the rubric (Vocabulary Count and Vocabulary Usage) was to measure students' productive use of science vocabulary in written form in a comprehensive manner. While the count of science vocabulary terms used in student writing was significant, vocabulary usage did not differ significantly between the experimental and the control groups. This finding could indicate a shortcoming of the curriculum, or it could be that, in the absence of an authentic audience for writing, students did not feel the need to define or explain the scientific terms they included in their writing.

Implications

A model for improving student writing in the context of an integrated curriculum unit, where content knowledge and literacy work hand-in-hand, introduces important implications. As teachers and students face increasing demands for improved achievement, especially in reading and math, quality time for the teaching of writing becomes rare. Yet literacy, and in many ways writing in particular, is a crucial component for success in the upper grades and beyond (Moje, 2007; Alexander & Jetton, 2002; Bransford, Brown, & Cocking, 2000). In fact, students with limited literacy abilities struggle with learning in school, especially in content areas such as science, and are more likely to drop out (Hammond, Linton, Smink, & Drew, 2007), thus limiting their ability to become informed citizens who are able to pursue the careers that are defining the twenty-first century, where jobs requiring specialized skills, training, and often, an advanced degree will dominate the new marketplace (U.S. Department of Labor, 2008; Levine, 2004). It is vital that educators have the means to teach students sophisticated literacy skills even within the compacted school day that is the reality of today's classrooms. An integrated science and literacy curriculum, such as the one described in this paper, may offer a solution for teaching students to communicate ideas clearly and effectively in writing. This curriculum also has the benefit of achieving dual aims—supporting students' literacy development as well as their content learning in science. An integrated approach maximizes the use of instructional time within a school day and allows both science content and literacy strategies to be taught.

LIMITATIONS

Although results suggest that integrating literacy and writing instruction with science supports writing development, it is important to recognize limitations in the design and implementation of this study. One such limitation was our inability to conduct classroom visits to collect observation data. Without such data, it was difficult to determine the extent to which fidelity of implementation across classrooms occurred. This may have influenced our results and introduced additional factors that may have had an effect on student performance. We attempted to address this limitation by administering a survey that included questions about what was taught and how much time was spent on various topics. This data gave us a moderate degree of confidence that instruction was content-comparable and that instructional materials in the experimental condition were adhered to within an acceptable degree of fidelity. Although relying solely on self-reports may not have been ideal in this situation, it was not possible to visit each classroom to triangulate data sources that may have also accounted for the effects reported.

Another limitation involved grouping the variety of different instructional approaches implemented within the control classrooms together in the analysis. Pre- and post-survey data collected from control teachers indicated that approaches in use could have potentially been more different than alike. Grouping these classrooms together may have not allowed us to characterize instructional approaches in the control classrooms adequately.

Implications for the Design of Future Studies

The findings of this study may inform further research and curriculum development pertaining to students' informational writing. The authenticity and purposefulness of integrating science with literacy, along with scaffolded instruction in writing, seems to allow students to learn important aspects of science writing. However, we remain curious about which particular elements of the instruction were most influential. Further research that allows us to isolate variables such as time spent writing, teacher modeling of writing strategies, or the impact of specific scaffolds offered, could provide descriptive information about outcomes for the students in the experimental group.

Pursuing this line of research would allow us to develop more targeted pedagogical information for teachers so that they might further improve their informational writing instruction. The more we learn about how these factors work in combination to help students become stronger writers, the better curricular modules we can offer.

Another critical question for further research is whether or not gains in writing transfer to other contexts. For example, if students are taught the crucial elements necessary for successful creation of one type of scientific writing, could this learning help them as they create other types of scientific writing? And, going further, could writing instruction in science have a positive effect on the informational writing that students engage in for other content areas as well? The rubric we designed to evaluate students' writing focused on general characteristics of informational writing; it is therefore conceivable that writing instruction in science could support transfer into other content areas.

Next Steps

This study explored important issues with regard to integrating science and literacy instruction. As we think forward about future studies, we are interested in looking more closely writing gains made by particular groups of students. For example, how effective is writing instruction embedded within science for academically diverse learners? Further investigation could help us to see how this kind of instruction affects different groups of students, and how we might adjust instruction to better address their varying needs.

The results of this study offer promising insights into a pedagogical approach that can help teachers address a vital area of educational concern: teaching today's students critical elements of informational writing. As emerging research suggests (Draper & Siebert, 2009; Greenleaf & Hinchman 2009; Shanahan & Shanahan, 2008), we need to teach students to become highly literate within content-specific domains. Through informational writing in science, students learn critical elements of writing, as well as skills and strategies that are specific to science: how to leverage evidence in support of an argument, use specialized language, and explain scientific concepts in a coherent and organized way. Although there is more work to be done to ensure that we understand why and how this approach yielded significant results in this study, we believe that integrating science and literacy, with an emphasis on writing instruction is a promising one that can be drawn upon to create more supportive and innovative curriculum programs in the future.

REFERENCES

Alvermann, D., Swafford, J., & Montero, M. K. (2004). *Content area literacy instruction for the elementary grades.* Boston, MA: Allyn & Bacon.

Alexander, P. A., & Jetton, T. L. (2002). Learning from text: A multidimensional and developmental perspective. In M. L. Kamil, P. Mosenthal, P. D. Pearson, & R. Barr (Eds*). Handbook of Reading Research*, Vol 3, pp. 285-310 Mahwah, NJ.

Bereiter, C., & Scardamalia, M. (2003). Learning to work creatively with knowledge. In E. De Corte, L. Verschaffel, N. Entwistle, & J. van Merrienboer (Eds.), *Powerful learning environments: Unravelling basic components and dimensions.* Oxford, UK: Elsevier Science.

Bransford, J. D., Brown, A. L., & Cocking, R. R. (Eds.). (2004). *How people learn: Brain, mind, experience, and school.* Washington, DC: National Research Council.

Carin, A. A., & Sund, R. B. (1985). *Teaching modern science* (4th ed). Columbus, OH: Merrill.

Carnegie Council on Advancing Adolescent Literacy [CCAAL]. (2010). *Time to act: An agenda for advancing adolescent literacy for college and career success.* New York, NY: Carnegie Corporation of New York. Retrieved on October 5th, 2009 from: http://www.carnegie.org/literacy/tta/pdf/tta_Main.pdf

Cervetti, G., Pearson, P. D., Bravo, M. A., & Barber, J. (2006). Reading and writing in the service of inquiry-based science. In R. Douglas, M. Klentschy, and K. Worth (Eds.). *Linking science and literacy in the K-8 classroom.* Arlington, VA: National Science Teachers Association.

Cohen, J. (1988). Statistical power analysis for the behavioral sciences (2nd ed.). Hillsdale, NJ: Erlbaum.

Cutler, L., & Graham, S. (2008). Primary grade writing instruction: A national survey. *Journal of Educational Psychology, 100,* 907-919.

Daniels, H., Zemelman, S. Steineke, N. (2007). Content area writing. Heinemann Press:Portsmouth, NH.

Draper, R., & Siebert, D. (2009). Content area literacy in mathematics and science classrooms. In S. R. Parris, D. Fisher, & K. Headley (Eds.), *Adolescent literacy, field tested* (pp. 105-116). Newark, DE: International Reading Association.

Driver, R., Newton, P., & Osborne, J. (2000). Establishing the norms of scientific argumentation in classrooms. *Science Education, 84,* 287–312.

Graham, S., & Perin, D. (2007). A meta-analysis of writing instruction for adolescent students. *Journal of Educational Psychology, 99*(3), 445-476.

Green, S. B., & Salkind, N. J. (2005). *Using SPSS for Windows and Macintosh: Analyzing and Understanding Data,* (Fourth Ed.). Upper Saddle River, NJ: Pearson.

Greenleaf, C., & Hinchman, K. (2009). Reimagining our inexperienced adolescent readers: From struggling, striving, marginalized, and reluctant to thriving. *Journal of Adolescent & Adult Literacy. (53)*1, 4-13.

Grigg, W. S., Lauko, M. A., & Brockway, D. M. (2006). *The Nation's Report Card: Science 2005* (NCES 2006–466). U.S. Department of Education, National Center for Education Statistics. Washington, DC: U.S. Government Printing Office.

Guthrie, J. T., Anderson, E., Alao, S., & Rinehart, J. (1999). Influences of concept-oriented reading instruction on strategy use and conceptual learning from text. *Elementary School Journal, 99*(4), 341-366.

Guthrie, J. T., & Ozgungor, S. (2002). Instructional contexts for reading engagement. In *Comprehension instruction: Research-based best practices* C. C. Block and M. Pressley (Eds). New York, NY: Guilford Press.

Hammond, C., Linton, D., Smink, J., & Drew, S. (2007). *Dropout risk factors and exemplary programs: A technical report.* Clemson University: National Dropout Prevention Center at Clemson University and Communities In Schools, Inc.

Hanrahan, M. (1999). Rethinking science literacy: Enhancing communication and participation in school science through affirmational dialogue journal writing. *Journal of Research in Science Teaching, 36*(6), 699-717.

Holliday, W. G., Yore, L. D., and Alvermann, D. E. (1994). The reading-science learning-writing connections: Breakthroughs, barriers and promises. *Journal of Research in Science Teaching, 31*(9), 877-893.

Klentschy, M., & Molina-De La Torre, E. (2004). Students' science notebooks and the inquiry process. In E. Saul (Ed.), *Crossing Borders in Literacy and Science Instruction* (pp. 161-189). Newark, DE: International Reading Association.

Krajcik, J. S., & McNeill, K. L (2007). Assessing middle school students' content knowledge and scientific reasoning through written explanations. Workshop presented at the Center for Assessment and Evaluation of Student Learning (CAESL) Conference. San Jose, CA.

Lee, C. D., Spratley, A. (2010). *Reading in the disciplines: The challenges of adolescent literacy.* New York, NY: Carnegie Corporation of New York.

Lemke, J. L. (1990). *Talking science: language, learning, and values.* Norwood, NJ: Ablex Publishing Corporation.

Levine, L. (2004). Offshoring (a.k.a. Offshore Outsourcing) and Job Insecurity Among U.S. Workers. CRS Report for Congress. Washington, DC: Congressional Research Service (CRS).

Littlefair, A. (1992). Reading and writing across the curriculum. In C. Harrison & M. Coles (Eds.), *Reading for real handbook* (pp. 83–104). London, UK: Routledge.

Martin, M. O., Mullis, I. V. S., & Chrostowski, S. J. (Eds.)(2004). TIMSS & PIRLS International Study Center, Chestnut Hill, MA: Boston College.

Moje, E. B. (2007). Developing socially just subject-matter instruction: A review of the literature on disciplinary literacy teaching. *Review of Research in Education. 31,* 1-44.

Moje, E. B., Ciechanowski, K. M., Kramer, K., Ellis, L. Carrillo, R., Collazo, T. (2004). *Working Toward Third Space in content area literacy: An examination of everyday funds of knowledge and Discourse. Reading Research Quarterly.* 39(1).

Morrow, L. M., Pressley, M., Smith, J. K., & Smith, M. (1997). The effect of a literature-based program integrated into literacy and science instruction with children from diverse backgrounds. *Reading Research Quarterly, 32*(1), 54-76.

Moss, B. (2005). Making a case and a place for effective content area literacy instruction in the elementary grades. *The Reading Teacher, 59*, 46–55.

Moser, B. K., Stevens G. R., & Watts C. L. (1989). The two-sample *t*-test versus Satterwaite's approximate *F* test. *Communication Statistics Theory and Methodology. 18*(39). 63–75.

National Center for Education Statistics (2006). *The nation's report card: Reading 2005 (NCES 2006-466).* Washington, D.C.: Institute of Education Sciences, U.S. Department of Education.

National Center for Education Statistics (2007). *The nation's report card: Reading 2006 (NCES 2007–496).* Washington, D.C.: Institute of Education Sciences, U.S. Department of Education.

National Center for Education Statistics (2010). *The nation's report card: Reading 2009 (NCES 2010–458).* Washington, D.C.: Institute of Education Sciences, U.S. Department of Education.

National Commission on Writing in America's Schools and Colleges. (2003). The neglected "R": The need for a writing revolution (No. 997548). New York, NY: College Board.

Osborne, J. (2010). Arguing to learn in Science: The role of collaborative, critical discourse. *Science, 328,* 463-466.

Palinscar, A. S., & Magnusson, S. J. (2001). The interplay of firsthand and text-based investigations to model and support the development of scientific knowledge and reasoning. In S. Carver & D. Klahr (Eds.) *Cognition and Instruction: Twenty-five years of Progress.* (151-194) Mahway, NJ: Lawrence Erlbaum.

Pappas, C. C., Kiefer, B. Z., & Levstik, L. S. (1999). *An integrated language perspective in the elementary school: An action approach* (3rd ed.). New York, NY: Longman.

Pappas, C. C., & Varelas, M. (2004). Promoting dialogic inquiry in information book read-alouds: Young urban children's ways of making sense in science. In E. Saul (Ed.), *Crossing Borders in Literacy and Science Instruction* (pp. 161-189). Newark, DE: International Reading Association.

Pearson, P. D. (2009, Dec.) From an instructional perspective. In S. Israel & G. Duffy (Chairs) *Research on comprehension and comprehension instruction: Where to go from here?* An invited session presented at the National Reading Conference. Albuquerque, NM.

Pearson, P. D., and Cervetti G. N. (2005). Reading and writing in the service of acquiring scientific knowledge and dispositions: In search of synergies. Paper presented at the Reading Research Conference the International Reading Association (IRA), San Antonio, TX.

Pearson, P. D., & Gallagher, M. (1983). The instruction of reading comprehension. *Contemporary Educational Psychology, 8,* 317–344.

Pearson, P. D., Moje, E., & Greenleaf, C. (2010). Literacy and Science: Each in the Service of the Other. *Science. 238*(5877). 459-463.

Prain, V. and Hand, B. (1996). Writing for learning in secondary science: rethinking practices. *Teaching and Teacher Education, 12*(6), 609-626.

Romance, N. R., & Vitale, M. R. (1992). A curriculum strategy that expands time for in-depth elementary science instruction by using science-based reading strategies: Effects of a year-long study in grade four. *Journal of Research in Science Teaching, 29*(6), 545-554.

Romance, N. R., & Vitale, M. R. (2001). Implementing an in-depth expanded science model in elementary schools: Multi-year findings, research issues, and policy implications. *International Journal of Science Education, 23*(4), 373-404.

Ruxton, G. D. (2006). The unequal variance t-test is an underused alternative to student's t-test and the Mann–Whitney U test. *Behavioral Ecology.* 688-690.

Shanahan, T & Shanahan, C. (2008). Teaching disciplinary literacy to adolescents: Rethinking content-area literacy. *Harvard Educational Review. 78*(1).

Schoenbach, R., & Greenleaf, C. L. (2009). Fostering adolescents' engaged in academic literacy. In L. Christenbury, R. Bomer, and P. Smagorinksy (Eds.), *Handbook on Adolescent Literacy Research.* New York, NY: Guilford Press.

U.S. Department of Labor (2008). Occupational outlook handbook 2008-2009 edition. Retrieved Nov. 3, 2009 from http://www.bls.gov/oco/ocos063.htm#

Vitale, M. R., & Romance, N. R. (2007). A knowledge-based framework for unifying content-area reading comprehension and reading comprehension strategies. In D. McNamara (Ed.) *Reading comprehension strategies: Theory, interventions, and technologies.* 73-104. New York, NY: Erlbaum.

Wang, J., & Herman, J. (2005). *Evaluation of Seeds of Science/Roots of Reading project: Shoreline Science and Terrarium Investigations.* CRESST, Los Angeles, CA.

Yore, L. D., Hand, B. M., & Prain, V. (2002). Scientists as writers. *Science Education, 86,* 672-692.

Yore, L. D., Hand, B. Goldman, S. R., Hildebrand, G. M., Osborne, J. F., Treagust, J. F., Wallace, C. S. (2004). New directions in language and science education. *Reading Research Quarterly, 39*(3), 347-352.

AUTHOR'S NOTE

This study was conducted with support provided by the National Science Foundation under Grant Numbers ESI-0242733, 0628272 and 0822119.

APPENDIX A - SCIENCE CONTENT AND WRITING RUBRIC

4- Exceeding expectations	The response shows a clear understanding and describes at least three main types of interactions light can have with materials. *Names three interactions of light with a material and describes all three of them by explaining what happens in that interaction and/or giving an example with a specific material* *Uses science terms: absorb, reflect, transmit, refract, block* *No misconceptions.*
3- Meeting expectations	The response shows a good understanding of the main types of interactions light can have with materials. *Merely names three interactions, using science terms for some.* *Or names only two interactions (using science terms) and describes one or both at the level of Level 4* *Or describes three interactions without using science terms for more than one (light makes things hot, light makes shadows, light goes through glass)* *Misconceptions OK (e.g., black felt doesn't transmit or reflect any light).*
2- Below expectations	The response shows a beginning understanding that light can interact with materials in one or more ways. **Describes one or two interactions of light with material, at a basic level, or describes how you can see (or not see) through a material.** *Possible interactions: transmit (or go through) absorb (or block), reflect (or bounce off) (or block), refract* *Does not need to use science terms.* *May describe transmission including translucent, transparent and opaque* *Just naming one or two interactions (using science terms)* *Misconceptions OK.*
1- Inaccurate under-standing	The response does not show understanding that light can have different interactions with materials. **Describes everyday experiences with light.** *May include incorrect use of terms like refract* *May say generic things like "light interacts with metal"* *May include other information about light NOT related to interactions with materials* *Light travels in straight lines, light comes from a source, we see with it, it helps plants grow, it keeps us warm, you can get sunburned from light.*

USING EVIDENCE FOR EXPLANATIONS: This dimension looks at <u>how well</u> the evidence provided <u>supports and</u> <u>explicates</u> the main points in the piece. This dimension is NOT concerned with scientific accuracy or source of the evidence provided. The light interactions mentioned need to be specifically paired with an example. For the pairing to count, the material needs to be named—glass, plastic, wood, etc. Use of the word "something" is not specific enough. The interaction needs to be named either with a vocabulary word (transmit, block, reflect, refract, absorb) or with a meaning centered phrase (bounce off, go through). Heat up and warming up count, as elements of absorption. Translucent and transparent are counted only if they further explain how light is transmitted and are paired with a specifically named material. The mention of shadows must be related to blocking and paired with a specifically named material. The use of "someone" or "object" is a specific enough example but "object" or "someone" must be linked to an interaction "blocks light." Opaque must be used in conjunction with blocking light. Colors can be mentioned as things (e.g., the color black absorbs all other colors but reflects black).

	1	2	3	4
Evidence	None of the interactions are supported with examples/evidence.	One interaction is supported with examples/evidence.	Two interactions are supported with examples/evidence	Three interactions are supported with examples/evidence.

WRITING ORGANIZATION: This dimension is not concerned with paragraph form, spelling, or readability of handwriting. This dimension looks at <u>how well</u> the writer conveys ideas.

	1	2	3	4
Intro-duction	The piece is too brief to have an introduction – it is only one or two thoughts. OR The beginning of the piece is difficult to understand. The reader is unable to follow what the student is intending to discuss.	An interaction is NOT mentioned at the outset. Launches right into examples and details without setting up what will be discussed.	One interaction is mentioned in the first sentence in the piece. (transmit, block, reflect, refract, absorb)	The first sentence states that light can interact with materials in multiple ways. AND Interactions are all further explained in some detail

WRITING ORGANIZATION: This dimension is not concerned with paragraph form, spelling, or readability of handwriting. This dimension looks at <u>how well</u> the writer conveys ideas.

	1	2	3
Clarity	It is difficult to grasp the meaning. Very few ideas can be understood. Clarity may be impeded due to one or more of the following: The relationships presented are difficult to understand. The piece is written as just a list of words. Syntax and word order interfere with the reader being able to understand ideas. Pronoun references are unclear. Several words used incorrectly, even very common words. Ideas are jumbled and many incomplete thoughts are strung together. Pieces are missing that cause the reader confusion.	Ideas are understandable but not always clearly communicated. Requires some inferences to be made in order to grasp meaning (Some ideas make sense while others do not). Clarity may be impeded due to one or more of the following: The context in which ideas are presented is lacking, making the flow of ideas hard to follow. Precise vocabulary is lacking. No distinction between main ideas and supporting details. Ideas are choppy and jump around.	Ideas in the piece are clearly communicated. All ideas can be understood. Clarity may be increased because: Transition words or phrases (for example, one idea is, next, finally, etc.) Ideas flow smoothly. The piece is well organized. Ideas are coherent.

WRITING ORGANIZATION: This dimension is not concerned with paragraph form, spelling, or readability of handwriting. This dimension looks at how well the writer conveys ideas.

	1	2	3	4
Conclusion	• The piece is too brief to have a conclusion – it is only one or two thoughts. OR • Piece is presented as just a list of words.	• Piece is more developed than just one or two thoughts. • The presentation of ideas just ends abruptly.	• The reader knows that the last example is coming because a signal word or phrase is used toward the end of the piece (the last example is, finally, last but not least, the last thing is)	• Ends with a general statement that brings the writing to a close (e.g. And that's what light does.)

VOCABULARY: This dimension looks at the extent to which the writer explained the interactions using the scientific words transmit, absorb, reflect, refract, and block. Additional science words used may be opaque, transparent, and translucent. For the purposes of this dimension, do not consider terms provided in the prompt (interact, light, material).

	1	2	3	4
Vocabulary Usage	• No science word(s) are used OR • Uses science word(s) BUT no definitions or examples were included.	• Science word(s) are used AND • Word(s) are explicitly defined. • NO examples are included.	• Science word(s) are used AND • Examples are used that show an understanding of the meaning of the word(s). • NO definitions are included.	• Science word(s) are used AND • At least one of the terms is explicitly defined • AND • Examples are used that show an understanding of the meaning of the word(s).

VOCABULARY COUNT: This score is a count of the number of words students used in their writing (32 words are the maximum possible). The target vocabulary taught in the unit are as follows: **absorb, block, characteristic, emit, energy, interact/interaction, lens, light, material, ray, reflect, refract, shadow, source, transmit, transform/transformation, travel, analyze, claim, data, diagram, evidence, explanation, investigate/investigation, observation/observe, predict/prediction, record, scientific community**

Developing a Professional Development Tool for Assessing Quality Talk about Text

Ian A. G. Wilkinson
The Ohio State University

Kristin Bourdage Reninger
Otterbein University

Anna O. Soter
The Ohio State University

Talk is a central feature of social-constructivist pedagogy, and researchers are beginning to understand those aspects of it that can be relied upon as either agents or signals of student learning. Research suggests that the quality of classroom talk is closely connected to the quality of student problem solving, learning, and understanding (e.g., Mercer, 1995, 2002; Nystrand, Gamoran, Kachur, & Prendergast, 1997; Wegerif, Mercer, & Dawes, 1999). This research indicates that there is sufficient reliability in language use to enable us to make valid inferences about the productiveness of talk for student learning outcomes (see also Applebee, Langer, Nystrand, & Gamoran, 2003). We acknowledge that the discourse-learning nexus is complex and highly situated. Nevertheless, we believe research in this area has reached a level of maturity where we can identify those aspects of discourse and attendant classroom norms that seem to shape student learning.

The purpose of this study was to apply this knowledge to the development of a tool to enable teachers to assess the quality of talk in classroom discussions about text, and to investigate the use of the tool as a means of supporting teachers' professional development in conducting discussions. The study was part of a larger project (Wilkinson, Soter, & Murphy, 2007), the long-term goal of which was to help elementary and middle school teachers use discussions as a means for promoting students' high-level comprehension of text. We use the term 'high-level comprehension' to refer to critical, reflective thinking about and around text. Borrowing from Chang-Wells and Wells' (1993) idea of literate thinking, we regard high-level comprehension as requiring students to engage with text in an epistemic mode to acquire not only knowledge of the topic, but also knowledge about how to think about the topic, and the capability to reflect on one's own thinking.

There have been other attempts to develop such a tool. Newman (1990) proposed a set of indicators of 'classroom thoughtfulness' to assess the teaching of higher-order thinking in high school social studies classes. Rueda, Goldenberg, and Gallimore (1992) developed the *Instructional Conversation Rating Scale* to estimate the extent to which a reading comprehension lesson approximated Goldenberg's (1993) model of instructional conversations. Similarly, Bender (1994) developed the *Seminar Teaching Guide,* a checklist to assess teacher and student behaviors in Paideia Seminars (Roberts & Billings, 1999). Roskos and colleagues (Roskos & Walker, 1997; Roskos, Boehlen, & Walker, 2000; Roskos & Boehlen, 2001) developed the *Instructional Talk Assessment Tool* to foster teachers' awareness and understanding of their talk in a reading clinic setting. There are also rubrics for assessing Accountable Talk in the *Instructional Quality Assessment* toolkit developed by Resnick and colleagues (Junker & Matsumara, 2006; Resnick, Matsumara, & Junker, 2006). The tools developed by Rueda, et al., Bender, and Rosko and colleagues are similar to the one described in the present study in that they can be used to rate videotaped lessons and were designed to be used as self and collaborative assessments by practitioners for purposes of professional development. Our intent in the present study was to develop an assessment tool that was more firmly grounded in theory and empirical research on discourse that might index students' engagement in high-level thinking and comprehension of text. By focusing exclusively on the quality of talk in discussions about text, we also hoped to develop a tool that would have applicability beyond any specific approach to conducting such discussions.

Our conceptualization of assessment derives from Wiggins' (1998) perspective on educative assessment; Wiggins and McTighe's (2005) notion of authentic assessment; and Stiggins, Arter, Chappuis and Chappuis' (2006) case for involving learners in the assessment process. These perspectives describe assessment as aimed at improving a learner's performance and understanding in the context of a realistic task and comprising a cycle of practice, feedback, learner-directed goal setting, and more practice. Overall, educative assessments are tools designed to 'teach' because they reveal to learners (in our case, teachers) the criteria that define a task or a desired outcome of learning and descriptions of the levels of quality related to that task.

Educative assessments assist learners to make progress toward a learning goal. For our purposes, an educative assessment should provide useful information for giving feedback and follow-up guidance to teachers, and it should enable teachers to make self-assessments of their performances, eliciting self-adjustments and goal setting for future practice. It should also be useable, meaning that it can be readily implemented and the information it provides is comprehensible to teachers. We used this conceptual framework to design our tool to assist teachers in learning how to conduct discussions to promote high-level comprehension of text.

Quality Talk about Text

As part of the larger project, we sought to identify indices of talk that might serve as proximal indicators of students' high-level comprehension. First, we reviewed the literature on classroom discourse and discussions to identify candidate indices. We looked for features for which there was good theoretical warrant for believing they were linked to high-level comprehension and good empirical research demonstrating that connection. Second, we investigated whether the indicators could be used to characterize the talk in nine approaches to conducting discussions that had potential to promote high-level comprehension of text. These approaches included: *Instructional Conversations* (Goldenberg, 1993), *Junior Great Books* (Great Books Foundation, 1987), *Questioning the Author* (Beck & McKeown, 2006; Beck, McKeown, Hamilton, & Kucan, 1997), *Collaborative Reasoning* (Anderson, Chinn, Chang, Waggoner, & Nguyen, 1998), *Paideia Seminars* (Billings & Fitzgerald, 2002), *Philosophy for Children* (Sharp, 1995), *Book Club* (Raphael & McMahon, 1994), *Grand Conversations* (Eeds & Wells, 1989), and *Literature Circles* (Short & Pierce, 1990). This process involved testing the indicators on 30 excerpts of discourse from published articles representing the approaches, establishing the reliability of coding, redefining coding categories, and modifying the coding as needed. We then applied the final coding scheme to analyzing four full transcripts of typical discussions from the nine approaches. Third, we developed a model of discussion, called Quality Talk (Wilkinson, Soter, & Murphy, 2010), built around these aspects of discourse, and tested the model in a range of elementary and middle school classrooms. These steps ensured that the indices could be used to analyze the discourse of free-flowing discussion about text and that they adequately described similarities and differences in various approaches to conducting discussions (see Soter, et al., 2008).

The discourse we identified as proximal indicators of high-level comprehension included question events and episodes of student talk. We coded authentic questions; questions that involved uptake; questions that elicited high-level thinking, defined as generalization, analysis, or speculation (Nystrand, Gamoran, Kachur, & Prendergast, 1997; Nystrand, Wu, Gamoran, Zeiser, & Long, 2003); and questions that elicited extra-textual connections. The latter included making connections to students' own lives or feelings (affective), to other texts or media (intertextual), and to knowledge or understanding established by a group in prior discussions (shared-knowledge) (Allington & Johnston, 2002; Applebee, et al., 2003; Bloome & Egan-Robertson, 1993; Edwards

Table 1. Discourse Indices of Quality Talk

Index	Notation	Description
Authentic Question	AQ	Where the person asking the question does not know the answer or is genuinely interested in knowing how others will answer (i.e., the answer is not pre-specified). Almost all student questions are authentic. An authentic question usually allows for a range of responses and generates several responses.
Uptake	⌐	A person asks a follow-up question about something that someone else said previously. Uptake is often marked by the use of pronouns (e.g., *"How did it work?," "What causes this?," "What city grew out of this?"*).
General-ization/ Analysis	GA	Student talk that shows evidence of high-level thinking in the form of *generalization* (building up ideas, tying things together, "what's the point") or *analysis* (breaking down ideas, "how or why").
Speculation	SP	Student talk that shows evidence of high-level thinking in the form of *speculation* (considering other possibilities, hypothesizing, "what if").
Elaborated Explanation	EE	Where a student explains her thinking in fairly detailed form to others. Elaborated explanations occur in a single turn where a student explains how she arrived at a conclusion by giving a step-by-step description or detailed account of how a conclusion was reached or how a problem might be resolved. They are elaborated descriptions of how things work, why some things are the way they are, or how they should be thought about. They include details of how to think about an issue and justification or rationale for thinking that way.
		Turns in which elaborated explanations occur are typically somewhat longer and more coherent than the average student turn, and contain at least one or more reasoning words (*because/'cause/cos, if, so, I think, agree/disagree, would, could, maybe/might/may be, like, but, how, why*).
		As the phrase 'elaborated explanations' suggests, students make some kind of claim and provide either two reasons to support it or one reason and evidence in support of the reason (e.g., *I agree with Joseph because he keeps annoying them by saying shut up and I think he is trying to just get them to let him play because they wouldn't let him play because he didn't have his glove*).

Index	Notation	Description
Explor-atory Talk	ET	A kind of 'co-reasoning,' where students (sometimes with the teacher) *over several turns* share knowledge, evaluate evidence, and consider options in a reasonable and equitable way. In essence, it is a way of using language to "chew on an idea," to think collectively, to 'interthink.' A key feature of exploratory talk is students giving reasons for their ideas or opinion. Hence, exploratory talk typically contains lots of reasoning words (*because/"cause/ cos, if, so, I think, agree/disagree, would, could, maybe/might/may be, like, but, how, why*).

E.g.

Joanna:	*Angelique, why do you think she wants to be a kid?*
Angelique:	*Because she likes to swim and she likes to be around a lot of kids.*
Tamika:	*And she likes playing a lot, with the kids and stuff?*
Angelique:	*Yes.*
Joshua:	*And I agree because if she wasn't swimming she'd probably be sitting back in the rocking chair. She's having a lot of fun, some fun like (the) children.*
Joanna:	*I think the same thing as Angelique was saying that she'd probably like to be a kid again, and um, probably she had a good life because she did a lot of stuff and you know how we, um, how we are now....*

(several turns deleted)

Brian:	*I disagree. I disagree with Angelique...'Cuz my grandma, she cleans up the House, she goes swimming and everything else, but I don't think she'd like to be a kid again.*
Angelique:	*Brian, that's different, but she still probably wants to be a kid again, this Grandma in the story.*
Brian:	*If I was that age, I wouldn't want to be a kid again because I'd have to go through all that, getting my license again, getting more money to get the house, then I've got to go get a job again, and everything over and over.*
Angelique:	*But that's probably what she wanted to do. It doesn't mean trying to be a kid again.*

Index	Notation	Description
Affective Response	AR	Student makes connection between the text and his/her feelings or his/her life (i.e., text-to-self) (e.g., *I felt, when I was little ...*).
Inter-textual Response	IT	Student makes connection between the text and other literary or nonliterary works, other works of art, or media, such as billboards, television, newspapers or magazines (i.e., text-to-text) (e.g., *In that other book we read ...*).
Shared-knowledge Response	SK	Student makes connection between current discussion and previous discussion the students have had, previous topics they have talked about, or previous knowledge they have shared (i.e., discuss-to-discuss) (e.g., *This reminds me of last week when we talked...*).
Reference to Text	RtT	Students refer to the text in order to bolster an argument or opinion.

& Mercer, 1987; Taylor, Pearson, Peterson, & Rodriguez, 2003). We also coded students' elaborated explanations (Chinn, O'Donnell, & Jinks, 2000; Webb, 1989) and engagement in exploratory talk (Mercer, 1995, 2000). Table 1 provides descriptions and examples of these indicators.

It is important to clarify how we think these aspects of discourse function. Authentic questions, uptake, and questions that elicit high-level thinking or extra-textual connections serve as indices of the social and epistemic interactions surrounding the utterances. They give students more control over the flow of information and more agency in the construction of knowledge and understanding. Following Nystrand et al. (2003), we view such questions as "sites of interaction" where participants' responses to questions reflect their understandings of the interactions as manifest in their discourse moves. Hence, these questions are best understood as 'question events' and coded based on what they elicit from students rather than on their form. Elaborated explanations and exploratory talk, on the other hand, serve more directly as indices of students' individual and collective reasoning about text. These are coded based on the presence of features demonstrating the coherence of an argument in support of a claim (in the case of elaborated explanations) and the sharing and co-construction of knowledge (in the case of exploratory talk).

Talk Assessment Tool for Teachers

We developed the Talk Assessment Tool for Teachers (TATT) to support teachers' professional development in learning to conduct discussions about text by helping them to make judgments about the quality of talk. We designed it to be used in the context of one-to-one coaching where the teacher and a 'discourse coach' viewed a video of a recently completed discussion and together completed the TATT. We sought to design a useable tool that was feasible to complete within the time constraints of teachers' schedules and provided information that was comprehensible to teachers so they could make self-assessments of their discussions. We hoped the tool would enable teachers to gain an overall understanding of the productiveness of the discussion for students' high-level comprehension and prompt their reflection on ways to enhance subsequent discussions.

The TATT is a paper-and-pencil instrument that the teacher, in conjunction with a discourse coach, completes in five steps. First, the teacher is prompted to state their goal for the discussion. Next, they select a 10-minute segment of the video they would like to analyze, view the segment, and make notes about the talk on a worksheet using the notation shown in Table 1. Then, they view the segment of video a second time and add notes to the worksheets. Based on their notes, they rate the quality of the talk on a 4-point scale using rubrics describing the incidence of discourse described earlier (we used a flower metaphor to emphasize the organic nature of discussions with the points on the scale denoted 'not yet,' 'emerging,' 'developing,' and 'blooming,' see Figure 1). Finally, they write responses to five questions to prompt reflection on the overall quality of the discussion and on ways to scaffold talk in subsequent discussions to promote high-level comprehension. At the back of the instrument is an appendix describing the discourse indicators (Table 1) and sample worksheet pages showing examples of other teachers' notations about talk in their discussions.

Although others have developed related instruments to assess teachers' implementation of classroom discussions, use of the TATT requires teachers to make high-level inferences about talk while viewing a video of discussion. The objectives of the present study were threefold: a) to investigate the usability of the tool; b) to examine the tool's educative value as a means of promoting

Figure 1. Sample Pages from TATT Rubric

Questions

Category	1 NOT YET	2 EMERGING	3 DEVELOPING	4 BLOOMING
Authentic	__ *None* of the questions are genuine or have no known answer; all questions are test questions (i.e. they have a known answer). Test questions dominate the discussion.	__ *Some* questions are genuine or have no known answer and some questions are test questions (i.e. they have known answers). There is a mix of questions.	__ *Many* questions are genuine or have no known answer. There are very few test questions.	__ *Almost all* questions are genuine or have no known answer. There are almost no test questions.
Uptake	__ *None* of the questions incorporate a previous student response (i.e. are follow-up questions).	__ *Some* questions incorporate a previous student response (i.e. are follow-up questions).	__ *Many* questions incorporate a previous student response (i.e. are follow-up questions).	__ *Almost all* questions incorporate a previous student response (i.e. are follow-up questions).
Analysis/ General-ization	__ *None* of the questions prompt students to tie ideas together (e.g., "What does the author mean by...?") or to break ideas apart (e.g., "Why do you think that?").	__ *Some* questions prompt students to tie ideas together (e.g., "What does the author mean by...?") or to break ideas apart (e.g., "Why do you think that?").	__ *Many* questions prompt students to tie ideas together (e.g., "What does the author mean by...?") or to break ideas apart (e.g., "Why do you think that?").	*Almost all* questions prompt students to tie ideas together (e.g., "What does the author mean by...?") or to break ideas apart (e.g., "Why do you think that?")
Speculation	__ *None* of the questions prompt students to consider alternative possibilities or to weigh up what might happen about topics or ideas related to the text (e.g., "What might happen..," "What if..")	__ *Some* questions prompt students to consider alternative possibilities or to weigh up what might happen about topics or ideas related to the text (e.g., "What might happen..," "What if.."). You only sometimes hear students say words or phrases such as "if..," "she would..," "I might...," "maybe..."	__ *Many* questions prompt students to consider alternative possibilities or to weigh up what might happen about topics or ideas related to the text (e.g., "What might happen..," "What if.."). You hear students say words or phrases such as "if..," "she would..," "I might...," "maybe..."	__ *Almost all* questions prompt students to consider alternative possibilities or to weigh up what might happen about topics or ideas related to the text (e.g., 'What might happen..,' 'What if..'). You often hear students say words or phrases such as "if..," "she would..," "I might...," "maybe..."

Textual Connections

Category	1 NOT YET	2 EMERGING	3 DEVELOPING	4 BLOOMING
Reference to Text	__ Students *do not* use text evidence to bolster an argument, support a position, or clarify ideas.	__ Students *once or twice* use text evidence to bolster an argument, support a position, or clarify ideas. You might hear the students say "On page x, it said....," "In the story, it said...."	__ Students *some* of the time use text evidence to bolster an argument, support a position, or clarify ideas. You might hear the students say "On page x, it said....," "In the story, it said...."	__ Students *many* times use text evidence to bolster an argument, support a position, or clarify ideas. You might hear the students say "On page x, it said....," "In the story, it said...."

Extra-Textual Connections

Category	1 NOT YET	2 EMERGING	3 DEVELOPING	4 BLOOMING
Affective Response	__ Students *do not* make connections between the text and their feelings or their own lives (i.e. text-to-self connections).	__ Students *once or twice* make connections between the text and their feelings or their own lives (i.e. text-to-self connections). You only sometimes hear students say "One time I...," "It made me feel ..."	__ Students *some* of the time make connections between the text and their feelings or their own lives (i.e. text-to-self connection). You might hear students say "One time I...," "It made me feel ..."	__ Students *many* times make connections between the text and their feelings or their own lives (i.e. text-to-self connections). You often might hear students say "One time I...," "It made me feel ..."
Inter-textual Response	__ Students *do not* make connections between the text and other specific texts, works of art, or other media (i.e. text-to-text connections).	__ Students *once or twice* make a connection between the text and other specific texts, works of art, or other media (i.e. text-to-text connections).	__ Students *some* of the time make connections between the text and other specific texts, works of art, or other media (i.e. text-to-text connections).	__ Students *many* times make connections between the text and other specific texts, works of art, or other media (i.e. text-to-text connections).
Shared Knowledge Response	__ Students *do not* make connections between the text and previous discussions they have had or previous knowledge they have shared (i.e. text-to-previous discussion connections).	__ Students *once or twice* make a connection between the text and previous discussions they have had or previous knowledge they have shared (i.e. text-to-previous discussion connections).	__ Students *some* of the time make connections between the text and previous discussions they have had or previous knowledge they have shared (i.e. text-to-previous discussion connections).	__ Students *many* times make connections between the text and previous discussions they have had or previous knowledge they have shared (i.e. text-to-previous discussion connections).

the professional development of teachers regarding their conduct of discussions; and c) to estimate the extent to which users could rate talk reliably using the 4-point scale and rubrics of the tool.

METHOD

Participants

Eight teachers and three discourse coaches participated in the study. The teachers volunteered to participate in a year-long study devoted to using classroom discussions to promote students' high-level comprehension of text. They included three fourth-grade and three fifth-grade teachers, one sixth-grade teacher, and one seventh-grade science teacher. Three of the teachers taught in a school located in a large suburban school district (34% of students classified as low income and 22% as minority). One teacher taught in a school located in a small-town school district (28% of students classified as low income and 13% as minority). The other four teachers taught in two Catholic schools located in middle- to upper-class neighborhoods with predominantly Caucasian students. All schools were in central Ohio. The coaches were two graduate students in education who had extensive experience teaching in elementary schools and supervising students in pre-service teacher education, and one faculty member in language and literacy education at The Ohio State University. Four of the teachers worked with one coach, three of the teachers worked with another coach, and one teacher worked with the third coach.

Professional Development Context

The TATT was developed over a one-year professional development program designed to support teachers' learning to conduct classroom discussions. Teachers participated in five 2.5-hour sessions at the beginning of the school year, three additional 2.5-hour sessions during the year, and in-class coaching approximately every two weeks. The purpose of the initial five sessions was to introduce teachers to the Quality Talk model for conducting discussions and to familiarize them with analyzing classroom talk. Teachers viewed videos of successful and not-so-successful discussions, analyzed transcripts of discourse showing traditional versus productive talk, and learned how to talk about talk (the meta-language of discussion). The purpose of the follow-up sessions was to engage teachers in collaborative problem-solving where they collectively viewed videotapes of their discussions and explored ways to enhance them. The purpose of the coaching was to provide teachers one-to-one assistance in conducting discussions. The TATT was an integral part of the coaching. Using the TATT, teachers made self-assessments of their discussion practices and coaches provided feedback in relation to the TATT assessment.

We videotaped discussions in all teachers' classrooms at four points during the school year. Discussions followed the Quality Talk model (Wilkinson, et al., 2010), which allows for considerable flexibility in how teachers conduct discussions. At each time point, the teacher read a story to the class, and/or students read a story independently or in pairs, before meeting to discuss the story in small groups with the teacher. The stories were at or above students' grade level and were provided by the research team. As a pre-discussion activity, some teachers had their students write their connections to the story on post-it notes or write questions about the story in their reading logs. Before the discussion started, the teacher reminded students of the ground rules they had established for their discussions (i.e., the norms for productive talk about text).

The role of the teacher in the discussions was to initiate the discussion with an authentic question about the story, to ask follow-up questions during the discussion, incorporating uptake, and gradually to cede responsibility for discussion to the students, monitoring the talk and interjecting as needed (see Reninger & Wilkinson, 2010). As a post-discussion activity, some teachers engaged students in a "debriefing" about the discussion, either asking students to summarize the different perspectives they had discussed about the story or to reflect on their participation and how well they adhered to the ground rules for discussion.

The role of the discourse coach was to support the teachers' understanding of productive talk about text. This was accomplished by promoting dialogue about the videotaped discussions using the TATT. The coaches built on the teachers' thoughts and comments with examples or points of clarification to promote deeper understanding, and they asked and answered questions to enhance the dialogue about the video or the concepts within the tool. For example, if a teacher made an observation about an aspect of discourse, such as an affective response on the part of a student, the coach might extend the teacher's observation with an example from the video or a teaching point that might help further understanding of the discourse. Overall, the coaches used the TATT as a mechanism to build on teachers' observations and questions, promoting dialogue about various aspects of productive discussions, high-level comprehension, and goals for future discussions.

Procedures

We developed the TATT across four time points using an action-research methodology. Students read and discussed texts chosen by the researchers at four times in the year: December (Time 1), February (Time 2), April (Time 3), and May/June (Time 4), and we videotaped these discussions. Approximately one week after each discussion, coaches met with their teachers to review the discussions. The meetings lasted approximately one hour and took place in the teachers' classrooms after school or in an empty classroom that had computer equipment available to watch the video. Following each time point, the research team met to consider revision to the tool in a series of trial-and-revise cycles.

The first version of the TATT was shown to participating teachers in December (Time 1). At this time, we simply solicited informal feedback from the teachers about the format of the assessment instrument. We also conducted a trial of the instrument with one of the teachers based on a 10-minute video segment of one of her discussions. The assessment was then revised and subjected to a series of further revisions over the next three time points. At these times, teachers and coaches reviewed a 10-minute segment of the teacher's videotaped discussion and independently rated the talk using the TATT. Following the ratings, the dyads discussed their responses in a collaborative effort to understand the nature of the student talk and to make goals for future discussions. The primary purposes of these sessions were to review discussion practices, to consider the students' discourse as it related to high-level thinking, and to offer feedback to encourage professional growth and understanding. A secondary purpose was to solicit teachers' feedback about the form, content, and usability of the assessment. As such, coaches asked questions about the teacher's perceptions of the format and the process of completing the assessment tool. Most coaching sessions were audio recorded. Data were collected during these sessions and used to inform our ongoing revisions in order to improve the usability of the assessment and increase agreement in scoring between raters.

Data Sources and Analysis

The data sources included 48 completed assessments from teacher-coach dyads (8 from teachers and 8 corresponding records from coaches) taken from the second, third, and fourth coaching sessions, 14 pages of indices of the digital audio files recorded during the professional development coaching sessions, approximately 20 pages of field notes, and approximately 15 pages of meeting notes from the researchers' and coaches' conversations about the assessment instrument.

To determine the usability and educative value of the TATT, we used qualitative data analysis. We read and reread the indices of the audio files from the coaching sessions, the completed assessment tools, and field notes, and inductively coded through constant comparison (Miles & Huberman, 1994) to develop codes describing what happened when coaches and teachers used the TATT and teachers' perspectives on the TATT. Our perspectives on educative assessment and learning framed the development of codes, providing the logic to our coding as we related cases in the data to concepts such as assisted performance, appropriation, scaffolding, discourse, and inquiry. For example, a code referred to as 'questioning' was used to describe the occurrences in the data of the teachers' inquiring about discourse features and discussion practices. The code 'rubric-descriptor' was used to describe instances in the data when teachers referred specifically to that part of the tool. A major assumption we made before coding took place was the notion that the assessment tool and the context in which the teacher-coach dyads collaborated could foster opportunities for learning about discussions and discourse.

As coding continued, we created data displays to help us refine the codes (e.g., the code, 'rubric-category' shifted to 'rubric-uptake,' a more specific label for what was happening). Data displays also helped us to examine patterns in the data, especially to assist with the process of identifying reoccurrences of codes across the data sources. At this point, we were able to group related codes together to formulate analytic categories. For instance, codes related to the tool itself (e.g., rubric-descriptor, rubric-uptake, reflection question) were collapsed to generate the category, 'tool mechanics.' At this point in the analysis we were able to determine core categories for the data. One core category derived from the data became labeled as 'coaching,' which comprised several codes to describe the instructional moves of the coach, such as 'explaining,' 'naming,' and 'modeling." Finally, we wrote hypothesizing memos (cf. Corbin, 1986) to account for any relationships between the core categories. For example, one relationship that emerged was between 'coaching,' 'teacher questioning,' and 'scaffolded idea' that we identified as a theme, *scaffolded thinking*. The identification of the core categories and their relationships provided the basis for the assertions made in the findings.

To estimate the extent to which users could rate talk reliably using the 4-point scale and rubrics of the TATT, we calculated the percentage of exact and adjacent (within 1-point on the scale) agreement between the teacher and coach's ratings across the eight dyads. We also calculated Weighted Kappas (Cohen 1968). Weighted Kappa provides a conservative estimate of reliability for ordered categorical data that includes a correction for chance agreement.

FINDINGS

Usability

Results showed that the combination and staging of the tool's major components—identifying the goal of the discussion, viewing and making notes on a segment of the discussion, rating the talk, and reflecting on the outcomes—was a manageable process. Each dyad at each time point completed the assessment tool in less than an hour, with the duration ranging between 25 and 50 minutes. Seven of the eight teachers reported variations on the theme of 'liking' the components and process of completing the tool. Since one of our objectives was to identify useable features of the tool, coaches were encouraged to ask questions at the end of the sessions with the teachers, such as, "What are your thoughts about the process of using the tool?," or "Which features of the tool are important to you or are not important," and "why?" In response to questions like these, almost all the teachers answered positively. The following quotations from the teachers reflect the kinds of comments almost all teachers made about the tool (all names are pseudonyms):

Elizabeth: I think the reflection questions at the end are good because they give me an idea of what I might want to do next time.... I like the rubric a lot.

Mandi: I think an important step [in the process] is comparing scores because it helps me stay objective.... I like this tool because it gives a place to start talking about discussion.

Gina: I like making notes before moving to the rubric, and it's good to have the cheat sheet [referring to the appendix as a resource to help make notes about the video].

Sandra: It's [the tool's] very manageable.

Indeed the positive feedback regarding the process of completing the tool was so strong that we made few design changes to the overall procedures or components of the tool.

Only one teacher commented indifferently about the components and process of using the tool. Laura disliked making notes and online judgments about the discussion while listening to and watching the video, saying, "It's too hard to catch everything...[so] I can't really do the rubric." As a result of this feedback (at Time 1), we suggested to Laura that she transcribe the segment of video before completing the rubric (which she did in Times 2-4).

Educative Value

Using the tool in conjunction with a coach seemed to support teachers' knowledge about discourse. We called this *scaffolded thinking*. An example of scaffolded thinking that reflects the teachers' emerging declarative knowledge of the discourse took place at Time 2, January 2005, between Gina (teacher) and Michelle (discourse coach). Gina and Michelle were discussing their assessments of the 10-minute video segment of the peer-led discussion, *Victor*, by James Howe (1995). They were using the rubric as a guide to talk about their assessments of the discourse features that they heard in the students' recorded discussion. The following excerpt of their conversation is about their discussion of the rubric category, 'high-level thinking,' which at Time 2 we referred to as analysis, speculation, and generalization.

Michelle: Let's look at the high-level thinking category—analysis, speculation, and generalization. We went to pulling it apart [referring to a change the research team had made for the name of this category on the rubric]. Excellent standard is: (*reads the descriptors from the rubric*) (pause).

Gina: I have to say 'yes' to that. I mean they didn't say, "the grass is green" or something basic, they were open-ended questions and deeper answers. This [high-level thinking] is easier when it's an open-ended question. You've got to have those authentic questions in order to get to this (referring to the descriptors for high-level thinking).

Michelle: Gina! Say that Monday night [in class]. That's it! That's a really big idea here. Authentic questions generate the kinds of high-level thinking we want to see kids using when they talk about their reading.

Gina: (laughing) Okay.

The excerpt demonstrates Gina's greater awareness of the interrelatedness of two major discourse features, authentic questions and high-level thinking. Authentic questions indeed generated more talk indicative of students' high-level thinking (see Soter, et al., 2008). This is an important example of scaffolded thinking because it shows how using the TATT in conjunction with the coaching promoted the teachers' thinking about the discourse of discussion.

Another example of scaffolded thinking occurred at Time 2, January 2005, between Diana (teacher) and Kathy (coach), discussing the goals of the discussion (the first page of the TATT). Diana asked Kathy if a goal for the discussion could relate to students working together in the discussions. The excerpt below illustrates Diana's developing understanding of an important aspect of discussions, the ground rules that support productive talk.

Diana: Do I really need a specific goal about the story? If we're supposed to be having specific goals then, (pause) I mean—

Kathy: (overlaps) That's a fine goal [referring to Diana's goal written on the tool about how students would work together]. Your goal might be about student relations and how they do with each other; it might not be about understanding the story, but it's still a goal.

Diana: Yeah, I mean I guess I'm not looking at the story as much here as I wanted to know more about the dynamics and how they're able to converse with one another.

Kathy: Hmm-hmm (agreeing).

Diana: I mean to me that [dynamics] has to come first before we get to the other stuff and I have to make sure they can work in groups. I'm trying to get them, uhm, so these guys are ready to discuss in any group.

Diana affirmed and built on Kathy's comment about establishing the norms for interaction among students when Diana used the word 'yeah' to signal she agreed with Kathy's position. We identified this interaction and its effect as scaffolded thinking because it seemed to demonstrate Diana's emerging knowledge about a prerequisite to any productive discussion, establishing the norms and ground rules of a good discussion. A major requirement for productive discussions is teaching students the ground rules for discussion, which helps establish the norms of productive talk (cf. Mercer, 2000).

Another dimension of scaffolded thinking was the way the TATT, in conjunction with the coach, prompted teachers' ideas for improving their discussion practices. A typical example of this occurred at the Time 3 coaching session, April 2005, between Sandra (teacher) and Michelle (coach). Sandra and Michelle had completed their discussion of their assessments on the rubric and had moved on to the reflection questions (the last page of the TATT) to discuss the goals for facilitating the next discussion. Michelle asked Sandra a question from the reflection page of the TATT, prompting an idea for pedagogy.

Michelle: Okay. For the next discussion what might be, what might you say are your next steps? (pause)…for your work.

Sandra: Well, definitely being the role of the challenger. You know, definitely—

Michelle: (overlap) I think that's going to push it [discussion] in the critical direction, uhm…, and whatever you do to work out that role, whether you get a phrase in your mind, or—

Sandra: (overlap) Exactly.

Michelle: That's how I do it. I get a phrase ready to go. (pause)…I get a phrase in my mind and that cues me in to challenge the group. Like, 'But what about…' So, whether you have a phrase or you can write what they [student group] say down. I think the challenger role will help push the group—

Sandra: Sure.

Michelle: Hmmm…I think the challenger role will support movement toward the critical-analytic (approach to discussion)—

Sandra: (overlap) Right. Okay.

In this exchange, the reflection section of the TATT and the coach prompted Sandra's thinking about an area she might work on in her next discussion. When Sandra said, "Well, definitely being the role of the challenger," she was drawing on what she and Michelle had discussed earlier in the session about exploratory talk, an element of discussion that requires claims and opinions to be challenged.

Reliability

Table 2 shows the percentage of exact agreement by each indicator for Times 2, 3, and 4. At Time 2, the TATT prompted teachers and coaches to rate all extra-textual connections together, whereas at Times 3 and 4 we subdivided these ratings into the different types of extra-textual connections (affective, intertextual, and shared-knowledge). By Time 4, the final form of the TATT yielded a mean exact agreement between raters of 68.8%. Authentic questions appeared to be the most difficult for users to rate reliably while the questions eliciting inter-textual responses were relatively easy for users to rate reliably. The incidence of extra-textual connections was quite low, so agreement between raters was relatively easy to obtain. These data suggest that teachers and coaches were able to reach a moderate level of exact agreement in ratings.

Table 3 shows the percentage of adjacent agreement by each indicator for Times 2, 3, and 4. By Time 4, the final form of the TATT yielded a mean agreement between raters within 1 point of 96.9%. Most indicators yielded adjacent agreement of 100%. These data suggest that teachers and coaches were able to reach a high degree of agreement between ratings within 1 point.

Table 2. Percentage of Exact Agreement by Indicator and Time

Indicator	Time 2	Time 3	Time 4
Questions			
Authentic	66.7	25.0	50.0
Uptake	33.3	50.0	62.5
High-Level Thinking	66.7	25.0	75.0
Extra-Textual Connections	66.7		
Affective response	na	62.5	62.5
Inter-textual response	na	62.5	87.5
Shared-knowledge response	na	50.0	75.0
Individual Reasoning			
Elaborated explanations	50.0	62.5	62.5
Collective Reasoning			
Exploratory talk	66.7	25.0	75.0
Mean	58.4	45.3	68.8

Note: na = not assessed

Table 3. Percentage of Adjacent Agreement by Indicator and Time

Indicator	Time 2	Time 3	Time 4
Questions			
Authentic	100	87.5	87.5
Uptake	66.7	100	100
High-Level Thinking	100	75.0	100
Extra-Textual Connections	100		
Affective response	na	87.5	87.5
Inter-textual response	na	100	100
Shared-knowledge response	na	87.5	100
Individual Reasoning			
Elaborated explanations	100	100	100
Collective Reasoning			
Exploratory talk	100	87.5	100
Mean	94.5	90.6	96.9

Note: na = not assessed

Table 4 shows the agreement between raters in terms of Weighted Kappas. The final form of the TATT yielded a mean Weighted Kappa of 0.48. Questions eliciting inter-textual responses showed the highest Kappa while elaborated explanations showed the lowest. The low to zero Kappas for questions eliciting shared-knowledge responses and elaborated explanations are somewhat spurious, as there was very little variability in ratings for these indicators (ratings of 1 or 2 for shared knowledge, 2 or 3 for elaborated explanations). According to Landis and Koch's (1977) criteria for interpreting the Cohen (1968) Kappa, these data show a moderate degree of agreement between ratings.

DISCUSSION

The purpose of this study was to develop a tool to enable teachers to assess the quality of talk in text-based discussions and to investigate use of the tool as a means of supporting teachers' professional development. Our findings regarding usability suggest that the components of the tool and the way in which the components were sequenced made sense to the participants. Teachers were able to rate the talk based on video of their discussions and they were able to complete the entire process in less than an hour. The latter is an important finding because other tools for assessing talk have required teachers to transcribe their discussions before analyzing them. Transcribing discussions is time consuming. Our findings also suggest that the tool had educative value when integrated into a professional learning context that involved one-to-one coaching. Use of the tool in this context facilitated teachers' scaffolded thinking that led to their consideration of ways to provide appropriate instruction about discussion to promote high-quality talk about text in their classrooms. In short, it appears the assessment tool helped teachers make reasoned judgments about the discourse of discussions that facilitates high-level comprehension.

Table 4. Weighted Cohen's Kappa by Indicator and Time

Indicator	Time 2	Time 3	Time 4
Questions			
Authentic	.68	nc	.46
Uptake	.25	.41	.63
High-Level Thinking	.57	.14	.75
Extra-Textual Connections	.60		
Affective response	na	.20	.48
Inter-textual response	na	.40	.76
Shared-knowledge response	na	.05	0
Individual Reasoning			
Elaborated explanations	.25	.40	.33
Collective Reasoning			
Exploratory talk	.74	.18	.43
Mean	.52	.25	.48

Note: nc = cannot be calculated, na = not assessed

The reliability attained at Time 4 suggests that the tool yielded ratings that had at least a moderate degree of reliability when used in conjunction with a discourse coach. We think this is also an important finding, as the judgments about the quality of talk based on the video required a high level of inference on the part of teachers. The changes in reliability of ratings over time were no doubt due to several factors, including the refinement of the instrument, increasing expertise in assessing the quality of talk by both teachers and coaches, and presumably the integrity of the discussions and the stability of the constructs being assessed.

It is important to note that the development and use of the instrument was embedded in the context of a professional development program designed to support teachers' learning to conduct classroom discussions. We believe that, as a result of this program, many teachers experienced a substantial shift in their knowledge and beliefs about the role of talk in learning and its potential benefit for students' high-level comprehension. While the TATT seems to have been instrumental in supporting the teachers' professional development, the overall professional development program was probably important in helping teachers acquire the necessary background knowledge to make inferences about talk and to use the TATT. Use of the TATT requires teachers to make high-level inferences about talk while viewing a video of discussion and these inferences are built on considerable background knowledge about discourse and discussions. The role of the discourse coach was also important in helping teachers make inferences about the productiveness of the discussions.

Our findings are consistent with those of other studies demonstrating the value of assessing discourse to enhance the quality of discussions and instructional talk (Bender, 1994; Roskos & Walker, 1997; Roskos, Boehlen, & Walker, 2000; Roskos & Boehlen, 2001; Rueda, Goldenberg, & Gallimore, 1992). The contributions of the present work are in the content and construct validity of the instrument—we relied on discourse features for which there were good theoretical and empirical warrants for believing they were linked to high-level comprehension. Moreover, the exclusive focus on the quality of the talk, rather than on practicalities of conducting discussion, means that the instrument has applicability beyond any specific approach to conducting text-based discussions.

Several caveats need to be mentioned in relation to the TATT. First, the tool should not be viewed as a finished product. Although the aspects of discourse featured as proximal indicators of high-level comprehension have a sound theoretical and empirical basis, the language of the rubrics and the manner in which the tool is used could benefit from further improvement to enhance reliability. Second, as alluded to earlier, the findings regarding usability, educative value, and reliability are specific to its use within the context of professional development and support surrounding the role of talk and the analysis of classroom discourse. We do not believe it should be used as a stand-alone instrument outside of this context. Third, although the use of the tool clearly prompted analysis of the discussions and reflection on subsequent discussions, we do not have data to show whether the scaffolded thinking that took place with the use of the tool actually influenced the teachers' subsequent discussions and students' high-level comprehension. Additional data are needed to address these issues.

In conclusion, our results suggest that the tool is usable, has educative value in professional development contexts, and that teachers are able to use the tool with sufficient reliability for assessment purposes in conjunction with professional support. For teachers who strive to support students' reading comprehension using discussion approaches, this assessment tool provides a means of examining the extent to which productive talk is manifest during discussions. The tool also facilitates teachers' consideration of the discourse practices of discussions that facilitate high-level comprehension of texts. The educative value of the TATT is important because we believe teachers who have knowledge of productive talk about text have a specialized capacity to support their students' engagement in high-level thinking about text during discussions. Deep understanding of, and the commitment to reflect upon, discourse that relates to high-level comprehension enables teachers to consider ways to incorporate such discourse into their discussion practices to promote students' understanding and learning.

REFERENCES

Allington, R. L., & Johnston, P. H. (2002). *Reading to learn: Lessons from exemplary fourth-grade classrooms.* New York, NY: Guilford Press.

Anderson, R. C., Chinn, C., Chang, J., Waggoner, J., & Nguyen, K. (1998). Intellectually stimulating story discussions. In J. L. Osborn, Fran (Ed.), *Literacy for all: Issues in teaching and learning* (pp. 170-186). New York, NY: Guilford Press.

Applebee, A., Langer, J., Nystrand, M., & Gamoran, A. (2003). Discussion-based approaches to developing understanding: Classroom instruction and student performance in middle and high school English. *American Educational Research Journal, 40,* 685-730.

Beck, I. L., McKeown, M. G., Hamilton, R. L., & Kucan, L. (1997). *Questioning the author: An approach for enhancing student engagement with text.* Newark, NJ: International Reading Association.

Beck, I. L., & McKeown, M. G., (2006). *Improving comprehension with Questioning the Author: A fresh and expanded view of a powerful approach.* New York, NY: Scholastic.

Bender, A. C. (1994). *Paideia seminar teaching guide: An assessment instrument to identify skills for effective seminar teachers.* Unpublished doctoral dissertation, University of North Carolina at Chapel Hill.

Billings, L., & Fitzgerald, J. (2002). Dialogic discussion and the Paideia Seminar. *American Educational Research Journal, 39*(4), 907-941.

Bloome, D., & Egan-Robertson, A. (1993). The social construction of intertextuality in classroom reading and writing lessons. *Reading Research Quarterly, 28,* 305-333.

Chang-Wells, G. L. M., & Wells, G. (1993). Dynamics of discourse: Literacy and the construction of knowledge. In E. A. Forman, N. N. Minick & C. A. Stone (Eds.), *Contexts for learning: Sociocultural dynamics in children's development* (pp. 58-90). New York, NY: Oxford University Press.

Chinn, C. A., O'Donnell, A. M., & Jinks, T. S. (2000). The structure of discourse in collaborative learning. *The Journal of Experimental Education, 69,* 77-97.

Cohen, J. (1968). Weighted kappa: nominal scale agreement with provision for scaled disagreement or partial credit. *Psychological Bulletin, 70,* 213-220.

Corbin, J. (1986). Coding, writing memos, and diagramming. In W. C. Chenitz and J. Swanson, *From practice to grounded theory: Qualitative research in nursing,* (pp. 102-132). Menlo Park, CA: Addison-Wesley.

Edwards, D., & Mercer, N. (1987). *Common knowledge: The development of understanding in the classroom.* New York, NY: Methuen.

Eeds, M., & Wells, D. (1989). Grand conversations: An exploration of meaning construction in literature study groups. *Research in the Teaching of English, 23*(1), 4-29.

Goldenberg, C. (1993). Instructional conversations: Promoting comprehension through discussion. *The Reading Teacher, 46*(4), 316-326.

Great Books Foundation. (1987). *An introduction to shared inquiry.* Chicago, IL: Author.

Howe, J. (1995). Victor. In J. Hurwitz (Ed.), *Birthday surprises: Ten great stories to unwrap.* (pp. 74-86). New York, NY: Beech Tree.

Junker, B., & Matsumara, L. C. (2006). *Beyond summative evaluation: The instructional quality assessment as a professional development tool* (CSE Technical Report 691). Los Angeles: National Center for Research on Evaluation, Standards, and Student Testing.

Landis, J. R., & Koch, G. G. (1977). The measurement of observer agreement for categorical data. *Biometrics, 33*, 159-174.

Mercer, N. (1995). *The guided construction of knowledge: Talk amongst teachers and learners.* Clevedon, England: Multilingual Matters.

Mercer, N. (2000). *Words and minds: How we use language to think together.* London, UK: Routledge.

Mercer, N. (2002). Developing dialogues. In G. Wells and G. Claxton (Eds.), *Learning for life in the 21st century: Sociocultural perspectives on the future of education,* (pp. 141-153). Oxford, UK: Blackwell Publishers.

Miles, M. B., & Huberman, A. M. (1994). *Qualitative data analysis.* Thousand Oaks, CA: Sage.

Newmann, F. M. (1990). Higher-order thinking in teaching social studies: A rationale for the assessment of classroom thoughtfulness. *Journal of Curriculum Studies, 22*, 41-56.

Nystrand, M. (1997). Dialogic instruction: When recitation becomes conversation. In M. Nystrand (with A. Gamoran, R. Kachure, & C. Prendergast), *Opening dialogue: Understanding the dynamics of language and learning in the English classroom,* (pp. 141-153). Oxford, UK: Blackwell Publishers.

Nystrand, M., Wu, A., Gamoran, A., Zeiser, S., & Long, D.A. (2003). Questions in time: Investigating the structure and dynamics of unfolding classroom discourse. *Discourse Processes, 35*(3), 135-198.

Raphael, T. E., & McMahon, S. I. (1994). Book Club: An alternative framework for reading instruction. *The Reading Teacher, 48*(2), 102-116.

Reninger, K. B., & Wilkinson, I. A. G. (2010). Using discussions to promote striving readers' higher level comprehension of literary texts. In J. L. Collins and T. G. Gunning (Eds.), *Building struggling students' higher level literacy: Practical ideas, powerful solutions* (pp. 57-83). Newark, DE: International Reading Association.

Resnick, L., Matsumara, L. C., & Junker, B. (2006). Measuring reading comprehension and mathematics instruction in urban middle schools: A pilot study of the Instructional Quality Assessment (CSE Technical Report 681). Los Angeles, CA: National Center for Research on Evaluation, Standards, and Student Testing.

Roberts, T., & Billings, L. (1999). *The Paideia classroom: Teaching for understanding.* Larchmont, NY: Eye on Education, Inc.

Roskos, K., Boehlen, S., & Walker, B. J. (2000). Learning the art of instructional conversation: The influence of self-assessment on teachers' instructional discourse in a reading clinic. *The Elementary School Journal, 100*(3), 229-252.

Roskos, K., & Boehlen, S. (2001). Enhancing teachers' awareness of their instructional talk in the teaching of reading. *Action in Teacher Education, 22*, 59-74.

Roskos, K., & Walker, B. (1997). A prototype tool for assessing instructional discourse in literacy teaching. In W. M. Linek and E. G. Sturtevant (Eds.), Exploring literacy (pp. 143-159). Commerce, TX: College Reading Association.

Rueda, R., Goldenberg, C., & Gallimore, R. (1992). *Rating instructional conversations: A guide* (Educational Practice Report 4). Santa Cruz, CA: National Center for Research on Cultural Diversity and Second Language Learning.

Sharp, A. M. (1995). Philosophy for children and the development of ethical values. *Early Child Development and Care, 107*, 45-55.

Short, K. G. and K. M. Pierce, Eds. (1990). *Talking about books: Creating literate communities.* Portsmouth, NH: Heinemann.

Soter, A. O., Wilkinson, I. A. G., Murphy, P. K., Rudge, L., Reninger, K., & Edwards, M. (2008). What the discourse tells us: Talk and indicators of high-level comprehension. *International Journal of Educational Research, 47*, 372-391.

Stiggins, R., Arter, J., Chappuis, J., & Chappuis, S. (2006). *Classroom assessment for student learning: Doing it right-using it well.* Portland, OR: Educational Testing Service.

Taylor, B. M., Pearson, P. D., Peterson, D. P., & Rodriguez, M. C. (2003). Reading growth in high-poverty classrooms: The influence of teacher practices that encourage cognitive engagement in literacy learning. *Elementary School Journal, 104*(1), 3-28.

Webb, N. M. (1989). Peer interaction and learning in small groups. *International Journal of Education Research, 13*, 21-39.

Wegerif, R., Mercer, N., & Dawes, L. (1999). From social interaction to individual reasoning: An empirical investigation of a possible socio-cultural model of cognitive development. *Learning and Instruction, 9*, 493-516.

Wiggins, G. (1998). *Educative assessment: Designing assessments to inform and improve student performance.* San Francisco, CA: Jossey-Bass.

Wiggins, G., & McTighe, J. (2005). *Understanding by design.* Alexandria, VA: Association for Supervision and Curriculum Development.

Wilkinson, I. A. G., Soter, A. O., & Murphy, P. K. (2007). *Group discussions as a mechanism for promoting high-level comprehension of text: Final grant performance report* (PR/Award No. R305G020075). Columbus, OH: Ohio State University Research Foundation.

Wilkinson, I. A. G., Soter, A. O., & Murphy, P. K. (2010). Developing a model of quality talk about literary text. In M. G. McKeown and L. Kucan (Eds.), *Bringing reading research to life* (pp. 142-169). New York, NY: Guilford Press.

The Nature of Texts Used in Five Academic Disciplines

Amy Alexandra Wilson
The University of Georgia

It has been more than 80 years since William S. Gray (1925) called for every teacher to be a reading teacher, yet after decades of research on and advocacy for content area literacy instruction, it remains absent from many secondary classrooms (Hall, 2005). The reasons offered for this absence are many, including institutional and systemic pressures that discourage people from teaching students to construct meanings from texts (O'Brien, Stewart, & Moje, 1995), preservice and inservice education that does not address how reading instruction can be adapted to meet the needs and interests of specific adolescents in specific contexts (Conley, Kerner, & Reynolds, 2005), and beliefs held by individual teachers that reading instruction is not their responsibility or that they are not qualified to teach reading (Donahue, 2000; O'Brien & Stewart, 1990). Moreover, generic comprehension strategies, often a mainstay in textbooks that offer advice to content area teachers (Conley, 2008), may not account for discipline-specific strategies for reading texts (Shanahan & Shanahan, 2008).

Siebert and Draper (2008) have offered another possible reason why content area teachers often do not use recommended approaches to literacy instruction: Many definitions of *literacy* implicitly assume that texts are primarily comprised of written words, without systematically addressing the multiple sign systems that are central to each discipline, such as numbers and symbols in mathematics. In accordance with the assertion that discipline-specific definitions of literacy must first be grounded in understandings of discipline-specific forms of texts (Wilson, in press), the purpose of this exploratory study of instruction in five classrooms was to document the types of representations used by sixth-grade teachers of five disciplines (earth science, English/language arts, mathematics, reading, and social studies) for 155 days. By recording the types of representations that middle school students were required to read as they engaged in these content areas, this study provides an account of how the nature of *texts*—defined broadly to encompass communication using any type of sign or combination of signs (Kress, 2003)—differed according to discipline. This exploratory study was not intended to produce generalizable findings, but rather to document patterns of representation used by the participating teachers. It was intended as a prerequisite, preliminary step toward conceptualizations of content area literacy instruction that account for the distinct ways that signs are used in each discipline.

THEORETICAL FRAMEWORK

Participants within academic disciplines seek to achieve discipline-specific outcomes such as writing a moving personal narrative or predicting natural phenomena (Siskin, 1994). What counts as an appropriate subject of study, how one comes to understand that subject, and how one demonstrates proficiency or makes legitimate claims in regards to that subject are all shaped by discipline-specific conventions and practices (Wineburg & Grossman, 2000). According to theories of social semiotics (Halliday, 1978; Hodge & Kress, 1988), academic disciplines, like other social configurations, are expressed and maintained through texts. Texts—such as a *coordinate plane* on the board with a *numeric/symbolic equation* written underneath it, or such as a *novel* with accompanying *questions* for *discussions*—reconstruct each discipline on an ongoing basis. As these texts form predictable patterns, they indicate what each content area encompasses and excludes.

Each text instantiates at least two aspects of a discipline: its *substance*, or a body of content, which may include subjects such as the poetic devices used in Shakespeare's sonnets, the order of operations, or the effects of World War II; and its *nature*, or "implicit messages" about "the aspects or properties of a subject that distinguish it as a discipline…the ways of knowing and pursuing knowledge…the questions and problems they examine, the ways in which answers are sought and validated," and the ways in which knowledge is communicated (McDiarmid, Ball, & Anderson, 1989, p. 196). For instance, science entails a longstanding tradition of using *equipment* (Rosenthal & Bybee, 1987), such as *thermometers* or *weighing scales* that measure *physical phenomena*. Students read these texts under the assumption that a proper domain of study in science is the physical universe, and an appropriate way to substantiate claims in regards to this domain is by conducting and reporting experiments that quantify or describe characteristics of these observable phenomena. In sum, texts instantiate both the *what* and the *how* of various facets of each discipline.

As these examples indicate, students regularly must make sense of many disciplinary texts that are non-linguistic in nature. Although its definition is contested, the concept of *mode* can be used to distinguish and classify these diverse forms of texts. According to Kress (2009), a mode is a socially fashioned resource used in representation and is provided by the social group in which one is participating. Examples of modes include written words, gestures, three-dimensional models, images, and spoken words. Modes may consist of subgenres. For instance, *instructions* and *novels,* although very different in form and purpose, may both be classified as *written words*, while *drawings* and *photographs* may both be classified as *images*. Despite significant differences across genres, modes are classified according to certain physical similarities. Drawings and photographs, for instance, both display information spatially and simultaneously, whereas *instructions* and *novels* are organized in part by a temporal sequence and have a set reading path as people read the lines and words (more or less) in a given order.

Many researchers (e.g., Kress, et al., 2005; Lemke, 2003; Prain & Waldrip, 2006) have studied how multiple forms of representation are integrated and used to communicate discipline-specific content, often by analyzing how gestures, written or spoken language, images, numbers, and other representations were used in specific lessons or texts, and by explaining how these modes contributed to or reflected students' understanding of content. Rather than asserting that multiple modes are important to an individual discipline in a specific lesson, however, the objective of this study was to open conversations on the relative importance of different forms of representation across content areas, and to offer an aggregated description of how teachers used modes in discipline-specific ways over time through showing the frequency with which these modes were used by content area teachers over the course of 1.5 school years.

METHOD

To provide this overall account of how modes were used across different content areas, this study examines the instruction provided by one team of sixth-grade teachers: an earth science and mathematics teacher who had taught for nine years and had earned Master's and Bachelor's degrees in teaching middle grades mathematics and science; a reading and language arts teacher who had taught for three years and had received a Bachelor's degree in secondary English education and a certification in reading instruction; and a social studies teacher who had taught for 25 years, 16 of which were in an elementary school, and who held a Bachelor's degree in elementary education and a Specialist degree in middle school education. This team was purposefully selected for the study based on its reputation for excellence throughout the surrounding region. Although students from their middle school qualified for free and reduced lunch at higher rates than other schools in this Southeastern rural area, the students on their team scored higher on end-of-year statewide tests than any other school in the district. Two of the teachers on the team had been nominated as Teacher of the Year and were known as leaders and innovators by district and school administration. It was hoped that their instruction would provide insight into the types of representation used by knowledgeable teachers who effectively supported students' learning in their disciplines.

Two types of data were collected and analyzed: *field notes* from classroom observations, which included a record of the teachers' essential questions or objectives for each day, and accompanying *artifacts*. For 155 days, the teachers' classroom instruction was observed: Reading, mathematics, and social studies were observed on "A days," while science and language arts were observed on alternating "B days," with each lesson lasting 1.5 hours. Artifacts collected from these lessons included print-outs from interactive white boards, handouts given in class, photographs of materials, and photocopies of textbook pages. Although the teachers were also interviewed once every four to six weeks, the 26 interviews were used to obtain background information and were not formally analyzed as a part of this study.

The field notes and artifacts were analyzed using a form of constant comparative analysis (Strauss & Corbin, 1998). Two coders, both of whom worked as instructors in a university's literacy program and who were former secondary teachers of English or history, independently read through randomly selected data points and noted patterns across data in regards to the types of representation that were used. Based on their initial readings and discussions, an articulated system of codes was developed, which defined the types of representations that were used (see Appendix for examples). The data were split into two overarching categories: (a) *non-linguistic texts*, or texts whose primary means of communication was not words; and (b) *genres of text in printed words,* or written texts. Examples of subcategories within these two categories included the following: *non-linguistic text: demonstration* and *photograph,* and *linguistic text: instructions* and *sentence.*

The field notes were divided into instructional episodes (Siskin, 1994), with each new episode delineated by one or both of the following: (1) a shift to a different instructional activity, often as indicated by the daily agenda written on the board, and often accompanied by the distribution of new materials; and/or (2) a new social configuration in the classroom, such as a shift from whole-class instruction to group work. For each instructional episode, a given representation was coded only once, even if it was used multiple times. After the data had been divided into instructional episodes, the author coded the types of representation used in all of the field notes and artifacts, while the second coder independently identified 15% of randomly selected data. The author and the coder identified over 80% of the same codes, but this percentage did not account for the times that they both agreed to assign data points with no codes. A science and mathematics teacher also read the findings related to mathematics and science instruction to confirm that the codes and results were credible to her.

This study was limited in at least two ways. Although linguistic and non-linguistic texts were reported separately, they were frequently used in conjunction with each other as spoken words mediated the connections between them. Because spoken words were not coded, the frequency tables provide a limited, simplified picture of how representations were used in classrooms. Second, students' homework, which oftentimes entailed textbook readings, also was not included as part of data analysis, and consequently the tables may not reflect with accuracy the times that these genres were used.

RESULTS

Earth Science

Lessons in earth science usually addressed causal or spatial relationships between observable physical entities or addressed the composition of these entities, as indicated by daily or weekly essential questions such as the following, *How do eclipses and phases of the moon occur? How does plate tectonics affect the earth's surface? Why do we have seasons? How does weathering and erosion affect the surface of the earth? How do rocks move through the rock cycle? What are minerals and their characteristics? What are the inner planets?* To help students answer these questions, Grace (pseudonym), the earth science teacher, relied heavily on iconic signs, or representations that bore a physical resemblance to the items they represented (Peirce, 1991), such as drawings, diagrams, photographs, objects, models, and demonstrations. As indicated by the frequency table (see Table 1), she relied on non-linguistic texts (n = 672) about 60% more than she relied on texts comprised primarily of written words (n = 394); moreover, earth science, more than any other academic discipline, was dependent on diverse iconic displays to represent key content.

An example will demonstrate how Grace used teacher gestures, the most common form of representation in the observed lessons, to help students answer part of the essential question, *What causes waves, currents, and tides?* One day, she began class by asking students if they could answer any part of that question, which was written on the board. One student stated that waves were caused by winds, including "how far it goes, how long it goes, and how strong the wind is." Grace elaborated on his answer, reiterating that waves' size was determined by: (a) the length or distance of the wind; (b) the duration of time of the wind; and (c) the strength, force, or speed of the wind. She referred students back to a previous lesson where she and the students had represented wind by "blowing" or moving across the room over a long distance, by moving for a long time, and by pursing their mouths and blowing with different degrees of force.

Grace then asked students if there were any other parts of the essential question that they could answer. One student rejoined, "Currents are caused by temperature and density." As part of elaborating and extending on his answer, Grace asked students about what affected density. One student said, "salinity," to which Grace responded, "Is water that has salt in it more dense

Table 1. Texts Used in Earth Science in 272 Instructional Episodes

Non-linguistic texts	Linguistic texts
Gesture: Teacher: 76	Instructions: 75
Diagram: 75	Multiple Choice Questions: 60
Drawing: 70	Questions: 57
Photographs: 63	Textbook Section: 52
Object: 43	Informational Paragraph: 45
Model: 35	List: 42
Demonstration: 34	Label: 26
Map: 32	Definition: 21
Gesture: Student: 30	Criteria: 8
Moving Image: 28	Article: 4
Table: 28	Narrative: 4
Embodied Representation: 25	
Graph: 24	
Nature: 24	
Measuring Instrument: 20	
Lab: 19	
Numbers/Symbols: 16	
Graphic Organizer: 11	
Number Line: 8	
Manipulative: 6	
Coordinate Plane: 3	
Symbols on Existing Text: 2	

or less dense?" She then reminded students of a demonstration they had done in which they had poured dyed salt water into clear tap water in a large clear plastic container, and she connected this demonstration to the formation of currents. Following further discussion about the essential question, Grace told her students that they were going to watch a video that would give them more information about waves. After students shared what they learned about water particles from the video footage, Grace and her students held the following interaction:

Grace: You were a bobber the other day. You're going to be a wave today. You're a water particle. I want you to stand and face me. There's energy coming from the dry erase board. [She gestures toward the board.] It causes you to go on your tiptoes and go down like this. [As Grace moves both arms to the left and then to the right in a circular motion, she stands on her tiptoes and squats, returning to a standing position.] We're going to do the wave. I should see the movement go this way, and then the next people will go up, and then the next people will go up. [Grace moves one outstretched arm with a pointed finger from left to right, indicating the direction in which she wants the "wave" to move when one student at a time will stand on his or her tiptoes and move in a circle.]

Student: Only if we can go whee like this! [Student makes a whee noise and moves his body up and down and from left to right, mimicking Grace's previous circular motion.]

Grace: You need to be standing here and when it gets to you, you go up and then back in a circle.

In this instructional episode, Grace and her students referred to multiple texts they had previously used in the classroom, including gestures, embodied representations, and demonstrations. Grace also used a variety of representations throughout this instructional episode, including teacher and student gestures and moving images in the video footage. The only printed words used or referenced in this episode, however, were the essential question. Other examples of Grace's gestures included showing students how ice wedging was a form of mechanical weathering that affected rocks (her arms represented the cracks in the rock that grew wider); showing the difference between divergent, convergent, and transform boundaries that are formed when tectonic plates come together (her hands represented the plates that came together in different ways); and showing how the Coriolis Effect influenced the movement of currents and winds (her hands indicated the direction of winds and currents over a globe).

Even the most commonly used genre of written words, instructions, referred its readers to other texts. For instance, Grace's students read instructions on how to design a moving model of sea floor spreading, on how much sugar they should add to water during a lab, and on how they should cut a chocolate-covered cherry in a "Pit of the Earth" activity that compared the cherry to the earth's layers. Textbook sections, too, were often used as supplements to nonlinguistic texts. In one lesson, students visited a series of mineral centers at which they investigated the different properties of various minerals. The instructions at each center directed students to taste, smell, observe, or scratch these minerals, and to put them in water and measure the water displacement. The instructions also required students to compare photographs in their textbooks to the minerals before them. Finally, the instructions required students to read a few paragraphs to reinforce and explain what they had observed. In other words, the photographs in the textbooks, the written words in the textbook, the measuring instruments, and the instructions were all supplementary tools to support students' reading of the focal text, the minerals.

English/Language Arts

As suggested by her daily or weekly essential questions, Shirley's (pseudonym) English language arts class was dedicated to language instruction in the dual areas of grammar and writing. Her most common essential question was *Do I know the parts of speech?*, with over half of the curriculum dedicated to related questions, such as *What are adverbs? Can I identify nouns and how they are used? What are prepositions? What are indefinite pronouns?* and *What are coordinating and correlative conjunctions?* Essential questions related to writing included *How can I use facts and opinions to persuade my audience? Can I show not tell? How can I plan the plot of my personal narrative? Will readers feel like they are in my story?* and *How do I need to edit my paper to make my meaning clear?*

To help her students accomplish these goals, Shirley used linguistic texts (n=359) more than twice as much as she used nonlinguistic texts (n=142), as indicated by Table 2. In accordance with her goal to teach the parts of speech, the most commonly used type of text was the sentence, and the most commonly used non-linguistic text was a series of symbols, such as arrows or letters (e.g., N for noun) that were used to annotate sentences by showing how words related to each other. Instructions, the second most common genre in her language arts classes, often indicated to students how they were to annotate or combine sentences.

Table 2. Texts Used in English/Language Arts in 216 Instructional Episodes

Non-linguistic texts	Linguistic texts
Symbols on Existing Text: 60	Sentence: 99
Drawing: 29	Instructions: 62
Graphic Organizer: 15	Word: 37
Table: 15	List: 37
Photo: 5	Multiple Choice Questions: 29
Embodied Representation: 4	Definition: 24
Gesture: Teacher: 4	Narrative: 22
Manipulative: 4	Questions: 13
Gesture: Student: 2	Essay: 9
Object: 2	Poem: 7
Coordinate Plane: 1	Writing Prompt: 7
Map: 1	Informational Paragraph: 4
	Label: 4
	Article: 2
	Letter: 2
	Criteria: 1

An example will serve to illustrate how Shirley used these types of texts in class. At the beginning of one period, students reviewed multiple choice questions that required them to combine sentences and to identify parts of speech. After getting one of the multiple choice questions wrong, a student asked Shirley why two sentences could not be combined with only a comma, to which she responded:

Shirley: I'm just going to do some short sentences. So if I have the boy ran, there's one sentence, OK, and if I want to join it with another sentence, the boy ran, the girl walked. [Shirley writes *The boy ran, the girl walked* on the whiteboard]. OK, now a lot of you are putting in the subordinating conjunction thing, but they didn't give you that option [on the multiple choice test]. It's just one of those punctuation and grammar rules, you can't just stick two sentences together with a comma and that will be enough. If you're using a comma, you need to have a conjunction with it. You can, however, stick them [points to two sentences on the board] together if you don't want to use a conjunction. The easiest way to put two sentences together is a semi-colon. But this word, this letter [points to *the* in *The girl walked*] stays lower case.

After students had reviewed the answers to the rest of the multiple choice questions in a similar fashion, Shirley distributed a handout with 10 sentences on which the students were required to identify the part of speech for each word. As another example of a grammar lesson in which the central text was a *word* or a *list,* students had to change an adjective such as *happy* to an adverb and to write a list of subordinating conjunctions.

As part of the second strand of Shirley's instruction, which entailed a focus on writing, students received a line shaped like a hook, drew a picture of their choosing around that line in which they added detail, and wrote "whatever they wanted to say to explain the picture." Shirley then explained to her students that adding detail in their illustrations was akin to the concept of adding detail in writing, and she asked students to revise their papers by adding descriptive words and sensory details from each of the five senses. For another writing lesson, students received photographs from magazines and brainstormed adjectives in groups to describe those images. Unlike in earth science, where images had to bear a fairly strict physical resemblance to the represented object in order to convey key concepts (e.g., the earth, sun, and moon had to be correctly aligned to illustrate a solar eclipse), images in language arts were not used as frequently and did not usually have to bear an accurate physical resemblance to a represented object of study. Linguistic texts, combined with symbols written on these linguistic texts, were instead the most commonly used forms of representation in this discipline.

Mathematics

Grace's mathematics class often was centered on how to solve different types of problems and how to represent mathematical concepts. Essential questions included *How do I find circumference and area? How do I write rules from tables? How do I measure to the nearest _____? How do I write and compare ratios? How do I solve equations? How do I solve problems involving probability?* and *How do I change units in the metric system?* To help students accomplish these goals, Grace used numbers and symbols fully twice as often as she used the most common type of written linguistic text, instructions (See Table 3). Due to their base-ten place values, numbers and symbols allowed students to perform the algorithms required by the essential questions, such as finding the surface area of a solid shape or such as changing fractions to decimals or percents. At times, these numbers and symbols may have referred to observable physical objects, such as money, but students also solved numerical problems with no observable physical referents, such as when they "simplified 6/10." Instructions told students what to do or explained to them how to do it, ranging from a brief one-word command such as *add,* to a series of steps on how to add, subtract, multiply, and divide fractions. Word problems provided students with scenarios that required them to use mathematical reasoning to solve various problems, while drawings (such as several pies divided into pieces to teach about subtracting fractions or such as a square divided into a hundred smaller squares to represent the concept of percent) enabled students to visualize concepts and to understand why and how numerical operations worked.

An example will illustrate how various sign systems were commonly used and integrated in this discipline. In a lesson whose essential question was *How did I find surface area?*, Grace began her

Table 3. Texts Used in Mathematics in 263 Instructional Episodes

Non-linguistic texts	Linguistic texts
Numbers/Symbols: 242	Instructions: 112
Geometric Shape: 88	Word Problem: 66
Drawing: 44	Questions: 34
Table: 37	Multiple Choice Questions: 32
Manipulatives: 33	Definition: 28
Gesture: Teacher: 27	Label: 20
Geometric Object: 25	List: 6
Measuring Instrument: 23	Criteria: 2
Symbols on Existing Text: 15	Informational Paragraph: 2
Graph: 14	
Coordinate Plane: 11	
Objects: 9	
Number Line: 8	
Photographs: 6	
Gesture: Student: 5	
Map: 3	
Graphic Organizer: 4	
Moving Image: 2	

instruction by unfolding an empty box of crackers as a model of a rectangular prism, and pointing to each flat rectangle on the folded-out box, showing how it corresponded to a drawn, folded-out rectangular prism on the whiteboard, whose background was a grid. She continued:

Grace: I'm going to find the surface area; I'm going to find this area of all the surfaces. Let's figure out the dimensions of each of these rectangles. I know this is hard to count so I'll tap for you. How long would this piece be right here? [Grace points to the top rectangle in the folded-out rectangular prism, and, moving her finger in a line that follows the bottom line of the top rectangle, she taps each square on the grid.]

The process continued as Grace pointed to each of the rectangles and asked the students to tell her its length and width, which Grace then labeled with an *l* or a *w*. After the students identified a length and width for each of the rectangles, Grace asked her students to find the area of each rectangle by saying repeatedly, "What's the area of this one? Length times width." As students answered each question, Grace wrote a number representing the surface area of each rectangle in the middle of that rectangle.

Grace then wrote the complete equation for finding the surface area of rectangular prisms to the side of the board "so that way we don't have to draw them out every time and add them up." As Grace added each number or letter to the formula, she pointed to the rectangle or line from

Table 4. Texts Used in Reading in 192 Instructional Episodes

Non-linguistic texts	Linguistic texts
Drawing: 22	Narrative: 51
Table: 12	Instructions: 29
Graphic Organizer: 11	Multiple Choice Questions: 27
Teacher Gesture: 10	Poem: 27
Embodied Representation: 9	Word: 25
Object: 8	List: 23
Photo: 7	Definition: 13
Student Gesture: 7	Questions: 13
Symbol on Existing Text: 3	Sentence: 13
Graph: 2	Novel: 11
Number/Symbol: 2	Informational Paragraph: 8
Manipulative: 2	Article: 6
Diagram: 1	Label: 4
Map: 1	Play: 4
Student Gesture: 1	Informational Book: 3
	Letter: 3
	Criteria: 2
	Essay: 1

which the number or letter came. At the end of this series of interactions, Grace wrote one label on the board, which served as the only four written words used throughout this instructional episode: *surface area rectangular prism*. This example demonstrates how spoken words, numbers and symbols, pointing, geometric shapes, and a geometric object worked together to convey a key mathematical concept with minimal reliance on written words.

Reading

Shirley's reading class primarily focused on three different strands. The most common strand entailed essential questions that drew students' attention to the form, structure, characteristics, or devices in a variety of literary and informational texts, such as *What are poetic devices? What are the elements of a story? What are important elements in Greek mythology? What are folktales?* and *What are the features of an informational text?* The second most common strand included questions related to comprehension strategies that students could use as they approached these texts, including questions such as *How do I utilize context clues? Can I infer information from a passage? How does a prefix affect a word's meaning?* and *Do I comprehend what I read?* The third strand asked students to summarize or reflect on specific content within literary texts by answering questions such as *What message do the Oompa Loompas send with their songs? What can we learn from the conflicts in part III?* and *What influenced each character in Maniac Magee?* To reach these goals, reading as a discipline entailed the reading of written linguistic texts (n=263) more than twice as much as it entailed the reading of non-linguistic texts (n=98) (See Table 4).

Although this overall result echoed the findings from English/language arts, the types of written linguistic texts used in reading class were different from those used in English. Whereas the most common type of text used in language arts was a single sentence, the most common type of text used in reading was a narrative, extending from several pages to several hundred pages. Unlike students' science or history textbooks, these novels, myths, and photocopied short stories usually did not include photographs, diagrams, or other iconic images, with examples such as the novel *Maniac Magee* (Spinelli, 1990) and numerous short stories.

An example will illustrate how Shirley provided instruction on the narrative texts that were a key staple of her discipline. To answer the essential question, *What is the plot summary of part I of Maniac Magee?*, Shirley began an instructional episode by saying:

Shirley: I don't want to keep on going [reading] because I want to summarize part one.

Student: 76 pages to summarize?

Shirley: It won't be as hard as you think. I'll show you why. At the top of each section, you need to write these words in order going from left to right. [Shirley wrote one word as the title to each of the four columns: Somebody, wanted, but, so]. Somebody, second section is wanted, third section is but, last section is so. Somebody wanted but so. All right, this is the tool you're going to use to help you summarize. And you all said 76 pages, that's a lot a lot of stuff that happened. But remember, in a summary, are you going to tell me every single little bitty detail? No, a summary is when you give me the main gist, the summary of what happened. So, let's start with this column [points to the column titled "Somebody]. Somebody. Give me a somebody in your story.

Student: Mars Bar.

Shirley: Mars Bar, sure. Great. So now we have one of the characters in the story. Over here on this side of the board [points to "Somebody" column], this is very important to have in a summary, don't you think? We need to have the characters. So here's one of our characters, Mars Bar. Now, what did Mars Bar want?

Shirley continued to solicit students' comments on the four columns, until she read the final summarizing sentence, "Mars Bar wanted to hurt Maniac because he was on the wrong side, but the lady with the broom and Amanda saved him, so Mars Bar didn't get to lay out Maniac and Mars Bar was spooked by Amanda and Mars Bar gets mad and wants revenge." She then asked students to use the heuristic, *Somebody wanted but so,* to summarize what happened to the other main characters in the story.

In other reading lessons, students discussed issues such as race, discrimination, social pressure, sadness, courage, and other themes in fictional texts, biographies, and—to a lesser extent—in informational texts about subjects such as World War II. Students made predictions and personal connections about these texts on wiki-pages. Photographs and other drawings occasionally served to illustrate the written words, but Shirley did not draw her students' attention to these images except to teach them about the features of informational texts.

Social Studies

Essential questions in Pamela's social studies class required students to understand factual information about the location, histories, resources, and economies of different countries, including questions such as *What countries are on the Balkan Peninsula? What is a czar? Name five resources found in Europe. Who was King Arthur? Name five unusual Australian animals.* and *Who are China's neighbors?* As in language arts and reading, linguistic texts (n=263) were over twice as common as non-linguistic texts (n=130) (See Table 5). The most common type of text used in this course was short-answer questions, such as those found in worksheets or at the end of textbook chapters, followed by multiple choice questions, which were also found in worksheets and on exams. While students responded to short-answer questions or multiple choice questions in 169 instructional episodes, they read extended texts, such as textbook sections and informational articles, in only 53 instructional episodes. The most common type of non-linguistic text was a map, which students read at the beginning of most periods as part of their Daily Geography Practice. Pamela also occasionally drew her students' attention to photographs in the textbooks when she read chapters aloud to the students.

Table 5. Texts Used in Social Studies in 179 Instructional Episodes

Non-linguistic texts	Linguistic texts
Map: 78	Questions: 110
Photo: 27	Multiple Choice Questions: 59
Drawing: 5	Textbook Section: 32
Graphic Organizer: 5	Article: 21
Graphs: 4	Instructions: 18
Moving Image: 4	Definition: 9
Diagram: 3	List: 8
Table: 3	Informational Paragraph: 2
	Number Line: 2
	Diagram: 1
	Letter: 1
	Model: 1

An example will illustrate the type of instruction found in Pamela's social studies class. One day, the essential question posted on the board was *How has Poland's economy changed?* Students entered the classroom, and used maps in their atlases to answer the questions: *1. What mountain range is located between the Black and Caspian Seas?*, and *2. Paraguay is to Bolivia as _____ is to Honduras.* After Pamela called on two students to share their answers, students completed an activity sheet on the British Isles that required them to write short answers to questions and to circle letters on multiple choice questions. Before the period was over, students exchanged their activity sheets with one another and graded each other's papers as Pamela called out the answers: "C, peat. D, farming, manufacturing. E, European Union. F, Gaelic, English. G, church. H, Dublin." The period ended after Pamela read the remaining answers.

DISCUSSION

Although this description of five subjects does not purport to be representative of academic disciplines in general, much of the content of these classes bears similarities to extant literature on the history and nature of each subject area. O'Halloran (1998), for example, asserted that numbers and symbols are often the primary sign system through which mathematicians solve problems that are central to the discipline, and others (Rotman, 2000; Sfard, 2000) have noted the abstract nature of numbers, by which signifiers are often seemingly cut off from any observable signified. Science, in contrast, is rich in a variety of iconic representations that display salient characteristics of the physical world (Lemke, 1998: Pauwels, 2006). In describing the origins of a branch of earth science, Rudwick (1976) concluded that it would be "both inadequate and pretentious" to call maps, diagrams, cross-sections, or other visual displays mere "visual aids" in this discipline (p. 149); instead, they are central to the generation and communication of scientific knowledge in this field.

Shirley's English/language arts instruction, too, was consistent with Applebee's (1974) assertion that English is characterized by several major strands, including instruction in grammar and writing. Grossman (1991) described the teaching of literature, including narratives and poetry, as central to the discipline of English, a definition that was later extended by others (e.g., Scholes, 1998) who noted that English/language arts also entails teaching about the forms, purposes, and characteristics of various types of texts as students read and write them. Although Shirley primarily focused on reading in reading class and on writing in English/language arts, she explained in interviews that she saw the two subjects as tightly related, but she divided them because she worked with the same group of students for both subjects. When taken jointly, however, her two classes focused on the reading and writing of different types of texts with an attention to the conventions, purposes, and forms of these texts.

The social studies class was perhaps the only class whose instruction did not resemble the conventions of an academic discipline to a considerable degree. Pamela, the only teacher who was not extensively prepared to teach in the content area that she taught, did not ask her students to read a variety of primary or secondary source documents by noting the source of the text, including the group and national affiliations of the authors that may have shaped the perspectives in the texts, nor did her students corroborate and compare the evidence across multiple texts as historians often do (Shanahan & Shanahan, 2008; Wineburg, 1991). Focal texts for many historians include a variety of written documents, with maps, monuments, photographs, music, and videos also being proper texts for study (Wineburg, 2000). Rather than exemplifying recommended disciplinary instruction in history, Pamela's instruction highlights a common thread found across all of the disciplines: an emphasis on the conventions of school, as evidenced by a heavy reliance on short-answer questions and multiple choice questions as a common genre. Indeed, these types of texts were used extensively across all of the disciplines, although historians, mathematicians, scientists, and literary analysts or authors may not typically answer short-answer questions or multiple-choice questions for others as a staple of their work.

IMPLICATIONS

Proponents of multimodality and social semiotics (e.g., Jewitt, 2008; Kress, 2003) have contended that all teaching and learning is multimodal, an assertion that is consonant with the instruction described in this study. Nonetheless, this study refines this assertion by showing how modes are not necessarily of equal importance across content areas. Instead, teachers used them to different extents and in different ways according to discipline-specific conventions. Although previous studies have shown how professional texts in a single discipline rely on multiple modes to convey meaning (e.g., Lemke, 1998; O'Halloran, 2005; Pauwels, 2006), or have shown how teachers use multimodal representations in individual units of instruction or on particular assignments (e.g., Kress, Jewitt, Ogborn, & Tsatsarelis, 2001), this study attempts to document more enduring and specific patterns of communication through quantifying how representations were used in five content areas over the course of 1.5 school years. This study substantiates the idea that pronounced discipline-specific patterns exist in the texts read by students, even for sixth-graders who have just left elementary schools to be taught (often for the first time) by people who have specialized degrees in their content areas.

Because this study was intended as a description of the instruction provided by one team of sixth-grade teachers, further large-scale research is needed to study the generalizability of these findings, including what constitutes a *text* in algebra, geometry, life science, earth science, American history, and so forth. Although a large body of research exists in regards to comprehension instruction on printed texts (National Reading Panel, 2000), this study raises additional questions in regards to how teachers might provide explicit comprehension instruction on multimodal texts. For example, how might teachers provide instruction on the reading of gestures, the leading form of representation used in earth science in this study? Would students' comprehension of these texts improve through asking clarifying questions, predicting, monitoring their comprehension, and summarizing (Palinscar & Brown, 1984)? If so, what form should their summaries take? Might the reading and writing of multimodal texts require a different type of literacy instruction than the reading and writing of printed texts? Moreover, how is *disciplinary literacy* shaped by what might be termed *school literacy*, or reading and responding to texts commonly used in schools, such as the multiple choice questions that are often used across disciplines?

In all disciplines except for the reading class, this case study challenges the notion that *literacy* primarily entails the reading and writing of extended written texts. By answering the call for more research on how and why uses and conceptions of *texts* vary according to discipline (e.g., Moje, 2008), this study hopes to contribute to future research on how conceptions of *literacy instruction* may consequently have to be individualized to each discipline to account for the combinations and patterns of texts that are used therein. This study suggests that it is insufficient for researchers to offer recommendations for literacy instruction based on the reading of print-based texts without rigorously accounting for how these written texts interplay with other modes to convey key content in each discipline.

REFERENCES

Applebee, A. N. (1974). *Tradition and reform in the teaching of English: A history.* Urbana, IL: National Council of Teachers of English.

Conley, M. (2008). Cognitive strategy instruction for adolescents: What we know about the promise, what we don't know about the potential. *Harvard Educational Review, 78, 84-108.*

Conley, M., Kerner, K., & Reynolds, J. M. (2005). Not a question of "should," but a question of "how": Integrating literacy knowledge and practice into secondary teacher preparation through tutoring in urban middle schools. *Action in Teacher Education, 27*(2), 22-32.

Donahue, D. M. (2000). Experimenting with texts: New science teachers' experience and practice as readers and teachers of reading. *Journal of Adolescent & Adult Literacy, 43,* 728-739.

Gray, W. S. (1925). A modern program of reading instruction for the grades and high school. In G. M. Whipple (Ed.), *Report of the National Committee on Reading: 24th Yearbook of the National Society for the Study of Education, Part 1* (pp. 21-73). Bloomington, IL: Public School Publishing Company.

Grossman, P. (1991). What are we talking about anyway?: Subject matter knowledge of secondary English teachers. In J. Brophy (Ed.), *Advances in research on teaching, Volume 2: Teachers' knowledge of their subject matter as it relates to their teaching practice* (pp. 245-264). Greenwich, CT: JAI Press.

Hall, L. A. (2005). Teachers and content area reading: Attitudes, beliefs, and change. *Teaching and Teacher Education, 21,* 403-414.

Halliday, M. A. K. (1978). *Language as social semiotic: The social interpretation of language and meaning.* London, UK: Arnold.

Hodge, R., & Kress, G. (1988). *Social semiotics.* Ithaca, NY: Cornell University Press.

Jewitt, C. (2008). Multimodal classroom research. *Review of Research in Education, 32,* 241- 267.

Kress, G. (2003). *Literacy in the new media age.* New York, NY: Routledge.

Kress, G. (2009). What is mode? In C. Jewitt (Ed.), *The Routledge handbook of multimodal analysis* (pp. 54-67). New York, NY: Routledge.

Kress, G., Jewitt, C., Bourne, J., Franks, A., Hardcastle, J., Jones, K., & Reid, E. (2005). *Urban classrooms, subject English: Multimodal perspectives on teaching and learning.* London, UK: RoutledgeFalmer.

Kress, G., Jewitt, C., Ogborn, J., & Tsatsarelis, C. (2001). *Multimodal teaching and learning: The rhetorics of the science classroom.* London, UK: Continuum.

Lemke, J. L. (1998). Multiplying meaning: Visual and verbal semiotics in scientific text. In J. R. Martin & R. Veel (Eds.), *Reading science: Critical and functional perspectives on discourses of science* (pp. 87-113). New York, NY: Routledge.

Lemke, J. L. (2003). Mathematics in the middle: Measure, picture, gesture, and word. In M. Anderson, A. Sáenz-Ludlow, S. Zellweger, S. Cifarelli, & V. V. Cifarelli (Eds.), *Educational perspectives on mathematics as semiosis: From thinking to knowing* (pp. 215-234). Ottawa, Canada: Legas.

McDiarmid, G. W., Ball, D. L., & Anderson C. W. (1989). Why staying one chapter ahead doesn't really work: Subject-specific pedagogy. In M. C. Reynolds (Ed.), *Knowledge base for the beginning teacher* (pp. 193-205). New York, NY: Pergamon.

Moje, E. B. (2008). Foregrounding the disciplines in secondary literacy teaching and learning: A call for change. *Journal of Adolescent & Adult Literacy, 52,* 96-107.

National Reading Panel. (2000). *Teaching children to read: An evidence-based assessment of the scientific research literature on reading and its implications for reading instruction.* NIH Publication No. 00-4754. Washington, DC: National Institute of Child Health and Human Development.

O'Brien, D. G., & Stewart, R. A. (1990). Preservice teachers' perspectives on why every teacher is not a teacher of reading: A qualitative analysis. *Journal of Reading Behavior, 22,* 101-129.

O'Brien, D. G., Stewart, R. A., & Moje, E. B. (1995). Why content area literacy is difficult to infuse into the secondary school: Complexities of curriculum, pedagogy, and school culture. *Reading Research Quarterly, 30,* 442-463.

O'Halloran, K. L. (1998). Classroom discourse in mathematics: A multi-semiotic analysis. *Linguistics and Education, 10,* 359-388.

O'Halloran, K. L. (2005). *Mathematical discourse: Language, symbolism, and visual images.* New York, NY: Continuum.

Palincsar, A. S., & Brown, A. L. (1984). Reciprocal teaching of comprehension-fostering and comprehension-monitoring activities. *Cognition and Instruction, 1,* 117-175.

Pauwels, L. (2006). Introduction: The role of visual representation in the production of scientific reality. In L. Pauwels (Ed.), *Visual cultures of science: Rethinking representational practices in knowledge building and science communication* (pp. vii–xix). Hanover, NH: Dartmouth College Press.

Peirce, C. S. (1991). In J. Hoopes (Ed.), *Peirce on signs: Writings on semiotic.* Chapel Hill, NC: University of North Carolina Press.

Prain, V., & Waldrip, B. (2006). An exploratory study of teachers' and students' use of multimodal representations of concepts in primary science. *International Journal of Science Education, 28,* 1843-1866.

Rosenthal, D. B., & Bybee, R. W. (1987). Emergence of the biology curriculum: A science of life or a science of living? In T. S. Popkewitz (Ed.), *The formation of school subjects: The struggle for creating an American institution* (123-144). London, UK: Falmer.

Rotman, B. (2000). *Mathematics as sign: Writing, imagining, counting.* Stanford, CA: Stanford University Press.

Rudwick, M. J. S. (1976). The emergence of a visual language for geological science, 1760-1840. *History of Science, 14,* 149-195.

Scholes, R. (1998). *The rise and fall of English: Reconstructing English as a discipline.* New Haven, CT: Yale University Press.

Sfard, A. (2000). Symbolizing mathematical reality into being, or how mathematical discourse and mathematical objects create each other. In P. Cobb, K. E. Yackel, & K. McClain (Eds.), *Symbolizing and communicating in mathematics classrooms: Perspectives on discourse, tools, and instructional design* (pp. 37-98). Mahwah, NJ: Lawrence Erlbaum.

Shanahan, T., & Shanahan, C. (2008). Teaching disciplinary literacy to adolescents: Rethinking content-area literacy. *Harvard Educational Review, 78,* 40-61.

Siebert, D., & Draper, R. J. (2008). Why content-area literacy messages do not speak to mathematics teachers: A critical content analysis. *Literacy Research and Instruction, 47,* 229-245.

Siskin, L. S. (1994). *Realms of knowledge: Academic departments in secondary schools.* London, UK: Falmer Press.

Spinelli, J. (1990). *Maniac Magee.* New York, NY: Little, Brown.

Strauss, A., & Corbin, J. (1998). *Basics of qualitative research: Techniques and procedures for developing grounded theory.* Thousand Oaks, CA: Sage Publications.

Wilson, A. A. (in press). A social semiotics framework for conceptualizing content area literacies. *Journal of Adolescent & Adult Literacy.*

Wineburg, S. S. (1991). Historical problem solving: A study of the cognitive processes used in the evaluation of documentary and pictorial evidence. *Journal of Educational Psychology, 83,* 73-87.

Wineburg, S. (2000). Making historical sense. In P. N. Stearns, P. Seixas, & S. Wineburg (Eds.), *Knowing, teaching, and learning history: National and international perspectives* (pp. 306-326). New York, NY: New York University Press.

Wineburg, S., & Grossman, P. (Eds.). (2000). *Interdisciplinary curricula: Challenges to implementation.* New York, NY: Teachers College Press.

APPENDIX
EXAMPLES OF CODES

Type of Non-linguistic Text

Diagram: A visual representation designed to explain or portray aspects of a phenomenon, often containing added textual features, such as arrows, lines, or labels, that show causes, processes, or relationships that are difficult to see with the unaided eye.

Embodied representation: Students' bodies represent the concept or person they are learning about.

Graphic organizer: Boxes or circles, connected by lines, which illustrate relationships between ideas.

Lab: Students' manipulation of two or more models, natural elements, or objects to investigate the results of the interaction between them.

Model: An object whose properties are designed to resemble something in the world or the solar system, usually on a smaller scale or larger scale.

Moving images: Video footage, computer-generated graphics, or cartoon animations, any of which are in constant movement on a screen, usually accompanied by sound.

Object: A tangible manmade item, often found as a regular part of a classroom setting, whose properties are used to contribute to the instructional objective.

Symbols on existing text: Lines, arrows, boxes, or other symbols are drawn on pre-existing texts.

Table: An organizational tool that uses headings, rows, and columns to summarize and relate information.

Teacher gesture: Teacher moves part of her body to convey a concept related to the instructional objective. The gesture must carry informational weight and not solely be to add emotive emphasis or to point to another type of representation.

Genre of Text in Written Words

Criteria: Standards by which something should be judged.

Definition: A brief statement that identifies or describes key characteristics of an object, phenomenon, or process.

Informational paragraph: A paragraph of one to five sentences in length comprised of descriptions and/or explanations about a single subject. A description is defined as an account of the properties of something, and an explanation is defined as an account of how or why something happens.

List: A series of words or phrases grouped together because their meanings are in some way related.

Multiple choice question: A question or an incomplete statement accompanied by a series of two to four choices, one of which correctly answers the question or completes the statement.

Question: A sentence in interrogative form whose purpose is to elicit an answer.

Word Consciousness in Practice: Illustrations from a Fourth-Grade Teacher's Classroom

Tatiana F. Miller
Ondine Gage-Serio
Judith A. Scott
University of California, Santa Cruz

This case study evolved out of the VINE project (*Vocabulary Innovations in Education*), a three-year study that explored vocabulary learning and teaching through word consciousness in fourth- and fifth-grade highly diverse classrooms. The VINE project sought to help teachers develop their own word consciousness and foster similar dispositions in their students, while at the same time providing opportunities for researchers to learn how teachers translate ideas from research into practice. Word consciousness is a generative approach to word learning. Instead of teaching selected words or word lists, teachers help students develop the capacity and desire to examine words in ways that draw on their existing word knowledge and transfer their learning to new words (Scott & Nagy, 2004). Word consciousness involves being reflective about the meanings and usages of words and phrases, using metalinguistic knowledge, being metacognitively aware of one's own processes for learning words, and enjoying word learning. The VINE intervention aimed to enhance student vocabulary knowledge, writing, and reading comprehension, particularly for English learners (ELs) and students who are traditionally underserved in schools, by raising teachers' word consciousness.

In this paper, we present a case study documenting how the VINE intervention impacted one teacher and his students, comparing his dispositions and practices from his year as a control teacher with those he developed in the following two years when he participated in the VINE professional development community. Analyses of interview and classroom observation data illustrate this teacher's development of word consciousness and instructional approaches used to foster word consciousness in students.

BACKGROUND AND RATIONALE

Vocabulary knowledge is critical to students' literacy development and reading comprehension and, in turn, their academic success in schools (NICHD, 2000; RAND, 2002). It becomes particularly important in upper-elementary grades when instructional goals involve reading to learn content using texts that typically contain unfamiliar, domain-specific vocabulary (Lapp, Flood, & Ranck-Buhr, 1995). For instance, Nagy & Anderson (1984) have estimated that students can encounter 88,533 different word families in texts in grades 3 through 9. It is therefore not surprising that vocabulary knowledge appears to be related to school success (Nagy & Herman, 1987) and is important for demonstrating growth and proficiency in academic arenas (Schleppegrell, 2004). One would be hard pressed to find any aspect of learning or assessment in schools that is not affected by, or dependent upon, understanding vocabulary.

Fostering students' word knowledge through instruction is vital for advancing students' academic achievement, since the type of vocabulary and discourse commonly found in school differs considerably from everyday vocabulary used in conversation (Gee, 2008; Scott, Nagy, & Flinspach, 2008; Snow, 2008). While important for all students, vocabulary instruction seems particularly important for those whose heritage or native language differs from English (Schleppegrell, 2004; Snow & Kim, 2007). Unfortunately, studies have shown that little time is devoted to vocabulary instruction, and teaching practices are often inadequate, lacking depth and substance (Baumann & Kame'enui, 1991; Scott, Jamieson-Noel & Asselin, 2003).

Anderson and Nagy (1992) were among the first to argue for a shift away from teaching particular sets of words towards generative approaches to word learning through the development of students' word consciousness. These approaches include playful encounters with words that arouse curiosity and interest in learning and using words, and the development of knowledge and dispositions for learning how word parts contribute to their meanings. Anderson and Nagy (1992) envision students exploring relationships in word families and developing a deep understanding and appreciation for words, through both formal lessons and teachable moments. Expanding on this theme, Scott (2004) advocates instruction which fosters word consciousness and argues that the development of word consciousness is fundamental to the process of accelerating vocabulary learning for students who depend on schools for acquiring academic language. She recommends integrating word consciousness throughout the curriculum to develop students' control over language use and their ability to negotiate the social language of schooling. Other researchers have also turned their attention to helping students become capable learners of words through metacognitive and metalinguistic awareness (Blachowicz, Fisher, Ogle, & Watts-Taffe, 2006; Bouleware-Gooden, et al., 2007; Graves, 2009; Lubliner & Smetana, 2005), through multifaceted curricular approaches taught by "real teachers" that explore how to cultivate students' knowledge and dispositions for becoming motivated, self-efficacious learners of words.

There is growing recognition of the potential for word consciousness to inform instructional approaches (Bauman & Kame'enui, 2004; Graves & Watts-Taffe, 2008; RAND, 2002; Wagner, Muse & Tannenbaum, 2007). The RAND report (2002) acknowledges that aspects of word consciousness are related to strategies for independent word learning, such as morphological awareness, generative knowledge of word schemas to infer meanings of unknown words, and awareness of cognate relationships between languages. However, research on word consciousness is relatively new, with several sources, including the RAND report (2002), calling for further study of its components, their interaction, and their relationship to other aspects of literacy development. The VINE project represents an effort to address this gap in knowledge. The contribution of this case study, in particular, is to examine how one teacher responded to VINE professional development designed both to raise his own word consciousness and to help him develop word consciousness in his students. This study explores the links between growth in the teacher's word consciousness and his changing teaching practices.

METHODS

Participants and Context

In the first year of the VINE Project, 2006–2007, 13 teachers were randomly assigned to either "control" or "intervention" groups. Control teachers allowed VINE researchers to study their class, but did not participate in professional development activities. Intervention teachers, on the other hand, met together with researchers throughout the school year. This group learned about word consciousness and vocabulary instruction from the researchers and from each other, and began to forge the VINE community. Using a staggered-entry design, initial control teachers later became intervention teachers, joining the first group of intervention teachers and researchers at the regular VINE meetings in the second year. This expanded VINE community continued to meet and work together through the third year of the study. The teacher described in this paper was a control teacher in the first year and an intervention teacher in subsequent years.

Buzz[1] is a fourth-grade teacher at Seaside Elementary[2], a K-5 public school located in a small city in coastal California. With over 18 years of teaching experience, Buzz has an active interest in research. He teaches from a sociocultural perspective, often integrating subject matter from a number of content areas into the design of his innovative, project-based curricula. In an interview held at the end of the first year as a control teacher, Buzz explained that his motivation for joining the study involved his search for a better vocabulary program that "should be part of every day, and just about everything." He had never found a program that he liked, and was frustrated that his vocabulary curriculum, whether purchased or original, wasn't meaningful to his students. He observed that his students often forget to use such words in their writing, and he regarded vocabulary teaching as "daunting," and teaching words one-by-one as "futile."

During Buzz's three years in the VINE Project, enrollment in his fourth-grade class ranged from 28 students in 2006-2007 to 26 students in 2007-2008 and 2008-2009. Seaside Elementary supports, through Title 1 funding, a considerable number of students who are either low-performing or who come from low-income backgrounds (in 2007-2008, 70.6% of students received free or reduced-price lunch[3]). The school also enrolls a large number of ELs, particularly children from Spanish-speaking homes. In the 2007-2008 school year, 57% of the students were designated ELs. Seaside entered year one of "Program Improvement" status for not meeting yearly growth targets in 2005-2006, a designation that Buzz felt created pressure for replacing integrated thematic instruction with district-adopted programs.

Buzz's participation in VINE professional development activities took place in his second and third years, the intervention years. When the first group of VINE control teachers became VINE intervention teachers, they joined the already existing group of randomly selected intervention teachers in professional development activities that focused on word consciousness. In early fall of the second year, they participated in a 1.5-day institute to introduce them to the concept of word consciousness, to develop a learning community with researchers and other VINE intervention teachers, and to engage in discussions and activities that could impact their classroom practice. Then they were asked to integrate word consciousness into their instruction in all subject areas throughout the rest of the year. This process was repeated in year 3 with a 2-day institute in the fall. The VINE intervention group came together at six-week intervals (approximately) as a "community of learners," in which both teachers and researchers co-constructed their understanding of word consciousness, and ways to foster metacognitive awareness about words in their classrooms.

All participants contributed their own expertise and knowledge to the discussion. Both teachers and researchers were active participants in and contributors to the discussions, sharing ideas and questions that centered on developing students' affinity for word learning. As Buzz puts it:

"…it was like a collaboration of equals, really. I felt like what I had to contribute was just as important as anybody else…I'm not afraid to share stuff that I've done …in the classroom here because it's a pretty safe environment to be in."

Data Sources

Throughout the project, the VINE researchers collected quantitative and qualitative data from both intervention and control teachers' classrooms. In this study, one researcher (the first author) was in Buzz's classroom frequently over the three years, videotaping 10 full school days, collecting data and conducting interviews. As she was also a fourth-grade teacher in Buzz's school district, they developed a collegial relationship, and often discussed Buzz's teaching philosophy, style, and practices. The primary data for this analysis includes transcripts of semi-structured, open-ended interviews conducted with Buzz at the end of each of the three years he participated in the project (see Appendix for interview protocols). Video and field notes from classroom observations were also analyzed. In the first year of the study, we collected video in the fall and spring with field notes from all teacher participants (intervention and control) for one full day. In the subsequent year, we recruited three "case study teachers" who were willing to be videotaped 4-6 times throughout each year for the remainder of the project and who represented different geographic areas. Buzz volunteered and was accepted as one of these case study teachers. His was the first case study analyzed because we had a greater amount of data on his practice and he had served as both a control and an intervention teacher.

Analysis

Interview transcripts were first analyzed for evidence of coding categories that aligned with the goals, hypotheses, and theoretical framework guiding the VINE project. These were generative categories that created affordances for identifying additional, emergent coding categories and patterns within them. Generative categories initially coded included: 'teacher's views of vocabulary teaching and learning,' 'examples of teaching practice,' and 'teacher's theory of word consciousness.' Sub-coding within these overarching categories allowed us to identify additional categories and patterns. For example, under the category 'views of vocabulary teaching and learning,' we added 'attitudes towards formal vocabulary lessons and word-level instruction,' 'awareness, and use of teachable moments in vocabulary instruction,' and 'an awareness of the teacher's or students sense of the affective nature of word learning' all of which emerged from the data. This approach to coding revealed patterns across the three years of interview data that provide a longitudinal comparison of the effects of participating in the VINE professional development. Responses and coding categories were examined for evidence of change in the teacher's understanding of word consciousness, and his conceptualization of classroom teaching practices that fostered students' word learning.

Once these patterns were identified in the interview data, additional analyses of classroom observations were conducted. In particular, when the teacher discussed in an interview something that was captured on videotape, these instances were located in the videotape and field notes were analyzed. These instances provide confirmatory evidence for the interview findings, provide qualitative illustrations of how his word consciousness developed over time, and how this development influenced his classroom practice. As this is a preliminary exploration of the data, we plan to carry out a full systematic analysis of the video in the future.

FINDINGS

Year One–The Control Year

In Buzz's year as a control teacher, he reported he had never heard of the term *word consciousness* before, but supposed it would include: (a) being conscious of words used while teaching, (b) assuming that students will not understand all of the vocabulary used by teachers, and (c) thinking about how to introduce words to students effectively. He explained that although he had never found a vocabulary program that he liked, he taught vocabulary and spelling once a week, in part to appease parents and to meet district expectations. He preferred to embed vocabulary instruction within his own curriculum. Rather than teaching arbitrary lists of words, he tailored instruction to meet students' individual needs, since they often "don't fit prepackaged programs." In discussing his own instruction, Buzz equated spelling with vocabulary lessons on several occasions, and observed that students did not use words from the district-adopted program in their unprompted writing. He viewed this as evidence supporting his assessment that testing students weekly on standard word lists was ineffective, as students didn't remember words after the test. A constant theme in Buzz's interviews across the three years was that he equated knowing a word with the ability to demonstrate its use in context.

During the first year, we found only one response for the category labeled "the affective domain of word learning," which relates to creating interest, curiosity, and a sense of enjoyment of word learning, and language play. After a videotaped observation of his class, Buzz commented that he "didn't really teach vocabulary today, as in a vocabulary lesson." But he went on to discuss how he had challenged a group of high EL students with an impromptu activity of solving anagrams. He commented that this was "a really good language development thing that keeps them motivated. If you only have ten minutes extra - let's do some anagrams, because I know you're going to like this and it's going to be good for you, and you're playing with words and all that." The videotape showed Buzz creating enthusiasm with comments like, "You'll never get this one." Playfully building more and more challenging anagrams, Buzz escalated the excitement by saying, "This is a UC [University of California] level [word]. You'll never get this." Feigning exasperation, he wrote down another exclaiming, "Now, PhD Level" to which the students asked, "What's that?" and Buzz answered, "It is as high as you can go!" In this game, the students were comfortable voicing their questions and were motivated by Buzz's playful challenge. It should be noted that no other evidence was found of teaching for metacognitive awareness of words in year one data.

Year Two–Participating in the VINE Community

In the second-year interview, Buzz exhibited a notable shift in his understanding of word consciousness, his thinking about teaching and learning vocabulary, and his incorporation of word consciousness into his practice. He described how, in addition to just being more conscious of the words he used, he actually found himself, while in the process of speaking to the class, changing the words he chose to use in order to communicate with more sophisticated language or with "good words they should know." He saw himself as more conscious of words he planned to use in designing curriculum and in lesson planning, thinking about words to introduce ahead of time, and relating learning to words that represent big ideas and concepts that he could return to frequently.

He also mentioned how he reached for the dictionary more often, looked for words students would understand, and that he was "looking at [his] word choice, hoping that they're going to pick up a lot more vocabulary, meaningful vocabulary. It's more specific language in some ways because I'm looking for words that really say what it is that I want to say." He began to see word consciousness as not only applying to his own conscious word choice and precision in meaning, but as transferring to students' vocabulary development, their word choice, and word consciousness as well: "[Kids are] thinking about word choice, and I've heard kids talking and change a word they normally would use to a new one that they learned that really is more accurate. For example, somebody might say, well, when I write this I want it to be more short or to the point, oh, *succinct*, that's what it should be, more succinct. [They are] using that word."

In describing how his understanding of word consciousness changed during his first year as an intervention teacher, Buzz explained that he began to see word consciousness as a framework for planning lessons and designing curriculum in all content areas. He reflected on how conversations with the researcher who observed him teach had made him aware of his language use and pedagogical moves in practice, helping him teach to identify and make use of teachable moments:

> VINE doesn't really have a program that says, 'here's your word consciousness manual,' so I was just kind of going along, and when I thought OK, let me start really planning lessons thinking about vocabulary no matter what it is, math or anything else, [it] just got more specific, I guess—refined. I think it was the first time you came in to film me, and you said 'Wow, you use a lot of really good vocabulary.' I wasn't even aware of that, so I started thinking about all of the things I was saying and doing, and it's almost automatic now, as I'm speaking. Like today, I didn't have it planned to talk about transitions, but it came up as we were doing something, and I thought OK, this is the time to do a little thing on transitions. So that's how it's changed, it's all just right here now [points to head].

Buzz also emphasized that the changes he made in moving from implementing a packaged vocabulary program to creating opportunities to make vocabulary learning more meaningful for students were substantial. Because he already used themes as an organizing principle in his classroom, he found it "really cool" and enjoyable to integrate those principles with word consciousness, especially in introducing key words and concepts, as he was able to "keep drawing them back whenever you need them." This not only illustrates how Buzz's growing sense of word consciousness influenced his planning as well as his general teaching strategies in year two, it shows how he was developing an affective disposition towards vocabulary teaching:

> Last year, I didn't really know what we were doing, I was just kind of winging it and going along, and the first of this year kind of the same. But all the sudden something started to click, and when I started thinking about words, contexts, concepts, then it became really fun to try to put it all together... and I think the way I'm doing it now is a lot more meaningful.

Finally, though Buzz still reported that he rarely taught discrete lessons on vocabulary, he described how he began to engage students in analyzing vocabulary, language, word meanings, and purposes for using particular words as part of his core curriculum. This represents a departure from his previous orientation towards word-level lessons being a waste of time, although the type of word-level instruction and lessons he developed are quite different than those typically found in published programs. For example, one unit from year two integrated persuasive writing and health sciences as part of an anti-tobacco campaign. Students analyzed advertising with this challenge from Buzz, "Let's analyze the language they're using, so you know what it is when you see it. You know exactly what it is they're trying to do." He wanted students to be able to critically analyze and evaluate the word choice and vocabulary used in advertising. The students then used these understandings about persuasive writing and the power of word choice to create anti-tobacco posters and to write letters to companies and newspaper editors. As a way to gain insight into the power of persuasive writing, students analyzed the language and vocabulary words found in real estate ads. In the quote below, Buzz noted that the emphasis he placed on words created a difference in students' use of new words in their conversations and writing, as well as developing an awareness that they enjoyed word learning:

> It made a difference to be a part of the VINE team and always talking about this consciousness thing…It made a really big difference actually, because it just made it more meaningful to me …Kids like to be able to use new words, and they like to use big words and they like to use cool words… [For instance] *quintessential*, I saw [it] come up a lot of times in their writing, and then what was cool [was that] I was able to stop and say. 'OK a lot of you are using *quintessential*. It's great, however, something has to BE *quintessential*. It's just not one of those stand-alone words… It's the idea of 'Let's look at this one word and really think about how it can be used.' It's just kind of fun to do that, and it's kind of what we're about, thinking about using words.

Videotapes and field notes from classroom observations in year two confirm Buzz's observations that students became more aware of the power of words as critical consumers and producers of advertising. When Buzz introduced the task of reviewing newspaper real estate ads for descriptive vocabulary, he asked the children to define *persuade*. He then led them through a scavenger hunt task to "find words that excite… Here's what advertisers do. See if you can tell what words excite people." As students worked collaboratively to post words on a giant semantic map on the board labeled: "Real Estate Words: How to Excite, " Buzz circulated among groups pointing out the word *gorgeous* to one student, and *exceptional value, spectacular, privacy,* and *spacious* to others. He then read off a list of words compiled by two girls adding, "We'll have to look some of these up… *Incredibly meticulous*, that one you want to circle, what does this word mean *quintessential?*" He challenged students to pick out which words excite interest in readers. In these activities, the students encountered all sorts of new vocabulary which they incorporated organically into subsequent tasks, rather than generating the lamented weekly spelling list. As Buzz noted, sometimes words such as "quintessential" required later refining. Nonetheless, it was obvious that the students attained a sense of the word from context and an awareness of its functions in writing and speech. These activities allowed students to make productive use of this new vocabulary in a relatively risk-free environment. Such experimentation provided students opportunities to discuss and later refine their knowledge.

Year Three–Further Developing Word Consciousness in Theory and Practice

By the end of year three, Buzz's understanding of word consciousness led to a deeper understanding of its underlying pedagogical framework, which influenced all aspects of his teaching. He moved beyond the themes that came out strongly in his year two interview, to a conception of word consciousness that included a "different perspective, a kind of a viewpoint looking at everything I do in terms of vocabulary…, and a way of relating to kids with that." Rather than focusing primarily on developing students' word choice, by the third year Buzz demonstrated awareness that an overarching theme of word consciousness was the development of a disposition that pays attention to words and their nuances. Buzz's instructional goals now included not only developing students' word choice, understanding, and use of vocabulary, but also fostering a disposition towards language and communication that included an interest in and a curiosity about words. While the curriculum he designed and implemented in year two on persuasive advertising and the power of words may have achieved this goal, in year three he showed a metacognitive awareness of how students' interest in the nuances of language and curiosity about the meanings and uses of words play a prominent role in word consciousness. The importance of this affective aspect surfaced for the first time in his third year interview:

> Games, to me that's a kind of a superficial way of looking at word consciousness. That's going to like "make it and take it" and here are some games that I've learned and I'm going to come back and all of the sudden I'm going to be more word conscious and so are my students. That's not the way I look at it. For me, it's just a way of looking at working with students and communicating with students that's different than I used to [do]. By really paying attention to all of the nuances of the word that you used, and having *them* eventually be that way also… doing things with word play or things where you really have an interest and a curiosity about words and more thought to it.

This attitude is also evident in a videotaped lesson where Buzz uses a photograph by Dorothea Lange of Florence Owens Thompson from the dustbowl era entitled *Migrant Mother*. Using a chart with column headings for parts of speech, Buzz invited students to describe the expression on Florence's face, creating a semantic word map on the board while also discussing nuances of the words students provided and identifying their syntactic form (e.g., adjectives included *impoverished, unhappy, poor* and *depressed*). He then asked the children, "What is she doing?" "Living a bad life" responded one child. Buzz read what they had constructed so far, "Depressed migrant mother is living a bad life" and elicited a prepositional phrase, "Where?" "In a pea pickers' camp" replied the students. When a child described her as "*worthless*," Buzz explained that she isn't *worthless* but that she may look like she feels that way. Then the students' created their own sentences describing the picture, identifying parts of speech in the process.

> I do spend more time thinking about how to integrate [word consciousness] into everything else that I'm doing, and all the different, as you referred to it, shades of meaning for words and I'm a lot more comfortable playing with that now. For example the Florence Thompson thing, and the words came out, *despair*, and *despondent* and all of that. I think that I can hold their attention and their interest playing around with that more than I used to be able to, just because I can make it interesting and meaningful to them to have an interest in really figuring out what would be really good words to describe the look on her face, for example.

In Buzz's third year he reported spending much more time thinking about how to integrate vocabulary into every aspect of his practice than he had in previous years. He also perceived himself as having a greater awareness of and capability for recognizing opportunities for word-level instruction and spontaneous teaching occasions in the moment, a process he saw as becoming more integrated into his teaching. In general, he valued time spent on teachable moments and used them to make pedagogical moves that supported word-level learning. As he said, "I just think my awareness is greater than it was before, that I can find more of those opportunities... easily ...so I think I'm better at it." When asked if he spent more time in general on vocabulary instruction, he responded:

> If I compare what I do now in terms of time on vocabulary compared to what I used to, probably yes. Well, I'll admit I used to do spelling tests and all that stuff a long time ago, but in a different way now. I spend more time, because I spend more time thinking about it, and I spend more time when it comes up, like today...

Buzz demonstrated a willingness to go in depth to facilitate students' understanding of vocabulary, particularly because he recognizes that "you can't assume kids know the meaning of any words. Like we said you can use words but really not know what they mean, just know that they fit in this context, just throw that in, and nobody ever questions that really, so it's just a perspective, and a way of looking at words and relating to kids with that." Specifically, he recognized that preliminary processes of word learning included risk taking with words where children might intuitively fit a word in context but not really understand its meaning. He was aware that facilitating word learning includes noticing a child's tangential understanding of a word and engaging them in a discussion that goes beyond its preliminary application to noticing the word and its precise usage in a particular context. In developing his own awareness of word consciousness, he became more attuned to the depth of understanding his students demonstrated and more aware of the incremental processes in word learning.

Buzz described how word consciousness came to life in his classroom, with students engaged in conversations about words, which he believes makes learning words more meaningful and "makes them want to use those words." Buzz saw his own developing word consciousness as influencing his practice, in turn supporting students' affective disposition towards word learning. He noted, for instance, that he was more playful in his conversations with students, and that he really enjoyed this because he realized that, "There's actually some really good learning going on during those moments that I never felt when I would give a [vocabulary word] list out. I always felt like, "Well I don't think this is worth anything but that's the way everybody does it and it's what parents want often, so, it's a waste of time, but here's an hour I'm going to waste of your time giving you this," So I never felt really good about it, now I do."

DISCUSSION

While there is much more data to mine from our observations and interviews with Buzz, this case study captures some of the changes that occurred in his disposition and practice as a result of his participation in the VINE intervention. Given that Buzz was an accomplished teacher with 18 years of experience, who had a strong sense of identity as a culturally responsive teacher, his complete turnaround from a dislike of vocabulary programs to "looking at everything [he does] in terms of vocabulary," is profound. These data from end-of-year interviews and videotapes illustrate how far this teacher changed in his practice regarding vocabulary instruction as a result of his involvement in two years of professional development in a collaborative community that focused on word consciousness.

Understanding of Word Consciousness

There is a growing sophistication in Buzz's interpretation of word consciousness and the vocabulary goals he held for both himself and his students. In the first year, he assumed that word consciousness included an awareness of words used while teaching; however, he was frustrated with programs provided by the district because he wanted to help students understand and remember words well enough to use them. He saw formal vocabulary instruction (which he equated with traditional spelling lessons and word lists) as a waste of time. While dissatisfied with his vocabulary instruction, he seemed unsure how to implement practices aligned with his social constructivist teaching philosophy. The only example of formal word-level instruction we observed in the videos involved an anagrams activity used as an impromptu time filler.

At the end of his first intervention year, Buzz had begun to develop a working theory of word consciousness that included substantially different goals for *both* himself and his students. He became more aware that his deliberate, selective attention to precise word choice in planning and while teaching could transfer to students' word choice and vocabulary development. He began to engage students in looking intently at a word in context and analyzing how it could be used. Not only were Buzz's views towards word-level instruction changing, he began to find evidence of students using key vocabulary words that he introduced in his curriculum, supporting his theory that his own focus on word choice was transferring to his students' word choices.

In his final year interview, Buzz's theory of word consciousness changed from focusing almost entirely on the role word choice plays in meaning to seeing word consciousness as a lens for teaching and learning. He articulated his enhanced goals for his students as he described how his own word consciousness provided him a framework and communication style. Modeling this practice for students would foster a similar meta-awareness and disposition towards the nuances of language and its use in his students. Addressing formal word-level instruction, he explained that he now spent more time thinking about how to integrate vocabulary into everything, providing numerous examples of word-level instruction. Ultimately, he saw paying attention to the uses of words with students and "having students eventually be that way" as a goal of developing his and his students' word consciousness. He recalled "aha" moments as he watched students actively engaged in using words, figuring out meaning and analyzing usage. He noted times during direct instruction when "students say something that makes him believe that they finally, really understand words they didn't know before."

Affective Dimension of Word Consciousness

Buzz began to see how word-level lessons and learning could be fun, playful, and "feel good" while "good learning is going on." He talked about making students interested in learning words, making learning words meaningful, motivating students to want to use and understand words and their contexts, and in these ways fostering their desire, intention, and motivation for learning words. This stands in stark contrast to the first year, in which no mention was made of fostering students' enjoyment, curiosity, or interest in learning words, let alone problem solving, understanding, or discussing word meanings. Students were motivated in their use of games that were engaging, but this was not seen as related to word meanings or the core curriculum.

In year two Buzz commented more frequently on his own enjoyment of teaching vocabulary, particularly in applying word consciousness to thematic instruction. He also attempted to develop student activities that made analyzing language game-like and challenging. In his interview responses at the end of year two, it is clear that Buzz attempted to cultivate fun in the curriculum he developed. However, he didn't explicitly incorporate the affective domain of word consciousness into the goals and outcomes for his instruction or student learning. While he was aware that students enjoy using new words, his efforts at creating fun, interest, and enjoyment centered around developing a fun or interesting context for students to use words within the curriculum rather than focusing on an interest or curiosity about words themselves.

While in year one the affective domain of word learning was absent in his articulated goals for instruction, and in year two were specific to providing a motivating context for learning in the curriculum, by the end of year three he characterized being curious, interested, and having fun as intrinsic to the processes of learning about words themselves and their meaning. Furthermore, he articulated how learning new words contributed to students' positive self-esteem as their confidence and capability grew in learning how to learn new words. Thus, by the end of year three, the affective domain of word consciousness played an integral role in his theoretical understanding of word consciousness, his goals for himself and his students, and his practice.

CONCLUSION

Research indicates that changing teacher attitudes and practices is not an easy task (Hammerness, Darling-Hammond, & Bransford, 2005). However, this study demonstrates that these did indeed change for Buzz over the two years he participated in the VINE Project. While more comprehensive analyses of teacher videotapes, interviews, and journals are still needed, we believe that the changes Buzz exhibited are not atypical for the VINE intervention teacher group. All of these teachers implemented word conscious activities in their classrooms and we were able to observe their enthusiasm as well as that of their students. Discussions of word consciousness at VINE meetings made teachers feel "recharged and more pumped up regarding word consciousness."(Journal entry March 7, 2008). A case study of another VINE intervention teacher shows similar growth, going from an interview in a previous year where she wanted to set aside dedicated time for studying vocabulary to an understanding that her "goal is to help the kids realize that 'vocabulary' doesn't mean 8:15-8:30; it means looking out for cool words no matter where you are or what you are doing" (Zeamer, Flinspach, & Scott, in preparation).

Student performance on a vocabulary test provides an additional source of evidence of the effects of the VINE project. Students in the intervention classrooms made significant growth when compared to students in the control classrooms, and the effort was particularly strong for those who were classified as English learners (Scott, Flinspach, Miller, Vevea, & Gage-Serio, 2009). A preliminary analysis of these data suggests that Buzz's students' performance on these vocabulary outcomes is similar to the growth made by the intervention group as a whole.

In this case study, we have presented an in-depth exploration of one teacher's practice and growth in understanding word consciousness by participating in a professional development program in which teachers met as a collaborative group with researchers for approximately 30 hours each year. This intervention influenced the pedagogical ideas and practices of a veteran teacher. We found there were changes in both his attitude toward vocabulary learning, and his everyday interactions with students, indicating that professional development through the collaborative community in the VINE project created a context that allowed this change to occur. With the emergence of word consciousness as an important area of vocabulary research, this case study points in a potentially powerful direction for both sudent and teacher growth.

REFERENCES

Anderson, R. C., & Nagy, W. E. (1992). The vocabulary conundrum. *American Educator 16*(3),14-18.

Baumann, J. F., & Kame'enui, E. J. (1991). Research on vocabulary: Ode to Voltaire. In J. Flood, J. Jensen, D. Lapp, & J. Squire (Eds.), *Handbook of research on teaching the English language arts* (pp. 604-632). New York, NY: Macmillan.

Bouleware-Gooden, R., Carreker, S., Thornhill, A., & Joshi, R. M. (2007). Instruction of metacognitive strategies enhances reading comprehension and vocabulary achievement of third-grade students. *The Reading Teacher, 61*(1), 70-77.

Blachowicz, C. L. Z., Fisher, P. J. L., Ogle, D., & Watts-Taffe, S. (2006). Theory and Research into Practice: Vocabulary: Questions from the Classroom. *Reading Research Quarterly, 41*(4), 524-539.

Gee, J. P. (2008). What is academic language? In A. S. Rosebery & B. Warren (Eds.), *Teaching Science to English Language Learners: Building on students' strengths* (pp. 57-70). Arlington, VA: National Science Teachers Association.

Graves, M. F., & Watts-Taffe, S. (2008). For the love of words: Fostering word consciousness in young readers. *The Reading Teacher, 62*(3), 185-193.

Graves, M. F. (2009). *Essential Readings in Vocabulary Instruction.* Newark, DE: International Reading Association.

Hammerness, K., Darling-Hammond, L., Bransford, J., with Berliner, D., Cochran-Smith, M., McDonald, M. (2005). How teachers learn and develop. In L. Darling-Hammond & J. Bransford (Eds.), *Preparing Teachers for a Changing World* (pp. 358-389). San Francisco, CA: Jossey-Bass.

Lapp, D., Flood, J., & Ranck-Buhr, W. (1995). Using multiple text formats to explore scientific phenomena in middle school classrooms. *Reading & Writing Quarterly, 11*(2), 173-186.

Lubliner, S., & Smetana, L. (2005). The effects of comprehensive vocabulary instruction in Title I students' metacognitive word-learning skills and reading comprehension. *Journal of Literacy Research, 37*(2), 163-200.

McKeown, M., Beck, I., Omanson, R., & Pople, M. (1985). Some effects of the nature and frequency of vocabulary instruction on the knowledge and use of words. *Reading Research Quarterly, 20*, 522-535.

Nagy, W. E., & Anderson, R. C. (1984). How many words are there in printed school English? *Reading Research Quarterly, 19*, 303-330.

Nagy, W., & Herman, P. (1987). Breadth and depth of vocabulary knowledge: Implications for acquisition and instruction. In M. G. McKeown & M. E. Curtis (Eds.), *The nature of vocabulary acquisition* (pp. 19-36). Hillsdale, NJ: Erlbaum.

National Institute of Child Health and Human Development. (2000). *Report of the National Reading Panel: Teaching children to read* (NIH Publication No. 00-4754). Washington, D.C.: U.S. Government Printing Office.

RAND Reading Study Group. (2002). Reading for understanding: Toward a research and development program in reading comprehension. Washington, DC: U.S. Department of Education.

Schleppegrell, M. J. (2004). *The Language of Schooling.* Mahwah, NJ: Lawrence Erlbaum Associates.

Scott, J. A. (2004). Scaffolding vocabulary learning: Ideas for equity in urban settings. In D. Lapp, C. Block, J. Cooper, J. Flood, N. Roser, & J. Tinajero (Eds.), *Teaching all the children: Strategies for developing literacy in an urban setting* (pp. 275-293). New York, NY: Guilford Press.

Scott, J. A., Flinspach, S. L., Miller, T. F., Vevea, J. L., & Gage-Serio, O. (2009). Vocabulary growth over time: Results of a multiple level vocabulary assessment based on grade level materials. Presented at the annual meeting of the National Reading Conference, Albuquerque, NM.

Scott, J. A., Jamieson-Noel, D., & Asselin, M. (2003). Vocabulary instruction throughout the day in twenty-three Canadian upper elementary classrooms. *Elementary School Journal, 103*(3), 269-286.

Scott, J. A., & Nagy, W. E. (2004). Developing word consciousness. In J. Baumann & E. Kame'enui (Eds.), *Vocabulary instruction: From research to practice* (pp. 201-217). New York, NY: Guilford Press.

Scott, J., Nagy, B., & Flinspach, S. (2008). More than merely words: Redefining vocabulary learning in a culturally and linguistically diverse society. In A. Farstrup & J. Samuels (Eds.). *What Research Has to Say About Vocabulary Instruction.* (pp.182-210) Newark, DE: International Reading Association.

Snow, C. E., & Kim, Y. S. (2007). Large problem spaces: The challenge of vocabulary for English language learners. In R. K. Wagner, A. E. Muse, & K. R. Tannenbaum (Eds.), *Vocabulary Acquisition: Implications for reading comprehension* (pp. 123-139). New York, NY: Guilford Press.

Snow, C. (2008). What is the vocabulary of science? In A. S. Rosebery & B. M. Warren (Eds.), *Teaching Science to English Language Learners: Building on students' strengths* (pp. 71-84). Arlington, VA: National Science Teachers Association Press.

Wagner, R. K., Muse, A. E., & Tannenbaum, K. R. (2007). Vocabulary acquisition: Implications for reading comprehension. New York, NY: Guilford Press.

Zeamer, C., Flinspach, S. L., & Scott, J. A. (in preparation). Reaping more than we sow: Focusing on teacher development in the VINE project. Will be available at: http://vineproject.ucsc.edu.

AUTHOR'S NOTE

The VINE Project was funded by IES Reading and Writing Education Research Grant Program #R305G060140 (U.S. Department of Education), FY2006-2009. This paper is the sole responsibility of the authors and does not necessarily reflect the opinions of the U.S. Department of Education. Correspondence should be addressed to the authors at the Education Department of the University of California Santa Cruz, 1156 High Street, Santa Cruz, CA 95064.

APPENDIX

Year One Questions–Both Intervention and Control Teacher Interviews

1. How typical was today in terms of how you go about teaching vocabulary?

   • [If no examples given from the day] Could you please give me an example or two?

   • [If no evaluation of their teaching is given] How successful do you think your vocabulary instruction was today?

2. What do you believe are the ways students learn new words or vocabulary?

3. What do you think are the best ways to teach vocabulary to students?

   • [If not clear from their response] What strategies have you found to be most effective?

4. Which strategies for teaching vocabulary do you think work particularly well with English learners?

5. [Skip if already covered] I'm now going to ask you about one particular strategy for teaching vocabulary to English learners—cognates. As you probably know, cognates are pairs of words in two different languages that are similar in meaning, form, and pronunciation because both members of the pair are derived from a common root in an ancestor language. An example is "pilot" in English and "piloto" in Spanish.

Do you use cognates to help your English learners master new vocabulary in English?

- [If so] How you do this.

- [If so, examples given?]

6. The VINE team tends to use the phrase "word consciousness" a lot when we talk about vocabulary instruction, yet we don't really know what, if anything, teachers understand when we use it. "Word consciousness" might be just jargon to you, or you may have a clear definition of the phrase. So, do you think you could describe "word consciousness" to another fourth-grade teacher?

- [If some sort of affirmative response] Then how would you describe "word consciousness" to your colleague?

- [If not] That is helpful for us to know. [Skip to question 9.]

7. Has your understanding of word consciousness influenced your teaching practice this year?

- [If some sort of affirmative response] How has it affected your practice?

- [If not, then skip to question 9.]

8. When teaching writing, do you try to help your students become more word conscious?

- [If so] Please explain.

9. In what ways was your vocabulary teaching today similar to, or different from, how you taught vocabulary at the beginning of the school year?

- [If the teacher mentions differences, then ask:] What influenced the change(s) you mentioned?

- [Ask probing questions]

10. Which resources have been most helpful to you in developing students' vocabularies?

- [If not addressed] Have any been helpful in developing the vocabularies of your English learners?

11. That's all. Is there anything else you'd like to add?

Year Two Questions—Intervention Teacher Interview

1. How would you describe "word consciousness" to another fourth-grade teacher?

- How would this look in a classroom?

2. Has your understanding of word consciousness changed this year? [Please explain.]

3. Tell me about the word consciousness activities that your students did this year. First, let's make a list of the word consciousness activities, and then you can tell me about each activity on the list.

- [Interviewer jots down all activities mentioned as a list. If interviewee makes no mention of teaching word consciousness during writing, ask specifically if there are writing activities to add to the list before continuing.]

[Go over each listed activity. Start discussion of each with something broad like, "Tell me about this one." For each activity, try hard to get all the following information:]

- [what?] What (exactly) was done?

- [purpose?] What was the purpose of this activity?

- [when?, frequency] When first tried? Done more than once? How frequently?
- [who?] (Typically) who was involved/who participated most? ELs' contribution? (If activity was repeated or continued over time, did more students participate later?)
- [outcome?] What did students learn? How do you know what they learned (evidence)?
- [word consciousness?] How does interviewee link this activity to word consciousness?
- [VINE] VINE influence? If so, in what ways did VINE influence this?

4. [ASK ONLY IF "cognates" WAS NOT one of the listed activities in question 3]

    Did you try Spanish-English cognates to help your English learners with vocabulary?
    - If so, how? [If no mention of VINE, ask if and how VINE influenced this.]

5. Which resources have been most helpful to you in developing students' vocabularies?
    - [If not addressed] Have any been helpful in developing the vocabularies of your English learners?

6. That's all. We've scheduled a retreat for all VINE intervention teachers on the weekend starting Friday, September 5th, and continuing through Sunday morning, Sept. 7th. Please mark your calendar now to save those dates for VINE. Is there anything else you'd like to add?

Year Three Questions–Intervention Teacher Interview

1. In reflecting back on your time as an intervention teacher in VINE, can you say how this Project has impacted your teaching?
    - [If interviewing a teacher who has previously been in the VINE Project as an intervention teacher the previous year]

    Is there anything special about the impact of the VINE Project on your teaching this year?
    - Do you spend more time teaching vocabulary/word consciousness now than before VINE?
    - When you've seen word consciousness come to life in your classroom, what kinds of things have worked well?
    - Have you adapted any word-consciousness strategies that have worked well?
    - Has your playfulness or enjoyment of words grown since joining the VINE intervention?
    - How has your playfulness or enjoyment of words influenced your teaching?

2. Have you noticed a change in the way your students approach reading, writing, or speaking since you introduced word consciousness into your classroom?
    - Do you attribute any of these changes to the students' growth in word consciousness?
    - Have you noticed any particular changes in your EL students?

3. What has been the biggest "Ah-ha!" moment about word learning for you?
    - Have you witnessed any "Ah-ha!" moments for your students?

4. I'm going to ask you about word consciousness and your teaching of ELs in specific ways. But first I'd like to know if, in general, introducing word consciousness to your class has influenced your teaching of ELs?

[If not mentioned] Did you teach about Spanish-English cognates?
[Probe about the following as time permits.]
[If not mentioned] Did you teach your ELs about Latin roots of English words?
[If not mentioned] Did you teach your ELs about word parts?
[If not mentioned] Did you teach your ELs about idioms?
[If not mentioned] Did you teach your ELs about the function of words and word parts in sentences?

5. How has VINE been different or similar to past professional development programs that you've participated in?

• What are VINE's strengths?

• What would you change if you were in charge of VINE?

FOOTNOTES

[1]The teacher wishes his name be used and that he be referred to as his colleagues and students refer to him.

[2]Pseudonyms are used to protect the privacy of participants.

[3]Source for this and all following school demographic information reported: School Profile, Education-Data Partnership, California Department of Education (2008).

Rare Words in Students' Writing
as a Measure of Vocabulary

Susan Leigh Flinspach
Judith A. Scott
University of California, Santa Cruz

Jack L. Vevea
University of California, Merced

> Knowing a word means knowing not only the meaning, but knowing the contexts
> in which that word is used; it means knowing related words and ideas; it means
> knowing when and where to use the word. Therefore, to assess word knowledge,
> we need to consider the behaviors and actions that demonstrate what it means to
> know a word (Harmon, Hedrick, Soares, & Gress, 2007, p. 138).

Assessing word knowledge through examination of the full scope of behaviors and actions that demonstrate what it means to know a word, as suggested by Harmon et al. (2007), sounds reasonable, but it is ambitious. Most assessments range from tasks asking students to identify a synonym or a definition for a decontextualized word to vocabulary items embedded in tests of reading skills (Pearson, Hiebert, & Kamil, 2007; Read, 2000). Taking the latter approach, for example, the National Assessment of Educational Progress (NAEP) recently developed items that produce reliable and valid vocabulary measures by functioning "…both as a measure of passage comprehension and as a test of readers' specific knowledge of the word's meaning as intended by the passage author" (National Assessment Governing Board, 2008, p. iv). Built on years of research documenting the strong link between vocabulary and reading comprehension (Davis, 1942; Freebody & Anderson, 1983; Just & Carpenter, 1987; National Institute of Child Health and Human Development, 2000; Whipple, 1925), the new NAEP assessment represents a leap forward in the study of what it means to know a word through the vocabulary-reading nexus.

Encouraging as recent progress has been, there are still gaps in the field of vocabulary assessment. Writing, for example, is an action or behavior that can demonstrate what it means to know a word, yet student writing is rarely considered a medium for the study of vocabulary. When scholars examine the words in students' writing, typically their purpose has been to assess the quality of the writing rather than the child's word knowledge. Word choice and word usage are important in the writing process (Culhan, 2003; Fletcher, 1993; Hayes & Ahrens, 1988; Samway, 2006), so not surprisingly, writing assessments draw on a variety of measures of word choice, word sequence, content words, number of words, word diversity, syllable length, word length, and word frequency (Deno, Marston, & Mirkin, 1982; Gansle, VanDerHeyden, Noell, Resetar, & Williams, 2006; Grobe, 1981; Olinghouse & Leaird, 2009). Despite their dependency on lexical attributes, these measures, and assessments based on them, reveal relatively little about students' vocabulary knowledge in the expressive dimension.

This paper makes an argument for studying vocabulary knowledge and growth through students' writing. It reviews the literature on vocabulary assessment both to provide a rationale for venturing into this relatively unmapped territory and to examine possible assessment tools. It then turns to one vocabulary assessment informed by this perspective—an analysis of the rare words in fourth-graders' personal narratives. A final section highlights the implications of this assessment for further study of elementary students' vocabulary in their written work.

LITERATURE REVIEW

Vocabulary Assessment and Word Learning in the Expressive Dimension

In their recent essay on vocabulary assessment, Pearson et al. (2007) criticize the vague use of the term "vocabulary" across distinct domains of words, across multiple text genres with varying vocabulary loads, and across the different dimensions of word learning needed to listen, speak, read, and write. The authors find that this undifferentiated notion of "vocabulary" leads to undifferentiated testing, which in turn fails to inform the educational community adequately about students' knowledge and skills, and about the relationship of prior knowledge, instruction, and skills such as comprehension to vocabulary learning. They recommend that the research agenda for the next decade pay greater attention to vocabulary distinctions, like the expressive versus receptive dimensions, and align assessments more specifically to reflect those distinctions (Pearson, et al., 2007, p. 294).

Current vocabulary assessments focus on the receptive dimensions of vocabulary (listening and reading), largely ignoring the expressive dimensions (speaking and writing) (Pearson, et al., 2007). Baumann, Kame'enui, and Ash note that "…expressive vocabulary requires a learner to know a word rather well before using it; not knowing a word is likely to result in the learner not using the word at all" (2003, p. 755). Thus testing the expressive dimension of vocabulary has the potential to inform researchers about how students master words by recalling and using them at will. In contrast, the word knowledge needed to complete receptive tasks varies in its demands; students can do some receptive vocabulary tasks without knowing the word at all by figuring out its meaning from the context (Baumann, et al., 2003). Consequently, current vocabulary assessments are limited in what they can say about the full trajectory of word learning.

Vocabulary scholars agree that "knowing a word" is not a binary variable; rather, word learning is a process. Several authors have suggested that word learning occurs along a continuum from "not knowing" to "knowing a word" (Beck, McCaslin, & McKeown, 1980; Carey, 1978; Clark, 1993; Kame'enui, Dixon, & Carnine, 1987; Stahl, 2003; Stahl & Nagy, 2006), and that correct word generation, production, or expression in speech and writing is evidence that a person is familiar with the meaning of the word.

> According to Beck et al. (1980) and Stahl, a word is really known when a child is able to retrieve that word from memory rapidly and use it correctly in an uninstructed context. This standard of knowing word meanings is akin to the standard we discussed earlier for expressive vocabulary (Baumann, et al., 2003, p. 756).

Receptive vocabulary assessments, especially in their current state, do not yield information about word learning near the end of this continuum.

With little information available about word learning and writing, those interested in expressive vocabulary assessment must look to studies of children's early word development as their point of departure. A review of that literature is beyond the scope of this paper, but it is important to include a few key ideas that may influence vocabulary use in writing. Bloom defines knowing the meaning of a word as having "1) a certain mental representation or concept 2) that is associated with a certain form" (2001, p. 17). So word learning can be viewed as a process of mapping a concept onto the right lexical form. The notion of "fast mapping" (Carey, 1978) explains a very efficient and rapid matching process that yields preliminary and tentative links between words and meanings in young children. Studies show that early word mapping is influenced by biological, psychological, and social factors, and that children tend to take new words as exemplars of taxonomies (Mayor & Plunkett, 2010), suggesting the importance of semantic relationships across words. Children's vocabularies grow incrementally; word knowledge tends to build gradually in complexity and completeness through additional exposures to a word and attempts to use it over time (Nagy & Scott, 2000). Word play and experimentation with words can demonstrate, and reinforce, the incremental nature of word learning (Bauman, Ware, & Edwards, 2007; Blachowicz & Fisher, 2004; Graves & Watts-Taffe, 2008; Scott, Skobel, & Wells, 2008).

Most vocabulary tests have been developed without reference to the nature of word learning (Scott, Hoover, Flinspach, & Vevea, 2008), yet Pearson et al. (2007) argue that incrementality should play a larger role in vocabulary assessment (p. 290). Scholars have studied incrementality through fairly discrete and decontextualized multiple-choice assessments that ask explicitly about, and test, levels of word knowledge (Dale, 1965; Paribakht & Wesche, 1997; Scott, et al., 2008) and that explore differing knowledge by varying the degree and type of contextualization across distractors and items on the same word (Stallman, Pearson, Nagy, Anderson, & Garcia, 1995). Although these instruments break new ground by incorporating the incremental aspect of word learning into assessments, they do not extend its study into the expressive dimension.

The literature assessing vocabulary instruction with measures derived from students' writing is piecemeal, but it can be divided into two approaches: 1) instruction explicitly designed to teach target words, and 2) instruction based on word-rich classrooms with word-conscious and word-learning strategies. In the first case, following instruction on target words, educators examine student writing for the frequency of the instructed words. Duin and Graves (1987), for instance, counted the number of target words in student essays both before and after instruction. Similarly, Papadopoulou (2007) compared a treatment group and a control group on the number of instructed words used in a story-writing exercise. Some teachers who teach target vocabulary in content areas like science and geography have examined vocabulary use in students' writing (notebooks, journals, and compositions) to evaluate knowledge and comprehension of the terms (Aschbacher & Alonzo, 2006; Gregg & Sekeres, 2006).

In a study of one word-rich classroom, Baumann and colleagues note that they integrated composition, and some assessment of the vocabulary embedded in writing, into their research plans to honor the teacher's belief in the importance of writing to literacy development (Baumann, Ware, & Edwards, 2007, p. 110). In this formative assessment, the pre- and post-test measures included parent and student questionnaires, a receptive assessment of listening vocabulary, the *Expressive Vocabulary Test* (Williams, 1997) to measure growth in spoken vocabulary, and, because of the ont_nameѕ?

teacher's beliefs about writing, the overall word count plus the number of low-frequency words used in students' writing samples. Their measures documented vocabulary growth using a comprehensive and strategy-driven approach to word learning.

Tools for Assessing Vocabulary Knowledge in Student Writing

Thanks to specialists in reading, speech, and writing, many word measures for use on texts currently exist. In the readability studies of the past century, researchers often counted the number of syllables per 100 words to determine the difficulty of reading passages (Stahl & Nagy, 2006). Many assessments of the quality of writing include the total number of words in the composition (Gansle, Noell, VanDerHeyden, Naquin, & Slider, 2002; Graham, Berninger, Abbott, Abbott, & Whitaker, 1997; Malecki & Jewell, 2003), and some employ measures based on the number of different words written (Gajar, 1989; Grobe, 1981; Morris & Crump, 1982; Olinghouse & Leaird, 2009) and on word size (Deno, et al., 1982; Gajar, 1989; Gansle, et al., 2002). As noted earlier, these measures have not been used to learn much about vocabulary or expressive vocabulary development.

The assessment goals of importance here include developing measures of students' growing familiarity with academic vocabulary in their writing and their ability to use such words expressively. Measures of curricular and instructional coverage, morphological complexity, word frequency, semantic networks, and conceptual difficulty would be promising measures for such assessments. Although researchers are working to capture some of these elements of word knowledge, measures of word frequency are readily available. Nagy and Hiebert (in press) caution that word frequency has, in the past, served as a proxy for word familiarity, conceptual difficulty, and other not-necessarily-related constructs because of its availability and ease of use. Hence word frequency may be a starting point for assessing vocabulary through writing, especially given the dearth of scholarly attention to the subject, but the field will be limited until a wider set of language and concept measures can be used.

Under the assumption that academic and literary words occur less frequently than other words in children's writing, word frequency measures can contribute to an understanding of expressive word learning. Word frequency has been measured in numerous ways, and the resources for constructing such measures are expanding rapidly. Early resources, generally lists of higher frequency words, include: Dale and O'Rourke's Living Word Vocabulary (Dale & O'Rourke, 1976); Finn's undistinguished word list (Finn, 1977); the Dale-Chall high-frequency list (Chall & Dale, 1995); and the Harris-Jacobson high-frequency list (Harrison, 1980). Several vocabulary researchers prefer the use of U values, a standardized measure of frequency per million words adjusted for variation in distribution, such as that found in the Educator's Word Frequency Guide (Zeno, Ivens, Millard, & Duvvuri, 1995). The U values allow researchers to compare the frequency of individual words or to set cut-off values that identify a set of frequent words or of rare words. Google and Wikipedia provide frequency information derived from online sources, and the Frequency Dictionary of American English is based on the prevalence of the words from the Corpus of Contemporary American English in several written genres and in speech (Davies & Gardner, 2010). Researchers who want to measure word frequency have options.

Unfortunately, there are problems associated with the use of word frequency. Stahl and Nagy (2006) note that word frequency measures distinguish neither idiomatic uses of words nor multiple meanings, so that, for example, "bear" meaning an animal, to carry, or to endure are conflated into one frequency. Often proper nouns are not differentiated from common nouns. Most frequency lists do not provide frequency values to help users understand differences among the words on the lists (Stahl & Nagy, 2006, pp. 19-20), although newer resources generally provide a frequency score for each word. The use of word frequency measures requires attention to these shortcomings.

Children's writing holds clues about their comprehension of words. Teachers can examine errors or experimentation in written work as indications of students' knowledge, and researchers could follow suit if they had the appropriate tools. Identifying and coding students' experimentation with language is not a vocabulary measure; however, the information gleaned from such coding may inform measure development for later assessments and provide insights about expressive word learning. It is included as part of the following rare-words assessment for that reason.

RARE WORDS IN FOURTH-GRADERS' PERSONAL NARRATIVES: A VOCABULARY ASSESSMENT

Based on personal narratives collected from fourth graders, this section presents an assessment of the word knowledge and growth that the students demonstrated in their writing. The assessment used a measure of word frequency that identifies the rare words in the writing samples. The assessment also included an analysis of the students' experimentation with rare words. The results and discussion highlight the need for more studies to advance the field of expressive vocabulary development through writing.

Data Collection and Analysis

The research participants, data, and analyses are part of the VINE (Vocabulary Innovations in Education) Project, a three-year study of the importance of word consciousness in vocabulary development. The study helped teachers create fourth-grade classrooms that celebrated rich language and approached word learning as a generative process. The intervention sought to improve vocabulary instruction by changing teachers' metalinguistic and metacognitive knowledge about word learning and their own engagement with words. The premise of the study was that teachers' heightened word consciousness would then nurture word consciousness in their students, which would lead, in turn, to greater student acquisition and use of academic language.

Instead of teaching specific sets of words, VINE intervention teachers designed their instruction to develop general understandings about how words work in English and to develop student dispositions to pay greater attention to word use. Teachers in VINE intervention classrooms met together as a collaborative learning community throughout the school year and shared ideas for building enthusiasm for word learning in their classrooms. See Miller, Gage-Serio, & Scott (in press, this volume) for a description of one VINE intervention teacher's word-conscious instruction.

The 2007-2008 VINE participants were 16 classroom teachers—8 intervention teachers and 8 control teachers without access to the VINE intervention—and their 381 fourth-grade students. These classrooms were in five school districts located in metropolitan and smaller-city settings of California. Forty-five percent of the fourth-graders spoke just English at home. Ten percent had more than one home language but had always been fluent in English. Thirty-two percent of the students were learning English, and ten percent had been reclassified as English proficient after having been English learners in school. The students came from backgrounds representing over 20 home languages, but 76% of the English learners were Spanish speakers. For this vocabulary assessment of the students' writing, the sample was delimited to the 300 fourth graders who took the narrative prompt in both the fall and spring and for whom the districts provided demographic and test-score data.

The vocabulary assessment draws on narrative writing collected during the 2007-2008 school year. The writing task asked students to compose a personal narrative in 30 minutes in response to the prompt: "Think about a memory that you would like to write about. It should be an event or experience you remember well and would like other people to read about." The research team administered the prompt in standardized fashion. The instructions suggested that students spend five minutes planning their piece, 20 minutes writing, and five minutes re-reading and revising, and the researchers reinforced these instructions with time cues and supplemental directions during the 30 minutes. Teachers generally remained in the room doing other work during the administration of the prompt, but some teachers helped answer questions, translated directions, or acted as scribes for students with restricting conditions. Spanish-speaking newcomers were allowed to write their narratives in Spanish, but those narratives were not used in the analyses. The prompts were administered in the fall of 2007 and again the following spring.

The rare-words measure described in this paper is a secondary analysis of the personal narrative data. Most of the 300 students wrote about a different memory in their fall and spring narratives. For example, in the fall one student wrote about her family's day at the beach, and in the spring her story was about a friend's birthday party at a pizza restaurant. Hence the academic and literary vocabulary that students used at each time period tended to be unrelated, limiting the possibilities for studying word learning. The VINE research team decided that a word-frequency measure might provide useful information about growth in academic vocabulary and the effectiveness of the study intervention despite the discontinuities created by topic.

The VINE research team developed a word-frequency measure based on the rare words identified by *The Educator's Word Frequency Guide* (Zeno, et al., 1995). The team set the cut-off for rare words at U value equal to 25 words per million in written text; words with U values of 25 or less were considered rare words. The team believed that this cut-off point would be sufficiently low to capture changes in word usage that demonstrated growth in word knowledge.

Teachers with experience deciphering developmental spelling helped clarify student writing and misspellings on the prompts. The prompts were converted into electronic documents and run through the word-frequency program to identify rare words. A researcher checked the computer results against the students' writing to delete unacceptable words (proper names, words with apostrophes, abbreviations, and nonwords). She also distinguished words like *Jade*, the gem, from *Jade*, a girl's name, and determined if *Sharks* referred to the marine animals or a sports team; the latter usages, respectively, were also dropped from the analysis. After these adjustments, the computer identified and summed the number of rare words in each piece of writing. The 300 students received a rare-words count for both their fall and spring narratives.

These data were analyzed using a three-level hierarchical linear model (HLM; Raudenbush, Bryk, Cheong, & Congdon, 2004). Fall to spring growth in rare words was estimated for each student at the lowest level of the HLM model. At the second level, differences in growth were investigated using English proficiency and home language as moderators. The third level recognized the nesting of children within classrooms and compared the intervention and control classrooms in the study.

To provide convergent evidence for the validity of the word-frequency results (American Educational Research Association, American Psychological Association, & National Council on Measurement in Education, 1999), the rare-word counts for the fall and the spring were correlated with three other measures from the students. The other measures were the students' performance on the fall and spring VINE Vocabulary Tests, their scores on the vocabulary subscale of the English Language Arts section of the California Standards Tests in 2007 (taken at the end of third grade) and in 2008 (taken at the end of fourth-grade), and their scale scores on the English Language Arts tests overall in 2007 (from third grade) and in 2008 (from fourth grade).

In order to maximize what might be learned about vocabulary development from the rare-words measure, a researcher examined and coded the identified rare words in their narrative contexts. She looked for examples of experimentation, defined as a marked or non-standard use of a rare word. Examples were coded as experimentation with semantic relationships, experimentation with lexical or morphological relationships, and/or experimentation with word choices.

RESULTS

On average, the 300 VINE fourth-graders in this analysis included 7.55 rare words in their fall narratives (s = 4.93) and 9.50 rare words in their spring narratives (s = 6.33). Their mean growth in rare words from fall to spring was 1.95 words, t_{598} = 5.429, p < .0001. As might be expected, students at different levels of English proficiency (English speakers, English learners, and fluent bilinguals) used dramatically different numbers of rare words, but there was no evidence of difference in their growth rates from fall to spring (χ^2 = 0.72 on 3 df, p = .870). Similarly, home language made no difference in rate of growth for these students (χ^2 = 1.44 on 2 df, p = .487). These results indicate that all fourth-graders' expressive knowledge of rare words grew fairly evenly over the school year.

The HLM analysis also compared students taught by VINE intervention and control teachers. Students in the intervention classrooms grew by 2.35 rare words, and students in the control classrooms grew by 1.57 words, but the difference was not significant (t_{597} = 1.144, p = .253). One of the assessment critiques made by Pearson et al. (2007) deals with the lack of alignment between different aspects of vocabulary and vocabulary assessments. Given that the rare-words measure was not particularly aligned with the VINE word-consciousness intervention, this finding, however disappointing, is not so surprising.

If the rare-words measure is indeed a measure of growth in the breadth of vocabulary knowledge of fourth graders, it should overlap with similar measures. Table 1 presents correlations between the students' rare-word counts in the fall and in the spring and their scores on three other vocabulary-related measures. The three other measures are the scores on the VINE Vocabulary Tests, the score on the vocabulary subscale of the English Language Arts test (California Standards Tests), and the scale score on the English Language Arts test (California Standards Tests). Students wrote the narrative prompt, took the VINE Vocabulary Tests, and took the standardized English Language Arts tests within a span of a month and a half during the spring of 2008, but the spring 2007 standardized tests were taken at the end of the students' third-grade year, several months before the fall 2007 VINE assessments. The time lag may help account for two of the lower correlations in the fall column of the table. For the tests taken at approximately the same time, the correlations range in value from .318 to .444. This is convergent evidence that the rare-words counts validly measure something about vocabulary growth in fourth graders.

Table 1. Convergent Evidence for the Validity of the Rare-Words Measure

Other Vocabulary-Related Measures	Correlation with Rare-Words Measure Fall 2007	Correlation with Rare-Words Measure Spring 2008
VINE Vocabulary Test Fall 2007	$r = .318$ (N=260, $p < .0001$)	
VINE Vocabulary Test Spring 2008		$r = .444$ (N=260, $p < .0001$)
Vocabulary Subscale, English Language Arts, California Standards Tests Spring 2007 (third grade)	$r = .255$ (N=273. $p < .0001$)	
Vocabulary Subscale, English Language Arts, California Standards Tests Spring 2008		$r = .338$ (N=291. $p < .0001$)
English Language Arts Scale Score, California Standards Tests Spring 2007 (third grade)	$r = .332$ (N=269, $p < .0001$)	
English Language Arts Scale Score, California Standards Tests Spring 2008		$r = .350$ (N=293, $p < .0001$)

The analysis of word experimentation in the narrative writing built on the rare-words measure. Only 35 of the 5115 rare words in this assessment were coded as clear examples of student experimentation with words. Each example was identified as a marked or non-standard use of a rare word in the narrative. These varied from "bestest" as in "...the first bestest person...," to "zephyr" in "...speaking of the whistle, Brenda blew the whistle harder than a zephyr of wind,...". Omitted from this analysis were experimentation at the phrase or multiple-word level ("in the crack of the sunlight morning" for "at the crack of dawn"), probable misspellings ("bread" instead of "breed" of hamster), slight orthographic irregularities (repeated references to "dye eggs" rather than "dyed eggs"), inflectional errors, and experimentation with words that were not identified as rare.

The examples were coded as experimentation with semantic relationships, experimentation with lexical or morphological relationships, and/or experimentation with word choice. In general, examples in the semantic category showed that the student both understood and misunderstood something about the meaning of the word—perhaps knowing only a partial meaning or another meaning not appropriate in the narrative context he or she had constructed. After describing a happy vacation disrupted only by a painful bee sting that caused her to faint, a girl concluded, "It turned out to be a very fun, hurtful vacation." In his story about the flag football season, one student wrote "versed" for "competed against." "I versed the Cheifs [*sic*] and Buccaneers that day. When I versed the Cheifs [*sic*], it was a close game!" Four of the semantic experiments occurred in written dialogue as proposed substitutes for "said." One child wrote that his mother "…pronounced 'well hurry up do you want to get a good parking spot [*sic*]' I pronounced back 'yes!' " Another described his mother's reason for allowing his sister to go on a ride at an amusement park, but not him: " 'She is big and your [*sic*] small,' my mom recommended." Thirteen of the 35 examples of rare-word experimentation were coded as exploring semantic relationships.

Eighteen of the examples reflect experimenting with lexical or morphological creations or mismatches, including the most common one, "humongous." A swimmer consistently used the word "components" for her opponents or competitors at a swim meet. One girl wrote "visibly" for "visibility" in her account of snorkeling in very clear water. Another described something as "near an algae infected river" rather than near an algae-infested one. A boy lunged for his little brother when the brother stole some of his Halloween candy, but he wrote, "I plunged at him with flames in my eyes…".

The third coded category, experimenting with word choice, consists of embellishments that fail to fit seamlessly into the narrative account. Some children, like the girl who wrote about the whistle being blown harder than "…a zephyr of wind," are playing with words. Others, though, seem to be adding modifiers solely to complicate their sentences. One boy wrote, "Finally the enthralling game started" without ever saying more to show that the game was indeed enthralling. Another described a long drive to a campground with his family and added, " 'We're here' I randomly hollered," where "randomly" leaves the reader guessing about the author's meaning. Although few, these examples of rare-words experimentation offer evidence important to the study of word learning.

DISCUSSION

This preliminary assessment of the vocabulary knowledge in fourth graders' narratives has both strengths and weaknesses. Its primary strength rests with its success in demonstrating that student writing is a promising vehicle for learning about vocabulary knowledge and development. The results add to what is known about the acquisition of expressive vocabulary—that both overall and across all subgroups, students' use of rare words increased in their narrative writing over the course of fourth grade. They also indicate that word-frequency measures in general, and the counting of rare words in particular, can be useful and valid tools for assessing the breadth of vocabulary that students employ in their writing. The analysis of rare-word experimentation provides evidence that some processes that characterize earlier word learning may also influence the words students write. The not-quite-right use of rare words suggests that the students' morphological, lexical, and semantic understandings are growing incrementally, with partial knowledge being mapped onto lexical forms. Thus the results from the assessment of rare words tantalizingly reveal the promise of putting greater focus on writing and writing measures in vocabulary assessment.

The convergent evidence for the rare-words measure presented in Table 1 is reasonable confirmation of the measure's validity. Vocabulary learning and vocabulary assessments are both multifaceted, and the results of any one vocabulary test should correlate with the results of another to the extent that the two measure the same thing. The rare-words measure is an indicator of the upper range of vocabulary breadth in writing. In contrast, two of the comparison tests in Table 1, the VINE Vocabulary Tests and the Vocabulary Subscale of the English Language Arts test (California Standards Tests), are based on receptive word knowledge across a broad continuum of fourth-grade words. The VINE Vocabulary Tests assess students' incremental knowledge of words (Scott, et al., 2008), and the Vocabulary Subscale focuses on students' understanding of concepts through knowledge of roots, affixes, derivations, synonyms, antonyms, and idioms (California Department of Education, 2002). In fourth grade, the English Language Arts scale score (California Standards Tests) includes vocabulary and a writing test, but it also covers an array of other literacy knowledge and skills (California Department of Education, 2002). Thus the overlap between the rare-words measure and any of the other measures in the table is limited. The correlations are sufficiently consistent and strong to provide convergent evidence for the rare-words measure; they are also sufficiently distinct to show that the measure adds new dimensions not tested by the other assessments.

The rare-words assessment also had flaws. Like other word-frequency indicators, the rare-words measure was insensitive to words with multiple meanings, which introduced error into the identification of rare words in the students' narratives. In addition, the rare-words measure relied on the word frequencies assigned by *The Educator's Word Frequency Guide* (Zeno, et al., 1995), and some words that are rare in the *Guide*, such as "pizza" and "mall," are not really rare for fourth graders. The U-value cut-off level distinguishing rare words from others was based on the authors' prediction about rare words in fourth-grade writing; it would be worthwhile to reanalyze the data using different cut-off levels to evaluate the accuracy of that prediction.

A final source of error came from the writing task itself. The assessment was a secondary analysis of VINE data collected for another purpose, and the writing prompt usually elicited completely different personal narratives in the fall and in the spring. Whereas the subject of a story does not necessarily influence the use of rare words, narratives about a horseback riding lesson or a field trip to a science museum tended to include more technical terms flagged as rare words than a story about a day spent shopping. In the future, researchers gathering data specifically for a growth analysis of vocabulary knowledge and use in student writing should consider developing tasks or prompts that encourage students to write about the same subject at both testing periods.

The VINE research team was hoping that the assessment would link the study's intervention to increasing use of rare words, but the greater rate of growth in the intervention classrooms was not significant. The generative word-learning strategies and word-rich activities characteristic of VINE intervention classrooms help students learn more words—both rare and not rare. A complete assessment of VINE vocabulary instruction would require multiple measures of word consciousness and vocabulary learning from multiple sources. In a VINE word-conscious classroom, increasing students' use of rare words is just one thread in the fabric of word learning.

CONCLUSIONS: IMPLICATIONS FOR THE FUTURE OF VOCABULARY ASSESSMENT

The results of the assessment support two conclusions about vocabulary assessment. First, the vocabulary knowledge encoded in student writing has been largely ignored by vocabulary researchers, a reality that has curtailed knowledge of vocabulary development and possibly of effective vocabulary instruction. Reading and writing are taught to most elementary students as complementary, mutually reinforcing skills. Both skills contribute to, and benefit from, word learning. Similarly, both present opportunities for vocabulary assessment that merit attention. The study and assessment of vocabulary in student writing is overdue.

Second, the measurement of written vocabulary is territory staked out and developed by several academic fields (writing, reading, and second-language acquisition to name a few) but not claimed by vocabulary researchers, who tend to focus on reading comprehension instead. Word-frequency measures, like the rare-words count in this paper, capture something about the breadth of students' expressive vocabulary knowledge, but other expressive measures based on words (word diversity, word length, number of syllables, total words, etc.) say remarkably little about an author's word knowledge. To learn more about vocabulary development through writing, scholars should lay aside the indicators of other fields and develop new measures to help them understand the instructional, lexical, morphological, and semantic attributes of the words in children's writing.

Pearson et al. wrote the following characterization of the field of vocabulary assessment today:

> …vocabulary assessment is grossly undernourished, both in its theoretical and practical aspects…it has been driven by tradition, convenience, psychometric standards, and a quest for economy of effort rather than a clear conceptualization of its nature and relation to other aspects of reading expertise, most notably comprehension (2007, p. 282).

Given this state of affairs, vocabulary researchers interested in assessment have much to do. The assessment presented in this paper suggests a promising new drection for this work.

REFERENCES

American Educational Research Association, American Psychological Association, & National Council on Measurement in Education. (1999). *Standards for educational and psychological testing.* Washington, D.C.: Author.

Aschbacher, P., & Alonzo, A. (2006). Examining the utility of elementary science notebooks for formative assessment purposes. *Educational Assessment, 11*(3 & 4), 179-203.

Baumann, J. F., Kame'enui, E. J., & Ash, G. E. (2003). Research on vocabulary instruction: Voltaire redux. In J. Flood, D. Lapp, J. R. Squire, & J. M. Jensen (Eds.), *Handbook of research on teaching the English language arts* (2nd ed., pp. 752-785). Mahwah, NJ: Lawrence Erlbaum Associates.

Baumann, J. F., Ware, D., & Edwards, E. C. (2007). "Bumping into spicy, tasty words that catch your tongue": A formative experiment on vocabulary instruction. *The Reading Teacher, 61*(2), 108-122.

Beck, I. L., McCaslin, E. S, & McKeown, M. G. (1980). *The rationale and design of a program to teach vocabulary to fourth-grade students* (LRDC Publication 1980/25). Pittsburgh, PA: University of Pittsburgh, Learning Research and Development Center.

Blachowicz, C. L. Z., & Fisher, P. J. (2004). Keep the "fun" in fundamental: Encouraging word awareness and incidental word learning in the classroom through word play. In J. F. Baumann & E. J. Kame'enui (Eds.), *Vocabulary instruction: Research to practice* (pp. 218-237). New York, NY: Guilford Press.

Bloom, P. (2001). *How children learn the meaning of words.* Cambridge, MA: MIT Press.

California Department of Education. (2002). *STAR CST blueprints, English language arts blueprints grades 2 to 11.* Retrieved from http://www.cde.ca.gov/ta/tg/sr/blueprints.asp

Carey, S. (1978). The child as word learner. In M. Halle, J. Bresnan, & G. Miller (Eds.), *Linguistic theory and psychological reality* (pp. 264-293). Cambridge, MA: MIT Press.

Chall, J., & Dale, E. (1995). *Readability revisited: The new Dale-Chall readability formula.* Cambridge, MA: Brookline Books.

Clark, E. V. (1993). *The lexicon in acquisition.* Cambridge, UK: Cambridge University Press.

Culhan, R. (2003). *6+1 Traits of writing: The complete guide grades 3 and up.* Northwest Regional Educational Laboratory. New York, NY: Scholastic.

Dale, E. (1965). Vocabulary measurement: Techniques and major findings. *Elementary English, 42,* 82-88.

Dale, E., & O'Rourke, J. (1976) *The living word vocabulary.* Elgin, IL: Field Enterprises Educational Corporation.

Davis, F. B. (1942). Two new measures of reading ability. *Journal of Educational Psychology, 33,* 365-372.

Davies, M., & Gardner, D. (2010). *A frequency dictionary of contemporary American English: Word sketches, collocates, and thematic lists.* New York, NY: Routledge.

Deno, S. L., Marston, D., & Mirkin, P. (1982). Valid measurement procedures for continuous evaluation of written expression. *Exceptional Children, 48,* 368–371.

Duin, A. H., & Graves, M. F. (1987). Intensive vocabulary instruction as a prewriting technique. *Reading Research Quarterly, 22*(3), 311-330.

Finn, P. J. (1977) Computer-aided description of mature word choices in writing. In C. R. Cooper & L. Odell (Eds.), *Evaluating writing: Describing, measuring, judging* (pp. 69–89). Buffalo, NY: State University of New York at Buffalo.

Fletcher, R. (1993). *What a writer needs.* Portsmouth, NH: Heinemann.

Freebody, P., & Anderson, R. C. (1983). Effects of vocabulary difficulty, text cohesion, and schema availability on reading comprehension. *Reading Research Quarterly, 18*(3), 277-294.

Gajar, A. H. (1989). A computer analysis of written language variables and a comparison of compositions written by university students with and without learning disabilities. *Journal of Learning Disabilities, 22,* 125–130.

Gansle, K. A., Noell, G. H., VanDerHeyden, A., Naquin, G. M., & Slider, N. J. (2002). Moving beyond total words written: The reliability, criterion validity, and time cost of alternative measures for curriculum-based measurement in writing. *School Psychology Review, 31,* 477–497.

Gansle, K. A., VanDerHeyden, A. M., Noell, G. H., Resetar, J. L., & Williams, K. L. (2006). The technical adequacy of curriculum-based and rating-based measures of written expression for elementary school students. *School Psychology Review, 35*(4), 435-450.

Graham, S., Berninger, V. W., Abbott, R. D., Abbott, S. P., & Whitaker, D. (1997). Role of mechanics in composing of elementary school students: A new methodological approach. *Journal of Educational Psychology, 89,* 170–182.

Graves, M. F., & Watts-Taffe, S. (2008). For the love of words: Fostering word consciousness in young readers. *The Reading Teacher, 62*(3), 185-193.

Gregg, M., Sr. fcJ., & Sekeres, D. C. (2006). My word! Vocabulary and geography learning. *Journal of Geography, 105*(2), 53-58.

Grobe, C. (1981). Syntactic maturity, mechanics, and vocabulary as predictors of quality ratings. *Research in the Teaching of English, 15,* 75–85.

Harrison, C. (1980). *Readability in the classroom.* Cambridge, MA: Cambridge University Press.

Harmon, J. M., Hedrick, W. B., Soares, L., & Gress, M. (2007). Assessing vocabulary: Examining knowledge about words and about word learning. In J. R. Paratore & R. L. McCorack (Eds.), *Classroom literacy assessment: Making sense of what students know and do* (pp. 135-153). New York, NY: Guilford Press.

Hayes, D. P., & Ahrens, M. (1988). Speaking and writing: Distinct patterns of word choice. *Journal of Memory and Language, 27,* 572-585.

Just, M. A., & Carpenter, P. A. (1987). *The psychology of reading and language comprehension.* Boston, MA: Allyn & Bacon.

Kame'enui, E. J., Dixon, D. W., & Carnine, R. C. (1987). Issues in the design of vocabulary instruction. In M. G. McKeown & M. E. Curtis (Eds.), *The nature of vocabulary acquisition* (pp. 129-145). Hillsdale, NJ: Lawrence Erlbaum Associates.

Malecki, C. K., & Jewell, J. (2003). Developmental, gender, and practical considerations in scoring curriculum-based writing probes. *Psychology in the Schools, 40*, 379–390.

Mayor, J., & Plunkett, K. (2010). A neurocomputational account of taxonomic responding and fast mapping in early word learning. *Psychological Review, 117*(1), 1-31.

Miller, T. F., Gage-Serio, O., & Scott, J. A. (in press). Word consciousness in practice: Illustrations from a fourth-grade teacher's classroom. *59th Yearbook of the National Reading Conference*. Oak Creek, WI: National Reading Conference.

Morris, N. T., & Crump, W. D. (1982). Syntactic and vocabulary development in the written language of learning disabled and non-learning disabled students at four age levels. *Learning Disability Quarterly, 5*, 163–172.

Nagy, W., & Hiebert, E. H. (in press). Toward a theory of word selection. In M. Kamil, P. D. Pearson, E. Moje, & P. Afflerbach (Eds.), *Handbook of Reading Research* (Vol. 4). New York, NY: Routledge.

Nagy, W., & Scott, J. (2000). Vocabulary processes. In R. Barr, P. Mosenthal, P. D. Pearson, & M. Kamil (Eds.), *Handbook of reading research* (Vol. 3, pp. 269-284). Hillsdale, NJ: Lawrence Erlbaum Associates.

National Assessment Governing Board (2008). *Reading framework for the 2009 National Assessment of Educational Progress*. U.S. Department of Education. Washington, D.C.: U.S. Government Printing Office.

National Institute of Child Health and Human Development, NIH, DHHS. (2000). *Report of the National Reading Panel: Teaching children to read: Reports of the subgroups (00-4754)*. Washington, D.C.: U.S. Government Printing Office.

Olinghouse, N. G., & Leaird, J. L. (2009). The relationship between measures of vocabulary and narrative writing quality in second- and fourth-grade students. *Reading and Writing, 22*(5), 545-565.

Papadopoulou, E. (2007). *The impact of vocabulary instruction on the vocabulary knowledge and writing performance of third grade students.* (Doctoral dissertation, University of Maryland). Retrieved from http://www.lib.umd.edu/drum/handle/1903/7649

Paribakht, T. S., & Wesche, M. (1997). Vocabulary enhancement activities and reading for meaning in second language vocabulary acquisition. In J. Coady & T. Huckin (Eds.), *Second language vocabulary acquisition* (pp. 174-200). Cambridge, UK: Cambridge University Press.

Pearson, P. D., Hiebert, E. H., & Kamil, M. L. (2007). Vocabulary assessment: What we know and what we need to learn. *Reading Research Quarterly 42*(2), 282-296.

Raudenbush, S. W., Bryk, A. S., Cheong, Y., & Congdon, R. T. (2004). *HLM 6: Hierarchical linear and nonlinear modeling*. Chicago, IL: Scientific Software International.

Read, J. (2000). *Assessing vocabulary.* Cambridge, England: Cambridge University Press.

Samway, K. D. (2006). *When English language learners write: Connecting research to practice, K-8.* Portsmouth, NH: Heinemann.

Scott, J. A., Hoover, M., Flinspach, S. L., & Vevea, J. L. (2008). A multiple-level vocabulary assessment tool: Measuring word knowledge based on grade-level materials. In Y. Kim, V. J. Risko, D. L. Compton, D. K. Dickinson, M. K. Hundley, R. T. Jiménez, K. M. Leander, & D. W. Rowe (Eds.), *57th Yearbook of the National Reading Conference* (pp. 325-340). Oak Creek, WI: National Reading Conference.

Scott, J. A., Skobel, B. J., & Wells, J. (2008). *The word conscious classroom: Building the vocabulary readers and writers need.* New York, NY: Scholastic.

Stahl, S. (2003). How words are learned incrementally over multiple exposures. *American Educator, 27*(1), 18-19.

Stahl, S. A., & Nagy, W. E. (2006). *Teaching word meanings.* Mahwah, NJ: Lawrence Erlbaum Associates.

Stallman, A. C., Pearson, P. D., Nagy, W. E., Anderson, R. C., & Garcia, G. E. (1995). *Alternative approaches to vocabulary assessment* (Report No. 607). Urbana-Champaign, IL: Center for the Study of Reading, University of Illinois.

Whipple, G. (Ed.). (1925). *The 24th Yearbook of the National Society for the Study of Education: Report of the National Committee on Reading*. Bloomington, IL: Public School Publishing.

Williams, K.T. (1997). *Expressive vocabulary test.* Circle Pines, MN: American Guidance Service.

Zeno, S., Ivens, S., Millard, R., & Duvvuri, R. (1995). *The educator's word frequency guide.* Brewster, NY: Touchstone Applied Science Associates.

AUTHORS' NOTE

Susan Leigh Flinspach, Education Department, University of California, Santa Cruz; Judith A. Scott, Education Department, University of California, Santa Cruz; Jack L. Vevea, School of Social Sciences, Humanities and Arts, University of California, Merced.

The VINE Project was funded by IES Reading and Writing Education Research Grant Program R305G060140 (U.S. Department of Education), FY2006-2009. This paper is the sole responsibility of the authors and does not necessarily reflect the opinions of the U.S. Department of Education.

Correspondence should be addressed to Susan Leigh Flinspach, Education Department, University of California, Santa Cruz, 1156 High Street, Santa Cruz, CA 95064. E-mail: flinspac@ucsc.edu

Romancing the Shown: A Study of Visual (and Gendered) Conversations in the Visual Texts of Fifth-Grade Students

Peggy Albers
Tammy Frederick
Georgia State University

Kay Cowan
The University of Tennesee at Chattanooga

In written stories, authors often infuse their lives into the very constructs of the plot, the characters, setting, and themes. Authors often write from their own experiences and beliefs, and young writers are apprenticed into such styles and techniques, writing about what they know. Artists, too, build their visual stories—narrative, expressive, informative, literary, and persuasive—through art elements and principles. Like artists, children tell stories visually all the time in English Language Arts (ELA) classes; they respond to literary texts, illustrate their own written stories, create artworks for parents, and so on. Through their interaction with the visual world, children internalize cultural symbols, concepts, and organizational patterns in artworks or visual images (Sonesson, 1988), and often reproduce traces of these texts—visual, compositional, or discursive—in their own visual texts (Albers & Frederick, 2009; Rowsell & Pahl, 2007), traces that offer glimpses into the discourse communities within which they identify, as well as evaluations of other discourse communities.

This interpretive study examined 38 visual texts, focused on perceptions of gender, created by fifth-grade students in a small rural southeastern school. We use the term "visual texts" (Albers, 2007) to denote texts created in ELA classes using art rather than the more commonly used term

Figure 1a and 1b. Anthony's and Karl's Representations of Girls as Gendered Beings, Respectively

"artworks," because the term artwork presumes a knowledge and experience of fine art, and/or training in processes and techniques associated with an art form (Efland, 1965), effort of time, money, study, and imagination (Winterson, 1995), and familiarity with the function and value of art (Berger, 2000). In short, artworks are visual texts, but not all visual texts are artworks. The following two research questions were investigated: What does a close analysis of visual elements suggest within and across visual texts?, and What messages do elementary children send about boys' and girls' experiences and interests through their visual texts created in English Language Arts classes?

We open this manuscript with two images created by Anthony and Karl, two fifth-grade boys, who, along with their classmates, visually expressed their beliefs about girls' interests and experiences after completing a unit of study that explored gender and racial stereotypes. Upon brief, but closer and side-by-side readings, Anthony's and Karl's drawings show remarkable similarity in composition, structure, and discourse. Compositionally, both boys draw specific objects that they associate with girls (unicorns, castles, rainbows, flowers) and both introduce spaceships. Both use graphite (pencil) as their primary medium; Karl added yellow and orange to his rainbow. Structurally, both centralize objects that discursively represent fantasy and love, especially noted through the unicorns, castles, and rainbows, objects that occupy the largest part of the text. Anthony's and Karl's visual texts are but two of 18 images constructed by fifth-grade grade boys, seven of whom conveyed similar content and contained similar visual elements.

This opening example gestures towards the analysis of visual texts that we undertook and which we make significant, for several reasons, the choices that children make when constructing meaning visually. First, like Fairclough (2003), we argue that the process of making meaning is multimodal and socially constructed, and that the relationship among and between words, images, sounds, gestures (and so on) is intertextual. Children's meanings are created not just by language but also by social images they see, read, and encounter in the world. Second, society believes that gender equity has been achieved, but gender studies suggest otherwise (Blackburn, 2007; Butler, 1990; Davies, 1993, 2000; Gurian & Stevens, 2005). Our study is situated in Davies' (1993) concept of male-female dualism and Butler's (1990) concept of gender as performativity; that is, our stance takes into account the interrelatedness of gender rules and regulations as "power regimes" in which gender is performed in normative ways (males are masculine and females are feminine) (Blackburn, 2007, p. 34). As bodies, we learn "appropriate patterns of desire" (Davies, 1993, p. 145), and bodies are often subjected within available discourses, and thus become the selves we take them to be. That is, bodies recognize themselves through "clichéd binaries (such as mind/body)" and bodies learn to recognize themselves through these binaries (Davies, et al., 2001, p. 170). And, third, the discourses regarding gender rules and regulations that children write into their visual texts have yet to be explored in depth by the field of literacy. We want to position art as a significant language through which visual messages are expressed daily in elementary classes, and which remain largely and uncritically read (Hobbs & Frost, 2003).

THEORETICAL FRAMEWORK AND RELEVANT LITERATURE

Kress (2003) argued "the world told" is vastly different from "the world shown" (p. 1). Thus, we ground our work theoretically in critical social semiotics and in visual discourse analysis (Albers, 2007). In social semiotics, systems cannot be viewed in isolation but must be studied as part of one's social practices, their motivations, their origins, and destinations. Social semiotics further stresses that the system and the product interact in a variety of ways in a range of social contexts (Hodge & Kress, 1988). We further define this theory as critical social semiotics in which attention is paid particularly to disrupting the commonplace, interrogating multiple perspectives, and realizing that attitudes and dispositions emerge from conscious engagement with social issues and languages with an understanding that there are alternate ways of being, and being reflexive (Albers, Vasquez, & Harste, 2008). In critical social semiotics, texts are in a dialectal relation with context; the text creates the context as much as the context creates the text. Meaning arises from the friction between the two (Halliday, 1985). Thus, texts can be critically examined to reveal discourses in operation and the contestation of meanings in institutions.

The world shown, especially as it relates to identity and gender, has become increasingly visible in the work of a number of scholars. Early research studies in gender and representation (McNiff, 1981; Reeves & Boyette, 1983) found that girls showed a great deal of interest in representing a highly detailed human figure that was quite well-proportioned, and often surrounded by a realistic, natural, or domestic environment. A masculine approach to the figure was described as individual, spontaneous, and animated. In contrast, boys were less interested in recording human figures in detail, and preferred to represent figures in imaginary scenes in which conflict, fantasy, and action with warriors, monsters, armies, and machines predominated (Duncum, 1989; Lark-Horovitz, Lewis, & Luca, 1967). Brent and Margery Wilson in the 1980s found that children do not simply copy (draw) objects from their environment but produce "the visual signs of the culture" (cited in Efland, 2002, p. 46), and thus, learn to make signs by observing others at work, and by reading and studying visual texts available in the culture.

Later studies of learners' positioned visual texts as culturally situated visual representations. Boyatzis and Eades (1999) found that pre-school and kindergarten children produced images often associated with the roles of men and/or women, and that even scribbles of the very young were "gender-stereotypical" (p. 634). McClure (1999) noted how society manufactures gender through language, and learners internalize that particular characteristics are associated with males and females. Tuman (1999) and Albers (1996), respectively, found elementary- and middle-grade participants reproduced gender-normative roles and included objects culturally associated with gender. These studies suggest a direct link between learners' visual renderings, conscious and unconscious semiotic practices, and a cognitive link to learning and their social environment.

METHODOLOGY

Overview of Study

This interpretive study involved the production and close readings of the visual texts of 38 fifth-grade students (female n=20, male n=18) in two classes, created at the end of a unit of study in which students studied stereotypes, including race and gender. We define this study as interpretive because, as researchers, we know, when analyzing any data, there is no objective reality which can be discovered (Geertz, 1983). As human beings who mediate, or make sense of, the world through our beliefs and experiences, we know that we have no direct access to reality and, as such, we must interpret data/phenomena through language—in this study—art and written language.

In a world dominated by visual texts, scholars, as noted earlier, increasingly recognize the importance of studying the visual in literacy research. We extend this literature by presenting both a method for analyzing visual texts that children produced in ELA classes, and the implications for literacy instruction. Image creation and interpretation, theorized and presented as a method, allows educators to see more clearly visible and invisible messages that are conveyed in the very texts that children produce in ELA classes, a method we believe must be a part of critical ELA instruction and practice.

Participants and Context of Study

Students were enrolled at Grasslands Elementary School (GES), a small rural school that lay outside a large metropolitan area in the South, and our entry into the school was seamless. Kay worked for 30 years as an elementary teacher of grades 1-6 and a reading specialist who worked with all content teachers to develop an arts-integrated approach to literacy and learning. The population of GES was approximately 70% European American and 30% of color, and represented a range of socio-economic backgrounds. Like other schools in the area, GES saw increasing diversity, and was concerned with issues that may arise, especially if teachers did not critically attend to them in their classes. Approximately eleven years ago, teachers began to introduce units of study that addressed gender and racial stereotypes. The students in this study had completed such a unit, and had explored through role-play, writing, art, and discussions gender and race stereotypes across a range of texts and content areas. Teachers noticed significant shifts in attitudes within the group, and as such, they were particularly interested in pairing with us to see the extent these attitudes shifted, with a focus on gender.

Procedures

To facilitate this study and ensure that both classes received the same information and directions, both classes of fifth-grade students were combined into one. Based on an earlier study (Robertson & Albers, 1994), before they drew, we asked them to view professional artworks with the names and genders of artists concealed, and to predict the gender of that artist, if possible, based on their interpretation of each composition. After a discussion of their responses, we asked students to respond to this prompt: "We'd now like you to step visually into the shoes of the opposite sex. We'd like you to draw what you consider to be the experiences and interests of the opposite sex." To take on gendered perspectives is commonplace in ELA classes. Through discussions, role plays, and writing, girls and boy are often asked to connect with literary characters, regardless of their sex. We saw this study as a way to locate this same connection in art. To create their visual texts, children used available classroom materials: paper, pencils, pencil colors, and crayons.

Data Collection and Analysis

Data included the 38 visual texts created by children, and the comments that they made on the actual texts. Data analysis was interpretive and semiotic in nature. According to Schwandt (1994), an interpretive approach provides insight into "the complex world of lived experience from the point of view of those who live it" (p. 118). Reality is assumed to be socially constructed, and the researcher is the conduit through which this reality is revealed. We treated these texts as part of the children's complex and lived world.

Our analysis was guided by research questions and literature in the field, and previous published analyses (Albers, Frederick & Cowan, 2009; Gee, 2005; Kress & van Leeuwen, 2006). Data analysis was done through visual discourse analysis (Albers, 2007) and was multifaceted and layered. Initially, we divided the visual texts into gender sets. We read each text holistically in each set in terms of semantics, noting which picture subjects (what the picture was about) were represented and how many times they were represented. We then read the structures within each text (Kress & van Leeuwen, 2006), paying particular attention to the graphic and syntactic information. We identified and analyzed size and volume of objects, placement of objects on the paper canvas (four quadrants, effective center of attention), colors used, and the intensity with which color was applied onto the paper (light pastel lines vs. thick dark lines), orientation of the canvas (vertical/horizontal). We also coded written text as part of the visual text. This close study of elements enabled us to note the textmaker's perception of the significance of the activity or object to the opposite sex. For example in Figure 2, the textmaker wrote, "Pacman. I saw a boy obsessed with Pacman." "Obsession," was expressed by Pacman's volume and size, central position, bright yellow color, and voracious eating action.

Figure 2. Girl's Representation of Boys' Interest

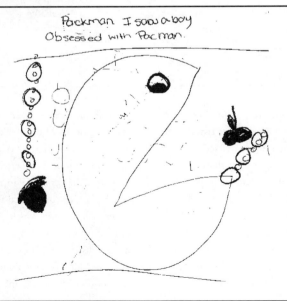

Visual discourse analysis also looks closely at children's use of cueing systems within their texts. We looked specifically for graphic information and Koch's concept of "recurrent pictorial elements" (cited in Sonesson, 1988, p. 38) or visual elements repeated within a text, or elements that cut across texts. For example, within his text, Anthony (Figure 3) used flowers as a recurrent visual element, curved lines to represent a rainbow, three turrets on the castle. Karl also represented similar content, and used recurrent visual elements of curved lines (rainbow), three turrets, and flowers. Across texts, we noted the graphic and structural similarity and differences of visual elements from one child's text to another. For example, both Anthony and Karl placed their castle with three turrets on the left hand side of the canvas, both of which have spaceships, viewed from below, atop one turret. Both include rainbows, flowers, smiling unicorns, objects associated with fantasy. When we noted that two texts contained a number of similar visual elements, we called this a visual conversation.

Figure 3. Karl's and Anthony's Visual Conversations

To corroborate this finding, we looked at the seating arrangement and organized the visual texts to reflect where children sat for this experience (Figure 4). This enabled us to consider how and to what extent students related to the content and to each others' texts (Cazden, 2001). The more visual elements that were shared, the stronger the conversation was between textmakers. Further, we noted to what extent we could determine who started the conversation and who took it on. This analysis of visual elements also helped us understand the extent to which these students integrated cultural information associated with objects (flowers = love), and which objects, concepts, and/or actions they associated with the opposite sex. When three or more texts contained similar elements and objects and/or picture subjects, we coded this as a discourse. For example, discourses on female experience and interests that emerged in boys' texts included fantasy, domesticity, beauty. We also studied how a textmaker intended a viewer to read his/her image, attending particularly to vectors

Figure 4. Visual Text Arrangement

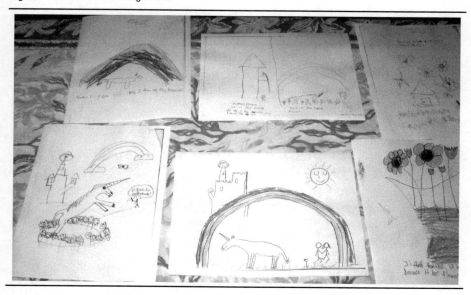

or where the eye moved (directionality), size and placement of object (to show interest), repetition (to show emphasis), representational conveyance of objects (likeness to real objects) or collections of objects that act as symbols or metaphors of abstract concepts (flowers, bucked teeth, lizard). This analysis enabled us to understand a textmaker's visual message about the interests and experiences of the opposite sex.

Limitations of the Study

With an increase of scholarship in visual text analysis (Albers, 2007; Cherney, Seiwert, Dickey, & Flichtbeil, 2006; Rowsell & Pahl, 2007), this study extends methods of analysis into children's visual texts, and we can assert that we are not "reading too much into the image." We also acknowledge that our reading is but one of many that could be made, with the same being said of any text including written. Based on our analyses of a large number of visual texts over the years, we are confident of our assertions about what is said visually in these texts.

FINDINGS

Two key findings emerged from our analysis.

Recurring Visual Elements Indicated that Identifiable Visual Conversations Occurred

We found that children engaged in visual conversations through their sharing of visual elements, including objects, colors, directionality of objects, orientation of objects, size, shape, and so on. That is, we noted that children often drew from each others' texts and integrated these elements into their own texts. The girls engaged in six distinct visual conversations around what they believed were boys' interests: video games, sports, cars, monsters/dragons, violence/war, and animals

Figure 5. Visual Conversations: Sharing of Visual Elements Across Texts

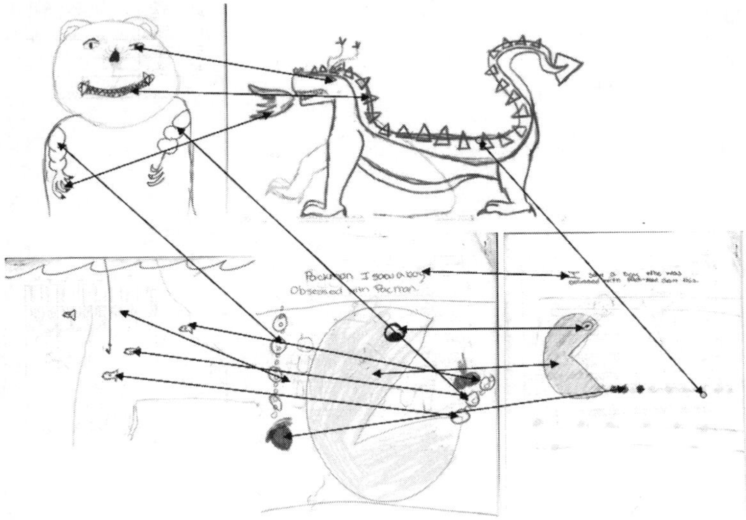

(reptiles). The boys participated in visual conversations in five distinct areas: fantasy, domesticity, beauty, romance, and caricature. Most children integrated elements from several children's texts to create their own. We drew arrows onto visual texts to show which elements were shared across texts; the more arrows that led to and away from a text, the more we saw this textmaker as starting the conversation. For example, in Figure 5, the textmaker who created the Pacman in the bottom middle picture started the conversation. The textmaker above and to the left used the design of attached circles, moving downward, to represent the arms of his character. The textmaker to the immediate left drew an underwater fishing scene. Both texts were drawn under something; the fish and fishing line were under water while Pacman was under written text. Further, the line moving from top to bottom of the image follows the same line as the blue circles on the left side of the Pacman. Diagonal lines of the fish under the water line up with the diagonal movement of the blue dots in Pacman. The textmaker immediately to the right integrated the same subject picture and objects, Pacman and the circles it consumed. Both pictures were in conversation with Pacman's act of eating, the eyes looking from left to right, and the use of yellow and purple. The textmaker who started the conversation took the perspective of a close-up; we know she is familiar with the game because she included specific fruit. The textmaker to her right added to this conversation by showing how Pacman moves within the video game.

The boys in this group also engaged in visual conversations in similar ways. They integrated visual elements, objects, concepts, language, orientation, directionality, color, and so on. Like the girls, there were boys who led their visual conversations.

Particular and Unified Discourses of Gender Emerged

To more carefully understand boys' and girls' representations, we also found that children represented particular and unified discourses of gender. That is, there were groups of students actively and visually communicating similar beliefs about interests and experiences of the opposite sex through and across their texts. When we noted that there were three or more texts that expressed similar interests and experiences of boys or girls, we saw this as a discourse, a unified expression of a social collective. We present two discourses as examples of this finding, fantasy-romance and beauty.

Fantasy and romance. Over half of the fifth-grade boys (10 of 18) engaged in a complex visual conversation around the discourse of romance: 10 contained flowers, 7 contained unicorns, and 5 contained rainbows, while 7 were set in castles or meadows. Seven out of the 18 texts intertextually related to the fantasy genre, imaginative, alternative, and strange (Kiefer, 2007). Figure 6 presents these seven texts, as this was the most visible and the strongest conversation that occurred across boys and girls.

Immediately noticeable were the shared visual elements that appeared across and between texts. In the 7 texts that contained unicorns, 5 had rainbows, all contained flowers, and 5 included a castle or home of some type. The unicorns' horns were emphasized in half of the texts through details such as rings on the horn, dark shading, and/or length. As the boys attempted to visually replicate what girls would be interested in, we found through careful analysis that their own interest in romance was revealed.

Textmaker 1 and 2 led the discourse of fantasy/romance with their highly detailed drawings of objects often found in fantasy as a genre; the other five textmakers integrated similar elements and objects in their own texts, only shifting slightly the conversations in their own way. Two discourses were evident in this conversation, fantasy as traditional and protective and fantasy as love and romance. Textmaker 1 understood fantasy and romance in more normative ways. In his text, the female is held captive in the castle and the male shouts to her, "expecto patronum!" ("I await a protector!"), and then moves in to save her. Objects like flowers, unicorns, and rainbows serve as cultural markers of romance, the imagined and happy life, and happy relationship. The castle,

Figure 6. Discourse of Fantasy/Romance

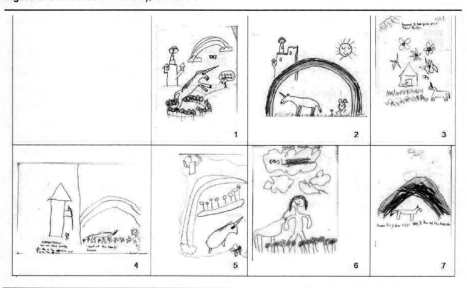

placed in the upper left hand quadrant, represents what we culturally know. It symbolizes strength (constructed of sturdy materials), and protection (tall and strategically located on hills), places where women can feel safe. Textmakers 4 and 5, in particular, took up this discourse through their choices and placements of objects very similar to that of Textmaker 1. Textmaker 5's visual text is a near replication of Textmaker 1's, as is Textmaker 4; however, he shifted this conversation slightly by representing the balcony scene from *Romeo and Juliet* rather than Textmaker's 1 allusion to Harry Potter. The clear, visible, and multiple integration of Textmaker 1's visual elements and objects into Textmakers 4 and 5's visual texts suggests that they align strongly with Textmaker 1's more normative discourse of romance and fantasy. We suggest that such acute observation and attempt to replicate the objects in another text indicated not only an interest in what these objects symbolized, but the discourses around which these objects have been culturally defined.

As the second leader in this conversation, Textmaker 2's discourse of fantasy focused on love and romance. Collectively, the objects in this visual text expressed romance, from the couple holding hands, to the single flower, to the smiling sun and unicorn, to the orange and yellow rainbow that serves to protect, not from enemies as in Textmaker 1's text, but to protect their love. As a cultural symbol of purity, elegance and charm, the unicorn, a central object in this visual text, is on equal plane with the couple, and because of this position, the couple takes on this symbolism. However, interestingly, the unicorn faces away from the couple and to the left, or the real/known, while the couple, hand-in-hand, walk away and toward the unknown. Such representation signified, for us, Textmaker 2's representation of walking away from childhood into young adulthood and the expectations placed on girls and boys in their move from elementary school to middle school. Textmakers 3 and 6 appeared to align themselves more closely with the discourse of romance and love. Textmaker 6's female in a field of flowers, accompanied by her unicorn, is happily dreaming, "Cool." He shifts the focus of the conversation from the love viewed through fantasy and into reality. His female figure has size and volume, and is the center of attention. Textmaker 3's free-floating flowers, the unicorn and the sun, in combination, focus on the house, where apparently the female resides. The flowers in this loving scene caress the home much like the singing birds circling Snow White in the Disney movie.

None of the other five boys took up Textmakers 1 and 2's addition of the spaceship on top of the castles, an object commonly associated with boys. With the spaceship as part of the castle, these two boys represented their own interest in science fiction rather than fantasy, a genre more associated with boys. We suggest that the inclusion of this object was a way for these two boys to masculinize the feminine, and thus participate freely in the conversation of romance/love, and could do so as boys, rather than as boys representing girls. As for the other five boys, we suggest their not including the spaceship may be related to maturity level and the possibility that they were not as ready to participate in this conversation. Rather, they chose to go along with Textmakers 1 and 2 in order to maintain solidarity; they had less to contribute to the conversation and may simply have been in agreement with the topic and willing listeners.

Discourse of beauty as counternarrative. Beauty as a counternarrative was taken up by three boys and one girl (Figure 7). There were two distinct ways in which beauty was represented: beautiful girls in designer clothing, and as a counternarrative—girls as exaggerations, distortions, and/or morphed figures. Figure 7 shows a distinct conversation taken up by the three male Textmakers, 1, 2, and 3.

Figure 7. Discourse of Beauty: Three Male Textmakers and One Female

There was no indication in these visual texts that they represented girls' interests or experiences, but represented how they saw girls. Unlike the boys' visual texts in Figure 6, these three boys saw girls not as objects of romance and fantasy, but as sexual objects. They drew clearly on facial and bodily features to position girls in a counternarrative to beauty, in unflattering ways, not to be viewed as objects of beauty, but as objects of ridicule. Facial features, eyes, mouth, lips, teeth, and hair were the objects of focus, and of exaggeration, morphing, or distortion. Textmaker 1 chose to exaggerate girls' features by elongating the eyes, very thin and curled up hair, and large lips that curved into a smile. The female on this paper is small and has little volume against all of the white space. This suggests a sort of reticence on this textmaker's part to fully commit to this perception of females. Textmaker 2 led this conversation through his use of bold orange, black, pink, and purple crayons. The face and hands were colored orange, and the application of the crayon was intense. Textmaker 2 focused a great deal on this area of the image. He morphed Santa Claus—"HO! HO! HO!"—with a witch, and in so doing erased any beauty that might be associated with females. The orange face, turned down and inward eyebrows, and the mustache above the half-smile bring attention to those features that often signal beauty, but instead again served as a counternarrative to beauty, with an intent to ridicule. Textmaker 3 carried on this conversation and added exaggeration to his female; her large rectangular teeth are bucked. Her eyes are empty circles, and hair straight and dull. Across the three texts, all females smile. The Textmakers were these smiles, boys vicariously engaging in their ability to present girls in unattractive ways, and also suggesting their inability to see themselves as partnered with or romancing them—yet. Textmaker 4, a female, engaged with the activity and drew a pretty girl, again a counternarrative to how she actually viewed how boys should view girls. Like the boys, she, too, focused on the facial features that highlight one's beauty. Textmaker 4's female has straight posture, perfectly coifed hair, green bright eyes, slightly upturned smile, and adorned with beautiful jewelry. On her text, she wrote, "I don't think that gender should have anything to do with the art. Not all boys draw cars, guns, hunters and policeman." Her conversation about how boys look at girls as objects of beauty ran counter to how these three boys really saw girls. Although only found in three visual texts, these visual elements in the boys' texts created a strong response in us. Female textmakers did not take up a discourse that positioned boys in negative ways.

DISCUSSION

Although visual texts had unique features, when studied carefully, recurrent and/or shared elements suggested that children dynamically engaged in both gendered and discursive visual conversations. They shared and replicated elements and objects that were fused with cultural symbolism (flowers = love), a sharing that became an issue of critical literacy and power (Lewison, Leland, & Harste, 2008). Although these children had experiences studying gender, as Davies et al. (2001) might argue, experience in this study was not defined by engagement with a topic. Rather, experience was defined in how children constituted each other as gendered subjects, "experiencing subjects" (p. 168) whose visual representations arose not just from authoritative positions of knowing about gender (what they have seen or felt), but also from what they sought to visually explain. They were recognizing gender through "clichéd binaries" (Davies, et al., 2001), and, at the moment of textmaking, were visually "improvising" these roles as gendered subjects within their doing of gender (Butler, 2004). In essence, they were taking up available discourses of gender, and visually representing the selves that they were taking each other to be. Studying objects and elements that cut across multiple visual texts enables educators to see how children are starting and taking up conversations, and how these conversations take shape and make discourses visible, both of which point to questions of power. Some children lacked confidence in their own experiencing (Textmaker 5), while others (Textmaker 1) more confidently constituted gender, and influenced those around them.

At the same time that these visual conversations indicated children's normative assumptions about gender roles, art as a language allowed them to take on aspects of gender that they might not in other spaces or languages. Butler (1990) argued that we all put on a gender performance, whether traditional or not. She continued that it is not a question of whether to *do* a gender performance, but what form that performance will take. Said differently, gender is not stable, but is flexibly performed, improvised, and situated by the context. Asking students to draw what they considered the interests of the opposite sex, we positioned them to see how this performance would look. Only one girl (Figure 7) saw this engagement as a sort of predictable gender performance—she drew what she knew boys would expect of her. Yet, by so doing, she engaged in the very performance that she worked against, thus, indicating the stronghold that discourses have around normative roles of males and females. As gender performance and through the genre of traditional fantasy, seven boys were able to participate in the discourse of romance. They moved away from binary thought and dualism, and towards multiple subject positions (Davies & Harré, 1990), without shame or ridicule in a world often ascribed to girls. We believe exploration of beliefs through art allows for such play and performance. Choosing to be different about it, Butler argued, might work to change gender norms and the binary understanding of masculinity and femininity.

From a critical perspective, this study provides some evidence that visual conversations raise questions about power relations that exist within the classroom—who has the power to start the conversation, who takes it up, and who is the subject of how representations are made? Textmakers 1 and 2 took up discourses of tradition and romance/love. Through their engagement with these two texts, five other boys uncritically took up these two positions, and thus, in some ways, silenced their own perspectives. The three boys who drew beauty as counternarratives entered into a discourse of power, one in which they saw themselves as able to take away beauty and replace it with what is not beautiful. Art as a language system, in this instance, allowed for subversive communication. These three boys were able to carry on a silent, but visible, conversation that positioned girls as sexual objects, but unattractive objects. Art afforded them a way to say "Girls are ugly" without writing or saying it, both of which may have gotten them into trouble. This study suggests that visual representations make visible the complex interplay among signifier (the form the sign takes) and signification (the concept represented), and the social and discursive practices that are part of classroom practices. Implied in this study is the need for visual texts to be collected and organized, and studied as conversations about aspects of humanity and life. When placed alongside each other, the discourses within compositions that children create are more easily discernible. Once these beliefs are made visible, educators and children can more critically interrogate these perspectives.

This study provides evidence that children's pictures must be taken seriously; they convey visible and invisible messages of their understandings of gender, experiences associated with it, and the power afforded to one sex over the other. By helping children read, analyze, and talk about the visual texts they create and, especially about size, volume, color, and design layout as well as context, they can learn to read their own as well as professionally generated texts with a more critical eye. In instances in which educators ask children to produce visual texts in conjunction with their understanding of a literary text, of informational texts or studies (like gender and race), or an original text, educators should be prepared to read and respond to this visual information. Further, educators should avoid saying, "Don't worry, I can't draw either" or "Don't worry about the art." To say such phrases suggests that art as a language has limited potential to communicate and be interpreted. This study shows otherwise.

Implications for Teaching and Curriculum

Like educators who have used critical literacy to address issues of power, agency, and voice in written texts, we want to argue for a critical framework for examining visual texts created in elementary and secondary language arts classes. First, we believe it is crucial to understand art as a visual language, and its potential to act on children and be reproduced as knowledge about someone or something. To understand visual language as such is to consider how it is learned (assumptions about messages conveyed through art), structural elements that comprise it, and strategies to become critical viewers and producers of visual texts. Rather than merely accept unconditionally children's representation of ideas, concepts, and perceptions as neutral, we want to suggest, like Kress (1988), that language, texts, and culture are intertwined, and that no visual representation is without interest or beliefs.

Second, educators can benefit from working with visual discourse analysis, a way of doing close readings that allow for a different interpretation of how children communicate—structurally, graphically, semantically, and pragmatically. We want to support such learning and suggest that the structure of all languages, including visual, dramatic, mathematic, music, and movement, should hold importance in reading, consuming, and critiquing messages within a range of texts. With children accessing the Internet at astronomical rates, creating multimedia projects, and participating in this multimedia world, they should be prepared to read, analyze, and produce messages with the intention and information of language systems.

Third, we also suggest that educators engage in ethical reflection of how classroom practices offer students experiences engaging with a range of texts, while at the same time, they are experiencing—improvising—subject positions within these texts, and producing knowledge informed by discourses. Visual discourse analysis provides educators and/or students a method by which they can study their texts, identify discourses, and engage in critical discussions about knowledge, representation, and power. When studied systematically, together they can begin to understand patterns that emerge across texts, develop strategies for critically viewing texts, and engage in important and critical discussions about social locations, identities, and cultural information associated with objects, contexts, and subject matters.

Implications for Future Research

It is our hope that this research precipitates further research into the role that visual texts play in learners' expressions of their beliefs and perceptions about the world. We especially encourage educators and researchers, located in a site in which children regularly create visual texts, to study them not only in the way that we have, but also across time and space. What more could be learned from children if we examined their visual texts created on day one of the fall term to the end of their school year? What markers of identity would we find or notice? What *other* aspects or information regarding their social and literacy practices would become apparent? Additionally, we hope that literacy and ELA researchers and educators will take a more serious and more critical look at the role of the visual arts, not just as a catalyst for strong writing or for development of comprehension in written texts, but as a language itself with opportunities for play and performance.

REFERENCES

Albers, M. M. (1996). *Art as literacy: The dynamic interplay of pedagogy and gendered meaning making in sixth grade art classes* (Doctoral dissertation), Indiana University, Bloomington, IN.
Albers, P. (2007). Visual discourse analysis: An introduction to the analysis of school-generated visual texts. In D. W. Rowe, R. T. Jiménez, D. L. Compton, D. K. Dickinson, Y. Kim, K. M. Leander, & V. J. Risko (Eds.), *56th Yearbook of the National Reading Conference* (pp. 81-95). Oak Creek, WI: NRC.
Albers, P., & Frederick, T. (2009). *Literacy (re)marks: A study of seven teachers' visual texts across time.* In V. J. Risko, D. L. Compton, D. K. Dickinson, M. Hundley, R. T. Jiménez, K. M. Leander, D. W. Rowe, & Y. Kim (Eds.), *58th Yearbook of the National Reading Conference* (pp. 112-128). Oak Creek, WI: NRC.
Albers, P., Frederick, T., & Cowan, K. (2009). Features of gender: A study of the visual texts of third grade students. *Journal of Early Childhood Literacy, 9*(2), 243-269.
Albers, P., Vasquez, V. M., & Harste, J. C. (2008). A classroom with a view: Teachers, multimodality and new literacies. *Talking Points, 19*(2), 3-13.
Berger, K. (2000). *A theory of art.* New York, NY: Oxford University Press.
Blackburn, M. V. (2007). The experiencing, negotiation, breaking, and remaking of gender rules and regulations by queer youth. *Journal of Gay & Lesbian Issues in Education, 4*(2), 33-54.
Boyatzis, C. J., & Eades, J. (1999). Gender differences in preschoolers' and kindergarteners' artistic production and preference. *Sex Roles, 41*(7/8), 627-637.
Butler, J. (1990) *Gender trouble: feminism and the subversion of identity.* London, UK: Routledge.
Butler, J. (2004). *Undoing gender.* New York, NY: Routledge.
Cazden, C. B. (2001). *Classroom discourse.* Portsmouth, NH: Heinemann.
Cherney, I. D., Seiwert, C. S., Dickey, T. M., & Flichtbeil, J. D. (2006). Children's drawings: A mirror to their minds. *Educational Psychology, 26*(1), 127-142.
Davies, B. (1993). Beyond dualism and towards multiple subjectivities. In L. Christian-Smith (Ed.). *Texts of desire: Essays on fiction, femininity and schooling* (pp. 145-173). London, UK: Falmer Press.
Davies, B. (2000). *(In)scribing body/language relations.* Walnut Creek, CA: Alta Mira Press.
Davies, B., Dormer, S., Gannon, S., Laws, C., Rocco, S., Taguchi, H. L., & McCann, H. (2001). Becoming schoolgirls: The ambivalent project of subjectification. *Gender and Education, 13*(2), 167-182.

Davies, B., & Harré, R. (1990). Positioning: The discursive production of selves. *Journal for the Theory of Social Behavior, 20*(1), 43-61.

Duncum, P. (1989). Children's unsolicited drawings of violence as a site of social contradiction. *Studies in Art Education, 30*(4), 249-256.

Efland, A. D. (1965). *The effects of perceptual training upon the differentiation of form in children's drawing* (Doctoral dissertation). Stanford University, Stanford, CA.

Efland, A. D. (2002). *Art and cognition: Integrating the visual arts in the curriculum.* New York, NY: Teachers College Press.

Fairclough, N. (2003). *Analysing discourse: Textual analysis for social research.* London, UK: Routledge.

Gee, J. (2005). *An introduction to discourse analysis: Theory and method* (2nd ed.). Abingdon, England: Routledge.

Geertz, C. (1983). *Local knowledge: Further essays in interpretive anthropology.* New York, NY: Basic Books.

Gurian, M., & Stevens, K. (2005). *The minds of boys: Saving our sons from falling behind in school and life.* San Francisco, CA: Jossey Bass.

Halliday, M. A. K. (1985). *An introduction to functional grammar.* London, UK: Arnold.

Hobbs, R., & Frost, R. (2003). Measuring the acquisition of media-literacy skills. *Reading Research Quarterly, 38*(3), 330-354.

Hodge, R., & Kress, G. (1988). *Social semiotics.* Cambridge, UK: Polity Press.

Kiefer, B. (2007). *Charlotte Huck's children's literature.* New York, NY: McGraw-Hill.

Kress, G. (1988). Language as social practice. In: G. Kress (Ed.), *Communication and culture: An introduction* (pp. 79-129). Sydney, Australia: UNSW Press.

Kress, G. (2003). *Literacy in the new media age.* New York, NY: Routledge.

Kress, G., & van Leeuwen, T. (2006). *Reading images: The grammar of visual design* (2nd ed.). New York, NY: Routledge.

Lark-Harovitz, B., Lewis, H., & Luca, M. N. (1967). *Understanding children's art for better teaching.* Columbus, OH: Merrill.

Lewison, M., Leland, C., & Harste, J.C. (2008). *Creating critical classrooms: K-8 reading and writing with an edge.* Philadelphia, PA: Lawrence Erlbaum Inc.

McClure, L. J. (1999). Wimpy boys and macho girls: Gender equity at the crossroads. *English Journal, 88*(3), 78-82.

McNiff, K. (1981). *Sex differences in children's art* (Doctoral dissertation). Boston University, Boston, MA.

Reeves, J. B., & Boyette, N. (1983). What does children's art tell us about gender? *Qualitative Sociology, 6,* 322-333.

Robertson, T., & Albers, P. (October, 1994). *Middle school adolescents' beliefs about art.* Paper presented at the annual meeting of Journal of Curriculum Theorizing Conference, Banff, Canada.

Rowsell, J., & Pahl, K. (2007). Sedimented identities in texts: Instances of practice. *Reading Research Quarterly, 42*(3), 388-404.

Schwandt, T. A. (1994). Constructivist, interpretivist approaches to human inquiry. In N. K. Denzin & Y. S. Lincoln (Eds.), *Handbook of qualitative research* (pp. 118-137). Thousand Oaks, CA: Sage.

Sonesson, G. (1988). *Methods and models in pictorial semiotics.* Report 3 from the Semiotics Project. Lund, Sweden: Lund University.

Tuman, D. (1999). Gender style as form and content: An examination of gender stereotypes in subject preference of children's drawing. *Studies in Art Education, 41*(1), 40-60.

Winterson, J. (1995). *Art objects: Essays on ecstasy and effrontery.* London, UK: J. Cape.

Redesigning Memoir: A Design-Based Investigation of Materiality and New Literacy Practices in an Elementary Classroom's Writing Workshop

Randy Bomer
Melody Zoch
Ann D. David
The University of Texas at Austin

It is widely understood these days that digital tools such as personal computers and digital environments such as the Internet are spurring literate people and communities to develop and sustain new literacy practices (Lankshear & Knobel, 2003; Leu, Kinzer, Coiro, & Cammack, 2004). Among many other things, new literacies demand new composing processes and knowledge of new forms of texts—texts that in fact work differently and must be designed more deliberately than most of us have been taught to do. For example, we know that many digital and multimedia texts employ varied modalities—such as sound, movement, and visual images—alongside print (Faigley, 1999; Kress, 2003; Kress & van Leeuwen, 2001; National Council of Teachers of English, 2005; Yancey, 2004). We know that texts in the current environment have a more deliberately designed (or re-designed) appearance, size, physical functionality, and use variously designed materials (The New London Group, 2000; Wysocki, Johnson-Eilola, Selfe, & Sirc, 2004). We know that texts that appear on networks such as the Internet often tend to be shorter, more fragmented, and do their development of ideas by linking to other texts, by the same author and by others (Barabasi, 2002; Faigley & Romano, 1995; Morgan, 2002; Weinberger, 2002). These changes present immediate challenges to educators, as many have noted. As the literacy practices that "count" shift, how do teachers make them available to students, even as curricula in older forms continue to prevail? How do we make the underlying practices available to students, rather than merely electronic tools? How is it possible to teach such practices even in situations where tools and technology are limited, non-functioning, or non-existent, which, like it or not, is still the state of things in many schools?

This study reports on a design-based inquiry in which researchers, one of whom was the classroom teacher, offered students experiences with three practices intrinsic to new literacies: linking, multimodality, and design. However, these experiences were undertaken with concrete materials—paper, string, markers, boxes, and other inexpensive and readily-available supplies. We made these choices for three reasons. First, the school did not have digital resources sufficient to the task. Second, we reasoned that children might construct understandings of abstracted, metaphorical tasks on computers more readily if they have had experiences with concrete instantiations of practices. And third, we believe that one educational opportunity afforded by technological shifts is that we need to pay more attention to underlying practices rather than focusing on techniques for operating particular devices and software programs.

We wanted to find out:

- What designs for composing invitations allow young writers to adhere to their rhetorical and aesthetic purposes (within a given curriculum) while also introducing linking, multimodality, and design as literacy practices?

- When textuality is opened to include linking, multimodality, and design, within a classroom that values students' intentions as writers, what do the finished products look like?

- What happens when non-electronic practices drawn from new literacies are introduced in material ways to a classroom pursuing a writing workshop curriculum of notebooks, literary genre studies, and test preparation?

- In what ways does a focus on the materiality of these literacy practices undertaken with concrete supplies permit or inhibit an identification of the practices as similar to or different from their instantiations in digital environments?

PERSPECTIVE/THEORETICAL FRAMEWORK

We view literacy as social, situated practice (Barton, Hamilton, & Ivanic, 2000; Scribner & Cole, 1981). If literacy in classrooms is viewed as sociocultural practice, then its development, even in individuals, may be viewed as a collaborative and concrete achievement. Researchers, then, must attend to the means by which actors in the activity systems of classrooms manage to work together to construct the details of learning. Such attention is aided by recent theoretical developments, stemming from new literacies and technological studies, as well as sociocultural, feminist, and queer theories, which make reading and writing visible as embodied and material practices (Bleich, 2001; Haas, 1996; Horner, 2000). That is, it is worth paying attention to the social and material things readers and writers are doing when they say they are reading and writing—the interactions, tools, artifacts, scripts, movements, positions, geographical spaces, language games, and forms of life that are involved. Reading and writing do not simply occur inside of heads. Reading and writing occur in fingers and hands, in sitting positions, on floors and in chairs, at a specific distance from other people, under particular lighting conditions and with sound waves of particular intensity (Leander, 2002; Rowe & Leander, 2005; Selzer & Crowley, 1999). They occur in the midst of particular social relationships and power relations (Clark & Ivanic, 1997; Lemke, 1995), at particular moments of individual life histories, and at specific geographic locations (Leander & Sheehy, 2004).

As stated above, we also draw upon research on technology and new literacies (Coiro, Knobel, Lankshear, & Leu, 2008) and on theory pertaining to digital composing, multimedia, and new forms of textuality in the field of composition (Bolter, 1991, 1998; George, 2002; Rice, 2008; Selfe, 1999; Selfe & Hawisher, 2004; Shipka, 2005; Wysocki, et al., 2004). In much of this work in higher education, scholars have been reminding their readers that emerging practices common to digital composing are still material, and that writing tasks employing concrete things like paper, ink, and string may be used to help students manipulate objects in order to build constructed understandings of practices on a computer, even though they may seem more ethereal or hidden (George, 2002; Shipka, 2005; Wysocki, et al., 2004).

METHODS

We selected a fourth-grade classroom for our study, and fourth-grade is the year of a writing test. We chose a school in a relatively disadvantaged section of a Southwestern city, which meant that access to digital devices in the building would be minimal. The school was 88% Latino, and

94% economically disadvantaged. This was a bilingual class, and all of the children spoke Spanish, though some were English dominant in school and among their friends. Our sampling, then, was purposive, in that new literacy practices would have to fit into an existing curriculum with substantial demands on time and attention, with students from a linguistic and ethnic group that experiences disproportionate vulnerability to school failure and other systemic disadvantage, and with no support for technological innovation. The children, we knew, brought substantial linguistic and knowledge resources to the classroom, and the teacher was skilled in purposeful code-switching in support of students' learning and also emotionally and ideologically supportive of children's multilingualism.

Melody, who was the teacher and also a member of the research team, employed a workshop design for her composition pedagogy. Students learned first to write about their most immediate thinking in writers' notebooks, and then to integrate these notebooks into other parts of their lives, such as experiences at home or on the playground. The notebooks, then, grew into tools for noticing and collecting and thinking. Later, when moving into specific genre writing invitations, students could read through the notebook for important themes from their own lives and experiences. These entries and themes were then developed through drafting and revision processes into finished examples of particular genres. Our research activity began after notebooks were under way, shortly before the first genre unit about memoir. The teachers on the fourth-grade team had selected memoir for two main reasons: because it valued students' lives outside school, their families and memories, and because it was close to the kind of writing they would be required to produce on the writing test in February.

We planned our research, drawing upon some of the principles of design-based research (Cobb, Confrey, DiSessa, Lehrer, & Schauble, 2003; Design-Based Research Collective, 2003; Reeves, 2000; Reinking & Bradley, 2008), which attempts to understand how well, how, and why a new design for activity works and seeks to understand the world in the process of attempting to transform it. This methodology is iterative, involving cycles of application and assessment, and it is attentive to responsiveness in process rather than hoping for a linear progression toward an outcome. Reeves (2000) states that design research begins with an analysis of practical problems by researchers and practitioners in collaboration, and moves from there to the development of solutions based on existing design principles and technological innovations. What follows that analysis and development is a number of iterative cycles of testing and refinement of those solutions in actual practice. These cycles lead researchers to reflect in order to produce "design principles" and enhance the ways they understand to go about implementing the solution.

Our team of practitioners and researchers (all four were experienced at both teaching writing and at research) began by reviewing literature on new literacy practices and collaboratively analyzing our own digital literacy processes in order to establish *linking, multimodality,* and *design* as the conceptualized practical problem with which we were engaging. We then designed collaboratively a set of two or three iterations of experiences pertaining to each of these practices; that is, we designed two to three lessons for each practice (two linking, three multimodal, two design) that could fit well within the memoir unit. Each of these lessons required us to assess student understanding and engagement with the practice, as well as assess the degree to which the practice advanced the students' purposes as they developed content for, composed, and revised their memoirs. Generally, design-based research should not be considered complete until the solutions have been tested in multiple sites or across multiple years (Design-Based Research Collective, 2003), but we are here presenting our findings from a single setting. Our solutions were iterative within this single overall cycle, but the whole cycle has yet to be re-tested.

Data analysis was conducted in two phases. In the first phase of our analysis we recast our narratives of "what happened with linking," "what happened with multimodality," and "what happened with design." We conducted close, visual analysis of multiple photographs of each child's composition, including fields in a database for: description, features, fonts, images, interactivity, materials, pathways, size, and text. We then proceeded to analyze more categorically in terms of the design/textual features of the finished products themselves and the relationships visible between those features and the practices as they exist in digital environments. In the second phase of analysis, we looked across cases in order to identify themes and characteristics that emerged. Using Tinderbox software as an analytical tool, we identified three categories from our initial first-level codes. The three categories to emerge were: Design of alphabetic text; Visual design; and Re-use and redesign, which are the categories in which we report our cross-case analysis below. What follows is a detailed description of a few of these artifacts and a cross-case analysis.

DATA SOURCES

Data collection lasted eight weeks in total. Data included photographic copies of students' writing in their writers' notebooks prior to the beginning of the cycle. During two preliminary class sessions, then the six writing workshop sessions in which we offered an iteration of the target practices, plus a museum trip, plus the celebration/publication event—10 events in all—we interviewed students as they worked, made field notes, and shot digital video with two cameras. At the end of each of these sessions, we made multiple sets of photographs of the artifacts produced during that session, and also of notebook entries and drafted revisions that occurred in between the major data collection events. At the final authors' celebration, where their work was displayed, we videotaped and made photographs of the artifacts and the interactions of students and others while they examined the objects.

Melody supplemented our collected data with observational data recorded when the rest of the team was not in the classroom and additional photos. In all, we have approximately 16 hours of video, 600 photos, and 90 pages of field notes. For this article, our analysis focuses on photos of the final objects and selected moments of students' composing practices.

RESULTS

Looking Closely at Selected Memoir Artifacts

Isaiah constructed his memoir (Figure 1) from a picture frame box, 8" by 6" by 1/2", which he cut along one of the 8" sides to allow the entire box to fold out, creating an open interior space as a user interface. He could close the memoir box with a long piece of ribbon running through the middle and holes on both sides. The memoir was designed to lie flat on a table surface while the reader should interact with it by lifting certain mobile components. One of the design decisions

Figure 1. Interior View of Isaiah's Memoir

Isaiah made was to pay considerable attention to the background and physicality of the main structure so when a reader picked up certain parts, there still remained on the inner surface of the box a cohesive memoir rather than blank cardboard. He used a mixture of photographs, colored paper, scrapbook paper, stationery, and stickers to create a colorful collage designed as a sort of playground for the reader's attention.

As a closed object, his memoir resembled a book or container for holding related objects. When opened completely, it was like the busy interface of computer software or Internet pages with choices about where to click and go. Several of the features in Isaiah's designed memoir were loose rather than tied together or glued down, such as a photograph of him with his brother and a map of his neighborhood. The outside was covered with scrapbook paper and he used die cut letters to make the title, "My Baby Brother." The design communicates multimodally through text, image, collage, movement, and texture.

Isaiah chose to break up his memoir about his baby brother. Some fragments were sequential and others stood on their own as smaller pieces of text. For example, on the main page Isaiah hand wrote "Manuel, Yo te quiero" ("Manuel, I love you"), and that fragment is non-sequential and can be read anytime in the reader's engagement with the text. Other sections require the reader to follow a sequential pathway (Kress, 2003). On the upper left-hand corner Isaiah placed a pocket decorated with Santa Claus stickers that operates as a container for small cards. Isaiah began the sequential narrative section of his memoir on one of these cards, labeled with the number one. Number two is hand written on a piece of blue computer paper pasted onto the bottom left corner with the text printed using a sans-serif font. He then continues the rest of his memoir on the rest of the cards inside of the pocket as the numbers indicate.

Parallel to this, Isaiah has written a shorter version of his memoir on the right-hand side on a square piece of blue paper tied to the edge along with other square pieces of paper. He used black ink to write this abbreviated form of the story. The third page of this collection of papers says "Escribe" (write), and he explained that this was for his readers to write back to him, and in particular, he had his mother in mind. This act of linking the sub-sections of his memoir, and the design of reader interactivity in the invitation to write in response and forge a path through the complex text, are examples of the literacy practices, sometimes thought of as native to digital spaces, that we worked to foster within this particular study of memoir.

There were two foldouts included in Isaiah's memoir, detached but fitting inside the box when closed. For the celebration, Isaiah displayed them both unfolded, placed above the box interface. One of the foldouts was a map of his neighborhood, which, he said, he included so the reader could see where his story took place. The other foldout contains a small book adjoined in the center that resembles an activity book. Part of it is an illustrated flipbook labeled "Flip-O-Rama," and it showed an incident when his brother hit him with a toy truck. Another part of this booklet contains storyboard frames where he told the story again through the genre of a comic book. The multimodal repetition of the story of his little brother throwing a toy truck and hitting Isaiah in the head seems like a near-obsessive re-narrating of the event, somewhat undercutting the sentimentality of the main text's protestations of love.

One interesting aspect of Isaiah's memoir was the way he dealt with interactivity. The complexity of how he designed his memoir and his use of multiple pathways (Kress, 2003) seemed to combine many of the strategies that other students in the class explored. Some used numbers to indicate a specific pathway while others indicated no specific or dictated pathways. This planned navigation was a design feature of many students' objects, with pathways thought through from beginning to end. The reading of Isaiah's memoir can begin with the outside, where the title is placed, and proceeds through the many available sections of the interior, sometimes author-planned, sometimes at the user's liberty. This outside-inside movement is similar to other decisions students made whose memoirs often moved from the exterior to the interior with text wrapping around the outside of the box.

Figure 2. Top View of Maria's Memoir

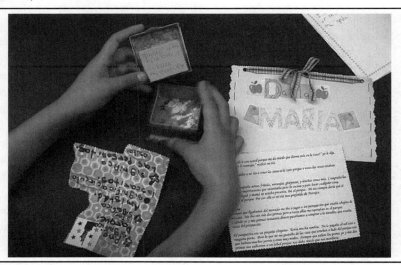

Maria wrote her memoir (Figure 2) about her aunt, whom she loved "as if she were [her] mother." Right away, Maria chose a small two-inch square box for her memoir. After spending time with the box and considering how to tell her story with it, she decided to type her memoir using an italic font on pink paper trimmed with a ruffled border created from using scissors with a decorative edge rather than a smooth cutting edge. Rather than placing the pink paper onto or inside of the box, Maria created a separate envelope to house the text. There is a metaphorical link, then, between the envelope and the box. Both combine to create Maria's memoir, like separate paragraphs combine to tell a story, but unlike writers working with traditional print paragraphs, the author opened up more possible paths for the audience to follow through her narrative.

Once those design decisions were made, Maria was able to focus her attention on the box and how to incorporate it. The result was the addition of more text, including the title, "Quiero a mi tía como fuera mi mamá" ("I love my aunt as if she were my mother") handwritten on a flap under the lid. Inside the box Maria placed confetti made from shapes punched out of art hole punchers, including a tree, a star, a circle, and a bear. To make these confetti signify more definitively, Maria created a legend that folds up inside of the box, and shows that each shape stands for something from the story. Quantities of each object represented their intensity or importance in the memoir. For example, the tree signifies the park and the star signifies friendship. With the inclusion of a legend, what at first appears to be an arts and crafts activity reveals deliberately composed and designed meanings and thoughtful, creative decision-making.

Alicia, like Maria, chose a small square box to tell her story, which also was fitting for her memoir (Figure 3). While Maria's box was made from cardboard and its lid came completely off the box, Alicia's box was wood with a hinged lid. The outside of her box contains a paw print and the title "When my dog died." In addition, Alicia made a strap from ribbon to carry the box. The inside of the box contains small square pieces of paper cut to fit inside the box with her story typed on them. The first card reads, "My dog Junior was white and he had brown spots too. He was so nice and I loved him. He was so little." The papers are all numbered in order to help readers know the correct sequence. Alicia designed her story so that readers would have to take out the papers and either cradle them in their hands or set them all out on the table. There is an overall effect of tininess, of a little, precious thing that begs close attention. Again, she chose multiple channels for her message. And while her cards are assigned an order, the links between them and among the cards and the box create a looser network of ideas than a more linearly structured written memoir would. Alicia, like Maria and Isaiah, began with her own memories, examined them through the lenses of multimodality, linking, and design, and composed rich and thoughtful memoirs.

Figure 3. Interior View of Alicia's Memoir

Table 1. Analysis of Students' Designed Objects.

Practice	Definition	Examples
Multimodality	Connections among fragments of text; composing into a network of small pieces; nonlinear relationships among sections of a single text	Using markers to enhance particular notebook entries while collecting memories for possible inclusion in the memoir.
		Illustrating a specific moment from the rough draft of the memoir as a way of going back into the text to infuse additional detail.
Linking	Purposeful or playful combinations of text, image, sound, interactivity; writing as materially made of color, size, shape; shifts of modality in the midst of composing and reading	Moving between important objects brought from home and conversations around those objects—linking home and school experiences—to collect memories for possible inclusion in the memoir.
		Manipulating post-it notes with pieces of a draft of the memoir to reorganize thoughts and add additional details.
Design	Conceptualization of the whole text as a working object; deliberate use of design elements and available resources for social effect; playful attention to user's experience of interacting with text	Using cropping-L's to focus in on particular pieces of photographs and write out of those redesigned images.
		Choosing particular materials for design of the final memoir from a varied assortment of papers, stickers, ribbons, boxes, markers, text, and images.

Cross-case Analysis

After conducting a close visual analysis of students' designed objects and noting the ways in which they took up different ways of designing, linking, and using multimodality, we began the third phase of analysis. This allowed us to look across cases and identify three new categories: Design of alphabetic text, Visual design, and Re-use and redesign. The definitions of each category are as follows. Design of alphabetic text refers to the print in and on the objects. The visual design of the objects represents the visual elements beyond alphabetic text. The re-use and redesign category addressed the ways in which community resources were integrated into the objects.

Design of alphabetic text. Though we viewed the complete objects as text, in all their varied modalities, our analysis led us to pay special attention to how each student designed the alphabetic text that formed part of the memoir. Because text is read in time, in some linear sequence or another, the layout of text on a three-dimensional object creates potential pathways for the reader, whether or not the author attempts to control the reader's movement from one section to another. Thus, the writer's decision about text placement in space has the potential to shape the reading experience of the viewer. These variations in the material design of the text force the writer to use diverse strategies of cohesion and intratextual reference. The gluing of a single long sheet inside a box, for example, created different language demands than did an array of small squares of text in a non-sequential order. Here, we describe these material, spatial decisions related to placement of paper with alphabetic text on them.

First, students made design decisions about where text was to appear: on the object itself, on paper attached to the object but stationary, or on paper that could be removed from the object and manipulated independently by the reader. These variable placements of text permitted different kinds of emphasis, relationships among parts, and interactivity for readers. Furthermore, when actually inscribing the text for their memoirs, they also made many decisions about the font, size, color, and form of the text. Some students handwrote pieces of text using various pencils, pens and markers, often in combination, for various visual effects. Some cut out words and letters from stationery. Others used computer-printed passages of text, often altered by being colored, cut, or otherwise changed to better fit the meaning and/or design of the memoir. With this broader range of materials available, students drew on a wider array of semiotic resources than is typically available in more traditional print texts found in schools.

Students also designed the ways their various text pieces hung together. Some created several parallel texts all related to the topic or theme of the memoir. The non-linear structure of these fragmented memoirs most resembled that of some forms of hypertext. Others chose a longer continuous piece written or printed either on a single piece of paper or several sequenced sheets or cards. These texts, more typically valued in school, tended to use cohesion strategies more akin to those common in print culture. Still others chose to incorporate both of these ideas with some small pieces of text and some larger, continuous pieces. Again, opening the possibilities for students allowed them to make choices and explore multiple ways of delivering their memoir to their audience.

The third decision we saw students making was in the way they expected the audience to interact with the object to reveal the text in time. Almost all objects required the reader to interact physically with them in order to read the alphabetic text. Some had to be turned around or sideways, or perpendicular, to make visible the various surfaces on which the text was written. In such cases, the entire text was not accessible from a single vantage point or at a single glance but rather had to be pursued across surfaces. Others had to be opened by either removing the lid or untying a string to get to the contents. Some required manipulation of various pieces of the object, sometimes attached to the rest of the object and sometimes detachable to reveal various pieces of text. Thus, the reader was required to take a more active role in the revealing of the text and choose a path through it.

In these material decisions about the design of alphabetic text, students mirrored decisions that designers make in creating online content. They designed the size and appearance of content, whether written or typed, on pieces of paper or glued to boxes, and how those pieces were to be linked, with glue, numbers, or less tangible links. They also considered how their audience would move through these pieces of text, allowing their audience more or less freedom by virtue of the overall design of the object. Similarly, Web designers choose carefully how much content is immediately available to the reader and in what ways the reader will access that content. Web designers often create sites that require readers to select from among a series of moves through the content to transact with the text (Krug, 2000). In this way, the students' work with readily-available school supplies closely mirrored decisions made by designers working in digital environments.

Visual design. Visual design is a part of all texts, even ones like this for the *NRC Yearbook*, in that there are choices of font, layout, color, size, and other elements. In this paper, those decisions are standardized in order to provide a common look among sections, to accommodate page limits in the *Yearbook*, and to project an image of academic authority. The students in the class we studied chose from a wider set of design possibilities and so more visual elements were part of their actual composing of meaning. In these objects, visual design elements included the selection of the container; the layering of paper, text, and color; and the appearance of images.

Creating a memoir, students began by choosing from a large selection of boxes their teacher made available. The design lesson Melody taught before they began work on the objects included other possibilities, including altered books and mobiles, but in this class, every student made their object from some kind of box, though the products ended up widely varied nonetheless. Some examples included shoeboxes, photo frame boxes, jewelry boxes, small papier-mâché boxes, and small wooden boxes. As students chose their boxes, they began composing within the possibilities of that container. With the shoeboxes, some students turned them on end, others left them with the bottoms on the table; some used the lids and others did not. The photo boxes were cut along various surfaces to allow different means to access the inside of the box. The papier-mâché and small wooden boxes, though small, were packed with meaning by using almost every available surface, inside and outside. One student brought a Barbie wardrobe box from home that gave her many different possibilities. These choices of container are similar to an individual's decisions or acceptance of an interface that will hold particular Web content. The decision to create a static Web page, blog, wiki, Facebook group, or something else, in part, guides the direction that content will take, as some things are possible in some spaces but not in others.

Once the choice of box was made, the students began covering the surfaces of the boxes. The materials available to them included scrapbook paper of various designs, stationery, magazines, and colored copy paper. While the choice of covering seemed quite individual, one constant across the class was students' decision to layer. Many covered a box in paper, and then added texts, images, stickers, ribbons, or more paper on top of that first layer. This was done both with boxes that had designs already (like the shoeboxes) and blank boxes. Often, a background layer (or series of them) provided a frame for an image or text, a ground against which the author could position a figure. Some of the layering was related to the revealing of the texts. Some design allowed for all texts to be visible and available at once. In other designs, the audience was required to move through the layers to gain access to all of the texts. Layering is a key element in communicating content in digital spaces, as it is for the writers who combine Google Earth with a narrative to create map memoirs. Anyone who has used Photoshop or Adobe Acrobat will recognize the term "layering" as a metaphor for visual composing processes in digital environments.

Like the decisions students were making about texts, the decisions about visual design mirror some types of thinking that occur in digital environments. Students had to decide what sorts of backgrounds would support their larger themes, then layer content—both textual and visual—over that background. They made decisions about the accessibility of textual frames and how readers were to move through those, like web designers creating frames within a page and hyperlinks between pages. Also, by selecting the particular container to hold their composition, the students were learning how to compose with a more extensive repertoire of expressive resources than is common in school-based writing experiences.

Reuse and redesign. The memoirs that the students produced demonstrated one of the key strategies of thinking in new literacies—the reuse and redesign of community resources (The New

London Group, 2000). Three examples of this are their surprisingly ubiquitous use of angel stickers, the numbering of pieces of text, and the employment of map foldouts. Each instance of reuse carried across a number of memoirs, and it represented a redesign that served the specific purposes of the author's particular memoir.

Angel stickers seemed to be the most prevalent reuse in the final memoirs. These stickers were one of several types that were available to the students, including American flags, small animals, and encouraging words (Good Job, Wow). The angel stickers appeared far more frequently in the final memoirs, and many seemed attached to memoirs about important people in the students' lives. Hernan includes four angel stickers on the surface of his memoir about his baby cousin. Monica includes the sticker on the lid of her box that has been framed in ribbon and includes a piece of stationery, cut out with pinking shears, that says "mother" in a cursive script. In this case, the angel is made a prominent feature on the outside of the memoir. Katarina's memoir includes one angel sticker on the exterior of the box, as well as a sticker that accents one of her mobile pieces of text.

Several students also wanted to guide their readers through their memoirs and so chose to label the various pieces of text with numbers in purple marker. Monica's memoir includes three small booklets of text that are held in the box. Each booklet is clearly labeled with numbers in purple ink. Erminda, who created scrolls instead of booklets, also labeled her pieces using scrapbook tags attached with ribbon. Sonia's memoir includes many frames of immoveable text attached to the box. These individual frames are labeled in pen, a different inscription technology than that of the rest of the text in the frame. It is possible these were labeled after they were attached and Sonia wanted to clarify the path her readers should take through her memoir.

Another technology that appeared repeatedly in the memoirs was map foldouts. The original classroom demonstration included an explanation that pieces of paper folded in this particular way were one way to make a map. Several students then appropriated the technology. Daniel created a very detailed map of the zoo where his memoir takes place. Each animal and enclosure is carefully labeled in both Spanish and English. Isaiah, as we described above, used the technology in a similar manner by creating a map of his neighborhood. Erminda redesigned the fold-out shape to make a storyboard of her memoir that relied mostly on pictures to tell the story. She also clearly labeled the various frames to guide the reader through this particular narrative within her memoir.

Each of these instances of reuse includes students taking a resource that was available to them—stickers, numbering, or a particular way to fold paper—and making it work for their particular memoir. Instead of being inhibited by the relatively limited range of compositional resources immediately available in the environment—paper, stickers, markers, glue, etc.—the final memoirs demonstrate a willingness to make those technologies work in innovative ways and express what the students wanted to say about their particular life story. This type of reuse and redesign is endemic to memes that move through social networking sites or the blogosphere—a particular snippet of video that is repurposed over and over again, a photo that appears to different effect on dozens of personal blogs, the attachment of a politician's face to an inappropriate body or context. The resource is widely available to everyone on the Internet, and particular composers employ it for particular purposes.

DISCUSSION

As literacy evolves in practice throughout diverse settings in people's lives, educators must wrestle with issues of: access to technological tools, how students construct understandings of digital literacy practices, availability of professional development, teacher willingness to take on new practices with which they have limited experiences, and many other obstacles to making valued electronic literacy practices available to all members of society. If the availability of one laptop per child is a goal, it is not just around the corner for students like the ones in this study. We know, moreover, that the availability of computers does not lead to high levels of composing work in classroom and school environments (Selfe, 1999). In the meantime, we need ways of helping students understand the basic ways with text that are valued in these new, significant environments.

The materials we used in this study are readily available in most schools and communities. They are not expensive, and they do not require maintenance or updating. While we would not argue that engaging linking, multimodality, and design in a paper-based way is identical to digital composing, we see no reason to delay making these underlying practices available to students, though we cannot from this study make claims about transfer. So to answer the question of what happens when practices drawn from new literacies are introduced into the classroom in materials ways, we argue that students engaged fully and meaningfully with the ideas and materials with which they are surrounded and composed memoirs perceived as beautiful by members of their communities. Further, an invitation to compose a memoir in this way allowed them to grapple, through aesthetic and design decisions, with complex rhetorical issues of audience and argument.

At the same time, the practices that many people refer to as new literacies are not limited to digital tools. It often is remarked that the school system lags behind the production of new literacy practices in digital environments outside school. This is undoubtedly true and likely to remain so. One of the difficulties often discussed is the reluctance of teachers to take up digital devices and software with which they are unfamiliar and which, except in the most affluent systems and even then only in peak years when equipment and software are quite new, often simply do not work well. However, many elementary teachers are pretty comfortable with getting their students to make things with construction paper, markers, boxes, glue and tape. It might be a helpful insight in teacher education, inservice and pre-service, that new literacies are practices that are newly common, newly digitized, newly legitimated, but that they also connect to rather familiar environments as well, including environments of childhood. Teachers for whom digital composing may, at the moment, still seem far off, may warm more quickly to investigations like the one we describe here, which can be integrated into existing practices, even with disadvantaged students, even in a year with a high-stakes writing assessment.

Many children like to construct objects, or at least they can, it seems, easily be led toward enthusiasm over such constructions. And written composition, in this study, borrowed that enthusiasm, as students wrote texts of substantial length, even as they were also busy with engineering in 3-D and the design of visual elements. The readers who visited the classroom on the day of the celebration manipulated hinged doorways that revealed text passages, tied and untied the bows that sealed the inside world of texts from the exterior, and turned these memoirs around to follow their stories. Their interactions with those texts had been designed well before, by authors reaching into the future.

REFERENCES

Barabasi, A. L. (2002). *Linked: The new science of networks*. Cambridge, MA: Perseus.

Barton, D., Hamilton, M., & Ivanic, R. (Eds.). (2000). *Situated Literacies: Reading and Writing in Context*. London, UK: Routledge.

Bleich, D. (2001). The Materiality of Language and the Pedagogy of Exchange. *Pedagogy: Critical Approaches to Teaching Literature, Language, Composition, and Culture, 1*(1), 117-125.

Bolter, J. D. (1991). *Writing Space: The Computer, Hypertext, and the History of Writing*. New York, NY: Erlbaum.

Bolter, J. D. (1998). The world wide web and new definitions of literacy. In D. Reinking (Ed.), *Handbook of literacy and technology: Transformations in a post-typographic world*. New York, NY: Erlbaum.

Clark, R., & Ivanic, R. (1997). *The Politics of Writing*. London, UK: Routledge.

Cobb, P., Confrey, J., DiSessa, A., Lehrer, R., & Schauble, L. (2003). Design experiments in educational research. *Educational Researcher, 32*(1), 9-13.

Coiro, J. L., Knobel, M., Lankshear, C., & Leu, D. J. (Eds.). (2008). *Handbook of research on new literacies*. New York, NY: Erlbaum.

Design-Based Research Collective, T. (2003). Design-based research: An emerging paradigm for educational inquiry. *Educational Researcher, 32*(1), 5-8.

Faigley, L. (1999). Material literacy and visual design. In J. Selzer & S. Crowley (Eds.), *Rhetorical Bodies* (pp. 171-201). Madison, WI: University of Wisconsin Press.

Faigley, L., & Romano, S. (1995). Going Electric: Creating multiple sites for innovation in a writing program. In J. Janangelo & K. Hensen (Eds.), *Resituating writing: Constructing and administering writing programs* (pp. 46-58). Portsmouth, NH: Boyton-Cook.

George, D. (2002). From analysis to design: Visual communication in the teaching of writing. *College Composition and Communication, 54*(1), 11-39.

Haas, C. (1996). *Writing Technology: Studies on the materiality of literacy*. New York, NY: Erlbaum.

Horner, B. (2000). *Terms of Work for Composition: A Materialist Critique*. Albany, NY: State University of New York Press.

Kress, G. (2003). *Literacy in the new media age*. London, UK: Routledge.

Kress, G., & van Leeuwen, T. (2001). *Multimodal discourse: The modes and media of contemporary communication*. London, UK: Arnold.

Krug, S. (2000). *Don't make me think: A common sense approach to web usability*. Indianapolis, IN: New Riders.

Lankshear, C., & Knobel, M. (2003). *New Literacies: Changing knowledge and classroom learning*. Buckingham, UK: Open University Press.

Leander, K. (2002). Polycontextual Construction Zones: Mapping the Expansion of Schooled Space and Identity. *Mind, Culture, and Activity, 9*(3), 211-237.

Leander, K., & Sheehy, M. (Eds.). (2004). *Spatializing literacy research and practice*. New York, NY: Peter Lang.

Lemke, J. (1995). *Textual Politics: Discourse and social dynamics*. London, UK: Taylor & Francis.

Leu, D. J., Kinzer, C. K., Coiro, J. L., & Cammack, D. W. (2004). Toward a theory of new literacies emerging from the Internet and other information and communication technologies. In R. B. Ruddell & N. Unrau (Eds.), *Theoretical Models and Processes of Reading* (5th ed., pp. 1570-1613). Newark, DE: International Reading Association.

Morgan, W. (2002). Heterotropes: learning the rhetoric of hyperlinks. *Education, Communication, and Information, 2*(2/3), 215-233.

National Council of Teachers of English. (2005). Multi-modal literacies. Retrieved August 1, 2010 from http://www.ncte.org/about/over/positions/category/media/123213.htm

Reeves, T. C. (2000). *Enhancing the worth of instructional technology research through "design experiments" and other developmental research strategies*. Paper presented at the American Educational Research Association.

Reinking, D., & Bradley, B. A. (2008). *On formative and design experiments*. New York, NY: Teachers College Press.

Rice, J. E. (2008). Rhetoric's mechanics: Retooling the equipment of writing production. *College Composition and Communication, 60*(2), 366-387.

Rowe, D. W., & Leander, K. (2005). Analyzing the production of third space in classroom literacy events. In B. Maloch, J. V. Hoffman, D. L. Schallert, C. M. Fairbanks & J. Worthy (Eds.), *Fifty-fourth Yearbook of the National Reading Conference* (pp. 318-333). Oak Creek, WI: National Reading Conference.

Scribner, S., & Cole, M. (1981). *The psychology of literacy*. Cambridge, MA: Harvard University Press.

Selfe, C. L. (1999). *Technology and Literacy in the Twenty-First Century: The importance of paying attention.* Carbondale, IL: Southern Illinois University Press.

Selfe, C. L., & Hawisher, G. E. (2004). *Literate lives in the information age: Narratives of literacy from the United States.* New York, NY: Erlbaum.

Selzer, J., & Crowley, S. (Eds.). (1999). *Rhetorical Bodies.* Madison, WI: University of Wisconsin Press.

Shipka, J. (2005). A multimodal task-based framework for composing. *College Composition and Communication, 57*(2), 277-306.

The New London Group. (2000). A pegagogy of mulitliteracies: designing social futures. In B. Cope & M. Kalantzis (Eds.), *Multiliteracies: Literacy Learning and the Design of Social Futures* (pp. 9-38). London, UK: Routledge.

Weinberger, D. (2002). *Small pieces loosely joined: A unified theory of the web.* Cambridge, MA: Perseus.

Wysocki, A. F., Johnson-Eilola, J., Selfe, C. L., & Sirc, G. (2004). *Writing new media: Theory and applications for expanding the teaching of composition.* Logan, UT: University of Utah Press.

Yancey, K. B. (2004). Made not only in words: Composition in a new key. *College Composition and Communication, 56*(2), 297-328.

A National Survey of Barriers to Integrating Information and Communication Technologies into Literacy Instruction

Amy C. Hutchison
Iowa State University

David Reinking
Clemson University

Even though computers and Internet connections are available in virtually all schools in the U.S. (Wells & Lewis, 2006), and despite the increasing influence of Information and Communication Technologies (ICTs) on every aspect of literacy (Leu, Kinzer Coiro, & Cammack, 2004), there is evidence that ICTs are not integrated widely into literacy instruction, especially in ways that authentically address new forms of literacy (Hutchison, 2009; Cuban, 2001; Leander, 2007; Russell, Bebell, O'Dwyer, & O'Connor, 2003; Stolle, 2008; Smerdon, Cronen, Lanahan, Anderson, Iannotti, & Angeles, 2000). That lack of integration expands the increasing gap between forms of literacy practiced inside and outside of schools (Hutchison & Henry, 2010). The serious implications of that gap are implicit in repeated, forceful calls for more integration of ICTs into literacy instruction, for example, through position papers and new standards emanating from leading professional organizations such as the International Reading Association (2009) and the National Council of Teachers of English (2008).

Towards understanding and addressing a lack of integration, researchers have tried to identify what barriers teachers face in integrating ICTs into their instruction (Bauer & Kenton, 2005; Ertmer, Addison, Lane, Ross, & Woods, 1999; Honan, 2008; Stolle, 2008; Warschauer, Knobel, & Stone, 2004; Zhao, Pugh, Sheldon, & Byers, 2002). The purpose of the present study was first to determine if there were common barriers to integrating ICTs into instruction identified in previous studies. Then, especially when that review revealed a host of mostly non-overlapping barriers, to analyze the results of a national survey toward clarifying which of these barriers, and perhaps others, literacy teachers perceived as inhibiting their integration of ICTs into their instruction. That information is useful because it could inform professional development and other interventions aimed at increasing integration.

Theoretical Perspectives

The rationale for this study and its use of survey methods is based on Labbo and Reinking's (1999) position that research related to integrating technology into instruction is more likely to influence practitioners when it is framed within one or more of the multiple realities in which they might be invested. That view suggests the need for data to determine how teachers define their reality in relation to integrating ICTs into instruction, including their perceptions about the barriers they face. Consistent with that view, teachers' subjective beliefs about what barriers inhibit their integration of ICTs into instruction are as important, and arguably more important, than more objective data about what barriers may or may not actually exist. Research supports this theoretical perspective. Specifically, teachers' beliefs have frequently been found to be a major influence on how teachers conceptualize and use technology in their instruction (Bruce & Rubin, 1993; Ertmer, 2005; Clark & Peterson, 1986; Windschitl & Sahl, 2002; Zhao, Pugh, Sheldon, & Byers, 2002).

In related work, Reinking, Labbo, and McKenna (2000) suggested that the integration of digital technologies into instruction may occur developmentally. They drew an analogy between the Piagetian concept of assimilation and accommodation in children's learning, suggesting that teachers may first assimilate ICTs into their existing instruction. Subsequently, after greater experience, they may more authentically accommodate ICTs by more fundamentally transforming their instruction. At least indirectly, the kinds of barriers teachers identify may suggest where as a group they fall on a continuum from assimilation to accommodation, as illustrated by the research reviewed in the subsequent section. Survey data also have the potential to track changes over time in teachers' perceptions about barriers, which may suggest changes in their instructional beliefs and practices, as well as the practical circumstances that affect the extent to which they integrate ICTs into their instruction.

Barriers Identified in Previous Research

Possible barriers to technology integration across the curriculum have been studied using qualitative methods (Honan, 2008; Stolle, 2008; Warschauer, Knobel, & Stone, 2004, Zhao, Pugh, Sheldon, & Byers, 2002), mixed methods (Bauer & Kenton, 2005) and surveys (National Center for Educational Statistics, 2003). Studies have investigated teachers in elementary, middle, and high schools.

However, only Honan (2008) has investigated barriers specific to literacy teachers. She conducted semi-structured interviews with four literacy teachers working with students in Grades 2 to 4 to determine barriers to using digital texts in their classrooms. In five full-day meetings, during which teachers engaged in discussions and reflections, she discovered three dominant barriers that inhibited authentic curricular integration of ICTs into instruction. First, teachers' responses indicated a lack of knowledge about students use of technology outside of school, which was problematic because it hindered teachers from using various digital texts. They believed students would be unfamiliar with such texts. A second barrier was a focus on technical, rather than literacy, skills, which was problematic because it led to more superficial integration consistent with what Reinking, Labbo, and McKenna (2000) referred to as assimilation rather than accommodation. A third major barrier was the focus on production of a digital products as a final or culminating project, which also shifted attention away from developing the skills, strategies, and dispositions associated with reading and writing digital texts. She also concluded that the placement of computers in a central computer laboratory inhibited integration because computers were not available in classrooms for use throughout the school day. Although informative, Honan's study, involved only four teachers in Australia and conclusions were based on her interpretations of teachers' responses rather than on directly querying teachers about what they perceived as barriers to integrating digital literacies into their instruction.

In another relevant study, Stolle (2008) gathered qualitative data from 16 high school English, social studies, and science teachers in the U.S. She examined the tensions, complexities, conceptualizations and practices of teachers in relation to technology. Her data included systematic observations, in-depth interviews, focus group interviews, response data interviews, and a researcher's journal. She identified four major tensions that affected integration of ICTs into instruction:

1. Lack of access to ICTs adequate for instructional tasks. For example, teachers were reluctant to assign homework that involved the use of ICTs because they believed that some students might not have access to necessary technologies outside of school. Further, teachers expressed that they lacked necessary equipment for in-class activities.

2. Insufficient knowledge of ICTs and how to use them. The teachers in the study did not believe that they were being taught how to effectively enhance learning with ICTs.

3. Teachers feared that ICTs threatened traditional literacy practices.

4. Uncertainty about the benefits of integrating ICTs into instruction and how benefits could be assessed.

Further, Stolle (2008) found that teachers often replicated existing literacy practices with technology instead of using technology in more innovative ways derived from the unique capabilities and uses of ICTs. Her study provides more nuanced insights into what teachers believe about ICTs. However, it was limited to high-school teachers in three different subject areas.

Bauer and Kenton (2005) conducted a mixed-methods study that illuminates barriers from another perspective. They focused on 30 teachers from several content areas who were identified as having technological savvy. Teachers in the study completed a questionnaire to identify their backgrounds and their experiences with, conceptions about, and use of computer technology. They also observed and conducted open-ended interviews with each teacher individually. Teachers reported the following barriers to integrating ICTs into their instruction: (a) lack of equipment or poorly functioning equipment, (b) time to use technology within a standard class period, (c) the varying levels of students' skills, (d) lack of teachers' skills in using digital technology, (e) scheduling computer lab time, (f) unavailability and incompatibility of software, and (g) Internet crashes caused by large numbers of students simultaneously searching Web sites. A questionnaire followed by observations in classrooms also revealed that teachers were most often simply using technology rather than integrating it meaningfully into instructional goals. However, it is not clear whether Bauer and Kenton's survey rigorously conformed to standards for survey development and administration. Specifically, they did not explain how the survey items were derived, nor did they report efforts to establish its validity and reliability. Further, they considered integration to be "a reliance on computer technology for regular lesson delivery" (p. 522), and seemed to consider any use of computers as evidence of integration. Thus, the findings and conclusions do not address specifically the issues investigated in the present study.

Warschauer, Knobel, and Stone (2004) conducted a qualitative study that did not specifically investigate the barriers teachers faced in integrating technology, but they did compare the use of new technologies among high schools in California serving respectively students from families of high- and low-socio-economic status. Based on the patterns they observed across the schools, they characterized the following difficulties teachers experienced in integrating technology into the school curriculum:

1. *Workability*, or how well equipment and networks function. For example, teachers voiced dissatisfaction with the need to plan back-up lessons in case the technology was not working properly.

2. *Complexity*, or the logistical challenges of integrating computers into instruction, such as taking students to the computer lab, dealing with different levels of skills in using the technology, and lack of access to computers at home for homework assignments.

3. *Performativity*, or an emphasis on skills rather than more meaningful application such as locating and evaluating search engine results. For example, teachers emphasized being able to measure performance of technology-related activities, which often undermined attention to more meaningful integration.

Their study did not explicitly address barriers to technology integration, but it nonetheless suggests broad categories into which barriers might fall.

Zhao, Pugh, Sheldon, and Byers' (2002) study parallels Bauer and Kenton's (2005) work because they investigated what factors facilitated or hindered the use of technology among teachers who had received a competitive technology grant, and who were presumably savvy users of technology. They conducted case studies with 10 of 118 teachers who had received funding for technology-related projects. The 10 teachers were selected on the basis of geographical location, grade level, and subject matter, and through systematic analysis were determined to be representative of the entire sample. They identified three domains, each with several factors that influenced the successful integration of technology into instruction among these teachers. The first domain included teachers labeled as *innovators* based on technology proficiency, pedagogical compatibility, and social awareness of the school culture. Importantly, they found that not only is understanding how to use equipment necessary, but also equally necessary is understanding the enabling conditions of certain technologies. For example, in addition to knowing how to instruct students to read and to send e-mail, a teacher must have access to a functional network, networked computers, e-mail software, and possibly software to filter inappropriate content. Pedagogical compatibility was deemed important because efforts to use technology were more likely to yield positive results when teachers' pedagogical approaches matched the technology and technological applications they chose to use. Awareness of school culture was also deemed important because interestingly they found that teachers who successfully integrated the projects into instruction understood school resources and how they were allocated and the priorities of colleagues in accessing and using them.

The second domain pertained to the *innovation*, or project itself. Factors in this domain were associated with how the selected project contributed to successful technology integration considering the project's distance from the school culture, from existing practice, from available technological resources and whether it depended on others and on the availability of technological resources.

The final domain was the instructional *context*. The school-related factors that influence the integration of technology were the organizational and technological infrastructure supporting integration and social support. Their study revealed 11 factors related to technology integration: technology proficiency, compatibility between teacher pedagogical beliefs and the technology, social awareness, distance from school culture, distance from existing practice, distance from available technological resources, dependence on others, dependence on technological resources, human infrastructure, technological infrastructure, and social support. However, their study was conducted with teachers who had received a technology grant, and thus were likely to have greater interest in, commitment to, and knowledge about digital technologies and their integration into the curriculum.

In a more dated study, Ertmer, Addison, Lane, Ross, and Woods (1999) examined teachers' beliefs about the role of technology in the elementary classroom. They collected survey, interview, and observational data from seven teachers in one elementary school, and categorized barriers to technology integration into first-order and second-order barriers. First-order barriers were those *extrinsic* to teachers, and included a lack of access to computers, lack of time, and lack of classroom help. Second-order barriers were those *intrinsic* to teachers, such as a teacher's beliefs or routines, lack of relevance, a mismatch with classroom management style, and a lack of teacher confidence about technology abilities.

Each of the studies reviewed here contributes to the base of knowledge regarding the barriers teachers face in using technology in a significant way. However, cumulatively they reveal limitations in our current knowledge about what barriers teachers face in integrating ICTs into instruction in general and literacy research in particular. Specifically, the studies are small scale. Most were conducted within only a single school. Further, only Honan's (2008) study of barriers to using digital text looked specifically at literacy practices. In addition, as illustrated in Table 1, which summarizes potential barriers to integrating ICTs into instruction across the studies reviewed, there is minimal overlap of the barriers identified and thus little consensus about what the barriers are to integrating technology into instruction. Therefore, a national study was designed and administered toward clarifying on a larger scale the barriers literacy teachers in particular face in integrating ICTs into their instruction. The survey included items that specifically addressed those barriers or categories of barriers indentified in the existing literature reviewed here.

Table 1. Comparison of Barriers to Technology Integration Reported in Previous Studies

	Honan (2008) [A]	Stolle (2008) [B]	Warshauer et al. (2004) [C]	Bauer & Kenton (2005) [D]	Zhao et al. (2002) [E]	Ertmer et al. (1999) [F]
Focus on technical rather than academic skills	X		X			
Emphasis on product as outcome	X					
Placement of computers in school setting	X			X		
Lack of equipment for desired tasks	X			X		X
Ability to use ICTs		X		X	X	
Fear of the Unknown		X				
Beliefs about the usefulness/benefit of ICTs		X				
Reliability of technology			X	X		
Logistical challenges such as varying skills & lack of home access			X	X		
Lack of time to implement ICTs during a single class period				X		
Fit of ICTs with teacher beliefs about learning					X	

continued from previous page

	Honan (2008) [A]	Stolle (2008) [B]	Warshauer et al. (2004) [C]	Bauer & Kenton (2005) [D]	Zhao et al. (2002) [E]	Ertmer et al. (1999) [F]
Teachers' awareness of school culture					X	
Distance of ICT innovation from existing school culture					X	
Distance of ICT from teachers' existing practice					X	
Amount of required dependence on others					X	
Human infrastructure supporting ICT integration					X	X
Existing technology infrastructure					X	
Social support for ICT integration					X	
Lack of time to plan for ICT integration						X
Ability to integrate ICTs into curriculum in a relevant way						X
Classroom management issues						X
Lack of teacher confidence in technological skill						X

METHOD

The data collected and reported here are part of a larger online survey addressing a broader range of questions and issues pertaining to literacy teachers' integration of ICTs into instruction. The full survey can be viewed at http://www.surveymonkey.com/s/W3BSDQL. It consists of 69 items soliciting responses on a Likert scale, 11 multiple-choice items, and eight open-ended items. Twenty-two items requesting that respondents identify barriers to instruction were the focus of the present investigation. The development and validation of the survey followed procedures and recommendations in the literature on survey development (Dillman, 2007; Rea & Parker, 2005) and conducting online surveys (Sue & Ritter, 2007). For example, development of the survey began by establishing the constructs that would be measured (Rea & Parker, 2005). The research questions, survey constructs, and findings from the review of the literature, were used to develop an initial pool of survey items. Items that were not found in a review of the literature were added to the survey in an attempt to better characterize the barriers that teachers experience by providing respondents with a wider variety of response options. A focus group interview with four teachers and a pilot survey involving 100 teachers were conducted to refine the initial survey items. After item revision was completed, item analyses were conducted on the items hypothesized to represent the constructs used to design the survey. Cronbach's alpha ranged from .92 to .96 on each of the constructs, indicating internal consistency. Therefore all items on the revised survey were retained on the final survey.

Participants. Participants were 1,441 predominantly literacy teachers who are members of a state or local council of the International Reading Association (IRA). Participation was solicited from IRA members, because (a) members are predominantly literacy educators, the target population of this study; (b) every state in the U.S. has a state affiliate comprised of local councils, thus representing the potential for a national sample; (c) many, but not all, of the state affiliates have e-mail distribution lists, or they have other means available to disseminate information about an online survey, and (d) there is precedent in the literacy research literature for using IRA members to gather data about literacy issues in classrooms (Baumann, Hoffman, Duffy-Hester, & Moon-Ro, 2000). In some states, leaders of the state IRA affiliate declined to invite their members to participate in the survey or did not have the means available to efficiently disseminate invitations to participate. In those cases, respondents were contacted through other organizations or list-servs such as the Connecticut Association for Reading, and the enhancing Missouri's Instructional Networked Teaching Strategies (eMINTS) network. Thirty-one states are represented in the survey from every major region of the U.S.

Procedures for administering the survey. Invitations to complete the online survey were disseminated in several stages and through multiple contacts during three months. The first contact consisted of sending a personal e-mail to the presidents and membership chairs of all the state IRA councils to inform them of the study, to request their cooperation in facilitating the study, and, if they consented, to make them aware that they would subsequently receive further instructions about how they could participate. The e-mail also informed them that if at least 15% of their members completed the survey, they would receive a customized report of the survey findings for their state. Five days after the first e-mail, a second e-mail contact was made with state presidents and membership chairs. The second e-mail suggested several ways state presidents could invite their members to complete the survey, and it included a sample invitation e-mail. The presidents were asked to send the invitation letter to their members through their e-mail distribution list, or to inform the researcher if an e-mail invitation was not a possibility. A reminder e-mail was sent to presidents who had not replied approximately a week after the second contact was made.

Twenty-three state presidents did not respond to either the first or second e-mail. Four state presidents declined to participate because they did not have an e-mail list or because of concerns about members' privacy. In these cases an e-mail with other options for announcing the survey and distributing the survey link, including posting to the organization's Web page and announcing the survey in their state newsletter was sent. After determining which state reading associations would not participate in the study, we e-mailed personal contacts in those states to request suggestions about how to distribute the survey effectively to the appropriate population and who might be contacted to facilitate dissemination through e-mail. These contacts led to participation in five additional states.

Data analysis. In the part of the survey relevant to the present study, teachers were asked to identify on a Likert scale the extent to which several potential barriers and challenges interfered with integrating ICTs into literacy instruction by responding to the following item: "Please indicate the extent to which you believe the following are barriers to integrating technology into your literacy/ language arts instruction," which was followed by a list of possible barriers derived from the studies reviewed in a previous section of this report. However, we added several barriers based on our many years experience working with literacy teachers and their efforts to integrate digital technologies into their instruction and/or that were pertinent to the focus of this investigation: lack of understanding about how to integrate technology into instruction, lack of professional development related to integrating technology into instruction, lack of understanding about how to evaluate students' ability to use ICTs, Internet texts being too difficult for students to read, and lack of time due to high-stakes testing.

RESULTS

Table 2 summarizes the responses to the survey item requesting that participants identify the extent to which each factor was perceived as a barrier to integrating ICTs into instruction. Values in bold indicate the one or two categories that reach a threshold of at least 50% of the respondents. The barriers are listed in an order from how quickly that threshold was reached beginning at "not at all" on the left side of the table to "a large extent" on the right side of the table. Thus, barriers at the top of the table are considered overall to be less of a barrier than those at the bottom of the table.

Table 2. Perceived Barriers to the Integration of ICTs into Literacy Instruction

Potential Barrier [Letters in brackets indicate that the item reflects a barrier found in the corresponding sources listed in Table 1.]	Not at all % (n)	Small Extent % (n)	Moderate extent % (n)	Large extent % (n)	Not applicable % (n)
I don't believe technology integration is useful [B]	**85.0** **(1225)**	9.6 (139)	1.9 (28)	1.3 (19)	2.2 (32)
I don't think technology fits my beliefs about learning [E]	**75.7** **(1091)**	16.0 (231)	4.1 (60)	1.8 (26)	2.4 (35)
I have difficulty managing the classroom when students are working on computers [F]	**56.9** **(820)**	28.0 (404)	7.1 (103)	3.4 (49)	4.8 (70)
I don't know how to use technology [B,D,E, F]	**51.6** **(744)**	29.9 (431)	11.9 (172)	3.9 (57)	1.9 (28)
I don't understand copyright issues [B,D,E]	**51.5** **(743)**	34.4 (496)	9.2 (133)	3.3 (48)	1.6 (24)
Lack of support from administrators [E]	**45.8** **(660)**	**24.5** **(354)**	16.3 (235)	11.6 (168)	1.9 (28)
I don't think technology is reliable [C,D]	**43.7** **(630)**	**37.9** **(547)**	12.1 (175)	3.8 (55)	1.8 (26)
I don't understand how to integrate technology into my literacy instruction	**41.9** **(604)**	**34.0** **(490)**	17.8 (257)	4.9 (71)	1.3 (19)
I think Internet text is too difficult for students to read	**40.4** **(583)**	**35.5** **(512)**	15.9 (230)	6.8 (98)	1.5 (22)

continued from previous page

Potential Barrier [Letters in brackets indicate that the item reflects a barrier found in the corresponding sources listed in Table 1.]	Not at all % (n)	Small Extent % (n)	Moderate extent % (n)	Large extent % (n)	Not applicable % (n)
I don't know how to incorporate technology and still teach content standards [A,C,F]	**39.3** **(567)**	**34.1** **(492)**	17.7 (256)	6.4 (93)	1.6 (24)
I don't know how skilled my students are at using technology [C,D]	**39.2** **(565)**	**39.7** **(573)**	12.3 (178)	6.2 (90)	2.6 (38)
Lack of incentives to use technology [E]	**38.9** **(561)**	**28.5** **(411)**	20.1 (290)	10.9 (158)	1.5 (22)
I have difficulty controlling what information students access online [B]	**34.4** **(496)**	**39.0** **(562)**	16.5 (238)	6.9 (100)	3.2 (47)
I don't know how to evaluate or assess students when they work online	**34.2** **(493)**	**38.9** **(561)**	18.2 (263)	5.9 (86)	2.7 (39)
I don't think I have time to integrate technology because of the amount of time required to prepare students for high stakes testing [F]	**29.1** **(420)**	**26.4** **(381)**	20.6 (297)	20.9 (302)	3.1 (45)
I don't have time to teach students the basic computer skills needed for more complex tasks [C,D]	**24.3** **(351)**	**30.8** **(444)**	21.3 (307)	20.9 (302)	2.7 (39)
I don't think I have enough time to prepare for using technology [F]	**21.7** **(313)**	**30.0** **(433)**	23.1 (333)	23.9 (345)	1.4 (21)
Lack of technical support [E,F]	19.5 (281)	**27.9** **(403)**	25.0 (361)	**27.2** **(392)**	0.5 (8)
Lack of professional development on how to integrate technology	17.9 (258)	**26.8** **(387)**	26.7 (385)	**28.1** **(405)**	0.5 (8)
Lack of access to technology [A,B,D,E,F]	17.7 (254)	**24.8** **(356)**	22.2 (319)	**35.5** **(511)**	0.0 (0)
Lack of time during a class period [D]	12.3 (177)	23.1 (333)	**27.3** **(394)**	**36.4** **(525)**	0.9 (12)

Note. Bold values represent the one or two largest values in each category reaching a threshold of at least 50% of the responses.

Lack of time during a class period was the most common barrier reported when considering the percentage of teachers indicating that a factor was a barrier to a moderate or large extent (63.7%), followed by lack of access to technology (57.7%), lack of professional development on how to integrate technology (54.8%), and lack of technical support (52.2%). A majority of the respondents indicated that all of the other factors were not a barrier at all or a barrier to a small extent.

Using a more liberal approach to determining the possible range of barriers, Table 3 lists, in descending order, the factors that at least 50% of participants listed as a barrier to some extent (small, moderate, or large) and compares these to barriers identified in previous studies or indicates if it is a barrier not previously reported.

Table 3. Barriers to Integrating ICTs Compared to Previous Studies

Identified as a barrier to a small, moderate, or large extent (% reporting as barrier)	Reported in Literature
Lack of time to implement during a single class period (86.8%)	Bauer & Kenton, 2005
Access to equipment (82.3%)	Honan, 2008; Stolle, 2008; Bauer & Kenton, 2005; Zhao, et al., 2002
Lack of professional development on how to integrate ICTs (81.6%)	Not previously reported
Lack of technical support (80%)	Bauer & Kenton, 2005; Stolle, 2008; Zhao, et al., 2002; Ertmer, et al., 1999
Lack of time to plan for using technology (76.9%)	Ertmer, et al., 1999
Necessity of teaching basic computer skills for more complex tasks (73%)	Honan, 2008
Lack of time to integrate due to high stakes testing (67.8%)	Not previously reported
Ability to evaluate student work using ICTs (63.1%)	Not previously reported
Difficulty controlling information students access online (62.4%)	Stolle, 2008
Lack of incentives for using technology (59.6%)	Zhao, et al., 2002
Lack of knowledge about how skilled students are at using technology (58.2%)	Bauer & Kenton, 2005; Warschauer, et al., 2004
Ability to integrate ICTs and still teach content standards (58.2%)	Ertmer, et al., 1999; Honan, 2008; Warschauer, et al., 2004
Difficulty level of Internet text (58.2%)	Not previously reported
Ability to integrate technology specific to Literacy instruction (56.7%)	Not previously reported
Unreliability of technology (53.8%)	Bauer & Kenton, 2005; Warschauer, et al., 2004
Support for integration (52.4%)	Zhao, et al., 2002

Using this more liberal approach resulted in an expanded list of possible barriers, although the same barriers emerged as most prominent in this list that emerged from taking a more conservative approach. The list in Table 3 also shows that several of the barriers reported by literacy teachers have not been reported previously. The following do not appear to be major barriers to integration of ICTs among literacy teachers, because more than 50% of respondents identified them as no barrier at all: Beliefs about usefulness of technology integration, fit of technology with beliefs about learning, difficulty of managing the classroom when students work on computers, knowledge of how to use technology, understanding of copyright issues.

DISCUSSION

From our systematic review of previous studies, it is clear that many diverse factors have been identified as barriers to integrating ICTs into instruction in general. That diversity of factors and the identification of many non-overlapping barriers (see Table 1) may be because of differences in the populations studied (e.g., teachers with different levels of technological expertise teaching different subjects), in the approaches to data collection and analysis (e.g., observations, case studies, interviews, surveys) and in technologies and their availability across time (the studies reviewed spanned almost 10 years).

Taken as a whole, then, the current literature provides no common core of a few barriers that inhibit integration of ICTs into instruction and thus provides little guidance about what course of action might be taken to increase integration by overcoming barriers. Further, only one of the studies reviewed (Honan, 2008) focused on barriers to integrating ICTs into literacy instruction. Thus, we conclude that a more focused, systematic approach to research is needed if the field is identify what barriers teachers most often face and to use that information as a foundation for addressing specific barriers and for increasing the integration of ICTs into literacy instruction. The existing research is ad hoc, local, not nuanced by subject area, and in some instances outdated. Researchers need to focus attention on identifying factors that are barriers to integrating ICTs into literacy instruction and to explore possible interventions that take into account those barriers. Given rapid changes in technology, it may also be useful to periodically monitor perceptions about barriers. Survey methods may be particularly useful to monitor changes in teachers' perceptions.

To move a step toward addressing these goals, the barriers identified in previous research were included in a national survey of literacy teachers aimed at increasing understanding various dimensions of integrating ICTs into literacy instruction. An analysis of that data indicated that literacy teachers, as a whole, did not perceive many of the barriers identified in previous research to be clear barriers to integrating ICTs into their instruction. That finding may be an encouraging sign and suggest progress. For example, unlike previous research, relatively few literacy teachers found the reliability of technology or the ability to use ICTs as a barrier, which may be due to the increasing availability of technology (e.g., one-on-one laptop initiatives and digital projectors), and to the increasing use of ICTs in the daily lives of teachers.

More importantly, a large majority of the teachers responding to this survey indicated that their own beliefs about technology and learning (75.7%) and their beliefs about integrating ICTs into instruction (85%) were not barriers even to a small extent. Thus, literacy teachers, as a whole may, perhaps contrary to common assumptions, be fundamentally open to efforts aimed at increasing integration of ICTs into their instruction. That finding has added importance because considerable research has shown that teachers' beliefs play a predominant role in how they conceptualize and use computer-based technologies in their teaching (Bruce & Rubin, 1993; Ertmer, 2005; Clark & Peterson, 1986; Windschitl & Sahl; 2002; Zhao, Pugh, Sheldon, & Byers; 2002). In particular, that finding also suggests that literacy teachers in general seem to be receptive to accommodating

ICTs into instruction (Reinking, Labbo, & McKenna, 2000). Knowing that literacy teachers are overwhelmingly supportive of integrating ICTs into instruction may also inform those who wish to engage them in professional development aimed at integrating ICTs into their teaching. Specifically, literacy teachers may not need to be convinced that ICTs are useful and that ICTs are potentially consistent with their goals for students' learning.

A majority of the participants indicated that their own knowledge about how to integrate technology into instruction was either not a barrier at all (39.3%) or was a barrier to only a small extent (31.4%). However, that item in particular begs the question of on what basis teachers are evaluating their own knowledge and how they define integration. For example, preliminary analysis of data from the larger study suggests that teachers may define integration more narrowly as technological rather than curricular integration. That is, to many literacy teachers, integration of ICTs into instruction may simply mean using the technologies associated with ICTs rather than teaching the skills, strategies, and dispositions necessary for their effective use. That possibility awaits further analysis of our data and ideally studies, for example, that interview teachers about how they define integration of ICTs into instruction.

On the other hand, using the more liberal standard for listing barriers in Table 3 (i.e., at least 50% of the respondents indicated that the items were a barrier to a small, moderate, or large extent), literacy teachers identified several barriers that were consistent with those identified in previous studies. Specifically, they perceived the following to be barriers: the ability to integrate ICTs into the curriculum, lack of planning time and time to carry out ICT activities during allotted time for instruction, diversity of students' computer skills, access to technology, lack of incentives to integrate ICTs into instruction, and lack of technical support. These barriers fall mainly into a category that Ertmer et al. (1999) refers to as extrinsic factors, which suggests that in teachers' views, much of the burden of achieving more integration of ICTs into literacy instruction falls more on curriculum developers, policy makers, and administrators and indirectly to researchers who could inform their efforts. Again, it would be useful to further explicate these barriers in future studies. For example, might teachers believe that a lack of incentives to integrate ICTs into instruction include the known fact that few high-stakes tests include an evaluation of students' abilities to use ICTs (Leu, 2006)? The finding that curricular integration is perceived as a barrier also suggests that professional development may need to provide more explicit guidance about how ICTs can be integrated into the language arts curriculum including perhaps developing generic instructional and curricular models aimed at specific goals and standards.

Other barriers that literacy teachers identified, but that were not identified in previous studies, support the previous conclusions. For example, literacy teachers identified the following as barriers: lack of school support for ICT integration, lack of means to assess students in that area, controlling access to information online (e.g., the necessity of using firewalls to prevent students from accessing inappropriate content), lack of professional development, lack of time to integrate due to high stakes testing, and a lack of understanding about how to integrate technology specific to literacy instruction. These barriers all imply the need for administrative support. However, many literacy teachers also perceived the difficulty of texts on the Internet to be a barrier to integrating ICTs into instruction, which suggests a topic for further research. Is the uncontrolled difficulty of texts on the Internet, as defined traditionally (e.g., by readability formulas), a barrier to engaging students with activities aimed at integrating ICTs into literacy instruction? Does the concept of defining texts as at a student's frustration, instructional, or independent levels apply to instruction involving ICTs? If not, how might teachers' perceptions be changed? These are topics for future research.

However, these interpretations, conclusions, and speculations must be tempered by the fact that they are based solely on survey data that only solicited teachers' perceptions and opinions, although, given our theoretical stance, perceptions are clearly important. Nonetheless, more systematic and detailed research is needed to determine if those perceptions are supported by observational data and if they are consistent with the views of administrators and policy makers. It would be informative, for example, to survey a national sample of educational administrators and policy makers involved in shaping literacy instruction to compare their views on integrating ICTs into literacy instruction. Such an approach would be consistent with multiple realities perspective cited as supporting the rationale for and methods of this investigation (Labbo & Reinking, 2000). Further, this study was conducted only with teachers who are members of the International Reading Association. Because the IRA has issued a position statement about the importance of integrating literacy and technology in the curriculum, teachers who are members of this organization may be more likely to integrate technology than teachers who are not IRA members. Thus, this sample may not be reflective of all literacy teachers.

It would also be informative for researchers to investigate interventions aimed at helping literacy teachers integrate ICTs into their instruction. Nonetheless, we believe the present study provides national data in the U.S. that can inform those efforts. We also believe that the present study highlights the need for more focused and systematic research and development aimed at furthering the integration of ICTs into literacy instruction.

REFERENCES

Bauer, J., & Kenton, J. (2005). Toward technology integration in the schools: Why it isn't happening. *Journal of Technology and Teacher Education 13*(4), 519-546.

Baumann, J. F., Hoffman, J., Duffy-Hester, A., & Moon-Ro, J. (2000). The First R yesterday and today: U.S. elementary reading instruction practices reported by teachers and administrators. *Reading Research Quarterly, 35*(3), 338-363.

Bruce, B. C., & Rubin, A. (1993). *Electronic quills: A situated evaluation of using computers for writing in the classroom.* Hillsdale, NJ: Erlbaum.

Clark, C. M., & Peterson, P. L. (1986). Teachers' thought processes. In M. C. Wittrock (Ed.), *Handbook of research on teaching.* New York, NY: Macmillan.

Cuban, L. (2001). *Oversold and underused: Computers in the classroom.* Cambridge, MA: Harvard University Press.

Dillman, D. A. (2007). *Mail and Internet surveys: The tailored design method* (2nd ed-2007 update.). Hoboken, NJ: Wiley.

Ertmer, P. (2005). Teacher pedagogical beliefs: The final frontier in our quest for technology integration. *Educational Technology Research and Development, 53*(4), 25-39.

Ertmer, P., Addison, P., Lane, M., Ross, E., & Woods, D. (1999). Examining teachers' beliefs about the role of technology in the elementary classroom. *Journal of Research on Computing in Education 32*(1), 54-72.

Honan, E. (2008). Barriers to teachers using digital texts of literacy classrooms. *Literacy, 42*(1), 36-43.

Hutchison, A. (2009). A national survey of teachers on their perceptions, challenges, and uses of information and communication technology. Ph.D dissertation, Clemson University, United States—South Carolina. Retrieved January 4, 2010, from Dissertations & Theses: A&I. (Publication No. AAT 3355144).

Hutchison, A., & Henry, L. (2010). Internet Use and Online Reading Among Middle-grade Students at Risk of Dropping Out of School. *Middle Grades Research Journal, 5*(2), 61-76.

International Reading Association (2009). New Literacies and 21st-Century Technologies: A position statement of the International Reading Association. Newark, DE: International Reading Association.

Labbo, L. D., & Reinking, D. (1999). Negotiating the multiple realities of technology in literacy research and instruction. *Reading Research Quarterly, 34*, 478-492.

Leander, K. M. (2007). "You won't be needing your laptops today": Wired bodies in the wireless classroom. In M. Knobel & C. Lankshear (Eds.), *A new literacies sampler* (p.25-48). New York, NY: Peter Lang.

Leu, D. J. (2006). New literacies, reading research, and the challenges of change: A Deictic perspective. In J. Hoffman, D. Schallert, C. M. Fairbanks, J. Worthy, & B. Maloch (Eds.) *The Fifty-fifth Yearbook of the National Reading Conference.* (1-20). Oak Creek, WI: National Reading Conference.

Leu, D. J., Jr., Kinzer, C. K., Coiro, J., & Cammack, D. (2004). Towards a theory of new literacies emerging from the Internet and other information and communication technologies. In R. B. Rudell, N. Unrau, (Ed.), *Theoretical models and processe of reading* (5th ed., pp. 1570-1613). Newark, DE: International Reading Association.

National Center for Educational Statistics. (2003). Internet access in public schools and classrooms: 1994-2002 Retrieved October 16, 2007, from http://nces.ed.gov/surveys/frss/publications/2004011

National Council of Teachers of English. (2008). Towards a definition of 21st century literacies. Urbana, IL: Author. http://www.ncte.org/about/gov/129117.htm

Rea, L., & Parker, R. (2005). *Designing and conducting survey research: A comprehensive guide.* San Francisco, CA: Jossey-Bass.

Reinking, D., Labbo, L. D., & McKenna, M. C. (2000). From assimilation to accommodation: A developmental framework for integrating digital technologies into literacy research and instruction. *Journal of Research in Reading, 23*, 110-122.

Russell, M., Bebell, D., O'Dwyer, L., & O'Connor, K. (2003). Examining teacher technology use: Implications for preservice and inservice teacher preparation. *Journal of Teacher Education 54*(4), 297-310.

Stolle, E. (2008). Teachers, literacy, & technology: Tensions, complexities, conceptualizations & practice. In Y. Kim, V. Risko, D. Compton, D. Dickinson, M. Hundley, R. Jiménez, K. Leander, & D. Wells-Rowe (Eds.), *Fifty-seventh Yearbook of the National Reading Conference* (pp. 56-69). Oak Creek: National Reading Conference.

Sue, V. M., & Ritter, L. A. (2007). *Conducting online surveys.* Thousand Oaks, CA: Sage.

Smerdon, B., Cronen, S. Lanahan, L., Anderson, J., Iannotti, N., & Angeles, J. (2000). *Teachers' Tools for the 21st Century: A Report on Teachers' Use of Technology.* Washington, DC: National Center for Educational Statistics.

Warschauer, M., Knobel, M., & Stone, L. A. (2004). Technology and equity in schooling: Deconstructing the digital divide. *Educational Policy, 18*(4), 562-588.

Wells, J., & Lewis, L. (2006). *Internet Access in U.S. Public Schools and Classrooms: 1994–2005* (NCES 2007-020). U.S. Department of Education. Washington, DC: National Center for Education Statistics.

Windschitl, M., & Sahl, K. (2002). Tracing teachers' use of technology in a laptop computer school: The interplay of teacher beliefs, social dynamics, and institutional culture. *American Educational Research Journal, 39*, 165-205.

Zhao, Y., Pugh, K., Sheldon, S., & Byers, J. (2002). Conditions for classroom technology innovations. *Teachers College Record, 104*(3), 482-515.

Becoming Literate in One's Heritage Language: Children's Situated Ethnic Identities and Their Motivation to Acquire the Discourse of Their Parents

Jung-In Kim
University of Colorado at Denver

Taehee Kim
Diane L. Schallert
The University of Texas at Austin

Children of immigrants and sojourners in this country often are enrolled in heritage language schools, *Saturday schools* in common parlance, to acquire the literate practices of their parents. Our goal was to understand the narratives of eight such children as they constructed their identities and expressed their motivation for participating in the discourse communities they encountered at school, in family, and at Korean language school. We approached these children's accounts informed by two literatures, the recently burgeoning work on identity and the well-established prolific area of research on achievement motivation.

IDENTITY AND MOTIVATION AS FRAMEWORK

The construct of *identity* (or, more recently, *identities*) is currently seen as useful in understanding how children develop their multiple literacy practices. In this perspective, individuals concurrently belong to many groups and take up and express diverse social identities in their interactions in these groups. Circumstances of time and situation allow different social identities to become salient (Pittinsky, Shih, & Ambady, 1999). Citing Canagarajah (1999), Perry and Purcell-Gates (2005) stated, "individuals have a range of available subject positions, and this subjectivity is fluid, dynamic, and negotiable" (p. 272). Similarly, Rogers (2004a) used Critical Discourse Analysis (CDA) to understand the narratives of 15 African-American adult learners across discourse communities, characterizing learners' *subjectivities* in various literacy contexts. Rogers used the term *subjectivities* to mean "the multiple, fluid, and unstable relationships that make up a person" (p. 276), contrasting it to a positivistic approach to identity as a fixed stable self. CDA allowed her to describe the construction and transformation of subjectivities as individuals participated in discourse communities across contexts and time.

Researchers have noted that one's language is a prominent indicator of identity (Fishman, 1977; Giles & Coupland, 1991), and that the development of one's heritage language is an important contributor to maintaining ethnic identity (Cho, 2000; Guardado, 2009; Leclezio, Louw-Potgieter, & Souchon, 1986; Lee, 2002). However, the relationship between language learning and ethnic identity seems complex. Children have been reported to hide their knowledge of their heritage language and culture, being afraid of being rejected by peers, teachers, and others who are from different ethnic groups (Cummins, 1984). Guardado's (2009) account of Spanish language heritage members of a Scout troop in Canada led him to highlight "the unpredictable nature of socialization processes and unstable character of identity" (p. 118), as illustrated by one of his participants who switched from English (her preferred dominant language) to Spanish depending on the group with whom she was interacting. Students often experience failure to develop their heritage languages in part because of the strong societal push toward English (Tse, 2001). Perry and Purcell-Gates (2005) argued for a position associated with Canagarajah (1999), Clayton (1998), and Giroux (1989), stating that "dominated actors are often aware of power relationships and are able to consciously make decisions" (p. 273) that include the appropriation of some dominant discourses and practices, as well as overt or covert resistance against those practices to preserve their identities. This is one poignant message from Anzaldúa's (1987) masterful narrative of living in the "la frontera" of the U.S. southwest.

Thus, a close examination of the discourse of learners might yield interesting insights about how they are enacting their multiple identities as they learn the language of their heritage. Indeed, several literacy researchers have recently argued for the utility of a critical approach to discourse as a tool in sociocultural analyses of any literacy learning situation (Gutierrez, 2008; Moje & Lewis, 2007; Rex, et al., 2010; Wohlwend, 2009). Moje and Lewis (2007) argued that learning involves not only participation in various discourse communities, but is also the process of becoming members of, resisting membership in, being marginalized from, or reshaping discourse communities. They argued for the utility of a critical discourse analysis of classroom discussions to examine "how social and power relations, identities, and knowledge are constructed through written and spoken texts in social settings such as schools, families, and communities" (p. 22). Thus, an individual's discourse reveals much about the cultural Discourses in which the person participates, and can be mined for constructions of identity and agency.

Turning now to the construct of motivation, we had begun with a strong interest in understanding why some of the children at the Korean language school seemed more engaged, more persistent, and happier to be there than other children. Having committed to an investigation of the multiple identities the children revealed, we were interested in connecting this identity work to the motivation the children expressed to learn their heritage language. Norton's (2000) call for more attention from second language researchers to the connection between identity and a more nuanced view of motivation is relevant to our own approach. Woodruff and Schallert (2008) proposed a grounded theory representing how motivation and self/identity processes were reciprocally intertwined and influenced students' emotions, cognitions, and behaviors. Their analysis pointed to an important implication of the interconnection between motivation and identity: As students' motivation shifted from more intrinsic to more extrinsic sources in a particular domain, the students experienced varying degrees of disidentification with the domain. Even more relevant to our project, Chen (2006) examined students' motivations and identities in the context of Chinese heritage language learning. She found that the ways that young learners of Chinese balanced their well-being goals and emotional reactions to language learning activities explained whether they attended Chinese school willingly, whether they were engaged in their learning, and whether they acknowledged or resisted their Chinese identity. In line with Chen, we wanted to explore Korean heritage language learners' experiences to understand relationships between their situated identities and their motivation to learn the language, taking sociocultural influences into account.

We had one overarching research question: What would a critical discourse analysis of the narratives of eight young people in a heritage language school teaching Korean reveal about the students' multiple, fluid, and unstable identities and their associations with their motivation to learn the literacy practices of Korean, their heritage language, as influenced by various sociocultural contexts? This question seemed important to guiding a look into the particulars of what happens when learning involves issues that touch on a learner's identity and that require, as all learning does, sustained motivation. The Korean language learning context for these young people living in the United States represented a place where they brought their different views of themselves and different reasons to learn, just as learners of any other domain bring their whole motivated self into the learning. We hoped that our study would allow a detailed look at how students expressed these motivational and identity processes in their actions and words.

METHOD

Participants

We collected data in one class in one Korean Saturday school in a mid-sized U.S. city. Of the 11 students in the class, eight agreed to participate. Two had a mother of Korean descent and a father of European descent, and perhaps less exposure to Korean in the home than the other six (see Table 1 for ages and other information). The pseudonyms we chose reflected how some children typically went by a Korean name whereas others typically used an English name, even though six of the children had names in both languages.

Setting

The Korean Saturday school rented space from a local public middle school to hold their classes. Because the space was borrowed, all materials had to be temporary, and the desks and bulletin boards had to be returned to their original state after every Saturday session. Korean school

Table 1. Demographics of Each Participant

	Sex	Age	Grade	Father's ethnic background	Mother's ethnic background
Minseong[1]	Female	13	7th	Korean	Korean
Katy	Female	13	8th	European American	Korean
Woojin	Male	11	5th	Korean	Korean
Boyeon	Female	13	7th	Korean	Korean
Jean	Female	10	4th	Korean	Korean
Seong-il	Male	11	5th	Korean	Korean
Junho	Male	13	7th	Korean	Korean
Tracy	Female	13	8th	European American	Korean

[1] All names are pseudonyms reflecting the language of the preferred name students wished to be called.

consisted of two sessions, a morning session of 90 minutes devoted to more academic topics, followed by lunch in the cafeteria (the children brought their own lunch), and a shorter afternoon session (60 mins.) devoted to more cultural, arts and crafts, and social issues. Speaking in Korean throughout the day was encouraged, but the children often reverted to English even during the academic session. In terms of their knowledge of Korean, as a rule the children had better listening comprehension than speaking production, and their ability to read and write Korean text, with its Korean characters, was nearly always quite low. In response to the goals of the school and the abilities of the students, the teachers seemed to take a positive encouraging approach rather than a strict or punitive approach, even though homework was assigned and activities that encouraged the use of Korean and that received corrections frequently occurred.

Data sources and collection. There were four sources of data: (a) classroom observations; (b) two interviews with each of the eight participants; (c) two interviews with the teacher; and (d) one interview with each of two parents (both mothers). For the classroom observations, two of us sat in on both sessions every other week throughout one semester (for a total of seven Saturdays), taking observation notes especially focused on the kinds of interactions in which the students engaged and any expression or body language that might reveal motivation.

The first student interviews took place at the beginning of the semester (during the lunch period of the first and second Saturdays), lasted 20 to 30 minutes, and involved open-ended questions about students' background and why they came to Saturday school (e.g., Why do you learn Korean? What has learning Korean been like for you?). The second interviews took place near the end of the semester. Compared to the first interviews, these were shorter (about 15 mins.) and more individualized, guided by questions we had derived from the first interview and our classroom observations that focused on student-teacher and student-student interactions (e.g., Why do you sit at the front of the class?). The teacher was interviewed once before the semester began and again after the semester had ended. We asked her about her goals for the class and her perceptions of each student in terms of motivation and improvement of Korean speaking and literacy skills. A topic that seemed important to her was the parents' role in their children's learning. Finally, two parents were interviewed once mid-semester and asked about their expectations for their children's learning and the kinds of interactions that went on at home about Saturday school. We also asked them the extent to which they spoke in Korean with their children relative to other languages. All interviews were audiorecorded and transcribed.

Data Analysis

Data were analyzed using constant comparative analyses from a grounded theory approach (Strauss & Corbin, 1998) and Critical Discourse Analysis (CDA). Although there are several examples of discourse analytic approaches available in the literature (Guardado, 2009; Ohara & Saft, 2003; Talmy, 2010), we chose for this report to base our analysis on Rogers (2004a) who, following Fairclough (2004), defined CDA as the systematic study of "ways of interacting" (genre), "ways of representing" (discourse), and "ways of being" (style) (p. 278). Table 2 lists definitions of Rogers' three main categories of CDA and provides examples of sub-categories as well as interview excerpts from our participants to illustrate these coding sub-categories. Underlining of particular words in the examples is meant to highlight the parts of the students' words that most clearly represented the category. Having used Rogers' analytic methods to code for genre, discourse, and

Table 2. Critical Discourse Analysis Coding Scheme with Excerpts from the Data

Codes/Definition	Excerpts from transcripts
Genres/text type: "the sort of language tied to a particular social activity" (Chouliaraki & Fairclough, 1999, p. 63) including markers to the organization of interactions	
Responding to interview questions Revoicing, Conversation building, Cohesion (parallel structure/ repetition)	*You know I know a lot of Korean...* *Because we are really close, and our families are really close...* *and then I can go by myself and I can study myself and I can stay there for five years.*
Discourse: "systematic clusters of themes, statements, ideas, and ideologies" (Luke, 2000, p. 456) as ways of representing the world by groups of individuals with some cultural connection	
Purpose of heritage language learning (a) for communication (b) to build relationships (c) for connection to one's culture	*O.k. my grandma, my Korean grandma, she often calls my mom and they talk, she never gets say anything to me.* *Because I kind of like to understand.* *It's kind of my background. I need to be expected to learn it.*
Ways of learning heritage language (a) through media	*... there is a yahoo Korea that tells about the Korean news...*
Practices of learning Korean at home	*My dad...we used to live in another house, and after we are done doing our homework, he would have to teach us Korean. Well I am not so sure about my sisters, but he would always teach me in Korean.* *Uhm, my dad... He told me to speak more Korean to her, because she is Korean.*
Purpose of any language learning (a) as a means to an end (b) interesting and as an end itself (c) for general education	*To get a good job when I get older.* *Because I think it is cool learning another language instead just learning about English, and only learning about America.*
Classroom practices of learning (a) Being right or wrong (b) Learning as either easy or difficult	*You have to write on a board and probably say it right. And I won one time with this girl, but then I lost.* *Uhm, at Korean school everything mostly is easy, but sometimes it is hard.*
Contrasting regular school and Korean language school	*Korean school is only one day of the week, so I sometimes forget. Usually at our school, we have to, we can touch everything and we can eat in our classrooms, only sometimes.*
Style: "domain closest to identity or ways of being" (Rogers, 2004b, p. 51), reflecting interpersonal choices in terms of language properties and aspects of grammar	
Affective statement (positive/negative/ neutral)	*I want to have a free Saturday,...* *It is fun...but sometimes it feels kind of dangerous over there.* *I feel normal. I don't feel bad, and I don't feel good. I feel ok.*
Action (physical/cognitive/lack of action/negative action)	*I go to Korean school...I want to improve in Korean. I am trying to speak Korean...Sometimes I forget, because Korean school is only one day of the week*

continued from previous page

Codes/Definition	Excerpts from transcripts
Cognition (positive/negative)	You know I <u>know</u> a lot of Korean, and I <u>know</u> a lot of English, too. They <u>don't know</u> really another language.
Tense (strong/less strong)	I feel <u>a lot more</u> home there… but inside I am <u>kind of</u> American, Well, 'cause Korean is my culture so <u>I guess</u>…
Modal verb (have to, can, should)	I <u>have to</u> speak to him (father) in Korean.
Identity	I think <u>my appearance is Korean</u>, but <u>inside I am kind of American</u>, and <u>Korean at the same time</u>. <u>Kind of like half</u>. <u>I was kind of hyper person</u>.
Positioning	Yeah, <u>me and my mom</u> will sit in front of the computer and watch random shows…
Ability (ability/lack of ability)	I am getting better at it. <u>I can read good</u> though. It is kind of <u>hard</u>.
Voice (active/passive)	My dad is, <u>want sending me</u> there to Korea… They <u>want me to</u> ----- expert Korean person.

style, we then related the discourse characteristics with the orientation and intensity of motivation the children expressed about learning Korean.

In our analysis of the ways the children expressed their motivation, we eventually recognized (or were influenced by our own familiarity with) *self-determination theory* (SDT), a particular form of achievement motivation theory. SDT assumes that intrinsic achievement motivation results from fulfilling the basic human needs for autonomy (freedom from imposition by others), relatedness (connection to others), and competence (knowledge and ability) (Deci & Ryan, 2002). Although SDT was not originally developed from a sociocultural approach, the theory acknowledges the importance of family, peers, teachers, and society's values and of their support of an individual's basic human needs for optimal motivational experiences. Different degrees of self-determination are said to depend on the extent to which reasons for acting apply: *intrinsic motivation*, engaging in an activity for its own sake, representing the most self-determined motivation, and four types of *extrinsic motivation*, engaging in a task to obtain a separate outcome. The four types of extrinsic motivation depend on different degrees of internalization: *integrated regulation*, motivated by more self-integrated reasons, *identified regulation*, motivated by identifying with an activity's underlying value, *introjected regulation*, motivated by internal pressures from valued others, and *external regulation*, motivated by contingencies overtly external to the individual. In general, it has been reported that children who are high on the less self-determined forms of regulation, such as introjected regulation, are likely to be anxious about school, to blame themselves for failure, and to experience less enjoyment in school, and to make less proactive response to failure (Ryan & Connell, 1989). We mention these categories because these labels were useful as we coded the interviews and observation notes. Also, we saw a good fit between critical discourse analysis and SDT because CDA relies heavily on markers of agency that could easily be related to SDT's autonomy continuum.

The trustworthiness of the data analysis came from the number of hours we spent at the school, the fact that what students said in the first interview and what we observed throughout the semester could be confirmed in the second interview, how the teacher's views of the students' language learning experience and motivation could inform our own sense of each student, and how the two parents we interviewed supplemented the students' views. We also used frequent conversations among the three of us (peer debriefing) to add to trustworthiness.

FINDINGS

Below we present the eight students, focusing on how our participants constructed their identities and were motivated to learn Korean. In Table 3, we organize the children along a continuum of motivation in the first column and different identities in the second.

Even though each student's motivation was often situative showing differences depending on context, it was still possible to identify characteristics of their motivation to learn Korean. And, even though according to self-determination theory, students can adopt various kinds of motivation across contexts, we saw the eight students as forming two groupings: one group with rather less autonomous, less self-determined motivation and the other group with more autonomous, more self-determined motivation.

Based on our analysis, we grouped the first four students in Table 3, Minseong, Katy, Woojin, and Boyeon, as displaying less autonomous motivation, what in SDT would be called *external* or *introjected regulation*. For these four students, the source of control, the reason for studying Korean, seemed to be externally derived, though the intensity of the motivation could vary from low (Minseong, Woojin) to moderate or high (Katy) levels of motivation.

Table 3. Type and Intensity of Motivation and Ethnic/Role Identity of the Eight Participants

Pseudonyms	**Motivation** Less autonomous motivation		
	Type/Source	**Overall Intensity**	**Ethnic/Role Identity**
Minseong	Didn't really think about it	Low	Korean American
Katy	To please mom	Moderate to High	Situated Korean & American
Woojin	To communicate	Low	"I am Japanese Korean"
Boyeon	To be a stewardess	Low to Moderate	"I am fully Korean"
Jean	Value it	High	"Wish I'd been born in Korea"
Seong-il	Because I am Korean	Moderate to High	"I am Korean, so I learn Korean"
Junho	to build relationships using Korean	High	"I am Korean with Korean people around me"
Tracy	I enjoy the language	High	Language lover

More autonomous motivation

By contrast, we identified the other four students, Jean, Seong-il, Junho, and Tracy, as a group with more autonomous internalized motivation, *identified regulation* or *intrinsic motivation* in the terminology of SDT. Although more autonomous, the motivation of this second group still came from different sources, like the first group of students, and again the intensity of the motivation seemed to vary, from moderate to high.

Minseong: "I Haven't Thought about That"

We begin with Minseong because she was the participant with the shortest answers and least engaged style during interviews. Although we group her with the less autonomously motivated students, we are less confident in this designation, acknowledging that her short responses could possibly be due to many other causes besides low motivation to learn Korean. Given this caveat, we can describe her as follows. Born in the United States, Minseong did not seem to feel pressure to learn Korean from her parents. Of all our participants, she seemed not to have given much thought about reasons to learn Korean, and gave us the most trouble in understanding her underlying reasons or motivation to learn Korean. Moreover, from her narratives and the inclusion of many uncertainty markers, such as "kind of" or "I guess" (style), we determined that she showed a low degree of motivation to learn Korean. (In our descriptions, the categories appearing in parentheses such as *style* or *discourse* represent the CDA terms defined in Table 2.) For example, when asked why she was learning Korean, she responded, "Because....umm..." When pushed to elaborate on her reasons for learning Korean, she reported that she was learning Korean because of her heritage (discourse): "Well, 'cause Korean is my culture so I guess..." and "Well, my parents are Korean so I guess they want me to learn, too."

Minseong did not seem to have given much thought about her ethnic identity. However, when given another chance to think about the question, she responded that she considered herself Korean American because she could speak some Korean and because of her heritage.

Minseong: I would say, like, Korean American... 'cause, I guess, I can speak some Korean and... uh. I am Korean and stuff...

Interviewer: Oh, you want to say you're Korean?

Minseong: Korean American.

Katy: "Pleasing My Mom"

Katy reflected a fluctuating identity of being American or Korean and seemed motivated to learn Korean mostly to please her mother, her one Korean parent.

Katy: Well, my mom, she wants me to learn Korean because we are going to Korea over the summer. So, like my mom also said, if I know more than one or two languages...

Even though she seemed to understand language learning as a purposeful activity (discourse), Katy's voice in expressing why she was learning Korean was passive in style because initiation came from her mother, revoicing her mom (genre), "like my mom also said." Thus, we saw her motivation as coming from an extrinsic source of regulation, *introjected* or *extrinsic regulation* in SDT, with Katy expressing a relatively passive reason for choosing to learn Korean.

Compared to the above statement "she wants me to learn Korean," when asked why she liked learning Korean, Katy replied, "It really makes my mom happy. I like to make my mom happy." Here, she seemed to be positioning herself with positive affect statements (style) about learning Korean, using the active voice in her verb choice (style). Her utterances led us to interpret that she saw learning Korean as important in building her relationship with her mother (discourse). This relationship building extended to the process she engaged in learning Korean:

Interviewer: Do you watch Korean dramas or movies?

Katy: Yeah, *me and my mom* will sit in front of the computer and watch random shows… like Korean doctor show.

Interviewer: Is it English subtitled?

Katy: It doesn't have any subtitles, but, sometime they use like a medical term, and they define it in Korean, so I try to learn it.

In using "me and my mom" as agents of the activity of watching Korean TV shows (discourse), Katy once again aligned her motivation with her mother (style), expressing positive affect (style), showing how she had internalized to some degree the motivation to learn Korean influenced by her mother. This is what SDT theorists would call *introjected regulation.*

Using active voice (style) and positive affect statements (style) in talking about her reasons for learning Korean as related to her mother, she identified herself as Korean (style). When asked why she thought it was important to learn Korean, she replied, "It's kind of, like, my background. I'm Korean. So, it just helps to know it." However, when she was asked later for her ethnic identity, she stated:

American. I'm proud to be Korean cause, it makes me different. But, there's a lot of American influence. Like, music, TV, and school, and stuff.

Here, Katy seemed to identify herself as American (style), recognizing the sociocultural influences from the culture. At this point, her ethnic identities seemed to be passively constructed (style) coming from outside: "makes me different," "American influence."

Katy seemed to construct her various situated identities within inconsistently supportive contexts where different values existed for becoming literate in Korean, leading to fluctuating motivation. There seemed to be some conflict between Katy's parents in their support for learning Korean. According to Katy, her father did not seem to "really care" if she spoke Korean. Even though Katy's mom seemed to value her learning Korean, she also was inconsistent in motivating her: "My mother always tells me if I need to quit, I'll quit, but then she gets mad at me" (genre; style). At her Korean school, too, Katy seemed to experience identity shifts, as she had changed from a classroom context in which the previous language teacher devalued her contributions to a context in which she was seen much more positively by her current teacher.

Woojin: "I'm Japanese Korean"

Woojin had lived in Japan for five years where his parents had immigrated before moving to the United States when he was 7 years old. Though born in Korea, his family and he seemed more comfortable with speaking Japanese rather than either English or Korean. Thus, he did not need to learn Korean to build a relationship with his parents, even though he seemed to see some value in learning Korean. We judged that he had some, but not strong, degree of what SDT would call *identified regulation* as his motivation for learning Korean, providing a sense that he valued knowing the language: "if I get to go to Korea, it might get useful… probably they wouldn't speak English," "I want to communicate with Korean people, and I want to live in a place that I know actually the language of." Woojin also mentioned that he was learning Korean because he had originally come from Korea, and, unlike Seong-il (see below), did not show any resentment that he could not yet speak Korean well.

Woojin reported that his parents did not seem to have high expectations about his learning of Korean, nor that they were putting much pressure on him. Compared to other students with Korean parents, Woojin seemed to get less exposure to Korean in his family: his father mostly spoke to him "about 75% Japanese and 25% Korean," even though his parents spoke mostly Korean to each other. Interestingly, he considered himself as Japanese Korean rather than either Korean American or Asian American. When probed, he denied several times the *American* label. Therefore, his construction of his identity seemed to depend on the language with which he felt most comfortable and the place he had spent most of his early years (Japanese), and with which his parents seemed to identify (Korean), rather than with English, a language he could speak as fluently as Japanese.

Boyeon: "I Want to be a Stewardess who Speaks both Korean and English"

As an immigrant to the United States since she was 7 years old, Boyeon seemed to reflect a sense of being Korean in her identity and seemed motivated to learn Korean to communicate with family and to get a job (stewardess) when she grew up (discourse). In SDT, such reasons for learning would indicate *identified regulation*, a valuing of the activity as a reason to learn.

> Boyeon: Why I came here [Korean language school] is because since I am from Korea, I have to learn Korean to communicate with my family in Korea, and my mom also said that if I want to get job it will be, like, more awesome if I speak Korean and English.

Yet, Boyeon reported that when her mom had signed her up for Korean school, she "got mad" because she did not want to wake up early on Saturdays, even though once she arrived at language school, she liked it. She also mentioned that she "has to" (style) talk to her parents in Korean. When asked about her mother's expectations for learning Korean, she said:

> She wants me to, like… she doesn't like to push me to learn Korean, but she wants me to learn Korean, and I don't like to wake up early, but I have to learn Korean.

We saw that Boyeon's mother had high expectations for her learning the language, even though she herself differentiated between her mother "pushing" and "wanting" her to learn Korean.

When Boyeon was asked to describe any difference between her "regular" school and Korean school, she reported, "in middle school there is, like, a lot of American people, and here there is Korean people, so it's comfortable, I guess" (discourse; style). Boyeon said that when she wanted to talk about something private with some Korean friends in public school, they always spoke in Korean. Though she had been in the United States for six years, she considered herself "a full Korean because both my parents are Koreans" (style). We saw her as on the borderline with the next four students who were more enthusiastic in their motivation and who seemed to perform identities more aligned with the valuing of Korean.

Jean: Value of Korean in her Future

The youngest of our participants at 10, Jean seemed motivated by the value she placed on learning Korean and by performing subjectivities that seemed much more Korean than American. In these narratives, we saw Jean as positioning herself with passive voice (style) in the context of her parents' strong urging to be able to speak Korean. At the same time, she voiced actively (style) her desire (style) to learn Korean, deeming the language as extremely valuable (discourse).

Jean: Because I am going to go to Korea this summer. And I have to go to school there. And they don't speak in English. ...and my parents are thinking about sending me when I am 15, and then I can go by myself, and I can stay there for five years.

Interviewer: Is it you or your parents who want you to go Korea and study?

Jean: Both.

Although her parents' controlling motivating style pointed to what would be called an *external regulation* in SDT, Jean's motivation also came from her strong desire to be able to communicate well once she found herself in Korea, a more internalized form of motivation (*identified* or *integrated regulation*) connected to a future goal and plan.

Interviewer: Why do you think that they (parents) want you to speak in Korean?

Jean: They don't know really another language. They want me to turn out like an expert Korean person. They kind of want us to act like we were born there...I didn't really want to be born here (U.S.)... and so I wanted to be born in Korea. I was actually born here, but when I go to Korea, I feel more at home.

Jean showed strong positive affect (style) toward Korea in general, unlike Katy, who showed positive affect only in the context of building her relationship with her mom by learning Korean. When she was asked which language she was encouraged to speak at home, she reported, "Just Korean. Just Korean," "I have to speak to him (father) in Korean," and "we have to call her (*mom* in Korean)" (style) even though "English is more comfortable" (discourse). Even at her American school, she seemed actively to situate herself as Korean, communicating with friends using Korean, as her father had advised. Both of Jean's parents seemed to show strong valuing of learning Korean with some degree of pressure on her consistently across time and contexts even within the broader U.S. culture, leading Jean to form identities that were relatively stable, and to experience more stable and strong motivation to learn Korean.

Interestingly, even though her parents' motivating style seemed even coercive, when asked whether she felt pressure from her parents, she said, "not really, it is kind of free." Our interpretation is that, as she already had a strong value or internalized motivation to learn Korean, her perception of her parents was more as a support encouraging her to learn Korean rather than as a constraining influence controlling and restricting her autonomy.

Seong-il: "I am Korean, so I'd Feel Guilty if I Didn't Learn Korean"

Seong-il's voice for learning and speaking Korean seemed relatively active (style), even though he seemed to have both kinds of motivation, more autonomous and less autonomous regulations. Most of all, he seemed to have a strong *integrated regulation*, motivated to learn Korean because

"I'm Korean and if I don't really know much about Korean, then I'm technically, not Korean, only in blood, not in…[trails off]" (discourse; style). As he was interviewed, he frequently stated what we interpreted as seeing the learning of Korean as purposeful and as a means to self-identifying as Korean (discourse). Interestingly, he also seemed to have *introjected regulation*, that is, being motivated to learn Korean by internal pressure to show others that he is Korean and that he is able to speak in Korean. When asked why he was learning Korean, he replied, "I'm learning Korean because I'm feeling I'm Korean, I need to know more about it rather than not knowing anything" (style). The interviewer went on to ask:

Interviewer: Because you are Korean that's why you feel like you have to learn Korean?

Seong-il: Not that I have to. I feel like it would be easier and like better… I'm saying basically, if I was Korean and someone came up to me, asking and say something in Korean, and I can't really say anything, I'll be pressured and feel guilty.

Seong-il perceived that his parents had an "expectation that I'll be knowing more Korean than before," but not a "high expectation." Compared to Jean or Katy who seemed to be studying Korean for the purpose of building relationships with their parents, we could see that Seong-il perceived less pressure from his parents to learn and speak Korean, as his parents were fluent in English. Seong-il reported that he thought his learning of Korean had really begun at age 7, when he had visited his grandparents in Korea. Now he perceived his current exposure to Korean to be very minimal, saying, "not really anywhere else other than here (Korean school)." At home, he reported speaking Korean to his parents "most of the time" (discourse), and his parents, more particularly his mother, spoke Korean to him.

In sum, Seong-il reported learning Korean as a way to build or support his strong Korean identity in the Unites States (discourse), an autonomous form of motivation in SDT.

Junho: Value of Korean in Building Relationships

With his Korean parents, Junho had immigrated to the United States when he was 5 years old. He stated that one purpose he had for learning Korean was to be recognized as the teacher's assistant (discourse), a practice that allowed teachers to reward the good progress of one or two children in each class of the school. A second purpose seemed more central and more frequently mentioned in his interviews: He wanted to learn Korean to build relationships and to communicate well with his family members and other Koreans with whom he interacted (discourse). Therefore, he seemed to have *identified regulation*, recognizing the importance of learning Korean with internalized value. When asked why he liked learning Korean, he stated:

Because I know more Korean, so, like, when I learn more Korean, I can speak to my grandmother when I talk to her on the phone. I understand way more. Now I can read Korean books, kind of. I try to read those baby books… I want to learn Korean so I don't forget it. So when I go back to Korea, I can still talk my cousins.

Junho stated that learning Korean helped him because "I won't be able to talk to my parents" without knowledge of Korean (discourse). Moreover, he stated that he "really enjoy learning Korean, because I get to talk with my parents more and comfortable more" (style), which led us to describe him with a combination of *integrated regulation* as well as *intrinsic motivation*.

Junho reported that his parents strongly valued learning Korean and communicated mostly in Korean at home: "they speak Korean but sometimes they speak English, but usually Korean, like, 90% of the time, and I speak back to them in Korean, like, 70%" and "they encourage me to speak it, but they don't actually tell me to speak Korean" (discourse). Asked about his parents' expectations for sending him to Korean school, he stated (style):

> The only reason they sent me here is so I learn, I'll be forced to learn how to read and write. I guess they try to teach me, but I have never kept reading and practicing. Here, I'm forced to read and write. I guess they want me to learn to read and write way faster.

Interestingly, when he talked about his "regular" school, he identified himself as Asian American rather than simply American or Korean American, referring directly to the pressure he felt from the stereotype to do well at school because he was Asian (discourse; style): "At school, I have to get A's. A is average for us. But here [Korean school], I can relax."

Tracy: The Little Linguist

Tracy represented the most autonomous, most strongly positive motivation for learning Korean. Also, because she was the one to initiate speaking Korean most of the time at home, as her Korean mother was fluent in English and her father did not speak Korean at all, we could see less pressure from them to speak Korean (discourse).

> Sometimes, when I come in, I will say "I am home from school" [in Korean] because I learned that, and then if I start speaking Korean to her, she will return in Korean. But she won't use too complicated sentences, and most of the time, English.

Tracy positioned herself as an active learner throughout her narratives with an active and agentic voice (style), associated with having *intrinsic motivation* to learning Korean:

> I think it is fun to be a translator (style). I think it is really fun because, when I went there [Korea], I was in the third grade, I could read signs, and I could find my way to the grocery store, and back to my aunt's apartment.

Unlike other students who seemed to be studying Korean because of their parents, Tracy showed strong intrinsic motivation for learning Korean attributable in part to her interest in learning languages and in part to her mother's autonomy-supportive motivating style. She was interested in learning Korean as an end in itself (discourse) rather than as a means to be able to communicate with Korean people (like Jean and Seong-il) or build relationships with parents (like Katy and Junho).

Interviewer: Your parents feel that you should learn Korean?

Tracy: My mom doesn't care. She doesn't really think I need to. But she doesn't object if I want to.

Interviewer: Then you are learning Korean just because you want to learn?

Tracy: Yeah, I don't need it for any part of my life, but I just want, I think it's fun to learn and it's interesting to learn.

Tracy seemed to perceive her ethnic identities slightly differently when she considered herself in different contexts. When first asked, Tracy said, "I consider myself as Korean, as I live a lot like a Korean," but when asked about her ethnic identity more directly, she said, "I think Korean

American, I always think of myself as half Korean. I always think Korean first." For Tracy, her identities and motivation associated with learning Korean seemed more stable and more generally positive, even though it was also interesting that she sometimes expressed frustration with the teacher's instructional style.

DISCUSSION AND SIGNIFICANCE

The analytic framework of Critical Discourse Analysis led us to see our participants as negotiating their identities in different ways associated with their motivation to learn Korean. The hallmark of this motivation and identity work was the situated and variable nature of how they saw themselves and what motivated them to learn their heritage language as revealed in their discourse. Using an analysis based on CDA, with its careful look at discourse markers of passivity, reason, positioning, and affect, allowed us to make a connection to one motivation theory, SDT, with its framework to account for the reasons people do what they do and sustain their actions. Through this analysis, we extended both frameworks, making CDA more directly aligned with motivational processes and making SDT more social, situative, and discoursal.

Interestingly, although all of the students at some point used the label "Korean," whether alone or in combination with "American" or "Japanese," to describe themselves, what they meant by the label was explained in greatly different ways depending on various values and goals they had for learning the literacy practices of Korean. Some saw the language as allowing for emotional bonds with Korean relatives, some for building relationship with their Korean parent, some to show respect to their Korean ethnic background, and some to enjoy the language itself. Intertwined with the influences that they perceived from their sociocultural milieu, these children's situated identities seemed connected to various types of motivation they had for learning Korean. As we came to understand their motivation, we saw the students as varying from an inchoate undifferentiated motivation (Minseong), to showing a more externally regulated motivation (Katy), to being motivated by the guilt of not knowing Korean (Seong-il), to wanting to learn the language as a means to a future job or opportunity for education in Korea (Boyeon), or simply because of the joy of learning the language itself (Tracy). Motivation seemed a part of the discourses that the students expressed, each taking up features of genre and characteristics of style that we identified in their utterances.

That students took on some sort of identification with being Korean did not necessarily mean that the kind or intensity of motivation to learn the language was coming solely from their ethnic identification. We could see that their motivation originated in diverse sources of meaning-making, such as through different ways of interacting with their family and the greater Korean community, or through pressure they adopted from within to learn Korean so as to avoid feeling guilty for not being able to do so. Although we have not yet fully explored the patterns by which issues of power and hegemony across language and culture were enacted, issues that a CDA analysis would usually highlight, we saw each of our participants working within multiple subjectivities and motivated to join or resist, overtly or more covertly, the different discourses in which they had the potential to participate. It is possible that the parents would have provided us a richer, more differentiated discourse about power and resistance than did the children. Because it was the children who found themselves at Saturday school, and it was they who had the task of learning Korean, we found their narratives interesting for the reasons they had for being there.

Conclusion

Our results should be of interest to literacy researchers and educators because of its account of the nuanced ways that identities and motivational processes supported students as they acquired language literacy practices appropriate to a second/bilingual setting. Whereas teachers may see their students as "good" students only when the students seem to engage willingly in the literacy tasks the teacher has put before them, the students for their part often face complex motivational and identity issues that make it difficult for them to approach classroom tasks willingly at all times. Understanding the challenges to self that students face may help educators take a more hopeful approach and give more supportive messages to support the students' motivational processes.

REFERENCES

Anzaldúa, G. (1987). *Borderlands/La frontera: The new mestiza*. San Francisco, CA: Aunt Lute Books.
Canagarajah, A. S. (1999). *Revisiting linguistic imperialism in English teaching*. Oxford, UK: Oxford University Press.
Chen, Y. (2006). *Balancing goals and emotional responses to learning Chinese as a heritage language*. Unpublished doctoral dissertation, The University of Texas at Austin.
Cho, G. (2000). The role of heritage language in social interactions and relationships: Reflections from a language minority group. *Bilingual Research Journal, 24, 369-384*.
Chouliaraki, L., & Fairclough, N. (1999). *Discourse in late modernity: Rethinking Critical Discourse Analysis*. Edinburgh, UK: Edinburgh University Press.
Clayton, T. (1998). Beyond mystification: Reconnecting world-system theory for comparative education. *Comparative Education Review, 42*, 479-496.
Cummins, J. (1984). *Bilingualism and special education: Issues in assessment and pedagogy*. Clevedon, UK: Multilingual Matters.
Deci, E. L., & Ryan, R. M. (Eds.). (2002). *Handbook of self-determination research*. Rochester, NY: University of Rochester Press.
Fairclough, N. (2004). Semiotic aspects of social transformation and learning. In R. Rogers (Ed.), *An introduction to Critical Discourse Analysis in education* (pp. 225-235). Mahwah, NJ: Erlbaum.
Fishman, J. (1977). Language and ethnicity. In H. Giles (Ed.), *Language, ethnicity and intergroup relations*. London, UK: Academic Press.
Guardado, M. (2009). Speaking Spanish like a Boy Scout: Language socialization, resistance and reproduction in a heritage language Scout troop. *The Canadian Modern Language Review/La Revue canadienne des langues vivantes, 66*(1), 101-129.
Giles, H., & Coupland, N. (1991). *Language: Contexts and consequences*. Pacific Groove, CA: Brooks/Cole Publishing.
Giroux, H. A. (1992). *Border crossings: Cultural workers and the politics of education*. New York, NY: Routledge.
Gutiérrez, K. D. (2008). Developing a sociocritical literacy in the third space. *Reading Research Quarterly, 43*(2), 148-164.
Leclezio, M. K., Louw-Potgieter, J., Souchon, M. B. S. (1986). The social identity of Mauritian immigrants in South Africa. *Journal of Social Psychology, 126*, 61-69.
Lee, J. (2002). The Korean language in America: The role of cultural identity in heritage language learning. *Language, Culture, and Curriculum, 15*(2), 117-133.
Luke, A. (2000). Critical literacy in Australia: A matter of context and standpoint. *Journal of Adolescent & Adult Literacy, 43*, 448-461.
Moje, E. B., & Lewis, C. (2007). Examining opportunities to learn literacy: The role of critical sociocultural literacy research. In C. Lewis, P. Enciso, & E. B. Moje (Eds.), *Reframing sociocultural research on literacy: Identity, agency, and power* (pp.15-48). Mahwah, NJ: Erlbaum.

Norton, B. (2000). *Identity and language learning: Gender, ethnicity, and educational change.* London, UK: Longman.

Ohara, Y., & Saft, S. (2003). Using conversation analysis to track gender ideologies in social interaction: Toward a feminist analysis of a Japanese phone-in consultation TV program. *Discourse & Society, 14*(2), 153-172.

Pittinsky, T. L., Shih, M., & Ambady, N. (1999). Identity adaptiveness: Affect across multiple identities. *Journal of Social Issues, 55*, 503-518.

Perry, K. H., & Purcell-Gates, V. (2005). Resistance and appropriation: Literacy practices as agency within hegemonic contexts. *Yearbook of the National Reading Conference, 54*, 272-285.

Rex, L. A., Bunn, M., Davila, B. A., Dickinson, H. A., Ford, A. C., Gerben, C., Orzulak, M. J. M., & Thomson, H. (2010). A review of discourse analysis in literacy research: Equitable access. *Reading Research Quarterly, 45*(1), 94-115.

Rogers, R. (2004a). Storied selves: A critical discourse analysis of adult learners' literate lives. *Reading Research Quarterly, 39*(3), 272-305.

Rogers, R. (2004b). A critical discourse analysis of literate identities across contexts: Alignment and conflict. In R. Rogers (Ed.), *An introduction to Critical Discourse Analysis in education* (pp. 51-78). Mahwah, NJ: Erlbaum.

Ryan, R. M., & Connell, J. P. (1989). Perceived locus of causality and internalization: Examining reasons for acting in two domains. *Journal of Personality and Social Psychology, 57*, 749-761.

Strauss, A., & Corbin, J. (1998). *Basics of qualitative research: Techniques and procedures for developing grounded theory* (2nd ed.). Thousand Oaks, CA: Sage.

Talmy, S. (2010). Becoming "local" in ESL: Racism as resource in a Hawai'i public high school. *Journal of Language, Identity, and Education, 9*(1), 36-57.

Tse, L. (2001). Resisting and reversing language shift: Heritage-language resilience among U.S. native biliterates. *Harvard Educational Review, 71*(4), 676-708.

Wohlwend, K. E., (2009). Damsels in discourse: Girls consuming and producing identity texts through Disney princess play. *Reading Research Quarterly, 44*(1), 57-83.

Woodruff, A. L., & Schallert, D. L. (2008). Studying to play, playing to study: Nine college student-athletes' motivational sense of self. *Contemporary Educational Psychology, 33*, 34-57.

Collaborative Robotics Engineering Projects: Managing Uncertainty in Multimodal Literacy Practice in a Fifth-Grade Class

Michelle E. Jordan
Arizona State University

At least I'm learning, but I'm not sure how all this stuff works…It interests me to finally notice something about technology. (Demetre)

I'm uncertain about everything in robotics because I'm new to robotics. (Satya)

Literacy and science educators alike would likely agree that literacy learning tasks are fraught with uncertainty associated with encountering new semiotic systems and complex practices in contexts ranging from learning to read and write a first language, to second language acquisition, to manipulating technological and digital literacies. Although theoretical discussions of uncertainty in academic settings have a long and venerable history (e.g., Bruner, 1986; Dewey, 1929), few researchers have explicitly and systematically examined what students do, their behaviors and strategies, as they attempt to manage uncertainty during literacy tasks (for exceptions see Covino, 1988; Feldman & Wertch, 1976; Langer, 1997). Because individuals often have difficulty managing uncertainty effectively (Doyle & Carter, 1984; Sorrentino & Roney, 2001), it seems important to understand the ways that students manage uncertainty in literacy contexts. This is especially true in today's complex hypertextual world where children, like Demetre and Satya, encounter new semiotic systems throughout their school lives.

The purpose of this study is to illuminate how upper elementary school students managed uncertainty elicited during engagement in multimodal literacy learning tasks. Specifically, I relied on observations and interviews of fifth-grade students learning robotics engineering. Working collaboratively, students built mechanical structures using LEGO parts (e.g., beams, axles) and programmed them using an iconic language that interfaces the computer with motors and sensors (e.g., light, touch) to allow robots to manipulate and maneuver through environments (e.g., deliver objects). Robotics projects offer students complicated multimodal experiences in which print literacies interact with hands-on production. I conceive of robotics activity both as *literacy writ small* where literacy events are confined to occasions "in which a piece of writing is integral to the nature of the participants' interactions and their interpretive processes" (Heath, 1982, p. 50) and, taking a step away from print, also as *literacy writ large*, arguing that children learning to think and talk like engineers and to comprehend and produce three-dimensional objects are participating in multimodal literacy events, experiencing the activity of science, and pursuing scientific literacy (Lemke, 1990; Palincsar, Anderson, & David, 1993).

This non-traditional literacy context was selected for my study because it offered an ideal space in which to investigate students' uncertainty management in literacy learning. Because robotics was new to all but one of the students in the class, it provided an opportunity to study uncertainty elicited from novelty of experience as well as uncertainty due to the complex intersection of sign systems in multimodal activity and high levels of ambiguity in production tasks. Because students worked collaboratively, their social practices and conceptions of literacy were made visible (Rowell, 2002), as were their strategies for managing uncertainty. The teacher of the class was known throughout the district for her expertise in robotics instruction. Also, in observations the year prior to the study, I noted that she incorporated the study and production of texts in multiple media daily in an effort to broaden her students' literacies (Kist, 2005).

THEORETICAL FRAMEWORKS

In this section, I first provide background on uncertainty and its management. I then provide a conceptualization of engagement in robotics projects as literacy acquisition and literacy practice, framing my argument in terms of multimodal conceptions of literacy.

Experiencing Uncertainty and Managing Uncertainty

Psychological uncertainty can be thought of as an individual's experience of being unsure, doubting, or wondering about one's own or others' knowledge, understanding, beliefs, or preferences about the past, present, or future, or about other aspects of the world. Sometimes considered a "cognitive feeling" (Clore, 1992), uncertainty is associated with both cognitive and affective responses (Wilson, Centerbar, Kermer, & Gilbert, 2005). Responses to uncertainty can be positive or negative, and they can impede or enhance thinking and action. Long-held beliefs and immediate attributions can influence one's response to uncertainty (Dweck, 2000; Thomas & McDaniel, 1990), and this can influence academic performance (Hodson & Sorrentino, 1997).

Uncertainty in academic contexts stems from multiple sources. Correct performance on learning tasks is not always clearly definable for learners in advance, and the possibility of failure to meet evaluation criteria is ever present (Doyle & Carter, 1984). Uncertainty is also likely to be elicited from task novelty (Herbst, 2003) and task complexity (Blumenfeld, Mergendoller, & Swarthout, 1987). The issues about which students experience uncertainty and the degree of uncertainty they experience depend also on how a task is perceived by students (Doyle, 1983), and student perceptions may depend on how tasks are framed by teachers (Engle & Conant, 2002; Hiebert, et al., 1996; Townsend, 1991).

By *managing uncertainty*, I am referring to behaviors students engage in to enable action in the face of uncertainty. Individuals often attempt to manage uncertainty by reducing it, but they may also ignore, maintain, or even increase uncertainty as they attempt to enable action and reach a goal (Babrow, Kasch, & Ford, 1998). Students across ages often fail to become uncertain when uncertainty would be appropriate and helpful for learning (Sieber, 1974). Furthermore, when students do experience uncertainty, they may attempt to reduce it as quickly as possible (Doyle & Carter, 1984). However, children as young as second grade are capable of recognizing and articulating their own uncertainty (Metz, 2004), and thus, possibly capable of regulating it.

Along with individual propensities (Kruglanski & Webster, 1996) and the nature of particular tasks, there are social aspects associated with uncertainty management. Characteristic and accepted ways of managing uncertainty tend to become established in different cultural groups (Goldsmith, 2001), and these are crucial for verifying membership in some communities of practice (Lingard, Garwood, Schryer, & Spafford, 2003). It seems logical that peer interaction would influence how individuals manage uncertainty, particularly during collaborative tasks. However, the effects of peer interaction on uncertainty management during literacy learning tasks are as of yet largely unexplored (but see Anderson, et al., 2001; Aukerman, Glasheen, & Riley, 2008). Understanding the ways students manage uncertainty must include understanding how they come to do so in the multimodal literacy communities in which they participate.

Collaborative Robotics Projects as Multimodal Literacy Acquisition and Practice

I investigated students' engagement in robotics engineering projects, an activity that entails multimodal literacy practices of various kinds, usually within a science education context. When we talk about science content literacy, we are often referring to how young students deal with science textbooks, trade books, charts, graphs, and maps. Literacy researchers have made important contributions to our knowledge about how children learn to read and produce such text (see, for example, Moss & Newton, 2002; Smolkin, & Donovan, 2004). However, science educators are not willing to have it that science is only learned through reading from print. By taking a multimodal literacy approach to robotics instruction, I am agreeing with those who would portray literacy as broadly inclusive of visual, gestural, kinesthetic and three-dimensional semiotic systems (Kress, 2003; Kress, Jewitt, Ogborn, & Tsatsarelis, 2001), and also with van Leeuwen's (2005) description of semiotic resources as actions and artifacts used to create and communicate cultural meanings from almost everything we do or make.

Multimodal, multiliteracy, and new literacy theorists (e.g., Lankshear & Knobel, 2006; Lemke, 2000; New London Group, 1996) share recognition of the immense changes to our social, personal, and work lives due to the emergence of digital technologies and the variety of text forms arising with them. In robotics engineering tasks, "technology and literacy have a transactional relationship" (Stolle, 2007, p. 57). What human beings engineer, create, and construct, and the ways they go about doing so, are constrained and enabled by the literacy tools at their disposal. Clearly, digital technologies have enabled robotics engineering to change everyday aspects of our lives, from the automated doorways allowing easy entry into public buildings, to tools used in the exploration of space, healthcare and warfare applications, and the assembly of automobiles and airplanes. Less clear is the potential of robotics learning to shape children's literacy development and identities.

Engineering is largely a new curricular area in elementary school classrooms, the *E* in the STEM disciplines. Robotics has recently become a popular way to introduce young students to engineering and computing, prompted in part by the ideas of Seymour Papert (1980) about how computer-based learning environments can support children's construction of knowledge. Robotics engineering as practiced in the observed classroom I observed consisted of building structures, writing programs, and testing. Each of these interdependent activities required its own multimodal literacy practices.

When talking about the act of building structures, it is easy to see how interacting with attendant texts such as building manuals is literacy practice. Even diagrams and sketches of plans for structures fit easily within Kress and van Leeuwen's (2006) conception of visual literacy. However, it is not as natural for literacy researchers to consider how designed structures and objects used in producing those structures can be "read." Discussions of multimodality are still often tied to the page, albeit the electronic page, confined to how two-dimensional images can be read alone or in conjunction with print text, or, when moved into three-dimensional contexts, are focused on modes of meaning in the arts such as sculpture and dancing (Albers & Harste, 2007). It is not so clear how physical objects used for pragmatic purposes also carry symbolic weight. Acquisition of such literacy involves how students move from looking at meaningless pieces (e.g., motors, gears) to looking at those same pieces for what they afford in a design that students can build (e.g., axles connect wheels to platforms; gear trains transfer energy between parts).

It may be relatively easy for literacy researchers to consider interaction with an iconic programming language as literacy practice. LEGO Mindstorms, the programming software utilized in the observed classroom, uses pictorial icons to represent programming actions (see Figure 1). The task of programming robots required readers and writers to recognize and differentiate among programming icons, integrate textual information from multiple places on the screen, negotiate interdependencies between power, duration, and direction, understand linear sequencing, and mentally imagine how program actions would be enacted in robot actions.

Figure 1. Program with Wait Blocks, Move Blocks, Light Sensor, and a Loop

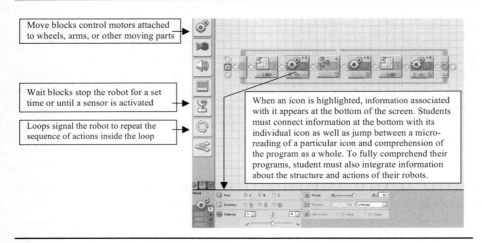

Literacy researchers acknowledge that the same meaning can be expressed in different semiotic modes and that meaning also resides in juxtapositions and transformations across sign systems (Siegel & Panofsky, 2009). Multimodal literacy activities in robotics engineering are interdependent in the sense of needing one another for full fruition. A constructed structure is not a robot, neither is a computer program. Only through interdependencies among multimodal texts do robots emerge. Learning to coordinate functionally among modes is paramount for scientific literacy (Kress, Jewitt, Ogborn, & Tsatsarelis, 2001; Lemke, 2000). Continuously testing and revising drafts of a robotics program to enable a built structure to act on its environment requires juggling modes. Visual imagery and translation between two-dimensional images and three-dimensional objects are key skills for comprehension and practice in this multimodal context.

METHOD

The data for this study were drawn from a larger research project that occurred across one school year. Using a qualitative, interpretive framework, I examined the ways students managed uncertainty as they struggled to acquire understanding of new sign systems and to learn to participate in multimodal literacy comprehension and production activities associated with instruction in robotics engineering.

Participants and Context

This study took place in a fifth-grade class in a suburban district in the southwestern United States. Participants included 24 students (15 boys, 9 girls) and their teacher, a White woman with 23 years of teaching experience and considerable expertise in project-based science and technology instruction. Students were diverse on several dimensions: five received special education services, three were identified as gifted-and-talented; ten were Black, seven White, five Hispanic, and two Asian; 33% of students in the school were economically disadvantaged.

Robotics instruction centered around three long-term projects assigned over the course of the school year. For the purposes of this report, I confine my discussion to analysis of data pertaining to the first project, when students were initially introduced to the semiotic sign systems associated with robotics. Students were assigned to mixed-ability groups of three and instructed to build a vehicle from a printed instruction manual and to program it to move forward, hit a wall, trigger a touch sensor to reverse direction, and land on a large X on the floor. The project took place across four months, in 14 sessions ranging from 40 to 90 minutes during which the teacher provided whole-class instruction and groups worked alone and with teacher support.

Data Collection

Rather than observe all students equally, I identified eight focal students selected for their diversity in demographics, academic achievement, and social skills as identified by the teacher. As these eight students were members of four of the eight collaborative groups, I closely observed half the class. I audiorecorded two to four groups each day, two of which I also videorecorded. Rotating among these groups, I wrote field notes in a small notebook and transcribed and expanded them, usually within 24 hours. I recorded my impressions, emotional responses, questions, and wonderings. I summarized whole-class activities and the groups' progress and added theoretical and methodological memos (Corsaro, 1982). I immediately began transcribing recordings to start making sense of the data.

Multiple semi-structured interviews (Spradley, 1979) with focal students occurred as early as possible after each robotics session, depending on availability, rotation, and whether I had specific burning questions for particular participants. I asked students about events from the immediately prior session, guided by field notes and rough transcriptions of recorded data (e.g., "What were you thinking when that happened?"). Interviews were audiorecorded and transcribed.

Additional data sources included photographs of structures and programming files, individual and group written work (e.g., written reflections), and teacher interviews.

Table 1. Multimodal Literacy Activities and Practices in the First Robotics Engineering Project

---

Building Structures

- recognizing, classifying, and naming (memorizing and creating vocabulary) pieces
- developing intuitions about how pieces fit together and physically connecting them
- recognizing common functional relationships among pieces and representing these through language and gestures
- reading and following procedures in a printed instruction manual (translating from 2-dimensional media to 3-dimensional media and examining equivalence, checking size by placing pieces against the page or counting bumps, turning physical pieces to match the orientation of pieces on the page)

Reading and Writing Programs

- using basic computer skills (e.g., open programs, locate palettes, click, drag)
- recognizing, naming, and associating icons with their functions (e.g., stop, wait, move)
- integrating information from different parts of the computer screen (e.g., recognizing that information at the bottom of the screen is associated with a specific icon and changes as you click on an icon, understanding that information contained in an icon changes when you change distance, power, direction, etc. at the bottom of the screen)
- understanding, comparing, and discussing methods for turning and translating these into robots' actions (e.g., stop on both sides versus slow down the motor on one side)
- reasoning about sequencing (e.g., recognizing the directionality of influence, labeling actions, programming in parts)
- comprehending and comparing systems for measuring distance (e.g., understanding that one rotation means one time around the wheel; translating between seconds, rotations, and degrees; predicting robot actions from understanding that wheel size changes distance traveled in one rotation,…)
- transferring a program from a computer to a robot (e.g., attaching to ports, understanding the relationship between an NXT and motors)
- accessing and utilizing programming instructions on the Mindstorms software

Testing: The Interface between Structures and Programs

- navigating the menu of NXT bricks (robot brain) to initialize a program
- developing intuitions about distance relative to measurement systems (i.e. rotations, degrees, seconds)
- choosing % battery power (link to speed, effect on turns, minimum needed)
- recognizing, discussing, and arguing about issues of precision (e.g., how precise is it possible to be, how precise do you need to be, is there one right answer?; using strategies and tools for increasing precision: partial rotations, tape, rulers, robot placement, stablizing wobbly wheels)
- recognizing issues of accuracy (experimenting with multiple runs of the same test)
- observing results of texts and hypothesizing about causal relationships; recognizing and discussing interdependencies between structure, distance, duration, power, etc.

Analysis of Data

I conducted an analysis of the literacy activities in which students engaged during the project simultaneously with an analysis of students' management of uncertainty, letting the two strands of inquiry inform one another. Examining whole-class and collaborative group data across the robotics project, I categorized activities, sequences of activities, and interdependencies among activities, conceptualizing them as literacy practice (see Table 1). I identified the semiotic resources used in this collaborative context, including traditional print texts and also digital, discursive, and three-dimensional "texts."

My analysis of uncertainty management was inductive, informed by prior research and by patterns that emerged from the data. I used the constant-comparative method (Corbin & Strauss, 2008) and analysis of discourse (Erickson, 1992; Wells, 2000) to construct an interpretive description of students' uncertainty management as they built, programmed, and tested their robots. Important in my interpretation were my understandings of linguistic uncertainty (Feldman & Wertsch, 1976; Lakoff, 1973), politeness (Brown & Levinson, 1978), communication (Brashers, 2001), and sociocultural theory (Wertsch, 1991). Using NVIVO, a qualitative analysis software, I analyzed transcripts and field notes, refining emerging categories and themes in several iterations by comparing and searching for negative cases of patterns of uncertainty management. Although uncertainty management was undoubtedly influenced by many outside actors (e.g., the teacher, other class members, family members), I limited my analysis to how students managed their uncertainty in conjunction with their collaborative group members.

Once I felt I had a good sense of the data, I selected two groups of students for closer examination. The examples for this report were drawn primarily from these groups: a group of three boys (Demetre, Nathan, and Luis) and a group of three girls (Satya, Kisha, and Kim) (all pseudonyms). I transcribed all audio data from these groups, incorporated information from other data sources to refine my summaries of their activities, and identified for deeper analysis events in which uncertainty was sustained for a significant amount of time by at least one group member while engaged in building, programming, or testing robots.

Peer review with colleagues ensured that data collected were congruent with the research objectives. After data were collected, I conducted member checking with the teacher of the class.

FINDINGS

Although not comprehensive, Table 1 demonstrates the rich range of semiotic meaning-making practices required of students as they worked to comprehend and produce the signs and sign systems of robotics. While building, programming, and testing their robots, students engaged in many practices involving multiple modes of representation (e.g., two-dimensional images in the instruction manual and in the programming environment, three-dimensional physical models and the obstacle course). Different modes were brought to the forefront during different activities and these modes interacted in different ways during different activities. Cognitive demands students faced in this setting included the ability to translate between multiple modes, recognize interdependencies among modes, and communicate about these in the language of science. Meaning was created by students through the complex interweaving among spoken and written language, physical actions such as gestures and manipulating materials, and interpretations of robots' actions.

In the remainder of the findings, I describe and illustrate with examples how students managed uncertainty associated with building, programming, and testing robots.

"It Looks Like a Churro": Managing Uncertainty While Building Structures

When building structures, student experienced uncertainty related to identifying materials and pieces and the typical functional relationships among them. Two uncertainty management strategies were particularly prominent while students were engaged in building activities: creating vocabulary and using the instruction manual as a source of authority.

Creating vocabulary. In addition to appropriating literacy practices modeled by the teacher, students also invented their own literacy practices for managing uncertainty associated with building structures. Although initial instruction by the teacher began with a lesson on the names of building pieces, students forgot many of the labels that the teacher had attached to pieces. Uncertainty about vocabulary was easily and smoothly handled by creating names for pieces based on attributes such as color ("give me a black"), size ("it's the 15"), or shape ("I think of it as a plus;" "It looks like a churro;" "Ok, now give me the L"). Created names seemed to spread quickly among the members of a group. One can easily imagine that building sessions might have bumped and jerked along if students had felt obligated to use the formal names for pieces. The fact that they were willing to create names that would satisfice and that they were able to engage in mind reading with one another about those names (Bloom, 2002) enabled students quickly to reduce their uncertainty and continue their work with minimum disruption.

Referring to the manual. Students began their work by referring to instructional manuals to build pre-designed structures step-by-step. The printed manual became the source of expertise that students turned to in reducing their uncertainty. Students learned to pay careful attention to the correspondence between the printed manual and the physical structure: turning the pieces in their hands to match the slant of pieces in the manual, placing pieces against the illustrations on the page, or counting the bumps on pieces to resolve uncertainty about sizing.

During one building session, Demetre had the manual and was trying to attach a motor to his group's developing structure. When he was unable to resolve his uncertainty about whether a piece was placed correctly by referencing the manual, Demetre addressed his group members, "Does it have this huge thing?" Nathan took the structure without referring to the manual, and moved the motor, saying, "I think you put it on the other side." He handed the structure back to Demetre, who looked at the page, skeptical. Without looking at the manual, Nathan asserted, "It should be right." Pointing back and forth between the manual and the structure, Demetre argued, "No, these two things should go together." Luis, who had also been referencing the manual, agreed. Finally, Nathan looked at the manual and said, "Oh, that's right," and Demetre proceeded to attach the motor in the correct spot. Demetre, who originally had expressed uncertainty, was the group member who also referred to the printed text for information, whereas Nathan, who did not seem to be experiencing uncertainty, did not do so until later, after his group members convinced him that he should be uncertain.

Not all building uncertainty could be resolved by referencing the authority of the manual. Students had to develop intuitions about the way pieces fit together by repetitious experience and through experimentation. During an early building session, Satya experienced difficulty correctly fitting together an axle and a motor. Uncertain about how to make progress, she and Kisha began sharing possible solutions, ranging from seeking the teacher's help to experimenting with their materials, finally hitting on a successful solution of trying a new axle and twisting it in.

"But Our Program was Good": Uncertainty Management While Programming

No step-by-step instruction manual was provided for programming. The teacher introduced students to the software and modeled programming practices. She conveyed the expectation that every group's program would "look a little different." Thus, text production was expected early in the literacy acquisition process, albeit with tight constraints. Decoding problems abounded. Students had difficulties differentiating between programming icons and navigating the complicated structure of the programming texts. They experienced varying amounts of uncertainty about their comprehension of programming icons and the association of icons with the motion of structures. They managed their uncertainty by requesting scaffolding of participation by their peer collaborators and by referring to the teacher's authority.

Most students demonstrated in their group discourse and in interviews that their comprehension of programs and programming was improving across the robotics project. Kim's progress in this area was less marked than that of her group members as evidenced in her talk, reflections, and interviews, which also revealed her uncertainty about programming. Kim initially exhibited a high level of participation in robotics but seemed increasingly hesitant to take an active role. Instead, she avoided uncertainty and the negative affect it created in her by turning the task over to her group members. On the rare occasions she requested a more central position, she managed her uncertainty by asking her group members to scaffold her participation.

One day in the middle of the project, Kim sat on the floor with Kisha as the group tested their robot's ability to run in a straight line for one meter, a feat that was proving difficult. Kim relayed information about programming changes to Kisha from Satya, who called them out from her place at the computer. After a few tests, Kim moved next to Satya and leaned in to watch her change the program. Finally, after a particularly successful and exciting test of the robot, Kim requested, "Let me try it now." Satya moved completely away from the computer to sit by Kisha and the robot while Kim sat behind the computer, looked at the screen, mumbled to herself, and called to Satya:

Kim: I'm typing... How many seconds do you want?

Satya: I don't know... like 17?

Kim: OK, 17 seconds. [she types it into the program] And then what do I do?

The session proceeded with Satya calling out changes to Kim, who typed them. Only near the end of the session did Kim initiate her own idea, "Wait, I know another one. Let me try."

In using the uncertainty management strategy of requesting scaffolding, Kim was still turning part of the task over to her group members but in a way that enabled her to take action that felt perfectly legitimate to her and to her group members. She told me later in an interview that she had wanted to program because she looked around and saw other groups having fun. Looking around to see what others are doing might be a strategy for managing uncertainty about what to do and about what one should be able to do in a new literacy context.

In addition to improving their comprehension of signs, students grew in their awareness of scientific issues related to programming. One such issue was sequencing. Students experienced uncertainty as they struggled to reason about sequencing of events. There were several examples in the data of students expressing the belief that an icon they added near the end of a program was "messing up" actions located before it. For example, Demetre said in an interview, "I think we put something in the second turn that's confusing with the first turn." This comment reveals a misconception about sequencing; the uncertainty that Demetre was experiencing was not about whether it was true that the second action icons were interfering with icons that came before them, the uncertainty he grappled with was why it was true and what they could do about it. Students' misconceptions led them to experience uncertainty about the wrong thing, and to manage their uncertainty by engaging the wrong actions.

Students had to develop legitimate engineering practices as identified by their teacher for testing sequences of programming actions. This involved recognizing that they should be uncertain at each step of programming and that they should resolve that uncertainty before programming the next action. The teacher had identified this as the correct strategy to use for engineering projects. After one instructional visit in which the teacher had reminded a group of boys (Demetre, Nathan, and Luis) about this practice, Nathan started the group's program from scratch. It became clear to Demetre that Nathan was rewriting the entire program at once rather than working action by action as suggested by the teacher. The following discussion ensued:

Demetre: You're only doing the same thing again?

Nathan: Yeah.

Luis: We have to.

Demetre: Oh, forget it.... I thought... I thought it was best to... do it a little bit different, you know?

Nathan: Yeah, but our program was good.

Demetre: Okay, we'll keep it.

For Luis, there was no uncertainty. His declaration "We have to" implies that he saw the possibilities for action as severely constrained. Likewise, Nathan expressed no uncertainty about his present course of action, which was to re-do the entire program. Demetre was the only group member to express doubt, which was brushed aside by his group members. Demetre gave in, perhaps because he was unable immediately to articulate clearly his concern. What is clear in this case is that the group member who expressed the most certainty and who was willing and able to take action quickly ended up with the upper hand in this situation, even though his actions clearly went against the teacher's suggestions about programming and testing step-by-step.

"Now It's Going to Work!": Uncertainty Management During Testing

Students experienced the most uncertainty while testing their robot's ability to maneuver through the assigned obstacle course. Continuously revising drafts required juggling multiple media (programs and structures) and interdependent variables. From their interpretation of the results of a failed test, students determined whether they needed to re-design either their structure or their program. Students showed increasing comprehension of the relevant issues that influenced the outcome of their tests (e.g., appropriate duration, amount of power, precision in placing the robot in the obstacle course). They were less clear about which variable had contributed to a particular test result, and their thinking was frequently fuzzy about how variables influenced test outcomes together. Under these conditions, students often managed uncertainty through trial and error experimentation, focusing on reducing uncertainty about what to do to achieve desired outcomes rather than addressing uncertainties about why results occurred. This is exemplified in Kisha's response when asked if she knew why her group's robot was curving off course: "Not really. But we're trying to fix it." As students struggled to understand the relationship between multiple, interdependent inputs on a testing output, the feedback they received was difficult to interpret. Students often found themselves having to make changes without fully understanding the relationships among the variables, and this influenced their uncertainty management strategies.

For example, early during the second day of programming, Demetre, Nathan, and Luis made several trips to the hall to test their robot, each time making a change in their program: shifting from measuring in rotations to measuring in degrees, lowering the power, taking out a *wait for completion* icon, and increasing the distance. All three group members made suggestions for changes. Their suggestions were accompanied by little to no explanation or analysis of the issues. When arguments arose about how to proceed, they were met with, "I know what I'm doing" or "This will work." Although the group as a whole could be said to be in a state of uncertainty about what the problem was and how to fix it, the group members themselves expressed great certainty. Heading out to test the latest change, Demetre would often make a positive prediction, "Now it's going to work." Although the expression was one of great certitude, these positive predictions may have been a strategy for managing uncertainty by ignoring it, a way to keep going in the face of not being sure what to do.

Only after multiple unfruitful tests did there seem to be a shift in the strategies the boys were using to manage uncertainty. Demetre's positivity was finally tempered by repeated experiences in which the results of testing did not match his confident predictions. Once again heading to the hall, his usual, "Now it's going to work" was followed by "Maybe. Please, please work." Finally, Demetre openly acknowledged the group's shared uncertainty.

Demetre: We need more something different. We just don't' know what it is.

Nathan: I told you, we need to do rotations.

Demetre: Rotations is not going to do any good.

Nathan: Yes it will.

Demetre: [turning to a student in a nearby group] Are you guys doing rotations? We're doing degrees.

Nathan: I told you, Ms. Chapman said we should always do it on rotations... OK guys, how are we going to get this to work?

Demetre: I have no idea.

Nathan: This thing is so complex!

Demetre: So complicated. (A few turns later, he continues). I'm going to go get the meter stick and we can just test it right here. [Demetre walks away to get the meter stick]

Luis: Let's do 100 rotations; that's what Satya did.

Nathan: I'm crazy, but OK.

Having exhausted their ideas about what to try, the group acknowledged their shared uncertainty and attributed it to the complexity of the task, something they previously had not done, choosing instead to experiment and hope for a positive outcome. They sought outside sources to enable action, Demetre and Luis looking to another group and Nathan referring to the authority of the teacher to justify his preferred plan of action. Demetre, seeming at last to realize they might be running many tests, brought closer to the computer the measuring stick against which they tested. Finally, Nathan acquiesced to Luis's proposal to adopt a solution from a nearby group. Although he did not have reason to believe the idea would work, he could not think of an alternative. Thus, experimentation continued with expanded options once the boys began openly expressing their uncertainty about what was happening, how to proceed, and the likelihood of success.

DISCUSSION

When examined as literacy practice, it becomes clear that this multimodal environment created rich affordances for semiotic meaning and knowledge construction by connecting three-dimensional materials and structures, a computer program, and the children interacting around these objects. The collaborative robotics engineering project observed in this study offered students diverse opportunities to engage in multiple and interactive literacy activities, both when considered as *literacy writ small* and as *literacy writ large*. Furthermore, different literacy activities associated with the robotics project offered different potentialities for students to experience uncertainty and facilitated the use of different strategies for managing uncertainty elicited from engagement in a complicated and unfamiliar scientific literacy context.

Across the three over-arching activities of building, programming, and testing their robots, students experienced and managed uncertainty associated with *literacy writ small* such as by producing their own linguistic products (creating vocabulary) to enable discourse about structural pieces when they were unsure of conventional labels, requesting peer confirmation about their reading of a source of authority (the print-based instruction manual) when uncertain about translating two-dimensional building instructions to three-dimensional structures, and seeking scaffolding of participation from their peers when uncertain about their comprehension and ability to manipulate a digital iconic programming language to produce a desired outcome. Students also managed uncertainty about *literacy writ large*, coming to recognize situations in which it is proper and necessary for engineers to be uncertain in order to make progress on a project (e.g., at each step of programming), learning how to include productive talk about uncertainty in their scientific discourse related to testing, increasing their attention to and willingness to argue about uncertainties concerning scientific issues such as sequencing, precision, and accuracy, and sharing possible solutions when uncertain about how to make progress with their project.

In a study involving middle and high school students, Doyle (1988) found that students tried to limit uncertainty in academic tasks across curricular disciplines, for instance, by requesting that their teacher re-define the task. However, I found little evidence that this was true for the students in my study. Students' psychological load of uncertainty stayed fairly constant rather than diminishing throughout the project. When students resolved uncertainty about one thing, their attention simply shifted to a new uncertainty. Doyle and Carter (1984) found that students experienced a great deal of uncertainty related to the possibility of failure to meet the evaluation criteria associated with academic tasks. However, students in my study spent little time worrying about this source of uncertainty. Perhaps the difference between previous findings and the findings of this study can be explained by the difference in ages of the participants, or it could be attributable to the evaluative context established by the teacher. However, it could also be that in a collaborative task setting the risk of failure is dispersed throughout the team, allowing students to concentrate on uncertainty about the activities of the academic project itself.

The importance of social support for managing uncertainty identified in other contexts (e.g., Brashers, 2001) was also found in this study. First, implementation of most uncertainty management strategies required supportive participation of some sort from one's group members. For example, Kim's request for scaffolding required that her group members provide information; Demetre was unable to act on his uncertainty about testing until that uncertainty had been taken up by his group members. Furthermore, collaborative groups seemed to have their own affordances and constraints on strategies through which it was acceptable for its members to manage uncertainty. For instance, it seems unlikely that Kim would have been able to implement her strategy for managing uncertainty by requesting scaffolding from group members had she been assigned to the group of boys (Demetre, Luis, and Nathan). So, not only characteristics of the literacy activities but also characteristics of the interactive social systems in which students participated in those activities were influential on uncertainty management.

Attempting to manage uncertainty with the help of one's peer collaborators was a double-edged sword. Expressing uncertainty carried the social danger of being considered less knowledgeable and being taken less seriously than group members who appeared completely certain of what needed doing and their own ability to get it done. For example, Demetre frequently found himself with little power in group decision-making as Nathan expressed self-assurance and took the upper hand in many group decisions. This was true even though Nathan appeared to have no better understanding of or prior experience in robotics projects than Demetre. However, the willingness to seek peers' help to manage uncertainty also seemed to catalyze students' use of resources for learning. Even as students used interaction with peers to reduce their own uncertainty, their attempts to do so led to the introduction of uncertainty in other group members. For example, Demetre's continued expressions of uncertainty about testing the robot eventually infected his peer collaborators and this spurred the group to seek information. Thus, the ways students attempted to manage uncertainty with peer support influenced how they engaged with the robotic project and their opportunities for learning from it.

Implications for Research and Practice

Findings from this study suggest that the experience of uncertainty and its management has a significant role to play in students' engagement in multimodal literacy tasks. However, further research is needed to determine the transferability of findings to other literacy tasks and contexts. Although beyond the scope of this study, a first look at the data related to the final robotics project in this class suggests that students used a wider range of strategies to manage uncertainty in the more open, creative task of designing their own robots. Furthermore, as Siegel and Panofsky (2009) argued, "understanding what people make of the space between modes depends on the activities, identities, and power at a particular moment in time" (p. 101). Although this study has identified interesting things about how students in this setting managed uncertainty, it is difficult to interpret the efficacy and effectiveness of students' choices without an analysis of what counted as knowledge and learning in this classroom. To fully understand the affordances and constraints of robotics engineering projects as multimodal literacy tasks, the influence of the teacher, classmates, and other aspects of the context need to be explored.

Believing that the same kinds of uncertainty management strategies used by students in the non-traditional literacy context observed in this study might manifest themselves in a wide variety of literacy learning tasks, I had as a broader goal for this study to help literacy researchers and educators begin to consider ways students manage uncertainty. If we knew more about how children manage uncertainty in a variety of literacy contexts, we might help them learn new strategies for managing uncertainty, to match strategies and situations successfully, and to implement strategies flexibly over a range of literacy contexts and thereby offer alternative paths for living in a complex, hypertextual world where uncertainty is a common experience as one engages in semiotic tasks.

REFERENCES

Albers, G. R., & Harste, J. C. (2007). The arts, new literacies, and multimodality. *English Education, 40*(1), 6-20.

Anderson, R. C., Nyuyen-Jahiel, K., McNurlen, B., Archodidou, A., Kim, S., Reznetskaya, A., & Gilbert, L. (2001). The snowball phenomenon: Spread of ways of talking and ways of thinking across groups of children. *Cognition and Instruction, 19*(1), 1-46.

Aukerman, M., Glasheen, G., & Riley, K. (2008, December). *The role of teacher and students questions in fostering third grade peer-to-peer discussions of literary texts.* Paper presented at the annual meeting of the National Reading Conference, Orlando, FL.

Babrow, A. S., Kasch, C. R., & Ford, L. A. (1998). The many meanings of *uncertainty* in illness: Toward a systematic accounting. *Health Communication, 10*, 1–23.

Bloom, P. (2002). Mindreading, communication, and the learning of names for things. *Mind & Language, 17*, 37-54.

Blumenfeld, P., Mergendoller, J., & Swarthout, D. (1987). Cumulative experience of task form: Its impact on students as thinkers and workers. *Journal of Curriculum Studies, 19*, 135-148.

Brashers, D. (2001). Communication and uncertainty management. *Journal of Communication, 51*(3), 477-498.

Brown, P., & Levinson, S. (1978). Universals in language usage: Politeness phenomena. In E. N. Goody (Ed.), *Questions and politeness: Strategies in social interactions* (pp. 256–289). Cambridge, UK: Cambridge University Press.

Bruner, J. (1986). The language of education (Chap 9, pp. 121-133). *Actual minds, possible worlds.* Cambridge, MA: Harvard University Press.

Clore, G. L. (1992). Cognitive phenomenology: The role of feelings in the construction of social judgment. In A. Tesser & L. L. Martin (Eds.), *The construction of social judgments* (pp. 133-164). Hillsdale, N.J.: Erlbaum.

Corbin, J. M., & Strauss, A. L. (2008). *Basics of Qualitative Research.* London, UK: Sage.

Corsaro, W. (1982). *Friendship and peer culture in the early years.* Norwood, NJ: Ablex.

Covino, W. A. (1988). *The art of wondering: A revisionist return to the history of rhetoric.* Portsmouth, New Hampshire: Boynton/Cook Heinemann.

Dewey, J. (1929). *The quest for certainty.* New York, NY: Minton, Balch, & Company.

Dweck, C. (2000). *Self-theories: Their role in motivation, personality, and development.* Philadelphia, PA: Psychology Press.

Doyle, W. (1983). Academic work. *Review of Educational Research, 53*, 159-199.

Doyle, W., & Carter, K. (1984). Academic tasks in classrooms. *Curriculum Inquiry, 14*, 129-149.

Engle, R. A., & Conant, F. R. (2002). Guiding principles for fostering productive disciplinary engagement: Explaining an emergent argument in a community of learners classroom. *Cognition & Instruction, 20*, 399-483.

Erickson, F. (1992). Ethnographic microanalysis of interaction. In M. D. LeCompte, W. Millroy, & J. Preissle (Eds.), *The handbook of qualitative research in education* (pp. 201-225). San Diego, CA: Academic Press.

Feldman, C. F., & Wertsch, J. V. (1976). Context dependent properties of teachers' speech. *Youth & Society, 7*(3), 227-258.

Goldsmith, D. J. (2001). A normative approach to the study of uncertainty and communication. *Journal of Communication, 51*, 514-533.

Heath, S. (1982). What no bedtime story means: Narrative skills at home and at school. *Language in Society, 11*(1), 49-76.

Herbst, P. G. (2003). Using novel tasks in teaching mathematics: Three tensions affecting the work of the teacher. *American Educational Research Journal, 40*(1), 197-238.

Hiebert, J., Carpenter, T. P., Fennema, E., Fuson, K., Human, P., Murray, H., & Wearne, D. (1996). Problem solving as a basis for reform in curriculum and instruction: The case of mathematics. *Educational Researcher, 25*(4), 12-21.

Hodson, H., & Sorrentino, R. (1997). Groupthink and uncertainty orientation: Personality differences in reactivity to the group situation. *Group dynamics: Theory, research, and practice, 1*, 144-155.

Kist, W. (2005). *New literacies in action: Teaching and learning in multiple media.* New York, NY: Teachers College Press.

Kress, G. (2003). *Literacy in the new media age.* New York, NY: Routledge.

Kress, G., Jewitt, C., Ogborn, J., & Tsatsarelis, C. (2001). *Multimodal teaching and learning: The rhetorics of the science classroom.* London, UK: Continuum.

Kress, G., & van Leeuwen, T. (2006). *Reading images: The grammar of visual design.* New York, NY: Routledge.

Kruglanski, A. W., & Webster, D. M. (1996). Motivated closing of the mind: Seizing and freezing. *Psychological Review, 103*, 263–283.

Lakoff, G. (1973). Hedges: A study in meaning criteria and the logic of fuzzy concepts. *Journal of Philosophical Logic, 2*, 458–508.

Langer, E. (1997). *The power of mindful learning.* Cambridge, MA: Da Capo Press.

Lankshear, C., & Knobel, M. (2006). *New literacies: Everyday practices & classroom learning.* Buckingham, UK: Open University Press.

Lemke, J. (1990). *Talking science: Language, learning, and values.* Norwood, NJ: Ablex.

Lemke, J. (2000). Multimedia literacy demands of the scientific curriculum. *Linguistics and Education, 10*(3), 247-271.

Lingard, L., Garwood, K., Schryer, C. F., & Spafford, M. M. (2003). A certain art of uncertainty: Case presentation and the development of professional identity. *Social Science & Medicine, 56*, 603-616.

Metz, K. (2004). Children's understanding of scientific inquiry: Their conceptualizations of uncertainty in investigations of their own design. *Cognition and Instruction, 22*(2), 219-290.

Moss, B., & Newton, E. (2002). An examination of the informational text genre in basal readers. *Reading Psychology, 23*, 1-13.

New London Group (1996). A pedagogy of multiliteracies: Designing social futures. *Harvard Educational Review, 66*(1), 60-92.

Papert, S. (1980). *Mindstorms: Children, computers, and powerful ideas.* New York, NY: Basic Books.

Palincsar, A. S., Anderson, C., & David, Y. M. (1993). Pursuing scientific literacy in the middle grades through collaborative problem solving. *The Elementary School Journal, 93*, 643-658.

Rowell, P. M. (2002). Peer interactions in shared technological activity: A study of participation. *International Journal of Technology and Design Education, 12*, 1-22.

Sieber, J. E. (1974). Effects of decision importance on ability to generate warranted subjective uncertainty. *Journal of Personality and Social Psychology, 30*(5), 688-694.

Siegel, M., & Panofsky, C. P. (2009). Designs for multimodality in literacy studies: Explorations in Analysis. *Yearbook of the National Reading Conference, 50*, 99-111.

Smolkin, L. B., & Donovan, C. A. (2004). Improving science instruction with information books: Understanding multimodal presentations. In E. W. Saul (Ed.), *Crossing borders in literacy and science instruction: Perspectives on theory and practice* (pp. 190-208). Newark, DE: International Reading Association; Arlington, VA: NSTA Press.

Spradley, J. P. (1979). *The ethnographic interview.* New York, NY: Holt Reinhart.

Sorrentino, R. M., & Roney, C. J. R. (2000). *The uncertain mind: Individual differences in facing the unknown.* Philadelphia, PA: Psychology Press.

Stolle, E. P. (2007). Teachers, literacy, and technology: Tensions, complexities, conceptualizations, and practice. *Yearbook of the National Reading Conference, 56*, 56-69.

Thomas, J. B., & McDaniel, R. R., Jr. (1990). Interpreting strategic issues: Effects of strategy and the information-processing structure of top management teams. *Academy of Management Journal, 33*, 286-306.

Townsend, J. S. (1991). A study of wondering discourse in three literature class discussions. (Doctoral dissertation, The University of Texas at Austin, 1991). *Dissertation Abstracts International,* AAT 9128380.

van Leeuwen, T. (2005). *Introducing social semiotics.* New York, NY: Routledge.

Wells, G. (2000). Modes of meaning in a science activity. *Linguistics and Education, 10*(3), 307-334.

Wertsch, J. V. (1991). A sociocultural approach to socially shared cognition. In L. B. Resnick, J. M. Levine, & S. D. Teasley (Eds.), *Perspectives on socially shared cognition* (pp. 85-100). Washington, DC: American Psychological Association.

Wilson, T. D., Centerbar, D. B., Kermer, D. A., & Gilbert, D. T. (2005). The pleasures of uncertainty: Prolonging positive moods in ways people do not anticipate. *Journal of Personality and Social Psychology, 88*(1), 5-21.

Local Literacies as Counter-Hegemonic Practices Deconstructing Anti-Spanish Ideologies in the Rio Grande Valley

Luz A. Murillo

The University of Texas-Pan American

DECONSTRUCTING ANTI-SPANISH IDEOLOGIES IN THE RIO GRANDE VALLEY

I am writing from the Rio Grande Valley, the birthplace of the Chicana poet and scholar Gloria Anzaldúa. According to the U.S. Census, 82.3% of households in Hidalgo County speak Spanish as a primary language, a figure which excludes the many Spanish speakers who regularly cross the border to study, shop, work, or visit with family in the different towns across the region. "The Valley," as it is known to residents, is also the birthplace and home of the future bilingual teachers with whom I work at a local university and whose attitudes towards Spanish and Spanish literacy are the focus of this paper. As an educational anthropologist, a professor of reading, a Colombian and relative newcomer to the Valley, and as a native speaker of a different and less criticized variety of Spanish, I am interested in how the uses (and non-use) of Spanish literacies shape and reflect the language and professional identities of future bilingual literacy teachers.

I encourage my students to talk to me in Tex Mex. They tell me that they speak like *pochos* and that "*aqui no hablamos bien ni inglés ni español*" ("Here we speak neither English nor Spanish well"). At the outset of our work together, most believe that local ways of speaking are incorrect and unacceptable in school because they have been taught for many years that code switching is emblematic of a kind of "linguistic disability" associated with poverty, illiteracy, and a lack of formal education. Few see themselves as multilingual or view the Rio Grande Valley as a multilingual place, as described by Anzaldúa (2007, p. 77):

> ...because we are a complex, heterogeneous people, we speak many languages. Some of the languages we speak are: 1) Standard English; 2) Working class and slang English; 3) Standard Spanish; 4) Standard Mexican Spanish; 5) North Mexican Spanish dialect; 6) Chicano Spanish (Texas); 7) Tex-Mex; and 8) Pachuco (called caló).

Thus, this study was motivated by my fascination with the ways my students speak and also by the fact that our university is located, almost literally, in Gloria Anzaldúa's backyard. She attended the local university as an undergraduate, where, she wrote "...all Chicano students were required to take two speech classes. Their purpose: to get rid of our accent" (2007, p. 76). Although I had first read Anzaldúa's work years before, re-reading her with my students helped me understand her ideas in new ways. For example, I didn't fully understand why students were reluctant to speak Spanish with me until after we had read together and discussed Anzaldúa's description of how Chicanas fear that conversation with Latinas will result in ridicule and shame. I undertook this study in order to learn better how to help my students become effective bilingual literacy teachers. To do this, I needed to reflect on the linguistic situation of the region and the language identities of its residents.

In addition to Anzaldúa, several scholars have helped me understand the linguistic situation of my students. Meyer (2009) uses the term "linguistic suffering" to explain a phenomenon that members of minority language communities face in United States schools. Gonzáles (2005) reflects on the "linguistic insecurity" many Latino students deal with on a daily basis in school, and Martínez (2006, p. 38) explains how Mexican American students' attitudes towards Spanish "conflate into an overarching ideological tension between language pride and language panic." These sociolinguistic phenomena influence the ways future bilingual teachers perceive the role of Spanish in school and their decisions to deliver (or not) literacy instruction in Spanish.

Bilingual teacher education is also a gendered space. In this particular region of the U.S.-Mexico borderlands, *mestizas* (women of mixed Mexican and indigenous heritage) comprise the great majority of the students in teacher preparation programs. Like Gloria Anzaldúa, nearly all of the practicing teachers currently working in public school classrooms in the Rio Grande Valley are *mestizas*, although this name is not one that many choose for themselves. When asked, my students refer to themselves as Mexican Americans or Mexicans. *"Aqui todos somos Mexicanos,"* they usually say. Locally, many people feel that *mestiza* and *Chicana*, the self-descriptors that felt right to Anzaldúa, are troubling words—labels that can cause problems and that are used to describe "troublemakers." They are labels that students are understandably anxious to avoid, perhaps because many have been raised in a system of silence and obedience. Thus, it has been very difficult for me to convince students that they shouldn't be afraid of professors, and that disagreements can be viewed as opportunities for learning rather than conflicts to be avoided. Only when they overcome the fear of speaking and sharing experiences in the classroom does it become apparent that most were raised in Spanish-speaking families. Because many students are also mothers or caregivers, they are often conflicted about the role of Spanish in the lives and education of their own children and families.

METHOD

This section describes the context of the study and the ways I collected the data reported in this study. The Lower Rio Grande Valley of South Texas has been described as one of the poorest regions in the country (Guerra, 2007; Richardson, 1999). However, following a period of residence here towards the end of his life, the ethnographer Henry Trueba described the Valley in very different terms:

> The Rio Grande Valley has unique socio-cultural and economic characteristics that make it a human laboratory and the training ground for the future of American society. What happens in the Valley now will soon, within a couple of decades, affect the rest of the country. Its rapid economic development, its fast demographic change, its ethnic, racial, and economic diversification, and its unique cultural profile make it the most fertile ground for the development of new intellectual leaders, with a realistic vision of the future and an educational mission of inclusion, academic excellence, and democratic participation (Trueba 2004, p.13).

While I agree with aspects of Trueba's analysis—the Valley is a place of much potential and hope—one has still to ask why the "mission of inclusion, academic excellence and democratic participation" is not more evident in the lives of local students preparing to become bilingual teachers. In a recent analysis, Richardson and Resendiz (2006) describe the "irrationalities" of the region. They argue that, following passage of the North American Free Trade Agreement (NAFTA) and the rapid increase in the number of *maquiladoras* situated on the Mexican side of the river, the profits of economic development have been channeled to the economic centers of the United States and Mexico. As a result, a large part of the region's population continues to be undocumented, unemployed, or underpaid; to suffer limited access to health and educational services, and to live in colonias, rural settlements lacking basic infrastructure such as potable water, drainage, and paved streets (Mier et al., 2008). These conditions have contributed to the emergence of an "underground employment economy" (Richardson & Resendiz, 2006, p. xiii) in which residents work in low-paying and seasonal jobs in agriculture, construction, and *pulgas* (flea markets), among others.

In summary, "the rapid economic development" described by Trueba and the "irrationalities" described by Richardson and Resendiz, are the economic bases that motivate a unique linguistic landscape (Shohamy & Gorter, 2009) where English, Spanish, and Tex-Mex co-exist, overlap, and complement each other. It is nearly impossible, for example, to find any town across the Rio Grande Valley where these languages are not simultaneously spoken and displayed in different varieties and combinations. This linguistic landscape constitutes the space in which future bilingual teachers develop their biliteracy skills and other funds of linguistic knowledge (Smith, 2001) embodied in the region's children and pre-service teachers alike.

During the semester before I began data collection, I piloted the methods and instruments used in this study with a Curriculum Language Arts class at the same university to ensure that they were appropriate tools for the context of this research. These included a weekly teaching log; students' autobiographical writing about Spanish and Spanish-language education; and interview questions focusing on students' Spanish literacy practices.

Observations of Bilingual Teacher Preparation Classes

In fall 2008, drawing on Philips' (1993) and Frank's (1999) orientations on classroom observation, I observed the teaching and learning that took place in a "pre-block" bilingual education course taught by my colleague, Matilde Sarmiento. The bilingual teacher education program is organized in four blocks, meaning that these students had yet to formally declare bilingual education as their undergraduate major. Each week, over the course of 14 weeks, I sat in the back of the classroom and took detailed notes of interactions among students and between the students and the professor. I was especially interested in observing the uses of Spanish during instruction and in the interactions among students. After each class, I reviewed and discussed my notes with Matilde in order to check the accuracy of my record of what she had said or taught. Afterwards, I polished my notes, compared them to the ideas of the authors I was reading for the study, added observer comments in a different color font as well as handwritten margin notes, and stored them for continuous analysis.

Instructor's Weekly Teaching Log

During this same semester, each class session was audiotaped. After class, Matilde wrote notes to capture her reactions to what she had taught that particular day, using the audio recording to ensure that her notes corresponded to the content and sequence of the lesson. In addition, these audiotaped classes were later transcribed and made available for my analysis, as were the fieldnotes occasionally taken by a project research assistant. The weekly teaching log, transcripts, and additional fieldnotes supplemented and enriched my understanding of classroom interactions.

Students' Autobiographical Writing about Spanish and Spanish-Language Education

To further the discussion of the role of Spanish in reading instruction and in school generally, each student wrote an autobiographical essay about his or her experiences with Spanish and English literacy. The course instructor agreed to incorporate this task as an in-class assignment, an arrangement that greatly facilitated data collection. In this exercise of "telling my own story" students were given the opportunity to narrate their experiences using Spanish at home, in their communities, and at school. In "narrating the self" (Ochs, 2001; Warshauer Freedman & Ball, 2004; Chase, 2009), students recounted and reflected on their stories of language marginalization during their school years, including their education at the university level. The depth of these narratives was fostered by the discussions generated in class and by the professor sharing her personal experience on the uses and maintenance of Spanish. Appendix A shows the guidelines students used to write their narratives.

In-Depth Interviews Focusing on Students' Spanish Literacy Practices

In spring 2009, as students moved into their next block, I conducted in-depth interviews with seventeen students in order to better understand the uses of Spanish literacy in their daily lives and their perceptions about how they planned to use Spanish when they become bilingual teachers. Despite initial reluctance to talk with me in and about Spanish, by the time of the interviews I had been able to create a sense of *confianza* (trust) (Gonzalez, Moll, & Amanti 2005) that enabled the participants to openly discuss their experiences with Spanish language and literacy. As students become more comfortable talking and writing about their own experiences, face-to-face interviewing was a powerful research technique (Haig-Brown 2006). The interview questions (Appendix B) were designed to give the students the opportunity to freely express their ideas about their experiences with and feelings about Spanish and Spanish literacy.

Using "Local" Literacies

During spring and fall 2009, I had the opportunity to teach several of the original participants in my classes. In search of possible counter-hegemonic practices, I began to include in my teaching children's literature and other works by authors from the Rio Grande Valley. In this way, I followed Gee's idea of "interventional ethnography" in which "you don't just describe what people do, you resource them in some way - give them new or expanded tools- and see what they do and how they do it" (St. Clair & Phipps 2008, p 7). I found that, although very few students were familiar with local authors or even with the concept of bilingual English–Spanish books, three texts proved especially relevant and evocative. Following our discussion of Anzaldúa's (2007) chapter "How to Tame a Wild Tongue," students read an article in which Juan Guerra (2007) describes his early life and education in the Rio Grande Valley. By reading Guerra's work and participating in a videoconference with him, students had the opportunity to discuss the linguistic contradictions experienced by many people in the region. The following account is one the students found compelling:

Few if any of us had learned any English by the time we had enrolled in first grade, where in my case, our teacher, Mrs. Rosales, a Mexican American who spoke Spanish fluently was forbidden by state law from speaking our language. Through the haze of time and a very young memory, I can still see Mrs. Rosales standing next to a bag of props sitting on her desk. She takes one out, shows it to us, and names it. "Apple," she says in her very best and distinct English accent. "Apple," she says again. "Repeat it after me, boys and girls." I look around, not sure what we're supposed to do. "Uhpull," a couple of children say. "Good," Mrs. Rosales responds. "Apple." And then we all join in and produce a crescendo of accented English: "Uhpull!" Not surprisingly, under the circumstances, my English-speaking ability developed slowly and imperfectly. As a matter of fact, my Spanish accent when I spoke English was so heavy that during my early teenage years several of my friends used to tease me about it. I became so annoyed with their taunting that I still recall making up my mind that I would one day speak English as well as the Anglos (Guerra, 2007, p. 143).

Several students commented on this passage, connecting Guerra's difficulties with English with those he later experienced in his high school Spanish class, where, according to his teacher, Guerra spoke "incorrect Spanish." During the videoconference, a student pointed out that "it is still the same. We are scolded in elementary school for speaking Spanish and then in high school we are scolded because we do not know how to read, write, and speak it."

After reading and speaking with Guerra, students listened to Rio Grande City native Xavier Garza read aloud from bilingual children's books he had written. Garza tells local stories and describes local practices in his books, and students were fascinated with books such as *Lucha Libre: The Man in the Silver Mask* (Garza, 2007), *Zulema and the Witch Owl* (Garza, 2009) and *Charro Claus and the Tejas Kid* (Garza, 2008). In his presentation and in his fiction, Garza switched between English, Spanish, and Tex-Mex, discourse patterns that are well known to the students in their homes but which they had not experienced before in school or at the university.

Finally, students read and listened to local author Daniel García Ordáz, whose poetry reflects the ways people speak in the Rio Grande Valley. García Ordaz teaches English in a local middle school, and, after we read his book *You Know What I'm Sayin'?* (García-Ordáz, 2006), he explained the importance of using local places and events in the writing process. In his remarks, he emphasized the idea that writing and reading have the greatest meaning when they are connected to our daily lives, as in this fragment from the poem "Why Come Nobody Tol' Me Dat?:

Why come nobody tol´me dat
There's more than one kind
of cereal, and ...no!...
it ain't called Corn Fléis!"
It's "Corn Flakes!"
And it ain't called "Pos Tóstis" either.
It's "Post Toasties!"
Why come nobody tol' me dat!

Following these readings and discussions with local authors, I asked students to interview their parents and other family members for the purposes of documenting and understanding the ways they use reading and writing in their daily lives (See Appendix C). Students expressed surprise that their parents used literacy in Spanish and in English in so many ways in their daily lives. For example, one young woman shared her mother's words:

> At work I read advertisements, instructions on cleaning products (in English). At home, I read the Bible, sales announcements, coupons, recipes, letters (in English and Spanish), subtitles of movies, children's stories, letters that you (her daughter) write to me. At work (I write) reports about group tasks for my co-workers and incidents that happen each day. I also write reports about failures in the system we use to record the hours we work. I write signs for the teachers like "Out of Order." At home, I write verses from the Bible, schedules, notes, shopping lists, letters, and requests."

These activities, although not included in the original research proposal, proved very powerful in raising students' consciousness about the importance of their own home/community language and literacy practices.

Data Analysis

I used the constant comparative method to develop categories that allowed me to compare and integrate the data in the light of theory (Glaser, 1965). To do this, I read and re-read my fieldnotes on a weekly basis, as well as the fall 2008 instructor's logs and the transcriptions of the interviews. I carefully read the students' autobiographies in order to identify recurrent events that helped me to create categories of analysis. In addition, as I read the family literacy interviews and listened to my students' presentations, I was seeking ideas related to my research questions. I triangulated these different sources of data to find consistency or patterns across different sources, not necessarily for achieving consensus, but to understand the multiple and overlapping perspectives offered by these different methods of data collection (Patton, 2001). I also checked my emerging findings with the participating teacher as well as a colleague with extensive experience teaching future bilingual reading educators at another border university. In these ways, I sought to understand and theorize the findings as they emerged over the course of the study.

To interpret these data, I relied on three main concepts related to aspects of multilingualism and language use in multilingual communities. First, I used Makoni and Pennycook's (2007) notion of disinvesting and reconstructing languages as a way to avoid looking at language in the Rio Grande Valley as "an autonomous system." As these scholars argue,

> Unless we actively engage with the history of invention of languages, with the processes by which these inventions are maintained, with the political imperative to work towards their disinvention and with the reformulation of basic concepts in linguistics and applied linguistics, we will continue to do damage to speech communities and deny those people educational opportunities (p. 21).

In addition to challenging the harmful myth of "monolithic" language (for example, viewing Spanish and English as separate entities), Makoni and Pennycook encourage us to incorporate local knowledge in order to understand language use in particular contexts.

Second, and expanding upon Makoni and Pennycook's call to reformulate views of language from the bottom-up (Hall, in preparation), I used Ruiz's concept of (minority) language as resource for schooling. In his essay, Orientations on Language Planning (1984), Ruiz analyzed the ways that language planners have viewed language as a problem, as a right, and as a resource. The participants' previous school experiences with language and views of language clearly fit the language-as-problem orientation described by Ruiz, and they contrasted strongly with the language-as-resource view of Spanish voiced by local authors and scholars such as Anzaldúa, Guerra, Garza, and García Ordáz.

Third, I drew on Smith's (2001) concept of funds of linguistic knowledge to understand the pedagogical potential of students' language practices in their households, local communities, and simultaneously in the global context of the border as a space of "accelerated economic development" (Trueba, 2004). These theoretical lenses allowed me to incorporate the works of literature produced by authors of the region, and also to pay close attention to my students' views about the uses of languages in the Rio Grande Valley.

FINDINGS

In this section, I present my findings in three categories: 1) the shared history of linguistic marginalization; 2) the diglossic nature of the Valley's linguistic environment; and (3) participants' new insights into the potential of Spanish for literacy instruction and learning.

Shared History of Linguistic Marginalization

One salient reaction to our work was students' sense of surprise that their own histories of linguistic marginalization were not unique but rather shared with many older relatives, classmates, and children now in schools. Students emphasized their emotions and the negative and positive memories about their experiences. One student wrote:

> In those days children who entered school with no English were expected to learn the school's language of instruction (English) as quickly as possible without help. I discovered quickly that I needed to learn the language (English) spoken in school. I felt my parents' language (Spanish) had no value in school. The school made my parents feel that they had nothing to contribute to my siblings and my education.

Another student wrote:

> My primary language is English. Although I grew up speaking both languages, I think I felt more comfortable using English. This comfort level was probably due to the fact that it's the language I used for the most part of my day. Growing up, I only used Spanish with my father and his side of the family…. My Spanish was and still is not perfect. My dad and other family members always laughed when I spoke Spanish. They would call me "Pocha". I did not feel bad about it, I just laughed. Now, I am more aware of the Spanish language and its implications. In junior high and high school, I always felt that I didn't know what a lot of words meant. I felt inferior to other people of a more affluent group. I felt like our family was loud and more Mexican than other Mexican families.

In order to foster a climate of possibility for Spanish in the classroom, we also read a chapter about language and schooling in Rio Grande Valley schools from Chad Richardson's (1999) book *Batos, Pochos, Bolillos and Pelados*. This reading, along with the others mentioned above, allowed us to see how contemporary attitudes toward Spanish are rooted in the history of marginalizing experiences faced by many Spanish speakers in the region.

The Diglossic Nature of the Valley's Linguistic Environment

For most of these *mestiza* student teachers, Spanish and Tex-Mex are the languages of intimacy, friendship, and the family, *"del chisme"* (gossip), just as it was for Anzaldúa. Most students reported speaking Spanish as their primary home language, as in the following account:

> Yeah, my first language is Spanish because at home that's all I speak with my parents; as I was growing up I picked up English because of school, we had no choice but to learn it; we didn't have an option; it is not like "you are going to get better at your first language while we give you the second" NOOO!!! We had no option, they gave us English....

In Matilde's classroom, with much encouragement, Spanish also served as the vehicle through which students expressed their emotions about the linguistic marginalization that many had suffered in school.

Very few of the students participating in this study had previously thought of Spanish as a language suitable for expressing knowledge or for developing academic literacies. Even after our close reading of counter-hegemonic texts, writing their language autobiographies, and participating in class discussions and the in-depth interviews I have described here, many students continued to express, explicitly or implicitly, anti-Spanish attitudes. For example, despite extensive reflection, some students continued to refer to Spanish as a problem that they and their future students must overcome. The following comment was typical:

> Because my first language is Spanish, the elementary school decided to drop me down two grades and I was placed in kinder[garten]..... For then on, I knew I had to overcome the obstacle of language. I learned English quick and now I think I've forgotten much of my Spanish.

These examples illustrate how the oppression of Spanish and the marginalization of those who speak it in school have been "normalized" within the educational discourse. Although many participants became more open to the possibility of speaking and writing in Spanish in the classroom, with the notable exception of those students who had received primary school education in Mexico, most remained insecure about their own abilities to actually teach in Spanish. Given these strong and entrenched practices of language marginalization, it is unrealistic to expect pre-service teachers to fully forge counter discourses by the time they step into classrooms of their own. The following quote from a student illustrates this point:

> ... it is like something when I see a professor yourself or any other ... It's just like, I feel like I have to talk to them in English and I am with my friends and I switch it back (to Spanish). That's how... es lo que me hicieron creer so asina pienso [that's how I was raised, so that's how I think], even at the store... I have to speak to the (the clients) in English. I guess it was like, if you speak to them in Spanish it's kind of disrespectful or you are not supposed to, so that is why I stick to that...

Participants' New Insights into the Potential of Spanish for Literacy Instruction and Learning

In Matilde's class, most students used Spanish to communicate amongst themselves before the professor walked in and also as they negotiated and formed group responses to questions posed in class. Without exception, students used English to communicate with the professor during the first weeks of class. Perhaps due to her ability to code-switch easily between English and Spanish, by mid-semester most of the students were responding orally to questions in the language the professor had posed to them. By the end of the semester, the class was essentially conducted in Spanish, and all student presentations were done in this language. Furthermore, most of the participants in this study chose to write their narratives in Spanish, although they had not been asked before to use "academic Spanish." The changes that took place in Matilde's classroom as a result of her bilingual teaching are reminiscent of what Warshauer Freedman and Ball (2004, p. 18), drawing on Baktin, have described in their research with preservice teachers as the "ideological becoming," in which struggles eventually lead to learning.

Regarding the participants' literacy autobiographies, as a native of South America, I was unprepared for the accounts of linguistic insecurity that featured so prominently in what students wrote about their own lives and educational experiences. Because I never experienced having my language banned from school, it was painful to read these accounts of systematic language marginalization, so similar to those described by Anzaldúa more than a quarter century ago. At times, I felt almost guilty for asking the students to reflect on these painful experiences, and I spent much time thinking about how best to support them. At the same time, I am also proud that we were able to create this space of reflection about language marginalization and what it means for the preparation of bilingual teachers and the development of Spanish literacy.

IMPLICATIONS AND NEXT STEPS

My students and I continue to confront these questions together, and, with colleagues, I struggle to develop counter-hegemonic pedagogies to help students reconnect with their personal language and literacy histories, and be able to use these as steps toward agency and change. In other words, we are developing ways of teaching that recognize the harm caused by deficit theories and that reject attempts to teach literacy through deficit practices. We refuse to continue to structure literacy teaching in ways that have silenced and marginalized generations of Spanish-speaking children in the Rio Grande Valley. Instead, we seek ways of educating that capitalize on local language resources in the development and practice of pedagogies of hope (Trueba, 1999). We have learned to recognize the borderlands as a space of linguistic and cultural hybridity (Ranker, 2009) and to celebrate the transidiomatic practices, "the communicative practices of transnational groups that interact using languages and communicative codes simultaneously" (Jacquemet, 2005, pp. 264-265), that characterize language as used in our students' homes and communities. Concerned with the future practice of bilingual educators, we are grappling with the question how should "... we teach bilingually in ways that reflect people's use of language and not simply people as language users?" (García, 2007, p. xiii). Using tools such as those presented in this study, literacy teacher educators can help students to regain the rights to their own languages as a step towards becoming teachers who will teach equitably and avoid reproducing injustices like those they experienced in school.

Despite these accomplishments, clearly we still have a long way to go in preparing bilingual teachers to warmly embrace the challenges of linguistic diversity in the classroom. This report of pre-service bilingual teachers' attitudes toward Spanish underscores the lasting harm done by discriminatory practices against Spanish speakers in the Valley. These findings support claims that language ideologies are persistent barriers to the transformation of negative experiences and feelings about Spanish literacy into tools that will help them teach bilingual children with academic rigor and cultural accommodation (Moll, 2009; Smith, 2001). Albright and Luke (2008) state that, in situations of linguistic marginalization, students and educators need to recover their right to speak in the languages they know, and as a consequence the right to use the literacies they grow up with.

A second implication for practice concerns the design of teacher preparation programs. In addition to the kinds of counter-pedagogies described above, opportunities to think and write about the role and potential of local literacies in the academic lives of multilingual learners should be introduced early and practiced throughout the course of study. It is important that we recognize that this "transcultural repositioning" (Guerra, 2007) cannot be accomplished in a single move, a single course, or perhaps even after a series of courses. After so many years of linguistic marginalization, it is a tremendous ideological task for immigrant and Mexican American students to (re)discover their own abilities, their voices and their academic strengths in their own languages. Theory will be important to this work. For example, my students' persistent belief that they speak an "inferior language" has recently led me to consider the "disinvention and reconstitution" of languages (Hall, in preparation; Makoni and Pennycook, 2007) as tools for moving us beyond dominant views of language and power and towards the development of more equitable and effective forms of literacy instruction.

A final implication concerns broadening pre-service teachers' views of literacy and multilingualism to include economic opportunity. As scholars document the importance of multiliteracies for the global economies of our era (Gee, 2008), a remaining task is to refocus curriculum on helping learners develop the literate proficiencies needed to succeed in the new economy. Although this study has stressed the importance of beginning with students' experiences and cultivating local and personal histories, counter-hegemonic teaching also involves steps to connect local literacies to the global and particularly to economic arrangements that clearly favor advanced bilingualism and multilingualism (Carreira, 2002). Considering the rich linguistic environment children grow up in the Rio Grande Valley, few regions in the United States have the same potential to foster biliteracy, or as much to gain from it, beginning with the preparation of bilingual teachers.

REFERENCES

Albright, J., & Luke, Allan (Eds.) (2008). *Pierre Bourdieu and literacy education.* New York, NY: Routledge.

Anzaldúa, G. (1987/2007). *Borderlands/La Frontera. The new mestiza.* San Francisco, CA: Aunt Lute Books.

Carreira, M. M. (2002). Portent of linguistic maintenance. *Southwest Journal of Linguistics, 21*(2), 37-53.

Chase, S. (2009). Narrative inquiry. Multiple lenses, approaches, voices. In Wendy Luttrell (Ed.)., *Qualitative educational research. Readings in reflexive methodology and transformative practice* (pp. 208-236). London, UK: Routledge.

Frank, C. (1999). *Ethnographic eyes: A teacher's guide to classroom observation.* Portsmouth, NH: Heinemann.

García Ordáz, D. (2006).You know what I'm sayin'? (2nd Edition). McAllen, TX: El Zarape Press.

García, O. (2007). Foreword. In Simon Makoni & Alastair Pennycook (Eds.) *Disinventing and reconstituting languages.* (pp. xi-xv.). Clevedon, UK: Multilingual Matters.

Garza, X. (2007). *Lucha libre: The man in the silver mask.* (English and Spanish version). Houston, TX: Piñata Press, Arte Público Press. (2008). *Charro claus and the Tejas kid.* (English and Spanish version). El Paso, TX: Cinco Puntos Pres. (2009). *Zulema and the witch owl/Zulema y la bruja lechuza.* Houston, TX: Piñata Press, Arte Publico Press.

Gee, J. P. (2008). *Social linguistics and literacies: Ideologies in discourse.* (3rd Edition). London, UK: Routledge.

Glaser, B. (1965). The constant comparative method of qualitative analysis. *Social Problems, 12*(4), 436-445.

González, N. (2005). Children in the eye of the storm: Language socialization and language ideologies in a dual-language school. In Ana Celia Zentella (Ed.). *Building on strength. Language and literacy in Latino families and communities* (pp. 162-174). New York, NY: Teachers College Press.

González, N., Moll, L. C., & Amanti, C. (Eds.). (2005). *Funds of Knowledge. Theorizing practices in households, communities, and classrooms.* Mahwah, NJ: Lawrence Erlbaum.

Guerra, J. (2007). Out of the Valley: Transcultural repositioning as rhetorical practice in ethnographic research and other aspects of everyday life. In Patricia Enciso & Cynthia Lewis (Eds.)., *Reframing sociocultural research on literacy: Identity, agency, and power* (pp. 131-162). Mahwah, NJ: Lawrence Erlbaum.

Haig-Brown, C. (1998/2006). *Resistance and renewal. Surviving the Indian residential school.* Vancouver, British Columbia, Canada: Arsenal Pulp Press.

Hall, C. J. (in preparation). *Bridging the paradigm gap: Cognitive contributions to plurilithic views of English and other languages.* Center for Languages and Linguistics, York St. John University, York, UK.

Jacquemet, M. (2005). Transidiomatic practices and power in the age of globalization. *Language & Communication, 25,* 257-277.

Makoni, S., & Pennycook, A. (Eds.). (2007). *Disinventing and reconstituting languages.* Clevedon, UK: Multilingual Matters.

Martinez, G. A. (2006). *Mexican Americans and language. Del dicho al hecho.* Tucson, AZ: The University of Arizona Press.

Meyer, R. (2009). Portraits, counterportraits, and the lives of children: Language, culture, and possibilities. In Jerrie Cobb Scott, Dolores Y. Straker, & Laurie Katz (Eds.)., *Affirming students' right to their own language* (pp. 54-67). New York, NY: Routledge & The National Council of Teachers of English.

Mier, N., Ory, M. G., Zhan, D., Conkling, M., Sharkey, J. R., & Burdine. J. N. (2008). Health related quality of life among Mexican Americans living in colonias at the Texas-Mexico border. *Social Science and Medicine, 66,* 1760-1771.

Moll, L. C. (2009). Mobilizing culture, language, and educational practices: Fulfilling the promises of *Mendez* and *Brown.* Unpublished manuscript.

Ochs, E. (2001). *Living narrative. Creating lives in everyday storytelling.* Cambridge, MA: Harvard University Press.

Patton, M. Q. (2001). *Qualitative evaluation and research methods.* Thousand Oaks, CA: Sage.

Philips, S. U. (1983/1993). *The invisible culture: Communication in classroom and community on the Warm Springs Indian Reservation.* Prospect Heights, IL: Waveland Press.

Ranker, J. (2009). Student appropriation of writing lessons through hybrid composing practices: Direct, diffuse, and indirect use of teacher-offered writing tools in an ESL classroom. *Journal of Literacy Research, 41,* 393-431.

Richardson, C. (1999). *Batos, pochos, bolillos and pelados.* Austin, TX: The University of Texas Press.

Richardson, C., & Resendiz, R. (2006). *On the edge of the law. Culture, labor & deviance on the South Texas border.* Austin, TX: The University of Texas Press.

Ruiz, R. (1984). Orientations in language planning. *NABE Journal, 8*(2), 15-34.

St. Clair, R., & Phipps, A. (2008). Ludic literacies at the intersections of cultures: An interview with James Paul Gee. *Language and Intercultural Communication, 8*(2), 91-100.

Shohamy, E., & Gorter, D. (Eds.). (2009). *Linguistic landscape: Expanding the scenery.* New York, NY: Routledge.

Smith, P. (2001). Community language resources in dual language schooling. *Bilingual Research Journal, 25*(3), pp. 251-280.

Trueba, E. (1999). Critical ethnography and a Vygotskian pedagogy of hope: The empowerment of Mexican immigrant children. *Qualitative Studies in Education, 12*(6), 591-614.

Trueba, E. (2004). *The new Americans. Immigrants and transnationals at work.* Lanham: Rowman & Littlefield Publishers.

Warshauer Freedman, S., &. Ball, A. F. (2004). Ideological becoming. Bakhtinian concepts to guide the study of language, literacy, and learning. In Arnetha F. Ball & Sarah Warshauer Freedman. (Eds.)., *Bakhtinian concepts to guide the study of language, literacy, and learning.* (pp. 3-33). Cambridge, MA: Cambridge University Press.

AUTHOR'S NOTE

The data presented in this research were collected thanks to a grant from the Department of Education initiative *Curricular Assessment for Successful Student Outcomes (CASSO)* and funded under the National Professional Development Program (CFDA 84 195 N) invitational priority 1 and 2, T195N070232.

APPENDIX A. AUTOBIOGRAPHICAL ESSAY*

Directions: This essay is to be about 4-7 double-spaced pages. Its focus is for you to share your memories, impressions, emotions, and the salient experiences that marked your journey toward becoming literate and biliterate, both at *home* and at *school*.

A. Include descriptions about how you started reading and writing in both Spanish and English. If you only speak English, describe the same learning process in this language.

B. Include memorable events that left an impression on you, both positive and negative.

C. How you were first exposed to reading and writing: in your L1/or L2? (Ojo: Many children growing up in the Valley have two first languages; if that was your situation, write about your first exposure to reading and writing in each language.)

D. Your essay should include experiences over the course of your life. For example, you might consider your experiences with writing before you began school, at primary school, middle school, high school, and at the university level.

E. Literacy is powerful and personal! Don't be afraid to share your feelings, your doubts, your joys and sadness, your accomplishments, etc. It's your story!

This essay experience will put you in closer touch with how you learned to read and write. Sometimes we forget how we struggled to learn, or the joys we experienced when reading and writing; so, it is with this intent that this assignment has been created. Thinking about thinking and learning raises our critical consciousness. Also, knowing who you are as a reader and writer can greatly enhance the ways you teach and help your future students to be successful readers and writers. As you reflect and write your literacy story, you might find it interesting to use some of the readings we are using in class to connect to your literacy experiences.

If You Can Write Your Own Life Story, You Can Write Your Own Happy Ending

From: The Talk Story project in Hawaii.

*I am grateful to Barbara Flores for sharing her expertise with students' autobiographical writing

APPENDIX B. PROTOCOL FOR PRESERVICE-TEACHER INTERVIEWS

Full name: _____

Age: _____

Sex: _____

Block: _____

Current address: _____

Phone: _____

E-mail: _____

Number of years studying in this university: _____

Are you employed? _____

How long have you been employed? _____

Where do you work?_____

Educational background: _____

I. <u>School</u>

   a. What made you decide to become a bilingual teacher?

   b. When did you decide to become a bilingual teacher?

   c. How many years have you been studying at the university level?

   d. How many of your classes in the bilingual program are taught in Spanish?

   e. Do you like to use Spanish at the university?

   f. Do you use Spanish at home or with your family?

   g. Do you use Spanish with friends?

   h. Do you use Spanish at work?

II. <u>Reading</u>

   a. What kinds of texts do you read in Spanish in your Bilingual Block classes?

   b. What kind of texts in Spanish do you read at home?

   c. What kind of texts in Spanish do you read at work?

   d. In your opinion, what is the best way for bilingual children to learn to read, in English or in Spanish? Why?

   e. In your opinion which is more important, reading in Spanish or reading in English? Why?

III. Writing

    a. How much time do you spend writing in Spanish each day?

    b. What kinds of texts in Spanish do you write in your Bilingual Block classes?

    c. What kinds of writing do you do in Spanish at home?

    d. In your opinion, how much time do you think people spend writing everyday in Spanish?

    e. Do you think this is more or less time than they spend writing everyday in English?

IV. Funds of Linguistic Knowledge

    a. In the community where you live now what kinds of texts do people read in their homes in Spanish? How do you know?

    b. Do you see Spanish in your community? e.g., restaurants, billboards, churches, offices, health centers, theaters, stores?

    c. Do you speak Tex-Mex?

Please take a few minutes to write anything else you think is important about you as a reader and writer of Spanish.

_____

_____

_____

Thank you very much for your time!

APPENDIX C. FAMILY LITERACY INTERVIEW*

In this assignment you will explore family literacy practices. Identify your participants: parents, grandparents, etc. Come up with a list of questions that will help you understand how your participants view and use literacy in their daily lives. Keep notes as you do your interview (you may also want to record it).

Possible Questions:

1. Do you like to read? Why or why not?

2. How much time do you spend reading and writing every day?

3. What sorts of things do you read in your work? In the household? In the community? (Textbooks, novels, poetry, magazines, newspapers, Internet, text messages, email, notes from friends, short stories, nonfiction, advertisement, checks, the Bible, etc.)

4. Did you go to school?

5. What languages do you speak? At home? At school? With your friends?

6. Do you enjoy writing? Why or why not?

7. How much time do you spend writing in your work? At home?

8. What sorts of things do you write in your work? At home? Reports, essays, short stories, poetry, lab reports, journals, music lyrics, text messages, emails, notes to friends, letters, lists, etc.

9. Did you see your parents reading at home? What sorts of things did they read?

10. Do you remember how did you learn to read?

11. What kinds of reading do you do in different subjects?

After the interview with your family, write up your findings in a 2-3 page <u>reflection</u>. You will turn in your interview notes (they can be hand written) **and** your reflection, which should answer the following question: **How do the readings relate to, support, and/or contradict what your interviewee(s) told you?**

Organization of the Reflection: You should follow these three steps:

1. Introduction to the participants: age, gender, home/family background, participants' occupation, education history, and any other relevant details;

2. Findings: What do the readings say and what does the participant say about literacy? How do the readings relate to, support, and/or contradict what your interviewees told you?

3. Your thoughts: What did you learn? What questions do you still have?

Be ready to discuss what you have learned. We will discuss our findings and reflections in class.

*Based on an activity shared with me by my colleague Janine Schall.

Literacy Learning in the Afternoon: A Study of Urban Adolescent Girls' Constructions of After-School Reading Groups

Jie Y. Park
University of Pennsylvania

The pedagogical practices and cultures of middle- and secondary-literacy classrooms often position adolescents as solitary, individual readers. An adolescent girl narrates a "typical" day of English class:

> Right now, we are reading the *Great Gatsby*. Usually we have to answer a question about the book. We have to connect it to a part of our lives or part of history. After like ten or five minutes, we finish and then people volunteer to read their answers.

Reading was commonly understood as a cognitive task, an "in the head encounter" with texts (Collins & Blot, 2003), and meaning was thought to be the product of individual reader-text interactions. However, almost three decades of research speaks to reading as a social process (Bloome, 1985). Research on out-of-school literacy practices of adolescents (Hull & Schultz, 2002; Mahiri, 2004) shows that students are reading together and forming informal reading groups—having conversations about and around a commonly read piece of "text"—on the bus, over the phone, and in notebooks, both paper and electronic. More recently, Moje, Overby, Tysaver, and Morris (2008) reported the range of reading and writing groups that students create, whether a formal book club that meets monthly or an informal group that discusses books during recess, lunch or homeroom. Students practice reading and literacy more broadly as social and relational. That is, literacy allows for the creation and sharing of real-life experiences and meaning.

This paper is based on a yearlong qualitative study of how 23 middle school girls attending an urban public school co-constructed and experienced an after-school reading group. The concept of "co-construction" has been widely used, yet there is a need for more studies that offer rich and complex images of exactly how co-construction happens among adolescent readers. In this paper, I explore how the girls took up different roles and responsibilities, established norms and rituals for the reading group, and negotiated the challenges of forming and sustaining the group. That is, what is the process by which they developed, participated in, and sustained the reading group? The reading group became a generative site for seeing adolescents as problem-posers, problem-solvers, decision-makers, negotiators, and architects of an after-school space for literacy learning.

REVIEW OF RELEVANT LITERATURE

In what ways might after- and out-of-school reading groups support adolescents' literacy learning? Several studies shed light on this question. Appleman (2006) found that high school, out-of-class reading groups led to a range of behaviors and practices: students offered a range of responses, including evaluative, aesthetic, descriptive and personal responses; students offered perspectives on themselves, on high school and on life in general; and, they addressed and listened to each other. Chandler (1997) formed, facilitated and studied a beach book club that met during the summers. Throughout the three-year study, she found that the high school students learned to listen and take seriously diverse perspectives and readings without adopting a relativist stance that any and all readings were equally valid. Hill and Van Horn (1995) studied a three-week summer book club for five middle school students at a juvenile detention center. The researchers wanted to study whether students would collaborate on group discussions, whether the book discussions would stimulate students' writing, and whether the discussions would change students' self-perceptions and perceptions of others. They found that students looked forward to coming to book club, wrote more frequently as a result of the book club, and saw themselves and family members differently.

Alvermann, Young, Green, and Wisenbaker (1999) studied four groups of primarily European American, middle-class, sixth to ninth graders who met at a public library after school. Two researchers facilitated four Read and Talk clubs. The authors found that students valued the social nature of the Read and Talk clubs and urged educators to imagine possibilities for different kinds of reading instruction that can foster a community among adolescents.

Broughton (2002) studied four sixth-grade girls as they read a novel centered on the experiences of two Mexican American children. The author focused on the ways that the girls—*in* and *through* reading and discussing a common text—performed and constructed their race, class and gender subjectivities.

The past decade has seen book clubs and reading groups appear on virtual spaces. Scharber (2009) studied an online book club organized for teens and preteens. Each day, the facilitator posted a question on the forum, inviting members to respond, read other students' comments, and discuss the book. The participants also could chat at a designated time. According to the author, students noted that the real-time chat was the best part of book club.

These studies and others (e.g., Smith, 2000; Vyas, 2004) capture the variation of work on reading groups and book clubs. Yet they are limited, for they often focus on reading groups that teachers, researchers, or other adult-facilitators designed for the adolescents. That is, very few studies have examined the ways that students take up the invitation to construct a reading group for themselves. Therefore several questions persist. Two at the center of this paper are: what happens when adolescents are intentionally positioned as constructors of an after-school reading group, and what is the process by which they create and participate in the group? In addition, few of the studies have expressly investigated the social practices that are part of reading and discussing texts (e.g., interactions and relationships). The research tends to focus on the individual reader and the responses of that individual reader as the unit of analysis. Hence, my work was guided by the suggestion (see Alvermann, et al., 1996) that literacy researchers both explore adolescent readers' social practices (e.g., ways that adolescents position each other and are being positioned; and ways that adolescents engage and relate to one another) as well as attend to adolescents' literacy practices and identities.

THEORETICAL FRAMEWORKS

My study drew upon two frameworks: literacy as a social, critical practice (Luke & Freebody, 1997) and learning as a social enterprise. According to Street (1995) and others, literacy is not merely a set of reading and writing skills, independent of social contexts, human relationships and ideologies. Rather, literacy is situated within and varied across social, cultural and institutional contexts. People live and function amid texts, coming to and taking up different literacy events. New Literacy Studies (Barton & Hamilton, 2000; Gee, 2000; Street, 1995) advanced the ways in which researchers study literacy to include a more explicit exploration of the social and cultural contexts which inform individuals' understandings and uses of literacy.

I also conceptualize literacy as a critical practice. Reading is not simply a matter of being able to offer "correct" interpretations and revise ones that are less relevant to the written text. Rather, readers should work to develop a stance that can critique the status quo and taken-for-granted worldviews (Kincheloe, 2004; Shor, 1999). People value and use literacy to generate different and deeper readings of themselves, of each other, and of their social and economic realities (Horton & Freire, 1990). Literacy is integral to exploring and interrogating ideas, experiences and meaning. Conceptualizing literacy as a social, critical practice means acknowledging that adolescents use literacy to position themselves and others; perform and enact different identities; claim social membership; and develop alternative readings of the word and world (Freire, 1987).

Literacy alone, however, cannot challenge individuals' habitual modes of thought. Underlying the framework of literacy as a social, critical practice is the significance of dialogue. It is through dialog and social interactions that knowledge gets challenged and reformulated (Bakhtin, 1986). Social constructivism (Bruffee, 1984, 1993; Vygotsky, 1986) presupposes that human beings are social. As such, learning occurs *in* and *through* social interactions. Knowledge is "socially constructed, contextualized, and in short the product of collaboration" (Lunsford, 1991, p. 4). A social constructivist perspective positions the girls as learning and generating knowledge, collaboratively and collectively.

Taken together, these frameworks present a way to theorize the reading groups as a site for students to experience and practice literacy as social and critical, and to extend, build on and complicate the knowledge that each person brings to the group.

PARTICIPANTS AND CONTEXT

In the study, a middle school literacy teacher, 23 seventh- and eighth-grade girls, and I participated in an after-school reading group. The girls attended a K-8 public school in a large Northeastern city. The school is 48% Black, 29% White, 13% Asian, and 9% Hispanic. Approximately 50 percent of students are eligible for free and reduced lunch. The participants reflected the racial, ethnic and socioeconomic diversity of the school. Of the 14 seventh graders, there were 7 White, 5 Black, 1 Asian, and 1 self-identified biracial student. Of the 9 eighth graders, there were 2 White, 4 Black, 1 Asian, and 2 self-identified biracial students.

Based on the girls' grade-level and after-school schedule (e.g., soccer practice, orchestra), the participants were assigned to one of three groups. There were two groups of seventh graders, and one group of eighth graders. Each group met biweekly to discuss a student-selected text (e.g., fiction, non-fiction, song lyrics). The meetings took place inside the school building, and lasted approximately an hour.

The middle school literacy teacher and I did not set an agenda for the reading groups, prepare discussion questions in advance, or impose participation frameworks, which allowed the girls to bring *their* questions and interests to the group. Describing the structure of the reading group, a seventh grader said, "We get to decide on the questions and we get to answer the questions instead of the adult supervising asking us questions or telling us the answer."

DATA COLLECTION AND ANALYSIS

As a researcher and co-facilitator of the reading group, I entered the site as a participant observer, negotiating the way I positioned myself vis-à-vis the teacher facilitator and girls. I used ethnographic (Hammersley & Atkinson, 1995) and case study (Merriam, 1998) methods to collect the following: fieldnotes and audio-recordings of all reading group meetings; fieldnotes of the girls' literacy class taken during weekly classroom observations; audio recordings and transcriptions of three rounds of student and teacher facilitator interviews; and artifacts and documents, including in-class student writings and class projects.

Each reading group met 12 times throughout the academic year (September 2008-June 2009). I observed and kept fieldnotes of all the reading group meetings. Although the meetings were audio-recorded and transcribed, I recorded the students' verbal and non-verbal behaviors, such as expressions, movements, postures, and eye contact. Observations also focused on the girls' interactions patterns with one another.

Weekly classroom observations began the second month of the study. I observed both the seventh and eighth-grade literacy class for 90 minutes each. Classroom observations focused on student interaction and participation patterns (i.e., who speaks when and to whom; who does not speak). I also documented the girls' literacy practices in school, such as their use of texts (i.e., what texts are read and discussed, and how); the ways that the girls positioned themselves and were being positioned as literacy learners; and the knowledge, questions and interests the girls brought to school.

Throughout the study, I conducted three rounds of semi-structured interviews with each girl. The interviews lasted approximately 30 minutes and took place either during school or after school. The first round of interviews focused on the girls' in-school and out-of-school literacy practices, expectations for the reading group, and reasons for deciding to participate. The second and third round of interviews focused on the girls' experiences of the reading group. All interviews were recorded and transcribed in their entirety.

Data analysis was ongoing and recursive. I did a focused reading of all data sources, noting patterns and regularities, and identifying possible ways that data could be chunked and coded. For each primary data source (e.g., reading group transcripts and fieldnotes, interview transcripts, fieldnotes of literacy class), I developed a set of open codes. The coding process was inductive; however, my research questions and theoretical frameworks informed my analysis. That is, guided by the theoretical framing and research questions, I identified what was important and relevant data for the purposes of the study

The codes were grouped into categories, including: references to students' own literacy practices in and out-of-school (e.g., reading habits and preferences, writing journals); references to friends and family members' literacy practices; references to in-school assignments, projects and tests; references to popular culture (e.g., movies, songs, television shows); responses to literary texts (e.g., evaluations, inter-textual connections); comments and perspectives on themselves or other people; comments and perspectives on social, political and economic realities; negotiations related to text-selection; roles and identities available to reading group members (e.g., leader, facilitator, question-poser, friend); instances of establishing and negotiating the norms and rules for the group; disagreements or differences between and among participants; and, descriptions of the reading group (e.g., "open," "free," "fun," "loose," etc).

Also, I coded for and paid particular attention to subjective, normative-evaluative and identity claims (Carspecken, 1996) that emerged during the reading group discussions. Prompted by the text and/or by their peers, the girls made statements about the way the reading group and participants should be (normative-evaluative claim), their social, cultural and historical locations (identity claim), and the fears, desires and feelings evoked by the text (subjective claim). For example, prompted by the novel, *Speak,* several of the seventh graders made identity claims about being part of the "popular" clique; or, while reading *Mick Harte Was Here,* the seventh graders made subjective claims, expressing sadness for the protagonist whose younger brother dies in an accident and fear for the safety of their own younger siblings.

As part of the analysis, I studied data from each reading group as well as data across the three groups, thereby working to generate an understanding of whether and how themes, ideas and issues resonated (or not) across the different groups. Data were triangulated using multiple sources of data, including transcribed student interviews, transcribed reading group sessions, classroom observation data, and student-produced documents and artifacts. I also asked participants for clarification whenever necessary, and asked each girl to articulate what she hoped to communicate to adults who might read this study. Rather than mere data validation techniques, these were part of doing research *with* adolescents, and not just on or about them.

RESULTS

The study's findings fall into two categories. The first category focuses on the range of responsibilities assumed by the seventh- and eighth-grade girls. The second category speaks to the tensions and challenges of creating and sustaining after-school, student-centered reading groups. The study's findings reveal the complex process by which adolescent girls developed and participated in an after-school reading group, thereby contributing knowledge about the ways in which students create and experience after-school spaces. These findings, I argue, are important to understanding after-school reading groups because they offer insight on how co-construction of a group and negotiation between and among adolescents actually happen.

Roles and Responsibilities for Reading Group Participants

Sid, an eighth grader, described the role of reading group participants as, "We're in charge of what we're saying, what we want to discuss, and what we want to read. Like we get to, we create everything. It's developed by us." Each of the three groups approached the task of constructing the after-school space differently. Each reading group developed its own method for selecting a text (e.g., voting, drawing names) and established norms for structuring their time together and the conversations (e.g., turn-taking, raising hands). For example, one of the seventh-grade groups decided to spend the first 15 minutes on Sharing Time. During Sharing Time, participants offered interesting facts about themselves (e.g., pet peeves and favorite books). Both seventh-grade groups decided to name themselves. The Tuesday group decided on Inspirational Readers, and the Thursday group on Secret Life of Literate Girls, after the novel they were reading at the time, *Secret Life of Bees*. Each group developed its own tone and rhythm, as well as its own set of rules—explicit and implicit—for organizing and sustaining conversations.

Data revealed that the girls brought different texts for the group to read; prepared discussion questions for the meetings; and asked questions for various purposes, including asking for clarification or prompting other girls to share perspectives on the text. Jessica prepared discussion questions for the reading group. Stephanie and Lauren worked to speak less, and not interrupt other members. During reading group, Stephanie would ask, "Am I talking too much?" and Lauren stated, "I just want to say, I like to interrupt people. It happens. I'll try to control it." For both girls, part of being a responsible group member was listening to others.

In the rest of this section, I will address what I identified as three primary responsibilities assumed by both seventh- and eighth-grade girls: responsibility to support each other; responsibility not to "ruin" the book; and responsibility to keep secret the stories and experiences that get shared at reading group.

"I need help to get into it": Responsibility to support each other. Analysis of data suggests that the girls took on the responsibility of supporting each other to navigate and make sense of challenging texts. The eighth-grade group had started reading Stephenie Meyer's *The Host*, a complex and lengthy science fiction novel. Before the girls started reading the novel, Veronica announced, "Yeah, but guys, like don't give up at the beginning. I am serious." Yet several students still experienced difficulty understanding the novel. Sue announced, "I need help to get into it [*The Host*]." Mary responded, "OK, We're in." Mary used "we" to signal that helping Sue is a collective and collaborative effort. A significant portion of the discussion was spent encouraging Sue.

Sue: I don't understand what I am reading. I just, I read it and two pages later, I don't remember what I read because I am not reading.

Mary: But what about the book, like you read some, what about that do you find not interesting?

Sue: Like it hasn't gotten exciting for me yet.

Yolanda: Cause it's not exciting. You're too little in the book.

Mary: Wait. What's happening? Read it out loud. Please.

Inez: "The electric bell rang, announcing another visitor."

Mary: Oh! I remember that. She, so you haven't got to the good part yet. You're at the part where she's like, living her life, boring life right now.

Inez: Yeah.

Mary: It will get more exciting if you read more. You are at the beginning.

Inez: You're like right at that point. Right there, it says Turn.

The conversation reflects the ways that the girls asked for support and assumed responsibility for helping each other to persist and continue reading, convincing each other that the book was worthwhile and interesting. Rather than dismiss Sue's confusion as unimportant, the girls offered support. For instance, stating, "You're like right at that point," Inez encouraged Sue. Yolanda tried a different approach. Stating "Cause it's not exciting. You're too little in the book," Yolanda affirmed Sue's confusion and frustration with the novel. In other words, according to Yolanda, Sue has good reason to find the book unexciting or uninteresting. The girls each assumed a different role: Inez cheered Sue, and Yolanda offered affirmation. Mary, however, assumed the role of question-poser. She asked, "But what about the book do you find not interesting?" The question is authentic. Mary expressed a genuine desire to understand the reasons that Sue finds the novel uninteresting and encouraged Sue to articulate those reasons. Mary made another important move. To be able to support Sue, the reading group should know the specific part of the novel Sue was reading. Hence, Mary asked Sue, "What's happening?" and Inez read aloud. Mary ensured that the reading group members were—literally and figuratively—on the "same page" as Sue.

The girls offer teachers valuable insight into the type of support that works for students. First, the reading group members did not force Sue to adopt positive views of *The Host*; instead, they encouraged and asked questions to get a better sense of Sue's confusion with the novel. They also did not ostracize Sue for not having the same level of understanding or enthusiasm for the novel. They did not evaluate others' comments as wrong or incorrect.

"We're not allowed to spoil the end": Responsibility not to ruin the book. Yolanda and Veronica often were the first students to finish a book. Given that the girls were not required to read a set number of pages every two weeks, and given that they had different reading practices, it was likely that one or two of the girls would finish the book before other members. This posed a challenge for the girls. Mary, an eighth grader, wondered, "But what if someone is really a slow reader, and like everyone is finished by the next meeting, but they're not?" The girls, however, thoughtfully navigated and negotiated such situations.

For instance, conversations such as the one below were not uncommon.

Amy: How about we go around a circle and say what page we are on, and what's going on. OK. I'll go first. I finished.

Clarissa: I kind of don't have the book, so I really didn't read anything.

Caitlin: I am at 92.

Helen: I need to get a copy of the book. They ran out at the book store.

Amy: Caitlin, what's going on where you're at?

The exchange among Amy, Clarissa, Caitlin and Helen took place during the seventh graders' meeting on the young adult novel, *Speak*. Amy assumed the role of leader and facilitator, addressing each of the girls. She asked Caitlin: "Caitlin, what's going on where you're at?"

The challenge was for the girls not to "ruin" the book for others. Across the three reading groups, the girls were careful not to reveal the conclusion. For example, the same seventh grade group debated whether or not to reveal the fact that Melinda, the protagonist of the novel, had been raped at a party.

Katherine: We're not allowed to spoil the end.

Karen: Yes, I want them to tell us what happened to her at the party. I don't like being kept from secrets. I don't like surprises.

Stephanie: I think we should only tell if everyone feels comfortable with this.

The girls eventually decided that they could openly discuss the rape of Melinda. According to Stephanie, knowledge of the rape would not "spoil" the story for other readers. She stated, "I don't think it really affects the storyline." The girls' concern for not spoiling the story for others suggests that they are adopting more of an aesthetic stance as readers (Rosenblatt, 1964). Taking an efferent stance means reading a text for the purpose of taking away information; taking an aesthetic stance means reading for the purpose of experiencing and living through the text. The girls recognized that reading can be a pleasurable experience and consciously avoided disclosing any information that could ruin that experience for other readers.

If one of the members missed a meeting or did not complete the reading, she made sure to ask others for a brief overview. For example, Carol, an eighth grader, had not prepared for the reading group meeting on *The Soloist*. She asked the group members, "Can you guys like keep me up, can you tell me what's it about?" It was not uncommon for the girls to make such a request. For example, Katherine, a seventh grader, wanted a summary of the book, *Dateable*.

Katherine: Before we start, can you summarize what happened so far cause I wasn't here.

Stephanie: It's not a novel. It's like an instruction book.

Knowing that they might not have the same knowledge and understanding of the text as the other members, Katherine and Carol took initiative and asked for summaries. Asking for updates and summaries, both girls were positioning the other members as knowledgeable and valuable resources.

"We keep what we say to us": Responsibility of confidentiality. The girls desired and constructed a reading group that was safe. Safe learning spaces have been conceptualized and discussed differently. For instance, Cochran-Smith (1995) argues that an overemphasis on safety can "eliminate conflict to the point of flatness, thus reducing the conversation to platitudes or superficial rhetoric" (p. 546). It is "safe" to avoid discussions of personal assumptions, prejudices and ideologies. Safe spaces, however, do not need to be neutral or flat. They can be spaces in which students feel valued and respected, and therefore better able to share vulnerabilities and painful stories, take intellectual risks, and interrogate—individually and collectively—ways of being, valuing and believing.

The girls created and maintained a safe space as a result of agreeing to do the following: be open (i.e., offer experiences, thoughts and ideas to the group); and keep reading group conversations confidential. According to Weis and Carbonell-Medina (2000), confidentiality allows people to reveal experiences that otherwise would not have been disclosed. The seventh- and eighth-grade girls needed assurance that they would not become the subject of school gossip. The girls saw the reading group as a space to share personal and family stories of pain, embarrassment or abuse. Before sharing the story of a family member who was sexually abused as a child, Jessica said, "I am asking you guys to keep this here." Jessica also revealed—in and through conversations—different facets of her upbringing, identity, and life. Rebecca, a classmate and friend, was taken aback to see Jessica so open. According to Rebecca, Jessica usually "keeps things to herself. She really don't say much."

Asked to describe the reading group during an interview, Rebecca commented, "Our group is about, we talk about not just the book. We can also put things on the table that are, um, sort of personal, but we keep what we say to us." The girls asked that the stories be kept within the group. Rebecca described the girls as both "putting things on the table" and "keeping what we say to us."

Openness and confidentiality are inextricably related: that is, openness cannot exist without the promise of confidentiality. In order to be open, girls needed assurance that they could reveal secrets and painful stories. The girls asked that the stories be kept within the reading group and among the group members.

Jessica was not the only student to share stories that might be seen as embarrassing, painful or "risky." Mary revealed both parents' mental health histories. Clarissa shared a poem she had written to process her grandfather's death. She shared details of seeing her grandfather on a breathing tube after undergoing surgery for lung cancer. Eventually, he died of pneumonia. She could not be at the hospital, so she composed and read aloud the following poem:

> Of course you know I love you. It's obviously true. And if you don't already know,
> I am going to miss you. I wish you could stay with us. It's hard to let you go. But
> I know it's best for you. So I'll go with the flow.

The girls articulated needing an environment in which they could be open and not fearful of becoming the subject of school gossip. During the last reading group meeting, Stephanie, a seventh grader, commented:

> I think it's important to have something where you can just talk, that it will really
> be confidential because you can trust in your friends, but not as much. Well, I
> think it's important to have something that's like confidential.

Ironically, the fact that the seventh graders were not all friends made it easier for Stephanie to talk, share and trust that they would keep the reading group conversations confidential. Rebecca recognized that it was risky to reveal oneself and "put things on the table." Such recognition might account for the way the girls valued each other and the stories told at reading group. The girls' honesty, vulnerability and trust were poignant and inspirational. They shared stories of parents' depressions and divorces, of death and violence, and of love, disappointment and loss.

Throughout the study I recognized the possibility that information shared during reading group might not be kept confidential. The girls signed a contract promising to keep the content of the reading group conversations private. Yet I could not help wonder, who was I to write about and make public the girls' lives and stories? Adolescent lives are increasingly scrutinized, commented on, written about and made public. There is an absence of critical analysis on the ways that adolescent students, particularly poor students and students of color are subject to the gaze of researchers and policy-makers. What was I doing when the girls disclosed their lives and experiences? What were *my* responsibilities—as a researcher, educator, reading group participant and woman?

Challenges and Complexities of After-School Reading Groups

In this section, I focus on the challenges of student-centered reading groups, including the messy process of text selection, influence of school cliques on the relationships between and among reading group participants, and instances in which certain participants felt ignored or marginalized.

"What if somebody picks a book and you thought it was kind of stupid?": Process of text selection. Given that each girl saw different purposes for the reading group, and had different identities as readers (e.g., good reader, slow reader), it is not surprising that participants wanted to read different books. The girls offered and then had to sort through a range of possible genres and titles. The girls

often put forth subjective claims as they recommended texts to the reading group. Recommending *A Summer of My German Soldier*, Jessica, a seventh grader, shared that she cried when she read the novel. All three groups established ground rules at the outset of the text-selection process. One seventh-grade group agreed not to read any books that belonged to a series. Stephanie later qualified the rule: "The thing about my rule is that sequels are allowed, but only if they make sense by themselves." The girls anticipated the negotiations and obstacles that are part of choosing books. For instance, Helen, a seventh grader, wondered, "Some people want to read *Harry Potter*, some people want to read *Clique*, and some people want to read. Like, I would want to read again, *Curious Incident of the Dog in the Night Time*. Yeah, it's a really good book."

Implicit here is the range and variation of titles adolescent girls like to read. That is, they do not all read *Clique*, *Gossip Girl* or even *Harry Potter*. Helen also acknowledged that readers' preferences change and evolve. According to Helen, she outgrew *Gossip Girl*. Helen wanted to try reading a classic and suggested *Emma*. All readers judge and evaluate books. Middle schoolers are no exception. Hence, Helen posed the question: What happens if and when some girls like a book that others find "stupid"? How do the members reconcile these differences and reach an agreement? Katherine, a seventh grader, proposed one solution: regardless of the number of votes, the group should not read a text if one member strongly opposed it.

"It's not a clique. We just happen to be friends": Popularity, cliques and reading groups. Stephanie and Amy's input and book recommendations were more valued than those of other seventh graders. Amy and Stephanie had recommended four of the five books that the group read throughout the school year. Was it mere coincidence that Amy and Stephanie were also identified as the most popular seventh graders at school?

Leaving the classroom and entering the after-school space of the reading group, the girls carried statuses as the "cool" or "popular" girl, and the power that those statuses afforded them. Coding for identity claims, I noted the ways in which seventh-grade girls positioned themselves and were positioned in relationship to the "popular" clique. For example, Amy identified as an "insider." However, many of the girls who belonged to the popular group did not see themselves as part of a clique.

Casey: It's not a clique. We just happen to be friends.

Stephanie: I don't like the concept that my little group of friends is a clique because cliques are exclusive and people feel left out. The thing is, if someone wanted to be friends with us, we would totally let you in Molly. If you would just, just come up to us, and be like, "Hey." And we'll be like, "Hey, Molly."

Aware that cliques are seen as exclusive, Stephanie resisted the particular label being placed on her group. According to Stephanie and others, anyone could be part of the group if she desired to do so. Close attention to the way Stephanie addressed Molly, however, reveals that the group still has the power to grant or deny membership. That is, the "we"—the group—gets to decide whether to "let in" Molly. The group does not extend invitations; rather, the girl who desires membership must approach the group. The girls outside to the "clique" simultaneously desired acceptance, yet were critical of its exclusionary practices. The study's findings suggest that students had more or less voice, power and status within the reading group. The social hierarchy that defined adolescents' status in school did not disappear completely in the after-school space.

"You're going to neglect someone's point of view": Reading groups as contact zones. Establishing rules for the reading group, Rebecca, a seventh grader, said: "Not to make anyone, like, make them feel like their ideas are bad." Several eighth graders made a similar normative-evaluative claim that reading group members *should* take seriously every book recommendation and value different perspectives. However, at times the after-school space became a contact zone (Pratt, 1991) as girls questioned and challenged each other, and worked to redefine group norms. For example, Carol, an eighth grader, recommended that the group read a murder mystery. The other girls, however, ignored Carol and her recommendation. Carol confronted the group, as shown in the transcript reproduced below:

Carol: I feel like it's going to continue that you guys are going to neglect someone's point of view.

Mary: No, we decided that at the beginning that we weren't going to ignore anyone's point of view.

Carol: But you did it, and I feel as though it's going to keep going.

The excerpt illustrates the tensions and struggles inherent in the process of collaboration, negotiation and community building. If the teacher-facilitator observed a student trying to articulate an idea or offer a perspective, she would often interrupt the discussion and say, "What did you want to say?" However, some girls' perspectives and opinions were still valued more than those of others. The reading group became a site of power negotiation, and student inclusion and exclusion. One common, mistaken assumption is that in a group of like-minded peers, every member is equally free to contribute and participate (Howard, 2001). Even among students, power relations determine whose voices are privileged, and whose readings are deemed more valid and meaningful. Thus, one must be mindful of the unequal distribution of power in social environments and spaces of learning (Howard, 2001; Trimbur, 1989).

DISCUSSION

Research on after- and out-of-school programs that motivate and inspire youth (e.g., Hull, 2003; Heath & McLaughlin, 1993) has identified the importance of adolescents' collective participation and collaboration. The effectiveness of out-of-school spaces of learning can be partly attributed to adolescents' involvement as co-constructors and collaborators working alongside invested adults. In these spaces, adolescents are positioned as problem-solvers, decision-makers, and agents of their learning.

Turning points 2000: Educating adolescents in the 21ˢᵗ century (Jackson, Davis, Abeel & Bordonaro, 2000) makes several recommendations for improving middle schools for all students, particularly low-income, students of color. The recommendations include extending learning beyond school hours and outside school walls through after-school programs. Because students spend 80% of their time out of school, how and where they spend that time has significant implications for improving literacy outcomes for adolescents (Miller, 2003). However, before supporting or designing after-school literacy programs, we need to identify the particular dimensions of after-school spaces that lead to student engagement and learning, know a good deal more about how students actually construct and experience these spaces, and most importantly, design learning environments *with* adolescents, not just for them. Only then can educators imagine and structure learning environments—both inside and out of schools—that can foster adolescents' literacy learning and engagement.

REFERENCES

Alvermann, D. E., Young, J. P., Weaver, D., Hinchman, K. A., Moore, D. W., Phelps, S. F., … Zalewski, P. (1996). Middle and high school students' perceptions of how they experience text-based discussions: A multicase study. *Reading Research Quarterly, 31*(3), 244-267.

Alvermann, D. E., Young J. P., Green, C., & Wisenbaker, J. M. (1999). Adolescents' perceptions and negotiations of literacy practices in after-school read and talk clubs. *American Educational Research Journal, 26*(2), 221-264.

Appleman, D. (2006). *Reading for themselves: How to transform adolescents into lifelong readers through out-of-class book clubs.* Portsmouth, NH: Heinemann.

Bakhtin, M. M. (1986). *Speech genres and other late essays* (V. McGee, Trans.). Austin, TX: University of Texas Press.

Barton, D., & Hamilton, M. (2000). Literacy as social practice. In D. Barton, M. Hamilton, & R. Ivanic (Eds.), *Situated literacies: Reading and writing in context* (pp. 7-15). London, U.K.: Routledge.

Bloome, D. (1985). Reading as a social process. *Language Arts, 62*(2), 134-142.

Broughton, M. A. (2002). The performance and construction of subjectivities of early adolescent girls in book club discussion groups. *Journal of Literacy Research, 34*(1), 1-38.

Bruffee, K. A. (1984). Collaborating learning and the "conversation of mankind." *College English, 46*(7), 635-652.

Bruffee, K. A. (1993). *Collaborative learning: Higher education, interdependence, and the authority of knowledge.* Baltimore, MD: Johns Hopkins University Press.

Carspecken, P. F. (1996). *Critical ethnography in educational research: A theoretical and practical guide.* New York, NY: Routledge.

Chandler, K. (1997). The beach book club: Literacy in the "lazy days of summer." *Journal of Adolescent & Adult Literacy, 41*(2), 104-116.

Cochran-Smith, M. (1995). Uncertain allies: Understanding the boundaries of race and teaching. *Harvard Educational Review, 65*(4), 541-570.

Collins, J., & Blot, R. (2003). *Literacy and literacies: Texts, power and identity.* Cambridge, U.K.: Cambridge University Press.

Freire, P. (1987). The importance of the act of reading. In P. Freire & D. Macedo (Eds.), *Literacy: Reading the word and the world* (pp. 5-11). South Hadley, MA: Bergin and Garvey.

Gee, J. (2000). The new literacy studies: From "socially situated" to the work of the social. In D. Barton, M. Hamilton, & R. Ivanic (Eds.), *Situated literacies: Reading and writing in context* (pp. 180-196). London, U.K.: Routledge.

Hammersely, M., & Atkinson, P. (1995). *Ethnography: Principles in practice* (2nd ed.). New York, NY: Routledge.

Heath, S. B., & McLaughlin, M. (1993). Ethnicity and gender in theory and practice: The youth perspective. In S. B. Heath & M. McLaughlin (Eds.), *Identity and inner-city youth: Beyond ethnicity and gender* (pp. 13-35). New York, NY: Teachers College Press.

Hill, M. H., & Van Horn, L. (1995). Book club goes to jail: Can book blubs replace gangs? *Journal of Adolescent & Adult Literacy, 39*(3), 180-188.

Horton, M., & Freire, P. (1990). *We make the road by walking: Conversations on education and social change.* Philadelphia, PA: Temple University Press.

Howard, R. M. (2001). Collaborative pedagogy. In G. Tate, A. Rupiper, & K. Schick (Eds.), *Composition pedagogies* (pp. 54-70). New York, NY: Oxford University Press.

Hull, G. (2003). Youth culture and digital media: New literacies for new times. *Research in the Teaching of English, 38*(2), 229-233.

Hull, G., & Schultz, K. (2002). *School's out! Bridging out-of-school literacies with classroom practice.* New York, NY: Teachers College Press.

Jackson, A. W., Davis, G. A., Abeel, M., & Bordonaro, A. (2000). *Turning points 2000: Educating adolescents in the 21st century.* New York, NY: Teachers College Press.

Kincheloe, J. L. (2004). *Critical pedagogy primer.* New York, NY: Peter Lang.

Luke, A., & Freebody, P. (1997). The social practices of reading. In S. Muspratt, A. Luke, and P. Freebody (Eds.), *Constructing critical literacies: Teaching and learning textual practice* (pp. 188-226). Cresskill, NJ: Hampton.

Lunsford, A. (1991). Collaboration, control, and the idea of a writing center. *The Writing Center Journal, 12*(1), 3-10.

Mahiri, J. (Ed.) (2004). *What they don't learn in school: Literacy in the lives of urban youth.* New York, NY: Peter Lang.

Merriam, S. B. (1998). *Qualitative research and case study applications in education.* San Francisco, CA: Josey-Bass.

Miller, B. M. (2003). *Critical hours: Afterschool programs and educational success.* Quincy, MA: Nellie Mae Education Foundation.

Moje, E., Overby, M., Tysaver, N., & Morris, K. (2008). The complex world of adolescent literacy: Myths, motivations, and mysteries. *Harvard Educational Review, 78*(1), 107-154.

Pratt, M. L. (1991). Arts of the contact zone. *Profession, 91,* 33-40.

Rosenblatt, L. M. (1964). The poem as event. *College English, 26*(2), 123-128.

Scharber, C. (2009). Online book clubs: Bridges between old and new literacies practices. *Journal of Adolescent & Adult Literacy, 52*(5), 433-437.

Shor, I. (1999). What is critical literacy? In. I. Shor & C. Pari (Eds.), *Critical literacy in action: Writing words, changing worlds* (pp. 1-30). Portsmouth, NH: Boynton/Cook-Heinemann.

Smith, S. A. (2000). Talking about "real stuff": Explorations of agency and romance in an all-girls book club. *Language Arts, 78,* 30-38.

Street, B. V. (1995). *Social literacies: Critical approaches to literacy in development, ethnography and education.* London, U.K.: Longman.

Trimbur, J. (1989). Consensus and difference in collaborative learning, *College English, 51*(6), 602-616.

Vyas, S. (2004). Exploring bicultural identities of Asian high school students through the analytic window of a literature club, *Journal of Adolescent & Adult Literacy, 48*(1), 12-23.

Vygotsky, L. S. (1986). *Thought and language* (A. Kouzulin, Trans.). Cambridge, MA: MIT Press.

Weis, L., & Carbonell-Medina, D. (2000). Learning to speak out in abstinence based sex education group: Gender and race work in an urban magnet high school, *Teachers College Record. 102*(3), 620-650.

Paths to Culturally Responsive Instruction: Preservice Teachers' Readiness Beliefs

Kathleen A. J. Mohr
Forrest Lane
Amie Sarker
University of North Texas

Efficacy has been a premise of many studies of teacher beliefs and their instructional practices (Labone, 2004; Raths & Raths McAninch, 2003; Taylor & Sorbel, 2001). Within Social Cognitive Theory, efficacy is often defined as "people's beliefs about their capabilities to exercise control over events that affect their lives" (Bandura, 1989, p.1). Self-efficacy beliefs are context specific and subject to change in that they can be affected by social influences. Thus, contextual and social factors may influence teachers' sense of capacity to make a difference.

Related research has documented that teacher beliefs influence their behaviors and that a sense of self-efficacy contributes to teacher motivation (Ashton & Webb, 1986). The relationship between teacher beliefs and instructional practices (Alderman, 2004; Risko, et al., 2008) has become especially important as student demographics and teacher expectations have changed. Contemporary teachers encounter numerous challenges in their efforts to provide productive learning opportunities for their students. In addition to federal mandates, high-stakes testing, and increasing expectations for Information Age competencies among students, teachers are required to meet the needs of increasingly diverse student populations.

One important aspect of today's teacher preparation and subsequent instructional success is teachers' beliefs about how well they can meet the needs of learners who lack English-language fluency or who come from markedly disparate cultural backgrounds. Some teacher preparation programs now include courses designed to help candidates develop skills for working with special populations, including English language learners and immigrants. Following professional discussion criticizing the schooling of minority students (Gay, 2000; Irvine, 1990; Ladson-Billings, 2000) some educational leaders have promoted the inclusion of more equitable and culturally sensitive instructional practices (Jordan, 1985; Vogt, Jordan, & Tharp, 1987). The recommendations of these and others typically include using students' cultural backgrounds to frame and support learning, help structure curriculum and classroom environments, and improve assessment, while providing ways for students to access and succeed in more mainstream conditions.

Preservice and inservice teachers generally report a lack of preparation to effectively teach students from culturally and linguistically diverse backgrounds (Knoblauch & Hoy, 2008; Ladson-Billings, 2000; Ruston, 2000). Although known by various terms, instruction that respects and utilizes the cultural differences among students is commonly referred to as "culturally responsive instruction." It is defined as "using the cultural knowledge, prior experiences, frames of reference, and performance styles of ethnically diverse students to make learning encounters more relevant to and effective for them" (Gay, 2000, p. 29).

In an attempt to better understand and monitor preservice teachers' perceptions of their ability to provide culturally responsive instruction, this study was designed to assess culturally responsive dispositions of students in similar courses required in their respective teacher education programs. Although there are several related terms in the extant literature, this study utilizes the following definition of culturally responsive pedagogy (Siwatu, 2007):

> An approach to teaching and learning that (1) uses students' cultural knowledge,... experiences, prior knowledge, and individual learning preferences as a conduit to facilitate the teaching-learning process,...(2) incorporates students' cultural orientations to design culturally compatible classroom environments,...(3) provides students with multiple opportunities to demonstrate what they have learned using a variety of assessment techniques,...(4) provides students with the knowledge and skills needed to function in mainstream culture while simultaneously helping students maintain their cultural identity, native language, and connection to their culture (cultural enrichment and competence). (pp. 1086-1087)

Siwatu's (2007) Culturally Responsive Teaching Self-Efficay Scale (CRTSE) aligns with a continuum of teaching practices, ranging from easy to difficult. In an initial study by Siwatu, respondents reported being "more efficacious in their ability to help students feel like important members of the classroom and develop positive, personal relationships with their students" (p. 1086). Siwatu deemed these items to be less challenging aspects of classroom instruction. Conversely, respondents in the Siwatu sample felt less ready to communicate with linguistically diverse students, particularly in their native languages, which would require some proficiency in languages other than English. Thus, those preservice teachers deemed themselves more prepared to build positive teacher-student relationships, characterized by trust, than to help students maintain cultural and language identities. This finding is somewhat intuitive when considering preservice teachers who represent a dominant, monolingual, culture.

Siwatu's research called for use of the CRTSE to compare students in different and more diverse programs to determine possible differentiation among preservice educators. This was the goal of the current study—to compare preservice teachers in different programs regarding their self-efficacy beliefs to be culturally responsive in their instruction.

The following research questions guided the current study:

1. How confident are preservice teachers in their readiness to provide culturally responsive instruction?

2. How do preservice teachers in two different programs compare in their perceived readiness to provide culturally responsive instruction?

3. How do preservice teachers in two different programs change in their perceived readiness to provide culturally responsive instruction during a semester course related to language and literacy development for culturally diverse students?

While advocates for more culturally sensitive instruction have called for changes in teacher education programs, until recently, most preservice teachers did not receive special training to work with culturally and linguistically diverse students (August & Shanahan, 2008). Now, however, teacher preparation programs are expected to incorporate more equitable and culturally sensitive programs for their preservice teacher candidates. Such programs are being scrutinized for their effectiveness and rivaled by alternative certification programs. These and other factors have caused teacher preparation programs to review and refine their programs and better monitor their candidates' paths of preparedness to teach all students well.

English language proficiency is highly related to school achievement, but culturally and linguistically diverse students are often acquiring English as a second language while working to meet grade-level content expectations. Language and literacy development are inextricably linked to student success and are key aspects of teacher training, especially at the elementary-grades preparation levels (Bean, 1997; Massey, 2002). Monitoring preservice teachers' perceptions of effectiveness should include both assessment of their cultural responsiveness and its relationship to teaching core subjects (Willis & Harris, 1997; Wolf, Hill, & Ballentine, 1999). Emphasizing aspects of and measuring attitudes related to cultural diversity can be productive components to teacher preparation programs and literacy courses within those programs. Teacher education programs that attend to the skills and attitudes of their prospective teachers are more likely to develop educators with strong efficacy beliefs that in turn correlate with their students' academic achievement (Linek, Sampson, Raine, Klakamp, & Smith, 2006).

METHOD

Context

The teacher preparation program targeted in this study is located in a region of north Texas that is characterized by large Latino populations and a montage of diverse urban, rural, and suburban schools. The program is committed to preparing teachers who are aware of cultural and linguistic diversity and equipped to sensitively differentiate instruction for all students. The program in this study made major revisions to its elementary teacher preparation program in 2000 and in 2002 initiated a program to prepare bilingual and ESL-certified teachers. The Bilingual/ESL program has grown considerably and received recognition by the TESOL organization in conjunction with its most recent NCATE review.

While department faculty have worked to infuse culturally and linguistically diverse teaching methods in various courses, faculty have especially focused on culturally responsive pedagogy in several literacy courses for candidates in both the Bilingual/ESL and Generalist programs. (These programs align with the state certifications. The term "generalist" refers to those seeking certification to teach in self-contained, elementary-school classrooms without a particular emphasis or specialization.) The required literacy-oriented courses in these two certification paths have afforded the opportunity to monitor the development of candidates in both programs with respect to their understanding of culturally responsive instruction.

Participants

In 2000, faculty worked together to design and deliver a new course, Language Arts for Linguistically Diverse Students, that exposes preservice teachers early in their major courses to the realities and needs of English language learners (ELLs). The course reviews social trends and the language processes of ELLs in contemporary schools. It also highlights legal requirements of classroom teachers with respect to ELLs and focuses on how to appreciate and simultaneously attend to literacy and language development in regular classroom settings. For example, one of the course objectives is to "delineate appropriate accommodations for ELLs in mainstream classrooms." Generalist candidates may take this course early in their teacher education sequence (and as one of their five literacy courses) so that they can begin to assume instructional responsibility for culturally and linguistically diverse students. For many preservice teachers, it is a wake-up call to realize that they are likely to have limited-English-speaking students in their classrooms and that they must be the professionals who assume responsibility for student success.

The Bilingual/ESL candidates differ from the Generalist candidates in that they have selected from the beginning to receive specialized training to effectively teach students who may speak another language at home and who may represent cultures that differ markedly from the school culture. The Bilingual/ESL candidates take six courses that target language and content development. It can be assumed that the Bilingual/ESL candidates differ in their orientation to student diversity, especially at the beginning of the teacher education course sequence. It is also expected that, given the focus of the department and the regional population, candidates become more culturally aware and sensitive during their coursework. Preservice students in several sections of these two courses were asked to participate in the study.

Instrument

Using the aforementioned definition, Siwatu (2007) developed the CRTSE based on related work that synthesized 27 performance standards gleaned from relevant research. The CRTSE is a 40-item survey that assesses preservice teachers' self-perceptions. The responses to the 40 items are summed to generate a total score, indicating the level of confidence to be culturally responsive in their teaching. Siwatu initially assessed undergraduate students at various stages in their teacher preparation (i.e., freshmen, sophomores, juniors, and seniors) within a largely homogenous population. For the current study, the survey was revised to use a 5-point Likert scale in order to align better with other assessment forms used to monitor candidates within the program.

Analyses

Preservice teacher candidates (representing both the Bilingual/ESL and Generalist programs previously mentioned) completed a modified version of the CRTSE at the beginning and end of literacy courses across two semesters. These programs differed considerably in size at the time of the study, so the sizes of the sub-samples are similarly disparate. Participant data were then analyzed using PASW version 17.0. Descriptive elements, including measures of central tendency, variance, and normality were calculated to assess the adequacy of the data and item performance.

An independent sample t-test was conducted to examine differences between the Bilingual/ESL and Generalist student samples at the beginning and end of the semester. T-values and standardized mean differences (effect sizes) were obtained to evaluate both statistical and practical differences. (Statistical significance allows the researcher to examine the probability of obtaining results from a given sample. Effect sizes provide a mechanism for evaluating the magnitude of the effect, allowing the researcher to place statistical differences in the context of practical importance in the literature.)

In addition, reliability and factor validities of the CTRSE were examined. Specifically, a principle components analysis was conducted to test the underlying theoretical structure of the CTRSE among two independent samples. This technique provides an empirical approach to synthesizing items into smaller subsets based on the interrelationships among observed variables (Gorsuch, 1983; Kieffer, 1999). Specifically, it allows researchers to "explain the most shared variance of measured variables using the fewest possible latent or synthetic variables," and provides a framework in which theoretical relationships can be better understood and utilized (Henson & Roberts, 2006, p. 394).

RESULTS

Table 1 shows the number of completed surveys at both junctures across the two groups (i.e., Bilingual/ESL and Generalist) along with descriptive statistics. (The instrument had reliability scores of no less than .950 in all administrations.) Normality was assessed by examining skewness and kurtosis values and was found to be within acceptable ranges suggesting a reasonably normal distribution of data. Variables were examined for missing data after which several cases were removed completely from the analysis based on the quantity of missing data for those participants. For isolated cases of missing data in normal distributions, Pedhazur (1997) suggests the mean as a reasonable substitute and this was used in the analysis. (The lower number of completed surveys for the Generalist candidates is due to the fact that one of the instructors failed to administer the survey in two sections of the course at the end of one semester.)

Table 1. Summary Pre and Post-Test Means & Standard Deviations of Responses to Modified CTRSE

	Bilingual/ESL Pretest (*N*=76)	Bilingual/ESL Posttest (*N*=68)	Generalist Pretest (*N*=151)	Generalist Posttest (*N*=92)
Total Score Mean	160.49	164.06 (+3.57)	146.80	170.72(+23.92)
Total Score SD	19.67	20.63	25.24	20.67
Range of Total Scores	129-193	82-198	62-200	101-200
Mean of Item Means	4.02	4.15 (+.13)	3.67	4.48 (+.81)
SD of Item Means	.36	.20	.26	.24
Range of Means	3.47-4.63	3.50-4.60	3.11-4.47	3.86-4.61

The salient findings of this pre- and post-course comparison of preservice teachers in two certification programs are somewhat confounding. At the beginning of the semester, Bilingual/ESL candidates were statistically higher on the CRTSE than the Generalist candidates at the beginning of the semester ($p < .001$) and with greater variance. The effect of this difference was moderate (d = .605) based on Cohen's qualitative guideline for effect size interpretation (Hinkle, Wiersma, & Jurs, 2003). However, post-test results indicate that Generalist candidates scored statistically higher (164.06 and 170.72 respectively) than the Bilingual/ESL candidates (t= -2.025., p=.045, *d*=.32). Additionally, variability increased for the Bilingual/ESL candidates, but decreased among the Generalist group.

In other words, while the Bilingual/ESL students showed a modest increase in their culturally responsive self-efficacy score (+3.57), the total mean score for Generalist candidates jumped markedly (+23.92), which was unexpected.

In order to compare the scores of these samples (using a 1-5 Likert scale,) with Siwatu's, the researcher team converted Siwatu's 100-point scale to correspond with the 1-5 scale. (The recalculation scores are noted in Table 2.) As shown, these groups' mean total scores were comparable to those in Siwatu's study at the end of their respective courses.

Table 2. Comparison of Scores from Siwatu's and the Bilingual/ESL and Generalist Populations

	Siwatu's Re-calculated Scores	Group 1 Bilingual/ESL	Group 2 Generalist
Mean Total Score	168.10 SD = 17.10	164.06 SD = 20.63	170.02 SD = 20.68
Mean Total	168.10 SD = 17.10	164.06 SD = 20.63	170.02 SD = 20.68
Range of Totals	113-198	82-198	101-200
Range of Means	3.55-4.65	3.50-4.60	3.86-4.61

In addition to the descriptive analyses, the researchers looked at specific survey items. The highest-mean items for the two groups in this study were similar and also reiterated the findings of Siwatu. These items were deemed by Siwatu as being "easier" aspects of culturally responsive instruction, but could be interpreted as more general teaching practices. For example, *#32 Help students feel like important members of the classroom* and *#20 Develop a personal relationship with my students*. (Same top high scores as in Siwatu's study.) The low-mean items for both groups related to more "difficult" or specific teaching practices: *#22 Praise ELLs phrases in their L1* and *#29 Design a lesson that shows cultural groups' contributions to mathematics*.

Interestingly, the mean scores for 8 of the 40 items among the Bilingual/ESL candidates decreased from beginning to end, while none of the mean scores for the Generalist candidates decreased. Only three of the Generalist items had means <4.0 at the end of the semester. The Bilingual/ESL candidates' scores included eight items with means <4.0, contributing to their generally lower scores at the end of the course. The three items that were most different between the Generalist and Bilingual/ESL groups at the beginning and end of the course deal with communicating to students' and their parents in the first language (Items 18, 22, and 31). Notably, these items require more than supportive instructional behaviors; they require specific linguistic skills that bilingual teachers would likely feel more ready to apply.

Given the mean differences between Billingual/ESL and Generalist students, the researchers found it prudent to test the validity of the CRTSE to determine the stability of the instrument's underlying theoretical structure. Two principal components analyses (PCA) with varimax rotation were used in the analysis. An orthogonal rotation strategy was used to improve the interpretation of the instrument and to remain consistent with rotation strategies used previously in the literature (Siwatu, 2007). The first PCA was conducted on Bilingual/ESL students while the second focused on students in the Generalist program.

Ten factors were initially extracted from the Bilingual/ELS sample using the Kaiser-Guttman rule (Eigenvalue >1) and explained approximately 76% of the variance across the items. The scree plot suggested the likelihood of three factors existing in the data. However, multiple criteria should be used in determining the number of factors to retain (Henson & Roberts, 2006; Keiffer, 1999). Therefore, parallel analysis and minimum average partial tests were used in the analysis (O'Connor, 2000; Velicer, 1976). Parallel analysis suggested three factors while minimum average partial tests suggested four factors be retained.

Two subsequent PCAs were performed for Bilingual/ESL students constraining for both three and four factors to identify the most interpretable structure. The factor pattern/structure matrix was examined for sufficient saturation of items on factors (>.3). The final solution included four factors explaining 57.55% of the variance across the items, which is beyond the recommended variance explained for factor analysis studies (Henson & Roberts, 2006). The items corresponding to the factors were interpreted as follows:

1. Getting information to connect to and meet the needs of students.

2. Communicating to students and parents in their native language.

3. Identifying negative bias in curriculum and assessments and building positive relationships.

4. Utilizing the variety in students' backgrounds and in instructional methods.

A principle components analysis was then conducted for Generalist sample. Eight factors were initially extracted using the Kaiser-Guttman rule (Eigenvalue >1) and explained approximately 72% of the variance across the items. The scree plot suggested that likely one factor existed in the data. Using multiple decision rules, parallel analysis and minimum average partial tests were conducted and suggested either two or six factors to be extracted. Several subsequent analyses were conducted constraining for two-six factors. Consequently, a decision was made to use the two factor solution based on the theoretical coherency and interpretability of the model which explained 51.82% of the variance in the items. The two factors were interpreted as:

1. Getting information and acknowledging cultural differences.

2. Student-centered concern and general practices.

While these interpretations are tentative, the analyses used suggest that the Bilingual/ESL preservice teachers have a more nuanced understanding of culturally responsive teaching than do Generalist education majors. For example, both groups consistently valued ways of getting information about their future students' cultural differences. But, the Bilingual/ESL candidates were more consistent in their responses related to using students' native language, differentiating instruction, and analyzing the curriculum and assessment practices for cultural sensitivity. The Generalist students were less similar in their responses to survey items considered to be more specific or more challenging than were the Bilingual/ESL students.

While expected, these findings might encourage teacher education programs to consider aspects of culturally responsive teaching that may need further explication and attention. Extended research is needed to clarify the issue of whether Bilingual/ESL majors perceive culturally responsive teaching as sets of specific skills and behaviors beyond the more general perspective that it is sensitive, student-centered instruction.

DISCUSSION

As indicated here, preservice teachers vary in their understanding of culturally responsive teaching. It is more than just "good teaching" (Au, 2009) and should progress towards more sophisticated beliefs and behaviors. The practical significance of these data is that even one course targeting culturally responsive pedagogy can impact preservice teachers' self-efficacy. However, there may be a false-positive effect in the marked increase in scores among these Generalist candidates. Generalist candidates may feel better about their preparedness, but be naïve in their understanding of students' needs. The Bilingual/ESL candidates may be more realistic about the complexities of effective instruction for culturally and linguistically diverse students and, thus, score themselves lower on such measures and with more consistency.

This is one interpretation of the principal components analyses—that initially, preservice teachers with more mono-cultural backgrounds may see culturally responsive teaching as a singular construct—being respectful of students, which corresponds with the student-centeredness espoused and promoted in their program. When they are made aware of the potential language and cultural differences among their prospective students, they recognize a need to be culturally sensitive and believe in their ability to provide such instruction. These analyses indicate that the Bilingual/ESL teacher candidates interpreted the items differently, as at least four factors, which include more knowledge of students' backgrounds, need for differentiation, and language skills other than English. Thus, there seems to be a disparity in these groups' perceptions about ways to differentiate instruction for students and meet their needs.

Given these results, it may be more useful for educators to consider culturally responsive instruction as a continuum of teacher skills, knowledge, and dispositions (Mohr, 2007; 2008). The continuum would include an array of teacher behaviors, ranging from basic or general (such as being welcoming) to more sophisticated actions (including praising students with statements in their native tongue). A continuum of skills could be tied to incrementally more sophisticated tasks that students complete in a set of courses. For example, preservice teachers could learn how to administer a learning style preference inventory or make observations of such among students in one class and explore the use of online translators to facilitate instruction in another. Using multicultural literature is another teacher practice that could range from using English-only texts with multicultural perspectives to being able to share a story in a different language (orally or via technology) depending on the skill level of the candidate and the related course assignment. In addition, teacher education language and literacy courses can include contrastive analyses of common languages used by student populations. For example, in the course for Generalists at this university, candidates must compare English and Spanish phonology, morphology, semantics, syntax, and pragmatics to determine language aspects that should transfer for Spanish-to-English learners and those areas that might require additional instruction. (A survey of predominant features of other languages is also provided.) In a different course, the Bilingual/ESL preservice teachers must plan mini-lessons that increase awareness and use of language features that transfer, such as cognates. The goal is to move students beyond the awareness of culturally responsive practices to implementation of specific methods and activities that "bridge students' homes and school success" (Au, 2009).

It makes sense that such tasks could be addressed in methods courses and in social studies and language arts courses, in particular. However, if cultural responsiveness is a developmental process, it is also important to monitor preservice teachers across several courses via, interviews, observation and empirical data. It is also important to monitor candidates' efficacy to provide culturally responsive instruction in early and late field experiences and beyond.

As indicated in Social Cognitive Theory, Bandura's (1997) perceptions of competence can predict future classroom behavior and are enhanced by experiences and competency in related skills. Thus, candidates who believe that they can successfully implement culturally respectful teaching practices and believe in the positive outcomes of their instruction may, in fact, be more effective as classroom teachers (Pajares, 2003). But, there appears to be a need for further delineation of culturally responsive instruction that helps to separate more general from more specific characteristics. If definitions and measures of culturally responsive teaching include many general teaching practices, such as building trust and fostering personal relationships, teachers and teacher candidates will likely continue to consider themselves ready to be responsive to student diversity. However, if increased emphasis is placed on more informed linguistic skills and deeper cultural understanding, via instruction and self-assessments, teacher candidates may, indeed, be more realistically prepared to meet the needs of all their students.

This study adds to a small, but growing body of literature that attends to teachers' abilities to provide culturally responsive instruction. Preparing and supporting teachers who are able to accept and maximize student diversity includes transforming preservice teachers' multicultural attitudes (Phuntsog, 2001; Villegas & Lucas, 2002), increasing their knowledge base (Hilliard, 1998), developing their skills to work with culturally diverse students (Leavell, Cowart, & Wilhelm, 1999), and giving them opportunities to hone their skills with diverse student populations. One way to attend to the transformation of teachers' beliefs and increasing their interest in developing knowledge and skills is to assess their perceptions of competency, also known as self-efficacy, for working with diverse student populations. While interpretation of self-reported data has its limitations, coupled with course-related tasks that help develop knowledge, skills, and dispositions, it is a means to understanding and developing the complex construct of culturally responsive pedagogy.

REFERENCES

Alderman, M. K. (2004). *Motivation for achievement: Possibilities for teaching and learning.* Mahwah, NJ: Lawrence Erlbaum.

Ashton, P. T., & Webb, R. B. (1986). *Making a difference: Teachers' sense of efficacy and student achievement.* New York, NY: Longman.

Au, K. H. (2009). Culturally responsive instruction: Application to multiethnic, multilingual classrooms. In L. Helman (Ed.), *Literacy development with English learners: Research-based instruction in grades K-6* (pp.18-39). New York, NY: Guilford.

August, D., & Shanahan, T. (Eds.). (2008). *Developing reading and writing in second-language learners: Lessons from the report of the National Literacy Panel on language minority children and youth.* New York, NY: Taylor & Francis.

Bandura, A. (1997). *Self-efficacy: The exercise of control.* New York, NY: W. H. Freeman.

Bandura, A. (1989, March). *Perceived self-efficacy in the exercise of personal agency.* Paper presented at the annual meeting of the British Psychological Society in St. Andrews, Scotland.

Bean, T. (1997). Preservice teachers' selection and use of content area literacy strategies. *Journal of Educational Research, 90*(3), 154-163.

Gay, G. (2000). *Culturally responsive teaching: Theory, research, and practice.* New York, NY: Teachers College Press.

Gorsuch, R. L. (1973). Using Bartlett's significance test to determine the number of factors to extract. *Educational and Psychological Measurement, 33,* 361-634.

Henson, R. K. (2006). Effect-size measures and meta-analytic thinking in counseling psychology research. *The Counseling Psychologist, 34*(5), 601-629.

Henson, R. K., & Roberts, J. K. (2006). Use of exploratory factor analysis in published research. *Educational and Psychological Measurement, 66,* 393-416.

Hilliard, A. G. (1998). *SBA: The reawakening of the African mind.* Gainesville, FL: Makare Publishing.

Hinkle, D. E., Wiersma, W., & Jurs, S. G. (2003). *Applied statistics for the behavior sciences.* New York, NY: Houghton Mifflin Company.

Irvine, J. J. (1990). *Black students and school failure.* New York, NY: Greenwood Press.

Jordan, C. (1985). Translating culture: From ethnographic information to educational program. *Anthropology and Education Quarterly, 16*(2), 102-123.

Kieffer, K. M. (1999). An introductory primer on the appropriate use of exploratory and confirmatory factor analysis. *Research in the Schools, 6*(2), 75-92.

Knobloch, D., & Hoy, A. (2008). "Maybe I can teach those kids." The influence of contextual factors on student teachers' efficacy beliefs. *Teaching and Teacher Education, 24,* 166-179.

Labone, E. (2004). Teacher efficacy: Maturing the construct through research in alternative paradigms. *Teaching and Teacher Education, 20,* 341-359.

Ladson-Billings, G. (2000). Fighting for our lives: Preparing teachers to teach African American students. *Journal of Teacher Education, 51*(3), 206-214.

Leavell, A. G., Cowart, M., & Wilhelm, R. W. (1999). Strategies for preparing culturally responsive teachers. *Equity & Excellence in Education, 32*(1) 64-71.

Linek, W. M., Sampson, M. B., Raine, I. L, Klakamp, K., & Smith, B, (2006). Development of literacy beliefs and practices of preservice teachers with reading specializations in a field-based program. *Reading Horizons, 46*(3), 183-213.

Massey, D. D. (2002). Personal journeys: Teaching teachers to teach literacy. *Reading Research and Instruction, 41*(2), 103-126.

Mohr, K. A. J. (2008, July). Cultural 3Rs: Do we know what they are and what they mean? Paper presented at the World Reading Congress of the International Reading Association, San Jose, Costa Rica.

Mohr, K. A. J. (2007, November). Preservice teachers' perceptions about reading instruction. Paper presented at the 57th meeting of the National Reading Conference, Austin, TX.

O'Connor, B. P. (2000). SPSS and SAS programs for determining the number of components using parallel analysis and Velicer's MAP test. *Behavior Research Methods, Instrumentation, and Computers, 32,* 396-402.

Pajares, F. (2003). Self-efficacy beliefs, motivation, and achievement in writing: A review of literature. *Reading and Writing Quarterly, 19,* 139-158.

Pedhazur, E. J. (1997). *Multiple regression in behavioral research: Explanation and prediction.* Fort Worth, TX: Harcourt Brace.

Phuntsog, N. (2001). Culturally responsive teaching: What do selected United States elementary school teachers think: *Intercultural Education, 12*(1), 51-64.

Raths, J., & Raths McAninch, A. (2003). *Teacher beliefs and classroom performance: The impact of teacher education.* Charlotte, NC: Information Age Publishing.

Risko, V. J., Roller, C. M., Cummins, C., Bean, R. M., Block, C. C., Anders, P. L., & Flood, J. (2008). A critical analysis of research on reading teacher education. *Reading Research Quarterly, 43*(3), 252-288.

Ruston, S. P. (2000). Student teacher efficacy in inner-city schools. *Urban Review, 32*(4), 365-383.

Siwatu, K. O. (2007). Preservice teachers' culturally responsive teaching self-efficacy and outcome expectancy beliefs. *Teaching and Teacher Education, 23, 1086-1101.*

Taylor, S. V., & Sorbel, D. M. (2001). Addressing the discontinuity of students' and teachers' diversity: A preliminary study of preservice teachers' beliefs and skills. *Teaching and Teacher Education, 17,* 487-503.

Velicer, W. F. (1976). Determining the number of components from the matrix of partial correlations. *Psychometrika, 41,* 321-327.

Villegas, A. M., & Lucas, T. (2002). *Educating culturally responsive teachers: A coherent approach.* New York, NY: State University of New York.

Vogt, L., Jordan, C., & Tharp, R. (1987). Explaining school failure, producing school success: Two cases. *Anthropology and Education Quarterly, 18*(4), 276-286.

Willis, A., & Harris, V. (1997). Preparing preservice teachers to teach multicultural literature. In J. Flood, S. B. Heath, & D. Lapp (Eds.), *Handbook of research on teaching literacy through communicative and visual arts* (pp. 460-469). New York, NY: Macmillan.

Wolf, S., Hill, L., & Ballentine, D. (1999). Teaching on fissured ground: Preparing preservice teacher for culturally conscious pedagogy. In T. Shanahan & F. Rodriguez-Brown (Eds.), *National Reading Conference Yearbook, 48* (pp. 423-466). Chicago, IL: NRC.

One Without the Other Isn't as Good as Both Together: A Theoretical Framework of Integrated Writing/Science Instruction in the Primary Grades

Vicki McQuitty
Sharon Dotger
Uzma Khan
Syracuse University

In *Crossing Borders in Literacy and Science Instruction* (2004), Wendy Saul reminds us that educational research, particularly research that crosses borders between disciplines, "is both messy and imperfect" (p. 3). "Messy imperfection" describes our experience as researchers and teacher educators attempting to integrate writing and science instruction. In the fall of 2008, we began several projects focused on K-2 inquiry science teaching (NRC, 2000) with writing integrated into the inquiry process. Our work quickly became messy as we realized we were integrating more than writing and science; we were integrating the different perspectives, concerns, and goals of literacy and science education. We realized we needed a theoretical framework to guide our thinking and the future empirical work we hoped to conduct. The purpose of this paper is to describe the framework we have developed.

Sharon and Uzma, science educators interested in elementary science teaching, approached our work with the goal of designing effective inquiry science instruction for K-2 classrooms. They viewed writing through a "writing-to-learn" lens (Bangert-Drowns, Hurley, & Wilkinson, 2004)—as a means of promoting students' science learning within the inquiry process. From their perspective, writing was a "thinking tool" that allowed children to record and reflect on the ideas they generated during inquiry. Vicki, a literacy educator and advocate of process writing (Calkins, 1994), recognized the value of writing to learn science concepts, but her perspective oriented her toward the process of composing texts for various audiences. She considered science writing a nonfiction genre students must learn to compose. In addition to these perspectives, we knew from previous experience that primary grade teachers sometimes approach writing in science as an opportunity to improve students' general writing skills. This perspective reflects the emphasis on literacy instruction in the primary grade curriculum (Worth, 2006), and it may lead teachers to focus on ELA benchmarks—complete sentences, spelling, mechanics—rather than science content when students write during science instruction.

As we reflected on these different perspectives, we realized that each represented a valid and valuable viewpoint. We wanted to ensure that writing supported students' science learning rather than science instruction simply providing topics for writing lessons. At the same time, we recognized that learning to write presents unique challenges for primary grade children that must be addressed throughout the curriculum. We began to ask: "How could we integrate our different perspectives into a single instructional framework that values both science and writing instruction, their goals, and their place within the curriculum?" While several models of integrated science/ writing instruction exist, (Klentschy, 2008; Powell & Aram, 2008; Wallace, Hand, & Prain, 2004), this work does not fully integrate writing-to-learn and learning-to-write research or attend to the particular needs of K-2 students.

This paper develops a framework of integrated writing/science instruction in the primary grades that encompasses the perspectives and purposes of both disciplines. We first describe the theoretical lens that guides our work and review four bodies of literature that have informed our thinking: inquiry science instruction, writing-to-learn science, process writing, and genre theory. We then bring this literature together into a framework of writing/science instruction and identify areas for future research. Throughout, we argue that writing instruction alone or science instruction alone is not as beneficial as both together.

THEORETICAL FRAMEWORK

In developing a framework of the writing/science process, we drew on Boix Mansilla, Miller, and Gardner's (2000) framework of interdisciplinary teaching. These scholars argue that interdisciplinary instruction requires careful treatment of each discipline and appropriate interactions between them. When integrating science and writing instruction, the integrity of each discipline, its purposes, and its goals must be maintained. This required us to address the research, theories, and concerns of both language arts and science education. Science educators want students to acquire science concepts, as well as understandings of and skills for scientific inquiry (NRC, 2000). Literacy educators want students to communicate using a wide range of strategies, for a variety of purposes, and with a wide variety of audiences (IRA & NCTE, 1996). We sought to design an instructional framework that simultaneously supports children's progress toward each of these goals.

Integrated writing/science instruction should also facilitate authentic and useful interactions between the two disciplines (Boix Mansilla, et al., 2000). The literature review that follows highlights the points of commonality and divergence between literacy and science education. We drew upon this literature to identify how the practices and goals of each discipline might facilitate the practices and goals of the other. For instance, the act of writing supports scientific learning while the act of learning science provides an authentic reason for learning to write. We attempt to design a writing/science framework that facilitates the most useful interactions between doing science and writing about science.

INQUIRY SCIENCE INSTRUCTION

Inquiry science instruction is a central tenet of the *National Science Education Standards* and an organizing framework for effective science teaching (NRC, 1996). Inquiry-based instruction engages students in many of the same activities and thinking processes as professional scientists by emphasizing students' active exploration of scientific concepts rather than didactic learning of established science knowledge (NRC, 2000). Critical reasoning, problem solving, and broad scientific understanding, as opposed to mastering disconnected facts, are the goals of inquiry-oriented science instruction.

When students participate in inquiry science, they define questions, propose hypotheses, plan and conduct investigations, gather evidence through observations, explain their findings based on explanation of the evidence, consider alternative explanations, and communicate their explanations to others (NRC, 2000). Through this learning cycle, children integrate process skills such as observation and experimentation with their scientific knowledge and reasoning. For example, students might decide to investigate earthworm habitats. They would hypothesize, based on their current knowledge, the types of habitats that earthworms might prefer and then design several habitats to test their hypotheses. Using observation, they would gather evidence to build a case for their explanation of earthworm "preferences." Throughout the investigation, they would consider and test alternative explanations and communicate those explanations both orally and in writing. Thus, inquiry allows children to learn science concepts while they also evaluate knowledge, construct scientifically based explanations, and communicate scientifically.

The teacher's role in inquiry science is to guide and facilitate learning (NRC, 2000). Rather than provide answers or tell students how to conduct their investigations, teachers provide materials, model science processes, ask questions to guide students' explorations, and raise issues to further students' thinking. For example, if students want to test a hypothesis, the teacher might guide a discussion about how to design a "fair" test. She might also ask leading questions, such as *What would happen if...*, in order to help students consider alternative possibilities.

WRITING-TO-LEARN SCIENCE

Writing-to-learn research within science education is grounded primarily in cognitive theories of writing (Wallace, et al., 2004). These theories posit that writers clarify, elaborate, and transform their understandings as they shape their compositions for specific rhetorical purposes (Klein, 1999). During writing, authors retrieve information about a topic from long-term memory and reorganize it to fit their communicative goals (Flower & Hayes, 1981). Organizing the information in a new way leads writers to see previously unnoticed connections between ideas, which facilitates their deeper conceptual understanding of the topic.

One particularly influential theory of writing-to-learn within science education is Bereiter and Scardamalia's (1987) *knowledge telling* and *knowledge transforming* models of writing. Knowledge telling occurs when writers retrieve their knowledge of a topic from memory and simply transfer that knowledge to paper. The author writes what she already knows and bypasses the reorganizing processes that facilitate learning. In contrast, writers engage in knowledge transforming writing by actively reworking their ideas as they write. This occurs when the writer simultaneously considers both the content of the text and how that content is communicated. As authors generate content, they clarify meaning through the language they use, while, at the same time, communicating that content through language facilitates their reflection on its meaning (Keys, 1999). Through the dialectical interaction between content and the language used to express it, flaws in the writer's thinking become apparent, are resolved, and learning occurs.

Drawing on these writing-to-learn theories, science educators argue that knowledge transforming writing can promote children's understanding of science concepts (Prain & Hand, 1996). Studies of writing during science indicate that writing can improve students' recall of science facts and understanding of scientific concepts (Gunel, Hand, & Prain, 2007; Mason & Boscolo, 2000) and promote their understanding of scientific questions, claims, and evidence (Wallace, et al., 2004). This work indicates that writing about science in everyday language, re-wording scientific ideas for different audiences (peers, parents, younger children), and writing in a variety of forms (letters, journals, explanations) enhances science learning. However, this research has been conducted exclusively with upper elementary and secondary students, so it is not clear if writing-to-learn impacts primary children's science learning in the same ways.

One type of knowledge transforming writing is science notebooks. Students use their science notebooks, much as professional scientists do (Yore, Hand, & Florence, 2004), to record their questions, observations, and reflections as they engage in scientific inquiry. Klentschy (2005), a leading proponent of science notebooks in elementary classrooms, proposes six notebook components that parallel the inquiry process: (1) the questions, problems, and purposes that guide the investigation, (2) predictions about what will occur, (3) a plan for how to conduct the investigation, (4) observations, data, and claims based on evidence collected, (5) an explanation of what the student learned, and (6) next steps and new questions. Within the context of these components, notebook writing takes many forms, including labels, sentences, drawings, tables, charts, and graphs (Klentschy & Molina-De La Torre, 2004).

Research on science notebooks in primary grades demonstrates that children tend to write about their lived experiences rather than scientific explanations. Students often write "narrative recounts" (Reddy, Jacobs, McCrohon, & Herrenkohl, 1998, p. 95) in their notebooks that describe the process of conducting the science investigation—the procedures they followed, the results they observed, and the social interactions that occurred among their group members (Mason & Boscolo, 2000). Young children may even include "imaginary worlds" in their notebooks, such as representing a classroom science activity involving sand and water by drawing a duck on a beach (Shepardson & Britsch, 2001). With instruction and practice, however, children begin to transition their science notebook writing from narrative to more argumentative forms (Mason & Boscolo, 2000). These argumentative forms are important because they mimic the process through which scientists generate scientific facts. The development of arguments rooted in claims and evidence is a key component of helping students experience science as a way of knowing the world.

Although science notebooks are considered a knowledge transforming writing task (Klentschy & Molina-De La Torre, 2004), students' narratives about their inquiry experience may be instances of knowledge telling (Mason & Boscolo, 2000). However, Shepardson and Britsch (2001) contend that recontextualizing scientific concepts through writing about imaginary or lived experiences may help children construct science understandings by linking new concepts to their prior knowledge. Unfortunately, it is not clear whether narrative writing in the science notebook facilitates children's learning of science concepts. More research is needed to examine how different types of notebook writing facilitate learning, which writing tasks best prompt students to transform their knowledge, and the learning benefits, if any, of scaffolding students toward writing scientific explanations.

PROCESS WRITING INSTRUCTION

Over the past 30 years, process writing instruction has emerged as an influential paradigm for teaching writing, particularly in elementary classrooms (Boscolo, 2008). Although teachers implement process writing instruction in different ways (Lipson, Mosenthal, Daniels, & Woodside-Jiron, 2000), several key features characterize this approach: prewriting, drafting, and revision activities; student-selected rather than teacher-assigned writing topics; writing for authentic purposes and audiences; and, more recently, using professionally authored texts as models for writing. While early process writing approaches deemphasized teacher instruction (Pritchard & Honeycutt, 2006), contemporary pedagogy includes the direct teaching of writing strategies (Calkins, 1994; Harris & Graham, 1996).

The defining feature of process writing instruction is its focus on the composing process and the recursive activities of prewriting, drafting, and revision. Prewriting instruction can involve a wide-ranging set of activities such as brainstorming, freewriting, concept mapping, and outlining (Graham & Harris, 2007). Alternatively, Calkins (1994) suggests children write in a "writer's notebook" (p. 24), a prewriting strategy used by some professional authors. Students record their thoughts, experiences, ideas, and observations in their notebooks and then develop those entries into drafts. Once children have drafted a piece, process writing instruction focuses on revision strategies, including having students evaluate their writing according to specific criteria (Hillocks, 1986) and peer revision in which students read others' drafts, note points of ambiguity, ask the author for clarification, and discuss how to revise the writing to make it more clear (Boscolo & Ascorti, 2004).

Process writing instruction also emphasizes that students write about self-selected topics, for audiences other than the teacher, and for purposes other than school. Students choose their own writing topics so they can write about personally meaningful subjects. They also write for "real life" audiences and purposes, such as a visitors' guide for classroom guests, letters to local advocacy groups, reports for the school newspaper, and narratives, poems, and nonfiction to share with friends and families (Calkins, 1994). Writing about self-selected topics for authentic audiences and purposes motivates children to deeply engage in writing and gives them control over the writing process. However, students sometimes struggle to identify personally meaningful topics and to generate the richness of content required to write about those topics in deeply meaningful ways (Overmeyer, 2005).

Process writing teachers often also use published texts, such as children's trade books, to teach the craft of writing (Calkins, 1994; Ray, 1999). Using a guided inquiry approach, they help children discover how professional authors structure their texts and use specific language strategies. For example, the teacher might read a text aloud and ask students to listen for examples of imagery. The class then discusses how the author created these "pictures" in the minds of readers, and students use those same strategies to create imagery in their own writing. Although this approach, like traditional writing instruction, uses model texts, students learn strategies for structuring text and language rather than imitating published authors' writing.

Process writing instruction in primary classrooms must address the unique challenges faced by young writers: learning conventions of print such as capitalization and punctuation, understanding how the alphabet represents speech sounds, learning about genres, and gaining skills, such as letter formation, needed to express their ideas fluently (Coker, 2007). Interactive writing (McCarrier, Pinnell, & Fountas, 1999), designed to help young children understand the writing process, provides a framework for teaching these emergent writing skills. In interactive writing, students and the teacher collaboratively compose a text, usually on chart paper positioned at the front of the classroom. The teacher models how to write and thinks aloud about her writing processes, and she invites children to add to the text as they are able. Through interactive writing, teachers explain and demonstrate writing strategies and conventions and scaffold students' understanding of how to write.

GENRE THEORY AND WRITING SCIENTIFIC GENRES

Genre theorists describe genres as typical forms of expression that have evolved through social action (Bakhtin, 1986). Genres, in this view, are social and functional in nature (Halliday & Hasan, 1989) because people communicate using specific forms that accomplish specific purposes in specific social settings. Distinctive genres arise in the various disciplines, within social and cultural groups, and among communities of practice, and these genres signal the community's norms, epistemology, and ideology (Berkenkotter & Huckin, 1993). Thus, genres can be conceptualized as culturally formed and culturally acceptable ways of speaking, writing, and thinking.

If genres embody the ways of thinking valued by a community of practice, then learning to write science can be understood as learning to think like a scientist (Morson & Emerson, 1990). Genre theorists contend that students should receive explicit instruction in the features of various genres and how to write them (Kress, 1999). They argue that academic genres, such as scientific writing, differ from those children learn in their homes and communities. This is particularly true for students from marginalized cultures whose home discourses differ markedly from the ones privileged in schools (Heath, 1983). To not explicitly teach genres disadvantages these students by blocking their access to the forms of communication and ways of thinking valued by the academic community (Delpit, 1988).

Despite genre theorists' compelling argument for genre instruction, Purcell-Gates, Duke, and Martineau (2007) found that explicitly teaching science genre features did not correlate with improved science writing for second- and third-graders except for second-grade procedural writing. Notably, writing for real purposes and audiences did correlate, for both grades, with improved informational and procedural texts. The authors suggest that the interaction between authentic writing and genre instruction, rather than genre instruction itself, may have explained second-graders' improved procedural writing.

Teaching scientific genres has stirred considerable debate among science educators. Because conventional genres are associated with knowledge telling tasks in which students write about established scientific concepts without linking them to the processes and data that generated them (Holliday, Yore, & Alvermann, 1994), traditional genres are often viewed as incompatible with inquiry-oriented instruction (Shymansky, Yore, & Good, 1991). In addition, some science educators criticize science genres as hegemonic and exclusionary. Hildebrand (1998), for example, argues that traditional science texts "construct science as masculine" (p. 348) and promote sexist and authoritarian conceptions of science. Others (Halliday & Martin, 1993; Keys, 1999), however, contend that scientific genres have arisen to encompass the purposes of the discipline and accommodate its unique communicative needs. These genres, then, make the enterprise of science possible and should be taught to students because they provide entry into the scientific community, its ways of thinking, and the discourses it uses.

In addition to providing access to scientific discourse, teaching conventional genres during inquiry instruction may also promote students' ownership of their scientific ideas (Keys, 1999). Because the unique features of science writing require students to explicate relationships between problems, observations, data as evidence, and knowledge claims, ideas that begin as speculation during inquiry must be transformed into complete, reasoned, and warranted arguments during writing.

WRITING SCIENCE/SCIENCE WRITING FRAMEWORK

While we are not the first scholars to attempt to integrate different perspectives on writing and science (Powell & Aram, 2008; Varelas & Pappas, 2006), our framework extends previous work by: (1) explicitly grounding the framework in the theoretical and research literature, (2) examining points of ambiguity and tension, (3) suggesting how teachers might facilitate each aspect of instruction, and (4) articulating how the framework accomplishes the purposes of both science and writing instruction. While it is embedded within the context of inquiry science instruction, we do not describe how students engage in inquiry because examples of the inquiry model are available elsewhere (Heuser, 2005; NRC, 2000). Instead, our framework highlights the two writing tasks in which students participate: science notebook writing and writing for authentic purposes and audiences.

Science Notebook Writing

Science notebook writing serves several purposes in the framework. First, it functions as a tool for learning science concepts. While evidence for the efficacy of writing-to-learn science generally (Gunel, et al., 2007) and science notebooks in particular (Vanosdall, Klentschy, Hedges, & Weisbaum, April, 2007) comes from upper grades, Klentschy (2008) suggests that notebook writing should support primary children's science learning as well. Although more research is needed into the forms of notebook writing that best facilitate young children's meaning construction, we contend that encouraging students to use self-selected combinations of writing and drawing may help them represent their understandings in personally meaningful ways (Shepardson & Britsch, 2001), thereby promoting learning.

Science notebooks are tools for learning, but notebook writing is also its own specialized genre. Though informal, its structure represents a particular way of thinking about scientific inquiry and science phenomena. Klentschy's (2005) notebook components, for example, require students to organize their thinking, via their writing, around the inquiry process and notions of data, claims, and evidence. Conceptualizing science notebooks as a genre of writing leads us to conclude that teachers should instruct young children in how to write in their notebooks. While empirical work has not demonstrated the efficacy of teaching science genres, we agree with genre theorists that explicit instruction may enhance students' abilities to write and think scientifically. Research also demonstrates that implementing science notebooks without teaching students how to use them will not result in science learning (Shepardson & Britsch, 2000). This finding further strengthens our belief in the value of teaching notebook writing.

Although there is no empirical evidence about how to best teach science notebook writing, Nesbit and colleagues (Nesbit, Hargrove, Harrelson, & Maxey, 2001) found interactive writing (McCarrier, et al., 1999) effective with primary grade children. The teacher introduced the notebook by reading a trade book about how scientists conduct their work. Students then participated in the inquiry process and together with the teacher recorded questions, predictions, observations, and explanations in a large, shared science notebook. As students became proficient at notebook writing, the teacher transitioned from whole class to individual notebooks. While this method of teaching notebook writing has not been empirically tested, we believe it may prove useful with primary children because it allows teachers to model emergent writing skills and explicitly demonstrate how to think and write scientifically.

As students mature, they need to move toward ever more sophisticated forms of scientific reasoning and writing in their notebooks. We propose that the narrative recounts primary children tend to write embody their scientific observations and should be viewed as an emergent form of collecting evidence. At the same time, because genre theory suggests that learning new ways of writing facilitates new ways of thinking, we propose teachers demonstrate and encourage increasingly scientific forms of notebook writing. For example, teachers can model how to give priority to evidence when writing the results of investigations and encourage students to record claims and evidence. Over time children may appropriate these new ways of writing into their notebooks (Mason & Boscolo, 2000; Wollman-Bonilla, 2000).

Science notebooks are learning tools within the inquiry process, but they are also prewriting tools within the writing process. We agree with Calkins (1994) that meaningful writing begins with "a state of readiness out of which one writes" (p. 24) rather than simply listing topics or brainstorming ideas. Like writer's notebooks, science notebooks offer a rich opportunity for children to ready themselves to write by providing fertile ground for idea generation. The ideas in the notebooks are inherently meaningful because students constructed them through hands-on experience. Science notebooks, then, address two challenges children face when writing: identifying a meaningful topic and generating rich ideas to put in their drafts.

Writing For Authentic Purposes and Audiences

Once students have generated ideas in their science notebooks, they begin to consider audiences and purposes for writing. Teachers support this process by asking children who might want to know about their inquiry (Powell & Aram, 2008), such as parents interested in what the class has learned or other children interested in the topic. Although more empirical evidence is needed from primary classrooms, writing for authentic audiences and purposes likely improves students' understanding of science concepts (Wallace, et al., 2004), motivates them to write and revise (Calkins, 1994), and possibly improves the quality of their science texts (Purcell-Gates, et al., 2007). We propose students write for a variety of audiences and purposes because this may give them a deeper understanding of the science content they are communicating (Gunel, et al., 2007) and teach them to communicate effectively with a variety of audiences for a variety of purposes (IRA & NCTE, 1996). For example, students might write a newsletter for their families about the science concepts they investigated, design informational books to share with other classes, or create field guides that other students can use to understand and explore scientific phenomena.

As students begin to draft their compositions, they will need to make decisions about content and structure. They may need to generate more content about the topic, which provides a valuable opportunity for them to extend their thinking through continued hands-on exploration of science concepts. At the same time, they must consider how to structure their texts. Process writing teachers suggest students examine published children's books to discover structures for their own writing (Ray, 1999). While we predict that science trade books may be useful models for children, we also recognize that the majority of these books present scientific "facts" and explanations (Ford, 2004) rather than structuring an argument around claims and evidence as scientists do (Keys, 1999). Of course, scientists also write explanations and facts, experimental procedures, essays, and descriptions of science phenomena (Yore, et al., 2004), and we contend children should also write in these forms and that trade books might be valuable models. However, if trade books serve as the *only* model of science writing, important scientific genres such as argumentation may never be taught in primary classrooms.

Successfully guiding students' decisions about audience, purpose, and genre for writing requires teachers to be clear about the goals of children's writing experiences. For example, writing a fictional story that includes science facts does not teach students to write in genres valued by the scientific community. While it may reinforce students' understanding of science facts, we contend that the features of more conventional science genres—logical presentation, linear organization, and explicit connections between concepts (Keys, 1999, p. 122)—facilitate deeper science learning than writing narratives. Writing stories, then, does not accomplish science education goals. However, narrative writing does accomplish goals valued by language arts teachers, and there may be benefits to having children write such stories. Because it may not be immediately clear the goals a particular writing task addresses, we encourage teachers to carefully assess the writing they assign to determine the goals it accomplishes.

Although the goals of writing within science education and literacy education are, at times, different, we do not view them as competing or believe teachers must choose one over the other. We assert that primary grade teachers can accomplish multiple goals by encouraging students to write about the same science concepts in both scientific and literary genres. Students may, for instance, write a report about their scientific inquiry and then write a poem that includes the concepts they learned through that inquiry. Writing the same content in multiple forms may facilitate science learning (Wallace, et al., 2004). It also allows children to examine how different communities of practice write for different purposes and why they value different genres.

Writing about meaningful content for authentic purposes and audiences provides motivation for children to revise their drafts (Calkins, 1994). Revision potentially serves several important purposes in the writing/science process. First, it creates another writing-to-learn opportunity because revisiting the original text allows students to reexamine and clarify the science concepts they included. In addition, children may learn revision strategies, how to communicate more effectively with their audience, and how to advance their texts toward their rhetorical goals. Teachers can support children's revision through peer feedback and providing criteria for evaluating and revising drafts (MacArthur, 2007), though only a few studies have demonstrated these strategies may be effective with primary grade children (Dauite & Dalton, 1993; Jasmine & Weiner, 2007; Sadoski, Willson, & Norton, 1997). More research is needed into how to guide young children as they revise their science writing.

AREAS FOR FUTURE RESEARCH

Although we have grounded our writing/science framework in the literature of science and literacy education, it is limited by the lack of empirical work in some areas. For example, it is currently unclear how different types of science notebook writing facilitate primary students' learning or if some writing tasks prompt learning better than others. As a result, we are uncertain the forms of writing teachers should encourage students to use in their notebooks. More research is needed on how primary children write in their science notebooks during inquiry and exactly what learning this writing facilitates.

It is also unclear how children's science writing evolves from emergent forms to more conventional scientific genres. While we do not hold to a developmental view of learning to write, it has become apparent in our work that kindergarten, first-, and second-grade children write science differently than older students. We grapple with the question, "What should we expect primary children to write in their science notebooks and in their final drafts?" A clearer understanding of how children grow as science writers would help us know how to scaffold them toward more sophisticated forms of scientific writing.

Another area that needs more research is how to best teach the unique features of science genres. While we propose in our framework that teachers explicitly teach science notebook writing, we based this suggestion on the theoretical literature because the empirical evidence is inconclusive. Given that the content of science and the genres used to communicate it are inextricably linked (Halliday & Martin, 1993), we suspect that teaching science genres will require simultaneously addressing the features of science writing and science content if children are to learn more than the surface features of science texts. We predict that interactive writing may prove useful for teaching primary students how to write scientifically, but this hypothesis must be empirically tested. Science trade books may also serve as useful models of science writing, but because children's authors tend to structure their texts differently than scientists, we need a better understanding of how these books impact students' understandings of scientific genres. However, we know of no studies that have examined the effects of trade books on children's science writing.

Our framework would also benefit from a better explanation of how writing for authentic audiences and purposes improves students' science learning, their writing skills, and their science texts. Our suggestion that primary students write for authentic audiences and a variety of purposes is based on research with upper elementary and secondary students, but it is unclear how audience and purpose affect primary children's science learning. While there is some evidence that writing for authentic audiences improves young children's informational and procedural texts (Purcell-Gates, et al., 2007), we need a better understanding of how this occurs and how teachers can structure authentic writing tasks.

Finally, we would like to see more research into how to help young children revise their science texts. Writing research indicates that providing criteria for evaluating and revising drafts improves students' writing (MacArthur, 2007), but this revision strategy has not been investigated with primary children writing science texts. Sutherland et al. (Sutherland, McNeill, Krajcik, & Colson, 2006) suggest that scientific explanations be evaluated for the strength of their claims, evidence, and reasoning. For example, a claim should provide an accurate and complete response to the question asked or problem posed, evidence should appropriately and sufficiently support the claim, and the reasoning should link claims and evidence through appropriate scientific principles. However, it is not clear if having young children revise their science texts according to these criteria will improve their scientific reasoning or their science writing.

CONCLUSION

Too often, in our experience, science instruction in primary classrooms is displaced by literacy instruction or co-opted as a platform to teach literacy skills with little attention to science learning. This deprives students not only of the opportunity to learn scientific concepts and ways of thinking but, ironically, also thwarts the literacy education goal of teaching nonfiction genres because authentic science writing cannot occur apart from the enterprise of doing science. At the same time, authentic scientific inquiry cannot occur without writing as a part of the process. This interdependence between doing science and writing science leads us to view integrated writing/science instruction as more than a good idea; it is critical to accomplishing the goals of both science education and literacy education.

Integrating writing and science instruction allows the strengths of each discipline to fill the gaps left by the other. Inquiry science instruction utilizes science notebooks to facilitate scientific learning and thinking, but it does not, particularly in the primary grades, attend to how students learn the rhetorical skills needed to effectively communicate scientific concepts to different audiences. Writing instruction fills this gap by offering a process model for teaching students to write. However, process writing and genre instruction do not adequately address the role of students' scientific knowledge in composing science texts. Inquiry science instruction provides a way for children to generate rich, personally meaningful understandings of scientific concepts that can form the basis of their science writing. In bringing together science and writing instruction, then, both are strengthened.

Our goal in this paper was to develop a framework of integrated writing/science that maintains the purposes of both writing and science instruction. While our framework accomplishes this, it does more than maintain the learning opportunities afforded by inquiry science and process writing. It extends them. Students write-to-learn science concepts as they use their science notebooks during inquiry, but drafting and revising texts to communicate scientific ideas to various audiences extends the opportunity to learn science content. Although other models engage students in communicating their science learning to outside audiences (Wallace, et al., 2004), we contend that specific instruction in structuring and revising science texts will promote science learning beyond simply writing for audiences without attention to rhetorical effectiveness. At the same time, science notebooks, generally absent from instruction in writing science genres, extend the writing process to include the meaningful generation of scientific ideas. Without science notebook writing, students have less opportunity to come to understand science in ways that allow them to write effective science texts. Thus, neither science instruction nor writing instruction alone can accomplish their goals as effectively without the other. One without the other simply isn't as good as both together.

REFERENCES

Bakhtin, M. M. (1986). The problem of speech genres. In *Speech genres and other late essays* (pp. 60-102). Austin, TX: University of Texas Press.

Bangert-Drowns, R. L., Hurley, M. M., & Wilkinson, B. (2004). The effects of school-based writing-to-learn interventions on academic achievement: A meta-analysis. *Review of Educational Research, 74*, 29-58.

Bereiter, C., & Scardamalia, M. (1987). *The psychology of written composition*. Hillsdale, NJ: Erlbaum.

Berkenkotter, C., & Huckin, T. N. (1993). Rethinking genre from a sociocognitive perspective. *Written Communication, 10*, 475-509.

Boix Mansilla, B. V., Miller, W., & Gardner, H. (2000). On disciplinary lenses and interdisciplinary work. In S. S. Wineburg & P. L. Grossman (Eds.), *Interdisciplinary curriculum: Challenges to implementation* (pp. 17-38). New York, NY: Teachers College Press.

Boscolo, P. (2008). Writing in primary school. In C. Bazerman (Ed.), *Handbook of research on writing: History, society, school, individual, text* (pp. 293-309). New York, NY: Lawrence Erlbaum.

Boscolo, P., & Ascorti, K. (2004). Effects of collaborative revision on children's ability to write understandable narratives. In L. Allal, L. Chanquoy & P. Largy (Eds.), *Revision: Cognitive and instructional processes* (Vol. 13, pp. 157-170). Boston, MA: Kluwer.

Calkins, L. M. (1994). *The art of teaching writing*. Portsmouth, NH: Heinemann.

Coker, D. (2007). Writing instruction for young children: Methods targeting the multiple demands that writers face. In S. Graham, C. MacArthur & J. Fitzgerald (Eds.), *Best practices in writing instruction* (pp. 101-118). New York, NY: Guilford Press.

Dauite, C., & Dalton, B. (1993). Collaboration between children learning to write: Can novices be masters? *Cognition and Instruction, 10*, 281-333.

Delpit, L. (1988). The silenced dialogue: Power and pedagogy in educating other people's children. *Harvard Educational Review, 58*, 280-298.

Flower, L. S., & Hayes, J. R. (1981). A cognitive process theory of writing. *College Composition and Communication, 32*, 365-387.

Ford, D. (2004). Highly recommended trade books: Can they be used in inquiry science? In E. W. Saul (Ed.), *Crossing borders in literacy and science instruction: Perspectives on theory and practice*. Newark, DE: International Reading Association.

Graham, S., & Harris, K. R. (2007). Best practices in teaching planning. In S. Graham, C. A. MacArthur & J. Fitzgerald (Eds.), *Best practices in writing instruction*. New York, NY: Guilford Press.

Gunel, M., Hand, B., & Prain, V. (2007). Writing for learning in science: A secondary analysis of six studies. *International Journal of Science and Mathematics Education, 5*(4), 615-637.

Halliday, M. A. K., & Hasan, R. (1989). *Language, context, and text: Aspects of language in a social-semiotic perspective*. Oxford, UK: Oxford University Press.

Halliday, M. A. K., & Martin, J. R. (1993). *Writing science: Literacy and discursive power*. Pittsburgh, PA: University of Pittsburgh Press.

Harris, K. R., & Graham, S. (1996). *Making the writing process work: Strategies for composition and self-regulation*. Brookline, MA: Brookline Books.

Heath, S. B. (1983). *Ways with words: Language, life, and work in communities and classrooms*. Cambridge, MA: Cambridge University Press.

Heuser, D. (2005). Inquiry, science workshop style. *Science and Children, 43*(2), 32-36.

Hildebrand, G. M. (1998). Disrupting hegemonic writing practices in school science: Contesting the right way to write. *Journal of Research in Science Teaching, 35*, 345-362.

Hillocks, G. (1986). *Research on written composition: New directions for teaching*. Urbana, IL: ERIC Clearinghouse on Reading and Communication Skills and National Conference on Research in English.

Holliday, W. G., Yore, L. D., & Alvermann, D. E. (1994). The reading-science learning-writing connection: Breakthroughs, barriers, and promises. *Journal of Research in Science Teaching, 31*, 877-893.

International Reading Association, & National Council of Teachers of English (IRA & NCTE). (1996). *Standards for the English Language Arts*. Urbana, IL: National Council of Teachers of English. Retrieved from http://www.ncte.org/standards

Jasmine, J., & Weiner, W. (2007). The effects of writing workshop on abilities of first grade students to become confident and independent writers. *Early Childhood Education Journal, 35*, 131-139. doi: 10.1007/s10643-007-0186-3

Keys, C. W. (1999). Revitalizing instruction in scientific genres: Connecting knowledge production with writing to learn science. *Science Education, 83*(2), 115-130.

Klein, P. D. (1999). Reopening inquiry into cognitive processes in writing-to-learn. *Educational Psychology Review, 11*, 203-270.

Klentschy, M. P. (2005). Science notebook essentials: A guide to effective notebook components. *Science and Children, 43*(3), 24-27.

Klentschy, M. P. (2008). *Using science notebooks in elementary classrooms*. Arlington, VA: National Science Teacher Association Press.

Klentschy, M. P., & Molina-De La Torre, E. (2004). Students' science notebooks and the inquiry process. In E. W. Saul (Ed.), *Crossing borders in literacy and science instruction: Perspectives on theory and practice* (pp. 340-354). Newark, DE: International Reading Association.

Kress, G. (1999). Genre and the changing contexts for English language arts. *Language Arts, 76*, 461-469.

Lipson, M. Y., Mosenthal, J., Daniels, P., & Woodside-Jiron, H. (2000). Process writing in the classrooms of eleven fifth-grade teachers with different orientations to teaching and learning. *Elementary School Journal, 101*, 209-231.

MacArthur, C. (2007). Best practices in teaching evaluation and revision. In S. Graham, C. MacArthur & J. Fitzgerald (Eds.), *Best practices in writing instruction*. New York, NY: Guilford.

Mason, L., & Boscolo, P. (2000). Writing and conceptual change. What changes? *Instructional Science, 28*, 199-226.

McCarrier, A., Pinnell, G. S., & Fountas, I. C. (1999). *Interactive writing: How language and literacy come together, K-2*. Portsmouth, NH: Heinemann.

Morson, G. S., & Emerson, C. (1990). *Mikhail Bakhtin: Creation of a prosaics*. Stanford, CA: Stanford University Press.

National Research Council (NRC). (2000). *Inquiry and the national science education standards: A guide for teaching and learning*. Washington, D.C.: National Academy Press. Retrieved from http://www.nap.edu/openbook.php?isbn=0309064767

National Research Council (NRC). (1996). *National science education standards*. Washington, D.C.: National Academies Press. Retrieved from http://www.nap.edu/openbook.php?record_id=4962

Nesbit, C. R., Hargrove, T. Y., Harrelson, L., & Maxey, B. (2001). Implementing science notebooks in the primary grades. *Science Activities, 40*(4), 21-29.

Overmeyer, M. (2005). *When writing workshop isn't working: Answers to ten tough questions*. Portland, ME: Stenhouse.

Powell, D. A., & Aram, R. J. (2008). Children publish in science as a way of knowing. In V. L. Akerson (Ed.), *Interdisciplinary language arts and science instruction in elementary classrooms: Applying research to practice* (pp. 79-103). Mahwah, NJ: Lawrence Erlbaum.

Prain, V., & Hand, B. (1996). Writing for learning in secondary science: Rethinking practices. *Teaching and Teacher Education, 12*, 609-626.

Pritchard, R. J., & Honeycutt, R. L. (2006). The process approach to writing instruction: Examining its effectiveness. In C. A. MacArther, S. Graham, & J. Fitzgerald (Eds.), *Handbook of writing research* (pp. 275-290). New York, NY: Guildford Press.

Purcell-Gates, V., Duke, N. K., & Martineau, J. A. (2007). Learning to read and write genre-specific text: Roles of authentic experience and explicit teaching. *Reading Research Quarterly, 42*, 8-45. doi: 1J.1598/RRQ.42.1.1

Ray, K. W. (1999). *Wondrous words: Writers and writing in the elementary classroom*. Urbana, IL: National Council of Teachers of English.

Reddy, M., Jacobs, P., McCrohon, C., & Herrenkohl, L. R. (1998). *Creating scientific communities in the elementary classroom*. Portsmouth, NH: Heinemann.

Sadoski, M., Willson, V. L., & Norton, D. E. (1997). The relative contributions of research-based composition activities to writing improvement in the lower and middle grades. *Research in the Teaching of English, 31*, 120-150.

Saul, E. W. (Ed.). (2004). *Crossing borders in literacy and science instruction: Perspectives on theory and practice.* Newark, DE: International Reading Association.

Shepardson, D. P., & Britsch, S. J. (2000). Analyzing children's science journals. *Science and Children, 38*(3), 29-33.

Shepardson, D. P., & Britsch, S. J. (2001). The role of children's journals in elementary school science activities. *Journal of Research in Science Teaching, 38*, 43-69.

Shymansky, J. A., Yore, L. D., & Good, R. (1991). Elementary school teachers' beliefs about and perceptions of elementary school science, science reading, science textbooks, and supportive instructional factors. *Journal of Research in Science Teaching, 28*, 437-454.

Sutherland, L. M., McNeill, K. L., Krajcik, J. S., & Colson, K. (2006). Supporting middle school students in developing scientific explanations. In R. Douglas, M. P. Klentschy, K. Worth & W. Binder (Eds.), *Linking science and literacy in the K-8 classroom* (pp. 163-181). Arlington, VA: National Science Teachers Association Press.

Vanosdall, R., Klentschy, M. P., Hedges, L. V., & Weisbaum, K. S. (April, 2007). *A randomized study of the effects of scaffolded guided-inquiry instruction on student achievement in science.* Paper presented at the Annual Meeting of the American Educational Research Association, Chicago, IL. Retrieved from http://www.nsrconline.org/pdf/Klentschy_07.pdf

Varelas, M., & Pappas, C. C. (2006). Young children's own illustrated information books: Making sense in science through words and pictures. In R. Douglas, M. P. Klentschy, K. Worth & W. Binder (Eds.), *Linking science and literacy in the K-8 classroom* (pp. 95-125). Alexandria, VA: National Science Teachers Association Press.

Wallace, C. S., Hand, B., & Prain, V. (2004). *Writing and learning in the science classroom.* Boston, MA: Kluwer.

Wollman-Bonilla, J. E. (2000). Teaching science writing to first graders: Genre learning and recontextualization. *Research in the Teaching of English, 35*, 35-65.

Worth, K. (2006). Introduction. In R. Douglas, M. P. Klentschy, K. Worth & W. Binder (Eds.), *Linking science and literacy in the K-8 classroom* (pp. xi-xv). Arlington, VA: National Science Teachers Association Press.

Yore, L. D., Hand, B. M., & Florence, M. K. (2004). Scientists' views of science, models of writing, and science writing practices. *Journal of Research in Science Teaching, 41*, 338-369. doi: 10.1002/tea.20008.

Exploring Two Content Area Teachers' Creativity and Use of Multiliteracies in Science and History

Jennifer J. Wimmer
Brigham Young University

Nancy T. Walker
University of La Verne

Thomas W. Bean
University of Nevada, Las Vegas

Adolescents "live in an increasingly multisensory world" (Semali & Fueyo, 2001, n.p.). They interact with multiple forms of communications media both in and out of school (O'Brien, 2006; Semali & Fueyo, 2001). While some adolescents may feel they have to "power off" their out of school literacies as they enter their classrooms, current research on multiliteracies demonstrates the possibilities for enhanced classroom learning (Kist, 2002, 2005, 2010). Out of school literacies often include what O'Brien (2006, p. 44) calls "multimediating"—denoting practices that involve semiotic designs typical of adolescents' video productions for YouTube audiences. These creative activities come into play in classrooms where teachers acknowledge students' out of school competencies. Students in multiliteracies classrooms are provided with opportunities to bring their out-of-school literacies into the classroom when presented with opportunities to collaborate, use technology, create, and explore their worlds in multiple forms. Multiliteracies encompasses those social practices used to understand, interpret, and create texts in print and non-print forms including multimedia, the Internet, and other non-print media (Bean, 2010).

Three theoretical lenses informed this research including: multiliteracies, discipline-based metadiscursive literacy, and creativity. We relied on the work of Lankshear and Knobel (2006) in defining multiliteracies as both paradigmatically and ontologically new. Therefore, we believe that literacy is a social practice and that multiliteracies involve technological advances as well as new ways of thinking about literacy. The latter part of the definition is particularly important in content area classrooms because of the long held view that content and literacy are separate entities. However, literacy scholars have begun to acknowledge that simply overlaying literacy strategies on content is not effective (Moje, 2008; Shanahan & Shanahan, 2008). In a recent article Elizabeth Moje (2008) argued that the important question that has not been asked in regards to content area learning is "What does literacy instruction do for learning in the subject areas?" (p. 96) As a result of this question, Moje suggested that educators engage in discipline-based metadiscursive literacy. Therefore, literacy is not viewed as a detached set of skills that are imposed on the content rather, it becomes a question of what types of literacies are needed to navigate, negotiate, and create specific content. When teachers integrate discipline-based metadiscursive literacy in their content areas they invite their students to learn "different knowledge and ways of knowing, doing, believing, and communicating that are privileged to those areas" (p. 99). Additionally, Moje called for research that examines how new media and multiliteracies practices potentially deepen disciplinary literacy practices.

O'Brien's (2006) studies of struggling readers with significant competence in digital literacies suggested that these students often find themselves marginalized in classrooms that rely on traditional content area texts. Presented with opportunities to produce multimedia, these same students excelled at handling complex issues of semiotic design in video and other multimedia productions. In addition, they navigated real and virtual text worlds with apparent ease. O'Brien (2006, p. 44) noted that "Few of the literacy practices they master in multimediating are ever officially sanctioned in school as literate competence." In addition, even accomplished readers may find a chasm between their out of school literacy practices in digital domains and their in school relegation to reading and recounting information from static textbooks.

Technology, specifically the Internet, allows teachers to use multiple texts/resources to engage students in learning (McNabb, 2006). Indeed, the use of multiple print and non-print resources is a key principle in recent studies and policy documents related to adolescent literacy (e.g., Sturtevant, Boyd, Brozo, Hinchman, Moore, & Alvermann, 2006), as well as studies of teachers' use of multiple resources in content area classrooms (Walker & Bean, 2005; Walker, Bean, & Dillard, 2010). The use of multiple texts/resources in the classroom has the potential to impact teachers' pedagogy and student learning (Bean, Wimmer, & Dunkerly, 2009).

In addition to the research on multiliteracies and discipline-based metadiscursive literacy, research on teacher creativity offered another important but often neglected lens in studies of multiliteracies-supported school sites. Teacher creativity refers to the development of unusual or novel lessons and units likely to serve as a jumping off point for creative student multimodal productions (Bean, 2010). We utilized Sawyer's (2006) definition of creativity to distinguish "big C such as works that are significant works of genius" from "little c which involve daily activities" (p. 27). Classroom creativity falls within the little c realm and rests on the degree to which an activity, unit, or lesson is novel (e.g., responding to an event in history by creating a plaster mask that is decorated to capture human emotions attached to an event like the atomic bomb in Hiroshima). Theoretical work on semiotics and design issues in computer environments (Norman, 2004, van Leeuwen, 2005), along with studies of creativity (Beghetto, & Kaufman, 2007; Craft, 2001; Runco, 2007; Sawyer, 2006), suggested that these multiliteracies settings jog teachers away from past comfort zones into ill-structured domains where creativity can flourish. For example, the science teacher chronicled in this study commented in an early interview that the use of multiliteracies "gives me creative impulses...not just me but my students as well." He was referring to the design of lessons that would captivate and model persuasive and interesting learning opportunities for his students both in presentation of the content and the projects assigned.

In a high-stakes assessment era, teachers may feel pressured to put multiliteracies practices aside and focus on print-based student outcomes. Because the work of multiliteracies and studies of teacher creativity are relatively new and ever changing, further research is needed to document the experiences of teachers as they begin to move toward "newer 'digital media-centric' " (O'Brien, 2006, p. 29) practices. Therefore, the purpose of this descriptive qualitative multiple case study was to explore two content area teachers use of multiliteracies and creativity in secondary content classes.

THEORETICAL FRAMEWORK

Teachers in secondary classrooms are incorporating multiliteracies practices that engage students in concept learning beyond simply reading and being assessed on narrow text comprehension (Kist, 2005, 2010; Walker & Bean, 2005). William Kist conducted multiple case studies across the United States and Canada in an effort to capture the everyday practices of teachers who were integrating multiliteracies into their classrooms. Kist (2002; 2005; 2010) identified five characteristics of multiliteracies classrooms that we used as a guide in developing the two case study profiles of a middle school science teacher and a high school history teacher. Kist's (2002; 2005; 2010) five characteristics of multiliteracies classrooms included:

- Daily work in multiple forms of representation
- Explicit discussions of the merits of using various symbol systems
- Metadialogues by the teacher who models problem solving
- A mixture of individual and collaborative activities
- Engaging contexts where students achieve flow states

Theories of teacher creativity suggested that in ill-structured domains (e.g., the Internet), there was space to try out new lesson strategies and that old ways of teaching relevant to traditional texts may need substantial modification to engage adolescent learners (McNabb, 2006; Smith & Wilhelm, 2006). Often labeled as constructivist learning or inquiry-based learning (Smith & Wilhelm, 2006), these forms of lesson and unit construction challenged teachers to go beyond canned lesson structures and text-based material. When students find themselves immersed in learning where they must deal with fuzzy, ill-structured domains in order to solve problems or construct something new, flow states are common (Csikzentmihalyi, 1990; Smith & Wilhelm, 2006). Indeed, this feeling of complete absorption in a school or classroom-based activity is all too rare, but it mirrors students' sense of competence and flow when they are working on hobbies or interests outside the classroom (Smith & Wilhelm, 2002). While these studies have shown positive student outcomes, Beghetto and Plucker (2006) expressed concern with the marginalization of creativity in schools. They noted, "When teachers feel pressured to cover vast amounts of content, for the primary purpose of raising standardized test scores, it is not surprising when they adopt teacher-centered practices that leave little room for creativity" (p. 319).

In the present study, both teachers alluded to elements of teacher creativity in classroom settings. Yet few studies at this point have examined the intersection of multiliteracies in content area classrooms and teacher creativity, as well as its perceived influence on student learning. Creativity is generally viewed as an important ingredient in problem solving at the individual and collective societal levels (Sak, 2004). Teachers serve as role models in this process and create classroom climates that encourage diverse thinking, critique, and creative production. In a review of research on creativity in education, Craft (2001) noted that past research centered on individual creativity, but there is a need for socioculturally grounded studies aimed at understanding specific strategies that encourage creativity. Thus, in the present study, we paid attention to how teacher creativity in lesson design and instruction fostered students' engagement in content area classrooms.

William Kist's framework for multiliteracies (2002; 2005; 2010), along with theories of teacher creativity (Craft, 2001; Runco, 2007; Sak, 2004) guided our observations, interviews, artifact collection, and interpretations of the two case study teachers' efforts to integrate multiliteracies in their teaching.

METHODS

Participants

This qualitative multiple case study (Merriam, 2009) examined two experienced teachers' multiliteracies practices and creativity in their content area classrooms. Because of limited resources and extensive time needed to examine the use of multiliteracies in different sites, we limited our study to two experienced teachers so that we could explore their instruction over time.

Through purposeful sampling (Creswell, 2007) we selected two teachers based on their vast experience, use of multiple texts/resources, and innovative teaching strategies. In addition, these teachers were willing to participate in our study, allowed us to observe them in their classrooms, and reflected on their teaching through interviews. Based on Kist's five characteristics, these two teachers charted new territory through their creative use of technology and other multiliteracies practices.

The first participant, Kevin, was introduced to us through his participation in a state-funded grant that focused on content area literacy, multiliteracies, and content area literacy strategies (Bean, Wimmer, & Dunkerly, 2009). He is a Caucasian male who has been a physical science teacher at a high-needs middle school in Southern Nevada for the past eight years. Kevin used multiliteracies practices in an effort to make science content accessible and relevant for his students. Project-based activities were designed to encourage and support students' understanding of the content.

The second participant, Oliver, was introduced to us by a teacher in an earlier study (Walker & Bean, 2004) when we expressed interest in continuing our work with experienced teachers who had familiarity with technology in their content area classrooms. Oliver was a history teacher at a high school in Southern California who utilized a smart classroom and multimedia to engage students in a deep understanding of history.

In order to situate ourselves in the context of this research, we briefly describe our biographies as co-researchers on this project before describing the data sources and analysis.

Researchers

The first author is a Caucasian female doctoral student at a Southwest university. She taught elementary school for seven years and has since worked with upper elementary and middle school teachers in the area of content literacy for the past four years. Her research interests lie in the intersection of content area literacy, new literacies, and teacher education. The second author is a Caucasian female professor employed at a West Coast university. She taught middle school for eight years, and her current research interests include content area reading instruction and adolescent reading motivation. The third author is a Caucasian senior adolescent literacy scholar at a southwest university. His current research interests include content area literacy instruction and young adult literature.

Data Sources

Given our interest in understanding how and why content area teachers used multiliteracies and creativity in the classroom, we constructed a descriptive qualitative multiple case study to describe the use of these practices in the classroom setting. Studying the use of multiliteracies practices and creativity by teachers during their classroom instruction allowed us to capture this phenomenon as it occurred in context (Marshall & Rossman, 2010).

We drew on four data sources that included 10 observations, field notes, classroom artifacts, and five semi-structured interviews collected over a nine-month time period. While classroom observations focused on instruction, field notes were focused on capturing the interaction of students as well as informal conversations between the teachers and researchers. Classroom artifacts included photographs of bulletin boards, Web site links, simulation materials, and student products. Finally, semi-structured interviews focused on educational history, teaching beliefs, and purposes for using multiliteracies to enhance and promote creativity. During this time, we shared, questioned, and triangulated data with the teachers.

Analysis

Pattern analysis (Yin, 2009) was used to analyze and interpret our data sets. Pattern analysis involved reading and rereading the transcribed field notes and interview transcripts, which were organized in data binders along with artifacts and photographs. This was followed by several meetings of the three researchers to discuss the transcripts, which were cross-referenced with the artifacts and photographs for types of multiliteracies practices.

Tentative categories were identified reflecting teacher content knowledge, content area strategy instruction, multiple resources, and critical literacy. These categories were coded and followed by additional readings of the data which led to meta-themes (Merriam, 2009) including the use of multiple texts and resources, classrooms as spaces for curricular creativity, and perceived student benefits.

Trustworthiness of the data was assessed by triangulating information from the data collection methods (specifically classroom observations, field notes, artifacts, and semi-structured interviews) and from the perspective of different participants (the researchers and teacher participants). In addition, we further triangulated the data with member checks (Merriam, 2009) conducted with key quotes from our transcripts and artifacts. These quotes captured the beliefs and practices of both teachers and included their respective rationales for technology use, along with references to pedagogical practices (e.g., simulations, videos). At the conclusion of this process we wrote descriptive case studies of each teacher's incorporation of multiliteracies practices and creativity to answer our research questions: How do these two teachers implement multiliteracies in their respective content areas? And, how does creativity influence these content area teachers' practice?

TWO CASES

Based on data analysis, three predominant themes were identified including: (a) Use of multiple texts and resources, (b) Multiliteracies classrooms as a space for creativity, and (c) Perceived student benefits. In the following section these themes are further explained through examples from the two teachers.

Kevin

Use of multiple texts and resources. Kevin's greatest concern was the complexity of his physical science content. When teaching a unit on nuclear energy he stated, "The biggest concern is the age appropriateness of the material. Especially when they are looking at nuclear energy, the atom, I mean that can be some pretty heavy reading." While multiple textbooks were available, they did not meet all of the students' needs. Kevin noted, "Some of the texts that we have are all activity based but no content, and then the content ones can be a little bit higher level than what our students are reading at." As a result Kevin provided opportunities for students to interact with a variety of texts and resources. For example, in the nuclear energy unit students engaged in reading print-based texts and online texts, watching videos, creating drawings, and composing PowerPoint presentations. Kevin was also aware that the use of multiple texts and resources could potentially confuse the students when information was contradictory. Therefore, classroom discussions were a large part of the class period. Kevin engaged the students in critical literacy as he taught them to question the texts and to support their findings with multiple sources.

Multiliteracies classrooms as a space for creativity. Kevin constantly sought to find a balance between student needs and interests and the demands of state and district standards. While these standards served as the foundation of his lessons he also noted, "I'm looking at [creating lessons that promote] student generated critical thinking or process type things that will develop their creativity." Kevin used the vast amount of resources available to him to construct engaging lessons that included presentations on the Promethean Board and hands-on science activities. Additionally, Kevin collaborated with his science colleagues in the creation of lessons. Kevin noted that he enjoyed observing his colleagues and discovering "How they do their lessons and how they have their classes set up and how they do group work because those are things that can impact me as a teacher and my creativity." As a result Kevin's lessons provided opportunities for students to explore scientific labs, observe content related video clips, and engage in student-led discussions. Kevin also provided opportunities for students to nurture their little c creativity through assignments. Kevin noted, "[Technology] allows the students to be more creative especially when they get to do PowerPoints and presentations...." With the support of guidelines and expectations, students were free to draw upon the multiple texts and resources in completing assignments.

Perceived student benefits. For Kevin science was not about passing chapter tests or about the memorization of facts. Kevin stated "[Science] is about relating to the real world. It's not magic... it lends itself to exploration and inquiry." Kevin sought to instill in his students an understanding of problem solving, exploration, and inquiry. He hoped that through group work and discussion, lab activities, and technology integration that he could engage his students in science content. Kevin noted:

> You know, there's a lot of speculation in preparing students for the future. But I think the biggest thing that I would like them to do is realize that there is a future. They need to be prepared for it and that's going to be knowing the reality around them.

Kevin believed that multiliteracies provided his students with an opportunity to explore the world around them. He also believed that multiliteracies would assist him in making the curriculum relevant to the students' lives. Kevin commented:

> At this time, I really want to make things more relevant to the students. Students may not realize why they're learning besides they have to learn it for some test and once they do that, to hell with it. So, I really would like to make it more relevant to them so they could see how it's applied in their daily life and then that way they can utilize it anytime in the future. [I am thinking about] starting to talk to them about the science of food…talk about elements or components of that, talk about the energy that's in there. It would be a very effective way to teach these students not only a skill, because they can go home and cook for their family and be a contributing member of the family, but also making it very relevant to them because now they can understand that "Whoa, there is science in a lot of things especially what I'm eating and how I'm preparing" and things like that.

Oliver

Use of multiple texts and resources. As a historian by hobby, Oliver translated this passion into his teaching by bringing in multiple resources to supplement the core textbook. Oliver used the textbook as a starting place but created learning situations that encouraged students to go beyond the textbook. As he explained, "When you go beyond the textbook, students know they have some knowledge that not everyone else has. Knowledge is power." When Oliver began his teaching career, he infused primary source documents into his instruction. Currently, using technology as a platform, Oliver accessed historical documents from the Internet in a series of PowerPoint lectures for each unit of study. Oliver did not resist the textbook but acknowledged that bringing in multiple sources provided a rich discussion in the classroom and deeper comprehension of the content. Furthermore, using the Internet as a source introduced another layer of instruction into his history classes. Students had to understand how to locate information that was reliable. According to Oliver, "Part of history is that you are only as good as where you obtain the information. Where is the information? Where is your source? You need to have a good source." Additionally, Oliver argued:

> The textbook is really based on a number of sources and for the students to really understand what is going on they don't always get [the textbook]. I can add so much in class. We were looking at a map of Africa in 1914 and you can see all of the countries and I had a question, "Why are there two independent countries? The answer is not in the textbook." I challenged the students to go find the answer and then we have a discussion about some of the sources for the information. You can make more connections. When you do this they really understand and the icing on that cake and in April when they take the state tests and for any question they will have more information and it will be cemented in their minds and I know this because I have juniors who discuss things and they will say "Oh, you told us that two days ago."

Multiliteracies classrooms as a space for creativity. While Oliver acknowledged that standards guided his teaching, he valued the amount of curricular space that he had in his classroom. This space allowed him to be creative in his instructional design and allowed for the integration of multiple sources in his lessons. This translated into PowerPoint lectures that incorporated art, music, literature, and geography in his history curriculum. Students in Oliver's classroom experienced a large variety of text in different formats and different contexts. Oliver used group discussions, debates, simulations, and paired discussions to explore the various forms of text brought into the classroom. At the beginning of every unit, Oliver considered lesson design in terms of:

> How many things can I do with this? You can bring in music from the late 19th century. A lot of kids learn about impressionism in middle school but they don't learn about modern art. You can incorporate cubism and Picasso. You can integrate poetry. There are so many possibilities.

This interdisciplinary approach along with the ability to access text from multiple sources provided a rich space for creativity. In Oliver's words, "I think it is essential to be creative. You have to ask yourself how you will reach students. Unless you try something new and different, you won't reach them."

Perceived student benefits. The strong visual support integrated into Oliver's lesson design increased student engagement in his classroom. Students were interested in the content and their work highlighted the level of interest and engagement. PowerPoints that involved art, music, and literature within a historical context captured the interest of many students in his classroom. One student in particular, who was doing poorly in other classes, was earning a B in Oliver's class because she was engaged and getting involved in the learning process. Oliver utilized a blog to stimulate student interest in the topics and increase discussion outside of the classroom. Blogs allowed discussion to continue, to go beyond the classroom, and to engage those students who are hesitant about speaking in class.

DISCUSSION

These two teachers approached the use of multiliteracies from a principled practices perspective (Sturtevant et. al., 2006) based on their years of teaching experience and the belief that they were adding to students' cultural capital. Although we set out to explore content area teachers' use of multiliteracies and creativity, the experiences of these two teachers shed light on a still dominant structure, that of the conventional classroom attempting to move into the future. For example, students continued to struggle to connect their out-of-school literacy lives to the classroom and find spaces where their practices were valued. Additionally, teachers continue to struggle to meet state and federal mandates while seeking to move forward with technology and create meaningful learning experiences for students.

The integration of multiliteracies into content area classrooms requires careful mentoring. Teachers must take time to nurture and understand students' little c projects, assist students in understanding when a creative project is inconsistent with domain knowledge and standards, and provide students with multiple opportunities to practice creative thinking and ideational code-switching (Beghetto & Kaufman, 2007). As Moje (2008) argued,

> A reconceptualized view of secondary school literacy suggests that a person who has learned deeply in a discipline can use a variety of representational forms—most notably reading and writing of written texts, but also oral language, visual images, music or artistic representation—to communicate their learning, to

synthesize ideas across texts and across groups of people, to express new ideas, and to question and challenge ideas held dear in the discipline and in boarder spheres. (p. 99)

If the goal of education is to empower students with the literacy knowledge, skills, and dispositions necessary to participate in their future lives, then technology is not something that can be an add on to a lesson every now and then; technology must be infused into the daily curriculum (Lankshear & Knobel, 2004). Additionally, educators must understand "literacy is more complex and involves learning a repertoire of practices for communicating and getting things done in particular social and cultural contexts" (Nixon, 2003, p. 407).

Through the use of multiliteracies, the teachers in this study used their creativity in both the planning and presentation of content to involve students in meaningful learning that promoted engagement. While many teachers use multiliteracies as a means to capture students' attention, we found that these two teachers used multiliteracies practices as a means to invite their students into the discourse of the content. The teachers provided opportunities for the students to read, write, and think like a scientist or historian (Moje, 2008). This occurred through the selection and evaluation of texts and resources as well as through the creation of projects and assignments.

This study was limited by the fact that we studied only two experienced teachers, yet we acknowledge that other teachers (both new and experienced) utilize multiple texts and resources in their classrooms in a highly creative environment. We also acknowledge that just because a teacher uses multiple texts and resources as well as multiliteracies there is no guarantee that student learning will be enhanced. For example, the two teachers in our study were well-versed in setting up learning scenarios where students constructed their own insights in highly engaged environments. Nevertheless, any curricular innovation is often more complex and demanding than it looks on the surface, and we argue that this holds for highly creative content teachers who incorporate multiliteracies into their classrooms.

By inquiring into the role that multiliteracies and creativity play in content area classrooms, we illuminated these practices for other teachers and classrooms. Furthermore, understanding beliefs and practices of teachers in classrooms deepens our knowledge of the complexities of teaching. Insights gained from this study will broaden the field by providing insight into the lives of teachers as they make curricular decisions that impact their students and themselves as professionals.

What have we learned about content area teachers' creativity and use of multiliteracies in their classrooms? Our work contributes to the fields of multiliteracies and creativity by identifying five teacher markers that are necessary to foster creativity in the classroom. First, classroom teachers need to possess solid, in-depth knowledge of their content. Second, curricular space must exist to allow for creativity to emerge. Third, peer collaboration provides a sounding board for expansion of ideas. Fourth, teachers must have the mindset that allows for flexibility, willingness, and novelty of ideas. Finally, teachers need to have access to multiple texts and resources that allow creative ideas to emerge in the classroom. These findings raise the following questions that should be addressed in future research: How do these markers and others define highly creative classrooms? What are the teacher and student outcomes of highly creative classrooms?

REFERENCES

Bean, T. W. (2010). *Multimodal learning for the 21ˢᵗ Century adolescent.* Huntington Beach, CA: Shell Education.

Bean, T. W., Wimmer, J. J., & Dunkerly, J. (2009). *Content area literacy in the middle school: Investigating professional development, interdisciplinary planning, and instruction across science, social studies, and English.* Paper presented at the 2009 Annual Meeting of the National Reading Conference.

Beghetto, R. A., & Kaufman, J. C. (2007). *Creativity in the classroom: Between chaos and conformity.* Paper presented at the 2007 Annual Meeting of the American Educational Research Association, Chicago, IL.

Beghetto, R. A., & Plucker, J. A. (2006). The relationship among schooling, learning, and creativity: "All roads lead to creativity" or "can't get there from here"? In J. Kauffman and J. Baer (Eds.), *Creativity and reason in cognitive development.* (pp. 316-332). New York, NY: Cambridge University Press.

Craft, A. (2001). An analysis of research and literature on creativity education. Research Report for the United Kingdom Qualifications and Curriculum Authority. Retrieved from National Curriculum website: http://www.ncaction.org.uk

Creswell, J. W. (2007). *Qualitative inquiry and research design: Choosing among five approaches* (2nd, Trans.). Thousand Oaks, CA: Sage Publications.

Csikszentmihalyi, M. (1990). *Flow: The psychology of optimal experience.* New York, NY: Harper & Row.

Kist, W. (2002). Finding "new literacy" in action: An interdisciplinary high school Western Civilization class. *Journal of Adolescent & Adult Literacy, 45*(5), 368-377.

Kist, W. (2005). *New literacies in action: Teaching and learning in multiple media.* New York, NY: Teachers College Press.

Kist, W. (2010). *The socially networked classroom: Teaching in the new media age.* Thousand Oaks, CA: Corwin.

Lankshear, C., & Knobel, M. (2004). Do we have your attention? New literacies, digital technologies, and the education of adolescents. In D. E. Alvermann (Ed.), *Adolescents and literacies in a digital world* (pp. 19-39). New York, NY: Peter Lang.

Lankshear, C., & Knobel, M. (2006). *New literacies: Everyday practices and classroom learning* (2nd ed.). New York, NY: Open University Press.

Marshall, C., & Rossman, G. B. (2010). *Designing qualitative research* (5th ed.). Thousand Oaks, CA: Sage Publications.

McNabb, M. (2006). *Literacy learning in networked classrooms: Using the Internet with middle level students.* Newark, DE: International Reading Association.

Merriam, S.B. (2009). *Qualitative research: A guide to design and implementation.* San Francisco, CA: Jossey-Bass.

Moje, E. B. (2008). Foregrounding the disciplines in secondary literacy teaching and learning: A Call for change. *Journal of Adolescent & Adult Literacy, 52*(2), 96-107.

Nixon, H. (2003). New research literacies for contemporary research into literacy and new media? *Reading Research Quarterly, 38*(3), 407-413.

Norman, D. A. (2004). *Emotional design: Why we love (or hate) everyday things.* New York, NY: Basic Books.

O'Brien, D. G. (2006). "Struggling" adolescents' engagement in multimediating: Countering the institutional construction of incompetence. In D. E. Alvermann, K. A. Hinchman, D. W. Moore, S. F. Phelps & D. R. Waff (Eds.), *Reconceptualizing the literacies in adolescents' lives* (2nd ed., pp. 29-46). Mahwah, NJ: Lawrence Erlbaum Associates.

Runco, M. A. (2007). *Creativity theories and themes: Research, development, and practice.* Burlington, MA: Elsevier Academic Press.

Sak, U. (2004). About creativity, giftedness and teaching the creatively gifted in the classroom. *Roeper Review,* 26. Retrieved from http:www/questia.com/PM.qst?a=o&se=gglsc&d=5006659719

Sawyer, R. K. (2006). *Explaining creativity: The science of human innovation.* New York, NY: Oxford University Press.

Semali, L., & Fueyo, J. (2001). Transmediation as a metaphor for new literacies in multimedia classrooms. *Reading Online,* 5 (5). Retrieved from http://www.readingonline.org/newliteracies/lit_index.asp?HREF=semali2/index.html

Shanahan, T., & Shanahan, C. (2008). Teaching disciplinary literacy to adolescents: Rethinking content-area literacy. *Harvard Educational Review, 78*(1), 40-59.

Smith, M. W., & Wilhelm, J. D. (2002). *"Reading don't fix no Chevys:" Literacy in the lives of young men.* Portsmouth, NH: Heinemann.

Smith, M. W., & Wilhelm, J. D. (2006). *Going with the flow: How to engage boys (and girls) in their literacy learning*. Portsmouth, NH: Heinemann.

Sturtevant, E. G., Boyd, F. B., Brozo, W. G., Hinchman, K. A., Moore, D. W., & Alvermann, D. E. (2006). *Principled practices for adolescent literacy: A framework for instruction and policy*. Mahwah, NJ: Lawrence Erlbaum.

van Leeuwen, T. (2005). *Introducing social semiotics*. London, UK: Routledge.

Walker, N. T., & Bean T. W. (2004). Using Multiple Texts in Content Area Classrooms. *Journal of Content Area Reading, 3*(1), 23-35.

Walker, N. T., & Bean, T. W. (2005). Sociocultural Influences in Content Area Teachers' Selection and Use of Multiple Texts. *Reading Research and Instruction, 44*(4), 61-77.

Walker, N. T., Bean, T. W., & Dillard, B. R. (2010). When textbooks fall short: New ways, new texts, new sources of information in the content areas. Portsmouth, NH: Heinemann.

Yin, R. K. (2009). *Case study research: Design and methods*. Thousand Oaks, CA: Sage Publications.

Language Ideologies of Mothers and Children in a Dual Language Program

Minda Morren López
Texas State University-San Marcos

We construct meanings or interpretations of our experiences and world in very complex ways, and ideologies are one manifestation of how we understand our experiences and the world around us. Ideologies are a "shared framework of social beliefs" that allow us to understand and interpret the practices of people and groups of people (van Dijk, 1998, p. 8). There has been an increased interest in ideologies in educational research in recent years, with much of the research focusing on ideologies in the curriculum (Apple, 1990) or the ideologies held by teachers (Bartolomé & Balderrama, 2001). Less attention has been devoted to research on the language ideologies of parents and their children and how these ideologies impact language and literacy practices. The focus of this paper is to examine the language ideologies of mothers and children and their influences on young emerging bilingual children's language and literate practices.

Language ideologies are sets of beliefs and attitudes related to language and language use (Woolard & Schieffelin, 1994) in both oral and written forms (Martínez-Roldán & Malavé, 2004). When people use language, they are also displaying their beliefs about language, making language ideologies visible through discourse. Ideologies are also manifest in practices and choices people make (López, 2008) but they are neither uniform nor fixed in families or groups (González, 2001). For example, language ideologies may be represented in decisions parents make about their children's education, such as what language to speak at home, what books to purchase, and enrollment in particular programs (such as generalist, transitional bilingual, or dual language). And a child's behaviors may reveal language ideologies when checking out a book from the library in Spanish or English or using a particular language for a written assignment. Studies have indicated that these practices and decisions made by parents, teachers, and students have consequences for student learning (Razfar, 2003). Although some scholars view language ideologies as consistently hegemonic (Bartolomé, 2008), others argue they can also be counter-hegemonic (Ricento, 2000) and may result in positive or negative outcomes for a student.

In this article, I examine the language ideologies of mothers whose children were enrolled in a Spanish-English Dual Language (DL) program and the impact of ideologies on the language and literacy practices of their children. I argue that the emerging bilingual children are heavily influenced by their mothers' ideologies and that young children are indeed beginning to formulate ideological stances regarding language. In addition, the ideologies of the mothers and their young children range across a continuum. The ideologies they express are not always hegemonic, are at times competing, and are often influenced by the participants' positionality.

REVIEW OF LITERATURE AND THEORETICAL PERSPECTIVES

Research on bilingualism shows the range of perspectives throughout the immigrant community in the U.S.. Some studies suggest immigrant parents are concerned about their children losing their mother tongue and encourage them to preserve it (Vásquez, Pease-Alvarez, & Shannon,

1994; Mushi, 2001), while other studies have found that immigrant parents push their children to learn English in order to avoid discrimination and obtain more opportunities in our largely monolingual society (Suarez-Orozco, & Suarez-Orozco, 2000; Worthy, 2006). For immigrant students in U.S. schools, the overwhelming experience in schools is a subtractive one (Valenzuela, 1999), where English Language Learners (ELLs) are forced to undergo native language loss and are pushed towards English and away from bilingualism. Currently, many policy makers are pushing for English as the mode of instruction in the United States, a result of *linguicism*, the "ideologies, structures and practices which are used to legitimate, effectuate, regulate and reproduce an unequal division of power and resources...on the basis of language" (Skutnabb-Kangas 2000, p. 30).

There is a growing number of educators and parents in the U.S. that reject the subtractive paradigm of pushing students towards English at all costs. One educational option based on an ideology of linguistic pluralism, where multiple languages are supported and taught, is Dual Language or Two-Way Immersion (Jeon, 2003). These programs resist educational homogenization and encourage bilingualism in a time when the U.S. is becoming an increasingly bilingual country but is fighting a monolingual ideology (Garcia, 2005). Nationally, Dual Language (DL) programs are growing exponentially. In 2000, there were 248 DL programs in 23 states and DC; in 2010 there were 359 programs in 28 states (Center for Applied Linguistics, 2010). This is an increase in reported programs at a rate of 45% in 10 years.

Most Dual Language programs share certain characteristics. First, the population of students includes some native English speakers and native speakers of another language (usually Spanish). These two groups study together most of the day (if not all), and students learn language through academic content instruction in both languages (Lindholm-Leary, 2001). In addition, a central goal is that all students become proficient in using two languages for communication and learning (Gomez, Freeman, & Freeman, 2005). In order to meet this goal, students must spend time in the program; most programs require that families commit to attend for at least five years (Lindholm-Leary, 2001).

The increase in popularity of Dual Language programs has resulted in increased studies of a wide range of various features such as design and implementation, student outcomes, instruction, and attitudes of parents and teachers. In their review of the research, Howard, Sugarman, and Christian (2003) discuss ways DL programs have reportedly been successful and directions for further research. Their report indicates a need for further examination of equity in DL programs, echoing the call made by Valdés (1997) over a decade ago. In her seminal work, Valdés (1997) cautions DL educators to attend to many different dimensions of power and intergroup relations, both on the micro and macro levels. There is often an imbalance between groups therefore, "What is at issue here is not an educational approach but intergroup relations, and the place of the powerful and the powerless in wider society" (p. 393). Educators are urged to confront the notion that language acquisition is incredibly complex and to be sensitive to the fact that language minority and language majority students often live in very different worlds and receive differential treatment even inside of programs designed for linguistic pluralism.

In light of Valdés' (1997) work underscoring the complexities of Dual Language programs, it is not surprising that students in such programs have shown a multiplicity of ideologies (González, 2005) with many differing and contradictory sets of beliefs regarding schooling, language, and literacy. In one salient example, Martínez-Roldán and Malavé (2004) studied young children in DL and found that a first-grade native Spanish speaker had formed a *cultural model* (D'Andrade, 1987; Gee, 1999) of Spanish speakers as lacking in intelligence. Because of this ideological stance, he was reticent to speak his native language of Spanish, even though he was enrolled in a DL program that supported Spanish language maintenance goals. He had not invested in an identity as a Spanish speaker, despite his parents' bilingualism and his own experiences in the DL program. Issues of identity, the sociopolitical context of bilingual education, and the overwhelming presence of English monolingualism in the United States are some of the many factors that influenced his actions and ideologies.

Because of these complexities of the relationship between language, society, and the education of both language minority- and language-majority-speaking children, I chose to use Critical Discourse Analysis (CDA) as both theory and method. Critical Discourse Analysis conceptualizes language as a multifaceted form of social practice and attempts to uncover the reciprocal influences of language and social structure (Fairclough, 1995; van Dijk, 1998; Wodak, 1989), exposing the often hidden ideological effects of language and power. By attending to both what is present and absent in discourse, this approach can expose patterns of beliefs and attitudes toward English and Spanish and point to possible ideological influences on students' beliefs and attitudes. This study attempts to contribute to our understanding of the complexities of DL programs and the language and literacy education of emerging bilinguals by examining the language ideologies of parents who serve as children's first language teachers and partners in literacy and tracing those ideologies to their children, through their language and literacy practices.

METHODS

The setting for this study was a public primary school with a Spanish-English Dual Language program. The school served grades PK-1 and was the first site of the DL program offered by this district as an option for both Spanish-speaking and English-speaking parents. The school also offered generalist English-only classes, English as a Second Language classes, and traditional bilingual education classes—making DL one choice of many. The 90-10 model was in its fifth year of implementation and gaining in popularity. This particular school district has a long history of bilingual education and established one of the first public bilingual programs in the state in the 1880s, albeit in German and English (Blanton, 2004). Although present-day demographics now include a population of roughly a third Latina/os and two-thirds Whites, this city of just over 50,000 people is still celebrated for its German heritage and retains its reputation as a German enclave. The reality is that now 30% of the residents speak Spanish, whereas only 3% speak German.

Participants

For this paper, I focus on three mothers and their children attending first grade in a Spanish/English Dual Language program, although my larger study focused on more than 200 teachers, five families, and two first-grade classes. The families in my study all came from different immigrant, ethnic, economic, linguistic, and social perspectives. These mother-children dyads from three families were chosen because they represent different language environments and ideologies across the spectrum of the continua, ranging from monolingual Spanish (Marisol and Mariana) to bilingual (Azucena and Julia) to monolingual English (Kathy and Cody). The participants are also representative of the population of DL programs, where a mixture of dominant Spanish speakers, dominant English speakers, and bilingual students is often cited as critical to their success (Lindholm-Leary, 2001). I chose to focus on participants from different language backgrounds and social positionings because I recognize that "there is a radical difference between a dominant speaker learning a second language and a minority speaker acquiring the dominant language" (Macedo, 1999/2000, p. 65). By selecting participants from a range of positions and backgrounds, the range of language ideologies represented in a DL program is made visible.

I also made the choice to interview mothers because of the influences they have on their children's language and literacy. Previous studies have shown that women from linguistically subjugated communities have the most responsibility for language maintenance (Zentella, 1987) and that mothers are strong influences on their children's attitudes for language learning (Brisk & Harrington, 2000; González, 2001) and bilingualism (Valdéz, 2006). The three mothers in this study range from a monolingual Spanish speaker (Marisol) to a bilingual Spanish/English speaker (Azucena) to a monolingual English speaker (Kathy). Table 1 shows the mothers and their children along a continua modeled after Hornberger's (1989) biliteracy continua. In Hornberger's model, the continuum ranges from monolingual to bilingual. However, it does not take into account the differences between a monolingual language minority speaker in the U.S. and a monolingual language majority (English) speaker in the U.S.. As Macedo (1999/2000) points out, this difference is important, and so I modified the continua to range from monolingual Spanish on the one side to bilingual in the middle and monolingual English on the other side.

The participant on the monolingual Spanish side of the continua, Marisol, was an immigrant from Mexico and a monolingual Spanish speaker. Her husband also emigrated from Mexico and they have three children. Marisol worked at home to care for the children and she felt fairly isolated. She could not drive and public transportation does not exist in this small community. In interviews, Marisol expressed a desire to learn English but had very few opportunities to do so because of many constraints. Her daughter, Mariana, was in the first grade during this study. Mariana was beginning to use English at times, but showed a strong preference for Spanish. Mariana also tended towards the monolingual Spanish end of the continua.

The family and mother with the most bilingual practices in this study was Azucena. She is from Mexico and worked as a secretary in a factory along the border, where she met her husband, who is originally from Pennsylvania. After they married, they moved to Texas and made a commitment to raise their two children with bilingual and bicultural practices. Her husband had learned Spanish as an adult and they agreed to speak primarily Spanish in the home. Their daughter, Julia, was already demonstrating leadership in the first grade as she was called upon by other students and teachers to be a language broker (Orellana, 2003). She skillfully moved between Spanish and English language and literacy practices and was one of the few students whom we observed choosing to engage in bilingual activities in school and home.

Kathy was on the monolingual English side of the continua. She is a White English-speaking American citizen originally from the East Coast. She and her husband are both engineers and moved to Texas for work. Kathy does not speak another language and talked in interviews about her unease in situations where people are speaking a language she does not understand. At the time of the study,

Kathy worked in the home (which is the same for all three mothers discussed here) and volunteered in the school. Her son, Cody, was in the first grade and although he was an accomplished bilingual/bilterate, he rarely chose to engage in bilingual practices. Cody expressed his dislike for Spanish and his desire to attend school in English exclusively. In first grade, Cody was already beginning to show a negative ideological stance towards Spanish and bilingualism.

Table 1. Mothers' and Childrens' Continua of Language and Literacy

Name (pseudonym)	Marisol	Azucena	Kathy
Dominant language	Spanish	Spanish	English
Primary language used in the home	Spanish with very limited English	Spanish with some English use in home	English with very limited Spanish use in home
Child	Mariana	Julia	Cody
Language behaviors at school	Somewhat bilingual; prefers Spanish	Very bilingual; language broker	Accomplished bilingual; prefers English
Spanish reading	On	Above	Slightly below
English reading	Below	On	Far above
Literacy practices	Observed only using Spanish for literacy activities at school and home	Frequently observed reading and writing in English and Spanish at home and school	Rarely chose Spanish literacy activities
Language and literacy continua	←------------- monolingual Spa	--------------- bilingual	------------------→ monolingual Eng

Data Collection and Analysis

My data sources consisted of field notes from observations at school and in homes, audiotaped interviews, and documentation of the material culture of the homes. Literacy artifacts were collected at school, including journal entries, written assignments, and literacy assessments. Over the school year I spent time as a participant observer in the two first-grade DL classrooms, averaging ten hours a week in the two classes. During that time I documented the teaching and learning practices in the two classes, including instructional techniques, student contributions and behaviors, language used, and literacy practices. As a Spanish/English bilingual and former DL teacher, I sought to respect all the norms and linguistic expectations of the program, such as separating English/Spanish according to teacher and using the language of instruction exclusively. At times this restricted my interaction with the students, so I decided to spend time "hanging out" with them during their lunch period, recess, and in the library. Towards the end of the school year I worked with students in various focus groups. In these groups we talked informally about their language and literacy interests and practices.

I also spent time talking to the mothers at school and at home. I interviewed them formally at least two times (in the language of preference of the participant) and spoke with them informally more frequently. At times I called or e-mailed the mothers and other times I went to their homes or chatted with them when they picked up their children from school. They sometimes invited me to their homes for coffee and they shared with me their children's work.

The data collection and analysis was ongoing over the course of eleven months and I used a constant comparison method (Strauss & Corbin, 1998) to track emerging themes. Critical Discourse Analysis as described by Fairclough (1995), Gee (1999), and van Dijk (1998) also informed my analysis and categorization of data. In particular, I examined language use and literacy events using four of Gee's (1999) six building tasks; activities, identity and relationships, politics, and views of the world. I then honed in on three of Gee's tools of inquiry—situated identities, Discourses, and cultural models—in order to learn how language ideologies might be evident in talk and practices. Next, I coded potential themes by culling out examples from participant observations, interviews, and written responses. All data was broken into data chunks and grouped by the emerging themes. When concepts and categories developed that were similar, I created typologies according to a three-step process outlined by Berg (2004). In this way I attempted to link social meanings or shared ideologies to practices and talk observed in the field, evident in interviews, and exemplified in literacy lessons and writing samples.

LANGUAGE IDEOLOGIES OF THE MOTHERS

The mothers' language ideologies were revealed in both their actions and their discourse, including enrolling their children in the DL program, making adaptations at home to foster bilingualism in their children, and in their talk about language and literacy practices. The mothers in this study expressed language ideologies that were at times congruent with the DL program and with each other and at other times were not. In this section I will outline the three mothers' ideologies and describe them in comparison to each other and in relation to the stated goals and enacted practices of the Dual Language program.

First of all, the mothers in this study went against the grain by enrolling their children in the Dual Language program at Presidio Primary. The program is voluntary and its stated goals are bilingualism and biliteracy for all children (López, 2008). Choosing the DL program was an important choice the mothers made that demonstrated a positive ideological stance towards bilingualism. In interviews, one question I asked the mothers was, "What are your reasons for enrolling your child(ren) in the DL program?" All three indicated that they chose DL because they believed their children, as bilinguals, would have advantages over monolingual children. These mothers described educational and occupational advantages as well as the ability to communicate with a wider audience. They also described the cognitive benefits such as vocabulary development and intellectual stimulation. Both Marisol and Azucena explained the importance of their cultural and linguistic roots. They believed that their children needed to understand where they came from and needed to be able to communicate with extended family members. These responses pointed towards language ideologies that supported bilingualism.

However, one response by Kathy showed a slightly different perspective. In an interview she expressed her discontent with public schools in the area because of their lack of rigor. She also said, "If the district offered a magnet program in math or science we would have enrolled our children in it. But since they don't offer any magnet programs, we thought this was the next best option." Her statement revealed that she viewed the intellectual stimulation of bilingualism in the Dual Language program as more important than the development of bicultural or bilingual competencies. Kathy was the only mother interviewed who expressed her view of the DL program in this way. All of the other mothers expressed a strong desire for their children to become bilingual and bicultural. This may be due in part to Kathy's social position as a middle-class, English-speaking citizen.

In addition to the important decision of enrolling their children in Dual Language, there were other actions the mothers engaged in that illustrated their positive ideologies towards bilingualism. All three reported that they read to their children in their dominant language and had done so since infancy. There were also displays of literate behaviors in all of the homes, including diplomas from educational programs, books, notebooks and workbooks, and letters. And in order to support their children's biliteracy development, the mothers made adaptations in their language and literacy practices at home. The adaptations were in some cases spurred on by school practices or by teachers' suggestions and although they may appear to be small, they demonstrate a desire on the part of the mothers to foster bilingualism and to support school practices. In order to foster more English at home, Marisol encouraged her children to watch television in English in 15 minutes each day. She indicated that this was something she could do despite the constraints she felt in regards to learning English and providing her children with more exposure to the language. On the other end of the spectrum and also a monolingual, Kathy encouraged her children to read for at least 15 minutes a day in Spanish. This change came about after a parent-teacher conference where the teacher suggested Cody needed to engage in more Spanish literacy activities at home. As a result, Kathy purchased children's literature and dictionaries in Spanish. In a similar fashion, Azucena also made adaptations in the family's routines and home practices in order to foster bilingualism at home. She relied on a large network of family and friends in Mexico to send her books, educational games, and software in Spanish. She provided these materials to her children so they could learn the language through play and also be current with cultural practices that their cousins in Mexico were experiencing. In addition, although she and her husband had originally made the decision to speak only Spanish at home, she felt that her children were lagging behind in English due in part to the lack of formal English literacy instruction in the DL program. As a result, she asked her husband to stop speaking Spanish at home and instead speak English to the children so they would begin to acquire English informally.

The changes these mothers made in their practices at home to meet the changing needs of their children in the DL program confirms previous studies that suggest Latina mothers adapt to new circumstances and add new practices to their own repertoires to help their children succeed in school (Gillanders & Jiménez, 2004; Reese & Gallimore, 2000). It also contradicts the common belief among many educators that Mexican immigrant parents are too busy surviving in this culture to care about their children's education or do not have the tools to help their children in school. The mothers who participated in this study, from both immigrant and non-immigrant backgrounds, did what they could at home to support the stated goal of bilingualism in the DL program, even when it meant adapting their own practices.

In many Dual Language programs, there is an ideology of "sequential literacy instruction" (Lindholm-Leary, 2001), the practice of teaching literacy in one language exclusively before teaching it in another. For this program, Spanish literacy was taught exclusively in grades K-2. There was no formal literacy instruction in English until third grade. The belief was that all students in the DL program would learn to read and write in Spanish at school and they would transfer these learned literacy skills over to English. This supports the notion of "spontaneous biliteracy" (Reyes, 2001) where students learning literacy in one language do not need formal literacy instruction in the other language because they naturally begin to transfer their skills and strategies from one language to the other without instruction. The problem with this view and practice in the DL program was that the Spanish-speaking parents wanted their children to learn English literacy skills before third grade. In order for this to happen, they needed their children to receive formal instruction in English literacy at school. Many parents, like Marisol, did not feel equipped to teach their children to read and write in English because they were not fluent in English. The English-dominant parents, however, were able to read to their children in English at home, providing some English literacy skills their children were not receiving in school yet. This ideology in practice created a situation where the English-dominant children were becoming biliterate in first and second grades but many Spanish-dominant children were not. The result was a divide between many of the Spanish-dominant and English-dominant mothers in their ideological stances of literacy instruction, their view of the program, and ideas about who it was benefitting the most. The result was that the Spanish-dominant mothers, like Marisol and Azucena, did not support sequential literacy instruction. English-dominant mothers, such as Kathy, did not find it problematic because their children were becoming biliterate in first grade.

LANGUAGE IDEOLOGIES OF THE FIRST-GRADE EMERGING BILINGUALS

The language ideologies of these three first-grade emerging bilinguals were made visible primarily through their literate and language behaviors, including in-class responses to literature with bilingual themes. The data suggests that children are indeed beginning to formulate ideologies, or "embryonic ideological discourses" (Martínez-Roldán & Malavé, 2004, p. 176). This term refers to the early development of the processes that eventually lead to the formation of concepts or ideologies. The complex mental activities that Vygotsky (1934/1978) calls *thinking in concepts* are not fully mature in the young child but are in an embryonic stage, just as these embryonic ideologies are not fully mature, but are developing. Although their stances may change over time, the children appear to be heavily influenced by their mothers' ideologies. In this section I will describe the three first-graders and provide examples of their discourse that reveal embryonic language ideologies. I will also discuss the potential impact their ideologies may have on students' literate practices.

Mariana

Spanish is Mariana's first language and both of her parents are monolingual Spanish speakers. At home, Mariana spoke Spanish almost exclusively and was exposed to English primarily when her mother turned the television to English for 15 minutes. At school, she spent the majority of her day in Spanish in the DL program. She received formal instruction in English for 30 minutes a day in English as a Second Language (ESL) and in extracurricular classes such as Physical Education, Computers, and Music.

After reading the bilingual children's book, *Pepita Habla Dos Veces/Pepita Talks Twice* (Lachtman, 1995), in class, Mariana wrote this response (note that written responses retain the students' invented spelling and syntax),

> *Yo soy como Pepita porque a mi no me gusta ablar en ingles. No mas me gusta ablar en espanol. A mi me gusta aser como Pepita.* [I am like Pepita because I don't like to speak English. I only like to speak in Spanish. I would like to be like Pepita.]

In the book, the protagonist, Pepita, decides she does not want to speak Spanish anymore because of the extra burden it places on her to be bilingual. As a result, Pepita stops speaking in Spanish at one point in the story. In her response, Mariana identifies with Pepita's desire to speak only one language and indicates her preference for Spanish.

A few months later, I talked to Mariana and some other girls in a focus group. I wanted to learn more about their social preferences, including who their friends were both at school and at home. I also asked about their language literacy practices. Mariana said,

> *Mis amigas hablan en español. Nada más me gusta leer en español porque inglés es muy difícil. También escribo en español porque mi lenguaje es español.* [My friends speak Spanish. I only like to read in Spanish because English is really hard. I also write in Spanish because my language is Spanish.]

In this response, she is identifying as a Spanish speaker. She describes her language as Spanish and that she associates with Spanish speakers. She also indicates that English is difficult for her, which may contribute to her language preference. Using Gee's (1999) building tasks and tools of inquiry for analysis, Mariana's behaviors and expressed views over time show she is engaged in identity and relationship building. Her pattern of language and literacy practices also demonstrate an ideological view of the world with a preference for Spanish. At the end of first grade, Mariana was reading on grade level in Spanish and below grade level in English. This is not surprising because of the curriculum of the DL program, where formal English literacy instruction did not occur until third grade. Perhaps because of a combination of factors such as the DL curriculum, her home language and family background, at the time of the study, Mariana expressed a monolingual ideology with a strong preference for Spanish.

Julia

Julia comes from a bilingual home and interacts with relatives in both languages on both sides of the U.S.-Mexico border. Their home is filled with bilingual books, software, games, and other materials. At school, Julia is instructed in the same way Mariana is, with no formal literacy instruction in English and 90% of the school day conducted in Spanish.

One day their classroom teacher read the Spanish translation of *My Name is Yoon/Me Llamo Yoon* (Recorvits, 2003). The story is about a young immigrant from Korea who struggles with literacy in English. The protagonist, Yoon, has a hard time understanding what her teacher is telling her and at one point compares the writing systems of Korean and English. The book illustrates the difficulty of adjusting to writing in a different language. In response to the book, Julia wrote,

> *Escribo en ingles cuando Yo estoy en clase de ingles. Con mi papá y unas veses con mi Hermano y con mi abuelita y abuelito. Y mi tía y tíos. Yo ablo en ingles. Porque ellos*

ablan en ingles. Escribo en español cuanbo yo estoy en mi clase y en mi casa. Y en mi abuelita casa y Mis primos y primas y tías y tíos. Y en la cafeteria nadamás Un poco y afuera yo ablo en español porque ellos hablan en español. [I write in English when I am in English class. With my dad and sometimes with my brother and my grandmother and grandfather. And with my aunt and uncles. I speak in English because they speak in English. I write in Spanish when I am in my class and at home. And at my grandmother's house and my cousins and my aunts and uncles. And in the cafeteria, just a little bit and outside I speak in Spanish because they speak Spanish.]

In her response, Julia shows that she has a high level of communicative competence. She knows that as a bilingual person, she will respectfully speak and write in the language of her interlocutors. She does not address the issue of difficulty, as Mariana did in her response, perhaps because Julia is already an accomplished bilingual, and possibly as a result of the many opportunities she has to interact in both languages with her extended family. Her skills and understanding of both languages were evident in teacher evaluations and also in conversations we had. After reading *The Cow that Went Oink!* (Most, 1990) with her in English during recess, I asked her if a cow in Mexico said the same thing as cows in Texas. She responded, "No, they say it like that, 'mau, mau' and in English they say, 'mooooo'." Julia pointed to an illustration in the book and said, "Oh, here he is sleeping. In Spanish we would say 'rrrrr,' but in English it's different; it's 'shhhh.' "

Julia shows a sophisticated understanding of linguistic features of English and Spanish and of communicative competence. At the end of first grade, Julia was reading above grade level in Spanish and on grade level in English. Although she did not receive any formal literacy instruction in English at school, Julia had multiple opportunities to interact in English at home. Unlike the first-grader in the Martínez-Roldán and Malavé (2004) study, Julia had a positive cultural model of Spanish-speaking bilinguals and her situated identities of home and school were not in conflict. Julia engaged in a Discourse (Gee, 1999) that integrated her cultural and linguistic values, resulting in a bilingual and biliterate ideological stance throughout the study.

Cody

Cody is a native English speaker, and both his parents are monolingual English speakers. His parents are highly educated and want a rigorous academic preparation for their children. His older sister was enrolled in the DL program as well as several of his friends from his neighborhood. Cody responded to *Pepita Talks Twice* (Lachtman, 1995) and focused on the idea of one language being tied to identity and aptitude, in similar ways that Mariana did. He wrote,

Yo no soy como Pepita porque yo no ayude a nadie, yo habla dos lenguas pero uno es mejor…una lengua es mejor porque casi toda mi viva yo habla ingles porque yo es ingles born… [I am not like Pepita because I do not help anyone, I speak two languages, but one is better…one language is better because most of my life I have spoken English because I am English born…]

His written response begins by clearing up any doubts about his willingness or need to help others with his bilingualism. Unlike a Spanish-speaking child who may need to translate for his or her parents, Cody lives in a world where language brokering skills are not needed. He also states that one language is better, and it is not clear if he means he is a more skilled English user or if he is indicating that one is indeed "better" in terms of prestige. As with Mariana, Cody ties language to identity when he states, "I am English born." We know that language is not a birthright, but for a young child learning in a DL program, it may be clear that the family you are born into does indeed influence your language skills and your opportunities in life.

Cody's response to *My Name is Yoon/Me Llamo Yoon* (Recorvits, 2003) indicates that he writes in Spanish only when told to do so. He may not see the value of Spanish in the world outside of school. He wrote,

> *Escribo en espanol cuando estoy en la escuela y habla español con mi maestra porque digo que nececito.* [I write in Spanish when I am in school and speak Spanish with my teacher because she tells me I have to.]

This writing is short and concise. Cody does not enjoy writing in Spanish, nor does he use Spanish with people in his family who speak Spanish, as in the case of Julia. Although he is in the DL program, he appears to have a view of Spanish that is less than favorable. In May of his first-grade year, he expressed his dislike for learning in Spanish when he exclaimed loudly in class, "I can't wait to go to second grade! We are going to be able to speak English!" Cody appeared to resist learning Spanish through his practices and his responses to literature. His responses and practices do not indicate he has internalized a cultural model of Spanish speakers as being less intelligent, but his worldview suggests that Spanish is not as relevant. His friends (identity and relationship bulding, Gee, 1999) are English speakers, and he prefers English for language and literacy activities. At the end of first-grade he was reading slightly below grade level in Spanish grade and at a fifth-grade level in English. He expressed a monolingual ideological stance that favored English.

DISCUSSION

Although all parents went against the grain and enrolled their children in an additive bilingual program, there were different degrees to which the mothers and children supported the ideologies of the DL program. As a result, children experienced different ideological stances and practices at home. This may be one reason why despite their participation in an additive bilingual program, not all of the children were enthusiastic about bilingualism and biliteracy. Of these three, the student who exhibited the most bilingual ideological stance was Julia, whose parents highly supported bilingualism in their practices as well as their d/Discourse. It appears that one of the strongest influences on the children's language ideologies were mothers' ideological stances and practices, confirming earlier studies that showed the strong influence of mothers on language maintenance, attitudes, and bilingualism in their children.

In this study, students who held more positive bilingual ideologies performed better in literacy in both languages. Those who tended towards monolingual (English or Spanish) language ideologies performed below grade level in literacy in at least one language at the end of first grade. The child in the middle of the continua, Julia, exhibited the most biliterate behaviors. She engaged in both Spanish and English literacy activities and often brought bilingual literacy materials to school. Julia's ideological stances towards language show someone who was not torn by two languages, nor by conflicting messages regarding who she was and what language she should speak. She did not find one excessively more difficult than the other, like Mariana found English to be. This is an important finding and should not be ignored by educators. Although we do not have control over attitudes and behaviors in the home, if we seek to foster bilingualism and biliteracy at school, as DL programs do, we should also actively work to foster positive attitudes about both languages.

There is another important dimension to this, however. Mariana viewed Spanish very positively and as a salient part of her identity, which is important for her continued development. Yet like her mother, English was difficult and appeared to be out of reach. She did not show an interest in English development at this time. It is possible that Mariana was not exhibiting a bilingual ideological stance in first grade because there were few opportunities for her to engage in authentic English practices both inside and outside of school. Perhaps if she had more opportunities to use English in all areas of language—listening, speaking, reading, and writing—she might have a more positive stance toward it. Many DL programs view the practices of language separation, sequential literacy instruction, and the majority of instructional time spent in Spanish in the early years as a way of countering the hegemonic powers of English in society. And Mariana may indeed become a bilingual and biliterate student soon. On the other hand, the lack of formal English literacy instruction may set her back and have long-term consequences for her schooling. With Mariana and other students like her, time will tell.

Like Mariana, Cody also exhibited a monolingual ideological stance in first-grade, but with a strong preference for English and what appeared to be a negative stance towards Spanish. He often refused to speak Spanish with adults or classmates during class time. Some might question the interpretations of his actions as a negative stance towards Spanish and think of them instead as "just being a kid" or "being a boy." Then again, there were other boys in his class who did not demonstrate such positions at all over the course of the year of study. In addition, Cody was one of the only students in the two first-grade classes who consistently rejected Spanish as a means of communication. Perhaps Cody understood his position in society as an English speaker and did not see the need for Spanish in his life. Or maybe he knew that his parents were more interested in his intellectual development than in his bicultural or bilingual abilities. Overall, the embryonic ideological stances of Cody and Mariana appeared to favor monolingualism, although from different social positions with a preference for different languages. What is important to note is that in first grade, the visible consequences as a result of their monolingual stances were minimal. However, if their embryonic ideologies become more fixed, Mariana will most likely face more social and educational challenges than Cody.

As noted previously by many prominent scholars of language and literacy education, DL programs are very complex learning environments where there is often an imbalance of societal power of participants due to immigration, socioeconomic, linguistic, and cultural factors. It has also been noted that too often, these programs do not attend to issues of equity. The ideological stances of the mothers in this study indicate that all of the families enrolled in DL went against the mainstream language ideology of English only and made adaptations in the home environment to support the developing bilingualism of their children. However, the families' educational needs and ideological stances differed in important ways and suggest that DL programs should focus more on intergroup relations while openly facing the challenges of educating students from diverse backgrounds. This could be done in many ways, through parent meetings and input, teacher training, and an official curriculum designed to infuse social justice.

The imbalance in societal power and opportunity was compounded in this DL program by the official policy and practice of sequential literacy instruction, which denies Spanish-dominant students formal English literacy instruction until third grade. The result was different literacy practices and achievement levels in first grade in the two languages, with English-dominant students having the advantage. In DL programs where immigrant parents do not have to choose between either maintaining their language or learning another, schools need to focus more on ensuring an equitable education for all students by carefully examining language and literacy practices and policies in DL programs during planning and implementation stages.

While this study captured participants' ideological stances at one point in time, it is important to note that ideologies are not static, but ever evolving and changing. For educators hoping to foster bilingualism and biliteracy in all students, we must take into account not only the different social positions of our students, but also the different ideological stances they are forming. These embryonic language ideologies have the potential to impact students either positively or negatively as they continue to attend school. As educators, it is time we acknowledge young students' developing ideologies and begin to consciously foster positive concepts about language, literacy, and learning that will promote emergent bilingual students' success.

REFERENCES

Apple, M. (1990). *Ideology and curriculum.* (2nd ed.). New York, NY: Routledge.

Bartolomé, L., & Balderrama, M. (2001). The Need for Educators with Political and Ideological Clarity. In Maria de la Luz Reyes & John Halcon (Eds.) *The Best for Our Children: Critical Perspectives on Literacy for Latino Students* (pp. 48 – 64). New York, NY: Teachers College Press.

Bartolomé, L. (2008). Introduction: Beyond the fog of ideology. In L. Bartolomé (Ed.) *Ideologies in education: Unmasking the trap of teacher neutrality* (pp. ix-xxix). New York, NY: Peter Lang.

Berg, B. (2004). *Qualitative research methods for the social sciences (5th ed.).* Boston, MA: Pearson.

Blanton, C. K. (2004). *The Strange Career of Bilingual Education in Texas, 1836–1981.* College Station, TX: Texas A&M University Press, 2004.

Brisk, M. E., & Harrington, M. M. (2000). *Literacy and bilingualism: A handbook for all teachers.* Mahwah, NJ: Lawrence Erlbaum Associates, Inc. Publishers.

Center for Applied Linguistics (2010). Directory of Two-Way Immersion programs in the United States. Downloaded January 30, 2010 from: http://www.cal.org/twi/directory/index.html

D'Andrade, J. (1987). A folk model in the mind. In D. Holland and N. Quinn (Eds.). *Cultural Models in language and thought* (pp. 112-147). Cambridge, UK: Cambridge University Press.

Fairclough, N. (1995). *Critical discourse analysis: The critical study of language.* New York, NY: Longman.

Garcia, O. (2005). Positioning Heritage Languages in the United States. *The Modern Language Journal, 89*, iii, 601-605.

Gee, J. P. (1999). *An Introduction to Discourse Analysis Theory and Method.* London, UK and New York, NY: Routledge.

Gillanders, C., & Jiménez, R. T. (2004). Reaching for success: A close-up of Mexican immigrant parents who foster literacy success for their kindergarten children. *Journal of Early Childhood Literacy, 4*(3), 243-269.

Gomez, L., Freeman, D., & Freeman, Y. (2005). Dual Language Education: A Promising 50-50 Model. *Bilingual Research Journal, 29*(1), 145-164.

González, N. (2001). *I am my language: discourses of women and children in the borderlands.* Tucson, AZ: University of Arizona Press.

González, N. (2005). Children in the eye of the storm: Language socialization and language ideologies in a dual-language school. In A. C. Zentella (Ed.). *Building on strength: Language and literacy in Latino families and communities* (pp.162-174). New York, NY: Teachers College Press.

Hornberger, N.H. (1989) Continua of biliteracy. *Review of Educational Research, 59*(3), 271-296.

Howard, E., Sugarman, J., & Christian, D. (2003). *Trends in Two-Way Immersion Education: A review of the research.* Baltimore, MD: CRESPAR/Johns Hopkins University.

Jeon, M. (2003) Searching for the rationale for two-way immersion program policies. In N. H. Hornberger (Ed.), *Continua of Biliteracy: An ecological framework for educational policy, research and practice in multilingual settings* (pp. 122-148). Clevedon, UK: Multilingual Matters.

Lachtman, O. D. (1995). *Pepita Talks Twice/Pepita habla dos veces*. Houston: Piñata Books.

Lindholm-Leary, K. J. (2001). *Dual Language Education*. Clevedon, UK: Multilingual Matters.

López, M. M. (2008). "Aquí en los Estados Unidos hablamos inglés....o, y español tambien": Students' Emerging Language Ideologies and literacy practices in a Dual Language primary program. *Dissertation Abstracts International, 69*(03), 312. (AAT 3303933)

Macedo, D. (1999/2000). The illiteracy of English-Only literacy. *Educational Leadership, 57*(4), 62-67.

Martínez-Roldán, C. M., & Malavé, G. (2004). Language Ideologies Mediating Literacy and Identity in Bilingual Contexts. *Journal of Early Childhood Literacy, 4*(2), 155-180.

Most, B. (1990). *The Cow that went Oink!* Boston, MA: Red Wagon Books.

Mushi, S. (2001) Acquisition of Multiple Languages among Children of Immigrant Families: Parents' Role in the Home-School Language Pendulum. *Supporting Immigrant Children's Language Learning*. ERIC ED459622

Orellana, M. (2003). Responsibilities of children in Latino immigrant homes. *New Directions for Youth Development, 100*, 25-39.

Razfar, A. (2003). Language ideologies in English language learner contexts: Implications for Latinos and higher education. *Journal of Hispanic Higher Education, 2*(3), 241-268.

Recorvits, H. (2003). *Me Llamo Yoon*. Barcelona: Editorial Juventud.

Reese, L. J., & Gallimore, R. (2000). Immigrant Latinos' cultural model of literacy development: An evolving perspective on home-school discontinuities. *American Journal of Education, 108*(2), 103-134.

Reyes, M. de la Luz. (2001). Unleashing Possibilities: Biliteracy in the Primary Grades, in M. de la Luz Reyes and John J. Halcón (Eds.) *The Best for Our Children: Critical Perspectives on Literacy for Latino Students* (pp. 96–121). New York, NY: Columbia.

Ricento, T. (2000). *Ideology, politics and language policies: Focus on English*. Amsterdam, Holland: John Benjamins.

Skutnabb-Kangas, T. (2000). *Linguistic genocide in education—or worldwide diversity and human rights?* Mahwah, NJ: Erlbaum.

Strauss, A., & Corbin, J. (1998). *Basics of qualitative research: Grounded theory procedures and techniques.* Newbury Park, CA: Sage.

Suárez-Orozco, M., & Suárez-Orozco, C. (2000). Some conceptual considerations in the interdisciplinary study of immigrant children. In H. Trueba and L. I. Bartolomé (Eds.), *Immigrant voices: In search of educational equity* (pp. 17-36). Lanham, MD: Rowman & Littlefield.

Vásquez, O., Pease-Alvarez, L., & Shannon, S. (1994). *Pushing boundaries: Language and culture in a Mexicano community*. Cambridge, MA: Cambridge University Press.

Valdés, G. (1997). Dual Language Immersion Programs: A cautionary note concerning the education of language minority students. *Harvard Educational Review, 67*(3), 391-429.

Valdéz, V. (2006). Mothers of Mexican Origin Within Day-to-Day Parent Involvement: Agency & Spanish Language Maintenance. *Dissertation Abstracts International, 67*(04), 340. (AAT 3217626)

Valenzuela, A. (1999) *Subtractive schooling: US–Mexican youth and the politics of caring*. Albany, NY: State University of New York Press.

van Dijk, T. A. (1998). Principles of critical discourse analysis, in J. Chesshire and P. Trudgill (Eds.) The Sociolinguistics Reader: Volume 2: Gender and Discourse. A Hodder Arnold Publication.

Vygotsky, L. S. (1978). *Thought and language* (A. Kozulin, Trans.). Cambridge, MA: MIT Press. (Original work published 1934)

Wodak, R. (1989). *Language, power and ideology. Studies in political discourse*. Amsterdam, Holland: John Benjamins.

Woolard, K., & Schieffelin, B. (1994). Language ideology. *Annual Review of Anthropology, 23*, 55-82.

Worthy, J. (2006) Como si le Falta un Brazo: Latino Immigrant Parents and the Costs of Not Knowing English, *Journal of Latinos & Education, 5*(2), 139-154.

Zentella, A. C. (1987). Language and female identity in the Puerto Rican community. In J. Penfield (Ed.), *Women and language in transition* (pp. 167-179). Albany: SUNY Press.

Story Club and Configurations of Literary and Cross-Cultural Insight Among Immigrant and Non-Immigrant Youth

Patricia Enciso
Allison Volz
The Ohio State University

Detra Price-Dennis
The University of Texas at Austin

Tati Durriyah
The Ohio State University

"I want to draw a map, so to speak, of a critical geography and use that map to open as much space for discovery, intellectual adventure, and close exploration as did the original charting of the New World—without the mandate for conquest." Morrison (1992, p.3)

If literary study with young people is ever going to be capable of creating new maps for intellectual, social, and self-discovery, as Morrison suggests, then the practice of making stories meaningful in school must be reconfigured. Such a change begins with the understanding that stories told or read in classrooms are associated with *prior narratives* that are situated in children's and teachers' experiences, other readings (of multiple text forms), and social discourses. Reading, in this view, is not a matter of 'getting meaning from the text'; it becomes what Ricouer (1983) calls a *configurational act,* calling upon readers to bring a collection of images, narratives, and experiences together into a complex whole (Smagorinsky, 2001).

Our research on storytelling with immigrant and non-immigrant students in a middle school setting is based on the concepts of configurational acts, Lee's (2007) Cultural Modeling theory, and Morrison's "critical geography." We argue that by documenting the ways a culturally heterogeneous group of students configure meanings for their own and others' oral stories we can construct new curricula and pedagogies that reflect and support the tacit knowledge they might bring to academic literary study. Our aim is to understand how children mobilize their knowledge of culturally specific stories in ways that relate to the disciplinary practices of literary study. We are aware, however, that like many mandated curricula, their literature curriculum limits configurations of meaning by overemphasizing identification and definitions of literary elements. Our second aim, then, is to understand how a "critical geography" of meaning is possible within the given curriculum and how the story club cultural data sets might be useful in constructing new curricular goals and practices that engage youth whose experiences, story forms, images, and linguistic practices are situated in diverse ethnic, racial, religious, and national identities.

We are addressing these questions through a multiyear, qualitative study of immigrant and non-immigrant middle school youth's storytelling and literary interpretations. Here, we report on a six month period between January and June 2009 when six to eight students met weekly in a lunchtime story club to share, question, and interpret stories based on everyday life at home and school, traditional oral narratives, movies, television programs, and events they remembered or were told that happened in cities, rural landscapes, and along refugee journeys before (and during) their first year of middle school. We focus on four ways students developed narrative content and configured meaning about their stories, themselves, and their shared experience in school: 1) Parallel storytelling, 2) Extended storytelling, 3) Joint storytelling, and 4) Reflexive and critical storytelling. We argue that these storytelling forms and the students' authority over and curiosity about one another's story content can be transformed for learning in the context of academic literary study if the curriculum is, likewise, transformed to become more oriented to story than the evaluation of isolated skills.

THEORETICAL FRAMES

Cultural Modeling

The configuration process is undoubtedly elusive for individual readers as they try to name what they know and understand about the ways a literary text works on their imaginations and emerging interpretations (Enciso 1996; 2004; Iser 1990). Lee (2007) addressed the gap between implicit and explicit knowledge of literary insights in her theory of Cultural Modeling. This theory argues for a systematic analysis of the practices and literary forms inherent in students' everyday language and popular media. This collection of practices is accompanied by a review and analysis of the discipline's cognitive and social demands and the routine problem solving inherent in the field of study—in this case literature. From this joint analysis, "cultural data sets" for literary study are created that show students the relationships between their prior narratives and the specific literary tropes, "habits of mind and dispositions" and "modes of argumentation" that accompany sophisticated, engaged literary analysis (Lee, 2007, p. 110-112). As Orellana and Eksner (2006) point out, Cultural Modeling is not a form of cultural matching that assumes people possess a static set of language forms that are then mirrored, for example, in familiar literary dialogue. Rather, Cultural Modeling "highlights the generative role of cultural funds of knowledge, and the specific ways in which one set of skills can be transformed for use in another setting" (Orellana & Eksner, p. 2).

Social Practices and Configurations of Meaning

Storytelling in story club was a new literacy practice in the school setting. This new practice was situated in the school's structures that typically isolated immigrant and non-immigrant students from one another during language arts education. Students' stories and storytelling practices were also told and reflected on in relationship with the school district's literature curricular guides and the accompanying surveillance of teaching and learning as teachers implemented question-answer protocols and skills assessments associated with standardized testing. Across the social practices (Luke 1995; Street 1995) of storytelling in story club and language arts education, we were interested in how students configured meaning when their own stories and processes of interpretation were encouraged.

Working within what Weis and Fine (2004) call a fracture or a place of possibility and change in an otherwise closed system, this research was informed by "an ethical belief that critical researchers have an obligation not simply to dislodge the dominant discourse, but to help readers and audiences [of the research] imagine where the spaces for resistance, agency, and possibility lie" (p. xxi). To this end, we constructed a hybrid or thirdspace (Gutiérrez & Baquedano-Lopez & Tejada 1999) during the school day, located in the school library, where we could engage children from across racial and ethnic groups in telling and interpreting their stories.

Narrative, Cultural, and Literary Sense-Making

In his analysis of the relationship between Vygotsky's concepts of thought and language, and literary understanding, Smagorinsky (2001) identifies two interdependent aspects of sense-making. The first is "sense" and can be understood as a "storm cloud of thought that produces the shower of words;" the second is "meaning" or what appears in a zone of articulation which becomes a represented, stable and unified form (p.275). As Smagorinsky argues, these two zones compose a meaningful whole. Sense, in this analysis, is changeable across situations, times, and people, while articulation can remain relatively constant. We propose that for participants in story club, a sense-orientation to language and literature developed in contrast with the dominant approach to learning that presented all narratives as "articulated" or finalized. In finalizing narratives, the landscapes of action and consciousness, as defined by Bruner (1990), are reduced to closed propositions and lose any potential for imagined scenarios, emotional changes, or transformations in perspective. Similarly, Daiute (2004) argues that children's "narrative texts represent an intersection of dialogues or 'moving relations' " (p.116), and can, therefore, be viewed as *sociobiographical activities* that are capable of capturing the tensions children experience between "cultural imperatives and responses to those imperatives" (p. 116). We find Daiute's analysis to be especially relevant to transnational narratives and the complex relations of discourse and power that students face in an articulated curriculum; that is, one which has predefined who is visible in a curriculum, who someone must become, and with what practices—to the exclusion of all other possible practices and stories. Configurational practices in story club were intended to create spaces for informal narrative production and interpretation that would allow us to document children's dynamic use of cultural resources for learning.

METHODS

Research Context and Mediated Learning Design

The youth in this study live in Alltown (pseudonym), a high poverty Midwestern community that had long been settled by African American and white Appalachian families. Over the past 10 years, new populations of Somali, Mexican, Central American, East Asian, and Caribbean families have established homes, places of religion and community centers. Although people express great pride in their working-class identities, children in our study also reported persistent narratives from peers and the media of exclusivity, superiority, and nationalism, leaving both immigrant and non-immigrant youth to defend their membership rights, in school, in the neighborhood, and in the state and nation.

Each week from December 2008 through early June 2009, children met with a teacher-researcher in their respective classrooms: a sixth-grade ESL class with eleven children (3 girls and 8 boys) from Cambodia, Somalia, Jordan, Kenya, Mexico, and the Dominican Republic; and a sixth grade Emotional Disorders class with 5 boys who identify with local African American and Appalachian communities.

The teacher-researcher also met weekly with the classroom teachers to select literature for study and coordinate the children's emerging interests and narratives with the district's curriculum and testing requirements. These weekly meetings with teachers became a significant "mediating space" (Engëstrom 1999; Moll 1990) for understanding the tensions between district curricular demands and children's narrative resources, their passion for local and transnational meaning in texts, and their interest in cross-cultural perspectives. In the related mediating space of story club, six case study participants (representing the diversity of the two groups) met during their lunchtime to tell stories.

All sessions were recorded with a high-definition digital camera and two or three digital audio recorders. Fieldnotes established a running account of changes in students' and teachers' use and reference to the increasing number of media, narratives, and artifacts children used to generate and interpret stories. Ongoing data analysis, informed by the guiding questions outlined above, focused initially on students' story topics and the uptake of stories across time. These topics were charted and key topics (e.g., ghost stories) were organized in a separate chart to indicate the sequence of tellings within and across story club sessions. Next, the audio and video data were reviewed to locate specific instances of storytelling confusions, collaboration, elaborations, silences, and transformations.

Four key practices of storytelling became evident in the data, based on several iterations of inductive analysis that included cross-referencing charts, specific instances of storytelling practices, fieldnotes, and video recordings. The four storytelling practices are described next along with an analysis of their potential for transforming literary study in middle school language arts education.

FINDINGS

Parallel Storytelling : Situating the Teller and the Told in the Literature Curriculum

From January through February 2009, a mandated districtwide curriculum for all middle schools focused on the memoir, *Of Beetles and Angels: A Boy's Remarkable Journey from a Refugee Camp to Harvard* by Mawi Asgedom (2002). The curriculum guide was informed by an underlying assumption that literacy skills can be directly and uniformly taught to children, regardless of their story knowledge, their histories and purposes for reading, or the story itself. These assumptions are evident in the language arts curriculum guides across urban schools.

The curriculum guide for Asgedom's memoir was structured by daily lessons that focused on predetermined questions, related and unrelated to the story. For example, the guide required the teacher to address the skills and standards for comparing and contrasting. Although the students were reading *Of Beetles and Angels*, with implicit comparisons available in the title, they were required to create a Venn diagram comparing tacos to kiwis. The cognitive task assumes universal world knowledge and requires no cross-cultural or literary interpretation. As a result, students and teachers are situated as strategy learners rather than as insightful interpreters of literary forms. In addition, their prior narratives and language knowledge were ignored, even when these would support configurations of metaphor and identity suggested by the story's title and themes. In a sense, the curriculum guide represents a parallel text that transforms Asgedom's story from a personal journey that was selected, presumably, to create greater understanding of immigrant experiences, to a series of isolated narratives used by students to perform literacy skills.

The official discourse of the curriculum guide also situates all readers and teachers as non-immigrant. SIOP or ESL lessons are designated at the end of the guide, but there is no mention of how to build upon or connect with students' immigrant experiences. For example, in Chapter 7, "Days of Mischief," Asgedom describes his boyhood perspective and antics related to the American celebration of Halloween. He recognizes the parallels to the Ethiopian celebration, Hoyo, Hoyo, when children run from one home to another shouting "Hoyo! Hoyo!" collecting treats, and eventually joining with the whole community for a feast. He also describes the racism, name calling, and fights he and his brother experienced as children in the small town of Wheaton, Illinois, where they tried to "turn the tables" and trick peers and adults at Halloween.

The curriculum guide for the chapter makes no mention of racism or exclusion. Instead, teacher and students' goals for reading are described in terms of the standards for being able to ask questions, summarize, define word meaning, practice pronunciation, and use organizational strategies to plan writing. Thus, the overall experience of literary reading is formulated as a practice of "conquest" whereby the story of racism remains unnamed, unaddressed, and, therefore, an unconfigured but highly relevant prior narrative—for both the author and the students.

Members of the story club followed the curriculum guide for Asgedom's memoir in their classrooms but also experienced more socially interactive literary study when Patricia Enciso led a weekly literature class. Of particular interest in our data analysis was a story, prompted by Asgedom's memoir, that Habiba told during class, and later retold during story club.

Habiba's parallel storytellling. As students in both classrooms listened to and discussed Asgedom's story, they talked about their experiences of racism on the playground, in shops, and within Alltown. Their analyses of racism included their uncertainties about who could be "legitimately" defined as American and how race and language interrupted a clear discourse for being designated American. In the midst of these discussions in the ESL classroom, Enciso directed the students' attention to the author's description of Halloween and invited students' stories of Halloween in America. Habiba, who identifies as Somali/Bantu, and who was still gaining confidence in extended use of English, responded immediately to my inquiry. She had rarely spoken in front of the whole group, and never at length. In story club, however, she had begun to initiate stories that were often elaborated on or explained by her peers.

The following summary of Asgedom's story is numbered to illustrate the correspondence of themes and events between his memoir and Habiba's story. Note that in both stories, the teller's immigrant status is acknowledged through relationships to place, family, and immigrant and non-immigrant community members' perspectives.

1. Mawi's family are, at first, the only Somali immigrants in Wheaton.

2. He hates the playground and afterschool fights based on racialized taunts.

3. Hoyo, Hoyo and Halloween share some similarities. Parents are skeptical of children's participation in American holiday traditions.

4. A local white woman intercedes on the children's behalf.

5. His parents were sick at times.

6. Some of the neighborhood and school peers taunted or called names; but others were more friendly and respectful.

7. Mawi and his brother found ways to steal and horde candy.

8. Mawi and his brother played tricks on other kids and adults during Halloween.

9. Mawi and his brother knew they had told a lie and were fearful of the consequences.

Prior to hearing Asgedom's narrative, Habiba told the following story (Bold font indicates associations with Asgedom's narrative.):

Enciso: This is about Halloween. Do you remember your first Halloween?

Habiba: Yes. I did. I was in a afterschool program,

1. and me and my brother was the only Somali in there.

2. **So people just bug us.** And then the teacher said we was going on a field trip on Halloween.

3. And then **we said we can't go.**

4. And she said she **would ask my mom** if you can go.

5. And she asked my mom but **she was sick.** So she asked my dad and my dad said yes. And then she **stopped the bad guys** and just took the people [who]

6. don't like, **don't tell people names**.

Enciso: So some people didn't get to go.

Habiba: Yes. Only seven got to go and three stayed home.

7. Enciso: Did you **get a lot of candy**?

   Habiba: Yeah.

8. **But my brother hide it from me.** And he took it to school every day. And when I ask him, he say, "Oh. Mommy just put it in the trash can." And then one day I saw it in his locker.

9. And I was like, **"You lie!"** "No. Those are my candies not your candies."

Habiba's story represents a valuable starting point from which to configure meaning about key events, relationships, and themes in Asgedom's story. Not only would this recentering of stories enable students to be situated as competent tellers and interpreters, the stories themselves, as others have argued, would be situated as cultural knowledge that contributes to configurations of meaning, belonging, and literary understanding (Campano & Ghiso in press; Martinez-Roldan 2005; Medina 2010).

Extended Storytelling: Jinns Across Time and Place

While parallel storytelling reflects children's tacit understanding of relationships among stories, extended storytelling points to the ways children attend to and configure meaning around diverse stories and prior narratives. Extended storytelling data helped us understand the tacit knowledge students bring to the process of framing, elaborating on, questioning, and eventually revising their interpretations of their own and others' culturally specific narratives. Such disciplinary knowledge can be transformed to guide more inclusive, "critical geographies" of meaning-making around multicultural literature study in classrooms.

During the first story club session, Tucker described a Cambodian figure named "Ya-Op," a ghost-monster who appears in the form of a disemboweled woman in the middle of the night and who eats babies. Tomás then described La Llorona, a spirit woman from the Mexican oral tradition, known in many versions to scare children who wander too close to rivers. Next, Habiba and Sara initiated a description of jinns or ghosts (as they initially called them) that can overtake a person's body and will. These initial tellings were soon to become the subject of extended configurations of meaning. From the first day of story club in January until our sixteenth meeting in June 2009, five to six stories were told per session, and jinns and ghosts were the subject of more than 30 stories.

Sara went on to say that the only way to defend against the ghosts is to know which lines to read from an ancient book of chants, that had been passed along in her family for generations. A young person, in particular, also needs help from an adult who will read passages from the Qur'an. She also told the story of a ghost that was extremely small, but troublesome, and lived in the walls of the house stealing food from people. But because of its size no one could follow it to exorcise it from the home. Her story concluded by explaining that the real name for the ghost is "jinn." Her peers listened attentively to her story—which was entertaining and familiar as a ghost story—and yet "hybrid" in the sense that it seemed to link a ghost story with religious practices. As evidenced in the following exchange, Sara and Habiba recognized their stories as connected to religious beliefs, while Tucker viewed *his* story, and therefore *their* stories as "just stories." At the same time, the introduction of a religious text in the jinn story prompted children to describe their bible reading and memorization experiences, and then to consider whether their religious practices and stories were "allowed" in school. In effect, this discussion opened the possibility that story club would not censor stories that mattered to them.

Enciso	Why do you think we don't hear these stories at school much?
Chris	Because we're not allowed to talk about it.
Tucker	Because we're not allowed to talk about it. (*All repeat*)
Sara	(Hand raised) Because they're religious...
...	
Tucker	These aren't religious stories. They're just stories.

We were aware that jinn stories could easily be misunderstood or colonized by prevailing ghost story narratives. For Habiba and Sara, and later, Hasana, jinns have a specific function within their daily lives and system of religious practices that do not intersect with ghosts as they are known through Hollywood films and other images of hauntings. This is not to say that the girls' interpretations of jinns were conclusive or finalized. Over time, they frequently questioned one another's understanding of the jinns' origins, forms of influence, and removal. However, it was many months before their stories were tacitly and explicitly interpreted by other students in terms of religious beliefs.

Initially, other story club members were interested in but did not try to elaborate on the girls' stories of jinns. Instead, they initiated their own stories about ghosts and scary movies. For example, on January 20th Sara elaborated on the value of ancestors, summoning spirits, and the mischief of jinns; and Habiba described the care that must be taken to protect babies from jinns. Parallel stories continued to develop around ghosts and supernatural sightings throughout the session. On January 27th, jinn stories were paralleled again by retellings of La Llorona, a more elaborated description of the Ya-Op, and a shared narrative about an Appalachian-origin ghost story called "Bloody Mary." Between early February and March, the children told fewer jinn stories but developed their understanding of one another's cultural traditions and religious beliefs, forming new insights about how their experiences are interrelated yet distinct (see Joint Storytelling).

In early May, Hasana joined the group, and told a story about being overcome when she saw a jinn and needed her brother's help to escape from it and then recite passages from the Qur'an. Habiba recounted a similar story involving a younger cousin, and Sara added that this experience had happened to her young cousin, too. Hasana argued that jinns are very scary because you could be taken away from your family; but "fun" because "you would be dancing all the time with them." Here she is referencing being overwhelmed or in a trance-like state when your body is inhabited by a jinn.

Following a round of stories about jinn encounters, and a retelling by Sara of the very small jinn behind a very small door, Chris, seated across from the girls, commented: "You guys are full of stories." To which Habiba replied, "We could tell stories like this for 24 hours."

Given the mounting evidence that the jinn stories were central to the girls' lives, Tucker asked if any of these jinns had ever been inside of *them*. All of the girls responded by saying no, but added that family members saw them and needed help. As the girls continued to question one another about jinns, there were several disagreements about how jinns come into being, and what size, shape and gender they can be. But they all agreed that they are most visible to children at nighttime. The light, they said, makes jinns melt away. This detail became relevant when Chris asked the girls directly if they believed the jinns are real.

Chris	Can I ask a question? Do you all actually <u>believe</u> that?
Habiba	Yeah. Of course it is real.
Hasana	We believe it <u>very well</u>.
Habiba	If you go to Africa and sleep there tonight, you will see them.
Sara	(laughs)
Habiba	I swear you will. And they will <u>freak</u> you <u>out</u>.
Hasana	It's true. If you go to Africa they will drive you <u>crazy</u>. Because Africa don't have these lights (raises her arm and hand toward the ceiling pointing to the fluorescent lights). And then they be scared of the light. Africa is <u>dark</u>.
Habiba	At night, when you sleep, it is dark.

Chris listened closely as did Tucker and Paul. But Chris began a story based on the irreconcilable values and practices associated with his Christian beliefs and his self-identified American Indian heritage. The following excerpt reconstructed for purposes of continuity in his storytelling, suggests that although he is telling a parallel story, he is extending the meaning of jinns as a religious story, not a familiar ghost story:

Chris	I believe what you said you believe in. But I don't believe in curses because my family's religious and I'm Indian so like we have a pow-wow... Like every three years. We go hunting and things in Washington [state]... Before we can get on our reservation, the shaman has to come out and bless the people that don't live on the reservation... We believe every person has a different animal spirit.

Even though the spirit Chris describes is benevolent, his tacit connections to the religious aspect of jinns is closer to themes and events of these stories than any others told so far. Similarly, Tucker told a story set in his contemporary Cambodian experience in the U.S. As a tacit extension of the need for a holy book and religious faith to overcome jinns, he reveals that by holding fast to religious beliefs he was protected from fear:

> Tucker   In Cambodia…my friends…if you didn't believe in a religion, you see weird
>   things like nightmares–if you're like atheist. But when I woke up, I was fine.
>   They're frightened but I was like what's the matter?

The extended storytelling associated with jinns began with limited points of reference for most story club members, then continued with shared narratives about ghosts, religious texts, and horror stories. In May, as the jinn stories were more personalized through Hasana's telling, the other participants began to recognize that indeed, for the girls, jinns are real. In turn, for the first time, the boys resituated and reconfigured the meaning of the jinn stories in alignment with a new set of narratives based on personal experiences of fear, protection, and religious practices. In addition, through their own storytelling, the boys tacitly situated jinn stories as belonging to culturally specific religious practices. Thus, the stories became open to new interpretations and possibilities for understanding human experience. For the first time in their storytelling arc, jinns had a place among other spiritual narratives and were no longer subject to a "map" that described a connected but "haunted" territory.

Story club data on extended storytelling suggest that as a culturally specific narrative evolves over time, the teller considers those details that are relevant to the group's interests; at the same time those listening work to situate the story, just as they might with unfamiliar literature. In story club however, the thinking and situating process is more available for questioning and development. Over time, the story club members were able to get to know one another and their beliefs as they also learned more about the meaning and implications of their stories. Similarly, in literature study, stories could be selected by students for rereading and interpretation across a year. Certainly, students are interested in sustaining a longer process of meaning configuration that invites multiple perspectives and first hand experiences on the same story content.

Joint Storytelling: Reconfiguring Stories for Alltown

In late January when La Llorona was told and explained again (to a new story club member) the students' discussion returned to the subject of Halloween. At this point in the collective history of story club, both groups had read Mawi Asgedom's story, and had been reading related stories including *Something About America* (Testa 2002), and *The Arrival* (Tan 2008). Their interest in and willingness to describe their lives across cultural differences had evolved into regular shared configurational inquiry about one another's lives and narratives in story club.

On February 3rd, the group briefly discussed their favorite stories told in story club, and Habiba was invited to retell the "First Halloween" story she had told in class. She constructed another extended narrative for the members of story club who were not members of her class. After finishing her story, Chris asked Habiba and Sara where they were from (for the second time) and if they did something like Halloween in their "…state …country." The girls explained their identities as immigrants who lived in Kenya (Habiba) as well as Jordan, Iraq, and the U.S. (Sara). They further explained that Eid is like Halloween because children could go to other people's houses and ask for money. Sara proudly described her best Eid when she gained more than $50 from her requests. As she put it, "The good thing about Eid is that the adults <u>have</u> to give you something. But the cheap ones just give you candy."

At that point, it seemed that Chris began to imagine his own participation in Eid. He repeated, "Fifty dollars!" Fifty dollars sounded like a good idea. Tomás also questioned the girls about the exact day of Eid and whether it overlapped with Halloween. The girls were not sure, and they were not clear, either about the point of the question. But Tomás reminded Chris that a nearby gas station and mini-mart was run by an Arabic-speaking gentleman. Then they both persisted in finding out more information about the practices around asking for money. Finally Chris announced that he and Tomás could plan to go to the Arabic-speaking gentleman on the last day of Eid and ask for money. Sara immediately countered that the boys could not speak Arabic. "Whatcha gonna do?" she asked. Tomás's face broke with a grin and he said, "I'll bring you all with me!"

Although their story was not retold in a completed form, the tellers had listened carefully to the culturally specific pieces of stories, reimagined their purposes and meaning in Alltown, and constructed a world where they would use one another's linguistic and cultural knowledge to outwit an unsuspecting adult. This is a wholly imagined scenario, unlike the stories traditionally told or shared as more familiar content. In many respects, joint storytelling represents the design and transformation of meaning described by the New London Group (1994) as vital practices in new literacy education.

In relation with Cultural Modeling, jointly constructed stories reveal the students' tacit knowledge about story structures such as setting, character perspectives, humor, and story resolution. In literary study, joint storytelling among immigrant and non-immigrant youth could invite socially created landscapes of consciousness and action that challenge students to interpret and anticipate how literary texts are formed and how they reveal information, as they also point to the ways students can value one another's experiences and knowledge.

Reflexive and Critical Storytelling

As students told stories, they also addressed what stories "do" and what they mean inside and beyond school. Their earlier exchange about religious beliefs, for example, raised questions for them (and the research team) about the place of those stories in school. Sara, Chris, and Paul explained the boundaries they experience around religious practices but continued to explore their meaning in everyday life:

Sara   Yeah. Sometimes we can ask the teacher if we can pray here. In that room (points) I think. We can go there if it's quiet.

Paul   Before I read the Bible I pray. And then me and my grandmother, she reads three chapters.

Chris   Just like I do.

By describing what they do around religious narratives at home, the students found common ground and a surprising degree of shared skepticism about the relative value of doing school work versus memorizing the Bible. In early March, Sara, Tucker, and Chris shared their mutual misery over memorizing extensive portions of religious texts.

Sara   I'm not even half-way.

Pat	She has to memorize it.
Chris	So do I!
Tucker	So do I.
Pat	No. She has to be able to recite it.
Chris	So do I!
Tucker	So do I!
Sara	If somebody asks you if. OK. If somebody asks you what. What like. What did you read on page 5? You have to say every single word.
Sara	And every word is so <u>complicated</u>. And. Really my father. All of my brothers and sisters finished. They don't even know the meanings of all the words. Some of the words are so complicated not many people know it. And it has so many different meanings you don't know what meaning it is.
Tucker	Then why read it?
Chris	Then why read it?
Sara	Because! You get a good deed if you finish it all.

They discovered, through their stories of reading religious texts at home, that this obligation was taken seriously by parents and extended family members, across their diverse religious traditions. And they, in turn, understood that this obligation had moral and lifelong implications for their well-being.

The cultural resources they accrued from one another during story club were also transformed in the same March session as they pursued a serious critique of school curricula. Chris argued that their education was missing the value of shared histories, languages, and interaction. In fact, he believed (incorrectly) that if he could enter the ESL classroom (a place he had deemed "uncool" a month earlier) he would have daily access to the multiple languages and viewpoints he had learned to value in story club:

Pat	How do you see the connection between the story club and learning to read in school and listening to stories?
Chris	It's whack. I think that we should be able to like. I think. Now it's a law. Well it's a law that they have [to learn Black History] because it's in our curriculum guide. When I was in like maybe in third, fourth-grade, we never learned about like Black history and stuff, and now it's <u>gotta</u> be part. We <u>have</u> to know about it. And I think it's not fair that only Black history is shown. But like not Hispanic or Arabic or Cambo- (Cambodian). All different cultures. It's just. It's just white and …
Sara	Just because something made history. And that, you know, doesn't mean that… Other people who have history other people don't know about.
Chris	No. And nobody really cares.

In the context of story club, and in the company of Sara, Tucker, and Tomás, Chris effectively challenged the injustice he saw in a curriculum that does not include students who do not relate to "American stories." And rather than introducing parallel stories as they had done earlier in story club sessions, the members built on one another's perspectives and critiques. Storytelling about stories that matter invite a serious meta analysis of the nature of stories and being a participant in school and home literacies.

DISCUSSION

A new, critical geography for literary study must begin with a more nuanced understanding of students' cultural knowledge. Parallel, extended, joint, and reflexive storytelling represent intercultural configurations of meaning and cultural knowledge that, we argue, can serve as cultural data sets for academic literary study. Each form of storytelling engaged students with the habits of mind and dispositions associated with literary reading, in some respects, while not fully addressing other aspects such as interpreting symbolism, story structures, or characterization. Parallel storytelling highlights students' tacit knowledge of theme and events; extended storytelling reveals students' deep interest in understanding others' stories beyond the familiar frames most often used for interpretation; joint storytelling shows the tremendous capacity of students to transform cultural and narrative knowledge for new designs of meaning; and reflexive and critical storytelling confirm that students want to know why stories matter to other people and how stories shape perceptions and values in a society.

The literature curriculum guide does not admit such exploration or revelation of students' cultural knowledge. Storytelling can only be recentered in the curriculum if configurations of meaning are valued over finalized meaning, and sense, the "storm cloud of thought," is encouraged as a beginning point for finding a way into and through literature. We argue that when young people are supported in sustained storytelling, they develop insight into the processes of forming meaning with others as they also playfully define the geography of their own and others' literary landscapes.

REFERENCES

Asgedom, M. (2002). *Of beetles and angels: A boy's remarkable journey from refugee camp to Harvard.* Chicago, IL: Megadee Books.

Bruner, J. (1987). *Actual minds, possible worlds.* Cambridge, MA: Harvard University Press.

Campano, G., & Ghiso, M. P. (In press) Immigrant students as cosmopolitan intellectuals. In S. Wolf, K. Coats, P. Enciso, and C. Jenkins (Eds). *The Handbook of Research on Children's and Young Adult Literature.* New York, NY: Routledge.

Daiute, C. (2004). Creative uses of cultural genres. In C. Daiute & C. Lightfoot (Eds). *Narrative analysis: Studying the development of individuals in society* (pp. 111-133). Thousand Oaks, CA: Sage. 111-133

Enciso, P. (1996). Why engagement in reading matters to Molly. *Reading and Writing Quarterly, 12*(2), 171-194.

Enciso, P. (2004). Reading discrimination. In S. Greene & D. Abt-Perkins (Eds.) *Making race visible: Literacy research for cultural understanding* (pp. 149-177). New York, NY: Teachers College Press.

Engeström, Y. (1999). Activity theory and individual and social transformation. In Y. Engeström, Y. R. Miettinen, & R-L Punamäki (Eds.), *Perspectives on activity theory* (pp. 19-38). Cambridge, UK: Cambridge University Press.

Gutiérrez, K. D., Baquedano-Lopez, P., & Tejeda, C. (1999). Rethinking diversity: Hybridity and hybrid language practices in the third space. *Mind, Culture, and Activity, 6*(4), 286–303.

Iser, W. (1990). *The act of reading: Toward a theory of aesthetic response.* Baltimore, MD: Johns Hopkins University Press.

Lee, C. (2007). *Culture, literacy, and learning: Taking bloom in the midst of the whirlwind.* New York, NY: Teachers College Press.

Luke, A. (1995). When basic skills and information processing just aren't enough: Rethinking reading in new times. *Teachers College Record 97*(1), 95-115.

Martínez-Roldan, C. (2005) The Interplay between Context and Students' Self-regulation in Bilingual Literature Discussions: A Case Study, *ISB4: Proceedings of the 4th International Symposium on Bilingualism*, James Cohen, Kara T. McAlister, Kellie Rolstad, and Jeff MacSwan (Eds), 1501-1521. Somerville, MA: Cascadilla Press.

Medina, C. (2010, January/February/March). "Reading Across Communities" in Biliteracy Practices: Examining Translocal Discourses and Cultural Flows in Literature Discussions. *Reading Research Quarterly, 45*(1), 40–60.

Moll, L (Ed.) (1990). *Vygotsky and education: Instructional implications and applications of sociohistorical psychology.* Cambridge, UK: Cambridge University Press.

Morrison, T. (1992). *Beloved.* New York, NY: Knopf.

New London Group. (1996). A pedagogy of multiliteracies: Designing social futures. *Harvard Educational Review, 66,* 60–92.

Orellana, M. F., & Eksner, J. H. (2006). Power in cultural modeling: Building on the bilingual language practices of immigrant youth in Germany and the United States. *National Reading Conference Yearbook, 55,* pp. 1-11.

Ricoeur, P. (1983). *Time and narrative* (Vol. 1; K. McLaughlin & D. Pellauer, Trans.). Chicago, IL: University of Chicago Press.

Smagorinsky, P. (2001). If meaning is constructed, what is it made from? Toward a cultural theory of reading. *Review of educational research, 71*(1), 133-169.

Street, B. V. (1995). *Social literacies: Critical approaches to literacy development, ethnography, and education.* London, UK: Longman.

Tan, S. (2007). *The arrival.* New York, NY: Scholastic.

Testa, M. (2005). *Something about America.* New York, NY: Candlewick Press.

Weis, L., & Fine, M. (2004). *Working method: Research and social justice.* New York, NY: Routledge.

Peritextual Discussions of Historical Fiction Picture Books

Suzette Youngs
University of Northern Colorado

Historical fiction picture books transport readers back in time through the use of text *and* visual images. In general, authors and illustrators of historical fiction picture books have 32 pages to blend together historical details and fictional elements to construct an engaging and historically accurate narrative. In order to do so, authors and illustrators take advantage of opportunities provided by peritextual features such as the cover, title page, author's note, endpages, and dust jacket to provide historical background information and to expand the written narrative (Higonett, 1998). I use the term peritextual because it refers specifically to information and elements contained within the book, whereas epitextual refers to elements and information outside the book such as books reviews and author interviews. The term paratext encompasses both terms; in other words, the peritextual and epitextual information equal the paratext (Pantaleo, 2003; Sipe & McGuire, 2006).

When readers attend to the peritextual features of historical fiction picture books, a greater understanding of an historical event becomes possible. Unfortunately, many teachers often miss the opportunities provided by the peritextual features to expand students' comprehension of historical events. By focusing on written text, visual images, *and* design elements of a picture book, readers are better positioned to take advantage of the meaning potential of these semiotic resources (Kress, 2003).

This article focuses on a study that explored students' interpretation and navigation of the peritextual features of historical fiction picture books. During the course of the study students' interpretations of the peritextual features and texts became more complex over time and students looked to the peritextual features as a potential resource for meaning. The peritextual features enhanced students' visual, literary, and historical understandings.

REVIEW OF RELATED LITERATURE

Multimodality and Picture Books

Picture books, including historical fiction picture books, are considered multimodal texts because they utilize more than one mode: namely image, text, and design to convey meaning. Illustrators draw upon visual design elements such as line, texture, shape, color, shape placement, character's gaze, and composition, to create images (Kress & van Leeuwen, 1996; Lewis, 2001). These elements also help to bring balance and unity as they convey the visual narrative across the entirety of the picture book (Sipe & McGuire, 2006). Written text is temporal and read sequentially, whereas image is simultaneous and read spatially (Kress, 2003). It is the consideration of text, design, *and* image that comprises picture book reading. This type of reading requires readers to have competency with both visual and textual systems of meaning to navigate the various modes available for interpreting multimodal texts (Kress & van Leeuwen, 2001; Unsworth & Wheeler, 2002). Interpretations of picture books become available to readers *because* they oscillate back and forth from text to image (Doonan, 1993; Lewis, 2001; Nodelman, 1988; Sipe, 1998, 2001). Readers then consider the meaning potential within each mode as well as across modes (Kress, 2003).

Historically greater weight has been given to written text in picture books than visual image (Anstey & Bull, 2006). Images are often considered support for what the written text is communicating (Kress & van Leeuwen, 2001). For example, when teachers do picture walks and turn to each image and ask students to predict what the text is going to communicate, image becomes a prompt for the written text. In other words, teachers use the images to make sense of text, rather than helping readers learn how to read visual images as a system of meaning in and of themselves. To garner the most from picture books, all modes must be considered, not one at the expense of the other. When readers attend to visual and textual cues provided by the author, illustrator, and publisher, a link is created between text-based and visual literacies (Anstey & Bull, 2006; Serafini & Ladd, 2008).

Peritextual Features

Because of the brevity of picture books, authors, illustrators, and publishers utilize all available space and draw from visual and textual systems of meaning within the pages of the peritext to communicate meaning (Higonnet, 1998; Nikolajeva & Scott, 2001). Genette (1997) describes the peritext as a feature that "mediates between the world of text and the world of publishing" (p. xviii). Peritextual features are "peripheral features" (Higonnet, 1998) that include, but are not limited to, the cover, title page, author's note, endpages, and dust jacket.

According to Sipe and McGuire (2006) peritextual features in picture books are constructed in ways that create a "unified effect" (p. 291). For example, endpages can be used to introduce the color scheme of a book and set the mood. All peritextual features work together to present a cohesive narrative. Nikolajeva and Scott (2001) write, "Endpapers can convey essential information, and pictures on title pages can both complement and contradict narrative. Since the amount of verbal text in picturebooks is limited, the title itself can sometimes constitute a considerable percentage of the book's verbal message" (p. 241). Pantaleo (2003) and Sipe and McGuire (2006) observed how children used the dust jackets, endpages, title pages, and dedications to make predictions and noticed how the peritextual information often extended stories because they included additional information not in the written narrative.

Attending to the peritextual features of historical fiction picture books helps set expectations for readers to become familiar with the storyline, characters, and historical event before reading the written narrative (Youngs, 2009). Peritextual features set the stage for the ensuing story and provide a sneak peek for readers (Sipe & McGuire, 2006).

In addition, important historical background information is often provided within the author's note and contained in the dust jacket. By attending to these features, readers are exposed to information about the historical event or time in history. They may also learn about the depth of research that was conducted in order to visually and textually create an authentic and accurate historical narrative. The information provided in the author's note can include details on what aspects of the text were fictional and which parts were taken from actual historical events.

Cultural and historical visual symbols are often introduced in the dust jacket or on the title page as cut out images (an image with no background detail) in historical fiction picture books. For example, in *A Place Where Sunflowers Grow* (Lee-Tai, 2006), there are cut out images on the dust jacket of Japanese Internment cabins and in *Home of the Brave* (Say, 2002), on the title page there is a cutout image in the shape of a bird in flight made from Japanese Internment tag internees were required to wear. These images introduce the reader to the story, but also invite readers to think beyond the literal to interpret the symbolic and inferential meanings the image might convey. The image of the tag might suggest flying home, freedom, or releasing of the past. Reading this image, as a symbol, requires readers to think metaphorically and to consider the cultural and historical significance the image might suggest (Albers, 2008; Nodelman, 1988).

Nikolajeva & Scott (2001) and Pantaleo (2003) suggest there is limited research on students' responses to peritextual features and children's responses to the multimodal nature of historical fiction picture books. Research on historical fiction has traditionally examined how historical fiction picture books can supplement the social studies curriculum to engage readers in critical discussions, historical thinking, and understanding (Levstik, 1989, 1993; Levstik & Barton, 2005; Roser & Keehn, 2002). This article extends the research base focusing on students' responses to the peritextual features and the multimodal nature of historical fiction picture books.

The research questions that guided this study were: 1) What types of responses do fifth-graders construct during their transactions with historical fiction picture books with purposeful instruction on genre, picture book design, and visual design elements?, 2) What types of responses do fifth-graders construct during their transactions with the peritextual features of historical fiction picture books?

METHOD

Context

This study was conducted over the course of four months in a fifth-grade classroom in collaboration with Emily (all names are pseudonyms), the classroom teacher. Emily was in her third year of teaching at the time of the study. Emily taught in a district where a core program was mandated, and at her school, fidelity to the program was expected. The reading block consisted of whole class instruction with core program anthology selections, small guided reading groups, and independent work. There were 26 students in the class at the time of the study. The ethnicity makeup of this class consisted of: 20 Anglo-European students; 2 African-American students; and 4 Hispanic students. This class had 2 students with an Individualized Education Program (IEP), 1 receiving English Language Learner (ELL) services, 5 students were reading below grade level, 18 were at grade level, and 3 were reading above grade level at the time of the study.

Phases of the Study

The study was conducted in three phases, the first being classroom observation of the literacy block. I positioned myself as a participant observer (Erickson, 1986) and audiotaped and transcribed lessons to gain an understanding of their literacy practices. During the second phase I conducted a series of 10 whole-class interactive read-alouds (Barrentine, 1996) with explicit demonstrations and learning experiences that helped readers become familiar with the genre of historical fiction, peritextual features, and visual design elements, and how to use these features in their meaning construction. The whole-class lessons lasted for two weeks, and during this time,

I worked in collaboration with the classroom teacher as she observed the read-alouds and kept observational notes on student responses and interactions.

During the third phase Emily returned to core program instruction and I met with small groups. Students were organized, with input from the teacher, into three small groups where there was a variety of reading abilities, but a balance of gender. I met with a different small group each day and read the same book to each group. One book was read each week and each meeting lasted 45 minutes. These small-group read-alouds extended the whole-class lessons as I facilitated the group discussion (Peterson & Eeds, 2007) and took advantage of teachable moments. My goal was to support students in their efforts and to help students take their discussions further than they would be able to go on their own. During the small groups students engaged in interactive read-alouds where they were invited to share ideas at any point to each other or to me during the read-aloud (Barrentine, 1996).

Book Selections

First, we purposefully chose historical fiction picture books around four major historical eras that Emily would later address in her social studies curriculum: 1) Japanese Internment; 2) The Holocaust; 3) Slavery; and 4) Civil Rights. Then, I chose picture books within those eras where the images were as compelling as the text. The text/image relationship in these books was considered enhancing as text and images each enriched the meaning of the other (Nikolajeva & Scott, 2001). The picture books also met the criteria for high-quality historical fiction as put forth by Temple, Martinez, and Yokota (2006): 1) author brings the setting to life for the reader; 2) historical details add to the story; 3) characters behave in ways that are congruent with the time period in which they lived and are realistic; and 4) conflicts in the story are plausible based on the time period (p. 368) (see *Appendix A* for a list of historical fiction picture books read with students).

Data Collection

Data collection consisted of audiotaped sessions of 10 whole-group and ten small-group read-alouds and discussions. All audiotapes were transcribed and analyzed, in addition, all whole-class read-alouds were videotaped and analyzed. All written responses to the picture books were copied and analyzed as well.

Data Analysis

The first level of analysis was completed by doing a chronological analysis of the entire data set. I used the conversational turn as the unit of analysis (Sinclair & Coulthard, 1975). During this analysis 2,669 student conversational turns were coded and analyzed. Each read-aloud transcript was read and a line-by-line analysis was completed. During open coding (Strauss & Corbin, 1998), concepts were constructed into categories. From the first level of analysis, five content categories were constructed. These categories represented the focus of the conversational turn; they were: Narrative Features, Historical, Connections, Peritextual Features, and Symbolism (see *Appendix B* for description and example of each).

During the second level of analysis all student conversational turns were coded using Serafini and Ladd's (2008) coding scheme for literal or inferential responses. Responses were coded as "literal" if the responses "focused on the literal text and images, and did not include interpretive references" and responses were coded as "inferential" or interpretive if the responses "went beyond the literal text and visual images" (Serafini & Ladd, pp. 12-13). This analysis revealed that 65% of the conversational turns were inferential.

The third level of analysis, utilizing axial and selective coding (Strauss & Corbin, 1998), was completed as I examined all interpretive responses more closely. Although the responses all matched the criteria for interpretive responses, they were not all similar in complexity. In an effort to describe these variations in complexity I coded the responses into levels of interpretive trajectory. I use the term trajectory because it means a path or progression or line of development (Trajectory). Trajectory describes the path these readers took in their progression to more complex interpretations.

Within the interpretive trajectory there are different levels of interpretation. The first two levels describe the literal responses students had to these books. Literal Naming is where a student named/ identified a word or image and made no inferential references and the conversational turn ended. Noticing is where a student noticed an image but is different from Literal Naming because the act of noticing led to inferential thinking and the conversational turn continued. Interpretive Naming were responses where a student named a visual design element or named a peritextual feature and that naming led to inferential thinking.

The next levels are the Micro Intratextual (within the book) and Micro Intertextual (outside the book). Micro refers to the close analysis represented by responses that were directed at what was happening on the page spread. Micro Intratextual responses refer to those that analyzed and interpreted the images and text within the page spread and inferred meaning. Yet they did not connect these interpretations to the meaning of the book as a whole within that conversational turn. At the Micro Intertextual level students connected ideas and aspects of the narratives to their own lives and to other literature. They made connections to things outside the book, but responses were directed at microanalysis of the page spread.

The last two levels are the macro levels of interpretation. Macro refers to the big ideas of a book and broad historical connections. At the Macro Intratextual level students understood the book as a whole in response to the details and aspects of the book came together. At the Macro Intertextual level students made broad historical or cultural connections and/or displayed historical understanding.

I then represented these levels of interpretation on an Interpretive Trajectory Chart (see Figure 1). The Interpretive Trajectory Chart represents all levels of interpretation, and indicates that all levels are important. This relationship is represented in the building block design of the chart. Each type/level of response acts as a building block to other levels and describes the variations in complexity in student interpretations. For example, a reader cannot interpret something they do not notice and understanding a text as a whole comes from analyzing the details as described in the hermeneutic cycle (Nikolajeva, 2005). Students noticed images at the Literal Naming level, analyzed meaning at the page level (Micro Interpretations), and projected those interpretations to make sense of the book as a whole (Macro Interpretations). Each level provides a foundation for the next and each were important for these readers to construct meaning with historical fiction picture books.

Lastly, during the fourth level of analysis I selected all conversational turns that were in direct relation to the peritextual features. I plotted each read-aloud upon the *Interpretive Trajectory*

Figure 1. Interpretive Trajectory Chart

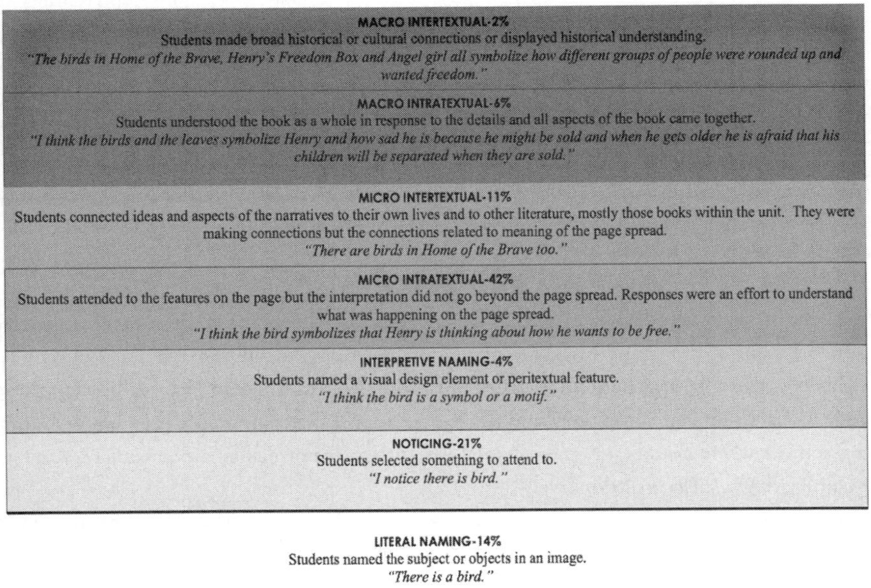

MACRO INTERTEXTUAL-2%
Students made broad historical or cultural connections or displayed historical understanding.
"The birds in Home of the Brave, Henry's Freedom Box and Angel girl all symbolize how different groups of people were rounded up and wanted freedom."

MACRO INTRATEXTUAL-6%
Students understood the book as a whole in response to the details and all aspects of the book came together.
"I think the birds and the leaves symbolize Henry and how sad he is because he might be sold and when he gets older he is afraid that his children will be separated when they are sold."

MICRO INTERTEXTUAL-11%
Students connected ideas and aspects of the narratives to their own lives and to other literature, mostly those books within the unit. They were making connections but the connections related to meaning of the page spread.
"There are birds in Home of the Brave too."

MICRO INTRATEXTUAL-42%
Students attended to the features on the page but the interpretation did not go beyond the page spread. Responses were an effort to understand what was happening on the page spread.
"I think the bird symbolizes that Henry is thinking about how he wants to be free."

INTERPRETIVE NAMING-4%
Students named a visual design element or peritextual feature.
"I think the bird is a symbol or a motif."

NOTICING-21%
Students selected something to attend to.
"I notice there is bird."

LITERAL NAMING-14%
Students named the subject or objects in an image.
"There is a bird."

Chart and analyzed the complexity of interpretations students made in response to the peritextual features. By plotting the conversational turns on the chart I was able to understand the interpretive trajectory within each read-aloud as well as the interpretive trajectory across read-alouds. Responses to the peritextual features comprised 17% of all conversations turns, thus representing a small yet interesting subset of the data.

RESULTS

Data analysis revealed that students' responses to peritextual features changed quantitatively and qualitatively over time. Not only did students attend and discuss the features in greater detail and length, but their interpretations became more complex. More specifically I constructed three major assertions about students' reading and understanding of the peritextual features of historical fiction picture books: 1) student responses to the peritextual features became more complex over time; 2) students looked to the peritextual features as a potential resource for meaning; and 3) students made intertextual peritextual connections of visual and historical symbols across historical events and picture books. Each assertion is described below and student responses to the peritextual features are taken from three historical fiction picture books that represent read-alouds from the beginning, middle, and end of the study. The books are listed in the order they were read during the study: 1) *So Far From the Sea* (Bunting, 1998), 2) *Angel Girl* (Friedman, 2008), and 3) *Henry's Freedom Box* (Levine, 2007) (see *Appendix C* for description of picture books).

Student Responses to the Peritextual Features Became More Complex Over Time

Analysis of the *Interpretive Trajectory* Charts for the three-read-alouds representing the beginning, middle, and end of the study and examination of all the read-alouds across the entire study revealed responses to peritextual features became more sophisticated over time. Analysis of the *Interpretive Trajectory Charts* revealed that the number of conversational turns related to these features increased over time from 26% in the whole-group read-aloud to 42% in the small-group read-aloud. Students spent more time discussing these features once they understood they were a potential resource to draw upon for constructing meaning. Over the course of the study students attended and analyzed these features to construct complex literary interpretations.

During the read-aloud of *So Far From the Sea* (Bunting,1998), the first book read in the study, 26% of the conversational turns referred to the peritextual features. Many of the turns were single topic strands suggesting students noticed something and then went on to another topic. In the vignette below, students responded literally as they named objects in the image because I asked them to tell me (Chambers, 1996) what they noticed, but they struggled to attach significance to their noticings. Also, it was not yet a literary practice to attend to the peritextual features for these students.

John: Um, there, it looks like the mountain looks like it's already snowed

S: Okay
(Researcher)

Emma: and there's big heavy clouds it's going to snow again maybe.

Anna: I noticed a difference between the two pictures is that the black and white one has only one kid but the colored one has two kids.

S: So what are you thinking about that?

Anna: I'm not sure.

In this excerpt, students focused on the text and images for literal understanding; the responses did not include interpretive references and students were unsure of how to construct meaning with the visual images or text on the cover. These comments are representative of the first two read-alouds before students began to understand the functionality of these features.

During the 10 whole-class read-alouds, I taught students about the peritextual features and visual design elements. Over time, students began to notice them and analyzed the use of various visual design elements within the peritextual features even more. At first I needed to bring these features and elements to the attention of the students but by the end of the study, as exemplified in the vignette below, students not only noticed the features but they began to attend and analyze their function and contribution to the story as a whole. During the last whole-class read-aloud of *Henry's Freedom Box* (Levine, 2007), students were engaged with the notion of demand (a character looks right at the viewer). On the jacket cover Henry is sitting with blue skies in the background and birds flying overhead. In the following vignette students share their interpretations:

Craig: He's looking right at us, he's trying to tell us that, that I'm going to be free no matter how long it takes me.

Isabella: It looks like he's happy and it kinda looks like he's free because the background's not all dark. It's bright and he doesn't look like he's trapped in a building where it's all dark and he's being beaten. And he can't get whipped and stuff.

Ellen: I was thinking, you know, to add on to what Isabella was saying, about the darkening… like the birds, maybe the lightest part is the freedom. And then as it gets darker, it's all the slavery, so that's why the birds are probably in the blue part.

Kyle: I would say, agreeing with everyone, the birds would mean freedom because a bird can fly anywhere it wants without delay.

Students analyzed another visual images on the cover, which helped them understand his plight, and details about slavery. Craig used the visual design element of demand to interpret what the character might be thinking or what the illustrator is communicating to the viewer through the use of demand. They also attended to the symbolic nature of birds and how they represent freedom and spirituality and observed the shading and lighting within the cover illustration. They attached symbolic meanings to these images and looked to darkness as slavery and bright blue as freedom. As they learned about peritextual features and visual design elements over the course of the study, their responses became more detailed and complex as they analyzed the visual design elements to make sense of the visual narrative. Interpretations of the peritextual features progressed from Literal Naming to Macro Interpretations. Students needed time and practice to become more familiar with the text, and the function of peritextual features before using them as a resource. The next two sections also provide examples of dialogue that demonstrate shifts in complexity. Students turned to the peritext to construct meaning in a variety of ways.

Students Looked to the Peritextual Features as a Potential Resource for Meaning

During these read-alouds, students engaged in discussions about the multimodal nature of historical fiction picture books as they alternated between text and image *and* between cover, jacket, and story. Students used the peritextual resources as a potential for constructing meaning and made intratextual connections. Because we attended to the jacket, cover, and title page before reading, students returned to these features during reading to enhance their understanding of the unfolding story.

In this next discussion students referred to the jacket and cover of *So Far From the Sea* (Bunting, 1998) to clarify events and purpose of certain visual images:

Emily: Um, on the back one is barbed wire fences and when you were reading it says all the barbed wire fences are gone.

Jake: It was like, that was like back in the day during World War II.

Sarah: The pictures were grey and white and these are colored.

Brendan: Um, uh, you said, they said that the barbed wire was gone, right here that looks like a piece of fence that's still there the pictures were taken at the same place but things were different then, right.

With more exposure to other historical fiction books and their peritextual features, students inferred what the images suggested in relation to the whole story. During reading, students often referred to various peritextual features as a resource to confirm or enhance an interpretation. For example, when reading *Angel Girl* (Friedman, 2008), students noticed that a picture in the story was similar to the image used on the cover. They observed a difference between the two, as one had a tear and one did not. While interpreting these differences, Anna referred to the author's note to defend her idea:

Isha: Is that a tear?

Craig: It's a tear.

Ellen: Why is she crying though?

S: Happiness? Maybe sadness that she won't see him anymore?

Anna: She just said, in the author's note, that it wasn't a cry of a sad beginning; it was of the happy ending!

Anna referred to the author's note and what she had to say about the story as a whole and used this information to construct meaning for this particular image and to challenge my interpretation. Observing the difference created a space for students to oscillate between text (author's note) and image (cover and image in the story).

Students also analyzed another cover of *Henry's Freedom Box* (Levine, 2007) to make sense of the setting. Students noticed where he was sitting and what it might mean for him:

Isha: I noticed the background, the bricks are fading and he's sitting on a bucket.

Craig: A wooden bucket.

S: Okay what are you thinking about this picture?

Braden: Like he's sad and he's just sitting there.

Jake: I am adding on to Isha's, because he is a slave it looks like he is surrounded by bricks—nowhere to go.

Looking at the cover and asking students what they noticed helped them analyze the visual cues that were available for meaning. The images guided them and the predictions they made were not wild or off topic, but rather grounded in the images available for interpretation. Over time students navigated the reading path, which included returning to or going ahead to various peritextual features to expand or confirm their interpretations.

Comparison of Visual and Historical Symbols Across Historical Events and Literature

Many illustrators and/or publishers include a cutout image on the title page or on the back covers. A cutout image is an image placed on white space with no background features. During our discussions I asked students what they noticed about the image and then what meaning it might hold for the rest of the book. We analyzed why that one image would be the most important to use over all the other images available. Responses demonstrated students' ability to think metaphorically as they analyzed the symbolic nature of the image and projected that meaning onto the book and other books which set up their expectations for reading. Students often referred to the cutout image throughout the read-aloud as well. Students connected these images across historical events and other peritextual features.

During the discussion of *Angel Girl* (Friedman, 2008), students attended to the cutout image on the back cover that included a picture of a boxcar and some barbed wire. They constructed symbolic meaning as they connected the train that transported Jewish people to concentration camps and the buses that transported the Japanese-Americans to internment camps. The illustrators used these images drawing from historical symbolism of the boxcars during the Holocaust, but students made the connection between the buses and then used these images to understand where the character was going and what the story was going to be about. Barbed wire was also recognized as a symbol of internment across texts and was included in books about the Holocaust and Japanese Internment. Students used these symbolic images to connect across the various books in the study. In the following vignette students discuss the cutout image of the train in *Angel Girl*:

Lori: There's a train, it's a cutout image.

Craig: She is going on a train and there's bared wire in the back so it's like Japanese internment.

Anna: I think she is in a camp but not a Japanese one.

Hannah: In that cutout image; it looks like her mom's like being taken away from her. And it looks like she is trying to follow with that little boy.

Kyle: It looks like you know the buses that take them there.

Isha: That looks like a train though that's taking them there.

S: The buses that took who where?

Nick: The Japanese, in *The Bracelet* they were taken away by buses so I think they are going to be taken away by trains.

S: Ok so you're connecting this train car to the buses. So tell me more about that.

Kyle: Because they go into the train so maybe they are going into an internment camp.

Hannah: Concentration camp.

From the very first read-aloud, students attended to the images of barbed wire and equated these images with containment and noticed these images were present in the books read about internment. Students connected barbed wire to internment and assumed she was going to an internment camp. They also connected buses and trains as ways of transporting people to camps and assumed characters were going to an internment camp, and then a student corrected as she stated a concentration camp. This discussion set the expectations for reading and opened dialogue for students to compare visual and historical symbols across historical events.

While reading *Home of the Brave* (Say, 2002), another book about Japanese Internment, students interpreted the meaning of the image of the Japanese Internment tag. This image was present in four of the picture books read. In the cutout image on the title page the tag is floating in the air and is folded suggesting the shape of a bird. I asked students to think about why that image might be so important that it is on the title page:

Braden: In the last story [*So Far From the Sea*] they had tags.

Jason: I think they are throwing down the tag because of their freedom.

Anna: I'm thinking maybe that one fell off and then it got blown away by the wind and got separated from its family.

Brittany: I think they got tired of it and they just ripped it off and they tried to run away.

Braden noticed and made a connection to *So Far from the Sea* (Bunting, 1998) and then students followed with three different interpretations as to why the tag might be there. All of the ideas were grounded in their developing understanding of Japanese Internment and the image acted as a point of entry into *different* interpretive responses.

Students also noticed different historical symbols that were on the cover. For example, on the cover of *The Bracelet* (Uchida, 1993), Brittany noticed: " She's not really happy, just like in *Home of the Brave*, she has one of those tags on and the suitcase is open and it's like they were told to bring only what they could carry." As students gained in background knowledge and became accustomed to looking *to* images as a resource for meaning, they made more connections and noticed patterns across historical contexts through their interpretations of various images.

Students read the title pages and cutout images and interpreted their meanings in multiple ways. The discussions about the cutout image required readers to attend to the visual, as they inferred meaning and enriched their understandings of the historical event. Students identified, named, and described what cutout images can suggest and used that information to construct multiple understandings that added to their progressing interpretations. Additionally, they noted how illustrators used title page scenes to extend the narrative.

DISCUSSION

Attention to the potential for meaning in the peritextual features and to the visual design elements acted as a point of departure for students to analyze and interpret the story at a deeper level. Students attended to these features and considered them as resources for meaning as seen in these discussions. They attended to both text and image within the peritext to establish their understandings before, during, and after reading the story. These discussions demonstrated multiple understandings and it became a literary practice within this interpretive community (Fish, 1980) to consider and consult with the peritextual resources when constructing meaning.

Nodelman (1988) suggested, "objects in pictures become meaningful in relation to the extent to which we notice them and single them out for special attention. The more we notice them, the more visual *weight* they have" (p.101). This study indicated that students gave more *visual weight* to the peritextual features because they attended to them in great detail. Students selected various images within the peritextual features and attributed symbolic meaning to them. Students described images like the suitcase, apple, tag, and cabins, and moved beyond the literal to infer and negotiate possible meanings (Serafini & Ladd, 2008). Analyzing the symbolic images and peritextual features created space for interpretation and promoted engagement with the book.

Making a shift to understanding multimodality and understanding three-meaning systems (visual, textual and design) rather than focusing solely upon the printed text for meaning (Kress & van Leeuwen, 2001) created opportunities for students to construct complex interpretations. Not only were images available as a resource for meaning but students appropriated the language of visual design (Kress & van Leeuwen, 1996), as seen when students discussed the importance and meaning of the cutout image. Readers did not rely on written text to carry *all* the meaning, but turned to text, image, and design to construct their interpretations.

Pantaleo (2003) suggested, "...teachers need to be aware of how these features contribute to the construction of meaning of the text" (p.75). We cannot show students what we are not aware of ourselves. As classroom teachers use historical fiction picture books to enhance their reading and history instructional practices, teachers need to understand how these books work and the resources that are available for interpretation within the peritextual features. If teachers and readers do not attend to these features, they are missing out on potential opportunities to enhance comprehension.

These peritextual discussions were much more about interpretation and negotiation than finding a main idea or a single interpretation (Nystrand, 1997). Reading powerful historical fiction picture books, where meaning is communicated through textual and visual narrative and peritext, is a way for teachers to introduce and engage in sophisticated dialogue with students that opens pathways for interpretation and expands students' visual, historical, and literary understandings.

REFERENCES

Albers, P. (2008). Theorizing visual representation in children's literature. *The Journal of Literacy Research, 40*(2), 163-200.

Anstey, M., & Bull, G. (2006). *Teaching and learning multiliteracies: Changing times, changing literacies.* Newark, DE: International Reading Association.

Youngs, S. (2009). *Literary, visual, and historical understandings: Intermediate readers respond to historical fiction picture books.* Unpublished doctoral dissertation, University of Nevada, Reno.

Barrentine, S. (1996). Engaging with reading through interactive read-alouds. *The Reading Teacher, 50*(1), 36-43.

Bunting, E. (1998). *So far from the sea.* New York, NY: Houghton Mifflin.

Chambers, A. (1996). *Tell me: Children, reading, and talk.* York, ME: Stenhouse.

Doonan, J. (1993). *Looking at pictures in picture books.* Stroud, UK: Thimble Press.

Erickson, F. (1986). Qualitative methods in research on teaching. In M. C. Wittrock (Ed.), *Handbook of research on teaching* (3rd ed., pp. 119-161). New York, NY: Macmillan.

Fish, S. (1980). *Is there a text in this class? The authority of interpretive communities.* Cambridge, MA: Harvard University Press.

Friedman, L. (2008). *Angel Girl.* Minneapolis, MN: Carolrhoda Books.

Genette, G. (1997). *Paratexts: Thresholds of interpretation.* (J. Lewan, Trans.). New York, NY: Cambridge Press.

Higonnet, M. R. (1998). The playground of the peritext. *Children's Literature Association Quarterly, 15,* 47-49.

Kress, G. (2003). *Literacy in the new media age.* London, UK: Routledge.

Kress, G., & van Leeuwen, T. (1996). *Reading images: The grammar of visual design.* London, UK: Routledge Falmer.

Kress, G., & van Leeuwen, T. (2001). *Multimodal discourse: The modes and media of contemporary communication.* London, UK: Routledge Falmer.

Lee-Tai, A. (2006). *A place where sunflowers grow.* New York, NY: Children's Book Press.

Levine, E. (2007). *Henry's freedom box.* New York, NY: Scholastic.

Levstik, L. (1989). Historical narrative and the young reader. *Theory Into Practice, 28*(2), 114-119.

Levstik, L. (1993) I wanted to be there: The impact of narrative on children's historical thinking. In M. Tunnell & R. Ammon (Eds.), *The story of ourselves: Teaching history through children's literature* (pp. 65-77). Portsmouth, NH: Heinemann.

Levstik, L., and Barton, K. (2005). *Doing history: Investigating with children in elementary and middle schools.* Mahawah, NJ: Lawrence Erlbaum Associates.

Lewis, D. (2001). *Reading contemporary picture books: Picturing text.* London, UK: Routledge Falmer.

Nikolajeva, M. (2005) *Aesthetic approaches to children's literature: An introduction.* Lanham, MD: The Scarecrow Press Inc.

Nikolajeva, M., & Scott, C. (2001). *How picture books work.* New York, NY: Routledge.

Nodelman, P. (1988). *Words about pictures: The narrative art of children's picture books.* Athens, GA: University of Georgia Press.

Nystrand, M. (1997). *Opening dialogue: Understanding the dynamics of language and learning in the English classroom.* New York, NY: Teachers College Press.

Pantaleo, S. (2003). "Godzilla lives in New York": Grade 1 students and the peritextual features of picture books. *Journal of Children's Literature, 29*(2), 66-77.

Peterson, R., & Eeds, M. (2007). *Grand conversations: Literature groups in action.* New York, NY: Scholastic.

Roser, N., & Keehn, S. (2002). Fostering thought, talk, and inquiry: Linking literature and social studies. *Reading Teacher, 55*(5), 416-26.

Say, A. (2002). *Home of the brave.* New York, NY: Houghton Mifflin.

Serafini, F., & Ladd, S. M. (2008). The challenge of moving beyond the literal in literature discussions. *Journal of Language and Literacy Education* [Online], *4*(2), 6-20. http://www.coe.uga.edu/jolle/2008_2/challenge.pdf

Sinclair, J. M., & Coulthard, R. M. (1975). *Towards an analysis of discourse: The English used by teachers and pupils.* London, UK: Oxford University Press.

Sipe, L. (1998). How picture books work: A semiotically framed theory of text-picture relationships. *Children's Literature in Education, 24,* 66-75.

Sipe, L. (2001). Picture books as aesthetic objects. *Literacy Teaching and Learning: An International Journal of Early Reading and Writing, 6*(1), 23-42.

Sipe, L., & McGuire, C. (2006). Picture book endpapers: Resource for literary and aesthetic interpretation. *Children's Literature in Education, 37,* 291-304.

Strauss, A. L., & Corbin, J. M. (1998). *Basics of qualitative research: Techniques and procedures for developing grounded theory* (2nd ed.). Thousand Oaks, CA: Sage Publications.

Temple, C., Martinez, M., & Yokota, J. (2006). *Children's books in children's hands* (3rd ed.). New York, NY: Allyn & Bacon.

Trajectory (n.d.). In *Oxford English Dictionary.* Retrieved January 15, 2010, from www.askoxford.com:80/concise_oed/trajectory?view=uk

Uchida, Y. (1993). *The bracelet.* New York, NY: Philomel.

Unsworth, L., & Wheeler, J. (2002). Re-valuing the role of images in reviewing picture books. *Reading, 36*(2), 68-74.

APPENDIX A

Children's Literature References

Bradby, M. (1995). *More than anything else.* New York, NY: Orchard.

Bunting, E. (1998). *So far from the sea.* New York, NY: Houghton Mifflin.

Bunting, E. (2002). *One candle.* New York, NY: Joanna Cotler Books.

Coleman, E. (1996). *White socks only.* Morton Grove, IL: Albert Whitman.

Deedy, C. A. (2000). *The yellow star.* Atlanta, GA: Peachtree.

Friedman, L. (2008). *Angel Girl.* Minneapolis, MN: Carolrhoda Books.

Hoagland Hunter, S. (2007). *The unbreakable code.* Flagstaff, AZ: Rising Moon.

Innocenti, R. (1985). *Rose Blanche.* New York, NY: Creative Paperbacks.

Johnson, A. (2007). *A sweet small of roses.* New York, NY: Aladdin.

Kirkpatrick, K. (1999). *Redcoats and petticoats.* New York, NY: Holiday.

Lee-Tai, A. (2006). *A place where sunflowers grow.* New York, NY: Children's Book Press.

Levine, E. (2007). *Henry's freedom box.* New York, NY: Scholastic.

Longfellow, H. W. (1990). *Paul Revere's ride.* New York, NY: Dutton.

Lorbiecki, M. (1998). *Sister Anne's hands.* New York, NY: Dial Books.

Lunn, J. (1998). *Charlotte.* Toronto, Canada: Tundra Books.

Miller, W. (2000). *The piano.* New York, NY: Lee & Low.

Mochizuki, K. (1993). *Baseball saved us.* New York, NY: Lee & Low.

Mochizuki, K. (1997). *Heroes.* New York, NY: Lee & Low.

Peacock, L. (1999). *Crossing the Delaware: A history in many voices.* New York, NY: Scholastic.

Polacco, P. (1994). *Pink and say.* New York, NY: Scholastic.

Rappaport, D. (1988). *The Boston coffee party.* New York, NY: Harper & Row.

Say, A. (2002). *Home of the brave.* New York, NY: Houghton Mifflin.

Siebert, D. (2003). *Rhyolite*. New York, NY: Clarion Books.
Turner, A. (1992). *Katie's trunk*. New York, NY: Aladdin.
Uchida, Y. (1993). *The bracelet*. New York, NY: Philomel.
VanderZee, R. (2003). *Erika's story*. New York, NY: Creative Editions.
Weatherford, C. (2005). *Freedom on the menu: The Greensboro sit-ins*. New York, NY: Puffin.
Wild, M. (1991). *Let the celebrations begin!* New York, NY: Orchard Books.
Wiles, D. (2001). *Freedom summer*. New York, NY: Atheneum.
Woodson, J. (2001). *The other side*. New York, NY: Putnam.
Woodson, J. (2005). *Show way*. New York, NY: Putnam's Sons.

APPENDIX B

Content Categories

Category	Description	Student Example
Narrative 42%	Responses that referred to narrative processes such as setting, characters, action, structure, mood, and themes.	"I think he went back in time. Maybe it's a dream. I think they're either orphans or their parents died there and they don't know where their home is. I think that they just got out of the camps."
Connections 24%	Intertextual Connections to other books, personal lives	"I think this is like right before they got sold or something like it said in *So Far From the Sea*—right before all the houses got auctioned."
	Intratextual Connections within the book	"Oh, on the front cover, that's them and then in the back it's the grandfather and his son."
Peritext 17%	Students named and used the peritextual features to construct meaning.	"The endpages look sandy to me... like freedom and the beach."
Symbolism 9%	Responses attended to the visual images or words that went beyond the literal descriptions. Students responded to the metaphorical nature of images and words.	"I think the birds represent freedom because they're free and can do whatever they want."
Historical 8%	Responses were related to historical events outside the text; students used a 21st century perspective, showed empathy, and shared historical facts and figures that were not mentioned in the story.	"Why did they [Japanese] bomb Pearl Harbor?" "Everybody was being rounded up and put in a camp." "Hitler made all the Jews wear the Star of David."

APPENDIX C

Description of Historical Fiction Picture Books

So Far From the Sea (Bunting, 1989) was the second book read aloud to the students. It was read in a whole-class setting where the students sat on the floor in front of me. This book is about Japanese Internment and tells the story about a family that returns to Manzanar Relocation Center to visit their grandfather's grave. The father tells his children of his experiences from the bombing of Pearl Harbor to being relocated to Manzanar. The illustrations and text flash back and forth from 1942 to 1972. 1942 is represented in black and white images and 1972 is represented in color.

Angel Girl (Friedman, 2008) was the 13th book read in the study and was read in a small group in a conference room at a round table during the third phase of the study. This book is about the Holocaust and tells the story of how a girl notices a boy in a concentration camp and risks her life to save his by bringing him apples to eat. After time passes they meet again and get married. This book has met with great controversy as the authors recently divulged that the events were not all true. The students and I read it as a piece of fiction, as the events seemed exaggerated.

Lastly *Henry's Freedom Box* (Levin, 2007) was the fifth and last (17th) book read in the study; students remained at their desks in rows at the request of the teacher because of time constraints. The data is drawn from the last read-aloud of *Henry's Freedom Box*. This story is about a slave named Henry Box Brown who mailed himself to freedom (Philadelphia) in a wooden box. The story tells of Henry's life as a child and how he was sold from his mother and later how his wife and children were sold from him. In the end, with the help of a kind doctor, he mails himself to freedom.

Peer and Teacher Talk in a First-Grade Writing Community: Constructing Multiple Possibilities for Authorship

María Paula Ghiso
Columbia University

Sociocultural and critical perspectives on literacy point to the limits of considering writing primarily through the physical representations writers produce. Any student's work is a partial view—not a singular, stable "voice," but a manufactured "story" (Kamler, 2001; Lensmire, 1998; Lewison & Heffernan, 2008). The writing artifact is in itself a construction that freezes fluid and multiple identities into a static representation. For young children, a piece may have very few words actually materialized on the page; the written piece alone is insufficient to denote the scope of students' artistic and intellectual expression or their varied authorial agendas. The words that do materialize stand in relation to the sizeable verbal composing that surrounds the physical production of texts, intellectual work which is often invisible in the finished product.

In this paper, which draws on data from a larger year-long ethnographic study, I explore the role of talk in the workings of a first-grade writing community in a large urban center. In this class, the teacher and her young students engaged with writing as an invested project embedded in social interaction, which was encapsulated in what they termed "writing that matters." Their teacher artfully orchestrated curricular invitations that encouraged students to value writing as a means of inquiring into and representing ideas considered important, relevant, or compelling— that "mattered"—and viewed young children as generators of knowledge about writing. The work of the writing community took place within and against a system of constraints that forwarded instrumental notions of writing, including high-stakes tests and the city's mandated curriculum, which promoted and enforced writing as a linear trajectory to a delineated endpoint. In the sections that follow, I examine the first graders' and their teacher's writing conversations in order to understand how students navigate the authoring process in relationship to the context of the classroom and their own resources and purposes for writing. These interactions are a rich site for conceptualizing school writing opportunities attuned to the range of students' social, creative, and intellectual authorial agendas.

THEORETICAL PERSPECTIVES

This study is situated within socio-cultural frameworks which contest bounded definitions of literacy as neutral skills. Street (1984) and other New Literacy Studies theories document literacy as "ideological," with practices embedded within particular contexts and influenced by issues of power and identity. Framed by this perspective, interactions around writing can be conceived as socially constructed and continually negotiated practices. In the writing process literature, students are viewed as writers with the ability to direct their work and draw on their experiences in the world for academic inquiries (Atwell, 1987; Calkins, 1994; Graves, 1983). A growing body of research adds to understandings of young children's literacy practices, exploring how early writers engage in critical literacy projects; they address issues of social justice and equity, ask questions of texts and of the world, and explore possibilities for moving from critique to social action (Edelsky,1999; Evans, 2005; Vasquez, 2004).

As Anne Haas Dyson (e.g., 1997, 2003) has documented, when young children navigate the process of writing in classroom spaces, they do so amid volumes of talk that signal their participation in a variety of communities, including families, friendships, and popular culture. In large part through the epistemic resources of these "unofficial" practices, students negotiate their social identities, engage in play, demarcate allegiances, and "remix" their experiences in relation to the school context. Dyson demonstrates the extent to which students' understandings of what it means to write is embedded in the talk students engage in alongside their writing, and emphasizes the need for the educational field to attend to children's exchanges as a way of supporting their writerly identities and negotiation of school literacy practices. The writing curriculum, she argues, must be made "permeable" to the linguistic, cultural, and popular culture resources of students. Following Dyson, I focus on students' conversations with each other during the writing time, which took place "away from the gaze of a teacher" (Laman, 2004), and attend to the relationship between this peer talk and teacher-students exchanges. The interactions of this first-grade writing community point to the possibilities for nurturing writing opportunities that are malleable to students' knowledge and their intellectual and social pursuits.

METHOD

Data and insights from this paper are derived from an ethnographic study of the "writing time" of a first-grade urban classroom for the duration of one academic year. Throughout this paper, the term "writing time," an emic label used by the teacher and students, differentiates this classroom structure from a writing workshop as described in the process literature (e.g., Calkins, 1994). While the writing time followed a workshop format (with brief opening whole-group conversations, work time, and sharing of writing), it was also informed by traditions of practitioner inquiry (Cochran-Smith & Lytle, 2001) and critical literacy, which significantly shaped the work of the writing community. The setting for this study was a first-grade class made up of 20 students: 16 were African American, 1 emigrated mid-year from West Africa, 1 was part Algerian, 1 was part Native American, and 1 was Caucasian. Their European-American teacher, Blanche (all names are pseudonyms), sought to imbue the curriculum with African-American history and literature as well as construct pedagogical invitations for students to draw on their diverse experiential and cultural knowledge.

Data collection consisted of audio-taped and transcribed writing conversations (including mini-lessons, conferences, and student sharing), fieldnotes of twice-weekly participant observation, samples of student writing at various stages of development, and interviews with the teacher and with 7 focal students whose work was representative of the class as a whole. I also reviewed school and federal guidelines (e.g., the school district Writing Plan, mandated curricula, and assessments) to understand the relationship between this writing time and broader performance standards and instructional requirements.

Throughout data collection, I wrote memos on salient aspects of the class' negotiations of writing, tentative patterns, and new and recurring questions. I began to note characteristics of the writing community, which ultimately were important themes in the study findings, such as children's roles as knowledge generators and the ways the teacher sought to position students as agentive. Talk about writing emerged as an area meriting further attention. For the section of the study that focuses on student and teacher talk, I began by reviewing all fieldnotes and transcripts from the writing time. As I discuss later in the paper, typically student-teacher interactions were bounded and relatively short (generally five to ten conversational turns), beginning when the teacher opened the conversation and ending when she moved on to another student. I assigned each of these student-teacher interactions a conceptual label (Strauss & Corbin, 1990) that represented the content of the conversation (e.g., structure, conventions, and classroom norms for writing). I looked within each student-teacher exchange at conversational turns (Sinclair & Coulthard, 1975) or groups of turns to note specific moves the teacher seemed to be making (e.g., modeling, making personal connections, linking to the work of other students, and fostering students' academic identities as writers). I also observed that students interacted with each other in more free-flowing and unbounded ways. This peer talk was thematic and recursive throughout the time students had to work on their pieces, bounded more by the beginning and end of the writing time or by topics of discussion than the strict delineations characteristic of student-teacher exchanges. I assigned stretches of talk (Beach & Philippot, 1999) conceptual labels that described the content of the peer conversations and students' moves in the exchanges (e.g., coauthoring, drawing, and performance of work). I returned to my data on classroom talk and re-read it alongside my codes in a recursive and iterative process (Bogdan & Biklen, 1992), and triangulated the resulting conceptual categories with interview data to represent the nature of and relationship between student-teacher and peer exchanges.

In the sections that follow, I examine and describe talk about writing within the classroom context. I intentionally begin with students' peer exchanges as starting points. Their interactions, though informed and enabled by pedagogical decisions, were not strictly a derivative of the teacher's understandings. I highlight a case representative of peer talk within the class in order to immerse the reader in this first-grade writing community and give a sense of students' multiple authorial purposes and varied semiotic resources not directly evident in their finished products or through student-teacher interactions. I then zoom out from this particular case example to unpack the role of the teacher in creating the conditions for viewing talk as a valued resource for authorship and to theorize the overlapping relationship between peer and student-teacher exchanges. I conclude by sharing insights garnered from students' negotiation of writing and the teacher's mediation of such opportunities for how we might structure the elementary writing curriculum to emphasize multiple possibilities for authorship.

A CASE EXAMPLE: NATASHA AND LONDYN

One mid-December morning, Natasha—sprawled out on the rug with a pencil and writing folder—was joined by her classmate Londyn, who commented that she was writing a story about her brother "doing mischief" with Natasha. In turn, Natasha revealed her intentions to write about a dog she used to play with, and proceeded to put the title of the story at the top of her page.

The writing paper Natasha had chosen for her work was divided into two parts: a lined section at the bottom, for words, and a blank section at the top, for the illustrations. At this point, Londyn reached over and flipped Natasha's page upside down, so that the drawing portion of the paper was at the bottom of the page, and told her, "Like this." Natasha wrote the title of the piece again on what had now become the top of the page and proceeded with her work.

In beginning their exchange, Londyn and Natasha made use of understandings about each other as writers and on collective knowledge generated by the writing community. They opened the conversation by disclosing the topics of their pieces. This content had resonance with themes made public in the class through whole-class discussions and sharing opportunities, and with notions of writing as a project that mattered to students and their classmates. Londyn's mischief story with her classmate and brother as characters was in part informed by the work of a peer, Kayla, who had just completed a five-chapter piece titled *How to Do Mischief,* detailing a variety of naughty scenarios in which she thwarted the authority of older siblings and parental figures. Natasha was a dog lover who had been writing about real and imaginary pets for the better part of the two months the children had been in school. Natasha and Londyn were familiar with the writings of other students in the class, including themes of interest to particular writers and their rationales for grounding their work in such topics, because these had been the explicit topic of conversations throughout the writing time. The expectation that writing "matters" and is connected to personal histories, interests, and experiences was the foundation for exchanges like Londyn's and Natasha's. Children took keen interest in each other's works and writing plans.

The class had also recently participated in an activity where they collectively sorted their work into portfolio containers. The class would sit in a circle on the rug, with Teacher Blanche holding a bin of student work in front of her. One by one, Blanche would lift different pieces from the overflowing pile—a good portion of which were pieces created during the writing time—and pass these artifacts of learning around the circle until they reached the student owner. The physical manipulation of pieces authored by the students built on familiarity with each other's work and added a layer of reflection regarding the practices of the class as a whole and the characteristics and talents of individual writers. As they handled each other's works, students would discuss them, noting patterns and particular features that stood out. Students would recall with glee the specific pieces of their classmates as these were passed around the circle, taking the opportunity to examine closely words and pictures or to read aloud particular phrases.

In the sorting activity that had taken place a few days prior to Londyn and Natasha's interaction, students had noted that Natasha "keeps her paper upside down," with the verbal text at the upper half of her paper and the drawings at the bottom, an orientation that was a reversal from that of the rest of the class. This characteristic of Natasha as a writer, brought out in a "procedural" activity like the sorting of work, was one that Londyn drew on in turning Natasha's paper to reflect her friend's preference regarding the material implements of writing. This action suggests Londyn's understandings of Natasha as a writer with individual characteristics and purposeful artistic choices. Londyn was able to read Natasha's work as an aspect of her authorial identity and use this information as a vehicle for relationship-building,

Once Natasha established the title of her piece, *My Dog Nicky,* in her preferred spot on the page as suggested by Londyn, she began to construct the illustration. As she drew herself petting Nicky,

Figure 1. Natasha's Illustration for Her Written Piece Titled My Dog Nicky

Natasha detailed the animal's characteristics and behavior, and recounted to Londyn stories about playing with the dog. The completed illustration shown in Figure 1 depicts Natasha and Londyn greeting and petting Nicky.

Not directly evident from the illustration is how the scene was collaboratively negotiated between the girls as they both decided on elements of the representation:

Natasha: I'm drawing you here [referring to the figure on the right of the page].

Londyn: You draw real good. How can you draw so good?

Natasha: I'll teach you. [Natasha points to her drawing of Londyn] Should I make a shirt or a dress?

Londyn: Long shirt.

[Natasha draws a bottom garment, and then a shirt above it]

Natasha: I like your hair when you have braids so I'm making you with braids.

[Natasha draws Londyn's head and hair]

Natasha: Do you want string on your shoes?

Londyn: [nods]

[Natasha draws shoelaces on her illustration. She shades the body of her drawing of Londyn, which she has placed directly in front of the dog in her picture.]

Natasha: Sometimes when something's in front of something else, I like to color that thing that's in front so that it looks like it's in front.

Having jointly established the particulars of Londyn as a character in Natasha's piece, the girls continued with their writing amid a range of exchanges: adding talk bubbles to their works while making intertextual connections to *Don't Let the Pigeon Drive the Bus* (Willems, 2003), which the teacher had read to them that morning; advising each other on spelling questions; sharing information about their lives, such as Londyn's upcoming "long visit" to North Carolina and her assurance to Natasha that she would return soon; and reading their work aloud to each other. When writing time drew to a close, they put away their works-in-progress for the day.

This scene is both a particular exchange and a commonplace occurrence in the life of the writing community. The girls discussed their pieces and worked together to write each other into their respective stories. Londyn constructed a narrative in which the two friends exact mischief on an unsuspecting older brother, writing: "When [Natasha] come over we seleup [sneaked] up on my big bruther." Natasha, meanwhile, created a scenario with her friend Londyn and a loved and recurring figure in her pieces, Nicky the dog. This inclusion of Londyn as a character took place through the visual medium of illustrations and with input from both girls.

Teacher Blanche's orchestration of classroom writing invitations provided openings for this type of collective visual and written composing to take place. The children's coauthoring and drawing practices were neither modeled nor necessarily privileged, but the writing curriculum could bend to accommodate their talents and preferences. Independent of instruction from the teacher, children relied on facilities with drawing, which allowed them to create sophisticated stories not constrained by their emerging mastery of spelling conventions. It is not surprising that students, writing on paper structured with a section for illustrations and reading picturebooks where the visual component works in synergistic relationship to the words, would use these semiotic resources as tools in designing their own pieces.

Interestingly, Natasha's constructed scenario featuring her friend and her pet are only present in the illustration portion of the work and not in the verbal text. The written words read:

> I miss my dog. Her name was Nicky. She was light brown. She was very curly but
> I loved to pet her. I loved Nicky a lot. So did her owner. I liked it when my mom
> and Nicky's owner's mom said Nicky could come down [to play].

Natasha's words describe her affection for a friend's dog she no longer visits, but do not mention Londyn, who is shown in the illustrations petting and greeting Nicky. The imaginative play and collaboration are not discernable from the written words alone; this suggests the importance of attending to the multiple modalities of writing and to children's interactions with one another around their texts so as to understand and support their multifaceted authoring practices.

Natasha's talent in drawing, admired by Londyn, became an opportunity to jointly create an intimate fictional scene and for Natasha to share her knowledge of the visual arts. Natasha invited Londyn to make decisions about her representation in the story and unpacked the various components of executing the drawing, such as what elements to incorporate or how to convey a sense of dimension and perspective. She made visible the intricacies of her decisions and created an occasion to take part in a shared endeavor. Natasha's identity as one who "draws real good" was well-known in the class and becomes a social resource. Natasha was a child who would typically gravitate to adults more than peers, so it is particularly meaningful that she could use her drawing abilities as a point of connection to a classmate.

Fiction was not a specific genre inquiry in the class, and the joint authoring and presence in each other's stories evident in Londyn's and Natasha's works were not explicitly discussed by the teacher or posed as a writing technique for students to try. Based on their own impulses and imaginative resources, most of the first-graders used fiction to play with reality and author alternative possibilities. Students constructed playful scenarios in their pieces that explored and assigned social roles, for instance, labeling certain students the "kids" and others the "parents" or making a peer the "teacher." They created stories where they traveled to far away lands or, like in Natasha's *My Dog Nicky*, to nearby out-of-school spots in the company of their school friends.

The exchanges between Natasha and Londyn, and that of their peers not highlighted here, invite us to consider writing as occurring within a range of collective arrangements, informed by the inquiries and projects of other students in the class, by the specific input of classmates, and by the children's social and creative energies. Both Natasha and Londyn were engaged in what we could consider their own "individual" works, in the traditional sense that each had chosen a topic and was pursuing it with vigor and dedication. Their subjects, however, were delicately connected and nested within layers of influence and relevance. Through inclusion in each other's works and coauthoring practices, classmates literally had the opportunity to intermingle with what mattered to their peers. Londyn and Natasha could best Londyn's older brother and play with Natasha's favorite pet, an imaginary world which had real-world relevance. Through interactions around writing decisions and in the fictional space, children built social relationships and used oral, visual, and written modes to author experiences that otherwise may be constrained by forces outside their control. The majority, if not all, of the students engaged in collaborative and imaginative authoring practices, as these became part of the culture of the class.

Writing workshop frameworks often emphasize personal narratives—centered on the idea of "writing from life"—which emphasize the importance of autobiographical accounts (Calkins, 1994, 2003). Imaginative works, however, are not impossibilities unrelated to reality. As Nigerian writer Chinua Achebe argues, "the truth of fiction" can provide insights for making "our way in the real world" (p.151). Natasha and Londyn's works are fictional instances with resonances to their understandings and desires—they make visible what the girls value and what they wish to happen in the world. Natasha's *My Dog Nicky* is multi-dimensional: The verbal text reads as a personal narrative of her affection for a pet, while the illustrations construct a shared imaginative world where she, her pet, and her friend can interact. The girls' conversations and the visual and written mediums are exploited as resources to create multiple representations that attend to school expectations for writing as well as the social dimensions of their work.

TALK AS A VALUED RESOURCE: RELATIONSHIP OF TEACHER-STUDENT AND PEER EXCHANGES

Natasha and Londyn's interactions, and that of their peers, did not occur in a vacuum, but were possible in part because of the affordances of the classroom setting, which provided a platform for inquiry and viewed talk as an integral component of authoring practices. Talk about writing was the foundation for the words that materialized on the page and for navigating understandings less visible in the finished product. Whether in individual arrangements or with the whole class, Teacher Blanche continually made this central belief explicit to students and created the conditions which fostered multi-dimensional peer interactions like that highlighted above. In an illustrative example from early in the year, she detailed the purpose of such talk, telling a student, "I want to help you make a plan, a plan for your writing. So what we're doing here is work, even though we're talking." Blanche frequently emphasized the expectation that children conceptualize their pieces before putting words down on the page and the guiding principle that discussion is part of the intellectual and creative work of writing.

In the following representative example of teacher-student interactions, Blanche dialogues with Natasha about her work-in-progress, a biography of her beloved gym teacher:

Teacher
Blanche: Natasha, what's the work you're doing as a writer this morning?

Natasha: Adding on to my biography of Teacher Rachel. She says things in a nice way.

T. Blanche: Natasha, this is a perfect place to put a little poetry in your biography. My father's voice is like booming canons, thundering [unintelligeable]. That's not like Teacher Rachel's voice, is it?

Natasha: It's soft like butterfly wings.

T. Blanche: Oh, Natasha, that's lovely. Get that down!

Figure 2. Relationship Between Teacher-Student and Peer Talk about Writing

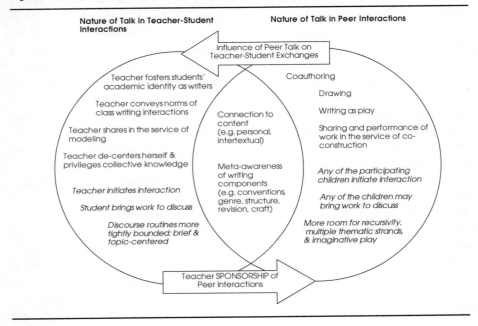

Blanche's interactions with students and the children's own social practices with one another around writing exist in a synergistic relationship. As suggested in Figure 2, teacher-student and peer talk exhibit both distinct features and overlapping characteristics.

Given Blanche's resonance with writing workshop approaches, it is not surprising that her talk in writing conferences fosters students' academic identities: Blanche made reference to the children as writers who plan their work and make deliberate creative and intellectual choices. This went hand-in-hand with explicit discussion of writing features such as genre, structure, revision, grammar and conventions, tone, etc., advancing a meta-awareness of the discipline which the children took up in their conversations with each other. In the biography conversation detailed above, Blanche conveys the intentionality of Natasha's writerly decisions and suggests altering the piece to include more poetry in its construction. At the heart of many teacher-student exchanges was the writing topic itself, with Blanche connecting to students' work through, for example, a laugh, a question on the subject, or the sharing of a connected story, such as the link between Blanche's father and Natasha's favorite teacher. The discussion of content and of components of writing occupies the shared space in the diagram, denoting that this type of talk was present in both teacher-student and peer conversations. In addition, Blanche conveyed the norms of classroom interaction during writing time: She exposed students to how writing conversations with the teacher typically go and orchestrated how time was spent, often encouraging children to dedicate sustained energy to thinking, planning, and discussion of ideas.

Blanche also engaged in talk that de-centered her own authority as a teacher. She encouraged students to recognize and draw on their own and each other's expertise in addressing issues they encountered in their writing (e.g., how to best express an idea or concept, how to overcome spelling challenges) and also in posing further inquiries through their writing. Blanche explicitly structured a writing environment where knowledge did not travel primarily from teacher to student, but was shared among the members of the classroom writing community. She urged students to be independent of the teacher's direction and to see peers as a valued resource for writing. Blanche frequently linked students' writing topics and shared connections between children's considerations for their work, even explicitly sending them to talk to one another in ways that highlight student expertise. Comments such as "If you want to know about [a topic], ask Peter" or "Take a look at what Khalil is doing" fostered intertextuality among students' works. The classroom writing time thus became less a site for furthering discrete projects and more a web of overlapping connections and potential influences.

As we saw with Natasha and Londyn in previous sections, when Blanche was not conferencing with students, they talked with each other, sharing their pieces and seeking out or providing feedback. The nature of this peer discourse, as denoted in the diagram, shares some features of the teacher's. In many instances there were concrete traces of the teacher's discourse in children's utterances, while at other times the influence was more conceptual and dispersed. The children's conversations, however, are not contained by what they witnessed the teacher doing—their interactions cannot be conceived of as strict socialization into norms delineated by the teacher, but rather as a unique and artful interplay between and among teacher and students. Features of the children's talk not present in teacher-student conferences are denoted in the right-hand side of Figure 2; these categories indicate peer conversations that were characterized by co-authoring, notions of writing as play, and attention to multiple modalities, such as use of the visual medium and sharing and performance of work in the service of co-construction.

As was evident in the exchange between Natasha and Londyn, the children frequently engaged in co-authoring and used writing as a vehicle for play, aspects which are neither modeled nor explicitly attended to by the teacher. Students formed permeable writing associations and jointly negotiated the parameters of collaborative authoring; they assigned roles, debated topics, and molded genres to suit their needs. Through writing they also crafted inventive scenarios featuring classmates and performed social relationships (akin to the interactions documented by

Dyson, 2008), creating stories which were at once imagined and also carried real-world effects in the immediate peer world. Though the students discussed the creative process with regards to the components of writing made explicit by the teacher (e.g., revision, craft, organization, etc.), they also incorporated semiotic modalities that were absent in the teacher's discourse. The children used visual and performative mediums as resources in their work, broadening classroom notions of what writing is and what purposes it can serve.

Several distinctions arise between peer exchanges and teacher-student interactions about writing that are related to the different locations, responsibilities, and agendas of teacher and students. Blanche purposely structured the writing time so that students were not approaching her with their work, but vice versa, thus creating opportunities for them to be independent of the teacher. As a result of this pedagogical decision, teacher-student exchanges exhibit patterns in interaction and use of particular terminology that forwarded students' academic identities as writers with individual and collective expertise. The teacher would initiate the conversation, typically by asking a variation of the question, "What's your plan today as a writer?", an opening that has resonance with writing conferences as described in the workshop literature (Calkins, 2003). The teacher and student then would go on to discuss some aspect of the work as related to creative and intellectual choices. Blanche's discourse positioned students as writers who have goals and plans for their pieces; student-teacher writing conferences were constructed not as an opportunity for students to "retell" a piece in its current instantiation, but to use the work as a platform for further inquiry into the topic or into specific writing techniques.

Since Blanche had to visit with as many children as possible during the writing time, teacher-student exchanges were usually brief (between five and ten conversational turns). More often than not, the writing conference between teacher and student had a principal topic or concept being discussed. It also typically followed a predictable interactional routine, with the teacher initiating the conversation and linking it to previous whole-group discussions, particular writing "challenges" featured by Blanche at the start of the writing time, or goals for writing as articulated by the student. For the most part, these conferences ended with praise for the child's work and/or a re-statement of what the student would focus on in his/her piece once the teacher moved on to a conversation with someone else in the class. Such teacher-student exchanges were influenced by Blanche's familiarity with characterizations of conferences in the workshop literature and in professional development experiences in which she had participated (Calkins, 1994, 2003), but also had important departures. For instance, Blanche often made reference to the collective writing of the class, whether by emphasizing resonance between the works of different students, recalling whole-group conversations based on children's writings, or explicitly recommending that students talk to one another about the content or structure of their work. This community orientation disrupted notions of writing as the individual trajectories of students (a feature of workshop approaches which has been critiqued in the educational literature; see Lensmire, 2000) and drew attention to the collective understandings and projects of the class.

The patterns in Blanche's discourse are not meant to imply that there was unilateral standardization in her responses to students, but rather that she intentionally structured her interactions in writing conferences so as to forward children's reliance on their own knowledge and that of their peers. Blanche's artfulness in talking with students and her respect for their autonomy adds to more conventional iterations of the writing process, which delineate a singular trajectory for taking on the socially ascribed identity of a "writer" and envision writing conferences as the means through which the teacher guides student work (e.g., Calkins, 2003; Fletcher & Portalupi, 2001). The workshop literature and curriculum guidelines portray the "writing process" as a predetermined course for authorship. Through her efforts to decenter her teaching and carve out a space for students to direct their own learning, as evidenced in her talk, Blanche instead created the conditions for children to take up multiple and diverse identities as writers.

As the case of Natasha and Londyn illustrates, the children's peer exchanges were grounded in engagement with particular pieces. Since students' talk about writing took place amid ongoing projects, there was shared motivation and initiative for beginning discussions about one's own work or that of a peer. Students were seated next to each other for the entirety of each day's writing time, and as a result their exchanges were more like recursive episodes than rigidly demarcated instances. They tended to inter-relate ideas and return to conversational threads instead of closing off one topic before beginning another. Peer interactions thus typically juggled multiple thematic strands over a longer span than the comparably brief exchanges students had with the teacher. The children navigated expectations of academic identities as authors with their own considerations and investments, resulting in improvisation and even a certain irreverence toward the act of writing.

It may be tempting to place the teacher-student and peer exchanges in a hierarchical relationship. Indeed, frameworks for writing differentiate between "official" classroom discourse around writing as orchestrated by the teacher and the "unofficial" resources students insert into school interactions (Dyson, 2003). This delineation attends to the ability of both teacher and student to shape the act of writing, while recognizing that the teacher's words and actions typically carry greater authority within the school setting. These observations, though accurate, can create an unnecessary dichotomy between teacher and students. Labeling the practices modeled and supported by Blanche as "official," with the young writers also drawing on "unofficial" resources, obscures a potentially more synergistic relationship. Blanche's discourse in student-teacher interactions did not necessarily run counter to the ways students interacted with each other. In fact, Blanche sponsored and helped construct the unique exchanges that occurred between peers. Through de-centering herself as a teacher, fostering students' identities as writers, and emphasizing collective knowledge, Blanche created a classroom environment that trusted and expected that students would devise their own ways of molding writing opportunities in collaboration with each other. These moments between students cannot be mapped onto a preconceived trajectory because they are outside of the teachers' deliberate mediation, but they are all part of the classroom community.

Peer conversations shape how classroom inquiries are constructed and can influence the extent to which writing curricula honor students' authorial purposes and "ways with words" (Heath, 1983), hence the arrow at the top of Figure 2. Conversations about writing which take place without the direction of the teacher offer insights into how students understand, negotiate, and create authoring practices, and suggest ways that student resources for writing might have an even greater presence in the curriculum.

CONCLUSION: TOWARDS A MULTIPLICITY OF AUTHORSHIP

In the context of young children's writing, considering their written work in relation to the surrounding talk makes visible the social energy and creative potential underlying any produced text. Situated within a community focused on "writing that matters," students' conversations about this work carried social investments and commitments. As such, children's authorial agendas had social as well as intellectual dimensions. Writing was embedded in relationships, and the children took seriously (and playfully) this type of project.

Student exchanges—of which Natasha and Londyn's interactions are only one example—disrupt portrayals of talk as primarily the pedagogical instrument of the teacher. The workshop literature emphasizes the importance of writing conferences as an opportunity to individualize teaching; from this perspective, the conference becomes shaped by attempts to discern what particular challenges students are taking on in their writing and how to best address an expressed need, reinforce a writerly behavior, or further develop a piece (Calkins, 2003; Fletcher & Portalupi, 2001). The first graders' conversations suggest that educators would also do well to pay attention to and learn from exchanges that occur outside the deliberate mediation of the teacher, and to create the conditions for such peer interactions to flourish.

The children's peer interactions unsettle the sacredness of texts when works are seen as the tangible endpoints of the process of writing. In this first-grade class, writing was never "done": Children's conversations with peers about their works emphasize how they navigated the construction of particular accounts, the stories left out of different representations, and the ways that "completed" pieces were pulled back into social interaction. This work was not in service of the text; it *made use of* the text to grapple with ideas, investigate the components of writing, and engage in social pursuits that often involved imagination and play. For the students, "play" and "seriousness" were not discrete modes, but simultaneous resources for creating meaningful writing. The children played with the genres highlighted in the class and made them porous to their experiences, knowledge, and social purposes. Natasha and Londyn imagined scenarios with real-world significance, and also used the "seriousness" of teacherly discourse for legitimizing play, giving authority to their social work.

The multimodality of authoring practices was a means for first-graders to access and represent the simultaneity of experience. The children drew on oral, visual, and written semiotic modes to achieve multiple purposes and address multiple audiences. They were able to explore and play with school conventions and navigate academic expectations while enacting and fortifying social bonds. Within their conversations, drawing, and writing, children could be both playful and serious, could attend to both their friend as an audience for the work and the expectations of the teacher. This multidimensional and situated conception of children's authoring practices challenges dichotomies between "school" and "out-of-school" contexts, allowing students to integrate their lives more fully within school spaces.

The children's exchanges make visible the creative and social dimensions of their work and the even greater possible influence these may have within the curriculum. Ideally, peer interactions can be a catalyst for a synergistic relationship that makes a space for and also more specifically supports notions of authorship as determined by the students. For instance, one might imagine a writing curriculum that highlights coauthoring, performance, and play alongside more "serious" articulations of the discipline. The peer exchanges are not only valuable insofar as they disclose how students grapple with writing invitations, but because these insights can themselves impact the types of authorial practices emphasized in classrooms.

AUTHOR'S NOTE

I would like to thank Gerald Campano and the *Yearbook* reviewers and editors for their thoughtful feedback on earlier drafts of this work.

REFERENCES

Achebe, C. (1988). The truth about fiction. In *Hopes and impediments: Selected essays* (pp. 138-153). New York, NY: Anchor Books.

Atwell, N. (1987). *In the middle: New understandings about writing, reading, and learning* (2nd ed.). Portsmouth, NH: Heinemann.

Beach, R., & Philippot, R. (1999, December). *Framing strategies in high school students' large group literature discussions.* Paper presented at the National Reading Conference 49th Annual Meeting, Orlando, FL.

Bogdan, R., & Biklen, S. (1992). *Qualitative research in education.* Boston, MA: Allyn and Bacon.

Calkins, L. (1994). *The art of teaching writing* (new ed.). Portsmouth, NH: Heinemann.

Calkins, L. (2003). *Units of Study for primary writing: A yearlong curriculum.* Portsmouth, NH: Heinemann.

Cochran-Smith, M., & Lytle, S. L. (2001). Beyond certainty: Taking an inquiry stance on practice. In A. Lieberman & L. Miller (Eds.), *Teachers caught in the action* (pp. 45-58). New York, NY: Teachers College Press.

Dyson, A. H. (1997). *Writing superheroes: Contemporary childhood, popular culture, and classroom literacy.* New York, NY: Teachers College Press.

Dyson, A. H. (2003). *The Brothers and Sisters learn to read and write: Popular literacies in childhood and school cultures.* New York, NY: Teachers College Press.

Dyson, A. H. (2008). The pine cone wars: Studying writing in a community of children. *Language Arts, 85*(4), 305-315.

Edelsky, C. (Ed.) (1999). *Making justice our project: Teachers working toward critical whole language practice.* Urbana, IL: National Council of Teachers of English.

Evans, J. (2005). *Literacy moves on: Popular culture, new technologies, and critical literacy in the elementary classroom.* Portsmouth, NH: Heinemann.

Fletcher, R., & Portalupi, J. (2001). *Writing workshop: The essential guide.* Portsmouth, NH: Heinemann.

Graves, D. (1983). *Writing: Children and teachers at work.* Exeter, NH: Heinemann Educational Books.

Heath, S. B. (1983). *Ways with words: Language, life, and work in communities and classrooms.* Cambridge, MA: Cambridge University Press.

Kamler, B. (2001). *Relocating the personal: A critical writing pedagogy.* New York, NY: State University of New York Press.

Laman, T. T. (2004). *"It's not like we're just playing, it's about learning stuff": A critical ethnography of children's social practices during literacy learning.* Unpublished doctoral dissertation. Bloomington, IN: Indiana University.

Lensmire, T. (1998). Rewriting student voice. *Journal of Curriculum Studies, 30*(3), 261-291.

Lensmire, T. (2000). *Powerful writing, responsible teaching.* New York, NY: Teachers College Press.

Lewison, M., & Heffernan, L. (2008). Rewriting writers workshop: Creating safe spaces for disruptive stories. *Research in the Teaching of English, 42*(4), 435-465.

Sinclair, J. M., & Coulthard, M. (1975). *Towards an analysis of discourse: The English used by teachers and pupils.* London, UK: Oxford University Press.

Strauss, A., & Corbin, J. (1990). *Basics of qualitative research: Grounded theory procedures and techniques.* Newbury Park, CA: Sage.

Street, B. (1984). *Literacy in theory and practice.* Cambridge, MA: Cambridge University Press.

Vasquez, V. (2004). *Negotiating critical literacies with young children.* Mahwah, NJ: Lawrence Erlbaum Associates.

Willems, M. (2003). *Don't let the pigeon drive the bus.* New York, NY: Hyperion Books for Children.

Experiments in Visual Analysis: (Re)positionings of Children and Youth in Relation to Larger Sociocultural Issues

Maureen Kendrick
Theresa Rogers
University of British Columbia

Kelleen Toohey
Elizabeth Marshall
Simon Fraser University

Harriet Mutonyi
Uganda Martyrs University

Chelsey Hauge
University of British Columbia

Marjorie Siegel
Teachers College, Columbia University

Jennifer Rowsell
Rutgers University

One of the most distinctive features of the 21st Century is the dominance of the visual and its relationship to multiple modalities of communication. Human experience is more visual and visualized than ever before (Mirzoeff, 1999). Visual communication is becoming less the domain of specialists, and more and more crucial in the domains of public communication (Kress & van Leeuwen, 1996), particularly as dominant modes of communication shift from page to screen (Snyder, 1997). Generating information about children's and youth's knowledge, and perceptions of their own lives and learning typically involves language-based modes, which may not build access to the multiple layers and complexities of their knowing. Visual representations have been utilized by researchers in various fields such as psychology and anthropology to learn more about participants' constructions of their worlds (e.g., Adler, 1982; Diem-Wille, 2001; Koppitz, 1984). Siegel and Panofsky argue literacy studies have taken a semiotic turn: "the unsettled status of the field appears to be a productive moment of experimentation, invention, and problem-posing as researchers design analytic approaches that draw on a range of theoretical frameworks relevant to their research interests, purposes, and questions... analyzing multimodality requires a hybrid approach—a blend or 'mash-up' of theories" (2009, p. 99). Similarly, Pahl and Rowsell assert that, in accessing the underlying meanings of multimodal practices, "we need not only to account for the materiality of the texts, that is, the way they look, sound, and feel, but also have an understanding of who made the text, why, where, and when" (2006, p. 2).

In this multi-authored collage, six researchers (Maureen Kendrick and Harriet Mutonyi, Theresa Rogers and Chelsey Hauge, Kelleen Toohey and Elizabeth Marshall) and two discussants (Jennifer Rowsell and Marjorie Siegel) explore the possibilities for the visual as a rich component of data collection and analysis in literacy as social practice research. These experimentations with visual analysis began as part of a multimodal interest group that included literacy scholars from two

Canadian universities: the University of British Columbia and Simon Fraser University. Although our work traverses diverse geographies, contexts, projects, and populations, what links our work is our interest in the affordances of the visual in sociocultural contexts. The three projects represented in this report include: a project involving the use of cartoon drawings as a tool for understanding Ugandan secondary students' health literacy, in particular, their conceptualizations of HIV/AIDS knowledge (Kendrick and Mutonyi); a project exploring the critical literacies and arts-integrated media practice, particularly video productions of Canadian urban youth (Rogers and Hauge); and an intergenerational bilingual and multimodal storytelling project explicitly designed to draw upon a Western Canadian school community's "funds of knowledge" (Moll & Greenberg, 1990) (Toohey and Marshall).

Drawing on three literacy research projects, we "experiment with blending different theoretical lenses" (Siegel & Panofsky, 2009, p. 99) to read the visual as a means of analyzing the (re) positioning of children and youth in relation to larger social issues; as a site of struggle within particular sociocultural contexts; as an alternate construction and coding of reality and identity; and as a site of audiencing that simultaneously includes the image-makers' and researchers' perspectives across private/public domains. These experiments in visual analysis demonstrate the need for broader sociocultural analytical/conceptual frameworks to more fully articulate and analyze what we think children and youth are doing with the visual as discursive resources.

A SOCIOCULTURAL STANCE

Across the three examples, literacy/ies are viewed as social practices rooted in conceptions of knowledge, identity, and being (Street, 2003). This perspective assumes the importance of understanding how literacy practices are embedded in other human activity—in social life and thought (Barton, 1994). The analyses are also informed by social semiotics, which, according to Kress and van Leeuwen (1996), is an attempt to explain and understand how signs are used to produce and communicate meanings across social settings from families to institutions. Signs created through visual representations such as drawings and digital images simultaneously communicate the here and now of a social context while representing the resources individuals have available from the world around them (Kress, 1997; Vygotsky, 1978). The meanings encoded in visual representations also reflect reality as imagined by sign-makers and influenced by their beliefs, values, and biases. Extending these socio-cultural analyses with perspectives on identity, agency, and subject positioning (Bakhtin, 1986; Holland, Lachicotte, Skinner & Cain, 1998) provides additional lenses through which to understand the available positions that children and youth take up in their multimodal work; particularly, how they appropriate and transform various discursive modes and resources to (re)position their own subjectivities (Davies & Harre, 1990; Holland, et al., 1998).

In the age of multimedia, literacy practices need to be recognized as necessarily changing and multiple, "where the textual is also related to the visual, the audio, the spatial, the behavioural... Meaning is made in ways that are increasingly multimodal in which written-linguistic modes of meaning are part and parcel of visual, audio, and spatial patterns of meaning" (Cope & Kalantzis, 2000, p. 6). From this perspective, it is argued that literacy learning, teaching, and research will require the development of a multimodal toolkit (Dyson, 2001; Jewitt & Kress, 2003; New London Group, 1996) that builds access to the complexity of literacy practices and discourse resources that constitute the contemporary social landscape (Luke, 2000). Three examples are offered as ways to begin thinking about how researchers and educators might draw on a range of theoretical paradigms and approaches to analyze the visual representations of contemporary children and youth.

EXAMPLE 1: UGANDAN STUDENTS' VISUAL REPRESENTATIONS OF HIV/AIDS KNOWLEDGE[1]
BY MAUREEN KENDRICK AND HARRIET MUTONYI

In this first example, the visual is analyzed as a tool for understanding students' health literacy in Uganda, specifically, their conceptualizations of HIV/AIDS knowledge. The study addresses the question: "How do secondary school students in Uganda use cartoons to represent their HIV/AIDS knowledge?" Senior 3 (Grade 12) biology classes from four eastern high schools were selected because of the focus on HIV/AIDS in the senior biology curriculum. The cartoons were collected as a subsidiary part of a larger study investigating adolescent students' understanding of the relationship between health literacy, HIV/AIDS, and gender in the context of Uganda (see Mutonyi, 2008). As part of a questionnaire on HIV/AIDS, they were asked to produce a cartoon-type message about HIV/AIDS. Specifically, "What would be your own slogan for HIV/AIDS? Illustrate in a cartoon form the message your slogan would convey about HIV/AIDS. Explain the message your cartoon is conveying." The analysis of the cartoon drawings was the focus of a University of British Columbia faculty-graduate student mentorship grant.[2]

Method of Analysis

In the interdisciplinary field of visual analysis, interpreters of visual images broadly agree that there are three sites at which the meanings of an image are made: the site of production, the site of the image itself, and the site of viewing (Rose, 2001). Many of the theoretical disagreements about visual interpretation relate to disputes over which of these sites is most important and why. From a sociocultural perspective, and in relation to the research reported here, Rose's three sites of meaning-making are viewed as inextricably connected and recursively relational to each other. Rose's framework in combination with an adaptation of Warburton's (1998) analytic framework is used to explore what the cartoons as mediated images might mean within the context of Uganda. The analysis traverses the sites of viewing/audiencing and production in relation to the image itself (Rose, 2001). The images were interpreted collaboratively and the students' own voices, evident in their written texts, were critical to this process. The analysis began with an *initial description* of the image (What visual and textual material is contained within the cartoon? Who and what is represented?), focusing on *immediate connotation* (What does the image/text signify in this context?), then *systemic connotation* (What is the place and status of the cartoon with respect to the communication system or systems it is part of?). Finally, *narrative threads* are established (For what/whom was the cartoon intended? What is the relationship between the cartoon and local/global discourses on HIV/AIDS?), which provide a synthesis across the three sites of meaning-making.

Developing a method of analysis in the study was particularly challenging because the images were produced in a non-Western context and dominant frameworks for visual analysis are based on the history of Western image-making (see e.g., Baldry & Thibault, 2006; Kress & van Leeuwen, 1996). The combination of analytic frameworks (i.e., Rose and Warburton) served to foreground the unique sociocultural context of Uganda, revealing visual narratives that were not initially evident (see also Mutonyi & Kendrick, 2009; in press). These narrative helped raise questions about the possible meanings of the cartoons in relation to broader theories and discourses on health literacy; identity; and personal, public and cultural constructions of HIV/AIDS.

Opondo's Cartoon

   Site of production. Uganda is considered the first African country to successfully reduce the rates of HIV infection in the larger populace (Stoneburner & Low-Beer, 2004; USAID, 2002). Public education campaigns have included various media for communicating messages about AIDS that are consistent with cultural ideologies (oral and written). Yet, discussion of HIV/AIDS issues directly related to sexual issues is generally taboo, and adults and youth do not talk easily about sexual matters in formal settings, particularly in the presence of outsiders (Nyanzi, Pool, & Kinsmen, 2001). The cultural practices associated with HIV/AIDS place considerable limitations on language, thus, at the site of production, a mode of representation that provided an atmosphere of safety and allowed students to express their knowledge of HIV/AIDS, sexuality, and social behaviour was required.

Figure 1. Opondo's Cartoon

   Site of the image. Opondo's cartoon is set outdoors amidst a heavy downpour (see Figure 1). There are three people: one wrapped in a condom, sheltered from the storm, the other two standing side by side in the rain without protection. The cartoonist uses metaphor to convey his message on HIV/AIDS prevention. The rain is labeled AIDS/HIV; the person wrapped in the condom is labeled "protected sex" whereas the unsheltered people are labeled "unprotected sex." The accompanying text reads, "To stay safe from HIV/AIDS simply abstain from sex or use condoms." Opondo's cartoon demonstrates his knowledge of condoms as protection from HIV/AIDS. The person wrapped in the condom does not appear wet while the ones without shelter are soaked, signifying their vulnerability to infection. The underlying narrative threads present two possibilities for the future: protected sex = no HIV/AIDS infection; unprotected sex = probable HIV/AIDS infection. The story he tells simultaneously provides a public message while also possibly serving as a private reminder to Opondo himself about the importance of practicing safe sex (or abstaining as his written text indicates). The metaphoric portrayal of condom use respects local cultural practices by presenting taboo topics of sexuality and sexual practices without being explicit. This cartoon shows a high level of creativity and cultural sensitivity in a message that moves beyond more common public media messages.

Site of viewing/audiencing. Reading the image as a whole text requires understanding how the various sign systems (e.g., visual and linguistic) work in relation to each other, that is, as fused rather than as separate systems. Opondo's cartoon is a highly effective metaphor comprised of multiple sign systems that work simultaneously to communicate his intended meaning and to open possibilities for viewer interpretation (e.g., in relation to the ambiguous nature of the image of the couple having unprotected sex). The cartoon format allows him to "talk" about sex metaphorically, which makes visible the kinds of "invisible" knowledge, experience, and emotion that for personal, social, and cultural reasons, he may have difficulty expressing through language alone. The cartoon is also an intermingling of cultural and personal narratives told to both public and private audiences that allow for the expression of a much fuller range of human emotion and experience than spoken or written communication alone (Kress & van Leeuwen, 1996; Lange, 2007). Of particular importance is how the cartoon serves to acknowledge the limits of language by simultaneously integrating and transcending taboo cultural practices around discussions of sexuality and condom use.

This example raises important questions about the potentials and limitations of visual modes of representation for understanding the relationship between students' own social histories and identities and their interpretation of public HIV/AIDS messages. The cartoon as a visual narrative allows us to understand Opondo's construction *and* critique of social reality, in particular how he simultaneously transcends and integrates local and global discourses on HIV/AIDS.

EXAMPLE 2: "TRACEI IS AWESOME": A FILMIC REPRESENTATION OF CONTEMPORARY GIRLHOOD
BY THERESA ROGERS AND CHELSEY HAUGE

In the context of a project exploring the critical literacies and arts-integrated media practices of urban youth (www.YouthCLAIM.ca), a young woman named Tracei made an "identity" video entitled "I am Tracei, hear me roar!" Identity videos were created as part of a workshop that extended the photojournalism activities of youth participating in a community anti-violence program. Tracei's video, through a series of still images, chronicled her transformation from a traditionally wholesome-looking young girl to a young woman with multicolored hair and facial piercings that, she said, conveyed her as "all crazy and older." In this video, she uses music from a third wave ska band (The Madd Caddies) entitled, "Mary Melody," to re-enforce her message. The coda is: "I showed you Tracie, now take it!"

Shortly after finishing this first video, Tracei sent us another video, entitled "Traceisawesome," from a site that hosts and shares images. The accompanying message was, "I wanted to share something with you." This second video, which is analyzed here, can be seen as a "publicly private film" (Lange, 2007) that provided a way to recognize an even more complex set of identity positions that Tracei took up in her life outside of the research relationship.

Figure 2. Tracei's Video

Arts-integrated media production in and out of schools provides a rich site for analyzing how youth exploit visual and multimodal resources to (re)position themselves in and through their work, and to make larger claims by engaging in cultural critique (Rogers, 2009; Rogers, Winters, LaMonde, & Perry, 2010). To analyze youth productions, the three-site approach developed for visual cultural analysis by Gillian Rose (2001), as discussed in the first study described by Kendrick and Mutonyi, is adapted here. The discussion of Tracei's film emanates from an analysis of the intersecting sites of production (creating the image), the site of the image itself, and the site of audiencing the image, which examines Tracei's video as an instantiation of a socio-cultural process of identity positioning.

The analysis also draws on theories of genre hybridity (Bakhtin, 1986; Biggs & Baumann, 1992) and multimodal intertextuality to understand how youth exploit cultural forms and layer various modes of expression into their work across these sites; and on current theories of social/ cultural identity, agency, and discursive subject positioning that posit identity work as both situated and fluid. For instance, Davies and Harre (1990) provide a useful perspective on the ways individuals position themselves and others in jointly produced storylines, and view the world in terms of the images, metaphors, and concepts from the perspective of the "discursive practice in which they are positioned" (p. 46). Holland et al. (1998), drawing on Bakhtinian theory, also illustrate how identities are formed (improvised) in the flow of historically, socially, culturally, and materially shaped lives. They emphasize the role of agency in this process as individuals shift—by hope, desperation or, most relevant here, play—from one set of socially and culturally formed subjectivities to another.

In terms of creating her film (site of production) Tracei referred to her passion for taking pictures and filmmaking, which she often did on her own and with friends; and she wanted the researchers to experience another, more complex rendering of her identity—one that is usually available only to her peers. The analysis of her film at the site of the image included analyzing the structure (scenes) and the use of technological tools, and the layering of genres and modes and embodied representations (see Rogers, et al., 2010 for details on this analytic approach). This film has three distinct scenes (see representative still images in Figure 2). The first scene includes two extended and close-up filmed shots of Tracei's bottom lip being pierced (first image). The second scene is a filmed shot of Tracei singing, laughing, and talking with a helium voice [to friends behind the camera who can be heard giggling], saying, "I don't know what to say. Hey you guys are putting pressure on me. What am I going to do? I'm gonna sit here an' cry making 'emo' songs, gonna die, this is gonna make me fall over. It's gonna hurt. I'm done" (second image). The third section of the film, which also serves as a kind of coda, is a mixture of print messages and photos of Tracei with her friends, and one still shot of her dressed in drag. This section begins with the text "the end" and continues with "This video was made to prevent the use of chemically made drugs" and "Kids learn about drugs before you think about using them…These kids didn't have a clue what they were doing." After several more photo sequences it ends with "save yourselves! Before it's too late" (third image).

How Tracei positions herself as a young woman throughout the three scenes becomes visible through this analysis of the use of discursive resources across three sites of production. In fact, this film is a fascinating representation of feminine subjectivity. The literal embodiment of expression and resistance to normalized feminine behaviour through piercings, hair color, and cross-dressing is evident. Drawing on popular culture and using new media provides her tools to parody gender identity and to engage in social commentary and critique (Buckingham & Sefton-Green, 1994): Her choice of music playfully draws on her interest in film and TV genres of horror. She uses the "Freaker's Ball" song by the 1970s rock band, Dr. Hook and the Medicine Show—itself a parody of the 1960s countercultural love-ins. The film becomes even more complex when she satirizes "emo" behaviour and appropriates discursive resources of popular media to parody Public Service Announcement (PSA) anti-drug messages. When asked about her use of print in her films she said, "words help get the point across. Some people can be totally oblivious but once they read it, they say 'oh, I get it.' "

Within this kind of identity and cultural work, adolescent bodies represent lived realities (Grosz, 1994); that is, the body is further inscribed with information about youth subjectivity and positioning in their work and in their lives. In this way, media is a particularly productive space for appropriating, refiguring, and imagining these embodiments (Ellsworth, 2005; Grosz & Eisenman, 2001). In fact, the fluid spaces between the body and media give the body "new forms of corporeality" (Ellsworth, 2005, p. 125-6).

Tracei's embodied visual production inscribes and repositions her in playful (parodic) and resistant ways to larger cultural narratives of gender; the images provide a private/public space for writing dissent on her body through piercing, the balloon performance, and presenting herself in drag. This dissent, in its representation of the complexity of girlhood and appropriation of stereotypes, cultural tropes, and a multimodal resources, can be seen as a form of private play as well as a more public counter-discourse of contemporary girlhood. As argued in Rogers and Winters (2010), and as demonstrated in this analysis, contemporary urban youth skillfully poach and play with a range of discursive and cultural resources to engage in or talk back to dominant cultural narratives about their lives and their social worlds.

EXAMPLE 3: "DEFEATING PURE EVIL": MULTIMODAL
REPRESENTATIONS OF "DIFFICULT KNOWLEDGE"[3]
BY KELLEEN TOOHEY AND ELIZABETH MARSHALL

In this example, one child's picture storybook from a larger intergenerational bilingual and multimodal storytelling project explicitly designed to draw upon a school community's "funds of knowledge" (Moll & Greenberg, 1990) is examined. The project took place in a classroom of 9- and 10-year-old mainly Punjabi Sikh English language learners on the west coast of Canada. The study included a Critical Discourse Analysis (van Leeuwen, 2008) of 19 multimodal and bilingual texts created by children for a school project. Below, a description of the study, a sample story and analysis, and some concluding thoughts are provided.

Figure 3. Jushinpreet's Story

Darshens great great great grandfather helped the gurus to defeat pure evil

As part of a larger study, one of the project teachers engaged with a group of children in an intergenerational storytelling project. She initiated this by mentioning to the children that very few of their grandparents came into the school for the 'noisy reading' half hour that took place in the school's primary wing, although it was almost always grandparents who dropped young children off at school. The teacher asked the children why they thought this might be, and the children said that maybe the grandparents didn't read English, and maybe they didn't understand the books available in the kindergarten. The teacher then suggested that the children might produce storybooks about the grandparents' lives as children, write them in English and Punjabi, and make them available to the kindergarten, so that the grandparents could come in and participate. The children were given cheap MP3 players and asked to ask their grandparents (in whatever language they were comfortable) to tell stories about when they were children. The children brought these recordings to school, selected, translated (and edited) the stories into storybook English, word-processed the stories, had relatives or the research assistants help them write the stories in Punjabi, illustrated them, recorded their readings of the stories in English and Punjabi onto CDs, and finally, included CDs in each of the bilingual storybooks. Nineteen storybooks of varying lengths were the result.

Means for analyzing mixed-mode representations are not as common as they are for analyzing written or spoken discourse. Van Leeuwen's recent (2008) work on theorizing mixed-mode representations was most helpful for this analysis. Van Leeuwen argued that "all texts, all representations of the world and what is going on in it, however abstract, should be interpreted as representations of social practices" (p. 5). Maintaining the distinction between social practice ("doing it") and representation ("talking about it") (p. 6), he argued that the task of the critical discourse analyst is to uncover social practices, recontextualized in representations. This recontextualization is important, because the location of a representation and its actors, its customary actions and resources, may be very different from the original context in which the social practice occurred. Thus the analyst must make explicit the features of each representation including: who is represented, what actions are involved, how such action is to be performed, what time and space constraints bear on the action, and what resources are involved (van Leeuwen, 2008, p. 7-12). In what follows, van Leeuwen's method is used to analyze one student's story.

Jushinpreet's Story

Though Jushinpreet entitled his book "Darshen as a soldier," he began his grandfather's story in childhood. His front cover included a military vehicle and a drawing of an (American) Navy Seal plane. The narrative began, "There was a boy named Darshen. He was walking and in his mind he was thinking of being a soldier [when] he grew up." Coming from a long line of soldiers, Jushinpreet tells us that Darshen's great great great grandfather "helped the gurus defeat pure evil," perhaps a reference to the beginnings of Sikhism in the 1600s during which time the Sikhs fought many battles with the central Mughal government. As seen in Figure 3, Jushinpreet illustrated his narrative with a smiling man wearing a turban and a labeled Nike jersey in the foreground, with another smiling (but probably dead) man with an "x'ed out" eye in profile in the background wearing a Champs jersey with a machete through his chest. The next pages of the story then go back to Darshen and his life, and end with his travel to Canada and his retirement.

To apply van Leeuwen's (2008) question, "How are the people depicted?" to this illustration, one might first consider perspective. The figure in the foreground, presumably the hero, most likely Darshen's great-great-great-grandfather, faces out to readers. The smiling dead man in the background is shown in profile. Pure evil (the enemy) is outside the picture frame, and is not identified with a human figure. Following van Leeuwen (2008), one interpretation is that the dead man and possibly pure evil in this drawing are objectivized, which he defined as "representing people as objects of our scrutiny, rather than as subjects addressing the viewer with their gaze and symbolically engaging with the viewer in this way" (p. 141). Such objectivization abstracts the story so that the tales of war in Jushinpreet's story seem heroic, bloodless, and almost people-less. Van Leeuwen (2008) also encouraged analysts to consider if figures are portrayed specifically or generically. On this page of the story, Darshen's great-great-great-grandfather is the agent and the patient (unspecified) is pure evil. In none of Jushinpreet's illustrations throughout the book is the villain moving. The hero is specific, and viewers are invited throughout to identify with the heroism of the grandfather, and his ancestors. The soldiers of pure evil are, on the other hand, an unseen and unspecified group.

Overall, Jushinpreet's grandfather's story represents a heroic vision of soldiering, and a rather abstracted vision of armed conflict. The social practices of soldiering, and the social practice of talking about soldiering with one's grandchild, are re-contextualized in school, a place where depictions of machetes through chests (and phrases like "pure evil") would usually not be permitted. Through his story, Jushinpreet brings home and community knowledge to school and not only his grandfather spoke about war; several other stories showed the violence of the Partition of India and Pakistan. One interpretation—and there other equally plausible explanations—is that this knowledge of violence and war exists uneasily in school and gets re-contextualized as something special, grandparents' stories, a "project." The attention given to the technologies of war (largely American) in it also presents a particular view of such conflict.

This project's stories as a whole demonstrated to us how reading, writing, and illustrating are not neutral practices; rather they are social tools used to re-contextualize and re-present in more than just this case, "difficult knowledge." The images the students created allowed them to convey traumatic material about topics such as war, which are often hard to represent in language. Like Jushinpreet, other children shared traumatic knowledge through their grandparents' stories that challenged school notions of appropriate conflict resolution, secularity, gender equity, cultural authenticity, and sunny childhoods. Pitt and Britzman (2006) argue that "difficult knowledge" might include "narratives of historical traumas such as genocide, slavery, and forms of social hatred and questions of equity, democracy and human rights" and highlighted "the problem of learning from social breakdowns in ways that might open teachers and students to their present ethical dilemmas" (p. 379). In this project children's multimodal productions highlighted the school as a contested socio-cultural site in which children's lives and their re-contextualizations of those worlds might become resources for children and teachers as well as the community.

COMMENTARY 1: (RE)POSITIONING AND (RE)READING LITERACY IN THE FACE OF THE VISUAL
BY JENNIFER ROWSELL

If you see the world as read and positioned through the visual, literacy looks different. Literacy at this moment in time is becoming far more visual. What this means in terms of literacy education is rereading assumptions about literacy learning: rereading our original epistemologies; rereading notions about 'reading' and 'writing'; and, perhaps most powerfully of all, rereading our methodologies for conducting literacy research. In other words, as literacy researchers, we are compelled to reread core issues of our vocation to ensure that they align well with visually dominant texts and environments.

What threads the three distinct research studies presented in this report is not only adopting visual methodologies as a more viable way forward, but also naturalizing an approach to materiality and multimodality that rereads epistemologies about literacy learning; rereads reading and writing; and rereads methodologies for investigating meaning making. To focus on the latter point, that of rereading research methods, researchers need to pay closer attention to issues of semiosis and materiality in texts along with sensory and embodied experiences that, quite naturally, even tacitly, occur when we see and experience images. Researchers such as Pink (2009) and Ingold (2007) remind us that there are wider possibilities for seeing and understanding everyday life that accounts for embodied experience. Accounting for embodied experience positions the multimodal and semiotic as sensory, as tactile and as felt in everyday life (Pink, 2009).

With the three research studies in mind, there is a participatory and sensory methodology embedded within each study. Through descriptions of Opondo's cartoon as expressive of his knowledge about HIV/AIDS and social behavior dealing with sexuality, there is a felt sense of the impact of HIV/AIDS on Ugandan youth (Kendrick and Mutonyi). Similarly, Tracei's story unravels through the optic of a short video that Tracei made wherein her visuals powerfully illustrate her embodied and sensory reactions to coming of age as a girl (Rogers and Hauge). Finally, the last analysis illustrates how a group of children came to terms with intergenerational events involving war and other traumatic episodes through digital stories (Toohey and Marshall). Each study throws into relief how such notions as modal choice, design, and remixing stories and ideas signal key information about participants' pathways into meaning and, broadly speaking, what inspires them to make meaning. To revisit core themes only possible through a participatory and sensory approach, in the first visual example, Opondo consolidates and critically frames knowledge and experience through art, drawing, and design. In the second example, Tracei's film-making resituates and repositions her within larger cultural narratives. In the third example, children come to terms with intergenerational trauma through enactment and modal compositions of family stories.

Place is experienced bodily and the mapping of place through visual methods such as video camera, photography, artwork, and audio recordings can call up memories of place that can be collectively shared in educational contexts. These sensory evocations of place are powerful tools for literacy learning. Whereas multimodality is useful, as Sarah Pink (2009) has written, there needs to be a sensory ethnographic understanding to respect what our students bring into the classroom, and what their artifactual knowledge could be.

COMMENTARY 2: ANALYZING VISUAL TEXTS AS THEORETICAL MASH-UPS
BY MARJORIE SIEGEL

Stretching beyond the limits of words, literacy researchers are beginning to reinvent the analysis of visual texts by blending visual and sociocultural theories to explore the rich panoply of literate practice. The examples of visual representation presented in this paper illustrate what can be known about literacy if we complicate the dominant assumption that texts are autonomous signifying structures. The recent history of literacy research could be read as a move toward theories (e.g., sociocultural, critical) and methodologies (e.g., ethnography, critical discourse analysis) that show how textual meanings are both local and global, socially situated and discursively produced. Yet, the initial efforts to analyze visual texts have tended to reinscribe the idea of texts as autonomous, disconnected from what Rose (2001) calls the sites of production and sites of audiencing. For example, Kress and van Leeuwan (1996) offer a grammar for reading images that they characterize as grounded in the history of Western image-making. However, the historical aspect of their work is often left behind in their construction of a "grammar," resulting in readings of visual texts that dislodge images from the social, cultural, and political contexts that shaped their production, interpretation, and circulation.

In each of the examples presented in this report, there is more to reading images than the grammar of visual design. In the study of what Ugandan youth know about HIV/AIDS, the visual metaphor produced by the student required the researchers to consider both local and global discourses about HIV/AIDS. The discourse of silence that has surrounded the HIV/AIDS pandemic has particular cultural meanings in Uganda that are essential to reading the cartoon. The condom serves as both a literal and metaphoric barrier against HIV/AIDS, but, as Kendrick and Mutonyi note, the taboos about speaking about sex contribute to the ambiguous representation of the couple in the unprotected sex image. The fusion of visual analysis with what are characterized as "narrative themes" serves to anchor the visual to the sociocultural. In doing so, this analytic "mash-up" offers "a view of text and meaning making that is interpreted, multimodal, socially performed, emplaced, and embodied" (Siegel & Rowe, in press).

A similar analytic blend is at work in the approach to visual analysis developed to produce a reading of Tracei's awesome film. Rogers and Hauge's analysis of the site of the image examines the structure of the film, the modes and genres, and the motifs, but goes beyond a structural analysis by tracing the intertextual connections from the site of the image to the site of production. Drawing on theories of social postioning and identity, they are able to show that the three seemingly disparate sections of the film—Tracei's lip piercing, playfulness with friends, and PSA-like texts declaring, for example, "This video was made to prevent the use of chemically made drugs"—work together as a counternarrative to the conventional discourses and subject positionings of Western girlhood. As these authors demonstrate, Tracei has not just produced a film, she has produced a film in which she plays with her identity, repositioning herself within the discourses of gender. The affordances of film multiply the resources available for this identity work, and vividly show the way in which multimodal texts are identity performances, entangled, embodied, and emplaced in time and space.

Finally, Toohey and Marshall's analysis of the texts produced by children and families at the intersection of home and school, offer another example of multimodal texts as assemblages of signs with local and global meanings. In their work, they describe the picture storybooks created from the stories that Punjabi Sikh family elders told their Canadian grandchildren as part of a school-sponsored project designed to tap and honor families' funds of knowledge. To analyze these texts, the authors trace the recontextualization of social histories narrated by Punjabi Sikh family elders into the multimedia texts, and show how these texts are shaped and reshaped by multiple global and local contexts. What this analysis makes visible are the ways in which family elders write themselves into new social positions for their Canadian grandchildren and their schoolmates. Even texts designed to tap the family's funds of knowledge cannot escape the history of schooling as sites of social regulation, regulating knowledge as well as bodies, so that what were intended as "family stories" become "something special" but do not count as knowledge for/in school. Instead, the multimodal texts shrink to fit what can be said, written, and drawn in school. Without an analysis that looked beyond the multimodal text as an autonomous structure, we would have missed the family story that matters.

FINAL THOUGHTS

The three visual examples, the cartoon, film, and digital story, are all places where meanings are created and contested in particular moments; each is "a constantly challenging place of social interaction" (Mirzoeff, 1999, p. 4). In relation to the research questions addressed within the three projects, the visual becomes a tool for understanding how children and youth momentarily *visualize* and *embody* their knowledge and experience of their everyday worlds. The use of discursive resources related to the visual (re)positions children and youth in relation to larger sociocultural narratives such as taboo cultural practices surrounding HIV/AIDS education, normalizing discourses of girlhood, and difficult knowledge of family social histories. Using these three examples, this group of authors calls for broader sociocultural, analytical, and conceptual frameworks to more fully articulate and analyze what children and youth are doing with the visual as discursive resources. Such frameworks will enable researchers and educators to reccognize and support visual practices as powerful literacies and tools of learning in and out of schools.

REFERENCES

Adler, L. L. (1982). Children's drawings as an indicator of individual preferences reflecting group values: A programmatic study. In L. L. Adler (Ed.), *Cross-cultural research at issue* (pp. 71-98). New York, NY: Academic Press.

Bakhtin, M. M. (1986). *Speech genres and other late essays*. Austin, TX: University of Texas.

Baldry, & Thibault, P. (2006). *Multimodal transcription and text analysis*. London, UK: Equinox.

Biggs, C., & Bauman, R. (1992). Genre, Intertextuality and Social Power. *Journal of Linguistic Anthropology, 2*(2), 131-172.

Buckingham, D., & Sefton-Green, J. (1994). *Cultural studies goes to school. Reading and teaching popular media.* London, UK: Taylor and Francis.

Cope, B., & Kalantzis, M., (2000). Introduction. In B. Cope & M. Kalantzis (Eds.), *Multiliteracies: Learning and the design of social futures* (pp. 3-8). London, UK: Routledge.

Davies, B., & Harre, R. (1990). Positioning: The discursive production of selves. *Journal for the Theory of Social Behaviour, 20*, 43-63.

Diem-Wille, G. (2001). A therapeutic perspective: the use of drawings in child psychoanalysis and social science. In T. van Leeuwen & C. Jewitt (Eds.), *Handbook of visual analysis.* (pp.119-133). London, UK: Sage.

Dyson, A. H. (2001). Where are the childhoods in childhood literacy: An exploration in outer (school) space. *Journal of Early Childhood Literacy, 1* (1), 9-39.

Harste, J. C., Woodward, V. A., & Burke, C. L. (1984). *Language stories and literacy lessons.* Portsmouth, NH: Heinemann.

Ellsworth, E. (2005). *Places of learning: Media, architecture, pedagogy.* New York, NY: Routledge Falmer.

Grosz, E. (1994). *Volatile bodies: Toward a corporeal feminism.* Bloomington, IN: Indiana University Press.

Grosz, E., & Eisenman, P. (2001). *Architecture from the outside: Essays on virtual and real space.* Cambridge, MA: MIT Press.

Holland, D., Lachicotte, W., Skinner, D., & Cain, C. (1998). *Identity and agency in cultural worlds.* Cambridge, MA: Harvard U. Press.

Ingold, T. (2007). *Lines: A Brief History.* London, UK: Routledge.

Jewitt, C., & Kress, G. (Eds.) (2003). *Multimodal literacy.* New York, NY: Peter Lang.

Koppitz, E. M. (1984). Psychological evaluation of human figure drawings by middle school pupils. Orlando, FL: Grune & Stratton, Inc.

Kress, G. (1997). *Before writing: Rethinking the paths to literacy.* London, UK: Routledge.

Kress, G., & van Leeuwen, T. (1996). *Reading images: The grammar of visual design.* London, UK: Routledge.

Lange, P. (2007). Publicly private and privately public: Social networking on YouTube. *Journal of Computer-Mediated Communication 13*, pp. 361–380.

Luke, A. (2000). Critical literacy in Australia. *Journal of Adolescent and Adult Literacies. 43*(5), 448-461.

Mirzoeff, N. (1999). *An introduction to visual culture.* London, UK: Routledge.

Moll, L., & Greenberg, J. (1990). Creating zones of possibilities: Combining social contexts for instruction. In L. C. Moll (Ed.), *Vygotsky and education* (pp. 319-348). Cambridge, MA: Cambridge University Press.

Mutonyi, H. (2008). *Health literacy, HIV/AIDS, and Gender: A Ugandan youth lens* (Doctoral dissertation). University of British Columbia, Vancouver, British Columbia.

Mutonyi, H., & Kendrick, M. (2009). Ugandan students' visual representation of HIV/AIDS knowledge. In C. Higgins & B. Norton (Eds.), *Applied Linguistics in the Field: Local Knowledge and HIV/AIDS.* Vol. Critical Language and Literacy Studies (pp. 38-62). Clevedon, UK: Multilingual Matters.

Mutonyi, H., & Kendrick, M. (in press). Cartoon Drawing as a Means of Accessing What Students Know About HIV/AIDS: A Case Study in Uganda. *Visual Communication Journal (Sage).*

New London Group. (1996). A pedagogy of multiliteracies: Designing social futures. *Harvard Educational Review, 66*, 60-92.

Nyanzi, S., Pool, R., & Kinsman, J. (2001) The negotiation of sexual relationships among school pupils in south-western Uganda. *AIDS Care 13*(1), 83–98.

Pahl, K., & Rowsell, J. (2006). Introduction. In K. Pahl & J. Rowsell, *Travel notes from the New Literacy Studies: Instances of practice* (pp. 1-15). Clevedon, UK: Multilingual Matters.

Pink, S. (2009). *Doing Sensory Ethnography.* London, UK: Sage Publications.

Pitt, A., & Britzman, D. (2006). Speculations on qualities of difficult knowledge in teaching and learning: An experiment in psychoanalytic research. In K. Tobin & J. Kincheloe (Eds.), *Doing educational research: A handbook* (pp. 379-401). New York, NY: Sense Publishers.

Rose, G. (2001). *Visual methodologies.* London, UK: Sage.

Rogers, T. (2009). Theorizing media productions as complex literacy performances among youth in and out of schools. In D.L. Pullen & D. Cole (Eds), *Handbook of Research on Multiliteracies and Technology Enhanced Education* (pp. 133-146). Philadelphia, PA: IGI Publications.

Rogers, T., & Winters, K. (2010). Textual play, satire and counter discourses of street youth 'zining practices. In D. Alvermann (Ed.), *Adolescents' Online Literacies: Connecting Classrooms, Media, and Paradigms* (pp. 91-108). New York, NY: Peter Lang.

Rogers, T., Winters, K., LaMonde, A., & Perry, M. (in press, 2010) From image to ideology: Analyzing shifting identity positions of marginalized youth across the cultural sites of video production. *Pedagogies: An International Journal,* 5(4).

Siegel, M., & Panofsky, C. P. (2009). Designs for multimodality in literacy studies: Explorations in analysis. In K. Leander, D. W. Rowe, D. Dickinson, R. Jiménez, M. Hundley, & V. Risko (Eds.), *58th National Reading Conference Yearbook* (pp. 99-111). Oak Creek, WI: National Reading Conference.

Siegel, M., & Rowe, D. W. (in press). Webs of significance: Semiotic perspectives on text. In D. Lapp & D. Fisher (Eds.). *Handbook of research on teaching the English language arts.* Urbana, IL: National Council of Teachers of English, Newark, DE: International Reading Association, and New York, NY: Taylor & Francis/Erlbaum.

Snyder, I. (Ed.). (1997). *Page to screen: Taking literacy into the electronic era.* Melbourne, Austrailia: Allen & Unwin.

Stoneburner, R. and Low-Beer, D. (2004) Population-level HIV declines and the behavioural risk avoidance in Uganda. *Science Magazine* 304, 704–718.

Street, B. (2003). What's 'new' in the New Literacy Studies? Critical approaches to literacy in theory and practice. *Current Issues in Comparative Education,* 5(2), 77-91.

USAID (United States Agency for International Development) (2002). *What Happened in Uganda?* Retrieved on 24 January 2004, from www.usaids/gov/ourwork/globalhealth/aids/countries/uganda.

Warburton, T. (1998). Cartoons and teachers: mediated visual images as data. In J. Prosser (Ed.), *Image-based Research: A Sourcebook for Qualitative Researchers* (pp. 252-262). London, UK: Routledge.

van Leeuwen, T. (2008). *Discourse and practice: New tools for critical discourse analysis.* Oxford, UK: Oxford University Press.

Vygotsky, L. (1978). *Mind in society: the development of higher psychological processes.* Cambridge, MA: Harvard University Press.

FOOTNOTES

[1] An expanded version of this example appears in Mutonyi, H., & Kendrick, M. (in press). *Journal of Visual Communication.*

[2] Kendrick, a Canadian, is faculty member at the University of British Columbia. Mutonyi, a Ugandan, was completing her PhD at the time of the study.

[3] Adapted from Elizabeth Marshall and Kelleen Toohey, "Representing family: Community Funds of Knowledge, bilingualism, and multimodality." Harvard Educational Review, v80:3 (Fall 2010). Copyright © by the President and Fellows of Harvard College. All rights reserved. Reprinted with permission. For more information, please visit www.harvardeducationalreview.org.